LIBRARY OF NEW TESTAMENT STUDIES

694

formerly the Journal for the Study of the New Testament Supplement series

Editor
Chris Keith

Editorial Board
Dale C. Allison, Lynn H. Cohick, Kylie Crabbe, R. Alan Culpepper,
Craig A. Evans, Jennifer Eyl, Robert Fowler, Juan Hernández Jr.,
John S. Kloppenborg, Michael Labahn, Matthew V. Novenson,
Love L. Sechrest, Robert Wall, Catrin H. Williams, Brittany E. Wilson

Jesus and YHWH-Texts in the Synoptic Gospels

Scott Brazil

LONDON • NEW YORK • OXFORD • NEW DELHI • SYDNEY

T&T CLARK

Bloomsbury Publishing Plc, 50 Bedford Square, London, WC1B 3DP, UK
Bloomsbury Publishing Inc, 1359 Broadway, New York, NY 10018, USA
Bloomsbury Publishing Ireland, 29 Earlsfort Terrace, Dublin 2, D02 AY28, Ireland

BLOOMSBURY, T&T CLARK and the T&T Clark logo are trademarks of
Bloomsbury Publishing Plc

First published in Great Britain 2024
Paperback edition published in 2025

Copyright © Scott Brazil, 2024

Scott Brazil has asserted his right under the Copyright, Designs and Patents Act,
1988, to be identified as Author of this work.

For legal purposes the Acknowledgments on p.xi constitute an extension
of this copyright page.

All rights reserved. No part of this publication may be: i) reproduced or transmitted
in any form, electronic or mechanical, including photocopying, recording or by means
of any information storage or retrieval system without prior permission in writing from the
publishers; or ii) used or reproduced in any way for the training, development or operation
of artificial intelligence (AI) technologies, including generative AI technologies. The rights
holders expressly reserve this publication from the text and data mining exception as
per Article 4(3) of the Digital Single Market Directive (EU) 2019/790.

Bloomsbury Publishing Plc does not have any control over, or responsibility for,
any third-party websites referred to or in this book. All internet addresses given
in this book were correct at the time of going to press. The author and publisher
regret any inconvenience caused if addresses have changed or sites have
ceased to exist, but can accept no responsibility for any such changes.

A catalogue record for this book is available from the British Library.

ISBN: HB: 978-0-5677-1395-7
PB: 978 0 5677-1399-5
ePDF: 978-0-5677-1396-4
eBook: 978-0-5677-1398-8

Series: Library of New Testament Studies, 2345678X, volume 694

Typeset by RefineCatch Limited, Bungay, Suffolk

For product safety related questions contact productsafety@bloomsbury.com.

To find out more about our authors and books visit www.bloomsbury.com
and sign up for our newsletters.

Contents

List of Tables	vi
List of Abbreviations	vii
Preface	x
Acknowledgments	xi
1 Backgrounds and Bearings	1
2 Matthew's Application of YHWH-Texts to Jesus	41
3 Mark's Application of YHWH-Texts to Jesus	71
4 Luke's Application of YHWH-Texts to Jesus	119
5 Realizations and Ramifications	165
Bibliography	181
Subject Index	203
Scripture Index	215

Tables

1.1	YHWH-Texts Applied to Jesus by NT Author	16
1.2	Luke's Fuller Allusion to Ezekiel's YHWH-Text	17
2.1	Cries to Jesus Reiterating Cries to YHWH	52
2.2	Probable OT YHWH-Texts Behind Matthew 25:31–32	65
3.1	Word Count Comparisons of the Synoptic Gospels	71
3.2	YHWH-Jesus Parallels in the Storms of Jonah and Mark	95
3.3	Parallels and Developments in Jesus' Parousia Predictions in Mark	112
4.1	YHWH-Texts in the Background of Luke 7:26–27	127
4.2	YHWH-Text Cluster behind Luke 20:17–18	159
5.1	List of Passages Addressed (or Paralleled) in this Study	166

Abbreviations

AB(C)	Anchor Bible (Commentary)
ABD	Anchor Bible Dictionary
AccRSMF	*Accademia: Revue de La Société Marsile Ficin*
AUSSJ	*Andrews University Seminary Student Journal*
BBR	*Bulletin for Biblical Research*
BDAG	Bauer-Danker-Arndt-Gingrich, Greek-English Lexicon (third ed., 2000)
BDB	Brown-Driver-Briggs, Hebrew-English Lexicon (1906 ed.)
BECNT	Baker Exegetical Commentary on the New Testament
Bib	*Biblica*
BN	*Biblische Notizen*
BogS	*Bogoslovska Smotra*
BSac	*Bibliotheca Sacra*
BSC	Bible Student's Commentary
BT	*Biblical Translator*
BTB	*Biblical Theology Bulletin*
CBQ	*Catholic Biblical Quarterly*
CGTC	Cambridge Greek Testament Commentaries
Chm	*Churchman*
ChrCent	*Christian Century*
ConcC	Concordia Commentary
CS	*Christian Scholar*
CT	*Christianity Today*
CTQ	*Concordia Theological Quarterly*
CTR	*Criswell Theological Review*
DSS	Dead Sea Scrolls
EBC	Expositor's Bible Commentary
EGGNT	Exegetical Guide to the Greek New Testament
EKK	Evangelishe-katholischer Kommentar
EKKNT	Evangelishe-katholischer Kommentar zum Neuen Testament
EQ or *EvQ*	*Evangelical Quarterly*
ETR	*Études Théologiques et Religieuses*
EvT	*Evangelische Theologie*
ExAud	Ex Auditu
GR	Gordon Review
HAR	Hebrew Annual Review
HB	Hebrew Bible
HBT	*Horizons in Biblical Theology*
Herm	Hermeneia
IBC	Interpretation: A Bible Commentary for Teaching and Preaching
ICC	International Critical Commentary
IDS	*In die Skriflig*

IJHSS	*International Journal of Humanities and Social Science*
Int	*Interpretation*
ISBE	International Standard Bible Encyclopedia
IVPNTC	InterVarsity Press New Testament Commentary
JETS	*Journal of the Evangelical Theological Society*
JJMJS	*Journal of the Jesus Movement in Its Jewish Setting*
JSJ	*Journal for the Study of Judaism in the Persian, Hellenistic, and Roman Period*
JSNT	*Journal for the Study of the New Testament*
JSOT	*Journal for the Study of the Old Testament*
JSP	*Journal for the Study of the Pseudepigrapha*
JTI	*Journal of Theological Interpretation*
JTS	*Journal of Theological Studies*
Kerux	*Kerux*
Logia	*Logia*
LS	*Louvain Studies*
LXX	Septuagint
MAJT	*Mid-America Journal of Theology*
MJT	*Midwestern Journal of Theology*
MT	Masoretic Text
NA	Nestle-Aland (Greek NT)
NAC	New American Commentary
Neot	*Neotestamentica*
NIB	New Interpreter's Bible
NICNT	New International Commentary on the New Testament
NICOT	New International Commentary on the Old Testament
NIGTC	New International Greek Testament Commentary
NIVAC	New International Version Application Commentary
NovT	*Novum Testamentum*
NS	New Series
NTL	New Testament Library
NTS	*New Testament Studies*
NZSTh	*Neue Zeitschrift für Systematische Theologie und Religionsphilosophie*
Phronema	*Phronema*
Pneuma	*Pneuma: Journal of the Society for Pentecostal Studies*
PNTC	Pillar New Testament Commentary
ProEccl	*Pro Ecclesia*
PRSt	*Perspectives in Religious Studies*
PTR	*Princeton Theological Review*
R-H	Rahlfs-Hanhart (edition of the Septnagint)
RelS	*Religious Studies*
RTR	*Reformed Theological Review*
Salm	*Salmanticensis*
SBJT	*Southern Baptist Journal of Theology*
SBL	Society of Biblical Literature
SBLSP	Society of Biblical Literature Seminar Papers
SCM	Student Christian Movement (Press)
SJT	*Scottish Journal of Theology*
SP	*Sacra Pagina*
ST	*Studia Theologica*

STRev	*Sewanee Theological Review*
Them	*Themelios*
ThTo	*Theology Today*
TJ	*Trinity Journal*
TMSJ	*The Master's Seminary Journal*
TNTC	Tyndale New Testament Commentaries
TP	*Theologie und Philosophie*
TTC	Teach the Text Commentary Series
TynBul	*Tyndale Bulletin*
USQR	*Union Seminary Quarterly Review*
VC	*Vigiliae Christianae*
VTeH	*Vetus Testamentum et Hellas*
WBC	Word Bible Commentary
WTJ	*Westminster Theological Journal*
ZECNT	Zondervan Exegetical Commentary on the New Testament
ZTK	*Zeitschrift für Theologie und Kirche*

Preface

This study examines the practice in the Synoptic Gospels of applying Old Testament (OT) passages to Jesus that originally referred to YHWH. Critical scholarship in the last two centuries has favored the theory that the Synoptics evidence a low (merely human) Christology in the primitive church, while John's Gospel displays a high (human and divine) Christology developed in the decades to follow. However, the YHWH-text phenomenon in the Synoptics contradicts that theory by revealing an early and united Christian understanding of Jesus as YHWH.

The introductory chapter explains the practice and significance of YHWH-texts applied to Jesus in the New Testament (NT). The importance of the divine name *YHWH* in the Hebrew Scriptures and its impact in the Greek Septuagint, as well as the uniqueness of the "Name" in OT Jewish monotheism, are introduced. Appellations of the divine name in the NT—primarily κύριος—are also examined. Following several NT examples of the YHWH-text phenomenon, the discussion turns to the significance of the phenomenon for Christological studies. The chapter surveys modern scholarship on the origin and meaning of Jesus as "Lord" as well as recent approaches in Jesus studies that interact with the YHWH-text phenomenon to varying degrees.

The meat of this biblical-theological study is found in its three respective chapters surveying the Gospels of Matthew, Mark, and Luke (chapters 2–4), which examine numerous clear and probable cases of OT YHWH-texts applied to Jesus. Each of the three chapters begins with a brief summary of the evangelist's Christological emphases, before exegeting various passages containing the YHWH-text phenomenon. The number of passages examined in each Synoptic Gospel may be considered complete, though not exhaustive. Each survey includes initial statements on the significance of the practice, anticipating more extensive remarks in the concluding chapter.

The final chapter highlights five realizations and five ramifications of the YHWH-text phenomenon in the Synoptics. The realizations focus on the frequency, diversity, and ubiquity of the practice, as well as its wide range of OT source material and its parallel to the NT practice of applying OT messianic texts to Jesus. Ramifications of the study include the early deliberate employment of YHWH-texts to Jesus, the likelihood that Jesus is the source of the practice, the high Christology of the Synoptics (rivaling that in John's Gospel), and the redemptive-historical metanarrative that Jesus is the divine interpreter and central figure of the Jewish Scriptures. In summary, understanding the prolific application of OT YHWH-texts to Jesus in the Synoptic Gospels cannot be neglected in biblical scholarship without truncating genuine NT Christology.

Acknowledgments

This project would not have been completed without the encouragement of my faithful wife, Elaine. Further household encouragement came from my mother-in-law, Constance Whitworth. My children, most of them grown but three still at home during the writing, have all experienced roller coaster life with a student-to-missionary-to-student-to-pastor-to-student (again!) father. Nathan, Jesse, Micah, Hannah, Sarah, Naomi, Seth, and Noah: may the Lord bless your lives greatly as you seek His face. Additionally, two beautiful weddings were pulled off to adorn the period of this project, and I am thrilled to welcome Nicole and Biez into our tribe.

I am honored to have had the readers of my original manuscript include NT and biblical-theological scholars Charles L. Quarles, Benjamin L. Merkle, and Dennis E. Johnson. Alysha Clark proved invaluable as an editor. Many thanks go to friends who encouraged the work, including Matt May, Mark Sessions, and Steve Bump. And I am very grateful to the Bloomsbury T&T Clark editors and staff for getting this project to print.

Immersing myself in this project constantly strengthened my heart's resonation with Peter, who may have said more than he realized: "Lord, to whom shall we go? You have the words of eternal life . . ." (John 6:68).

To Jonathan Davis

Thank you, dear brother.

1

Backgrounds and Bearings

The Phenomenon of YHWH-Texts Applied to Jesus and Its Significance

A peculiar phenomenon in the New Testament (NT) is its practice of applying to Jesus of Nazareth various Old Testament (OT) texts originally referring to YHWH,[1] the biblical creator of the cosmos and divine redeemer of Israel. A clear example of this phenomenon is found in Heb 1:10–12, a description of God's "son" (identified as Jesus in 2:9) as the eternal and imperishable creator of the created and perishable universe. The passage is a quotation of Ps 102:25–27, which, in its original context, refers to YHWH as the eternal and imperishable creator. Thus, the subject of the original OT text is YHWH, while the subject of the same text as quoted in the NT is Jesus.[2] And since the writer to the Hebrews had already made this kind of interpretive maneuver in his book (cf. Heb 1:6; Deut 32:43 LXX), it is apparently his deliberate practice and not a careless oversight.

Such a conscious calculation appears to be the case as well in the canonical Gospels: Matthew, Mark, Luke, and John. As this study in the Synoptics shall demonstrate, the phenomenon of applying YHWH-texts to Jesus is common enough to be understood as their deliberate practice and, therefore, as a phenomenon their readers would have been expected to recognize.[3] Historically, John's Gospel has been distinguished from

---

[1] See discussion below on the meaning and usage of "YHWH" for the God of Jewish monotheism. For a standard general article on the divine name, see Henry O. Thompson, "Yahweh," *The Anchor Bible Dictionary* 6:1011–12.
[2] Cf. C. John Collins, "How the New Testament Quotes and Interprets the Old Testament," in *Understanding Scripture*, ed. Wayne A. Grudem, C. John Collins, and Thomas R. Schreiner (Wheaton, IL: Crossway, 2012), 191.
[3] Proving intent in authors and recognition in readers can be elusive. However, the two examples of quotations just given from Hebrews display explicit intent on the part of the author to use YHWH-texts for proving that Jesus is greater than angels (the highest created beings), who are called to worship Jesus (Heb 1:6). Thus, the use of YHWH-texts in this context shows an expectation by the author that his readers will understand his point: Jesus is both God's Son and God (YHWH) himself. Although some scholars balk at the idea that first-century monotheistic Jews would ever identify Jesus as YHWH, others have pointed out that Second Temple Judaism was ripe for combining the two-fold promise of the coming Davidic messiah with the personal coming of the Lord (YHWH). That those parallel promises were fulfilled in the same person was a central tenet of the new Christian movement. For more explanation of Jewish expectation during the Second Temple period, see, for example, the summary of N. T. Wright's work later in this chapter. Cf. N. T. Wright, *The New Testament and the People of God* (Minneapolis, MN: Fortress, 1992), 475–76; N. T. Wright, *Jesus and the Victory of God* (Minneapolis, MN: Fortress, 1996), 651–53.

the Synoptics as reflecting a higher Christology formulated decades after they were written. This study will question that distinction while examining the YHWH-text phenomenon in Matthew, Mark, and Luke.

The significance of this NT phenomenon lies in connecting the identity of YHWH in the OT and the identity of Jesus in the NT. The OT texts are rooted in a Jewish monotheistic worldview focusing on the God whose self-revealed "name" is *YHWH*. His lordship is absolute as creator, sustainer, redeemer, judge, king, and other divine roles. The NT writings are also rooted in a Jewish monotheistic worldview. And yet, there, it is often the "Lord" Jesus Christ who is portrayed as creator, sustainer, redeemer, judge, king, and other divine roles.[4] Hypothetically, the coexistence of two levels of lordship is a logical possibility for interpreting the data (cf. a parallel with Ancient Near East covenantal arrangements between suzerain "kings/lords" and their vassal "kings/lords"). In fact, a common hermeneutic in modern biblical scholarship is to distinguish between the absolute divine lordship of the biblical God and a derivative, merely human lordship of the NT Christ.[5] But does the phenomenon of YHWH-texts applied to Jesus support—or even allow—such a creator-creature distinction between YHWH and Jesus? In particular, do the texts of the Synoptic Gospels allow it? The evidence, this study seeks to show, suggests not. Rather, the purpose of the practice appears to be the deliberate identification of Jesus with and as YHWH.

Examination of this phenomenon as practiced in each of the Synoptic Gospels (cf. chapters 2–4) will seek to establish and confirm its significance. At this point, however, some explanation of the basis and direction of this study will seek to clarify the subject at hand and to justify its value for current Christological conversations.

What Are Old Testament "YHWH-Texts"?

In 1990, a valuable dissertation was completed by David B. Capes entitled, "Paul's Use of Old Testament Yahweh-Texts and Its Implications for His Christology."[6] The results of his work showed that when Paul quoted OT passages referring to the God of Israel—who was identified in each OT context by the divine name, *YHWH*—he applied those passages either to God or to Jesus in equal measure, in fact, seven times each.[7] In other words, it is not only astonishing that "Yahweh texts"[8] are applied to Jesus at all, but that

---

[4] Or, as John M. Frame, *Systematic Theology* (Phillipsburg, NJ: P&R Publishing, 2013), 450, describes the same observation, "The most concise, and arguably most fundamental, summary of OT teaching is 'Yahweh is Lord.' But the NT, over and over again, represents Jesus as Lord in the same way that Yahweh is Lord."

[5] R. Daniel Kirk's, *A Man Attested by God* (Grand Rapids, MI: Eerdmans, 2016), is a recent version of this view. Kirk argues throughout this extensive work that Jesus is never depicted as pre-existent or divine in the Synoptics, but rather as an ideal human figure.

[6] David B. Capes, "Paul's Use of Old Testament Yahweh-Texts and Its Implications for His Christology" (PhD diss., Southwestern Baptist Theological Seminary, 1990), subsequently published *in substantia* as *Old Testament Yahweh Texts in Paul's Christology* (Tübingen, Germany: Mohr Siebeck, 1992; repr. 2017, Waco, TX: Baylor University Press).

[7] E.g., Capes, *Old Testament Yahweh Texts in Paul's Christology*, 160.

[8] Capes has since preferred to use the term "YHWH texts" over "Yahweh texts" for four reasons: "First, YHWH has become a standard way of referencing the divine in scholarly discourse. Second, the use

Paul does so just as frequently and as readily as he applied such texts to God in general. Before examining the work of Capes and others on the divine lordship of Jesus more carefully, it will be necessary to lay some groundwork on the importance of the divine name in the Hebrew OT, its varied transmission into Greek translations of the OT, and the ubiquitous nature of YHWH-texts applied to Jesus in the NT.

The Importance of the Divine Name in the Old Testament

Moses' encounter with God at the burning bush, particularly the interchange described at Exod 3:13–15, serves as a key revelatory event in the early record of ancient Israel. In response to Moses' question about the "name" by which God should be identified to the Israelites, God first replied, אהיה אשר אהיה ("I am who/that I am"; 3:14a), before simplifying to אהיה ("I am"; 3:14b), and then calling himself what would become the most common form of the divine name, יהוה (transliteratively, *YHWH*; 3:15b). YHWH then further identified himself as "the God of your fathers—the God of Abraham, the God of Isaac, and the God of Jacob" (3:15b), capping the name-series with the claim that the entire series (or, at minimum, the nearest name-referent, *YHWH*) answers Moses' inquiry: "this is my name forever and my memorial to all generations" (3:15c). Thus, the particular and fundamental answer to Moses' question about God's name was that it is eternally "YHWH."

While scholarly debate continues on how best to translate the initially revealed name-phrase, אהיה אשר אהיה, and its simplification, אהיה, it is generally thought that אהיה is etymologically related to the verb *to be*, היה.[9] Thus, the explanatory form of God's personal name may be translated along the lines of "I am who/that I am" or "I will be who I will be,"[10] and the simplified form as "I am." These descriptors are immediately tied to the Tetragrammaton ("four letters"), יהוה, used most frequently in the OT as the personal name of God. Apparently, therefore, following the train of thought in Exod 3:14–15, the explanatory meaning of God's name (אהיה אשר אהיה) and its summary (אהיה) is encapsulated in the well-known form of God's personal "name" (יהוה). If so, then the name of God appears to underscore both his transcendentally eternal existence and his immanently relational presence (see discussion in the next section).

---

of four block capitalized letters visually approximates the tetragrammaton (literally, 'four letters'). Third, we cannot say for certain which 'vowel' sounds would have been associated with the tetragrammaton, and therefore we cannot know how the faithful might have pronounced it (on the odd occasion when they did). Finally, I want to demonstrate clearly the respect I have for Jews and Christians who regard the divine name as sacred." See, David B. Capes, *The Divine Christ* (Grand Rapids, MI: Baker Academic, 2018), xv. His reasons are persuasive. However, the hyphenated form, "YHWH-text," is preferred in this study, since *YHWH* is being used adjectivally as part of a singular concept.

[9] See, for example, Raymond Abba, "The Divine Name Yahweh," *JBL* 80.4 (1961): 328; Zev Garber, "Teaching the Shema (Torah and Testament): Text, Translation, Tradition," *BTB* 48.3 (2018): 144; Thomas Edward McComiskey, "God, Names Of," in *Evangelical Dictionary of Theology*, ed. Daniel J. Treier and Walter A. Elwell, 3rd ed. (Grand Rapids, MI: Baker Academic, 2017), 350; Jacques Vermeylen, "Name," *Encyclopedia of Christian Theology* 2:1093; Robert J. Wilkinson, *Tetragrammaton: Western Christians and the Hebrew Name of God* (Leiden; Boston: Brill, 2015), 9–10.

[10] McComiskey, "God, Names of," 351, prefers the rendering, "I am (the) One who is."

Ultimately, knowing the precise meaning of the divine name does not change the fact of its frequent connection to Jesus, though it could deepen an understanding of that fact. The more fundamental point being established here is that *YHWH* is the personal name of the God of the Hebrew Scriptures, so that a *YHWH-text* may be understood as any OT passage referring to YHWH, whether his personal name is explicitly written or demonstrably implied by the context.

Occurrences of YHWH in the Hebrew Old Testament

The Tetragrammaton, יהוה (along with a few less-common forms of the divine name),[11] occurs well over 6,000 times in the Hebrew/Aramaic Scriptures.[12] This is more than twice the use of the most common and generic word for "God," אלהים. As noted above, Exod 3:14–15 is a key text in the explanation of the divine name. But, while 3:14 is the first explanatory treatment of the divine name, 3:15 is not the first use of the Tetragrammaton, which already occurs 165 times in the book of Genesis and anticipates the expanded divine disclosure with a variety of occurrences in Exod 3:2, 4, 7. In fact, use of the divine name is nearly ubiquitous in the OT. The lengthy books of Jeremiah and the Psalter contain the highest number of occurrences—726 and 695, respectively— while even the smallest prophetic book, Obadiah, contains seven occurrences of the divine name. Only three of the thirty-nine canonical books lack the Tetragrammaton (Esther, Ecclesiastes, Song of Solomon), although cases can be made that YHWH is presupposed in the text or background of each.[13]

While the precise meaning of the divine name remains controversial, a firm case can be made that its implied relation to the copulative "to be" in Exod 3:14–15 emphasizes that the unique, eternal, self-existing God also discloses his "being" (existence) in the world he created.[14] This can be seen particularly in occurrences of *theophany*—the manifestation of his divine presence.[15] The unconsumed "burning" bush is a prime example of theophany, especially considering its context as the event in

---

[11] See discussions by Jacob A. Loewen, "The Names of God in the Old Testament," *BT* 35.2 (1984): 204; Wilkinson, *Tetragrammaton*, 28.

[12] Harris cites the Hebrew Bible count from *BDB* (217b) as 6,823 occurrences. Cf. Murray J. Harris, *Jesus as God* (Grand Rapids, MI: Baker, 1992), 24. See also, R. Kendall Soulen, *The Divine Name(s) and the Holy Trinity* (Louisville, KY: Westminster John Knox, 2011), 10.

[13] The God [*Elohim*] mentioned numerous times in Ecclesiastes can be none other than YHWH, based on his role as creator (e.g., 3:10–13) and connections to the temple (e.g., 5:1) and the monarchy (e.g., 1:1). And while even "Elohim" is not mentioned in the other two books, Song of Solomon has often been understood allegorically as a metaphor for YHWH and his people, while Esther appears to contain several acrostics of the divine name. See Ethelbert William Bullinger, ed., *The Companion Bible* (Grand Rapids, MI: Kregel, 1990), Appendix 60. In any event, the three are not only shorter works of the OT but topically less likely to use the Tetragrammaton than many other OT books. So, the absence of the divine name in three of thirty-nine books does not negate the pervasiveness of the name in the OT canon.

[14] Kavin Rowe, "Romans 10:13: What Is the Name of the Lord?," *HBT* 22.2 (2000): 159, similarly argues, "Third, there is no disjunction between the divine name and the divine being. The divine subject was present in his name. Thus YHWH is not some *thing* which is called the name of God, but is rather the one Lord himself" (emphasis Rowe).

[15] Cf. David W. Baker, "God, Names Of," *Dictionary of the Old Testament: Pentateuch*, 363; Roch A. Kereszty, *Jesus Christ*, rev. and updated ed. (New York: Alba House, 2002), 166; McComiskey, "God, Names Of," 351.

which YHWH discloses his personal name. But it is by no means the only theophanic self-disclosure of the OT.

The creation account, for example, describes the Spirit of God's localized act of "hovering over the waters" before shaping a formless earth (Gen 1:1–2). Also, when Adam and Eve disobeyed God, they heard the "sound of YHWH Elohim traversing the garden in the wind of the day," an apparent judgment theophany (3:8).[16] Other significant theophanies include the glory-cloud presence of YHWH during the Exodus (Exod 13:21–22), which was manifested in storm-fiery display and deafening noise at the giving of the Law on Sinai (18:16–19).[17] Also, Moses was allowed the unique but safely diminished view of the "back" of God as his manifest glory (כבד) passed by (33:22–23), a glory which lingered in its effect on Moses' face (Exod 34:5–30; cf. 2 Cor 3:7–18). Significantly, this unique and dangerous theophany was the occasion of YHWH revealing his divine name in doublet and with extended interpretation (34:6–7), upon which disclosure Moses "quickly bowed his head toward the earth and worshiped" (34:8a). The glory of God would later evidence his dwelling in the tabernacle (משכן, "dwelling place") and temple (היכל, "palace, great house") or house of YHWH (בית יהוה), where access to YHWH's "presence" would be granted to the high priest alone upon the ground of, and for the sake of, sacrificial atonement. (This localized or manifest presence of YHWH would later be summarized by the Rabbinic term, *shekinah*, meaning "settling, dwelling.") In Scripture, the theophanic presence of YHWH could also be manifested as the "Angel of YHWH/Elohim" (often identified as YHWH/God himself: e.g., Gen 31:11–13; Exod 3:2–6; Judg 6:11, 14, 20–24) or as the "Angel of His Presence" (Isa 63:7–9).

Significantly, the "name" and the "presence" of YHWH conceptually overlapped and became characteristic features of God's covenants with his people.[18] The expressed promise of YHWH's presence, YHWH's name, and/or YHWH himself dwelling with his people became the central promise of redemptive covenantal arrangements.[19] Statements such as "I will be with you" or "I will be your God, and you will be my people," are frequently used as shorthand markers of God's covenantal/relational presence with his delivered/redeemed people.[20] These promissory markers can be seen

---

[16] Cf. Meredith G. Kline, "Primal Parousia," *WTJ* 40.2 (1978): 245–80. Kline's understanding of Gen 3:8 that the noise heard by Adam and Eve was a theophanic whirlwind of YHWH's coming in judgment, rather than a gentle breeze and divine stroll through the Garden, appears to fit the context and terminology best. In any case, the scene depicted is clearly meant to be understood as an early theophanic visitation of YHWH.

[17] Abba, "The Divine Name Yahweh," 325, rightly connects the divine Name with both the theophany in Exod 3 and the glory-cloud theophanies during and after the Exodus.

[18] J. Ryan Lister, *The Presence of God* (Wheaton, IL: Crossway, 2015), 179, notes, "God is essentially saying, 'You have my name, which, more importantly, means you have me.' The reality of God's identity is intimately tied to his presence. And why is he present? He is present to deliver. The name Yahweh, therefore, is more than just a proper name; it is an expression of divine character that centers on his being redemptively present with and for a people."

[19] Cf. Lister, *The Presence of God*, 171–79.

[20] Charles D. Isbell, "The Divine Name היה as a Symbol of Presence in Israelite Tradition," *HAR* 2 (1978): 101, 116, writes, "The basic thesis to be advanced is simple. Whenever היה appears in a context of divine action or promise, its theological significance as a symbol of divine presence far exceeds its simple syntactic function as a first person singular verbal form . . . . The self-disclosure of Yahweh plainly included the willingness to speak a personal word about himself, to put himself on the spot promissorily and openly. It included his readiness to say, 'I will be with you'; 'I will become God to you.'" Cf. Lister, *The Presence of God*, 179.

particularly in the Abrahamic Covenant (e.g., Gen 17:8), the Mosaic Covenant (e.g., Exod 29:45), and the New Covenant (e.g., Jer 31:33). Significantly, YHWH used his divine name in such contexts to identify himself as the covenant-initiating, covenant-keeping God, whose presence ensured the fulfillment of his promises.[21]

Furthermore, promissory markers of divine presence, such as, "I will be with you" or "I will be your God, and you will be my people," appear to reflect the meaning-laden self-identity in the divine name, *YHWH*.[22] If so, he who is eternally self-existent chooses by redemptive-covenantal means to exist in manifest presence with his people. YHWH promised to dwell *with* and, ultimately, *in* his people (cf. Lev 26:11–12; Ezek 37:26–27), particularly in the person of his Holy Spirit (cf. Isa 44:3–5; Ezek 36:26–28). Ultimate redemption for his people, the trusting remnant, would come when YHWH himself comes (cf. Zech 2:10–13; Mal 3:1–3; 4:1–6). His eschatological appearance would be the final and climactic disclosure of his presence, indeed, the disclosure of himself.

The name *YHWH*, therefore, appears to be revelatory of both God's transcendence and immanence.[23] YHWH is transcendently absolute as the eternal self-existent creator of the universe, and he is immanently personal as the ever-present, yet soon-to-appear, deliverer and judge. Salvation and judgment would be consummated "when he comes."[24] This coming of YHWH, frequently associated with "the Day of YHWH (יהוה יום)," occupies large tracts in the OT prophets.[25] They frequently employ prosecutorial indictments and warnings against both Israel and the nations, as well as promise messianic redemption for both Israel and the nations. Yet they present their cases in light of the future coming/day of YHWH, prototyped in Gen 3:8. The personal return and manifest presence of YHWH is viewed as the radical cause of future change for all humanity and, indeed, all creation. Thus, the prophetic corpus in particular emphasizes an unfinished narrative which anticipates its completion at the personal return of the One whose identifying name/title is *YHWH*.[26] This revelatory metanarrative in the Jewish Scriptures is, of course, foundational to the significance of the NT writers—particularly the biographers of Jesus—applying OT YHWH-texts to Jesus.

---

[21] Cf. McComiskey, "God, Names of," 351.

[22] Cf. Isbell's overlapping argument for God's identity and promissory presence in the use of אהיה in Isbell, "The Divine Name אהיה as a Symbol of Presence in Israelite Tradition," 101–18.

[23] Cf. Abba, "The Divine Name Yahweh," 327; Máire Byrne, *The Names of God in Judaism, Christianity and Islam* (London; New York: Continuum, 2011), 24.

[24] Cf. Abba, "The Divine Name Yahweh," 327–28.

[25] The exact phrase, יהוה יום, occurs at least fifteen times in the Prophets, while similar expressions using יום are even more numerous. The concept is especially strong in Isaiah, Jeremiah, Ezekiel, Joel, Amos, Obadiah, Zephaniah, Zechariah, and Malachi. Cf. Joel D. Barker, "Day of the Lord," *Dictionary of the Old Testament Prophets*, 132–43; Craig A. Blaising, "The Day of the Lord: Theme and Pattern in Biblical Theology," *BSac* 169 (2012): 3–19. Significantly, Mark D. Vander Hart, "The Transition of the Old Testament Day of the LORD into the New Testament Day of the Lord Jesus Christ," *MJT* 9.1 (1993): 8, observes, "it should be clearly noted that the Day of YHWH is one in which YHWH is seen as the sole Actor."

[26] See discussion below on the contributions of N. T. Wright. Cf. Lister, *The Presence of God*, 247.

Appellations of YHWH in the Greek Old Testament

Roman Hellenization of lands in and around Palestine brought the inevitable need for a Greek translation of the Hebrew Scriptures. Initial efforts in Alexandria, Egypt, in the third century BC reportedly focused on translating the Torah, while a number of later efforts produced translations eventually covering the entire OT (likely) by the mid-first century before Christ.[27] Although some modern scholars are careful to distinguish the Old Greek (OG) of early translation efforts from later versions, tradition would come to label the general collection of Greek translations of the Hebrew Scriptures originally produced during the third to first centuries BC as the *Septuagint* (LXX).[28]

Scholars question the extent to which the LXX manuscripts available today came from Jewish or Christian scribes. In surviving manuscripts copied by Christian scribes, the divine name is translated over 6,000 times by the Greek word for "lord," κύριος (*kurios* or *kyrios*, depending on which transliterary schema is preferred), likely chosen because scrupulous Jews frequently had been substituting the Hebrew, אדני (*adonai*, "Lord"), for the sacred Tetragrammaton.[29] θεός (*theos*, "God"), is also used to translate the Tetragrammaton in available LXX manuscripts, but much less frequently.[30] Would the Jews have used these titular appellations as substitutes for the revered divine name? Or is the practice in the vast majority of known LXX manuscripts a Christian invention? Scholars have long known that κύριος is used for יהוה by both Josephus and

---

[27] Cf. Karen H. Jobes and Moisés Silva, *Invitation to the Septuagint*, 2nd ed. (Grand Rapids, MI: Baker Academic, 2015), 17–32; Pavlos D. Vasileiadis, "The God *Iao* and His Connection with the Biblical God, with Special Emphasis on the Manuscript 4QpapLXXLevb," *Vetus Testamentum et Hellas* 4 (2017): 26.

[28] From the Latin, *septuaginta* ("seventy"), frequently abbreviated by the Roman numeral LXX. The title is short for *Interpretatio septuaginta virorum*, or "the translation of the seventy men," in reference to the seventy-member (or seventy-two-member: six translators from each tribe of Israel) translation team of the Pentateuch in third century BC Alexandria. Many scholars, however, find this tradition suspect. For more detailed accounts of the traditional origins of the LXX, see, Henry Barclay Swete and Richard Rusden Ottley, *An Introduction to the Old Testament in Greek*, 2nd ed. (Cambridge, Cambridge University Press, 1914), 1–28; Jobes and Silva, *Invitation to the Septuagint*, 17–24.

[29] Ferdinand Hahn, *The Titles of Jesus in Christology* (London: Lutterworth, 1969), 71–72, has written, "It is, however, overwhelmingly probable that the κύριος of the LXX presupposes that אֲדֹנָי was already in existence as a term of replacement.... But the use of Kyrios as a description of God raises no problem, because the term was an obvious translation of the *Qᵉrê* אֲדֹנָי, and furthermore the LXX use had probably already become fully established in Jewish and Christian churches of the Hellenistic sphere; this will no doubt explain the penetration of the LXX formula in those contexts with κύριος." Edwin Keith Broadhead, *Naming Jesus* (Sheffield, England: Sheffield Academic, 1999), 136, adds, "Within pre-Christian Palestine, Jews probably spoke of Yahweh in Hebrew as *'ādōn*, in Aramaic as *mārê* and *māryā*, and in Greek as κύριος." And, R. Kendall Soulen, "The Name of the Holy Trinity: A Triune Name," *ThTo* 59.2 (2002): 249–50, draws further implications: "I would argue that, far from being moribund, the Tetragrammaton is alive and well in the New Testament. It has not been buried beneath periphrastic speech anymore than it is buried today among reverent Jews who intentionally refrain from pronouncing it. On the contrary, the Tetragrammaton directs the logic of the New Testament's identification of God the way that magnetic north directs the needle of a compass. For those with ears to hear, the unspoken Tetragrammaton speaks on every page."

[30] Harris, *Jesus as God*, 24–25, offers these figures: "Although the tetragrammaton יהוה occurs some 6,823 times in the Hebrew Bible (BDB 217b), it is rendered by θεός in the LXX only 353 times. These instances are scattered sparsely throughout all four sections of the LXX, although the equation יהוה = θεός sometimes occurs frequently in particular sections.... But, as noted above, by far the most common LXX rendering of יהוה is (ὁ) κύριος (6,156 instances)."

Philo, but the copies we have of these Jewish authors date after Christ and, therefore, could have been doctored by Christian scribes.[31]

The answer is not a simple one, because the available Greek manuscripts of confirmed Jewish origin are a very small minority[32] and often retain the Hebrew Tetragrammaton for the divine name.[33] Significantly, however, there is at least one manuscript among the Dead Sea Scrolls (DSS) of the divine name being transliterated into Greek with ιαω (at Lev 3:12 and 4:7),[34] showing that at least one Jewish scribe prior to Jesus believed that the Tetragrammaton could be transliterated/interpreted without defiling the divine name.[35] This occurrence also implies that the name of YHWH still may have been pronounced orally by at least some Jews in the late Second Temple period, although this remains inconclusive.

More importantly, however, are cases in which the Jewish translators of the DSS used various appellations for the Tetragrammaton (or other forms of the divine name).

---

[31] See, for example, George Howard, "The Tetragram and the New Testament," *JBL* 96.1 (1977): 70–71; James R. Royse, "Philo, Κυριος, and the Tetragrammaton," in *Heirs of the Septuagint*, ed. David T. Runia, David M. Hay, and David Winston (Atlanta, GA: Scholar's Press, 1991), 183.

[32] Greek manuscripts compose just three percent of all discovered manuscripts among the Dead Sea Scrolls, according to Emanuel Tov, "The Greek Biblical Texts from the Judean Desert," in *The Bible as Book*, ed. Scot McKendrick and Orlaith A. O'Sullivan (London: British Library; New Castle, DE: Oak Knoll Press, 2003), 97.

[33] See, François Bovon, "Premiéres Christologies: Exaltation et Incarnation, Ou de Pâques â Noël," *ETR* 85.2 (2010): 195; Howard, "The Tetragram and the New Testament," 65; Garber, "Teaching the Shema," 144; Ben Witherington III and Kazuhiko Yamazaki-Ransom, "Lord," *Dictionary of Jesus and the Gospels*, 528.

[34] Emanuel Tov, "The Greek Biblical Texts from the Judean Desert," 102, among others (see next footnote), points out that document 4QpapLXXLev^b has ΙΑΩ for the divine name. Cf. Jobes and Silva, *Invitation to the Septuagint*, 184.

[35] There is varied speculation about what precipitated the use of ΙΑΩ for the divine name in this pre-Christian Greek translation of this Hebrew text in Leviticus. Tov, "The Greek Biblical Texts from the Judean Desert," 112–13, believes it "reflects the earliest attested stage in the history of the LXX translation, when the name of God was represented by its transliteration, just like any other personal name in the LXX." Martin Rösel, "The Reading and Translation of the Divine Name in the Masoretic Tradition and the Greek Pentateuch," *JSOT* 31.4 (2007): 424–25, speculates, "it seems clear to me that from the very beginnings of the translation of the Pentateuch, the translators were using κύριος as an/the equivalent for the Hebrew name of God, following a principle of replacing the sacred name with the word אדני. In a Jewish monotheistic milieu, this development is easily understandable, since the use of a *name* as a means of identifying (and distinguishing) one god from others was now no longer needed—there was but one God. And yet obviously this practice was not generally accepted in Judaism, as the later replacement by the Hebrew *tetragrammaton* shows. From even later sources we also know that there were circles that pronounced the name of God as ΙΑΩ, and that not merely for magical reasons. This custom must have been considered extremely unusual, if not heretical, in the eyes of those Jews and Christians who were used to calling upon God using the title 'Lord' (κύριος or אדני). Therefore, the ΙΑΩ readings in the biblical manuscript 4QLXXLev^b are a mystery still awaiting sound explanation. What can be said, is that such readings cannot be claimed to be original." Michael Antony Hylton, "Reflections on the Use of the Name Yahuwah (Yahweh) or IAO in the Early Church Communities," *International Journal of Humanities and Social Science* 3.4 (2013): 96, believes that "Kurios is conspicuous by its absence in the early years of the Church up until 150 AD .... [and speculates that] Iao has been in use in the early church much more than perhaps we would have suspected." Frank Shaw, *Earliest Non-Mystical Jewish Use of Ιαω* (Leuven, Belgium; Walpole, MA: Peeters Publishers, 2014), 257, concludes that the evidence is too uncertain to espouse whether יהוה, ΙΑΩ, or κύριος is original to the LXX. But he is confident that the use of ΙΑΩ in "mystical sources such a magical papyri, gems, and metal tablets, or Gnosticism ... did not

Hebrew terms for "Lord" and "God" were often surrogates for the divine name (even in *Greek* translations!), but so were symbols and spaces—providing evidence that at least some Jewish scribes had scruples not only about pronouncing the divine name but also translating it into Greek.[36] Thus, while there is no confirmed pre-Christian case of substituting *kurios* for YHWH in the LXX, the practice of substituting titles and other appellations is certainly pre-Christian, likely having roots in the Exilic period.[37]

It is now generally acknowledged that there was no universal scribal standard for translating the Tetragrammaton into Greek.[38] But the known variety of practices during the later Second Temple period (and beyond) vindicates the standard practice of using *kurios* for YHWH in the LXX manuscripts now available.[39] Thus, whether or not the common practice of using "Lord" for the divine name in the vast majority of known LXX manuscripts is primarily of Jewish or Christian origin, its basis is certainly of

---

really begin in any earnest until the second century" and, thus, "has no connection with the use of ΙΑΩ in the DSS." See also, Frank Shaw, "The Transition of Ιαω from Non-Mystical to Mystical Use and Its Implications for Scholarship," *BN* 176 (2018): 65, 72. Pavlos D. Vasileiadis and Nehemia Gordon, "Transmission of the Tetragrammaton in Judeo-Greek and Christian Sources," *Accademia: Revue de La Société Marsile Ficin* 18 (2019): 22, note and speculate that "a re-evaluation of the available evidence has led to a new consensus that the Old Greek contained either a Greek form of the Tetragrammaton (like ιαω) or the four Hebrew letters of the divine name. The Tetragrammaton was replaced with κc (κυριος) and θc (θεος) in copies of the Septuagint by Christian scribes in the 2nd century, although it persisted in some manuscripts until as late as the 10th century. Hence, the New Testament may have also originally contained the Tetragrammaton in Greek or Hebrew script. Although no surviving text of the Greek New Testament has been found containing the Tetragrammaton, it has been reconstructed in many New Testament verses by translators and scholars."

[36] Howard, "The Tetragram and the New Testament," 65–66, notes that Hebrew forms of the Tetragrammaton preceded Greek surrogates, even in Greek translations. Norm Mundhenk, "Jesus Is Lord: The Tetragrammaton in Bible Translation," *BT* 61.2 (2010): 56, describes more of the variety found in Greek translations and suggests that *kurios* became the prominent appellation of *YHWH* in later LXX texts because of the common Jewish practice of substituting *Adonai* for *YHWH*. Rösel, "Reading and Translation of the Divine Name," 419, 424–25, acknowledges that no known pre-Christian LXX manuscript can be shown to have kurios in the place of YHWH, but he, nevertheless, argues that kurios would have been used in the original LXX translations. Vasileiadis and Gordon, "Transmission of the Tetragrammaton in Judeo-Greek and Christian Sources," 15, 22, note that "the Tetragrammaton has been transmitted in Greek mainly by (a) nontranslation, (b) semantic translation, and by (c) conversion of scripts that includes both transliteration and transcription," but that the most recent scholarly consensus finds the introduction of kurios for YHWH to have been "by Christian scribes in the 2nd century."

[37] Hylton, "Reflections on the Use of the Name Yahuwah (Yahweh) or IAO in the Early Church Communities," 92, however, finds "that *adon* or *adonai* for which the Greek *kurios* is a translation is rarely used as a substitute for the tetragrammaton in the dead sea scrolls." See, also, the discussion by Vasileiadis and Gordon, "Transmission of the Tetragrammaton in Judeo-Greek and Christian Sources," 15.

[38] Vasileiadis and Gordon, "Transmission of the Tetragrammaton in Judeo-Greek and Christian Sources," 15, write, "For a number of reasons already discussed elsewhere, 'there is no unique or universally "correct" rendering of the Hebrew Tetragrammaton in Greek.' Instead, there is evidence for more than a hundred different renderings of the Tetragrammaton in Greek, including both transcriptions and transliterations." See also, Vasileiadis, "The God Iao and His Connection with the Biblical God," 29–30, and, Tov, "P. Vindob. G 39777 (Symmachus) and the Use of the Divine Names in Greek Scripture Texts," 7–8.

[39] Curiously, Rösel, "Reading and Translation of the Divine Name," 425, goes even further, arguing from the variety of pre-Christian translations that κύριος was most likely original in the oldest Greek translations.

Jewish origin, and its practice appears to have been common when Christians penned the NT.[40] This view is further supported from scholarly consensus that most OT quotations in the NT appear to be from LXX texts rather than from known Hebrew texts.[41]

Thus, the evidence suggests that *kurios* likely became a common substitute for *YHWH* in Greek translations of the Hebrew-Aramaic Scriptures by the time of the NT.[42] In any case, the standardized use of *kurios* for both YHWH and Jesus in all ancient Greek NT MSS becomes highly significant.

Jewish Monotheism and YHWH's Uniqueness in the Shema

The uniqueness of the divine name reflects the uniqueness of the OT God. Despite recent claims that (at least Second Temple) Jewish monotheism was not absolute but embraced gradients of divinity, the OT Scriptures portray YHWH in a category by

---

[40] Wilkinson, *Tetragrammaton*, 88, writes, "it appears prudent to conclude that there was no one way of way of [sic] presenting the Tetragrammaton or its substitutes in the Greek Biblical texts of the time of the Apostle Paul. But importantly, the evidence of anticipations of the Palestinian *Qere* in the LXX Prophets and the usage of Philo prevent us from excluding *tout court* the presence of *kurios* in Jewish Greek biblical manuscripts." Broadhead, *Naming Jesus*, 136, finds the discussion complex but the scales tipped with the likely factor that "[w]ithin pre-Christian Palestine, Jews probably spoke of Yahweh in Hebrew as *'ādōn*, in Aramaic as *mārê* and *māryā*, and in Greek as κύριος." Richard Bauckham, *Jesus and the God of Israel* (Grand Rapids, MI: Eerdmans, 2008), 190, is convinced that Paul, for example, "could not have been unaware of the function of *kurios* as representing the Tetragrammaton."

[41] Cf. Hylton, "Reflections on the Use of the Name Yahuwah (Yahweh) or IAO in the Early Church Communities," 92; Pavlos D. Vasileiadis, "Exodus 3:14 as an Explanation of the Tetragrammaton: What If the Septuagint Rendering Had No Platonic Nuances?" *BN* 183 (2019): 106. Mundhenk, "Jesus Is Lord," 57, writes perceptively, however, that it is likely "the readers of the Jewish scriptures understood that the Tetragrammaton should be replaced with a word meaning 'Lord,' whether in Hebrew or in Greek. If that is true, then it was not (just) because of LXX that NT writers used *kurios* when quoting from the Old Testament. If they were quoting from LXX, they would certainly use *kurios*. But even if they happened to be using the Hebrew text (as they apparently did at times, whether actually referring to a manuscript or quoting from memory), whenever they came to the Tetragrammaton they would have read *'Adonai*. When translating the passage into Greek, they would have naturally rendered *'Adonai* as *kurios*. There is therefore no basis for arguing that NT writers used *kurios* because they were in some way misled by their reliance on LXX. *Kurios* would be the natural term to use even if they were quoting directly from the Hebrew and translating into Greek as they did so. Furthermore, even when referring to some manuscripts of LXX, they would have been reminded every time they saw it that the word they were writing as *kurios* was actually the Tetragrammaton.... This is an extremely important point for theologians and translators to consider. It means that in the development of early Christian theology, the Jewish point of view which required the replacement of YHWH by *'Adonai* can no longer be looked at as just an unfortunate curiosity of Jewish tradition. On the contrary, it was precisely this requirement which led to the Tetragrammaton being read as 'Lord' both in the Hebrew and in the Greek. Early Christians called Jesus 'Lord,' and frequently applied OT passages referring to *YHWH*/Lord to Jesus. It seems clear that the use of this common term is a key factor in the identification of Jesus with God by the early Christians."

[42] Although Vasileiadis, "Exodus 3:14 as an Explanation of the Tetragrammaton," 122, thinks that the scribal convention of using *nomina divina* to mark the divine name and titles may not have been practiced until the common era, he nevertheless points out that the use of *kurios* for YHWH occurred "in Jewish non-biblical literature since around the second century BCE"—more evidence that both Second Temple Jews and first generation Christians would have at least recognized, if not practiced, the convention of using *kurios* to represent the divine name.

himself.⁴³ Pagan gods are exposed as no gods at all, while YHWH is the only creator of all things.⁴⁴ Although heavenly and human agents are at times given god-like functions, they are distinguished from YHWH as his creaturely representatives and servants.⁴⁵ Even exalted beings (heavenly angels, human kings) are not worshiped with biblical approval.⁴⁶ Rather, the creator-creature divide is consistently maintained throughout the biblical record, in which YHWH is the central character and the ultimate sovereign of all that he created.

The creator–creature distinction is notably protected in the central representative creed of Judaism, the *Shema*, succinctly declared in Deut 6:4–5:

> Hear, O Israel: YHWH our God, YHWH [is] one. And you shall love YHWH your God with all your heart and with all your soul and with all your might.

The *Shema*'s emphasis in triplicate of the Tetragrammaton ties the divine name not only to the central imperative of God's covenant claim upon Israel ("you shall love YHWH"), but also to his own unique deity (YHWH "our God" is "one"). His personal relations and exalted identity show a combination of both immanence and transcendence in his nature. As N. T. Wright observes, the Jewish monotheism of the OT is both a *creational* (transcendent) and a *covenantal* (immanent) monotheism.⁴⁷ But it is YHWH's transcendent divinity which makes him unique to Jewish monotheism; he does not claim to be the top of a pyramid of divine beings, but to be the "sole creator and sole ruler" of all other beings and things.⁴⁸

Implications of OT monotheism for the NT understanding of Jesus will be addressed in more detail later with examination of the Synoptic Gospels. But two more points deserve mention here. First, the clearest intertextual OT passage to the *Shema* does not occur until one of the latter prophets: "YHWH will be king over all the earth.

---

[43] Richard Bauckham, *God Crucified* (Grand Rapids, MI: Eerdmans, 1998), 10–11, summarizes Jewish monotheism as, "YHWH, the God of Israel, is sole Creator of all things and sole Ruler of all things." Contra Adela Yarbro Collins, "The Worship of Jesus and the Imperial Cult," in *The Jewish Roots of Christological Monotheism*, ed. Carey C. Newman, James R. Davila, and Gladys S. Lewis (Leiden; Boston: Brill, 1999), 236; J. R. Daniel Kirk, *A Man Attested by God*, 2–4, 99; Paula Fredriksen, *When Christians Were Jews* (New Haven, CT: Yale University Press, 2018), 186–87.

[44] Richard Bauckham, "Biblical Theology and the Problems of Monotheism," in *Out of Egypt*, ed. Craig G. Bartholomew et al. (Bletchley, Milton Keynes, UK; Grand Rapids, MI: Paternoster Press; Zondervan, 2004), 212, observes, "The other category of 'gods' consists of the gods of the nations, reduced to the status of powerless nonentities by the biblical texts' insistence on YHWH's uniquely supreme power, and ridiculed as 'non-gods' and 'nothings'." Cf. Nathan MacDonald, *Deuteronomy and the Meaning of "Monotheism*," 2nd ed. (Tübingen: Mohr Siebeck, 2012), 95–96.

[45] P. Maurice Casey, "The Deification of Jesus," in *1994 Seminar Papers*, ed. Eugene H. Lovering Jr. (Chicago, IL: Scholars Press, 1994), 699–701, however, argues that both the Danielic Son of Man, and the Pauline Jesus in Phil 2:6–11 are not presented as having "full deity." More recently, J. R. Daniel Kirk, *A Man Attested by God*, e.g., 1–4, 44–47, has argued that the Synoptics never portray Jesus as divine/God but as an "idealized human figure." Larry W. Hurtado, *Ancient Jewish Monotheism and Early Christian Jesus-Devotion* (Waco, TX: Baylor University Press, 2017), 215–16, points out, however, that exalted human agents and angels, unlike Jesus, are never worshiped approvingly.

[46] Cf. Hurtado, *Ancient Jewish Monotheism and Early Christian Jesus-Devotion*, 178, 183; Bauckham, "Biblical Theology and the Problems of Monotheism," 212.

[47] See, N. T. Wright, "Jesus and the Identity of God," *ExAud* 14 (1988): 44–45.

[48] Again, Bauckham, *God Crucified*, 10–11.

On that day YHWH will be one and his name one" (Zech 14:9).[49] Alluding to the *Shema*, this prophecy describes not only the future relation (immanence) of YHWH to all his creation but the future oneness/uniqueness (transcendence) of his name, prompting the question: Since YHWH was already declared in the *Shema* to be the sovereign God who is "one," how will he become "king" and his "name" become "one" after the Exile? Zechariah's context (14:1–21) answers this question by describing the future in terms of cosmic judgment and renewal in the coming "day of the LORD (YHWH)," an expectant stance shared generally by the Prophets (e.g., Isa 11; Joel 2; Zeph 3; Mal 4).[50]

Second, the Jewish monotheism of the *Shema* is assumed and retained by the Christian-penned NT, no doubt because the founder of Christianity and his first disciples were steeped in Jewish monotheism.[51] When Jesus was asked to identify the greatest commandment, he not only cited the imperative to love God, but, according to Mark's account, he included the basis of the greatest command of the Law, which is the identity of the Lawgiver from the *Shema*: "Hear, O Israel, the Lord our God, the Lord is one" (Mark 12:29).[52] *Shema*-connected monotheism is affirmed throughout the NT (e.g., Matt 4:10; 1 Cor 8:4–6; Jas 2:19). Thus, the NT affirms the "Jewish monotheism" of YHWH in continuity with the OT and its definitive expression in Jewish history.[53]

---

[49] Daniel I. Block, "How Many Is God? An Investigation into the Meaning of Deuteronomy 6:4–5," *JETS* 47.2 (2004): 208–9, writes, "Given the theological and confessional weight of the Shema' it is remarkable how faint are its echoes in the OT. And when it is finally sounded, it breaks out of the parochial and ethnocentric box of Moses' original utterance with a supranational boom. After almost a thousand years of history in which the Shema' proved to be 'more honored in the breach than in the observance,' after the horrors of destruction and exile had signaled the suspension of the covenant blessings (586 BC), and after Yahweh had revisited his people only 'in small measure,' we hear the only certain OT echo in Zech 14:9."

[50] The prophetic "day of the Lord" appears to see its fulfillment in the day of the Lord Jesus Christ, according to NT writers. Many scholars have made the connection, including, C. E. B. Cranfield, "The Witness of the New Testament to Christ," in *Essays in Christology for Karl Barth*, ed. T. H. L. Parker (London: Lutterworth, 1956), 78–79; Oscar Cullmann, *Early Christian Worship* (Philadelphia, PA: Westminster Press, 1953), 91–92; Robert M. Bowman and J. Ed Komoszewski, *Putting Jesus in His Place* (Grand Rapids, MI: Kregel, 2007), 230.

[51] Esteban J. Hidalgo, "The Shema Through the Ages: A Pre-Modern History of Its Interpretation," *Andrews University Seminary Student Journal* 2.2 (2016): 18, writes, "The use of the Shema by NT writers also affirms early Judaism's concept of the universal oneness of God (cf. Mark 12:29–30, 32–33; Gal 3:20; Jas 2:19). Jesus accepted the common understanding of the Shema during his day as seen in an evaluation of the Great Commandment pericope in the Synoptics (Mat 22:34–40; Mark 12:28–34; Luke 10:25–28). Jesus quoted the Shema as the 'first and greatest commandment,' in keeping with the tendency among Jewish teachers of his day to search for the central, unifying tenets of the Torah."

[52] Bauckham, "Biblical Theology and the Problems of Monotheism," 227–28, also finds an allusion to the *Shema* in John 10:30 and in Jesus's subsequent "oneness statements" with the Father (10:38; 14:10, 11, 20; 17:21, 23).

[53] Soulen, *The Divine Name(s) and the Holy Trinity*, 34–35, writes of 1 Cor 8:5–6, "This passage is both a confession of Christian faith and an evocation of Judaism's primal confession, 'Hear, O Israel: The LORD is our God, the LORD alone.' Paul's aim is not to 'break' with the Shema, but to express its truth in a new way, by placing the figure of Jesus Christ *inside* the ancient confession, as it were.... Jesus Christ's participation in God's uniqueness is emphasized by applying eye-catching orthography not only to the 'one God,' as we might expect, but also to 'one Lord, Jesus Christ.'" Cf. Bauckham, "Biblical Theology and the Problems of Monotheism," 224.

Appellations of the Divine Name in the Gospels

As noted earlier, by the time of the NT writings, the Tetragrammaton was being replaced in Greek translations of the Hebrew Scriptures primarily with the titular appellation, κύριος. Although some scholars have argued that early versions of the Gospels likely utilized either the Hebrew Tetragrammaton, Hebrew surrogates (such as אדני, "Lord"), or Greek transliterations of the divine name, the evidence for this is questionable, and the fact is that no ancient manuscripts with these options are known today. Until such a manuscript appears, it remains clear that the first-century church typically substituted κύριος (or, much less frequently, θεός) as a Greek appellation for the God of the OT, who had revealed himself as YHWH.

The Gospels also use surrogates such as "King" and, especially, "Father" to refer to the holy God of OT background, YHWH. The title, *Father*—primarily in the speech of Jesus—sees a wide range of usage: "(the) Father," "my/your Father," "(Our) Father who is in heaven/heavenly Father," "holy/righteous Father," "the living Father," "One who is your Father," "Abba, Father." The practices of circumlocution and illeism by Jesus both underscore the use of surrogate titles as appellations for the divine name.[54] Therefore, the interpreter should recognize that the absence of the Tetragrammaton in the Gospels (as well as the rest of the NT) is only literal. The divine name is represented extensively by Greek appellations, which amount to interpretive translations. Thus, the NT authors anticipated their largely Jewish readership "hearing" the divine name behind an appellation or other descriptor from the OT background.

Κύριος *as the Primary Appellation of the Divine Name*

Although "Father" is used frequently in the Gospels as a title for God by Jesus (expectantly, for one who claimed filial cognizance of being "the [unique] Son" of God), it is not the most frequently used appellation for God in the NT as a whole. Rather, *kurios* and *theos* are more numerous overall. However, when OT YHWH-texts are quoted and alluded to in the NT, *kurios* is by far the favored term of translation.[55] This titular appellation possesses great significance for this study, as long as interpreters recognize that many OT YHWH-texts are referenced in the NT without the term *kurios*. Of greater importance is whether an identifiable OT YHWH-text is clearly applied to Jesus—regardless of whether *kurios* is employed.

---

[54] Illeism is the use of the third person to refer to oneself—a category of indirect surrogate language. Ervin Roderick Elledge, "The Illeism of Jesus and Jahweh: A Study of the Use of the Third-Person Self-Reference in the Bible and Ancient Near Eastern Texts and Its Implications for Christology" (PhD diss., Southern Baptist Theological Seminary, 2015), especially, 156, 187–89, notes that YHWH, far more often than any other OT figure, uses the convention of illeism, while Jesus is the only figure in the NT to use it (cf. "Son," "Son of Man," "Son of God," "Christ," "Lord," etc.), an apparently deliberate allusion to the divine practice.

[55] Cf. Martin Hengel, *Studies in Early Christology* (London; New York: T&T Clark, 2004), 380–81; Capes, *Old Testament Yahweh Texts in Paul's Christology*, 39–50; Crispin H. T. Fletcher-Louis, *Christological Origins*, vol. 1 of *Jesus Monotheism* (Eugene, OR: Wipf & Stock, 2015), 10.

Other Designations of the One God in the Gospels

As mentioned, various substitutionary titles other than *Lord*—such as *God, King, Father*, and circumlocutions like *the Most High* or *Heaven*—may be employed by NT authors referencing the God who is self-named "YHWH" in the OT. Circumlocutions use distinguishing associations, as in "the kingdom of *heaven* [=God]" (Matt 3:2) or "*the living* Father" (in contrast to dead or false fathers/gods; John 6:57).[56] But readers must recognize that a reference to a YHWH-text may employ no title at all. The NT may simply apply to Jesus qualities or actions that are unique to YHWH. A case in point appears to be Jesus's "walking on the sea" (cf. Mark 6:48, 49), which brings to mind the description of YHWH's uniqueness in Job 9:8, "who alone stretched out the heavens and treaded the waves of the sea." Whether or not this example may be identified as a YHWH-text applied to Jesus will be confirmed later. But it serves to alert readers to the probability that the term *kurios* (or any other name/title for God) is not required to be present in a NT text that applies an OT YHWH-text to Jesus.

The Phenomenon of Old Testament YHWH-Texts Applied to Jesus

The example above of Jesus walking on the sea indicates one probable occurrence of a YHWH-text being applied to Jesus in Mark. The example presented in the opening of this chapter—Heb 1:10–12 quoting Ps 102:25–27—is even more easily defended.[57] And the examples mentioned from Capes's work demonstrate the phenomenon in the Epistles of Paul. This suggests that at least three NT authors—Mark, the author of Hebrews, Paul—show evidence of the practice. Is the practice embraced by a much wider scope of NT authors? Even in a cursory overview, it appears to be so.

---

[56] Cf. R. Kendall Soulen, "'Hallowed by Thy Name!': The Theological Significance of the Avoidance of God's Name in the New Testament," in *Strangers in a Strange Land*, ed. Lucy Lind Hogan and D. William Faupel (Lexington, KY: Emeth Press, 2009), 145–46; R. Kendall Soulen, "Jesus and the Divine Name," *USQR* 65.1–2 (2015): 50–53.

[57] Dennis E. Johnson, *Him We Proclaim* (Phillipsburg, NJ: P&R, 2007), 185, comments, "The title 'Lord' (*kyrios*) appeared in the sixth (and longest) of the seven Old Testament citations leading up to this exhortation. Whereas the series opened with texts showing the Son's superiority to angels (1:5, citing Ps. 2:7 and 2 Sam. 7:14; cf. also Heb. 1:6 'the firstborn' and 1:8 'the Son'), in the later Scripture citations the Son is not only accorded divine titles (1:8 'O God'; 1:10 'Lord') but also credited with the divine task of creation and the divine attribute of immutability (1:10–12, citing Ps. 102:25–27). The latter truth—the fact that, whereas earth's foundations will perish and the heavens will wear out, 'you are the same, and your years will have no end' (Heb. 1:12)—becomes a recurring motif in Hebrews' proclamation of Christ. Most explicit is the echo of Psalm 102:27 in the epistolary conclusion that the preacher has appended to his sermon, in which the hearers are reassured that even though one generation of beloved leaders has passed from the scene, 'Jesus Christ is *the same* yesterday and today and forever' (Heb. 13:8)" (emphasis Johnson). The equating of Jesus with YHWH can also be visualized in the chiastic structure of the immediate context, showing the intertwined status of Jesus as both Davidic King and God:

Jesus's Superior "Name" as both Davidic and Divine
A Conceptual Chiasm of Hebrews 1:5–13

A – The Son's Status as Davidic King (cf. Ps 2:7; 2 Sam 7:14)	Heb 1:5
B – The Son's Status as God (cf. Deut 32:43; Ps 104:4)	Heb 1:6–7
C – The Son's Status as Divine Davidic King (cf. Ps 45:6–7)	Heb 1:8–9
B' – The Son's Status as God (cf. Ps 102:25–27)	Heb 1:10–12
A' – The Son's Status as Davidic King (cf. Ps 110:1)	Heb 1:13

Its Ubiquity in the New Testament

A brief survey of the NT reveals that at least seven of the nine NT authors demonstrate the practice of applying OT YHWH-texts to Jesus.[58] Examples above from Paul and the author of the Epistle to the Hebrews have already been mentioned.

Additionally, the four Evangelists may be included in their united use of the same OT text(s), which they all implement to identify Jesus as YHWH (and John the Baptist as the messenger sent before YHWH to prepare the way for his coming).[59] The OT passage primarily in view is Isaiah 40:3: "A voice cries, 'In the wilderness prepare the way of YHWH.'" The Evangelists are united in quoting this YHWH-text and placing Jesus in YHWH's position, as the one for whom the "voice" (John the Baptist), prepared the way (cf. Matt 3:1–13; Mark 1:1–9; Luke 3:1–22; John 1:19–34). Although some scholars dispute that all the Evangelists understood Jesus to be the manifest presence of YHWH promised in Isa 40:4, their joint application of the same text to Jesus (and to John as forerunner of YHWH) is uncanny if any of the Gospel writers did *not* perceive Jesus as fulfilling the quoted text in the position of YHWH. In any case, this study shall briefly touch on other representative examples in the following section and shall thoroughly examine numerous examples in each Synoptic Gospel in the following three chapters.

Furthermore, in the NT, Peter demonstrates the phenomenon. First Peter 3:14–15 is a clear allusion to Isa 8:12–14, in which the people of God are urged not to fear their adversaries but to "honor YHWH as holy." Peter makes the same contrast urging believers not to fear their adversaries but to "honor Christ as holy." This application of a YHWH-text to Jesus is likely not a mistake or coincidence, because Peter had just (1 Pet 2:8) applied the same Isaianic passage (Isa 8:14) to Jesus as the "stone of stumbling and rock of offense," a description of YHWH in its original OT context.

If these cases or others of applying YHWH-texts to Jesus are legitimate, then the seven most-prolific NT authors (granted traditional authorship)—Luke, Paul, John, Matthew, Mark, author of Hebrews, Peter—are united in demonstrating the phenomenon. Only James and Jude seem not to contain obvious cases of the practice.[60] But as the two least-prolific of the nine NT writers, this pattern makes reasonable sense. Note the pattern in Table 1.1, in which *many* refers to "clearly more than five" and *few* refers to "apparently two to four."

---

[58] Cf. Carl Judson Davis, *The Name and Way of the Lord* (Sheffield, England: Sheffield Academic Press, 1996).

[59] Davis, *The Name and Way of the Lord*, 92–93, argues, "it is unlikely that these Greek speaking Jews could read τὴν ὁδὸν κυρίου messianically. Furthermore, evidence of the closeness between the phrase τὴν ὁδὸν τοῦ κυρίου and τὴν ὁδὸν τοῦ θεοῦ exists in Acts 18.25 and 26."

[60] Christfried Böttrich, "'Gott Und Retter': Gottesprädikationen in Christologischen Titeln," *NZSTh* 42.3 (2000): 230–31, however, makes the case that "the judge at the door" in Jas 5:9 equates the coming Lord Jesus with the "the only lawgiver and judge" (i.e., YHWH) in 4:12, the "God" already referenced in 2:19. It may be that "the judge at the door" has an OT YHWH-text(s) for its basis in the mind of James. If so, then here would be yet another YHWH-text application to Jesus, making James the eighth of nine NT writers to employ the phenomenon.

Table 1.1 YHWH-Texts Applied to Jesus by NT Author

NT Author	Percentage of NT by Greek Word Count	Occurrences of YHWH-Texts Applied to Jesus
Luke	27.5	many
Paul	23.5	many
John	20.4	many
Matthew	13.3	many
Mark	8.2	many
Author of Hebrews	3.6	few
Peter	2.0	few
James	1.3	?
Jude	0.3	?

If the same author wrote Luke and Acts, then Luke penned 27.5 percent of the NT by word count. This affords him the highest probability of demonstrating the phenomenon of applying YHWH-texts to Jesus—assuming it was a settled and accepted practice among the apostolic writers. The point is this: if the NT authors were united in their understanding of Jesus as the self-disclosure of YHWH promised in the OT, then the more each author wrote, the more likely he might be to demonstrate such an understanding by applying YHWH-texts to Jesus.

And that is precisely what the pattern supports. New Testament writers who penned at least 8 percent of the NT appear to include many (5+) occurrences of the phenomenon; writers who penned from 2 to 4 percent of the NT appear to have few (2–4) occurrences; and writers who penned less than 2 percent appear not to have demonstrated the phenomenon in any obvious way. These data are tentative, of course, at least in part until the Synoptics have been carefully surveyed in the following chapters. But, if Table 1.1 has any accuracy, then the general pattern—that the more a NT writer contributed to the canonical corpus the more likely he was to employ the practice of applying OT YHWH-texts to Jesus—is transparently true.

Its Presence in the Canonical Gospels

Defining the Gospels' genre is somewhat controversial among NT scholars. Propositions range from historical biography to religious myth. Perhaps the best understanding of what the Evangelists intended, however, may be described as "theological biography." Expressed and implied intentions from the Gospels' texts include both (biographical) documentation and (theological) interpretation of the life of Jesus. This double lens of the *theological* application of YHWH-texts to the *historical* Jesus may distinguish the canonical Gospels from the non-canonical gospels of the first two centuries.

Occurrences of YHWH-texts applied to Jesus in the Synoptic Gospels shall be demonstrated in the following chapters. But an introductory word is pertinent here: the phenomenon occurs in a variety of fashions which seem to reflect the personal preferences and theological emphases of the Evangelists. Although overlap is certain— and arguably inevitable, due to their unity of genre and subject matter—each Evangelist does not slavishly copy another but frequently expresses his own perspective and differs in the arrangement of his materials, resulting in a variety of ways that YHWH-texts are utilized in the disclosure of Jesus's identity.

For example, although all four Evangelists[61] see fulfillment in the prophecy of Isa 40:3 and/or Mal 3:1 with the public appearance of Jesus (with John the Baptist as his forerunner), the identification each one makes between YHWH and Jesus may be viewed on a continuum from the more subtle implication in John's account to the more straightforward identification in Mark's account. The distinctive intent and style of each Evangelist comes out in unique explications of the YHWH-text phenomenon.

Numerous other examples will be addressed later, but singular cases may be offered here from each Gospel writer. (1) More than any other Evangelist Matthew cites Jesus using the formulaic divine address, κύριε κύριε, in reference to himself (Matt 7:21, 22; 25:11). Each occurrence highlights Matthew's focus on Jesus's eschatological teaching that he, as the Son of Man, will be mankind's final judge. In the OT, only YHWH is addressed by the doublet, "kurie, kurie" (LXX), and has absolute judicial authority at the Final Assize. (2) In Mark, while all the Synoptics record Jesus calling himself "Lord of the Sabbath" (Matt 12:8; Mark 2:28; Luke 6:5), an implied identification with YHWH who is the creator and owner of the Sabbath (Exod 31:12–17), only Mark records Jesus pre-empting the claim with the authoritative interpretation, "The Sabbath was made for man, not man for the Sabbath," highlighting a common Markan focus on Jesus's interpretive authority. (3) In Luke 19:10, the third Evangelist is not content to parallel Matthew's abbreviated reference in 18:11 (only some manuscripts; see discussion of Luke 19:9–10) to Ezek 34:16 of YHWH's claim to seek the lost. Rather, he quotes Jesus as tying in more of Ezekiel's context (Table 1.2).

Table 1.2 Luke's Fuller Allusion to Ezekiel's YHWH-Text

Ezekiel 34:12, 16	Matthew 18:11	Luke 19:10
"I [YHWH] will seek out My sheep, and I will save them.... I will seek the lost."	"The Son of Man came to save the lost."	"The Son of Man came to seek and to save the lost."

Whether Matthew had written 18:11 and the parable of the lost sheep beforehand or not, Luke's version demonstrates an independent understanding with a more complete application of a YHWH-text to Jesus. (4) Although "I AM" statements of Jesus are found in the Synoptics (e.g., Matt 14:27; Mark 14:62; Luke 22:70),[62] John's

---

[61] J. Massingberd Ford, "'He That Cometh' and the Divine Name (Apocalypse 1, 4. 8; 4, 8)," *JSJ* 1.2 (1970): 145–47, points out another fourfold Gospels parallel that potentially identifies Jesus with YHWH: "It is Psalm 118 which all four evangelists accommodate to Jesus as He enters Jerusalem (Matthew 21, 9, Mark 11, 9, Luke 19, 38 (compare 13, 35) and John 12, 13)." James R. Harrison, "Modern Scholarship and the 'Nature' Miracles: A Defense of Their Historicity and Affirmation of Jesus' Deity," *RTR* 72.2 (2013): 89–90, 101, similarly finds Jesus's assumption of YHWH's prerogatives in multiple-attestation miracle accounts.

[62] P. Maurice Casey, *From Jewish Prophet to Gentile God* (Cambridge: J. Clarke & Co.; Louisville, KY: Westminster/Knox Press, 1991), 26, overlooks this fact and, therefore, arrives at a regrettable conclusion: "The 'I am' statement at John 6.35, 48 is only one of a group of such statements.... The synoptic Jesus does not make statements of this kind. If the Jesus of history did in fact make them, the omission of every one of them from the synoptics is simply incomprehensible."

Gospel contains a seven-fold fullness of occurrences, making their emphasis a distinguishing characteristic of the Fourth Gospel. Scholars have noted in them, particularly in John 8:58, apparently deliberate allusions to YHWH's giving and explanation of his name in Exod 3:14–15.

Thus, it appears that the four Evangelists not only practiced the phenomenon of applying OT YHWH-texts to Jesus, but each did so in unique ways that show some independence from the others. Confirmation of their personal styles and emphases, as well as some interdependence, will unfold to a greater degree as each of the Synoptics is examined in the subsequent chapters.

The Significance of the Phenomenon for Christological Studies

The ever-broadening sea of Christological studies can be daunting to navigate.[63] Traditional categories of Christ's person and work as found in Scripture are no longer the focus in many scholarly circles. This study, however, focuses on the biblical teaching of Christ as found intertextually between the Old and New Testaments. Furthermore, the application of OT YHWH-texts to Jesus in the Synoptic Gospels narrows the scope drastically. However, even this specific topic touches on a number of overlapping issues, such as Jewish monotheism, the divine name/Tetragrammaton and its translation, Septuagintal origins and transmission, the NT use of the OT in both Hebrew and Greek, theophanies, divine agents, incarnation, pre-existence, dual natures (divine and human), the use of *kurios* in the LXX and NT, and the meaning of Christ's lordship in the Scriptures.[64] While studies on these topics and more may factor into the discussion of this study, past scholarship that is most relevant revolves around the origin and meaning of Jesus as Lord. This is the case because the Jewish practice of substituting "Lord" for "YHWH," the primary LXX and NT term for *Lord* (κύριος), and the NT meaning of Jesus's *lordship*, largely interact with the practice of applying YHWH-texts to Jesus.[65]

---

[63] Charles A. Gieschen, "Confronting Current Christological Controversy," *CTQ* 69.1 (2005): 3, before surveying modern Christological views, likewise states, "The past two centuries, in fact, have witnessed Christological controversies that rival and surpass those early ones."

[64] Paul J. Achtemeier, "Gospel Miracle Tradition and the Divine Man," *Int* 26.2 (1972): 188, discussed another related, but now rightfully abandoned, christological question: "Did the early Christian tradition—which underlies and which has received written form in our New Testament Gospels and epistles, and which, as the language alone testifies, was intended for the Hellenistic world at large—also use the hermeneutical device of divine man in interpreting the figure of Jesus? That is, did early Christology attempt to understand and present the earthly Jesus by making use of motifs belonging to the Hellenistic concept of *theios anēr*?" R. T. France, "Development in New Testament Christology," in *Crisis in Christology*, ed. William R. Farmer (Livonia, MI: Dove Booksellers, 1995), 63–64, asks the more vital question for biblical Christology: "Was the increasingly sophisticated Christology of the New Testament authors (and still more of subsequent Christian discussion) due to the addition of new ideas which substantially changed the underlying understanding of Jesus, or was it simply working out more explicitly what was already there?"

[65] Douglas J. Moo, "The Christology of the Early Pauline Letters," in *Contours of Christology in the New Testament*, ed. Richard N. Longenecker (Grand Rapids, MI: Eerdmans, 2005), 188, of the Pauline corpus writes, "If 'Christ' is Paul's most common designation of Jesus, 'Lord' is his most important . . . . The importance of the title in Paul's letters can be gauged from such texts as Rom 10:9, where the

Thus, since an historical survey of scholarship on how the Gospels apply YHWH-texts to Jesus would contain relatively few key figures, and since the larger question of Jesus's lordship and divinity may be greatly affected by the phenomenon, a survey of modern scholarship on *Jesus as Lord* may prove valuable. Additionally, this section will address the general neglect of YHWH-texts in critical views of Jesus and the Gospels, as well as affirm the importance of YHWH-texts for wider Christological discussions.

Modern Scholarship on the Origin and Meaning of Jesus as Lord

Prior to the Enlightenment of the eighteenth century, biblical scholarship from the Patristic writings through the Reformation generally perceived and promoted the deity of Jesus Christ as a doctrine detected in the canonical Scriptures and expressed in the historic creeds.[66] But with the exaltation of human reason and scholastic skepticism over Scripture, the biblical texts and teachings began to be questioned or jettisoned altogether. In particular, the canonical Gospels became objects of "higher criticism" with the presupposition that the supernatural Jesus they describe cannot be accepted as historically true by the modern mind. "Lessing's Ditch,"[67] which assumes an impassable divide between empirical reason and unverifiable "historical truth" (anticipating the later distinction between "the Jesus of history and the Christ of faith")[68] has continued to be a widely held

---

confession 'Jesus is Lord' summarizes Christian commitment (see also Rom 14:9; 1 Cor 12:3)." Cf. I. Howard Marshall, *The Origins of New Testament Christology* (Downers Grove, IL: InterVarsity Press, 1976), 97; Vincent Taylor, *The Names of Jesus* (London: Macmillan, 1953), 68; Robert W. Yarbrough, "Jesus Christ, Name and Titles Of," in *Evangelical Dictionary of Biblical Theology*, ed. Walter A. Elwell (Grand Rapids, MI: Baker, 1996), 409.

[66] Colin Brown, "Quest of the Historical Jesus," in *Dictionary of Jesus and the Gospels*, ed. Joel B. Green, Jeannine K. Brown, and Nicholas Perrin, 2nd ed. (Downers Grove, IL; Nottingham, England: IVP Academic, 2013), 719, suggests that Christian scholarship before the Reformation could be called "the quest for the theological Jesus," who is "construed within the context [of] the belief systems of Christian tradition."

[67] Cf. Gotthold Ephraim Lessing, "On the Proof of the Spirit and of Power," in *Lessing: Philosophical and Theological Writings*, ed. and trans. H. B. Nisbet from the German, 1777 (Cambridge; New York: Cambridge University Press, 2005), 87, (in)famously wrote, "This, this is the broad and ugly ditch which I cannot get across, no matter how often and earnestly I have tried to make the leap. If anyone can help me over it, I beg and implore him to do so. He will earn a divine reward for this service. And so I repeat what I said above, and in the same words. I do not deny for a moment that prophecies were fulfilled in Christ; I do not deny for a moment that Christ performed miracles. But since the truth of these miracles has ceased altogether to be proved by miracles still practicable today, and since they are merely reports of miracles (however undisputed and indisputable these reports may be), I do deny that they can and should bind me to the least faith in the other teachings of Christ." John M. Frame, *A History of Western Philosophy and Theology* (Phillipsburg, NJ: P&R, 2015), 222, analyzes, "The deists simply rejected Scripture because they thought only natural revelation was credible. Lessing is more specific. He rejects any foundation of Christian faith based on historical events. But of course, this means that he, like the deists, rejects the gospel, a message of good news about historical events. Later generations of theologians would talk much about 'Lessing's ditch' and would try to reply to it. Orthodox theologians did not admit to a problem here. For them, our faith is based on history, but not on an autonomous analysis of history. God has spoken to us in Scripture, and we authenticate the Scripture not by an autonomous analysis of its history, but by Scripture's self-testimony illumined by the Holy Spirit."

[68] Scholars generally attribute the first expression of this distinction to Martin Kähler, *The So-Called Historical Jesus and the Historic, Biblical Christ* (Philadelphia, PA: Fortress Press, 1964), trans. Carl E. Braaten of *Der songenannte historische Jesus und der geschichtliche, biblische Christus* (Leipzig: A. Deichert, 1896). Kähler writes of a distinction between *historisch* and *geschichtlich*, a problem for English translators who attempt to show the differing nuances.

presupposition of modern critical scholarship. That assumption has spawned various "quests for the historical Jesus" in the nineteenth and twentieth centuries and predisposed scholarly opinion in many quarters against recognizing any "historical Jesus" who could have disclosed himself as both man and God.

The (First) Quest for the Historical Jesus

The first so-called "quest of the historical Jesus" during the period 1778–1906, which is roughly in line with the evaluation of Albert Schweitzer,[69] included some of the most radical approaches to understanding Jesus and the Gospels. Hermann Samuel Reimarus's posthumously published work (released by G. E. Lessing in 1774–78), *Apologie oder Schutzschrift für die vernünftigen Verehrer Gottes* ("An Apology or Defense for the Rational Worshipers of God"),[70] is generally viewed, following Schweitzer, as kicking off historical Jesus research. Reimarus described the NT presentation of Jesus as an apostolic fabrication not in line with the aims of their deceased teacher.[71] The historical Jesus, he believed, was a Jewish preacher of a soon-to-come kingdom whose expectations failed when he was killed. His disciples stole his body in order to propagate the claim of a resurrected Christ and thereby salvage the movement.[72]

David Friedrich Strauss's *Das Leben Jesu, kritisch bearbeitet* (*The Life of Jesus, Critically Examined*, German edition, 1835)[73] is also significant among early attempts to uncover the historical Jesus. Strauss posited that the miracles of Jesus were embellished myths. Influenced by Hegelian philosophy, Strauss viewed Jesus not as uniquely divine, but as a symbol that all humanity is one with God.[74]

The works of William Wrede on the "messianic secret" (*Das Messiasgeheimnis in Den Evangelien*, 1901)[75] and Schweitzer himself on "life of Jesus research" (*Vom Reimarus zu Wrede: Geschichte der Leben-Jesu-Forschung*, 1906; retitled for English publication as *The Quest the Historical Jesus*)[76] mark a close to the "First Quest" era. Wrede challenged the historical accuracy of Mark's Gospel and argued that Jesus never claimed to be the messiah.[77] Schweitzer, while decrying liberalism's failed attempts to

---

[69] The phrase was popularized by the English title of Albert Schweitzer, *The Quest of the Historical Jesus: A Critical Study of Its Progress from Reimarus to Wrede*, trans. W. Montgomery (London: Adam & Charles Black, 1952).

[70] A relatively early English translation of Lessing's compilation of Reimarus can be found in Hermann Samuel Reimarus, *Fragments from Reimarus*, ed. Charles Voysey, trans. anonymous (London; Edinburgh: Williams and Norgate, 1879; repr. Lexington, KY: American Theological Library Association, 1962). For the first translation of Reimarus's most pertinent essay, see, Hermann Samuel Reimarus, *The Goal of Jesus and His Disciples*, trans. George Wesley Buchanan (Leiden, Netherlands: Brill, 1970).

[71] E.g., Reimarus, *The Goal of Jesus and His Disciples*, 62.

[72] Cf. Reimarus, *The Goal of Jesus and His Disciples*, 84, 95–96, 130.

[73] David Friedrich Strauss, *The Life of Jesus, Critically Examined* (Philadelphia, PA: Fortress, 1973).

[74] E.g., Strauss, *The Life of Jesus, Critically Examined*, 780.

[75] Cf. William Wrede, *Das Messiasgeheimnis in Den Evangelien*, 2nd ed. 1913 (Göttingen: Vandenhoeck & Ruprecht, 1963).

[76] Albert Schweitzer, *Von Reimarus Zu Wrede* (Tübingen, Germany: J. C. B. Mohr [Paul Siebeck], 1906). The full English title was *The Quest of the Historical Jesus: A Critical Study of Its Progress from Reimarus to Wrede*.

[77] Cf. William Wrede, *The Messianic Secret*, trans. J. C. G. Greig (Cambridge and London: James Clarke & Co., 1971), 215, 230.

find the historical Jesus, promoted a Jesus who first taught an imminent apocalypse, revised his mistaken view when the Son of Man did not return, then willingly sacrificed himself to shorten the misery caused by that failed return.[78] Nor did Jesus, a mere man, rise bodily from his grave. For Schweitzer, "in the last analysis, our relation to Jesus is mystical."[79]

Since the approaches of these and many other "lives of Jesus" scholars ruled out *a priori* any possibility of Jesus's divinity, there appeared little or no acknowledgment from First Questers that the Evangelists (except, perhaps, John) portrayed a Jesus who was self-aware and self-disclosing as God/YHWH in the flesh. Critical studies focused on demythologizing the Jesus of the Gospels, such that scholarship seemed largely unaware of its resulting "historical Jesus" losing any substantial likeness to the biblical portrayals. Scholars tended to discover a "Jesus" more like themselves and their assumptions than like the portraits painted in the Gospels.[80]

Despite the rise and influence of critical views of Jesus during the eighteenth and nineteenth centuries, however, there were some scholarly works which not only pointed out the divine claims of Jesus, but even noted some uses of OT YHWH-texts applied to him in the canonical Gospels. These include works by British statesman Ambrose Serle (1804), who claimed that the divine name, YHWH, is applied to each person of the trinity;[81] Yale Hebrew Scholar Alexander MacWhorter (1857), who connected the OT divine name to titles of Jesus such as the "the coming one" and "Lord";[82] and professor of theology at the University of Göttingen, Theodore Zahn (1894), who noted, for example, that Rom 10:13 applies YHWH-text Joel 2:32 to Jesus as the one who answers prayer and receives worship.[83]

Wilhelm Bousset's Theory and Critical Responses

The tide of higher critical scholarship, however, was unabated. And in the period sometimes designated as the "no quest" era, there appeared, in the view of many scholars, the most influential work ever written on the life of Jesus, Wilhelm Bousset's *Kyrios Christos: Geschichte Des Christusglaubens von Den Anfängen Des Christentums Bis Irenäus* (English edition, *Kyrios Christos: A History of the Belief in Christ from the*

---

[78] Henry B. Clark, "Albert Schweitzer's Understanding of Jesus as the Christ," *The Christian Scholar* 45.3 (1962): 236–37, defends Schweitzer's view of a mistaken, merely-human Jesus.

[79] Albert Schweitzer, *Geschichte Der Leben-Jesu-Forschung*, 2nd ed. (Tübingen, Germany: J. C. B. Mohr [Paul Siebeck], 1913), 641: "Im letzten Grunde ist unser Verhältnis zu Jesus mystischer Art." See also, Schweitzer, *The Quest of the Historical Jesus*, 399.

[80] Cf. William Baird, *From Jonathan Edwards to Rudolf Bultmann*, vol. 2 of *History of New Testament Research* (Minneapolis, MN: Fortress, 2003), 234: "In short, scholars dedicated to historical research had constructed a nonhistorical Jesus—a Jesus who mirrored their own presuppositions."

[81] Ambrose Serle, *Horae Solitariae*, 3rd ed. (London: J. Mills, 1804), 6, writes, "The title Jehovah ... is applied to the Father, as *Creator*, in Isa. lx. 16, and lxiii, 7–9; to the Son, as *Redeemer*, in Isa. lx. 16, and lxiii. 7–9; to the Spirit, as the *divine Agent*, Isa. lxi. 1–3; to the three Persons together, or Trinity in Unity, Deut. vi. 4" (emphasis Serle).

[82] See, Alexander MacWhorter, *Jahveh Christ, or, The Memorial Name* (Boston, MA: Gould and Lincoln, 1857), 141–43.

[83] See, Theodore Zahn, *Die Anbetung Jesu Im Zeitalter Der Apostel*, 5th ed. (Leipzig, Germany: Deichert's Publishing House, 1910), 320–21. For an English translation of the first edition, see, Theodore Zahn, "The Adoration of Jesus in the Apostolic Age," trans. C. J. H. Ropes, *BSac* 51 (1894): 314–30, 389–406.

Beginnings of Christianity to Irenaeus).[84] Originally published in 1913, *Kyrios Christos* occupies a watershed position in Christological studies.

Essentially, Bousset argued that the discerning scholarly eye can see that the Jesus of the canonical Gospels is a Hellenized embellishment (with miracle stories) of an earlier messianic picture of Jesus.[85] This is evidenced particularly in the titular use of κύριος ("Kyrios") for Jesus in the NT. For Bousset, the borrowing of the Greek term and concept of κύριος for Jesus led the Hellenistic Christian community outside Palestine to read the divine lordship of Jesus back into the OT, something that the monotheistic Jewish Christians in Jerusalem would never have attempted. He writes,

> Now it becomes clear that it was no accident that we did not encounter the title Kyrios on Palestinian soil in the gospel tradition. Such a development would not have been possible here. This placing of Jesus in the center of the cultus of a believing community, this peculiar doubling of the object of veneration in worship, is conceivable only in an environment in which Old Testament monotheism no longer ruled unconditionally and with absolute security.... I have already disputed that people in the Hellenistic primitive communities had read the title κύριος out of the Old Testament. It certainly has its own roots. But after this designation for Christ had once been adopted, people naturally read it into the Old Testament and connected the sacred name of God with Jesus of Nazareth.[86]

For Bousset, the faster-growing Pauline communities eventually outstripped the more traditionally Jewish "Johannine enclave" with a developing doctrine of Jesus as Kyrios.[87] It did not take many decades before "[t]he spirit of unconquerable and stalwart Old Testament monotheism [was] transferred to the Kyrios worship and the Kyrios faith!"[88] Bousset sought to support his thesis by turning particularly to the Apostolic Fathers and Apologists. Interestingly, he noticed that Second Clement actually cites the speech of an OT YHWH-text as coming from the mouth of Jesus.[89] But for Bousset, this and other language about Jesus in the early generations of the church was a natural development of the Hellenistic Christian mindset, not an understanding and imitation of the Jewish Apostolic teaching, and it resulted in a blurring of the distinction between God and Christ.[90]

Although Bousset was hailed by Rudolf Bultmann[91] and others of the "no quest" period of the early twentieth century, he was not without significant critics. Geerhardus Vos responded by saying that Bousset conveniently avoided discussion of passages

---

[84] Wilhelm Bousset, *Kyrios Christos: A History of the Belief in Christ from the Beginnings of Christianity to Irenaeus*, trans. John E. Steely (Nashville, TN: Abingdon, 1970). For a German edition, see, Wilhelm Bousset, *Kyrios Christos: Geschichte Des Christusglaubens von Den Anfängen Des Christentums Bis Irenäus*, 5th ed. (Göttingen: Vandenhoeck & Ruprecht, 1965).
[85] E.g., Bousset, *Kyrios Christos*, 98, 103.
[86] Bousset, *Kyrios Christos*, 147, 149.
[87] Cf. Bousset, *Kyrios Christos*, 287.
[88] Bousset, *Kyrios Christos*, 151.
[89] Bousset, *Kyrios Christos*, 319.
[90] See, for example, Bousset, *Kyrios Christos*, 317, 382–84.
[91] See Rudolf Bultmann, "Introductory Word," Bousset, *Kyrios Christos*, 7–9.

challenging his thesis.⁹² J. Gresham Machen pointedly observed that Bousset's hypothesis largely ignored the Book of Acts as containing "the only extant narrative of the early progress of Jerusalem Christianity"⁹³ and fumbled the evidence in 1 Corinthians 16:22 of a primitive Aramaic (i.e., *Jewish* Christian) confession of Jesus as "Lord."⁹⁴ Alfred Rawlinson agreed with this last observation, writing famously, "The phrase *Maran tha* is in fact the Achilles' heel of the theory of Bousset."⁹⁵

Subsequent Quests for the Historical Jesus

Despite these criticisms, Bousset's theory thrived until, roughly, the time of the so-called "new (or, second) quest" of the historical Jesus inaugurated by Günther Bornkamm⁹⁶ and Ernst Käsemann⁹⁷ in the 1950s. Although they had been disciples of Bultmann, they opposed his complete bifurcation between a largely unknowable "Jesus of history" and a largely mythical "Christ of faith" by rethinking the criteria for what could be considered historically reliable in the NT accounts.⁹⁸

It was Oscar Cullmann, however, who more strongly asserted the identity of the historical Jesus with the Christ of the Gospels. For Cullman, the commonly juxtaposed concepts of *Historie* and *Geschichte* were bested by the approach of *Heilsgeschichte*. History and theological interpretation did not necessarily contradict each other, but could be mutually informative. Thus, the central Christian belief that Jesus is Lord could again be understood, not as an evolving theological construct developed later from Hellenistic thought, but as a teaching that actually originated from Jesus himself.⁹⁹ Cullmann saw the primitive church applying OT YHWH-texts to Jesus soon after the resurrection.¹⁰⁰ But he was just one representative in a tide of scholarship flowing

---

⁹² Geerhardus Vos, "The Kyrios Christos Controversy," *PTR* 15.1 (1917): 33: "Bousset passes by in silence the pericope about the Messiah being David's Lord." Regarding usage patterns of κύριος in the Gospels, Vos argues against Bousset, 49, "The attitude of all three Evangelists appears to be determined by considerations of tact and is not the result of historical evolution."
⁹³ J. Gresham Machen, *The Origin of Paul's Religion* (Grand Rapids, MI: Eerdmans, 1925), 285.
⁹⁴ Machen, *The Origin of Paul's Religion*, 301.
⁹⁵ A. E. J. Rawlinson, *The New Testament Doctrine of the Christ* (London: Longmans, Green and Co., 1926), 236–37. Cf. Matthew Black, "The Christological Use of the Old Testament in the New Testament," *NTS* 18.1 (1971): 9–10.
⁹⁶ Cf. Günther Bornkamm, *Jesus von Nazareth* (Stuttgart, Germany: W. Kohlhammer, 1956).
⁹⁷ Cf. Ernst Käsemann, "Das Problem Des Historischen Jesus," *ZTK* 51 (1954): 125–53.
⁹⁸ For a synopsis of form-critical guidelines often used in identifying "authentic" sayings of Jesus, see, Robert H. Stein, "The 'Criteria' for Authenticity," in *Gospel Perspectives*, ed. R. T. France and David Wenham (Sheffield, England: JSOT Press, 1983), 225–63. Cf. Craig L. Blomberg, *The Historical Reliability of the Gospels*, 2nd ed. (Nottingham, England; Downers Grove, IL: Apollos; IVP Academic, 2007), 310–11.
⁹⁹ Oscar Cullmann, "'Kyrios' as Designation for the Oral Tradition Concerning Jesus," *SJT* 3.2 (1950): 183, writes, "I agree indeed with the great majority of scholars that 1 Cor. 11.23 deals with a tradition through the Church, and not with a vision; but I should like to explain the fact that Paul refers it back to the *Lord* rather in terms of the whole complex of *paradosis* in the New Testament. I should like to show that, seen in this connexion, the designation *Kyrios* not only points to the historical Jesus as the chronological beginning of the chain of tradition, as the first member of it, but accepts the exalted Lord as the real Author of the whole tradition developing itself in the apostolic Church. Thus the apostolic *paradosis* can be set directly on a level with the exalted *Kyrios*. The *Lord* is Himself at work in the tradition of His words and deeds through the Apostles; He works through the apostolic church" (emphasis Cullmann).
¹⁰⁰ Cf. Cullmann, *Early Christian Worship*, 91–92; Cullmann, *The Christology of the New Testament*, 217–19, 234–35; Cullmann, "All Who Call on the Name of Our Lord Jesus Christ," 13.

against Bousset, Bultmann, and the bifurcation of a Palestinian Jesus from a Hellenistic Jesus[101]—as well as against the skepticism of "Lessing's Ditch" and the bifurcation of the historical Jesus from the Christ of faith.[102]

However, despite the concurrent trend in biblical theology since the 1970s[103] to move away from the atomization of biblical texts and to understand the Gospels as historically-informed narratives, some scholars continued to practice a severe brand of form criticism intent on identifying and separating editorial layers within the Gospels. Members of "The Jesus Seminar" of the 1980s and 1990s, in particular, sought to redefine various criteria of authenticity in order to determine the probabilities of Jesus making any of the statements found in the canonical Gospels and the Gospel of Thomas.[104] Their findings suggested that very little of the canonical Gospels contain the authentic words of Jesus.[105] Judged by their criteria,[106] the Jesus of The Jesus Seminar is virtually unknowable historically and certainly did not consider himself to be the

---

[101] C. H. Dodd, in particular, should be noted for his parallel studies in the NT use of OT and his defense of the view that early Christianity was only minimally influenced by Hellenism but greatly influenced by Jesus's own use of the OT. See, for example, Dodd, *According to the Scriptures* (London: Nisbet and Company, 1952), 27, 110, 115, 136.

[102] Representative works critical of Bousset's theory to varying degrees include Taylor, *The Names of Jesus*; Werner Kramer, *Christ, Lord, Son of God*, trans. Brian Hardy (Chattam, UK: SCM Press, 1966); I. Howard Marshall, "The Development of Christology in the Early Church," *TynBul* 18 (1967): 77–93; Marshall, *The Origins of New Testament Christology*; Hendrikus Boers, "Where Christology Is Real," *Int* 26.2 (1972): 300–327; Black, "The Christological Use of the Old Testament in the New Testament," 9–10.

[103] The 1970 publication often viewed as marking the demise of a "biblical theology" based on the presuppositions of higher criticism is Brevard S. Childs, *Biblical Theology in Crisis* (Philadelphia, PA: Westminster, 1970). Since then, a flood of "biblical theologies" have been written from positions which recognize significant redemptive-historical unity within each canonical book, within each Testament, and/or within the Bible as a whole.

[104] The findings of the Jesus Seminar are laid out in Robert Walter Funk and Roy W. Hoover, eds., *The Five Gospels* (Toronto; New York: Macmillan, 1993). See also, Robert Funk, "The Jesus Seminar and the Quest," in *Jesus Then & Now*, ed. Marvin Meyer and Charles Hughes (Harrisburg, PA: Trinity Press International, 2001), 130–39.

[105] A few examples of the Seminar's skepticism—one for each Evangelist—include the following from Funk and Hoover, *The Five Gospels*, 60: "[Mark 4:39–41] ... *Rebuking wind & wave*. The words ascribed to Jesus in this story would not have circulated independently during the oral period; they reflect what the storyteller imagined Jesus would have said on such an occasion", 199–200; "[Matt 14:1–33] ... *Loaves & fish for 5,000. Jesus walks on the sea*. None of the words attributed to Jesus in these stories falls into the category of aphorism, parable, or witty reply. As a consequence, the Fellows were unanimous in their view that the relatively few sentences quoted from Jesus were the creation of the storyteller. Like storytellers in all cultures and ages, the evangelists invented words appropriate for the occasion and put them on the lips of their characters. This accounts, in some measure, for the large number of sayings designated black in the four narrative gospels", 380; "[Luke 20:41–44] ... *Son of David*. The sophistry involved in this argument over a citation of Ps 110:1, a favorite of the early Christian movement, was judged by the Fellows to be alien to Jesus, who did not ordinarily cite scripture. He also did not argue by manipulating words in the text and, so far as we know, he did not concern himself with questions about who the messiah was", 439; "[John 11:25–26] ... *Resurrection & life*. Jesus is credited with another I AM saying in connection with the resurrection of Lazarus (11:25). As we have noted in the cameo essay on the I AM sayings (p. 419), these formulations were widely used in the ancient Near East as speech attributed to God or the gods. There are also precedents in the Hebrew and Greek Bibles. In the Fourth Gospel they are the work of the author; they did not originate with Jesus" (emphasis Funk and Hoover).

[106] Cf. Funk and Hoover, *The Five Gospels*. Their criteria are supplemented by what is labeled "the seven pillars of scholarly wisdom," 3–5: "The first was the distinction between the historical Jesus, to be uncovered by historical excavation, and the Christ of faith encapsulated in the first creeds. The

"Lord" he is called throughout the NT. Their extreme skepticism, however, has been criticized by many.[107]

Apart from The Jesus Seminar and other higher critics, scholars of an alternate "third quest" have joined the Christological discussion. Their movement, in tandem with current trends in biblical theology, does not *a priori* separate the Christ of faith from the Jesus of history. Rather, it sees the canonical Gospels as historical-theological literature intending to communicate the truth of history with interpretive significance. In their view, no scholar may hope to discover the real Jesus by rejecting outright any of the biblical data devoted to disclosing who he is.

Recent Scholarship on Jesus: Hurtado, Bauckham, Wright, Hays, Capes

Whether they would consider themselves to be "third questers" or not, several scholars of the current generation have made notable contributions to Jesus research. The following interpreters, in particular, have advanced historical-theological conclusions closely related to the thesis of this study: Larry Hurtado, Richard Bauckham, N. T. Wright, Richard Hays, and David Capes. Although they maintain emphases unique to themselves and disagree with one another on some details, they are united in rejecting the central premise of Bousset and in recognizing to varying degrees the deliberate application of OT YHWH-texts to Jesus in the NT.

Larry W. Hurtado (1943–2019) produced a wealth of studies on Christology, most notably on the early Christian worship of Jesus. He promoted what he saw in the NT and other early Christian writings as a "binitarian pattern" of devotion to both God and Jesus.[108] Remarkably, according to Hurtado, the first Christians enthusiastically

---

second pillar consisted of recognizing the synoptic gospels as much closer to the historical Jesus than the Fourth Gospel, which presented a 'spiritual' Jesus.... The recognition of the Gospel of Mark as prior to Matthew and Luke, and the basis for them both, is the third pillar. A fourth pillar was the identification of material Matthew and Luke have in common beyond their dependence on Mark.... The liberation of the non-eschatological Jesus of the aphorisms and parables from Schweitzer's eschatological Jesus is the fifth pillar of contemporary scholarship.... A sixth pillar of modern gospel scholarship, to be explored subsequently consists of the recognition of the fundamental contrast between the oral culture (in which Jesus was at home) and a print culture (like our own).... The seventh and final pillar that supports the edifice of contemporary gospel scholarship is the reversal that has taken place regarding who bears the burden of proof. It was once assumed that scholars had to prove that details in the synoptic gospels were *not* historical.... The current assumption is more nearly the opposite and indicates how far scholarship has come since Strauss: the gospels are now assumed to be narratives in which the memory of Jesus is embellished by mythic elements that express the church's faith in him, and by plausible fictions that enhance the telling of the gospel story for first-century listeners who knew about divine men and miracle workers firsthand. Supposedly historical elements in these narratives must therefore be demonstrated to be so" (emphasis Funk and Hoover).

[107] A few representative responses critical of the Jesus Seminar include N. T. Wright, "Five Gospels but No Gospel: Jesus and the Seminar," in *Crisis in Christology*, ed. William R. Farmer (Livonia, MI: Dove Booksellers, 1995), 115–57; Luke Timothy Johnson, "The Jesus Seminar's Misguided Quest for the Historical Jesus," *ChrCent* 113.1 (1994): 16–22; Frank S. Thielman, "Evangelicals and the Jesus Quest: Some Problems of Historical and Theological Method," *Chm* 115.1 (2001): 61–73.

[108] E.g., Larry W. Hurtado, *Lord Jesus Christ* (Grand Rapids, MI: Eerdmans, 2003), 2–7; Larry W. Hurtado, *One God, One Lord*, 3rd ed. (London; New York: Bloomsbury T&T Clark, 2015), xv; Hurtado, *Ancient Jewish Monotheism and Early Christian Jesus-Devotion*, 100.

practiced binitarian devotion while remaining committed Jewish monotheists.[109] However, in this "mutation" of Christian monotheism, Jesus is considered to be both the direct expression of God and the chief agent of God. On the one hand he does God's will as God's servant, and on the other hand he is the recipient of prayers and divine veneration reserved for God alone:

> I have argued that in the earliest Christian texts we have evidence of a programmatic incorporation of Jesus in the beliefs and devotional practice of Christian groups, constituting an apparently novel "mutation" of ancient Jewish monotheism that is expressed in a distinctive "dyadic" devotional pattern. That is, in early Christian texts we have a strong affirmation of the uniqueness of the one God, combined with a programmatic incorporation of Jesus along with God in beliefs and in core, identifying ritual practices. In short, there are two distinguishable but linked figures, God and Jesus, in early Christians' religious discourse and practice, and yet they clearly seem to have thought of themselves as loyal to one God, and saw their reverence of Jesus as obedience to the one God.[110]

Hurtado delineated six features in the devotional practices of the early church which indicate and incorporate reverence to Jesus within their Jewish monotheism: "(1) hymnic practices, (2) prayer and related practices, (3) use of the name of Christ, (4) the Lord's Supper, (5) confession of faith in Jesus, and (6) prophetic pronouncements of the risen Christ."[111] Perhaps most notably for this study, however, is Hurtado's recognition that the NT writings, particularly the Pauline corpus, occasionally apply OT YHWH-texts to Jesus.[112]

Richard Bauckham (b. 1946) maintains that a high Christology existed in the early church before any of the NT was penned.[113] As for the NT documents themselves, he proposes that they contain a "Christology of divine identity" in which Jesus is not *added* to the identity of God but *included* in the divine identity without violating Jewish monotheism.[114] The supremely monotheistic creed of the *Shema* is actually used in passages such as Rom 11:36, 1 Cor 8:6, and John 10:30 for the inclusion of Jesus in the identity of God. Concerning 1 Cor 8:6, Bauckham writes,

> [Paul] is redefining monotheism as christological monotheism . . . . The *addition* of a unique Lord to the unique God of the Shemaʿ would flatly *contradict* the uniqueness of the latter. The only possible way to understand Paul as maintaining

---

[109] E.g., Hurtado, *Lord Jesus Christ*, 3.
[110] Hurtado, *Ancient Jewish Monotheism and Early Christian Jesus-Devotion*, 143.
[111] Hurtado, *One God, One Lord*, 105.
[112] See, for example, Hurtado, *One God, One Lord*, 133, 156–57; Hurtado, *Lord Jesus Christ*, 112; Hurtado, *Ancient Jewish Monotheism and Early Christian Jesus-Devotion*, 89–94.
[113] See esp., Richard Bauckham, *God Crucified* (Grand Rapids, MI: Eerdmans, 1998), 27; Richard Bauckham, *Jesus and the God of Israel* (Grand Rapids, MI: Eerdmans, 2008), 19.
[114] Cf. Bauckham, *God Crucified*, viii, 78; Bauckham, *Jesus and the God of Israel*, 19, 28, 101; Richard J. Bauckham, "Christology," *Dictionary of Jesus and the Gospels*, 127, 129; Richard Bauckham, "The Incarnation and the Cosmic Christ," in *Incarnation*, ed. Niels Henrik Gregersen (Minneapolis, MN: Fortress, 2015), 31–32.

monotheism is to understand him to be including Jesus in the unique identity of the one God affirmed in the Shemaʽ. But this is, in any case, clear from the fact that the term "Lord", applied here to Jesus as the "one Lord", is taken from the Shemaʽ itself. Paul is not adding to the one God of the Shemaʽ a "Lord" the Shemaʽ does not mention. He is identifying Jesus as the 'Lord' whom the Shemaʽ affirms to be one. Thus, in Paul's quite unprecedented reformulation of the Shemaʽ, the unique identity of the one God *consists of* the one God, the Father, *and* the one Lord, his Messiah.[115]

Bauckham further asserts that Jesus cannot be reduced to a mere agent or intermediary, because he is described in terms appropriate to God alone.[116] He believes that the deity of Jesus was not a Hellenistic development[117] but a recognition by the Jewish eyewitnesses of Jesus's resurrection.[118] Church Fathers after the Apostles through Nicaea "did not develop [a fully divine Christology] so much as transpose it into a conceptual framework constructed more in terms of the Greek philosophical categories of essence and nature."[119] The fact that all of the NT contains a high Christology is evidence of its first-generation acceptance in the church. Form criticism and historical Jesus approaches have failed in part, says Bauckham, because they have not reckoned with differences between oral and written transmission.[120]

One of the few to go beyond merely mentioning the phenomenon of OT YHWH-texts applied to Jesus, Bauckham actually constructs lists of occurrences, mainly in the Pauline corpus, but he notes a few cases in the Gospels, as well.[121]

Nicholas Thomas (N. T.) Wright (b. 1948), perhaps better known for his defense of the controversial "New Perspective on Paul," has made significant contributions to the study of Jesus. Wright shows how slippery the term *historical* has been in historical Jesus studies and seeks to orient the interpreter to the claims of Jesus's resurrection by the earliest Christians within the milieu of second-Temple Jewish and pagan Gentile worldviews.[122] Wright is a severe critic of the new (second) quest approaches to the

---

[115] Bauckham, *Jesus and the God of Israel*, 28 (emphasis Bauckham).
[116] Cf. Bauckham, "Biblical Theology and the Problems of Monotheism," 211–12. Bauckham, "Christology," 129, writes, "It is not enough to say, with some scholars, that Jesus exercises God's authority as his human agent, for as the passages in the OT cited above show, the prerogatives that Jesus claims are intrinsic to God's identity, inalienable aspects of what distinguishes God from all his creatures."
[117] E.g., Richard Bauckham, "Jesus, Worship Of," in *Anchor Bible Dictionary*, ed. David Noel Freedman (New York: Doubleday, 1992), 3:812–19.
[118] E.g., Richard Bauckham, *Jesus and the Eyewitnesses: The Gospels as Eyewitness Testimony*, 2nd ed. (Grand Rapids, MI: Eerdmans, 2017), 146, 290, 297, 508.
[119] Bauckham, *God Crucified*, viii.
[120] E.g., Richard Bauckham, "The Gospel of John and the Synoptic Problem," in *New Studies in the Synoptic Problem*, ed. P. Foster et. al. (Leuven; Paris; Walpole, MA: Peeters, 2011), 658–59; Bauckham, *Jesus and the Eyewitnesses*, 297–98, 611–12, 615.
[121] Bauckham, *Jesus and the God of Israel*, esp., 186–88, 219–21.
[122] See, N. T. Wright, *The Resurrection of the Son of God* (Minneapolis, MN: Fortress, 2008), 12–14, where Wright identifies five different ways in which scholars speak of "history" and its cognates: (1) as event, (2) as significant event, (3) as provable event, (4) as writing-about-events-in-the-past, and (5) as what modern historians can say about a topic. Cf. Wright, "Jesus and the Identity of God," 44–46; N. T. Wright, "The Biblical Formation of a Doctrine of Christ," in *Who Do You Say That I Am?*

historical Jesus of the 1950s to 1960s, as well as of The Jesus Seminar of the 1980s to 1990s.[123] In their stead, he proposes a "third quest" that seeks to give due to the Jewish eschatological context of Jesus's life and teaching.[124] In contrast to critical scholarship "lopping off" theological elements of the Gospels in the name of a supposed objectivity,[125] Wright points to a pervasive Jewish expectation of the personal coming/presence of YHWH for the deliverance of Israel in tandem with the arrival of the Jewish messianic king.[126] When Jesus came on the scene, says Wright, he was fully cognizant of this dual Jewish eschatological expectation and identified the arrival of God's rule and God's presence as being *in himself*.[127] Jesus thus lived as the embodied presence of YHWH, the fulfillment of Torah (divine authority) and Temple (divine presence).[128] Jesus himself is the climax to Israel's history:

> What Jesus has done, the evangelists are saying, is to bring to its climax not simply the chain of the stories of individual faithful Jews but the whole history of Israel. The gospels are therefore the story of Jesus *told as the history of Israel in miniature*: the 'typology' which is observed here and there by critics is simply a function of this larger purpose of the evangelists.[129]

Beyond a mere self-understanding, this theological stance was purposefully disclosed to his audiences by Jesus's performance of works that only YHWH can do.[130] He came,

---

Christology and the Church, ed. Donald Armstrong (Grand Rapids, MI: Eerdmans, 1999), 48, 65–66; N. T. Wright, "Jesus' Self-Understanding," in *The Incarnation*, ed. S. T. Davis, D. Kendall, and G. O'Collins (Oxford: Oxford University Press, 2002), 56–57.

[123] Cf. N. T. Wright, "The New, Unimproved Jesus," *Christianity Today* 37.10 (1993), esp. 24–26. Also, Wright, "Five Gospels but No Gospel," 146, criticizes, "One cannot tackle serious historical problems by taking them to bits and voting on the bits one by one. The only way forward must be the way of serious historiography, and one may search *The Five Gospels* from cover to cover in vain for such a thing. There are a good many people engaged in serious historical study of Jesus at the moment, but the Seminar in its corporate identity (as opposed to some of its individual members) cannot be reckoned among their number."

[124] Cf. Wright, *Jesus and the Victory of God*, 35, 80–83. And Wright succinctly summarizes, 123, "The Third Quest . . . correctly highlights Jewish eschatology as the key to understanding Jesus"; and again, 653, "I suggest, in short, that the return of YHWH to Zion, and the Temple-theology which it brings into focus, are the deepest keys and clues to gospel Christology."

[125] See, Wright, *The New Testament and the People of God*, 95.

[126] Cf. Wright, "Jesus and the Identity of God," 48; Wright, "The Biblical Formation of a Doctrine of Christ," 61; Wright, "Jesus' Self-Understanding," 56; N. T. Wright, "One God, One Lord," *ChrCent* 130.4 (2013): 22.

[127] Cf. Wright, "Jesus and the Identity of God," 46, 52–53; Wright, "The Historical Jesus and Christian Theology," 410; Wright, "The Biblical Formation of a Doctrine of Christ," 63–64, 66. Wright, "Jesus' Self-Understanding," 53, pointedly asks, "Can you have a serious Christology without having Jesus aware of it? This sounds like the sort of question one might set in a final degree examination, but it is actually a serious question facing our whole enterprise. One might suppose that the lower one's Christology, the less Jesus' awareness of it matters, but this is illusory: if Jesus was a human being and nothing more, part of the picture will precisely be that he was aware of being a human being and nothing more."

[128] Cf. Wright, "Jesus and the Identity of God," 46, 53; Wright, "The Historical Jesus and Christian Theology," 410; Wright, "The Biblical Formation of a Doctrine of Christ," 64–65; Wright, "Jesus' Self-Understanding," 57.

[129] Wright, *The New Testament and the People of God*, 401 (emphasis Wright).

[130] Cf. Wright, "Jesus and the Identity of God," 53; Wright, "The Biblical Formation of a Doctrine of Christ," 64–66; Wright, *The Resurrection of the Son of God*, 733.

then, as no mere intermediary—no mere messianic claimant like the contemporary failures who made no claims of divinity—but as YHWH incarnate, the one God of monotheistic Judaism.[131]

For Wright, such a Christological monotheism can be traced back only to Jesus himself.[132] Unfortunately, however, many critical scholars have *a priori* ruled out divine acts such as the resurrection as historically impossible—based on reductionist presuppositions of what may be considered historical—and subsequently cannot account for the immediate rise and spread of Christianity.[133] The approach of "critical realism," in which the meaning of the Evangelists' stories is found within their grander narrative and worldviews, is Wright's corrective to the abuses of both critical reductionism and naïve realism.[134]

According to Wright, all four Evangelists assume Jesus was divine.[135] And, while it is not crucial to his argument, Wright notes that a feature of their portrayals of Jesus is the phenomenon of OT YHWH-texts being applied generally to Jesus.[136] He sees Paul, however, as demonstrating the phenomenon more clearly by incorporating Jesus into the Jewish monotheistic *Shema* from Deut 6.[137]

Richard B. Hays (b. 1948) champions the intertextuality of the OT and NT, finding that the Gospels are built on an OT substratum.[138] He has written extensively on the

---

[131] E.g., Wright, "The Biblical Formation of a Doctrine of Christ," 48, writes, "I believe it is certain, historically, that Jesus believed himself to be the Messiah; but I believe it is also certain, that he radically redefined that role around his own dramatically different sense of vocation. If Jesus was the Messiah, he was quite unlike what most if not all of his contemporaries—including John the Baptist and the Twelve—were expecting in such a figure. But the point I particularly wish to make at this preliminary stage is a different one. As far as we can tell, none of the other would-be Messiahs in the first century thought for a moment that they were in any sense 'divine'; nor did their followers predicate any such thing of them." And Wright, "One God, One Lord," 23, commenting on 1 Cor 8:6, adds, "Jesus is not a 'second God'; that would abrogate monotheism entirely. He is not a semidivine intermediate figure. He is the one in whom the identity of Israel's God is revealed."

[132] Cf. N. T. Wright, *The Climax of the Covenant* (Minneapolis, MN: Fortress, 1993), 129; Wright, *The New Testament and the People of God*, 251; Wright, "Jesus and the Identity of God," 44–48.

[133] Cf. Wright, *The New Testament and the People of God*, 81, 93–95; Wright, *Jesus and the Victory of God*, 17–18. See esp. Wright, *The Resurrection of the Son of God*, 12–28, where he discusses five senses of "history" used and confused by scholars and thereby critiques various figureheads of critical theories. Also, see his discussion of Jesus's resurrection as historical (e.g., 686, 696, 712), summarized on 717: "The claim can be stated once more in terms of necessary and sufficient conditions. The actual bodily resurrection of Jesus (not a mere resuscitation, but a transforming revivification) clearly provides a *sufficient* condition of the tomb being empty and the 'meetings' taking place. Nobody is likely to doubt that. Once grant that Jesus really was raised, and all the pieces of the historical jigsaw puzzle of early Christianity fall into place. My claim is stronger: that the bodily resurrection of Jesus provides a *necessary* condition for these things; in other words, that no other explanation could or would do. All the efforts to find alternative explanations fail, and they were bound to do so" (emphasis Wright).

[134] E.g., Wright, *The New Testament and the People of God*, 61, 66.

[135] E.g., N. T. Wright, "Pictures, Stories, and the Cross: Where Do the Echoes Lead?," *JTI* 11.1 (2017): 49, 68.

[136] Cf. Wright, *Jesus and the Victory of God*, 600–4; Wright, "The Biblical Formation of a Doctrine of Christ," 63–65.

[137] Cf. Wright, *The Climax of the Covenant*, 125–29; Wright, "The Biblical Formation of a Doctrine of Christ," 56–57; Wright, "One God, One Lord," 22–23.

[138] Cf. Richard B. Hays, *Echoes of Scripture in the Gospels* (Waco, TX: Baylor University Press, 2016), 10, 166–67. Similarly, see Richard B. Hays, *Reading Backwards* (London: SPCK, 2015), 14.

NT use of the OT, using the categories of quotations, allusions, and echoes.[139] Hays has promoted the phrase "reading backwards" to emphasize how NT writers have connected pre-figural OT content to Jesus and his people.[140] The Evangelists, however, were not *inventing* these connections but *discovering* them as providential links from God, the author of history.[141] The story of Israel builds to a climax in Jesus, who replaces the Temple and "assumes and transforms" Israel's Torah and worship.[142] The narrative structures and purposes of the canonical Gospels are witness-bearing testimonies in history, demonstrating (unlike the non-canonical "gospels," such as *Thomas* and *Judas*)[143] their connection to, and fulfillment of, the OT.[144]

For Hays, Jesus and his works are revelatory, as can be seen in his portrayals by all four Evangelists.[145] The Gospels are united in identifying Jesus as the embodied presence of Israel's God, whose divine visitation is not through a mere intermediary.[146] Jesus's divine identity is demonstrated by his self-revelation, which can be seen in both Jesus's authoritative teaching in the role of God and in his performance of works which only God can do.[147] For Hays, Jesus is "the glory-bearing *eikon*," sharing the divine

---

[139] Hays, *Echoes of Scripture in the Gospels*, 10, explains, "These terms are approximate markers on the spectrum of intertextual linkage, moving from the most to the least explicit forms of reference. Generally speaking, a 'quotation' is introduced by a citation formula (e.g., 'as it is written'), or it features the verbatim reproduction of an extended chain of words, often a sentence or more, from the source text. An 'allusion' usually imbeds several words from the precursor text, or it at least in some way explicitly mentions notable characters or events that signal the reader to make the intertextual connection. It is difficult to separate the concept of allusion from notions of authorial intentionality; the meaning of a text in which an allusion occurs would be opaque or severely diminished if the reader failed to recognize the implied reference to the earlier text. 'Echo' is the least distinct, and therefore always the most disputable, form of intertextual reference; it may involve the inclusion of only a word or phrase that evokes, for the alert reader, a reminiscence of an earlier text. Readers who hear the echo will discern some semantic nuance that carries a surplus of significance beyond the literal sense of the text in which the echo occurs; ordinarily, however, the surface meaning of the text would be intelligible to readers who fail to hear the echoed language."

[140] See, for example, Hays, *Reading Backwards*, 2–3, 15–16, 77–78; Richard B. Hays, "Figural Exegesis and the Retrospective Re-Cognition of Israel's Story," *BBR* 29.1 (2019): 38–39.

[141] Cf. Hays, *Reading Backwards*, 37; Hays, "Figural Exegesis and the Retrospective Re-Cognition of Israel's Story," 43–44.

[142] E.g., Hays, *Reading Backwards*, 15–16, 45, 82, and, here, 87: "It is not accurate, then, to say that Jesus nullifies or replaces Israel's Torah and Israel's worship life. Rather, he *assumes* and *transforms* them" (emphasis Hays).

[143] See, Richard B. Hays, "Can Narrative Criticism Recover the Theological Unity of Scripture?," *JTI* 2.2 (2008): 211.

[144] Cf. Hays, *Reading Backwards*, xi, "the Gospel narratives are not simply artful edifying fictions; rather, they are testimony. The aim of these lectures is to listen carefully to their acts of narrative witness-bearing and to discern the ways in which their testimony is the product of a catalytic fusion of Israel's Scripture and the story of Jesus."

[145] Cf. Hays, *Reading Backwards*, 104; Hays, "Figural Exegesis and the Retrospective Re-Cognition of Israel's Story," 43.

[146] E.g., Hays, *Reading Backwards*, 48, 53–54, 67; Hays, *Echoes of Scripture in the Gospels*, 167–68; and, here, 175: "*Matthew highlights the worship of Jesus for one reason: he believes and proclaims that Jesus is the embodied presence of God and that to worship Jesus is to worship YHWH*—not merely an agent or a facsimile or an intermediary" (emphasis Hays). Cf. Hays, "Figural Exegesis and the Retrospective Re-Cognition of Israel's Story," 40, 46–47.

[147] E.g., Hays, *Reading Backwards*, 31, 70–71; Hays, *Echoes of Scripture in the Gospels*, 170, 174.

identity as the divine *kurios* of Israel.¹⁴⁸ Jesus identifies as the "I AM" of the Tetragrammaton,¹⁴⁹ claiming exaltation with God and receiving worship.¹⁵⁰

In support of these views, Hays often identifies cases of OT YHWH-texts applied to Jesus in the Gospels.¹⁵¹ The phenomenon becomes more apparent when one recognizes the common NT practice of *metalepsis*—the echoing of bits of the OT to make typological connections (particularly) to Jesus.¹⁵² Unfortunately, the atomization of NT texts by critical scholars tends to promote the neglect of such intertextuality, rendering some critics "tone-deaf."¹⁵³ For Hays, the intertextual connections discovered by "reading backwards" show just how extensively the apostolic community as a whole shared a high Christology.¹⁵⁴

David B. Capes (b. 1955) wrote his 1990 doctoral dissertation on "Paul's Use of Old Testament Yahweh-Texts and Its Implications for His Christology."¹⁵⁵ He more recently prefers the term "YHWH texts"¹⁵⁶ to describe the phenomenon of NT writers quoting

---

[148] See, Richard B. Hays, *Echoes of Scripture in the Letters of Paul* (New Haven, CT: Yale University Press, 1989), 153; Hays, *Reading Backwards*, 62, 69; Hays, *Echoes of Scripture in the Gospels*, 63.

[149] Hays addresses the phenomenon as it is often overlooked by others in Mark's Gospel: Hays, *Echoes of Scripture in the Gospels*, 72–73; Hays, *Reading Backwards*, 26.

[150] Cf. Hays, *Reading Backwards*, 53, 69. Hays, *Echoes of Scripture in the Gospels*, 167, clarifies, "The action of the disciples in worshiping Jesus (προσεκύνησαν αὐτῷ) is only one of numerous incidents in this Gospel [of Matthew] where various characters are depicted in the posture of worshiping him ... 2:2, 11 ... 8:2 ... 9:18 ... 15:25 ... 20:20 ... 28:9 ... 18:17.... Now, to be sure, the verb προσκυνεῖν possesses a certain ambiguity. It can in some contexts mean 'pay homage, bow down,' without necessarily implying a divine status of the one who receives the gesture of homage. Several of these Matthean passages might be understood in such a sense, particularly in the cases of those who come to Jesus as postulants. Yet in view of Matthew's portrayal of Jesus as 'God with us' and his use of the verb in settings where it unmistakably narrates an appropriate human response to Jesus' epiphanic self-manifestation (14:33, 28:9, 28:17), it is hard to deny that, in and through these references to worshiping Jesus, Matthew is identifying him as nothing less than the embodied presence of Israel's God, the one to whom alone worship is due, the one who jealously forbids the worship of any idols, images, or other gods."

[151] E.g., Hays, *Reading Backwards*, 20, 49–50; Hays, *Echoes of Scripture in the Gospels*, 63, 69–73; Hays, "Figural Exegesis and the Retrospective Re-Cognition of Israel's Story," 39.

[152] Cf. Hays, *Echoes of Scripture in the Gospels*, 11: "Metalepsis is a literary technique of citing or echoing a small bit of a precursor text in such a way that the reader can grasp the significance of the echo only by recalling or recovering the original context from which the fragmentary echo came and then reading the two texts in dialogical juxtaposition. The figurative effect of such an intertextual linkage lies in the unstated or suppressed points of correspondence between the two texts."

[153] Cf. Hays, "Can Narrative Criticism Recover the Theological Unity of Scripture?," 197. Hays, "Figural Exegesis and the Retrospective Re-Cognition of Israel's Story," 46–47, writes, "through their pervasive evocations of Israel's Scripture, both subtle and overt, the Evangelists portray Jesus as the embodiment of Israel's God. This finding flies in the face of two centuries of NT criticism that have argued, as Bart Ehrman asserts in one of his recent popularizations, that 'The idea that Jesus was divine was a later Christian invention, one found, among our Gospels, only in John.' This is a conclusion that can be reached and defended only by readers who are tone-deaf to the scriptural intertexts that form the theological foundation of the Gospels."

[154] E.g., Hays, "Figural Exegesis and the Retrospective Re-Cognition of Israel's Story," 47; Hays, *Echoes of Scripture in the Gospels*, 171–72; Hays, *Reading Backwards*, 72.

[155] Capes, "Paul's Use of Old Testament Yahweh-Texts and Its Implications for His Christology" (PhD diss., Southwest Baptist Theological Seminary, 1990), published later as *Old Testament Yahweh Texts in Paul's Christology* (Tübingen, Germany: Mohr [Paul Siebeck], 1992; repr., Waco, TX: Baylor University Press, 2017).

[156] See, Capes, *The Divine Christ* (Grand Rapids, MI: Baker Academic, 2018), xiv–xv.

or alluding to various OT passages that refer to God with the divine name, *YHWH*.[157] Capes demonstrates beyond dispute how frequently "YHWH texts" are applied to Jesus in Paul.[158]

The theory of Bousset and his followers is found to be in error by Capes, not only because there is no evidence of a Christological disparity between the earliest Palestinian Jewish and Hellenistic Jewish converts to Christianity,[159] but because Second Temple Jewish monotheism was varied and robust enough to embrace Christological monotheism.[160] This is especially the case, says Capes, because Jewish mediation traditions and the corporate personality concept prepared the way for early Jewish Christians to associate Jesus with God, and *as* God.[161] The identification of Jesus with God, disclosed by Jesus himself, simply needed a defining revelatory event, which was more than fulfilled by the resurrection and exaltation of Jesus,[162] the primary catalyst for devotion to Jesus as the object of prayer and worship by first generation Christians.[163]

Capes argues that the Pauline letters, comprising many of the earliest Christian documents, are proof positive of a high Christology *prior* to Paul.[164] After all, Paul's life overlapped that of Jesus, so Paul's writings cannot be dismissed as distant memory of events long past.[165] Rather, they display the highest possible Christology decades before the period in which many critical scholars believe John developed his high Christology.[166] The Aramaic "maranatha" saying of 1 Cor 16:22 evidences a pre-Pauline

---

[157] Cf. Capes, *Old Testament Yahweh Texts in Paul's Christology*, 3; Capes, *The Divine Christ*, xiv.

[158] As mentioned earlier, Capes identifies at least seven quotations of YHWH-texts in the Pauline corpus alone: Rom 10:13; 14:11; 1 Cor 1:31; 2:16; 10:26; 2 Cor 10:17; 2 Tim 2:19. See, Capes, *Old Testament Yahweh Texts in Paul's Christology*, 115–48. Cf. Capes, *The Divine Christ*, 86, for a quick-reference chart of YHWH-text quotations and allusions in Paul.

[159] Cf. Capes, *Old Testament Yahweh Texts in Paul's Christology*, 23.

[160] Cf. Capes, *The Divine Christ*, 42–43, 163–64.

[161] Capes, *Old Testament Yahweh Texts in Paul's Christology*, 29–30, 32, explains, "[T]he Old Testament views man as extending beyond the individual to encompass a corporate reality. Likewise, it portrays God in corporate categories which are adopted and expanded in the intertestamental period so that he appears in many manifestations including 'the angel of the Lord,' the divine 'Word' (e.g., Isa 9:8; 55:10–11), and 'Wisdom.'.... Given this background and the expectation that Yahweh would come to deliver Israel, Ellis concluded that 'the followers of Jesus would have been prepared, wholly within a Jewish monotheistic and "salvation history" perspective, to see in the Messiah a manifestation of God ....' Thus, pre-Christian Jewish monotheism should be seen as a different entity from later rabbinic monotheism due to the Hebrew concept of corporate personality." In light of Hurtado's findings, Capes suggests, 169, "that early Christians not only worshiped Jesus *alongside God*, they worshiped him *as God*" (emphasis Capes). See also pages 173–74.

[162] Cf. Capes, *The Divine Christ*, 43, 49.

[163] E.g., Capes, *Old Testament Yahweh Texts in Paul's Christology*, 46–47, 168–69; Capes, *The Divine Christ*, 182–83, 187.

[164] E.g., Capes, *Old Testament Yahweh Texts in Paul's Christology*, 50, 164–67; Capes, *The Divine Christ*, 21–22, 49.

[165] Cf. Capes, *The Divine Christ*, 155.

[166] Capes, *Old Testament Yahweh Texts in Paul's Christology*, 181–83, writes persuasively, "Paul's Christological use of Yahweh texts calls into question the construct that Christianity moved from a 'low' Christology, represented by Paul's letters, to a 'high' Christology, represented by the Fourth Gospel.... Most interpreters agree that several decades separate the composition of Paul's letters from the writing of the Fourth Gospel. As one reads the Gospel and letters attributed to John, it is apparent that what is in danger of being lost is not the divinity of Jesus but his humanity. Therefore, the author insists that only deceivers and anti-Christs deny that Jesus came in the flesh (John 1:14; 1

and Palestinian origin,[167] exaltation hymns (such as Phil 2:6-11 and Col 1:15-20) declaring Jesus as "Lord" imply a pre-settled and self-evident community perspective of Christ as divine,[168] and Paul's reworking of the *Shema* places Jesus within the divine identity.[169] All of these features point to a radical shift in Paul's perspective from an avowed Jewish monotheist and staunch enemy of Christ to a bold proponent of Christological monotheism and lordship. Paul himself admitted to and accounted for the shift as a result of meeting the risen κύριος, a term that Paul applied as easily to Jesus as he did to God the Father.[170] In fact, says Capes, no other title in Greek could better associate Jesus with YHWH.[171] This is evident in the fact that OT passages referring to the Jewish expectation of the coming (presence/visitation) and day of the Lord *YHWH* are applied in the NT to the coming (presence/visitation) and day of the Lord *Jesus*.[172]

The primary contribution of Capes's work is the NT application of YHWH-texts to Jesus in the Pauline corpus. After citing numerous examples, he concludes that the phenomenon is not an anomaly but a common practice in Paul.[173] But he is also well aware of the practice in the canonical Gospels, which, in turn, he finds as evidence that Jesus himself is the source of the practice picked up by Paul and the Evangelists.[174] It must be acknowledged that reading Capes's work was an influential factor in the decision to undertake this study and to explore just *how* evident and significant this practice is in the Synoptic Gospels.

John 4:2–3; 2 John 7); true believers continue to hold to that important doctrine. The problem facing John then is a Christology which is too high, a Christology which, among certain circles, denies Jesus' humanity. Since this is true, it is difficult to understand how some interpret early Christianity and its most prominent spokesman, the apostle Paul, as representing a 'low Christology.' Or, to put it another way, could Paul's 'low Christology'—as some would have it—have evolved so quickly to a Christology which denied Jesus humanity? The evidence from Paul's letters and particularly his use of Yahweh texts suggests that he identifies Jesus as Yahweh manifest and thus his Christology is already 'high.'"

[167] Capes, *Old Testament Yahweh Texts in Paul's Christology*, 46–47, 165; Capes, *The Divine Christ*, 49.
[168] Cf. Capes, *Old Testament Yahweh Texts in Paul's Christology*, 165; Capes, "YHWH and His Messiah," 132; Capes, *The Divine Christ*, 161.
[169] E.g., Capes, *The Divine Christ*, 77.
[170] Cf. Capes, *Old Testament Yahweh Texts in Paul's Christology*, 116 with 160; Capes, *The Divine Christ*, 86.
[171] Capes, *Old Testament Yahweh Texts in Paul's Christology*, 89, argues, "For Paul, κύριος became the Christological title par excellence for referring to final things such as (a) the Day of the Lord, (b) the coming of the Lord, and (c) the final judgment.... Yet he knew that many of these functions belonged primarily to Yahweh in the Old Testament. It may be concluded therefore that one reason for Paul's use of κύριος as a Christological title was to apply to Jesus concepts and functions originally reserved for Yahweh in the Old Testament. No other Christological title could serve to associate Jesus so closely with Yahweh."
[172] Cf. Capes, *Old Testament Yahweh Texts in Paul's Christology*, 89; David B. Capes, "Intertextual Echoes in the Matthean Baptismal Narrative," *BBR* 9 (1999): 44; Capes, *The Divine Christ*, 42–43, 182–83.
[173] Cf. Capes, "YHWH and His Messiah," 137. Capes, *The Divine Christ*, 173, writes, "It may be one thing to 'slip up' and link Christ with God's name in a single text; but Paul programmatically read texts containing the divine name in relation to Jesus over and over again in a variety of contexts. And we should not forget that Paul was reading these texts in relation to a man of recent history, not a religious figure from two thousand years ago. This is a remarkable development that took place within only a few years of Jesus's execution."
[174] Cf. Capes, *Old Testament Yahweh Texts in Paul's Christology*, 179–80; Capes, *The Divine Christ*, 178–83.

Recent Scholarship and the Niche of This Study

Sketches of the previous five contemporary scholars have demonstrated a challenge to the critical trend advanced by Bousset and others. No longer can it be maintained without serious contradiction that the foundational Christian concept summarized in the primitive creed, "Jesus is Lord," was a late Hellenistic development of schismatic Christians in the generations after Christ. Rather, the evidence shows it was the sudden and ubiquitous realization of the earliest Jewish Christians, likely triggered by their experience of seeing the risen Christ. According to the studies of Hurtado, Bauckham, Wright, Hays, and Capes, the view of Jesus as divine Lord by those who knew him takes better account of the NT canonical writings during the Second Temple period than does the presumptive higher critical view of most historical Jesus studies in the last two centuries.

The contributions most pertinent to this study from each of these five scholars, with the risk of oversimplification, may be summarized as follows: Hurtado emphasizes the "binitarian" worship of the Messiah by the first Christians, who viewed Jesus as both God's chief agent and God's equal. Bauckham demonstrates how the apostolic generation of Christians included (rather than added) Jesus into the divine identity without contradicting concurrent Jewish monotheism. Wright explores the OT in light of Second Temple Judaism and finds that expectations of the coming human Messiah can only be understood in tandem with the expectations of the personal coming of YHWH—both trajectories finding fulfillment in Jesus. Hays discovers that the quotations, allusions, and echoes of the OT found in NT authors, who were "reading backwards," reveal their united opinion of Jesus as the embodiment of Israel's God. And Capes most explicitly demonstrates the deliberate use of YHWH-texts in application to Jesus, particularly in the Pauline corpus, but also noted to exist in the Gospels.

The works of Hays and Capes are the publications most closely related to this study. But there are significant differences, as well. In following the Evangelists as they "read backwards," Hays discovers as one important feature the application of OT YHWH-texts (and, more generally, YHWH-characteristics) to Jesus. He notes the phenomenon often in his book on the four Gospels.[175] The primary difference between Hays's work and this study is that Hays's work is fundamentally an exercise in intertextual hermeneutics that includes several examples of the YHWH-text phenomenon within its wider presentation, while this study shall focus on the YHWH-text phenomenon in the Synoptics to provide a more complete picture of its practice and ramifications.

The work of Capes is specific and complete in evaluating OT YHWH-texts, but with a focus on the Pauline corpus rather than the Gospels. Another difference between Capes's work and this study is necessitated by the difference in genres: the didactic nature of the Pauline corpus means that most occurrences of YHWH-texts are specified (or clearly implied) quotations, while the narrative nature of the Gospels incorporates relatively more allusions and echoes.

---

[175] I.e., Hays, *Echoes of Scripture in the Gospels*.

For example, it is part of Paul's didactic argument to quote (YHWH-text) Joel 2:32 (in Rom 10:13) to prove his theological assertion that one must call upon Jesus as Lord (= YHWH) to be saved. Paul's connections are often explicit, due to the more didactic nature of his epistles. By comparison, it is necessary for the Evangelists merely to narrate the Pharisees' accusation of blasphemy against Jesus's claim to forgive sins (Mark 2; Matt 9; Luke 5) in order to alert the reader by *allusion* to recall texts such as Ps 103:3 or Jer 31:34, which attribute to YHWH alone the divine prerogative of forgiving sins. Thus, the different approaches (mostly quotations in Paul; mostly allusions/echoes in the Evangelists) are better explained as a matter of genre differences (didactic epistles vs. biographical narratives) rather than as later editorial changes or even authorial preferences. These differences in corpus and genre further imply that there is an important niche for this study to fill.

The Neglect of YHWH-Texts in Critical Views of the Historical Jesus

It is difficult to account for the nearly wholesale scholarly oversight of OT YHWH-texts applied to Jesus in the past two centuries apart from the power of critical presuppositions. If one prescribes to the history of religions school (*Religionsgeschichtliche Schule*) as championed by Bousset, Bultmann, and others, then the assumption of a long historical development for the central Christian doctrine that Jesus is Lord (= YHWH) is taken in stride without consideration of the YHWH-text phenomenon. If the occurrence of a YHWH-text applied to Jesus is even noticed, the critical scholar may wish to explain it away as careless editorial work or as propaganda by a later-generation Christian scribe. In any case, the relative absence of comments on a phenomenon so ubiquitous in the NT suggests that it is easier for one to discover what is assumed to exist than what is assumed cannot exist.[176] There seems to be no other explanation for the gross neglect of the YHWH-text phenomenon by most critical scholars of the historical Jesus.

The Importance of YHWH-Texts in Christological Discussion

But the use of YHWH-texts for Jesus by at least seven of the nine NT authors cannot be ignored without truncating the Christological picture of the NT. And the frequent practice of the phenomenon in all four of the canonical Gospels (to be confirmed in the earlier three in this study) cannot be neglected without leading scholars to a "Jesus" detached and strangely different from the Jesus of those who set out to narrate his unique life. The topic of this study, then, becomes in important piece of Jesus's portrait, because the Gospels assume eyewitness knowledge of Jesus in the earliest narratives of his life.[177] And if the earliest biographers of Jesus all employed the use of YHWH-texts

---

[176] E.g., P. Maurice Casey, *From Jewish Prophet to Gentile God: The Origins and Development of New Testament Christology* (Louisville, KY: Westminster/John Knox, 1991), and J. R. Daniel Kirk, *A Man Attested by God* (Grand Rapids, MI: Eerdmans, 2016), similarly argue that Jesus is not portrayed with divine identity in the Synoptics. However, their interpretive assumptions (see later discussions) compel them either to overlook or to downplay YHWH-texts applied to Jesus.

to portray his identity, then they become a unified non-ignorable source of revelation of primitive Christology.

It seems vital, therefore, to reverse the assumptions of the *Religionsgeschichliche Schule*, form criticism, and other critical approaches that tend to neglect the interpretation of particular NT texts within their meta-narratival context. Rather than assume, for example, that the Nicene Creed is the product of a lengthy transformation of the "historical Jesus" into the divine Christ, it makes better sense to recognize that Nicaea was attempting to summarize in the language of its time the biblical witnesses to (the historical) Jesus. Similarly, the modern interpreter must question the presuppositions of his own time as much as those of past centuries and ask: What is the meaning of the text in its own time? The four hundred "silent years" prior to Jesus and during Greco-Roman domination are pregnant with Jewish expectation of God's promised coming for deliverance, which had been dangling unfilled from the last OT prophecies. So, if Jesus and the Evangelists applied OT YHWH-texts to a carpenter's son out of Nazareth, then readers of the NT are obliged to tune in to the phenomenon and ask what it all means.

Interpreting New Testament Uses of the Old Testament

The NT use of the OT has received much attention in recent hermeneutical and biblical-theological studies.[178] And while there is little consensus on the best interpretive methods and terminology for classifying usages, recent discussions on the topic may provide some help in orienting the methodology of this study.

The impact of Richard B. Hays's work is undeniable and provides a good point of

---

[177] Contrast this eyewitness storyline with the *Gospel of Thomas*, which, as a collection of 114 sayings, appears unsuccessful as a narrative. Bart D. Ehrman and Zlatko Pleše, eds., *The Apocryphal Gospels* (New York: Oxford University Press, 2011), 307–8, who think *Thomas* may have had access to early oral teachings of Jesus, nevertheless detect a heavy flavor of Gnosticism in *Thomas* when compared to the Synoptic Gospels: "The Gnostic orientation is especially signaled by the repeated emphasis on the need for saving 'knowledge' . . . found implicitly even in sayings where the term 'knowledge' or its verbal equivalent are not explicitly found. . . . Possibly it is best to say that both Thomas and the Synoptics had access to sayings of Jesus in the oral tradition and included the sayings in the forms familiar to them. If so, this raises the possibility that in some of the sayings of Thomas we may have access not just to later versions of Jesus' teachings, but to the actual teachings themselves—at least for those sayings that do not reflect the later concerns of whatever form of Gnostic thought underlies much of the Gospel." But this argument appears contradictory. If *Thomas* exhibits a "Gnostic orientation" with "later concerns" not found in the Synoptics, then it is self-evidently more distant from Jesus's teachings both chronologically and theologically. Simon Gathercole, *The Composition of The Gospel of Thomas* (Cambridge; New York: Cambridge University Press, 2012), 267–70, rightly argues that, while *Thomas* appears to draw from the Synoptic accounts, it lacks their Semitic substratum.

[178] E.g., R. V. G. Tasker, *The Old Testament in the New Testament*, 2nd ed. (London: SCM Press, 1954); S. Lewis Johnson, *The Old Testament in the New* (Grand Rapids, MI: Zondervan, 1980); R. T. France, *Jesus and the Old Testament* (Grand Rapids, MI: Baker, 1982); Walter C. Kaiser Jr., *The Uses of the Old Testament in the New* (Chicago, IL: Moody, 1985); Hays, *Echoes of Scripture in the Letters of Paul*; Richard N. Longenecker, *Biblical Exegesis in the Apostolic Period*, 2nd ed. (Grand Rapids, MI: Eerdmans; Vancouver, Canada: Regent, 1999); Steve Moyise, *The Old Testament in the New*, 2nd ed. (London: Bloomsbury T&T Clark, 2015); G. K. Beale, *Handbook on the New Testament Use of the Old*

entry.[179] He identifies a general three-fold distinction between quotations, allusions, and echoes—with the latter category assigned "seven tests" to help identify a true echo.[180] Gregory K. Beale finds much of Hays's work commendable, but says "one could reduce Hays's seven criteria to five" and prefers to classify echoes within a continuum of various kinds of allusions.[181] Unhappy with both approaches, Stanley E. Porter argues for more specific categories: formulaic quotations, direct quotations, paraphrases, allusions, and echoes (properly defined).[182] Anticipating Porter's concern for greater definition, and predating Hays's work, Richard T. France had also attempted to make careful distinctions in "Appendix C: A Table of Uses of the Old Testament Attributed to Jesus in the Synoptic Gospels" of his classic work, *Jesus and the Old Testament*.[183] France distinguishes between six classes, but freely admits, "A measure of arbitrariness in the classification is inevitable."[184]

Porter would like to limit such arbitrariness, and he is keen on requiring a series of at least three shared words (assuming use of the LXX) to distinguish a quotation from a paraphrase. He reasons,

> One word, without a formula citation (or equivalent introduction), may simply be a coincidence, and even two words may be a coincidence, since with two words it is difficult to establish what their relationship is. With three words, however, it is less likely that one has a coincidence, and the three form a minimal unit of determinable syntax and conceptual relation.[185]

On the surface, Porter's careful delineation might be considered a reasonable interpretive restriction or hermeneutical rule of thumb. But, as will become evident, there are multiple cases of two-word "quotations" that are decidedly not paraphrases, let alone mere allusions. Furthermore, titular references to Jesus in the Gospels may sometimes be more than allusive. That is, certain names, titles, and other unique OT references to YHWH, when deliberately applied to Jesus, have *citation force*; they are

---

Testament: Exegesis and Interpretation (Grand Rapids, MI: Baker Academic, 2012); Stanley E. Porter, *Sacred Tradition in the New Testament* (Grand Rapids, MI: Baker Academic, 2016). Collins, "How the New Testament Quotes and Interprets the Old Testament," 185–86, points out that intertextual allusion was already practiced within the OT corpus and the NT writers continued the practice as self-conscious heirs of Israel's story.

[179] See especially, Hays, *Echoes of Scripture in the Letters of Paul*; Hays, *Echoes of Scripture in the Gospels*.
[180] Hays, *Echoes of Scripture in the Letters of Paul*, 29–32.
[181] Beale, *Handbook on the New Testament Use of the Old Testament*, 35. See also the helpful discussion in Johnson, *Him We Proclaim* (Phillipsburg, NJ: P&R, 2007), 199–217, on five categories of "Old Testament texts that are interpreted by New Testament authors as fulfilled in Jesus."
[182] Porter, *Sacred Tradition in the New Testament*, 34–46.
[183] France, *Jesus and the Old Testament*, 259.
[184] France, *Jesus and the Old Testament*, 259. He distinguishes between the following classes:
   A. Verbatim quotations with introductory formula.
   B. Verbatim quotations without introductory formula.
   C. Clear verbal allusions.
   D. Clear references without verbal allusion.
   E. Possible verbal allusions.
   F. Possible references without verbal allusion.
[185] Porter, *Sacred Tradition in the New Testament*, 35.

beyond allusive, because of their *verbal exclusivity to YHWH*. The very lack of consensus among scholars in pinpointing differences between quotations, allusions, echoes, and several possible subcategories demonstrates a natural ambiguity and overlapping of categories. Added to this is the substantial difference from modern writers that the biblical writers appeared not to make such hard distinctions between quotations and allusions, but simply referred to the OT in various creative and complementary ways.

Despite the modern tendency to place more weight on formal quotations over other NT uses of the OT,[186] numerous allusions and echoes may carry as much referential weight as any formal quotation.[187] A more important criterion than the categorical *form* of a reference is the exegetical *confirmation* that the speaker and/or writer of a given NT passage is deliberately calling attention to an identifiable OT passage or cluster of passages. The real question is whether a substantive connection would have been clear to the author and, therefore, likely deliberate. On this approach, the number of quotations, allusions, and echoes of OT YHWH-texts applied to Jesus is not artificially limited by searches for formal quotations alone.

The recognition that allusive references may carry citation weight—particularly in narrative texts—is notable for interpretation. It understands that the Jewish metanarrative of the entire OT is the foundational interpretive context for understanding the Gospel narratives.[188] When the Evangelists are recognized as portraying Jesus as the *telos* of Israel's story, then the vast OT worldview—with YHWH at the center creating the universe, redeeming the fallen world through tiny Israel's great Messiah, and culminating human history with his own visitation in redemption and judgment—becomes the context for understanding the words and works of Jesus in the Gospels. The way NT writers use OT texts to trace biblical-historical themes to their consummation is decisive for understanding their contributions. And this is unequivocally the case when NT authors apply OT YHWH-texts to Jesus.

This study, therefore, will seek to approach each Synoptic Gospel with a sensitivity to hearing OT reverberations of any classification in the author's narrative description of Jesus. While formal quotations (citations) may sometimes offer more certainty that deliberate intertestamental connections are being made, many informal quotations and

---

[186] Longenecker, *Biblical Exegesis in the Apostolic Period*, xvi–xvii, for example, is overly reluctant to identify quotations and allusions not explicitly identified by the NT authors.

[187] Similarly, France, *Jesus and the Old Testament*, 14–15, states, "We shall not confine our attention to formal quotations of the Old Testament. The tendency to do so has marred some recent work, for it inevitably results in an incomplete picture. To discover how Jesus understood and used the Old Testament, we must go beyond verbatim quotations, whether introduced by a set formula or not, to include references to Old Testament teaching or events, verbal allusions, and even, in a few cases, significant actions which seem to have been intended to call attention to prophecies of the Old Testament. The importance of the less formal allusions in particular is that they often betray the Old Testament models around which the speaker's or writer's thinking formed itself and in many cases they are deliberately framed to suggest a particular Old Testament passage or idea."

[188] C. H. Dodd, *According to the Scriptures* (London: Nisbet and Company, 1952), e.g., 31, 57, 61, notes that NT quotations of the OT often assume the wider OT context and imply a "common pre-canonical tradition" of Gospel-related OT texts, or testimonies (*testimonia*) that the early Christians referenced as the *kerygma* to support and explain the Gospel facts around Jesus's life, death, and resurrection.

allusions may be identified as equally certain in their authorial intent. "Echoes," by definition, do not demonstrate certainty of authorial intent but, nevertheless, are often valuable as purveyors of an authorial worldview that finds no contradiction in connecting Jesus to YHWH-texts. Although they may be at times difficult to distinguish without authorial disclosure, both conscious and subconscious connections—determinate quotations/allusions and indeterminate echoes—attest to the same Christological worldview: Jesus fulfills the personal promises and prerogatives of YHWH. He occupies YHWH's shoes, from the perspective of the Evangelists.

Summary of the Content and Format of This Study

In summary, this study sets out to demonstrate that the Synoptic Gospels frequently utilize OT passages originally applied to YHWH, the unique God of Jewish monotheism, and reapply them to Jesus. While some modern biblical scholars have detected this phenomenon to varying degrees, many others—often employing critical assumptions to the biblical texts—have dismissed occurrences as late editorial misapplications or have ignored the phenomenon entirely. Thus, a vast pool of biblical data characterizing first-century Christology is often neglected. This study seeks to rectify that neglect and to resubmit a significant body of evidence into modern Christological discussions.

The uniqueness of this study, when compared with the published works of David B. Capes, is that Capes has concentrated his efforts on the Pauline epistles, while this study will focus on the Synoptics. The uniqueness of this study, when compared with the published words of Richard B. Hays, is that Hays's work in the Gospels has concentrated on hermeneutical issues, such as "reading backwards," and does not attempt a complete review of YHWH-texts applied to Jesus, while this study will focus solely on YHWH-texts applied to Jesus in the Synoptic Gospels and will indeed seek to be reasonably complete.

Methodologically, each of the Synoptics will be surveyed in canonical order for the practice of applying OT YHWH-texts to Jesus. Due to the relative extent of the Gospel narratives, exegesis of each pertinent passage will be restricted to what is necessary to demonstrate with certainty or relative likelihood that the Evangelist in question was deliberately placing Jesus in the position of YHWH by the application of an OT text or combination of texts. Thus, while classifications such as Hays's quotations, allusions, and echoes may at times be distinguished, taxonomic categories will be considered as secondary and sometimes irrelevant to the phenomenon under examination. The key question to be answered for each case examined is whether or not the Evangelist in view makes Jesus the referent of OT texts originally referring to YHWH. After many significant occurrences in the Synoptics have been identified and discussed, several ramifications shall be identified addressing the significance of OT YHWH-texts applied to Jesus in the Synoptic Gospels.

2

Matthew's Application of YHWH-Texts to Jesus

Did the Evangelists deliberately apply OT YHWH-texts to Jesus? An author's intent and motive can be difficult to prove, unless there is overwhelming evidence from which to infer their existence. In the case of YHWH-texts used for Jesus, their ubiquity among the Gospels would evidence a conscious deliberation on the part of each Evangelist. The following three chapters shall seek to show how the Synoptic Gospels of Matthew, Mark, and Luke each display the phenomenon as a pervasive practice and, therefore, as a deliberate practice, leading to several significant ramifications.

Matthew's Christology

The earliest manuscript collections show Matthew's Gospel arranged as the first of the four canonical Gospels. This arrangement may be based in part on the Church Fathers' belief that Matthew's Gospel was written first.[1] Perhaps more significantly, however, Matthew may have been placed in the first position for theological reasons, largely because of its numerous overt connections to the OT.[2] Matthew, at least as much as any other Gospel, emphasizes the continuity of Jesus's story with the story of Israel and Israel's God.[3] In grand fashion, Matthew picks up the hanging expectations and loose ends of the unfinished OT metanarrative to find their fulfillment and *telos* in Jesus.[4]

---

[1] Presentations on what the earliest Church Fathers (from Papias to Augustine) believed about the composition of Matthew relative to other Gospels include John William Wenham, *Redating Matthew, Mark & Luke* (Downers Grove, IL: InterVarsity Press, 1992), 116–35; F. David Farnell, "The Synoptic Gospels in the Ancient Church: The Testimony to the Priority of Matthew's Gospel," *TMSJ* 10.1 (1999): 53–86. For an early history (first through fifth centuries) of controversies surrounding which Gospels were authoritative for the church, see David L. Dungan, *A History of the Synoptic Problem* (New York: Doubleday, 1999), 11–141.

[2] Joel Kennedy, *The Recapitulation of Israel* (Tübingen, Germany: Mohr Siebeck, 2008), 22, pursuing a parallel line of thought, rightly observes, "Undoubtedly, the entirety of Matthew's Gospel is a work of theological interpretation and presentation of Jesus Christ, and his use of the Old Testament in this regard is a key component in his theology. The Christology is saturated with Old Testament scriptures, themes, and traditions; and the use of the Old Testament is vitally connected to the Christological perspective Matthew sets forth."

[3] Cf. N. T. Wright, *The New Testament and the People of God* (Minneapolis, MN: Fortress, 1992), 396; W. F. Albright and C. S. Mann, *Matthew*, AB (Garden City, NY: Doubleday, 1971), xxvi.

[4] Martin C. Spadaro, *Reading Matthew as the Climactic Fulfillment of the Hebrew Story* (Eugene, OR: Wipf & Stock, 2015), 24, observes, "Some of these early documents were given the highest possible standing, even being referred to as Scripture (2 Peter 3:16). Even within the concluding apocalyptic of Revelation a command can be found to write it down (Rev 1:11), and it even emphasized the inviolability of the document itself (Rev 22:18–19). The author of Matthew certainly was encultured

Whether the OT reader comes to the end of the Hebrew/Aramaic canon (usually, the historical book of Chronicles in the Masoretic Text) or to the end of Greek translation collections (usually, the prophetic book of Malachi), one can readily see that both are ably and conspicuously picked up for continuation by Matthew's account of Jesus. In the First Gospel, Jesus is portrayed as the climax of Israel's story and, indeed, of God's personal intervention in Israel specifically and in the created world generally.[5] The end of the Historical Books (Chronicles) anticipates both divine deliverance from the Exile and the installment of the Davidic king.[6] And the cumulative end of the Prophets (climaxing with Malachi) anticipates both the arrival of YHWH with his "Day" of judgment/salvation and the arrival of God's unique human agent, the Messiah/Servant of YHWH.[7] Matthew picks up these dual "coming" themes by showing historical continuity in Jesus by his messianic genealogy (Matt 1:1–7) and prophetic fulfillment in Jesus by YHWH's arrival in Israel (Matt 1:18–2:6; 3:1–17; cf. commentary below). While all of the Evangelists make similar OT connections to Jesus, Matthew's connections tend to be more conspicuous, especially in light of his early and frequent use of "fulfillment formula" quotations.[8] In fulfillment of the OT metanarrative, Jesus is both the promised Davidic shepherd-king and the eschatologically-present divine Savior/Judge.[9]

---

with this same viewpoint; his document, should it have been written to extend the Hebrew metanarrative, was written to be Scripture. It would seem that the early church accepted the writer's assessment of his own work." Alternatively, see Ulrich Luz, *Matthew 1–7*, Hermeneia, trans. James E. Crouch, rev. ed. (Minneapolis, MN: Fortress, 2007), 13, 49–50, for an expression of the common critical view that Matthew's focal purpose was on ethical behavior as shaped by a later-generation Matthean community.

[5] Stephen J. Wellum, "From Alpha to Omega: A Biblical-Theological Approach to God the Son Incarnate," *JETS* 63.1 (2020): 90–92, writes, "As Israel's history unfolds, it becomes evident that God alone must act to accomplish his promises; he must initiate in order to save; he must unilaterally act if there is going to be redemption at all.... If one approaches and reads Scripture on its own terms (i.e., according to its self-attestation, categories, content, metaphysical-theological framework, unfolding storyline, etc.), then we will conclude that the entire Bible gives us the highest Christology imaginable." Cf. Wright, *The New Testament and the People of God*, 397–98; Richard J. Bauckham, "Christology," in *Dictionary of Jesus and the Gospels*, 2nd ed., ed. Joel B. Green, Jeannine K. Brown, and Nicholas Perrin (Downers Grove, IL: IVP Academic, 2013), 129.

[6] Cf. Graham A. Cole, *The God Who Became Human* (Downers Grove, IL: Apollos; InterVarsity Press, 2013), 95.

[7] Larry W. Hurtado, "YHWH's Return to Zion: A New Catalyst for Earliest High Christology?," in *Ancient Jewish Monotheism and Early Christian Jesus-Devotion*, ed. Larry W. Hurtado, April D. DeConick, and David B. Capes (Waco, TX: Baylor University Press, 2017), 88–89, writes, "In short, the NT comfortably presents Jesus both as the direct expression of God in redemptive purposes (e.g., 2 Cor 5:19; Col 1:19), and as the unique agent of God (e.g., 1 Cor 8:6; Col 1:20), and it distorts the evidence to play up the one emphasis and play down the other." Cf. Mark D. Vander Hart, "The Transition of the Old Testament Day of the LORD into the New Testament Day of the Lord Jesus Christ," *MJT* 9.1 (1993): 3–4. For a developmental view, see Joachim Gnilka, *Jesus Christus Nach Frühen Zeugnissen Des Glaubens* (Munich Kösel-Verlag, 1970), 89, who speaks of a "transfer" of YHWH's name and day to Jesus and sees application of the term *kurios* to Jesus beginning after the diaspora.

[8] Matthew's fulfillment quotations have long been recognized as a hallmark of his Gospel. For a classic discussion on this feature, see Krister Stendahl, *The School of St. Matthew and Its Use of the Old Testament*, 2nd ed. (Philadelphia, PA: Fortress Press, 1968), 97–127. For a thematic approach of Matthew's focus on Jesus as the personal fulfillment of the OT, see the study by Kennedy, *The Recapitulation of Israel*.

[9] Cf. David R. Bauer, *The Gospel of the Son of God* (Downers Grove, IL: IVP Academic, 2019), 244.

The high Christology of Matthew's Gospel has been the subject of numerous studies. Without denying the humanity of the Davidic messiah, various Matthean themes emphasize the deity, or divine identity, of the man Jesus. Although he is God's unique chief agent, in Matthew he is also worshiped as God's equal, welcoming and not rejecting that worship.[10] Although he is located in the human promissory ancestry of Abraham and David, he is also identified as the Son of God.[11] He was not adopted by God, but "came" from God.[12] His coming/presence—emphasized in Matt 1:23 by the name Emmanuel—fulfills the divine coming/presence promised by YHWH.[13] Indeed, Jesus saw himself as the locus of God's presence, the true tabernacle/temple.[14] His

---

[10] Joshua E. Leim, *Matthew's Theological Grammar* (Tübingen, Germany: Mohr Siebeck, 2015), 15, 28, argues that the Matthean narrative determines the meaning of the term "worship" and that the Father-Son depiction requires the worship of Jesus to be understood by the readers as being at the same level as the worship of the Father. Richard B. Hays, *Echoes of Scripture in the Gospels* (Waco, TX: Baylor University Press, 2016), 167, also argues that Matthew's emphasis on the worship of Jesus cannot be less than the worship of God. Larry W. Hurtado, *Ancient Jewish Monotheism and Early Christian Jesus-Devotion* (Waco, TX: Baylor University Press, 2017), 388, writes of Matthew's Gospel, "we see a clear programmatic effort to heighten the homage given by people to the earthly Jesus."

[11] Bauer, *The Gospel of the Son of God*, 129, notes how Matthew's Gospel is structured around "Son of God" confessions. Stephen J. Wellum, "The Deity of Christ in the Synoptic Gospels," in *The Deity of Christ*, ed. Christopher W. Morgan and Robert A. Peterson (Wheaton, IL: Crossway, 2011), 82, argues, "the only way one can make sense of this reciprocal/mutual knowledge of the Son is in categories that are antecedent to Jesus becoming Messiah. Why? Because it is nigh impossible to think of Jesus' knowledge as merely a consequence of his messianic mission; it has to be tied to pre-temporal, even eternal relations. That is why 'sonship' cannot merely be reduced to functional categories. Rather, as George Ladd has argued, sonship precedes messiahship and is in fact the ground for the messianic mission." N. T. Wright, *The Resurrection of the Son of God* (Minneapolis, MN: Fortress, 2008), 729, further asserts that references to Jesus's sonship in the NT would have triggered thoughts of divine claims in the Greek culture of the day.

[12] See, for example, Wellum, "The Deity of Christ in the Synoptic Gospels," 64; Wright, *The Resurrection of the Son of God*, 733. For an expression of the adoptionist view, see Ferdinand Hahn, *The Titles of Jesus in Christology* (London: Lutterworth, 1969), 113–14.

[13] Like many, Craig L. Blomberg, *A New Testament Theology* (Waco, TX: Baylor University Press, 2018), 352–53, sees the presence of God in Jesus as a major Matthean theme: "By continuing and including 'they will call him Immanuel' and then explaining the meaning of the name as 'God with us,' he is highlighting the presence of God in Jesus. It hardly seems coincidental, therefore, when Matthew's last verse presents Jesus promising always to be with his disciples even 'to the very end of the age' (28:20). He has bookended his narrative with the image of Jesus as God personally present with his people. Matthew also highlights Jesus as God's presence with his people in 8:23–27 (even while sleeping in the midst of the storm), in 10:40–42 (when one helps a 'little one,' one is helping Jesus), in 12:6 (in the presence of something greater than the Temple, the place of God's dwelling), in 14:22–33 (in coming to them walking on the water), in 17:17 (in staying with 'this generation' despite its perversity), in 18:20 (where two or three are gathered in his name he is with them), in 25:34–40 (in ministering to the marginalized disciples, one ministers to Jesus), and in 26:29 (in the fellowship of the coming heavenly banquet)." Cf. Rikk E. Watts, "Immanuel: Virgin Birth Proof Text or Programmatic Warning of Things to Come (Isa 7:14 in Matt 1:23)?," in *From Prophecy to Testament* (Peabody, MA: Hendrickson, 2004), 92–113. Ulrich Luz, *The Theology of the Gospel of Matthew*, trans. J. Bradford Robinson (Cambridge; New York: Cambridge University Press, 1995), 31–32, ties God's presence in the OT historical books to the Immanuel motif in Matthew.

[14] N. T. Wright, *Jesus and the Victory of God* (Minneapolis, MN: Fortress, 1996), 653, goes so far as to suggest "that the return of YHWH to Zion, and the Temple-theology which it brings into focus, are the deepest keys and clues to gospel Christology." Wright, "Jesus' Self-Understanding," in *The Incarnation*, ed. S. T. Davis, D. Kendall, and G. O'Collins (Oxford: Oxford University Press, 2002), 56–57, adds, "The Temple has for too long been the forgotten factor in New Testament Theology. Omit it, and you will spend a lifetime in titles, 'figures,' and other unsatisfying by-paths. Make it central, and the whole picture will come into focus.... Thus, as I have often said, when Jesus came to Jerusalem the place wasn't big enough for both of them, himself and the Temple side by side."

authority is equal to God's authority.[15] His glory is that of God.[16] His power over both the natural and the supernatural is that of God.[17] His name is that of God (YHWH).[18] Matthew does not hesitate to give Jesus uniquely divine titles and descriptors.[19] Jesus is

---

[15] The divine authority of Jesus has been recognized from several angles. Like many, Daniel Doriani, "The Deity of Christ in the Synoptic Gospels," *JETS* 37.3 (1994): 342, points to Jesus's "I say to you" phrase as equivalent to the common OT line, "thus says the Lord." R. Alan Culpepper, "Fulfilment of Scripture and Jesus' Teachings in Matthew," *IDS* 49.2 (2015): 4, notes that Jesus's unique authority is a significant Matthean theme. Jack Dean Kingsbury, "The Title 'Kyrios' in Matthew's Gospel," *JBL* 94.2 (1975): 248, argues that Matthew's use of "kyrios" for Jesus is to attribute divine authority to him. Cf. Dennis Edward Johnson, "Immutability and Incarnation: An Historical and Theological Study of the Concepts of Christ's Divine Unchangeability and His Human Development" (PhD diss., Fuller Theological Seminary, 1984), 432–37; Sigurd Grindheim, *God's Equal* (London; New York: T&T Clark, 2011), 163–67.

[16] Günther Juncker, "Jesus and the Angel of the Lord: An Old Testament Paradigm for New Testament Christology" (PhD diss., Trinity Evangelical Theological Seminary, 2001), 376, notes that the glory of Jesus resembles the glory of God in Daniel 7, while Jesus does not resemble Moses and Elijah. Dale C. Allison Jr., "The Embodiment of God's Will: Jesus in Matthew," in *Seeking the Identity of Jesus*, ed. Beverly Roberts Gaventa and Richard B. Hays (Grand Rapids, MI: Eerdmans, 2008), 131, finds divine glory evidenced even in the concluding words of Jesus in the First Gospel: "The speaker is like the ark of the covenant, where God dwells (Num 10:35–36), or like the Angel of the Lord, who fully represents God (Genesis 18–19), or like the Son of Man enthroned at God's right hand, whose rule is 'everlasting' (Dan 7:13–14). Matthew would probably have been sympathetic with the ancient Christians who identified Jesus with God's 'glory' (1133, כבוד = δόξα, *doxa*; see, e.g., John 1:14 and Heb 1:3). The presence of the Deity is the presence of Jesus, and vice versa."

[17] Bauer, *The Gospel of the Son of God*, 253, observes, "When supplicants cry out to Jesus, 'Lord, have mercy on me [us]' (Mt 7:21, 22; 24:42; 25:11, 37, 44) they are employing the same phrase repeatedly directed to Yahweh in the Psalms (Ps 6:2; 9:13; 25:16; 26:11; 27:7; 30:10; 31:9; 41:4, 10; 51:1; 57:1; 86:1). When Jesus heals those who appeal to him as 'Lord,' we remember that, according to Psalm 103:3 it is Yahweh the Lord who 'heals all your diseases.'" Doriani, "The Deity of Christ in the Synoptic Gospels," *JETS* 37.3 (1994): 343, notes that Jesus's miracles are carried out by his own authority. In his classic study, J. Gresham Machen, *The Origin of Paul's Religion* (Grand Rapids, MI: Eerdmans, 1925), 153–54, writes, "For the Gospels, taken as a whole, present a Jesus like in essentials to that divine Lord who was sum and substance of the life of Paul. The Jesus of the Gospels is no mere prophet, no mere inspired teacher of righteousness, no mere revealer or interpreter of God. He is, on the contrary, a supernatural person; a heavenly Redeemer come to earth for the salvation of men." See also, pages 158–59.

[18] Simon J. Gathercole, *The Preexistent Son* (Grand Rapids, MI: Eerdmans, 2006), 65–68, writes that, in Scripture, "a 'name' is a matter of identity and not merely function," and demonstrates how Jesus's name in Matthew is identified with YHWH's name. Cf. Hurtado, *Ancient Jewish Monotheism and Early Christian Jesus-Devotion*, 612–13. The actual given name, *Jesus*, which means "YHWH saves" or "YHWH is salvation," is emphasized in Matthew and connected to YHWH's OT promises to save. Cf. James Orr, "Jesus Christ," *International Standard Bible Encyclopedia*, ed. James Orr (Grand Rapids, MI: Eerdmans, 1956), 1626; I. Howard Marshall, "Jesus Christ, Titles Of," in *New Bible Dictionary*, ed. James D. Douglas (Downers Grove, IL: InterVarsity Press, 1982), 584; Everett F. Harrison, "Jesus," *Baker's Dictionary of Theology*, ed. Everett F. Harrison, Geoffrey William Bromiley, and Carl F. H. Henry (Grand Rapids, MI: Baker, 1960), 297.

[19] One major divine title/function in Matthew is of Jesus as eschatological Judge. Cf. Christfried Böttrich, "'Gott Und Retter': Gottesprädikationen in Christologischen Titeln," *NZSTh* 42.3 (2000): 231; Maarten J. J. Menken, "The Psalms in Matthew's Gospel," in *The Psalms in the New Testament*, ed. Steve Moyise and Maarten J. J. Menken (London; New York: T&T Clark, 2004), 69–70. Simon J. Gathercole, "The Trinity in the Synoptic Gospels and Acts," in *The Oxford Handbook of the Trinity*, ed. Gilles Emery and Matthew Levering (Oxford; New York: Oxford University Press, 2011), 58–59, points out that, among other things, Jesus takes on the divine prerogatives of election and forgiveness of sins. See also statements of Jesus's assumption of divine functions by R. T. France, "The Worship of Jesus: A Neglected Factor in Christological Debate?," in *Christ the Lord*, ed. Harold H. Rowdon (Leicester, England; Downers Grove, IL: InterVarsity Press, 1982), 28, and Benjamin B. Warfield, *The Lord of Glory* (New York: American Tract Society, 1907), 93–94.

subtly and not-so-subtly "Lord" in Matthew.[20] A high Christology runs deeply through the entire Matthean narrative.

What such "divine identity" themes reveal is a settled narrative stance in the first evangelist's worldview. Elements of divine identity are not tacked onto the biography of Jesus here and there, but rather permeate the Matthean presentation. It is no wonder, then, that Matthew would naturally and liberally apply OT YHWH-texts to Jesus within his account. If he believed the Lord Jesus to be the embodiment of YHWH,[21] then he would have recognized YHWH-texts as descriptions of the "Lord" Jesus. The following passages in Matthew's Gospel demonstrate how the first evangelist utilized numerous OT YHWH-texts in his theological biography of Jesus to underscore his divine identity.

Matthean Cases of Old Testament YHWH-Texts Applied to Jesus

Matthew 1:23

The introduction and birth narrative of Jesus in Matthew's Gospel contain several allusions to Jesus's divine identity (some noted in this chapter's conclusion), but the Isa 7:14 quotation in Matt 1:23 is perhaps the boldest identification of Jesus as YHWH in the first chapter: "All this took place to fulfill what the Lord had spoken by the prophet: 'Behold, the virgin shall conceive and bear a son, and they shall call his name Immanuel,' which means, *God with us*" (Matt 1:22–23).

While critics of Matthew's hermeneutical move here claim that the original context of the Isaian prophecy refers to the birth of one called *Immanuel* through a young woman living in King Ahaz's day, the Isaian context does not demand it, and, rather,

---

[20] The title *Lord* (κύριος) is clearly significant in Matthew. While it does not appear as often as it does in Luke's Gospel, it's substitution for the divine name in Jewish writings of the Second Temple period and Matthew's application of YHWH-texts to Jesus imply that it is a divine title when used of Jesus. Although the word is fluid in meaning, that may be exactly why it is given to Jesus in Matthew's theological biography as both man and God. D. A. Carson, "Christological Ambiguities in the Gospel of Matthew," in *Christ the Lord*, ed. Harold H. Rowdon (Leicester, England; Downers Grove, IL: InterVarsity Press, 1982), 110–11, finds that an ambiguity in Matthew's use of both κύριος and προσκυνέω permits not anachronism but a fuller understanding of the terms in Matthew's day. Ned Bernard Stonehouse, *The Witness of Matthew and Mark to Christ* (Philadelphia, PA: Presbyterian Guardian, 1944), 254, also sees in the very "flexibility" of the term a consciously implied divinity when used of Jesus. Kingsbury, "The Title 'Kyrios' in Matthew's Gospel," *JBL* 94.2 (1975): 248, sees "at least three levels" in Matthew's employment of *kurios*: as conventional ("sir"), as a title for God, and as having "christological coloration." Francis Wright Beare, *The Gospel According to Matthew* (San Francisco, CA: Harper & Row, 1982), 42, while less inclined to attribute divinity to Jesus, could say, "It is apparent from this that Matthew feels that there is something more than ordinary courtesy involved when Jesus is addressed as Kyrie—it verges on the Christian cultic sense of 'Lord Jesus'. Only when they appear before him for judgement do the condemned call him Kyrie (7:22; 25:44), and then it is to hear him pronounce their doom." But others conclude that Matthew "virtually identifies the two" (Bauer, *The Gospel of the Son of God*, 254) or shows "that there is a blurring here of the lordly identity of Jesus and of Yahweh in the OT" (Gathercole, *The Preexistent Son*, 245).

[21] Statements that Matthew portrays Jesus as the embodiment of YHWH include those of Francois P. Viljoen, "The Superior Authority of Jesus in Matthew to Interpret the Torah," *IDS* 50.2 (2016): 2, and Hays, *Echoes of Scripture in the Gospels*, e.g., 103, 167. It must be emphasized, however, that Matthew also portrays Jesus as the embodiment of Israel; see, Kennedy, *The Recapitulation of Israel*, 225. This dual theme is only natural if Jesus is to be viewed as both divine and human, thus embodying all that qualifies him to be the mediator between God and man.

implies otherwise.²² Broader contextual features in Isaiah point to the Immanuel-figure as a future king in the Davidic line who also possesses divine qualities and the identity of YHWH.²³ And for Matthew, the ambiguity of YHWH's term in Isa 7:14 for *the maiden/virgin* (העלמה) as the one bearing the Davidic son—and YHWH's promise of personal presence in the eschaton—are proof enough for him that Jesus "fulfills" the promise of "God with us," not merely that Jesus is God's agent/ambassador to us.

Jesus's being called *Immanuel* theologically escalates the significance of his being called *Jesus*. Matthew underscores both appellations in a display of Hebrew parallelism to drive home the identification of Jesus as YHWH. He shall be called "Jesus," Matthew first points out, "for he shall save his people from their sins." Since the name *Jesus* literally means "YHWH saves," Matthew exegetes from the name that it is YHWH himself who shall save YHWH's people from their sins (Matt 1:21).²⁴ The parallel addition of the "name" *Immanuel* simply reinforces that Jesus is not merely another OT Joshua (who bore the same name), but rather YHWH in person, "God with us."²⁵ And while neither the name *Immanuel* nor the quotation of Isaiah 7:14 contain the Tetragrammaton, the Isaian context prophesied YHWH's personal coming/presence (9:1–7; cf. 35:1–10; 40:3–5), and the Matthean context had just identified Jesus as bearer

---

[22] John D. W. Watts, *Isaiah 1–33*, WBC (Nashville, TN: Nelson, 1999), 139–41, is one who believes that a NT christological interpretation of Isa 7:14 "ignores the rightful demands of contextual and historical exegesis." John Oswalt, *The Book of Isaiah: Chapters, 1–39*, NICOT (Grand Rapids, MI: Eerdmans, 1986), 211–12, however, recognizes that "no child born to a young woman in Ahaz's day is proof of God's presence in all times. But if a virgin overshadowed by God's Spirit should conceive and give birth, it would not only be a sign of God's presence with us. Better than that, it would be the reality of that experience. So Ahaz's sign must be rooted in its own time to have significance for that time, but it also must extend beyond that time and into a much more universal mode if its radical truth is to be any more than a vain hope. . . . This emphasis upon the mother and the corresponding de-emphasis of the father's role cannot help but be suggestive in the shaping of the ultimate understanding of the sign. No man sired by a human father could be the embodiment of 'God with us.'"

[23] Cf. Gary V. Smith, *Isaiah 1–39*, NAC (Nashville, TN: B&H, 2007), 211–16; Oswalt, *The Book of Isaiah: Chapters 1–39*, 203–14. It is often overlooked by critics of Matthew's use of Isa 7:14 that the promised Davidic son (called *Immanuel*) is further described in subsequent Isaian texts as ruling the world (8:5–10), being called "mighty God, everlasting Father" (9:6), and sitting on the Davidic throne forever (9:7). These prerogatives would not apply to Ahaz's immediate son, nor Isaiah's son, nor any other maiden's son of Isaiah's day. Matthew and those in his readership familiar with the Immanuel prophecy within the entirety of the Isaian document would understand the significance of the Immanuel name as consonant with the promise that YHWH would visit and be personally present with his people in the eschaton (cf. Isa 35; 40).

[24] Cf. Charles L. Quarles, *Matthew*, EGGNT (Nashville, TN: B&H Academic, 2017), 21–22; Jacques Guillet, "Jesus (Name Of)," *Dictionary of Biblical Theology*, ed. Xavier Léon-Dufour, trans. Joseph R. Sweeny (New York: Seabury Press, 1973), 264–65.

[25] Guillet, "Jesus (Name Of)," 264–65, surmised, "The name which He received at circumcision, as every Jewish child did (Lk 1,31; 2,21; Mt 1,21.25), was not exceptional in Israel (cf. Si 51,30). But since in this infant God becomes Emmanuel, 'God with us' (Mt 1,23), God accomplished in Him the promise made to the first Jesus, Joshua, to be with Him and to reveal Himself as 'Yahweh the Savior' (Dt 31,7f). . . . The name of Jesus has become the proper name of the Lord. When Israel called on the name of the Lord to find salvation (Jl 3,5), it pronounced the name that God had given Himself, Yahweh, the name which is always with His people to deliver them (Ex 3,14f). This name evoked a personality extraordinarily emphatic and vigorous which it would have been vain to wish to constrain or flatter. The name of Jesus evokes the same divine omnipotence, the same invulnerable vitality, but with the traits that are familiar to us; and we discover ourselves in the presence of someone who has given Himself to us forever and who belongs to us." Cf. Charles L. Quarles, *A Theology of Matthew* (Phillipsburg, NJ: P&R, 2013), 20.

of the divine Name possessing in himself divine initiative and power (1:21).[26] The child Mary would bear was to be called *Jesus*, "YHWH saves," because "he (Jesus) would save his (Jesus's) people from their sins." If Matthew had meant to portray Jesus merely as YHWH's agent rather than the embodiment of YHWH himself in 1:21 and, therefore, 1:23, then as an avowed monotheist Matthew failed to note that vital distinction.[27]

Further verification that the *Immanuel* "name" implies YHWH's personal presence in Jesus can be seen within the literary structure of Matthew's Gospel. The promise of Jesus's own presence with his/God's people (even when he is physically absent) bookends the Gospel (1:23; 28:20) and arises as a vital theme within its body (18:20), emphasizing that Jesus is the locus of God's promised presence.[28] Thus, Matthew's Gospel *en toto* boldly takes its position as the continuation of the OT metanarrative of YHWH's personal visitation and dwelling with his people being "fulfilled" in Jesus.[29] The purpose of the Matthean application of Isa 7:14—contextually interpreted in Isaiah as the personal coming/presence of YHWH with his people—to Jesus in Matt 1:23 is to underscore Jesus as the embodiment of YHWH.[30] If there is any doubt that Jesus is being portrayed with the divine identity of YHWH in this radical opening from the

---

[26] R. T. France, *The Gospel of Matthew* (Grand Rapids, MI: Eerdmans, 2007), 49, notes how Matthew's use of the Isaian prophecy implies YHWH's incarnational presence in Jesus.

[27] W. D. Davies and Dale C. Allison, *A Critical and Exegetical Commentary on the Gospel According to Saint Matthew*, vol. 1 (London; New York: T&T Clark, 2004), 217, however, speculate, "The evangelist could have believed Jesus to be the fullest embodiment or vehicle of the divine purpose and love and yet have perceived him as less than God (cf. Lk 1.68; 7.16; Mt 11:25–30)." Bauer, *The Gospel of the Son of God*, 241, recognizes a divine claim in light of the larger context. And many more commentators understand Matthew to be portraying Jesus as the personal presence and embodiment of YHWH. E.g., Herman N. Ridderbos, *Matthew* (Grand Rapids, MI: Regency Reference Library, 1987), 30; Donald A. Hagner, *Matthew 1–13*, WBC (Nashville, TN: Word, 1993), 21; Craig S. Keener, *A Commentary on the Gospel of Matthew* (Grand Rapids, MI: Eerdmans, 1999), 97.

[28] Luz, *Matthew 1–7*, Hermeneia, 96, among others, notes, "with the last verse of his Gospel...Matthew has created an inclusion that marks out a basic theme: the presence of the exalted Lord with his church establishes him as Immanuel, as God with us. Thus the Jewish Christian Matthew has put his story of Jesus in an extremely high christological perspective." Curiously, Luz continues, "Although he did not identify Jesus with God, he probably implied that in him Jesus is the form in which God will be present with his people and later with all nations." Others, however, apparently see a contradiction in Luz's caveat and interpret the passage within the Gospel's overall structure precisely as Matthew identifying Jesus with God. See, Quarles, *Matthew*, 22, 352; Hays, *Echoes of Scripture in the Gospels*, 162–63.

[29] Keener, *A Commentary on the Gospel of Matthew*, 67, sees Matthew's Immanuel theme as continuing the OT theme of YHWH's *shekinah*, or glory-presence: "like John, Matthew emphasizes Jesus' deity to monotheistic readers. Whereas John uses especially the image of Wisdom to develop his Christology, however, Matthew also focuses on the Shekinah. Although Matthew elsewhere articulates Wisdom Christology...he frames his Gospel with the portrait of Jesus as the present, saving God. Jesus is not only God present with his people (1:23), after his exaltation as Son of Man (28:18) equal to the Father and divine Spirit (28:19) and virtually omnipresent (28:20); Jesus is God's presence among his people (18:20), fulfilling a function Jewish teachers ascribed to the Shekinah, God's presence." David B. Capes, "Intertextual Echoes in the Matthean Baptismal Narrative," *BBR* 9 (1999): 44, further ties the Immanuel theme of YHWH's visitation/presence to Jesus's baptism.

[30] Crawford Howell Toy, *Quotations in the New Testament* (New York: Charles Scribner's Sons, 1884), 3, appears to interpret the embodiment metaphorically when he writes, "But the spiritual significance of the name, the spiritual presence of God with men, was realized more and more perfectly as Israel grew in knowledge, and most perfectly in Jesus of Nazareth, who most truly embodied the divine, and became the redeemer of men." Others, however, recognize that Matthew did not portray Jesus's presence as symbolic but as the literal embodiment of YHWH: e.g., Craig L. Blomberg, "Matthew," in *Commentary on the New Testament Use of the Old Testament*, ed. G. K. Beale and D. A. Carson (Grand Rapids, MI: Baker Academic; Apollos, 2007), 5; Hays, *Echoes of Scripture in the Gospels*, 163, 175.

First Evangelist, he dispels that ambiguity with the following transparent application of YHWH-texts to Jesus.

Matthew 3:3

While there are numerous allusions to Jesus's divine identity in Matthew's opening two chapters and, perhaps for some, an ambiguous application of a YHWH-text to Jesus at 1:23, the ambiguity is quickly dispelled in the formula quotation of Matt 3:3 referencing Isa 40:3, among other texts. It is also an example of the same YHWH-text(s) being applied to Jesus in all four Gospels (Matt 3:3; Mark 1:3; Luke 3:4; John 1:23).[31] Isaiah's text reads, "A voice cries, 'In the wilderness prepare the way of the LORD [MT: יְהוָה; LXX: κυρίου]; make straight in the desert a highway for our God.'" Astonishingly, Matthew's Gospel equates the crying "voice" to that of John the Baptist and the way of "YHWH" to the way of Jesus.

Scholars of all stripes acknowledge Matthew's equation of YHWH with Jesus (as heard from the lips of the Baptist),[32] but some find it to be a misapplication of the text. F. W. Beare, for example, concludes that the quotation is penned "in disregard of its original meaning.... But we must not judge [the NT writers] by our standards of scholarly investigation; they used the methods of their own time. Scientific exegesis and historical criticism in anything like our sense was quite unknown to them."[33]

Both OT and NT contexts, however, appear to be quite cogent when the latter is viewed hermeneutically as the fulfillment of the former. In Isaiah, the exiles are told that YHWH himself would come to their people on the occasion of great repentance— the meaning of the metaphor about making straight paths for YHWH's arrival.[34] Thus, the preaching of repentance by John the Baptist in the previous verse (3:2) is not a mere parallel or "spiritualization" of Isaiah's meaning, but rather a direct fulfillment

---

[31] Leon Morris, *The Gospel According to Matthew* (Grand Rapids, MI: Leicester, England: Eerdmans; InterVarsity Press, 1992), 54, makes the significant observation, "The use of the same prophecy in the other Synoptists indicates that this was an accepted practice among the Christians, not something peculiar to Matthew." Cf. Mark D. Vander Hart, "The Transition of the Old Testament Day of the LORD into the New Testament Day of the Lord Jesus Christ," *MJT* 9.1 (1993): 13.

[32] Of course, a few commentators neglect mentioning the connection altogether. Ulrich Luz, *Das Evangelium Nach Matthäus (Mt 1–7)*, EKK (Zürich, Einsiedeln, Köln: Benziger Verlag; Neukirchen Verlag, 1985), 145, has sparse comments on the verse, mentioning that all the formula quotations of Matthew apply to Jesus, but saying nothing else about the content of this quotation. Crawford Howell Toy, *Quotations in the New Testament* (New York: Charles Scribner's Sons, 1884), 19, writes of the "striking parallelism of the two periods" in view, which "in both cases there is a preparation for the great act." But he fails to acknowledge that Jesus is being portrayed here in the role of YHWH.

[33] Francis Wright Beare, *The Gospel According to Matthew* (San Francisco, CA: Harper & Row, 1982), 90. Cf. W. D. Davies and Dale C. Allison, *A Critical and Exegetical Commentary on the Gospel According to Saint Matthew*, ICC (London; New York: T&T Clark, 2004), 293, who describe Matthew's use of Isaiah as parallel to the hermeneutic of the Dead Sea Scrolls, and as a "thorough reinterpretation which disregards original context." Cf. Emerson B. Powery, *Jesus Reads Scripture* (Leiden, Germany: Brill, 2003), 102.

[34] Cf. D. A. Carson, "Matthew," in *The Expositor's Bible Commentary*, vol. 9, ed. Tremper III Longman and David E. Garland, rev. ed. (Grand Rapids, MI: Zondervan, 2010), 130; Quarles, *A Theology of Matthew*, 162; Thomas R. Schreiner, *The King in His Beauty* (Grand Rapids, MI: Baker Academic, 2013), 436.

of it. This is significant, because the Isaian prophecy does not predict the coming of a mere agent or representative of YHWH, but the coming of YHWH himself.[35] And, as D. A. Carson notes, Isaiah's clear reference to YHWH "is applied to Jesus without any sense of impropriety"[36] by the Baptist (and thus by Matthew). The quotation in Matt 3:3, therefore, is unforced and makes the best sense of both OT and NT contexts when the coming of Jesus is understood as the coming of YHWH.[37] Additional supporting comments may be found in the discussions of the parallel passages of Matt 3:3 in Mark 1:2–3 and Luke 3:4–6 (and related passages in Luke 1:17, 76; 7:26–27).

Matthew 7:21–22; 25:11

The next application of YHWH-texts to Jesus appears to be the double doublet in 7:21–22, which is found in Jesus's own teaching. Twice in the same passage Jesus applies to himself the vocative doublet "Lord, Lord" (κύριε, κύριε) to expose the attempted self-justification of false disciples at the final Judgment. (He uses the doublet a third time in the same vein in Matt 25:11.) The double vocative is allusive to numerous occurrences of the same combination in the LXX. Its unique use for YHWH in the LXX adds weight to its application by Jesus as a title for himself. Whenever the same vocative doublet is found in the LXX it is always with reference to God, and, in particular, as a form used in place of the Divine name.[38] Of the sixteen occurrences of κύριε κύριε in the LXX of canonical OT books, all refer to the Divine name: most translate the combination "Adonai YHWH," a few translate "YHWH Adonai," and at least one translates "YHWH" alone. But the doublet in the LXX never refers to anyone but YHWH.[39]

---

[35] Cf. Edward W. Eckman, "The Identification of Christ with Yahweh by New Testament Writers," *Gordon Review* 7.4 (1964): 147–48; John M. Frame, *The Doctrine of God* (Phillipsburg, NJ: P&R, 2002), 653; R. T. France, *The Gospel of Matthew*, NICNT (Grand Rapids, MI: Eerdmans, 2007), 105. Curiously, however, Craig L. Blomberg, "Matthew," in *Commentary on the New Testament Use of the Old Testament*, ed. G. K. Beale and D. A. Carson (Grand Rapids, MI: Baker Academic; Apollos, 2007), 12, admits, "Nothing in the immediate context of Isa. 40 suggests that Isaiah is referring to anyone other than Yahweh himself returning to Israel as king," but then proceeds to argue that other more distant indicators in Isaiah point to Yahweh "revealing himself through a specially anointed agent." Blomberg seems unclear on whether the "agent" may still be YHWH.

[36] D. A. Carson, "Christological Ambiguities in the Gospel of Matthew," in *Christ the Lord*, ed. Harold H. Rowdon (Leicester, England; Downers Grove, IL: InterVarsity Press, 1982), 109.

[37] Cf. Adolf Schlatter, *Der Evangelist Matthäus* (Stuttgart: Calwer Verlag, 1963), 59: "Für Mat. geschieht das Kommen Gottes durch das Kommen des Christus" [For Matthew the coming of God occurs through the coming of the Christ].

[38] Quarles, *A Theology of Matthew*, 142, notes, "This double vocative appears eighteen times in the Septuagint. Every single occurrence is an indisputable reference to Yahweh, and most occurrences translate the combined title and name *Adonai Yahweh*." Jason A. Staples, "'Lord, Lord': Jesus as YHWH in Matthew and Luke," *NTS* 64 (2018): 13, adds, "It bears repeating that this double formulation specifically arose to designate the distinctive Hebrew אדני יהוה and was employed despite a scribal tendency to eschew repetition.... The double κύριος thus distinctively marks the presence of the name to the Greek reader, making it clear that the formula in question is directly referring to the God of Israel by the special name." Cf. Quarles, *Matthew*, 75; Robert M. Bowman and J. Ed Komoszewski, *Putting Jesus in His Place* (Grand Rapids, MI: Kregel, 2007), 160.

[39] Cf. Quarles, *A Theology of Matthew*, 142.

The contexts of Jesus's application of the doublet support this understanding of their use. In Matt 7:21, κύριε κύριε is spoken to Jesus as the Judge who decides who will enter the kingdom of heaven. Who else but YHWH can determine who enters the heavenly kingdom? In 7:22, κύριε κύριε is addressed to Jesus as the one in whose "name" the false disciples claimed to have prophesied and performed miracles. To what other "name" but *YHWH* would anyone in Jesus's audience have thought to appeal at the Great Assize?[40] In the following verse, 7:23, Jesus makes it clear that his relational knowledge of people ("I never knew you") is the vital watershed of Final Judgment, and that it will be his own personal pronouncement ("depart from Me") that determines the eternal destinies of all people.[41]

Similarly, in 25:11 (Jesus's third use of the phrase in Matthew), κύριε κύριε is spoken to Jesus by the careless bridesmaids to whom he replies, "I do not know you," and leaves them locked out of the marriage feast (i.e., his eternal kingdom). In every case, Jesus uses the vocative doublet as a self-attesting name/title that not only refers to the unique name/title for YHWH[42] but applies to himself in contexts equivalent to those applied to Yahweh in the OT. Thus, according to his own usage in Matthew, Jesus is YHWH the Judge,[43] in whose identifying name and relational knowledge is the divine source of eternal salvation. According to Jesus, no hypocrite who merely claims loyalty to the divine name shall escape Jesus's own all-knowing judgment as the κύριος.

Strikingly, as Jason A. Staples notes, every occurrence of κύριος up to this point in Matthew has been used as a title for God (including at 3:3, where it is further applied to Jesus), following septuagintal usage of κύριος for יהוה.[44] Applying the doublet to Jesus would likely have sent a strongly message to the readers of the First Gospel that

---

[40] Stephen J. Wellum, "The Deity of Christ in the Synoptic Gospels," in *The Deity of Christ*, ed. Christopher W. Morgan and Robert A. Peterson (Wheaton, IL: Crossway, 2011), 76, notes, "Scripture is clear: judgment is the work of God alone (Deut. 1:17; Jer. 25:31; Rom. 2:3, 5–6; 14:10; 1 Pet. 1:17).... In fact, Jesus' verdict and sentence determines each individual's destiny as either eternal punishment or eternal life (Matt. 25:46...). Exercising divine judgment is implicit evidence of Jesus' self-understanding that he is in unique relation to his Father and has divine authority to do the very works of God."

[41] France, *The Gospel of Matthew*, 294, writes, "[Jesus] presents himself as the one who decides who does and does not enter the kingdom of heaven, and even more remarkably the basis for that entry is people's relationship with him, whether or not *he* 'knew them.' Further, the essence of their rejection from the kingdom of heaven is that they must go away *from him*. This pericope therefore stands alongside 25:31–46 in making the most exalted claims for Jesus as the eschatological judge and the personal focus of salvation" (emphasis France).

[42] Robert A. Peterson, "Toward a Systematic Theology of the Deity of Christ," in *The Deity of Christ*, ed. Christopher W. Morgan and Robert A. Peterson (Wheaton, IL: Crossway, 2011), 197, notes the following connection: "Viewed against its background in the law, the words 'prophesy in your name' in Matthew 7:22 identify Jesus with the God of the Old Testament.... The name of Jesus is used in place of the name of Yahweh." Cf. Staples, "'Lord, Lord': Jesus as YHWH in Matthew and Luke," 19.

[43] Cf. Simon J. Gathercole, *The Preexistent Son* (Grand Rapids, MI: Eerdmans, 2006), 246–47; A. H. McNeile, *The Gospel According to St. Matthew* (Grand Rapids, MI: Baker, 1980), 96; Ned Bernard Stonehouse, *The Witness of Matthew and Mark to Christ* (Philadelphia, PA: Presbyterian Guardian, 1944), 254.

[44] Staples, "'Lord, Lord': Jesus as YHWH in Matthew and Luke," 15, notes, "It is surely no accident that Matt 7.21-2 involves the first uses of κύριος referring to Jesus in the Gospel after using that term eleven times to refer to God before this passage. The use of the double form for the first application of κύριος to Jesus thus ensures that the reader does not miss the theological implications of that term, signaling that this κύριε is not a rudimentary 'sir.'"

Jesus's divine identity (as YHWH) is not in question but is even emphasized.⁴⁵ The claim of F. Hahn and others⁴⁶ that "[a]t first the title κύριος did not imply the divinity of Jesus,"⁴⁷ rings hollow in light of the LXX background and what the first readers would likely have understood by the doublet. Staples better explains the doublet's use and meaning as emphasizing the divine lordship of Christ and "setting the tone" for the rest of the book.⁴⁸

Matthew 8:25 and Similar Cries

In Matthew 8:25, Jesus's disciples in a storm-tossed boat cry out, "Lord, save!" (Κύριε, σῶσον). Some commentators understand the cry to be innocuous or merely natural to the circumstance. But, several factors point to the two words as applying a class of OT YHWH-texts to Jesus. First, the disciples call out "Lord" rather than *teacher, master, Jesus*, or other titles and names.⁴⁹ Second, the readership of Matthew has already been prompted by the clear quotation at 3:3 and the blatant doublet at 7:21–22 that "set the tone" for the use of κύριος for Jesus in all subsequent passages. Third, the deity of Jesus has already been emphasized by allusions in other previous passages (e.g., 1:1, 18, 20, 21, 23; 2:2; see below in the conclusion). Fourth, the nature of the request itself implies that the use of the κύριος title anticipates a YHWH-like response. How was a teacher (even, healer) supposed to "save" twelve grown men—some with a lifetime of experience on the sea—from perishing in a great storm on Galilee? The request appears nonsensical, unless by "Lord" a divine figure was being addressed.⁵⁰

Likewise, fifth, an additional stream of similar requests for mercy are also YHWH-unique. In other words, they assume the cultic worship of YHWH as the only one with the authority and power to relieve suffering and danger.⁵¹ And yet, the same cultic request for mercy is expressed to Jesus in the NT. Sixth, the actual response of Jesus confirms his divine power. He does not appeal to YHWH but acts as YHWH in stilling the storm (and in his subsequent response to each additional "Lord" request.) The disciples emphasize Jesus's personal power and authority in their astonished response,

---

⁴⁵ Cf. Staples, "'Lord, Lord': Jesus as YHWH in Matthew and Luke," 14.
⁴⁶ Cf. Davies and Allison, *Matthew 1–7*, 716, who find in the term at most "a messianic figure." Even Herman N. Ridderbos, *Matthew*, BSC (Grand Rapids, MI: Zondervan, 1987), 153, overlooks the significance of the double vocative as an allusion to YHWH-texts.
⁴⁷ Ferdinand Hahn, *The Titles of Jesus in Christology* (London: Lutterworth, 1969), 91, 113.
⁴⁸ Cf. Staples, "'Lord, Lord': Jesus as YHWH in Matthew and Luke," 15: "By using the double form here, Matthew thereby sets the tone for when characters call Jesus by the more ambiguous single κύριος later in the Gospel."
⁴⁹ In Mark the vocative is Διδάσκαλε (4:38), and in Luke it is the doublet Ἐπιστάτα, ἐπιστάτα (8:24). Carson, "Christological Ambiguities," 109, sees this as an example of "reportorial freedom" in line with "the already predicted 'divine majesty' of Jesus."
⁵⁰ Craig L. Blomberg, *Matthew*, NAC (Nashville, TN: Broadman, 1992), 150, writes, "[T]he focus of this passage remains squarely Christological—on who Christ is, not on what he will do for us. One who has this kind of power can be no less than God himself, worthy of worship, irrespective of when and how he chooses to use that power in our lives."
⁵¹ Cf. Jack Dean Kingsbury, *Matthew* (Philadelphia, PA: Fortress, 1975), 110–11. Although Beare, *The Gospel According to Matthew*, 341, believes that Matthew's usage reflects a later development of the church, he writes, "Kyrie, 'Lord', would by itself mean no more than 'Sir'—a respectful form of address; and it is so used in Mark, but here it clearly has the force of a cult title." Cf. Blomberg, *Matthew*, 150.

"What sort of man is this, that even winds and sea obey him?" (8:27).[52] And seventh, the OT is clear that YHWH is the exclusive master of wind and waves.[53]

Regarding certain cries (thus, prayers) for help to Jesus as "Lord," Simon J. Gathercole makes the case that they have a distinctive OT background that may be understood only as addresses to YHWH.[54] The comparisons in Table 2.1 are based on a table in Gathercole's work:[55]

Table 2.1 Cries to Jesus Reiterating Cries to YHWH

Sample texts [LXX]	Greek OT/NT comparisons	Literal translation
Ps 12:2 [11:2]	Σῶσόν, με, κύριε	Save me, Lord
Ps 106:47 [105:47]	σῶσον ἡμᾶς, κύριε ὁ θεὸς ἡμῶν	Save us, Lord our God
Ps 118:25 [117:25]	ὦ κύριε, σῶσον δή	O Lord, save indeed
Matt 8:25	Κύριε, σῶσον	Lord, save
Matt 14:30	Κύριε, σῶσον με	Lord, save me
Ps 6:2 [6:3]	ἐλέησόν με, κύριε	Have mercy on me, Lord
Ps 30:10	ἐλέησόν με, κύριε	Have mercy on me, Lord
Ps 41:4 [40:5]	Κύριε, ἐλέησόν με	Lord, have mercy on me
Ps 41:10 [40:11]	σύ δέ, κύριε, ἐλέησόν με	You, Lord, have mercy on me
Ps 86:3 [85:3]	ἐλέησόν με, κύριε	Have mercy on me, Lord
Ps 123:3 [122:3]	ἐλέησον ἡμᾶς, κύριε, ἐλέησον ἡμᾶς	Have mercy on us, Lord, have mercy on us
Matt 15:22	Ἐλέησόν με, κύριε	Have mercy on me, Lord
Matt 17:15	Κύριε, ἐλέησόν μου τὸν υἱόν	Lord, have mercy on my son
Matt 20:30	Ἐλέησον ἡμᾶς, κύριε	Have mercy on us, Lord
Matt 20:31	Ἐλέησον ἡμᾶς, κύριε	Have mercy on us, Lord

Cries for salvation and for mercy are two streams of requests to YHWH as "Lord" in the OT that are applied to Jesus as "Lord" in the NT. While it may be difficult to determine if the original speakers (and Matthew as author) deliberately quoted from particular OT texts, the cries in each context are too critically desperate to be cries for human assistance. Matthew's characters call out to Jesus as OT characters called out to God.

Matthew 9:2

Jesus's declaration to the paralytic, "Your sins are forgiven," brought accusations of blasphemy[56] from some scribes, because these words from Jesus are expected to be the

---

[52] Cf. Carson, "Christological Ambiguities," 109.
[53] Cf. Carson, "Matthew," 254; David L. Turner, *Matthew*, BECNT (Grand Rapids, MI: Baker Academic, 2008), 372; Hays, *Echoes of Scripture in the Gospels*, 166–67; W. D. Davies and Dale C. Allison, *A Critical and Exegetical Commentary on the Gospel According to Saint Matthew (Matthew 8–18)*, vol. 2, ICC (London; New York: T&T Clark, 2004), 75.
[54] Gathercole, *The Preexistent Son*, 245. However, he more modestly refers to these as "echoes" rather than quotations or allusions.
[55] Gathercole, *The Preexistent Son*, 246. Quarles, *Theology of Matthew*, 144, notes a similar list and includes another category of requests.
[56] Harrington, *The Gospel of Matthew*, 121, writes, "The technical biblical meaning of blasphemy consists in misusing the divine name Yahweh (see Lev 24:15–16; Num 15:30). By declaring the man's sins forgiven, Jesus usurps the divine prerogative of forgiving the sins of others," although "usurps" seems misleading as a term for asserting one's prerogative.

words of YHWH in the eschaton.[57] The Markan account makes explicit what is implied in Matthew: "Who can forgive sins but God alone?" (Mark 2:7).[58] Forgiveness of sins was known as a key component of the new covenant (Jer 31:34), in which YHWH promised the houses of Israel and Judah, "I will forgive all the guilt of their sin" (Jer 33:8; cf. Isa 40:2).

Here in Matt 9:2 Jesus speaks with the voice of YHWH to one of his own "sons": "Take heart, my son; your sins are forgiven." The declaration was not of a future forgiveness, but expressed in the present tense, taking immediate effect.[59] Neither was it transferred through the agency of a mere prophet or messenger,[60] but it was granted directly.[61] As the only acting subject on this occasion, Jesus made it clear that he had authority in himself both to heal the paralytic and to forgive his sins.[62]

Matthew 11:10

Jesus here formally cites an OT passage(s) to identify John the Baptist as the messenger coming before and preparing the way of God. Jesus's focus on John's identity and a perceived silence from Jesus with regard to himself prompted C. S. Macfarland to deny that Jesus is applying any OT passages to himself here.[63] But more recent scholarship is

---

[57] Quarles, *A Theology of Matthew*, 172, ties Jesus's authority to forgive to his (divine) identity as eschatological Judge.

[58] Douglas R. A. Hare, *Matthew* (Louisville, KY: John Knox, 1993), 100, claims, "The narrative does not identify who Jesus is. The self-designation 'the Son of man' does not relieve the mystery for the audience but only heightens it. The story by no means implies that the critics are right, that is, that Jesus claims to be God. In the Hebrew Scriptures, prophets function as messengers of God's forgiveness (II Sam. 12:13; Isa. 40:2). Christian readers know, however, that the one who here demonstrates his authority to communicate God's pardon is the one whose life will be poured out for many for the forgiveness of sins (26:28)." The passages Hare cites do not prove his point. II Sam 12:13 indeed describes Nathan the prophet giving David the message that YHWH has forgiven David. But Nathan is not self-designated "the Son of Man" with his own authority to forgive sins. And Isa 40:2 functions (much like Jer 33:8) as a prophetic promise of forgiveness from YHWH in the future new covenant. Jesus, however, was pronouncing forgiveness to the paralytic at the moment of healing—with both healing and forgiveness coming from Jesus as their divine source.

[59] Cf. Donald A. Hagner, *Matthew 1–13*, WBC 33A (Nashville, TN: Word, 1993), 232; Morris, *The Gospel According to Matthew*, 217.

[60] Schreiner, *The King in His Beauty*, 438, comments, "Jesus did not qualify his words by saying that it was actually God who forgave the sins of the paralytic. Instead, he emphasized his own authority as God."

[61] Davies and Allison, *Matthew 8–18*, 91, write, "9.6 states clearly enough that the Son of man does indeed have authority on earth to forgive sins. So Jesus does more than announce God's forgiveness.... It seems best to take our clue from Mark's text: 'Who is able to forgive sins but God alone?'.... In Mark and, we may think, in Matthew, Jesus has taken to himself a divine prerogative. He has made himself out to be more than an intermediary. He has acted not as a channel of forgiveness but as its source (cf. Jn 10.33)."

[62] Timothy J. Geddert, "The Implied YHWH Christology of Mark's Gospel: Mark's Challenge to the Reader to 'Connect the Dots,'" *BBR* 25.3 (2015): 331, writing of the parallel passage in Mark, writes applicably to this passage as well: "The whole point of Jesus' argument was that his own power to heal demonstrated his *own* authority to forgive. The only actor in this text has been Jesus, and Mark's narrator implies that Jesus is worthy of the praise *as* God, however much or little the characters in the story see it that way" (emphasis Geddert). Cf. Harrington, *The Gospel of Matthew*, 121–22; Blomberg, *Matthew*, 154.

[63] Cf. Charles S. Macfarland, *Jesus and the Prophets* (New York; London: G. P. Putnam's Sons, 1905), 192–93.

generally united that this citation of Jesus deliberately implies his own equation with YHWH.[64] In fact, it is precisely in Jesus's filling of the role of YHWH that the intended eschatological meaning of the cited text(s) is fulfilled.[65]

The citation is largely taken from Mal 3:1,[66] though a case can be made that Jesus incorporated Exod 23:20 in his view, as well.[67] In Malachi YHWH says, "Behold, I send my messenger, and he will prepare the way before me." The wording seems to be a paraphrastic recapitulation of Exodus 23:20, in which YHWH had promised the wandering children of Israel, "Behold, I send an angel (messenger) before you to guard you on the way and to bring you to the place that I have prepared." Thus, in Exodus, the messenger (Angel of YHWH) goes before Israel to the place prepared by YHWH. In Malachi, the messenger goes before YHWH to prepare the way of YHWH. Now in Matthew 11:10, Jesus identifies John the Baptist as that messenger of preparation in Malachi, which means that Jesus identifies his own coming with the coming of YHWH. Jesus occupies the place of YHWH in both OT passages.

This trajectory is made all the more interesting by Jesus's change in the pronouns. Whereas in Malachi YHWH says that his messenger will prepare the way before "me," in Matthew YHWH says his messenger will prepare "your" way before "you." Thus, in Jesus's paraphrase YHWH both sends and appears as another: Jesus. By the second person pronouns Jesus both distinguishes himself from the divine Sender of the messenger (John) and takes the position of YHWH as the one for whom the messenger prepares the way. Furthermore, if Jesus is also harkening back to the Exodus passage, then "he identifies the Messiah with Yahweh, as Exod. 23.20–23 identifies the 'angel' with Yahweh."[68] Carson writes,

---

[64] Cf. Morris, *The Gospel According to Matthew*, 279–80; Craig S. Keener, *A Commentary on the Gospel of Matthew* (Grand Rapids, MI: Eerdmans, 1999), 338; Hagner, *Matthew 1–13*, 305; Robert Horton Gundry, *The Use of the Old Testament in St. Matthew's Gospel* (Leiden, The Netherlands: Brill, 1967), 225; France, *Jesus and the Old Testament*, 155; James B. DeYoung, "The Function of Malachi 3.1 in Matthew 11.10: Kingdom Reality as the Hermentutic of Jesus," in *The Gospels and the Scriptures of Israel*, ed. Craig A. Evans and W. Richard Stegner (Sheffield, England: Sheffield Academic, 1994), 71–73; Carson, "Matthew," 306–7; David B. Capes, *Old Testament Yahweh Texts in Paul's Christology*, 180; Blomberg, "Matthew," 40. Other nuanced explanations that emphasize Jesus as the agent of YHWH without denying his identity as YHWH include, Larry W. Hurtado, *One God, One Lord*, 3rd ed. (London; New York: Bloomsbury T&T Clark, 2015), 251; Ridderbos, *Matthew*, 215.

[65] Cf. Gundry, *Use of the Old Testament in St. Matthew's Gospel*, 224–25.

[66] Cf. DeYoung, "The Function of Malachi 3.1 in Matthew 11.10," in *The Gospels and the Scriptures of Israel*, ed. Craig A. Evans and Richard W. Stegner (Sheffield, England: Sheffield Academic, 1994), 69; Carson, "Matthew," 306–7; Keener, *A Commentary on the Gospel of Matthew*, 338; Ridderbos, *Matthew*, 215.

[67] Cf. Davies and Allison, *Matthew 8–18*, 250: "The combination of Exod 23.20 with Mal 3.1 was not a Christian innovation. It can also be found in Jewish texts (see Stendahl, *School*, p. 50).... Mal 4.5–6 interprets Mal 3.1 as a prophecy about Elijah. Our text does the same (cf. 11.14). It thus makes John the Baptist (= Elijah) the messenger preparing the way for Jesus. (The OT has 'my messenger before me,' 'me' being Yahweh. Matthew's σοῦ is Jesus. So Jesus has replaced Yahweh: 'the way of God is the way of Christ' (Schlatter, p. 363)."

[68] DeYoung, "The Function of Malachi 3.1 in Matthew 11.10," 71. He adds, 72–73, "[T]he 'Lord' and the 'messenger of the covenant' are one and the same person. Clearly the 'Lord' is divine; he is the one described as 'the Lord you are seeking,' which answers to Mal. 2.17: 'Where is the God of justice?' Also he is said to 'come to his temple,' which must be Yahweh's (Zech. 1.16). The last title, 'Messenger [or Angel] of the covenant,' is unique in Scripture but reminiscent of Exod. 3.6, 14.19 and especially 23.20. This angel is Yahweh himself, the preincarnate Christ (cf. Exod. 33.15; Isa. 63.9). The covenant

[T]his periphrastic rendering makes Jesus' identity unambiguous.... Even if Malachi 3:1 had been exactly quoted, the flow of the argument in Matthew demands that if John the Baptist is the prophesied Elijah who prepares the way for Yahweh (3:3; cf. Lk 1:76) or for the Day of Yahweh (Mal 4:5–6), and John the Baptist is Jesus' forerunner, then Jesus himself is the manifestation of Yahweh and brings in the eschatological Day of Yahweh.[69]

Thus, Matthew's narrative here clearly portrays Jesus as the fulfillment of Malachi's YHWH-text.

Matthew 11:28

In Matt 11:28 Jesus appears to quote the promise of YHWH to the Israelites in Exod 33:14 as his own promise: "and I will give you rest." The conjunction, second person pronoun, and word order argue for a strict translation of the Hebrew into Greek [:יִתְחֲנֻהַ לָךְ = κἀγὼ ἀναπαύσω ὑμᾶς],[70] increasing the plausibility that Jesus had the promise of Exod 33:14 in mind when he spoke. If so, then he likely expected his audience to recall the same promise.[71]

The contexts of both passages increase this probability. In Exod 33, YHWH called the people of Israel to leave Sinai for Canaan and promised that he would drive out the wicked inhabitants of the Promised Land. Yet, YHWH said he would not go with the Israelites, lest he should consume them for their wickedness. Moses interceded for the nation within the Tent of Meeting, wherein YHWH then responded to Moses, "My presence will go with you, and I will give you rest" (v. 14). Thus, the promise is of divine presence en route to divine rest. Jesus could hardly mean anything different, although the "rest" of Exod 33 on the surface likely implied peace and safety from enemies in Canaan. The same words from Jesus imply spiritual rest—salvation—both present and future.

This is confirmed by the immediate context in Matthew. In 11:25, Jesus thanks his Father for hiding the importance of Jesus's mighty works from the "wise" and revealing it instead to "little children" by his "gracious will," a description of sovereign

---

must be the New Covenant (Jer. 31.31–34). Hence, the 'Lord' and 'the Messenger of the covenant' are titles for one, divine person. He is also related to Yahweh." Cf. Gundry, *Use of the Old Testament in St. Matthew's Gospel*, 225.

[69] Carson, "Matthew," 307. Cf. Morris, *The Gospel According to Matthew*, 279–80.

[70] The change from the feminine singular pronoun in Hebrew to the masculine plural pronoun in Greek is easily accounted for when it is recognized that YHWH's promise of rest was for the nation of Israel (a collective feminine singular concept in Hebrew). Thus, what Yahweh promises (typologically) for the old covenant people of God Jesus promises (anti-typologically) for the new covenant people of God. Some commentators note a connection back to Exod 33: e.g., Turner, *Matthew*, 305; Hagner, *Matthew 1–13*, 323; Davies and Allison, *Matthew 8–18*, 285, 287.

[71] Carson, "Matthew," 322, sees Jesus's promise as an "echo of Jeremiah 31:25." This is surely right. But the new covenant promise of Yahweh, "I will refresh the weary soul" [הִפְעִיע שָׁפֵן יְתִיוֹרָה], is more closely an echoed (paraphrased) by Matthew's next verse: "you will find rest for your souls" [καὶ εὑρήσετε ἀνάπαυσιν ταῖς ψυχαῖς ὑμῶν] (11:29). The phrase in Matt 11:28, however, is closest to that in Exod 33:14. Nevertheless, the same trajectory runs through all of these verses to the ultimate rest given by Jesus in the new creation (cf. Heb 3–4).

grace in the salvation of God's true people.[72] Jesus then describes the universal rule he possesses by the Father's will and the reciprocal nature of his relationship with the Father, such that Jesus, too, sovereignly chooses to whom he reveals the Father.[73] It is with this background that he extends the promise of "rest" to all who are burdened. But the character of those who actually receive the Jesus-granted rest is marked by their response to Jesus himself: "Come to me. . . . Take my yoke upon you, and learn from me . . . and you will find rest for your souls" (11:28–29).[74] The ones who "shall find rest" are those who personally attach themselves to their "meek" leader (anticipated by Moses), so that he would grant them soul-rest. The glaring difference between Moses and Jesus, however, is that Jesus does not relay YHWH's promise to grant rest in Canaan, but directly promises to grant rest in himself.[75]

Matthew 12:8

Having taught that he provides rest for the burdened (Matt 11:28) and that he surpasses the value of the temple (12:6),[76] Jesus astonished the Pharisees by issuing another theologically charged claim: "For the Son of Man is Lord of the Sabbath" [κύριος γάρ ἐστιν τοῦ σαββάτου ὁ υἱὸς τοῦ ἀνθρώπου]. Thus, temple worship and Sabbath rest are intertwined in Jesus. As John M. Frame notes of the OT God, "It is his house, as the Sabbath is his day."[77] Furthermore, Jesus bolsters his claim of lordship over the Sabbath by identifying himself as the "Son of Man" (the occupant of God's throne in Dan 7:13–14) and placing κύριος in the first position to emphasize his exalted role as the Sabbath's Lord.[78] Jesus identifies himself with the unique prerogatives of YHWH.[79]

---

[72] Cf. Rudolf Schnackenburg, *The Gospel of Matthew* (Grand Rapids, MI: Eerdmans, 2002), 110.
[73] Benjamin B. Warfield, *The Lord of Glory* (New York: American Tract Society, 1907), 93, writes insightfully of the ontological import of Jesus's claim here: "Our Lord represents Himself as the sole source of the knowledge of God and of the divine grace, because this is the relation in which He stands essentially to the Father—a relation of complete and perfect intercommunion. The assertion of the reciprocal knowledge of the Father and Son, in other words, rises far above the merely mediatorial function of the Son, although it underlies His mediatorial mission: it carries us back into the region of metaphysical relations. The Son is a fit and perfect mediator of the divine knowledge and grace because the Son and the Father are mutually intercommunicative. The depth of the Son's being, we are told, can be fathomed by none but a divine knowledge, while the knowledge of the Son compasses all that God is; from both points of view, the Son appears thus as 'equal with God.'" Cf. Gathercole, *The Preexistent Son*, 248–49.
[74] Cf. Hagner, *Matthew 1–13*, 323.
[75] Davies and Allison, *Matthew 8–18*, 286–90, find multiple comparisons.
[76] Ridderbos, *Matthew*, 230, notes well the connection between Jesus as greater than the temple and as Lord of the Sabbath. Hays, *Echoes of Scripture in the Gospels,* 168, adds, "What could be greater than the temple other than the one to whom it is dedicated, the one who is worshiped in it? Matthew's argument is in effect this: if Jesus is 'God with us,' then his presence sanctifies the labors of those who work to serve him, even on the Sabbath. Indeed, if Jesus is 'God with us,' then his personal presence now takes the place of the temple where the presence of God was formerly thought to dwell."
[77] Frame, *The Doctrine of God,* 654.
[78] Grant R. Osborne, *Matthew*, ZECNT (Grand Rapids, MI: Zondervan, 2010), 454, notes the significance of this as well: "The 'Lord' (κύριος) is in the emphatic position and stresses the fact that Jesus has absolute authority over the Sabbath as cosmic Lord and the final interpreter of Torah."
[79] Perplexingly, Hare, *Matthew*, 133, asserts, "Here as everywhere in Matthew it is a mysterious self-designation that makes no assertion about Jesus' identity." Davies and Allison, *Matthew 8–18*, 316, find the claim so incredible that they deny its authenticity by suggesting a probably Markan editorial comment.

The background of Jesus's claim is the creation in Genesis, after which God rested, for God's creation "rest" is the basis of his Sabbath command (cf. Gen 2:3; Exod 20:8–11).[80] YHWH's institution of the Sabbath/Seventh, patterned after his own seventh-day rest, means that he is the Sabbath's originating authority and that the Sabbath belongs to him. This is explicitly claimed when YHWH calls the weekly observances, "My Sabbaths" (cf. Exod 31:13; Lev 19:3, 30), and when both he and his people call the seventh day observance "a (holy) Sabbath to Yahweh" (cf. Exod 16:23; Lev 23:3).[81] Thus, for Jesus to claim for himself the position of "Lord of the Sabbath" would be nothing short of blasphemous, if he were anyone but YHWH. The title in this passage functions as one of the strongest indicators of Christ's deity in the Scriptures.[82] "Lord" in this context cannot mean a lesser lord than YHWH, but rather implies that Jesus is the Sabbath institution's initiating source and absolute authority.[83] The ownership and regulation of the Sabbath exist as divine prerogatives; Jesus claims those prerogatives for himself.[84]

Matthew 14:25–27

The next passage contains a complex of allusions to texts formerly used of YHWH and now applied to Jesus. Gathered together, they emphasize that Jesus is to be identified as YHWH. In Matt 14:25, the disciples experience another storm on Galilee, but this time without Jesus in the boat. Instead—and this seems to be implied as being by design since Jesus had told them to get in the boat and go on ahead of him (14:22)—Jesus comes to the rescue of the disciples "walking on the sea" [περιπατῶν ἐπὶ τὴν θάλασσαν]. And the same act is described from the disciples' point of view in 14:26, implying the phrase's significance for understanding this event. In the OT, it is YHWH "alone" who walks on the sea (see esp., Job 9:8; cf. Job 38:16; Ps 77:16, 19; Isa 43:16; Hab 3:15).[85]

---

[80] Cf. France, *The Gospel of Matthew*, 463.
[81] France, *The Gospel of Matthew*, 463, writes, "Not only is the Son of Man greater than David and the temple, but he is 'Lord' of the institution which is traced in the OT to God's direct command (Gen 2:3), enshrined in the Decalogue which is the central codification of God's requirements for his people, and described by God as '*my* Sabbath' (Exod 31:13; Lev 19:3, 30; Isa 56:4, etc.; cf. the recurrent phrase 'a Sabbath to/for Yahweh,' Exod 16:23; 20:10; 35:2, etc.). Against that background to speak of humanity in general as 'lord of the Sabbath' would be unthinkable; to speak of an individual human being as such is to make the most extraordinary claim to an authority on a par with that of God himself" (emphasis France). Cf. Rusty N. Small, "What Was Spoken Through the Prophet Isaiah: Matthew's Use of Isaiah to Reveal Matthew's Christology" (PhD diss., Southeastern Baptist Theological Seminary, 2012), 216; Quarles, *Matthew*, 124.
[82] Cf. Kingsbury, *Matthew*, 106; Quarles, *A Theology of Matthew*, 145; Gathercole, *The Preexistent Son*, 248.
[83] Hagner, *Matthew 1–13*, 330, writes, "The Son of Man, i.e., Jesus, is said here to be the 'Lord of the Sabbath' in the sense that he has the sovereign authority to decide what loyalty to the Sabbath means. . . . If something greater than the temple is present, then here is also someone greater than the sabbath." Cf. Frame, *The Doctrine of God*, 654.
[84] Cf. Robert L. Reymond, *Jesus, Divine Messiah* (Phillipsburg, NJ: P&R, 1990), 66; McNeile, *The Gospel According to St. Matthew*, 170.
[85] Job 9:8 (LXX: ὁ τανύσας τὸν οὐρανὸν μόνος καὶ περιπατῶν ὡς ἐπ' ἐδάφους ἐπὶ θαλάσσης), which has the closest wording to Matt 14:25, emphasizes that YHWH "alone" (both MT and LXX use the modifier) made the heavens and walks on the sea. Cf. Harrington, *The Gospel of Matthew*, 224; Blomberg, "Matthew," 50.

Furthermore, as Schnackenburg notes, "the power of water is an image of menace and might (Pss. 18:16; 32:6; 69:2)."[86] It stands as a barrier between God's people and God's promises (cf. the Red Sea and the swollen Jordan River at each end of the wilderness wanderings)[87] until YHWH intervenes and reveals his lordship over its power. Like YHWH, Jesus walks on the waves of the sea,[88] and like YHWH, Jesus reveals his power over his creation by calming the storm.[89]

Moreover, like YHWH, Jesus takes the divine name upon himself. His initial words to his disciples while walking toward them on the sea are of profound economy: Θαρσεῖτε, ἐγώ εἰμι· μὴ φοβεῖσθε. Three staccato phrases are bracketed with two sharp commands ("have courage" and "don't be afraid"), which frame the reason to obey Jesus's commands: "I AM." Some scholars doubt that Jesus is applying a form of the OT divine name to himself,[90] but many others have pointed out numerous contextual clues that speak otherwise.[91] It is no small factor that Jesus assumes YHWH's commands into his self-identity. The command "Do not fear" is commonly known as the most frequent command of God in Scripture[92]—typically given to those who experience his favorable presence.[93] Jesus appears to be requiring what YHWH requires when he is present to save.

---

[86] Schnackenburg, *The Gospel of Matthew*, 144.
[87] Cf. Harrington, *The Gospel of Matthew*, 226; Davies and Allison, *Matthew 8–18*, 504.
[88] Kirk, *A Man Attested by God*, 250–51, represents a number of scholars who argue that Peter's brief walk on water (Matt 14:28–33) negates the view that Jesus shares in the divine identity simply because he walked on water. But the Evangelist emphasizes a categorical contrast so that no reader will miss it: Jesus never calls upon YHWH but behaves as YHWH. He controls who can join him in the suspension of natural laws and "commands" Peter to come to him in response to Peter's request for permission. Jesus unilaterally saves Peter from drowning after Peter's prayer-cry for supernatural intervention. The entire scene reveals Jesus as the source of divine power and authority to tread the waves of the sea. Kirk fails to connect what Jesus does in this event with what YHWH alone can do in Job 9:8, the clearest background text. Cf. Joshua Leim, "Theological Hermeneutics, Exegesis, and J. R. Daniel Kirk's *A Man Attested by God*," *JTI* 15.1 (2021): 31.
[89] Cf. Harrington, *The Gospel of Matthew*, 226; Blomberg, "Matthew," 50; Davies and Allison, *Matthew 8–18*, 506.
[90] Cf. Hare, *Matthew*, 168–69. W. F. Albright and C. S. Mann, *Matthew* (Garden City, NY: Doubleday & Company, 1971), 182, admit that there is some deeper meaning to the passage, but deny the event actually happened as described.
[91] E.g., Keener, *A Commentary on the Gospel of Matthew*, 406; Quarles, *A Theology of Matthew*, 169–70; Donald A. Hagner, *Matthew 14–28*, WBC (Dallas, TX: Word, 1995), 423; Harrington, *The Gospel of Matthew*, 227; Geddert, "Implied YHWH Christology," 333; Davies and Allison, *Matthew 8–18*, 506; Blomberg, "Matthew," 50.
[92] One such online list of occurrences appears in Felix Just, "'Have No Fear! Do Not Be Afraid!'" *Catholic Resources for Bible, Liturgy, Art, and Theology*, 15 June 2021, http://catholic-resources.org/Bible/HaveNoFear.htm. Quarles, *A Theology of Matthew*, 170, notes as well, "The command 'Do not be afraid' (Matt. 14:27) reinforces the nuance of divine self-disclosure, since the singular form of Jesus' command is the familiar way in which Yahweh addresses the patriarchs and the nation of Israel (Gen. 15:1; 26:24; 28:13 [Septuagint]; 46:3; Isa. 41:13). This is all the more likely in the context of Peter's cry, 'Lord, save me' (Matt. 14:30), which, like the cry in 8:25, is reminiscent of cries to Yahweh in the Old Testament."
[93] Schnackenburg, *The Gospel of Matthew*, 145, connects Jesus's use of the Tetragrammaton with the common Yahwistic command not to fear: "The sovereign 'It is I' (in the Greek, 'I am') is not merely a formula of identification, but divine self-revelation, in the same way that Yahweh so often presents himself in the Old Testament (and even more clearly in the Gospel of John). God's protective nearness is communicated in Jesus' appearance."

Thus, in a brief span of three verses in Matthew, (1) Jesus walks on the sea as YHWH "alone" can do, (2) Jesus issues commands that epitomize the commands of YHWH (and reduce to nonsense if uttered by a mere man), and (3) Jesus identifies himself by a well-known Greek allusion to the tetragrammaton. It would seem probable, then, that Matt 14:25–27 constitutes a deliberate attempt by Jesus (and in Matthew's recollection of Jesus) to portray himself as the self-expression of YHWH.[94]

Matthew 16:27

Here is another case of multiple allusions with partial quotations of OT YHWH-texts used to identify Jesus as YHWH. In the short space of this verse, Jesus affirms his future coming (1) as the divine Son of Man from Daniel, (2) as the master of God's angels, (3) as embodying the *shekinah* of YHWH, and (4) as the eschatological Judge of mankind. Verse 28 adds the feature that he comes (5) as the ruler of God's kingdom. The stacking of these roles of Jesus is not meant to depict a mere representative of YHWH, but YHWH himself. It will be instructive to briefly examine each of these features of the text in turn.

First, Matthew's readers have seen Jesus use his favorite self-designation,[95] "the Son of Man," ten times before this verse, but the importance of the title is greatly advanced here. If there were any question beforehand as to the background of Jesus's meaning of the title, he clarifies it here with the "coming" of "the Son of Man" in God's "glory" and "kingdom." These features solidify that Jesus is referring to himself as the exalted figure of Dan 7:13–14 to whom the Ancient of Days confers his eternal and universal dominion.[96] The Danielic description of the Son of Man is so exalted that he appears to take on the role of the Ancient of Days—a clear alternate title for YHWH. In fact, the LXX version of Daniel more closely identifies the two figures, implying equality.[97] The Ancient of Days and the Son of Man share the same absolute authority.

---

[94] Blomberg, "Matthew," 50, writes, "Jesus' self-revelation to the disciples (14:27) can be translated 'It is I,' but literally it reads *ego eimi* ('I am'), a probable allusion to the divine name in Exod. 3:14." Even Beare, *The Gospel According to Matthew,* 322, admits, "This mode of speech is frequently attributed to Jesus in the Gospels. In LXX, it is generally a self-proclamation of God."

[95] Cf. Osborne, *Matthew*, 307. William Hendriksen, *Exposition of the Gospel According to Matthew* (Grand Rapids, MI: Baker, 1984), 406, arranges a chart of all Synoptic occurrences with notations showing how the term is used in contexts of the humiliation and/or exaltation of Jesus.

[96] Cf. Darrell L. Bock, "Son of Man," in *Dictionary of Jesus and the Gospels*, ed. Joel B. Green, Jeannine K. Brown, and Nicholas Perrin, 2nd ed. (Downers Grove, IL: IVP Academic, 2013), 900.

[97] The central issue is whether the Old Greek version understands the Son of Man to be taking his seat/throne "like" the Ancient of Days does or "as" the Ancient of Days himself. Is it possible that the ambiguity of the LXX allows for both ideas of equality and identity? Benjamin E. Reynolds, "The 'One Like a Son of Man' According to the Old Greek of Daniel 7,13–14," *Biblica* 89 (2008): 70–80, ably presents the hermeneutical options. And while arguing for two distinct personages, he nevertheless sees their intrinsic similarity as well. Charles L. Quarles, "Lord or Legend: Jesus as the Messianic Son of Man," *JETS* 62.1 (2019): 111, notes, "Although some scholars argue that the Septuagint reading is a product of unintentional scribal error which mistook ἕως for ὡς, most critics now conclude that the original Greek translation equated the Son of Man and Ancient of Days to express a carefully thought-out interpretation of the Aramaic text."

Second, the Son of Man is possessor of YHWH's angels. Carson writes, "They are his angels. He stands so far above them that he owns them and uses them."[98] This ownership is claimed by Jesus as a matter of course and without any hint of delegation or transference (cf. 24:31). In fact, transference seems out of the question, since the Creator of the angels will always be their owner and master. Furthermore, for Jesus to say that he, the Son of Man, will "come with his angels" in the Father's glory is to assume the role of YHWH, whom Zech 14:5 predicts will "come with all his holy ones." If Jesus is pulling from Zechariah as well as from Daniel, then the coming of the Son of Man is confirmed to be simultaneously the coming of YHWH.[99]

Third, for the Son of Man to come in his Father's "glory" is a clear reference to the OT *shekinah*, or manifested divine presence of the glory-cloud of the Exodus and in the Tabernacle/Temple.[100] Thus, Jesus's coming in glory is a coming in the manifest presence of God. It is a visible display and confirmation of Jesus as Immanuel, "God with us" (Matt 1:23). Here, the glory is of the Father. Later, Jesus will call the same glory his own with an even clearer reference to "the Son of Man coming on the clouds of heaven with power and great glory" (24:30).[101] This seems to imply that the *shekinah* (as well as the angels) belongs equally to the Ancient of Days and the Son of Man. "Jesus thus will come into his own visible, divine majesty, and not just that of the Father."[102]

Fourth, another partial quotation of a YHWH-text(s) applied to Jesus is found in Jesus's claim that he, the Son of Man, will "repay each person according to what he has done." If this is not a general allusion to several OT texts asserting the same truth, then it may be a quotation of a specific text, such as Ps 62:12 (or Prov 24:12).[103] By any connection, the pertinent point is that Jesus here assumes the role of YHWH as the divine eschatological Judge.[104]

Fifth (to contextually include verse 28), for Jesus as "the Son of Man" to "come" in "his kingdom," he not only alludes again to the exalted figure who takes his heavenly throne, but he claims kingship of God's kingdom. (That Jesus appears to refer to the Transfiguration of the following passage that "some standing here will see" does not negate the further eschatological implications of his prediction.) The kingdom handed over to him is eternal and universal. It is the jurisdiction of YHWH. The universal reign and realm belong to the Ancient of Days and to the Son of Man simultaneously.

---

[98] Carson, "Matthew," 431. McNeile, *The Gospel According to St. Matthew*, 247, also notes, "Only Mt adds αὐτοῦ after ἀγγέλων, emphasizing the divine authority of the glorified Christ; cf. xiii. 41, xxiv. 31."

[99] Cf. France, *The Gospel of Matthew*, 639.

[100] Cf. J. A. Dennis, "Glory," in *Dictionary of Jesus and the Gospels*, ed. Joel B. Green, Jeannine K. Brown, and Nicholas Perrin, 2nd ed. (Downers Grove, IL: IVP Academic, 2013), 313. Osborne, *Matthew*, 638, adds, "The idea of the 'Son of Man' . . . returning 'in the glory of his Father' reflects Dan 7:13–14 (cf. Rom 6:4), God's 'glory' (δόξα) includes both his Shekinah glory (the glory 'dwelling' among his people) and the ineffable glory, majesty, and splendor of the enthroned God of Isa 6 and Ezek 1."

[101] Cf. Carson, "Matthew," 431; John Nolland, *The Gospel of Matthew*, NIGTC (Grand Rapids, MI: Eerdmans; Paternoster, 2005), 694.

[102] Dennis, "Glory," 313.

[103] Cf. Maarten J. J. Menken, "The Psalms in Matthew's Gospel," in *The Psalms in the New Testament*, ed. Steve Moyise and Maarten J. J. Menken (London; New York: T&T Clark, 2004), 69; France, *The Gospel of Matthew*, 639; Carson, "Matthew," 431.

[104] Nolland, *The Gospel of Matthew*, 694, notes, "In 6:4, 6, 18 (cf. 20:8) it is the Father who rewards. To reward each according to his or her works or deeds is a function regularly attributed to God." Cf. France, *The Gospel of Matthew*, 639; Osborne, *Matthew*, 638.

Just one of these connections alone might render less certain the evidence that Jesus applied OT YHWH-texts to himself in this passage. But his use of a wide-reaching series of quotations and allusions of YHWH-texts marshals multiple witnesses to testify strongly of his divine self-identity.

Matthew 18:20

As Jesus looked ahead to the formation of his Church, he promised his disciples that he would be present "in their midst" for their congregational self-judgment (church discipline).[105] The phrase reflects the concept—if not specific OT texts, such as Num 35:34 or Joel 2:27[106]—that YHWH dwelt and shall dwell in the midst of his people.[107] Furthermore, it lies clearly within the thematic trajectory between the Gospel's introduction of Jesus as "God with us" (1:23) and Jesus's final promise "I will be with you always, even to the end of the age" (28:20).[108] These bookends, and Jesus's promise here in 18:20 to be in the midst of even two or three of his followers, appears to be the new covenant fulfillment of YHWH's old covenant promises to be savingly present with his people. This is no mere promise to be in his disciples' memories or aspirations. Jesus's promise can only be fulfilled in all his redeemed people if he is divinely omnipresent.[109]

Furthermore, this gracious sort of divine presence is experienced only by those who gather in Jesus's "name"—implying the authority of his divine person/identity.[110] The authoritative name of *YHWH* is present in the name of *Jesus*, which literally means "YHWH saves."[111] Being "in their midst" is a word of comfort to his disciples,

---

[105] Carson, "Matthew," 457, notes, "It is a truism of the biblical revelation that God's presence stands with the judges of his people (Ps 82:1). Here as elsewhere, Jesus takes God's place. Jesus will be with the judges."

[106] Many commentators suggest that a statement in *Aboth* 3.3—"Two that sit together occupied in Torah have the Presence in their midst"—is the background for Jesus's claim in Matt 18:20. (Cf. Albright and Mann, *Matthew*, 221; Beare, *The Gospel According to Matthew*, 381; Morris, *The Gospel According to Matthew*, 471, Schnackenburg, *The Gospel of Matthew*, 178; Turner, *Matthew*, 446.) But, while the parallel is fascinating and was possibly known by Jesus, he is more likely drawing from the OT promises of YHWH to be with his eschatological people.

[107] J. R. Daniel Kirk, *A Man Attested by God* (Grand Rapids, MI: Eerdmans, 2016), 380, also overlooks these YHWH-texts when he suggests that Matthew understands Jesus to be promising his presence "as a brother who is a fellow subject of God rather than as God himself."

[108] Cf. Quarles, *A Theology of Matthew*, 154.

[109] As Hagner, *Matthew 14–28*, notes, "This presence of Jesus should not be understood as a metaphor (as in the case of Paul's statement in 1 Cor 5:4) but is the literal presence of the resurrected Christ, in keeping with the promise to be articulated in 28:20 (cf. 1:23b)."

[110] Cf. Gieschen, "The Divine Name," 146.

[111] Turner, *Matthew*, 750, comes close to connecting Jesus's name to the divine name. Dieter Böhler, "Mose Als Empfänger Der Offenbarung Des Namens JHWH Und Urheber Des Namens 'Jesus,'" *TP* 89.4 (2014): 589, sees a connection between the name *Jesus/Joshua* and the Tetragrammaton, but postulates that Moses is the author of the name of his successor and that Matthew follows that tradition in positing Jesus as a second Joshua. It is unclear, however, whether Böhler sees implications for Jesus's deity with YHWH's name being used as the ground for Jesus's name. Quarles, *Matthew*, 352, notes concerning Matt 28:19, "The phrase 'the name' is prob. used in typical Jewish fashion to refer to the divine name Yahweh." If he is correct, then Jesus seems to be anticipating that meaning here in 18:20, which lies in the same trajectory of divine presence passages in the First Gospel (1:23; 18:20; 28:19–20).

because this is what YHWH does and promised to do for his redeemed eschatological people.[112]

Matthew 21:16

When the chief priests and scribes heard "children crying out in the temple, 'Hosanna to the Son of David!' they were indignant" (Matt 21:14). Jesus's response to them in 21:16 is an explicitly cited excerpt from Ps 8:2 (LXX 8:3): "Out of the mouth of infants and nursing babies you have prepared praise." The Hebrew text has "established strength" (עֹז יִסַּדְתָּ) rather than "prepared praise" (κατηρτίσω αἶνον, LXX). Thus, it is more likely that Jesus was citing from the LXX (or from an unknown Hebrew text behind it). In fact, LXX Ps 8:3 (R-H) and Matt 21:16 (NA[28]) agree verbatim: ἐκ στόματος νηπίων καὶ θηλαζόντων κατηρτίσω αἶνον.[113]

The key to interpreting Jesus's response to the complaint of the religious leaders that he did not stop the children from shouting hosannas to him as the Son of David is his appeal to a YHWH-text in a Davidic psalm. In Psalm 8, David juxtaposes God and man.[114] And although David stands amazed that God would adorn man as his highest creation, only YHWH possesses glory "above the heavens"—evidenced even in his "prepared praise" from the lowliest of the human race, "infants and nursing babies." Jesus will not stop the children's hosannas to him as David's Son because this, he asserts in his rebuke of the religious leaders, is exactly what they ought to have expected from this Davidic psalm. Ironically, Jesus's religious critics have placed themselves in the position of YHWH's enemies by opposing his praise from children.[115] "The Lord our Lord"— יְהוָה אֲדֹנֵינוּ (Ps 8:1 MT); Κύριε ὁ κύριος ἡμῶν (Ps 8:2 LXX)—has indeed prepared praise for himself, and that is precisely why Jesus receives the children's praise. Carson calls this citation response from Jesus

> a masterpiece. It not only provides a biblical basis for letting the children go on with their exuberant praise, thus stifling, for the moment, the objections of the authorities; but, at the same time, it also encourages thoughtful persons to reflect, especially after the resurrection, that Jesus is saying more than first meets the eyes.

---

[112] Morris, *The Gospel According to Matthew*, 471, summarizes well: "[T]he presence of Jesus is 'the Divine Presence.'"

[113] Toy, *Quotations in the New Testament*, 55, believes that Matthew erred in following the LXX, but "the meaning which Jesus puts into the words is substantially the same as that of the Psalmist." Other scholars show no qualms about the LXX as a source, especially since the citation is exact. Cf. J. Samuel Subramanian, *The Synoptic Gospels and the Psalms as Prophecy* (London; New York: T&T Clark, 2007), 107; Menken, "The Psalms in Matthew's Gospel," in *The Psalms in the New Testament*, ed. Steve Moyise and Maarten J. J. Menken (London; New York: T&T Clark, 2004), 71–72; Hagner, *Matthew 14–28*, 602.

[114] France, *The Gospel of Matthew*, 789–90, notes, "The most striking feature of this quotation, however, is the bold assumption by Jesus that what the psalm says about the praise of God (in distinction from mere human beings, Ps 8:4) is applicable to the children's praise of him ... the fact that the children in the psalm vindicated *God* against his enemies remains strongly suggestive, particularly when this quotation follows an action of Jesus which could be seen as 'the LORD' coming to his temple (Mal 3:1)" (emphasis France).

[115] Cf. France, *Jesus and the Old Testament*, 789–90.

The children's 'Hosannas', after all, were not being directed to God, but to the Son of David, the Messiah. Jesus is therefore not only acknowledging he is the Son of David, but he is daring to justify the praise of the children by applying to himself a passage of the Scripture referring exclusively to God.[116]

Thus, Jesus here applies to himself a YHWH-text in which YHWH is worshiped.[117] It seems apparent that Jesus himself possessed a high Christology.[118]

Matthew 21:42–45

In Matthew 21, Jesus uses another complex of OT passages referring to YHWH to apply to himself. After telling the chief priests and elders of the people (21:23) a parable exposing their rejection of the Messiah (21:33–41), Jesus first refers them to Ps 118:22–23 ("The stone that the builders rejected has become the cornerstone"), then pronounces the judgment upon them that God's kingdom will be taken away from them, and finally refers them (in a paraphrase) to two parallel passages in the Prophets, Isa 8:14–15 and Dan 2:34, 44–45, by saying, "the one who falls on this stone will be broken to pieces; and when it falls on anyone, it will crush him." Thus, the first frame is a formally cited direct quotation of a stone-passage, while the second frame is a complex of at least two other stone-passages.

In Matthew's context, Jesus is always the stone. He is rejected, he is the cause of stumbling, and he breaks and crushes the stumblers. In Psalm 118, the stone is possibly YHWH, who is the prime subject of the Psalm, though it is more likely the psalmist himself, who is rescued by YHWH from his rejection.[119] If the latter is the case, then the rejected psalmist appears to prefigure the Messiah (and/or the people represented by the Messiah).[120]

In Matthew's second frame of quotations, however, the "stone" is clearly YHWH in the Isaiah passage and a "stone cut by no human hand" in the Daniel passage. It appears that Jesus applies all the "stone passages" to himself, because he occupies the roles of both Messiah and YHWH (and a stone cut without human hands).[121] It appears again that Jesus had no hesitation to occupy the position of YHWH.[122]

---

[116] Carson, "Christological Ambiguities," 110.
[117] France, *Jesus and the Old Testament*, 151–52, writes forcefully, "Jesus' use of the verse depends on its applicability to the children's praise of *him*, and to *his* adversaries. Unless he is here setting himself in the place of Yahweh, the argument is a *non sequitur*" (emphasis France).
[118] Blomberg, "Matthew," 70, is reticent to attribute too much to the text. In a later work, however Blomberg, *Matthew*, 316, writes, "[T]he children are praising Yahweh, so Jesus again accepts worship that is reserved for God alone. Truly, one greater than the temple is here (12:6)." R. T. France, "The Worship of Jesus: A Neglected Factor in Christological Debate?," in *Christ the Lord*, ed. Harold H. Rowdon (Leicester, England; Downers Grove, IL: InterVarsity Press, 1982), 28, notes, "[I]n Jesus' use of Old Testament texts and imagery we find the same tendency to put himself in the place of God, not ostentatiously, but almost incidentally, as if it were a perfectly natural substitution." Cf. Menken, "The Psalms in Matthew's Gospel," 72.
[119] Cf. Nancy L. DeClaissé-Walford, Rolf A. Jacobson, and Beth LaNeel Tanner, *The Book of Psalms* (Grand Rapids, MI: Eerdmans, 2014), 868.
[120] Cf. Leslie C. Allen, *Psalms 101–150* (Nashville, TN: Nelson, 2002), 167–68.
[121] France, *Jesus and the Old Testament*, 152–53.
[122] France, *The Gospel of Matthew*, 818.

Matthew 24:35

When Jesus claimed that his words were more abiding than heaven and earth, he was alluding to OT descriptions of YHWH and YHWH's words.[123] In Ps 102:26 (Heb 101:27), the eternity of "God" (v. 24, *Elohim*, who is called *YHWH* nine other times in the Psalm) is contrasted with the temporality of the earth and the heavens, which "will perish ... and will pass away" (ויחלפו ... יאבדו).[124] In Matt 24:35, Jesus alluded to this contrast when he affirmed that heaven and earth "will pass away" (παρελεύσεται), unlike his own words, which "will surely not pass away" (οὐ μὴ παρέλθωσιν). Additionally, Jesus's emphasis on the eternality of his words likely alludes to another YHWH-text, Isa 40:8 ("God" in v. 8 is called "YHWH" in v. 7), in which the eternality of God's word is contrasted with the temporality of grass and flowers, symbols for mortal humanity (40:7).[125] Thus, Jesus placed his teaching authority on the divine side of the Creator–creature distinction.

In fact, Jesus heightened the contrast beyond the OT expressions.[126] Whereas Isaiah claimed that God's word was unlike perishing vegetation (40:7–8), Jesus claimed that his own words would outlast all creation (Matt 24:35)—a characteristic of God himself (Ps 102:26).[127] Whereas Isaiah grounded his claims in the speech of YHWH (cf. Isa 40:1, 5), Jesus grounded his claims in himself ("my words").[128] Significantly, Jesus's allusion to Isa 40:8 recalls the same prophetic context from which Matthew had earlier applied a YHWH-text to Jesus: "prepare the way of YHWH" (40:3; cf. Matt 3:3). Original Jewish-Christian readers of Matthew's Gospel likely realized that Jesus was here confirming his identity as YHWH. Isaiah 40:1–11 had predicted the personal coming and glorious revealing of YHWH, whose word lasts forever. Matthew, likewise, portrays Jesus in the role of YHWH as the coming One (3:3, 11–13), who revealed his glory (17:1–13), and whose words last forever (24:25).

---

[123] France, *The Gospel of Matthew*, 930, similarly writes, "such language is used to affirm the permanence of God's covenant faithfulness (Isa 51:6; 54:10; Jer 31:35–36; 33:20–21, 25–26)." The point here is that nothing innately outlasts the created universe but the Creator. Cf. W. D. Davies and Dale C. Allison, *A Critical and Exegetical Commentary on the Gospel According to Saint Matthew*, vol. 3 (London; New York: T&T Clark, 2004), 368.

[124] Only a few commentators mention Ps 102:25–27 and/or Ps 119:89 as possible referents to Jesus's claim in Matt 24:35. Cf. Nolland, *The Gospel of Matthew*, 990; Carson, "Matthew," 569; Turner, *Matthew*, 585. For good reason, nearly all commentators who recognize an OT background for Jesus's claim opt for Isa 40:8 as the clearest referent (see discussion below). But Ps 102:25–26 is also a likely part of the background with its parallels to Matt 24:35 of "the earth" and "the heavens" predicted to "be changed or pass away."

[125] Many scholars have noted an allusion in Jesus's claim for himself in Matt 24:35 to Isaiah's claim for YHWH in Isa 40:8. Cf. Capes, *Old Testament Yahweh Texts in Paul's Christology*, 179; Carson, "Matthew," 569; Erickson, *The Word Became Flesh*, 446; France, *Jesus and the Old Testament*, 151; Hagner, *Matthew 14–28*, 715; Harrington, *The Gospel of Matthew*, 342; Hays, *Echoes of Scripture in the Gospels*, 169; Nolland, *The Gospel of Matthew*, 990; Davies and Allison, *Matthew 19–28*, 368; Turner, *Matthew*, 585.

[126] So, France, *The Gospel of Matthew*, 930: "Here an even stronger formula asserts the permanent validity of the word of Jesus himself." Cf. Erickson, *The Word Became Flesh*, 447.

[127] Cf. France, *Jesus and the Old Testament*, 151; Erickson, *The Word Became Flesh*, 447.

[128] Cf. Carson, "Matthew," 569; Hagner, *Matthew 14–28*, 715; Osborne, *Matthew*, 900. Turner, *Matthew*, 585, concludes, "Jesus's words are equivalent to the words of God, as eternal and authoritative as God himself (Isa 40:8; Ps. 119:89)."

Previously, Jesus had declared his coming to be for the fulfillment of the Law and the Prophets (5:17) and had demonstrated a unique teaching authority with binding commandments (cf. 5:1–2; 7:21–29) reminiscent of Torah, which he himself said would not pass away until heaven and earth "shall pass away" (5:18; παρέλθῃ).[129] Thus, Jesus characterized his own words as (at least as) enduring as the Law, which, in turn, he portrayed as more enduring than creation.[130] What mere mortal—even among privileged agents such as Moses and Elijah (cf. 17:3–5)—could in any sense make the claim of Matt 24:35 with Ps 102:26 and Isa 40:8 as background?[131] It is difficult to justify Jesus's use of these YHWH-texts for himself, unless he is YHWH.[132]

Matthew 25:31–32

These two verses repeat OT connections Jesus had made in 16:27–28, but Jesus here seems to widen the net to include more YHWH-texts that he applies to himself and his work. Table 2.2 is a comparison to the probable references:[133]

Table 2.2 Probable OT YHWH-Texts Behind Matthew 25:31–32

Zechariah 14.5 / Daniel 7:9 / Joel 3:2	Matthew 25:31–32
Z: Then YHWH my God will come, And all the holy ones with him. D: And the Ancient of Days took his seat . . . his throne was fiery flames . . . . J: I [YHWH] will gather all the nations. . . And I will enter into judgment with them	When the Son of Man comes in his glory, and all the angels with him, then he will sit on his glorious throne. Before him will be gathered all the nations, and he will separate people . . . .

Admittedly, some connections are more conceptual than verbal, though there are still multiple verbal similarities in Jesus's words to the Zechariah and Joel passages. The key to seeing the connections, however, lies in what Jesus was claiming for himself and to recognize that his claims are the exclusive rights and prerogatives that YHWH had

---

[129] Nolland, *The Gospel of Matthew*, 988–90, argues compellingly that the "words" of Jesus refer to all his speech/teachings and not merely to his most recent eschatological prediction. In light of Matt 5:17–18 and this passage, Jesus clearly views his own speech as authoritatively equivalent to that of YHWH. Cf. Davies and Allison, *Matthew 19–28*, 368; Harrington, *The Gospel of Matthew*, 342; Keener, *A Commentary on the Gospel of Matthew*, 590; Turner, *Matthew*, 585.

[130] Davies and Allison, *Matthew 19–28*, 368, believe, even more, that Jesus's speech "sets him above Torah." Cf. Osborne, *Matthew*, 900. Others see Jesus's combined claims in Matt 5:17–18 and 24:35 as emphasizing his equal authority with God (Turner, *Matthew*, 585) or with the Mosaic Law (Nolland, *The Gospel of Matthew*, 988–89).

[131] Richard B. Hays, *Reading Backwards* (London: SPCK Publishing, 2015), 47, writes, "If we ask ourselves who might legitimately say such a thing, once again there can be only one answer: we find ourselves face-to-face with the God the Old Testament." France, *Jesus and the Old Testament*, 151, calls Jesus's "stronger" contrast "a daring one."

[132] Cf. Osborne, *Matthew*, 900. For a defense of why the next passage on Jesus's limited knowledge does not contradict his implied deity in this passage, see Blomberg, *Matthew*, 365, and the discussion of the parallel passage in Mark 13:31.

[133] These three passages are generally recognized by scholars as the specific bases for Jesus's claims in Matt 25:31–32. Cf. Capes, *Old Testament Yahweh Texts in Paul's Christology*, 180; France, *Jesus and the Old Testament*, 159; Quarles, *A Theology of Matthew*, 163–64; Erickson, *The Word Became Flesh*, 448–49.

already claimed for himself in these passages.¹³⁴ The Zech 14:5 context is an eschatological vision that climaxes in the coming of YHWH (with all the "holy ones"), living waters flowing from Jerusalem, and YHWH's universal reign in which "YHWH will be one and his name one" (14:9). The Dan 7:9 context includes an eschatological vision of the Ancient of Days taking his flaming judgment seat while "ten thousand times ten thousand stood before him; the court sat in judgment, and the books were opened" (7:10). And the Joel context is an eschatological vision of the fortunes of Judah and Jerusalem restored and the nations gathered for judgment before YHWH because of their treatment of his people.¹³⁵

While the apocalyptic details and timelines of these three passages may be up for debate, there is one pertinent feature they share: they are all "Day of YHWH" judgment texts that Jesus appears to apply to himself.¹³⁶ In Matt 25:31–32 (and following), Jesus claims that he will come in his glory with all the angels and sit on a throne of glory before a gathering of all nations as their judge, separating and sending them into one of two eternal destinies. The Jewish Scriptures had made clear that all of these eschatological actions were the exclusive work of YHWH, but Jesus quotes and alludes to such prominent YHWH-texts in order to apply them to himself.¹³⁷

Matthew 26:64

Nearing the end of the Gospel (and the account of the end of Jesus's earthly ministry), there has been an increase in Jesus's teaching on eschatological matters, particularly his return in judgment. This verse advances that teaching, only his words this time are not directed to his disciples but to his adversaries who would presume to be his judges by condemning him to death. When the high priest (with the Jewish high council) binds Jesus on oath "by the living God" to answer whether or not he is God's Son and Messiah (26:63), Jesus finally responds with unexpected candor: "(It is as) you say. Nevertheless I tell you, from now on you will see the Son of Man sitting at the right (hand) of Power and coming on the clouds of heaven" (26:64).

Although "the Power" is "a reverent substitution for the divine name,"¹³⁸ the distinction Jesus makes between himself and YHWH does not preclude their identity as well. This is because, as he has now shown multiple times, in his use of YHWH-texts Jesus can apply them to himself as either YHWH's peer or YHWH himself.¹³⁹ Just as the Danielic Son of Man figure can be distinguished from—as well as identified

---

[134] Cf. Hagner, *Matthew 14–28*, 742; Wellum, "The Deity of Christ in the Synoptic Gospels," 76.
[135] Hays, *Echoes of Scripture in the Gospels*, 170–71, sees an allusion to an additional YHWH-text applied to Jesus in this pericope: Prov 19:17.
[136] Cf. Capes, *Old Testament Yahweh Texts in Paul's Christology*, 180; France, *Jesus and the Old Testament*, 158–59.
[137] Cf. Warfield, *The Lord of Glory*, 142–43; Quarles, *A Theology of Matthew*, 163–64; France, *Jesus and the Old Testament*, 156; Keener, *A Commentary on the Gospel of Matthew*, 602–3; Hagner, *Matthew 14–28*, 745.
[138] Quarles, *Matthew*, 327, following BDAG (262b–263c 1.a). Cf. France, *The Gospel of Matthew*, 1028.
[139] D. A. Carson, *The God Who Is There* (Grand Rapids, MI: Baker, 2010), 109–10, uses the language of "God's peer" for Jesus in discussing the prologue of John's Gospel.

with—the Ancient of Days, so Jesus, in identifying himself as the Danielic Son of Man, both distinguishes himself from and identifies himself as YHWH. In terms of Matt 26:64, Jesus claims both that his position is at YHWH's right hand (cf. Ps 110:1) and that his coming is as YHWH on the clouds (cf. Dan 7:13; Exod 39:5; Nah 1:3).

Matthew 28:18–20

The close of Matthew's Gospel is the "Great Commission" of Jesus to his disciples. But it is far more than a commission; it is a crescendo of the pattern seen throughout the Gospel of YHWH-texts being applied to Jesus. In this passage three applications stand out: (1) Jesus's claim in 28:18, "All authority has been given to me in heaven and on earth," (2) Jesus's claim in 28:19 to be possessor of the "name" he shares with the Father and the Spirit, and (3) Jesus's claim in 28:20, "I am with you always."

(1) As many commentators have pointed out, Jesus's claim of universal authority is likely another reference to his identity as the Danielic[140] Son of Man who receives an eternal kingdom over all the nations of the earth (Dan 7:13–14).[141] "All authority" implies divine authority, especially recognizing the epexegetical phrase, "in heaven," as a designation of God's dwelling place. To have authority in heaven is not to possess authority over God (that is not possible) but to possess authority as God. In the exalted, post-suffering state of God the Son, he has been reinstated, as it were, to his rightful reign over the universe. His authority includes the prize of his saving kingdom, which continues to expand in its number of the redeemed.[142] Jesus has been given all authority in heaven and earth, and thus his great commission will succeed. "Mission is possible because Jesus is potent."[143] One may say that Matthew's Son of Man is distinct from the Ancient of Days, yet simultaneously say that the two (as Father and Son) share divine authority as YHWH.

(2) Of course, the concept that Jesus as the Son can be distinguished from the Father yet be divine is a fundamental part of Trinitarian doctrine, which finds amazing expression in the very next verse. In Matthew 28:19, the same Jesus who has all authority commands his disciples to make more disciples, which includes "baptizing them in the name of the Father, and of the Son, and of the Holy Spirit." Here is the "three-in-one" doctrine of trinitarianism, emphasized by the use of the singular "name"—a probable

---

[140] This connection between the Danielic Son of Man and Jesus's claim in Matt 28:18 is commonly noted among the commentators. E.g., Harrington, *The Gospel of Matthew*, 414; Turner, *Matthew*, 689; Blomberg, *Matthew*, 431; Keener, *A Commentary on the Gospel of Matthew*, 716.

[141] Cf. Schlatter, *Der Evangelist Matthäus: Seine Sprache, Sein Ziel, Seine Selbständigkeit*, 797, who points out that Christ's unlimited power over all earthly events is found in his heavenly authority: "Einzig von der ἐξουσία Jesu wird gesprochen, durch die er der Wirkende ist. Die unbegrenzte Macht über das, was auf der Erde geschieht, hat er deshalb, weil er sie im Himmel hat. Sein Wirken vermittelt das göttliche Wirken [Only the ἐξουσία of Jesus is mentioned, by which he is the one acting. He has unlimited power over what happens on earth because he has it in heaven. His action mediates the divine action]."

[142] Similarly, Hagner, *Matthew 14–28*, 886; Carson, "Matthew," 594–95.

[143] Turner, *Matthew*, 689. Xavier Léon-Dufour, "Jesus Christ," *Dictionary of Biblical Theology*, 268, adds: "Jesus is the Lord of history (cf. Mt 28,20). . . . He shares the divine omnipotence (Mt 28,18)."

allusion to the divine name, YHWH (Exod 3:14–15).[144] (What other "name" from the Scriptures would Father, Son, and Spirit share?)[145] Father, Son, and Spirit together having one "name" implies that they must be considered as one entity (or being), though they are simultaneously identified as three personages.[146] Again, Jesus (as well as the Father and the Spirit) is YHWH, since he identifies himself by the divine "name."

(3) The promise of Jesus to be with his people is easily recognized as YHWH's repeated OT promise to be with his people (e.g., Isa 41:10; 43:2).[147] YHWH was outwardly present with his old covenant people, Israel (e.g., Deut 31:6), except when he/his glory "departed" because of Israel's faithlessness (Ezek 10), and he promised to be inwardly present with his eschatological people in the Spirit-effected New Covenant (e.g., Ezek 36:25–29). Elsewhere, Jesus and the NT writers make it clear that Jesus mediates and effects this New Covenant (Luke 22:20; Heb 9:15; cf. Matt 26:28), which guarantees inward changes and divine presence (Heb 8:10–12; cf. Jer 31:33–34). But here in Matthew that presence is asserted as the basis and guarantee for Jesus's people fulfilling the Great Commission. Jesus in fact emphasizes that he is the fulfillment of YHWH dwelling with his people: "Behold, I myself am with you [ἰδοὺ ἐγὼ μεθ' ὑμῶν εἰμι]." This assertion appears to be that of YHWH fulfilling his longstanding promise to initiate his saving presence with his new covenant people.[148]

Conclusion

This survey in Matthew's Gospel of OT YHWH-texts applied to Jesus is complete enough to demonstrate the ubiquity of the practice. Many other connections between Jesus and YHWH can be made which imply the high Christology of Jesus's divine identity. To note just a few early examples,

---

[144] Cf. Quarles, *Matthew*, 152.

[145] Charles A. Gieschen, "The Divine Name in Ante-Nicene Christology," *VC* 57.2 (2003): 144, writes compellingly, "As a Jew who was writing for Jewish followers of Jesus, this author would certainly understand the name of the Father to be the Divine Name. The challenging part of this formula for a Jew is that the singular Divine Name is also possessed by the Son and the Holy Spirit. This understanding of 'the name' in Matthew 28.19 as the Divine Name, however, anchors the reality of the Son and Holy Spirit in YHWH who had revealed himself over centuries of time, especially in the history of Israel. If the Son and the Holy Spirit can be identified with the sacred and revered name YHWH, then the Jew can worship the Son and Holy Spirit together with the Father as YHWH (cf. Matt 28.17)."

[146] Cf. Warfield, *The Lord of Glory*, 94–95.

[147] Cf. Hays, *Echoes of Scripture in the Gospels*, 171; Hagner, *Matthew 14–28*, 888–89. Quarles, *A Theology of Matthew*, 153, notes, "Jesus' promise is a verbatim repetition of the promise of Yahweh in Haggai 1:13: 'I am with you, declares the LORD.' . . . [and] reminiscent of many other Old Testament texts . . . (Gen. 26:24; 28:15; Ex. 3:12; Josh. 1:5, 9; Isa. 41:10; 43:5; Jer. 1:19; 15:20; 42:11; Hag. 2:4)."

[148] Cf. Hays, *Echoes of Scripture in the Gospels*, 171; France, *The Gospel of Matthew*, 1119. Harrington, *The Gospel of Matthew*, 416, summarizes well: "It is possible to view Matt 28:16–20 as a summary of the whole Gospel. Jesus whose story has been told throughout the Gospel appears as the risen Lord who is worthy to be approached in an attitude of homage or worship. The teacher par excellence commissions his disciples to carry on his teaching mission. The Son of Man affirms that all authority has been given to him. The son of God directs that the Gentiles be baptized in his name. And 'Emmanuel' (see Matt 1:22–23) promises to be with his followers until the end of the present age. Thus many of the major Christological motifs developed in the course of the Gospel return at a mature level in Matt 28:16–20."

1:1   How the book of the "genesis" of Jesus may imply that he is the Creator.
1:18 How Jesus's conception by the Spirit of God implies his divine nature.
2:2   How this and other verses showing the worship of Jesus imply his deity.
2:6   How the context of the Micah 5:2 quotation implies the Christ is YHWH.
2:15 How this divine pronouncement of Jesus's sonship implies his deity.
3:11 How Jesus's giving of, and baptizing by, the Holy Spirit implies his deity.
3:12 How his winnowing fork, threshing floor, and wheat show his judgeship.

And this list would surely increase with twenty-five more chapters of potential OT YHWH connections from Matthew's text.

But this study of Matthew's Gospel has already examined at least seventeen passages containing roughly twice that many occurrences of the astonishing phenomenon of OT texts pertaining to YHWH being applied to Jesus. The frequency of the texts examined—as well as the promising potential of more of them—implies that the concept of Jesus as YHWH, the divine Savior, the God-Man, permeated the intentional writing of Matthew. Even more, the author depicts a Jesus whose own teaching is the source of that understanding.

In view of this chapter's examples, the application of OT YHWH-texts to Jesus can be acknowledged as a regular phenomenon in Matthew's Gospel. Matthew has created a theological biography that breathes with all the complexities of its main Character as one who himself quotes and alludes to dozens of OT passages by his teaching and actions, regularly identifying himself as YHWH and YHWH's equal. From beginning to end Matthew's theological record does not evidence a developing doctrine but a thoroughly settled viewpoint. He has anticipated the theological beachhead of the Johannine prologue—"In the beginning was the Word, and the Word was with God, and the Word was God"—and has produced the same doctrine unfolding from nearly every scene. In particular, with his use of OT YHWH-texts applied to Jesus, Matthew has continued the OT story of YHWH by showing that he has come in the person of Jesus.

3

Mark's Application of YHWH-Texts to Jesus

Biblical scholarship during the last century-and-a-half has strongly favored Markan priority, which is usually advanced under the "two-source theory" proposing that the Gospel of Mark and hypothetical Q (*Quelle* = "source") were the two primary sources used to compile the Gospels of Matthew and Luke.[1] Certainly, Mark's Gospel displays significant differences from Matthew and Luke. It bypasses any genealogy or birth narrative of Jesus and appears to end abruptly without describing any of Jesus's resurrection appearances as found in the other Gospels. For these and other editorial choices Mark is noticeably shorter than the other Synoptic Gospels (see Table 3.1).

Table 3.1 Word Count Comparisons of the Synoptic Gospels

	Word count (NA^{27})	Percentage of the NT
Gospel of Luke	19,482	14.12
Gospel of Matthew	18,346	13.29
Gospel of Mark	11,304	8.19

Numerous other factors could be cited in support of Markan priority.[2] However, the most commonly accepted solution to the "Synoptic problem" still lies within the realm of the hypothetical and likely has little if no impact on the subject of this study.[3] Rather, the deliberate choices and differences between the Evangelists must be evaluated within each overall narrative presentation of Jesus, despite textual influences.[4] What Mark

---

[1] A fairly typical example among recent scholars accepting Markan priority and the two-source theory may be found in Joel Marcus, *Mark 1–8*, ABC (New York: Doubleday, 2000), 57: "Mark, then, probably did not draw on other Gospels in composing his narrative. He wrote before Matthew, Luke, John, and Thomas did; and even if it were correct (as it probably is not) to call Q a Gospel, Mark seems not to have used that document."

[2] See, e.g., Eckhard J. Schnabel, *Mark* (Downers Grove, IL: IVP Academic, 2017), 3–4.

[3] In this vein, one can appreciate the comments of R. T. France, *Divine Government: God's Kingship in the Gospel of Mark* (London: SPCK, 1990), 4: "I do not subscribe to the simple 'Who-copied-whom?' approach to the Synoptic Problem. I suspect that the situation was a good deal more complex and less tidy than that. I think we may better understand Mark, Matthew and Luke as at least partially parallel developments of a widespread Jesus tradition in different parts of the Roman Empire, though with a great deal of cross-fertilization which at some points took the form of the exact reproduction of written accounts of sayings and events."

[4] Similarly, Morna D. Hooker, "'Who Can This Be?' The Christology of Mark's Gospel," in *Contours of Christology in the New Testament*, ed. Richard N. Longenecker (Grand Rapids, MI: Eerdmans, 2005), 83.

wrote and how he wrote it (e.g., often with more intercalation, irony, and personal details than the other Evangelists) are more valuable than knowing if he wrote before or after Matthew.[5] Every canonical Evangelist—and Mark is no exception—wrote a theological biography[6] of a Character who embodied "the good news." Mark makes this especially clear in his opening statement. There is no doubt that Mark pursued his own shape and themes in his Christological agenda.[7] The pertinent question remains in this chapter: does Mark, as a part of his Christological agenda, clearly and unequivocally use OT YHWH-texts to describe the person and work of Jesus in his Gospel?

Mark's Christology

It is nearly impossible to deny that the central theme of Mark's Gospel is the identity of Jesus as the "Son of God."[8] The claim is thrust forward in the (likely) Jewish-Christian author's opening (1:1) and reaffirmed by the (likely) Gentile centurion at the book's

---

[5] Cf. Nicholas Perrin, "Mark, Gospel Of," in *Dictionary of Jesus and the Gospels*, ed. Joel B. Green, Jeannine K. Brown, and Nicholas Perrin, 2nd ed. (Downers Grove, IL: IVP Academic, 2013), 555; Henry Barclay Swete, *Commentary on Mark* [repr. of *The Gospel According to Mark*, London: Macmillan, 1913] (Grand Rapids, MI: Kregel, 1977), lxxv; Paul J. Achtemeier, "Mark, Gospel Of," in *The Anchor Bible Dictionary*, ed. David Noel Freedman (New York: Doubleday, 1992), 546; Schnabel, *Mark*, 6.

[6] So, Craig L. Blomberg, *Jesus and the Gospels*, 2nd ed. (Nottingham, England: Apollos; Downers Grove, IL: InterVarsity Press, 2009), 122, who believes that all the Gospels are best described as theological biographies. Willi Marxsen, *Mark the Evangelist*, trans. James Boyce et. al. (Nashville, TN: Abingdon, 1969), 65, famously concluded that Mark "does not write from a biographical interest, but … a kerygmatic interest," paralleling the common critical bifurcation between the Jesus of history and the Christ of faith. Thorsten Moritz, "Mark, Book Of," in *Dictionary for Theological Interpretation of the Bible*, ed. Kevin J. Vanhoozer (London: SPCK; Grand Rapids, MI: Baker Academic, 2005), 480, takes a more recent view that Mark generally followed the "ancient *bioi*." Others argue that the *bioi* genre of the first century has similarities with Mark, but that Mark is significantly distinct from contemporary Greco-Roman hero accounts. Hans F. Bayer, *A Theology of Mark* (Phillipsburg, NJ: P&R, 2012), 11, writes (following Paul Barnett), "While classical *bios*-accounts observe the way in which an important figure dies, including the dying person's last words, nowhere besides the canonical Gospels is there the notion that the goal of the main character's life was to die." Similarly, Mark L. Strauss, *Mark*, ZECNT (Grand Rapids, MI: Zondervan, 2014), 27; M. Eugene Boring, *Mark: A Commentary* (Louisville, KY: Westminster John Knox, 2006), 22.

[7] This is not to sacrifice history for theology in one's agenda. Morna Hooker, *The Gospel According to St. Mark* (Peabody, MA: Hendrickson, 1991), 4–5, short of the extreme position of Marxsen, nevertheless thought that Mark's preaching agenda meant his readers should not "insist that his presentation is an accurate historical record of what Jesus did and said." On the other hand, Jack Dean Kingsbury, *The Christology of Mark's Gospel* (Philadelphia: Fortress Press, 1983), 41–43, was critical of the critics who imposed Hellenistic ideals onto Marcan themes: "In principle, however, any thesis that dictates that the interpretive key to Mark's Christology is to be found outside the Second Gospel may be said to be suspect from the outset…. From the time of Wrede to the present, scholars have interpreted Mark along tradition-critical lines. That is to say, they have first reconstructed the development of early Christianity within its first-century environment and then have assigned Mark its place within this development and have read it in this light. Such attempts to reconstruct the course of early Christianity in the world in which it arose are of course necessary. The art of approaching a document with such a tradition-critical scheme, however, consists in not permitting the scheme to predetermine the message of the document."

[8] So, Vincent Taylor, *The Gospel According to Mark*, 2nd ed. (New York: St. Martin's Press, 1966), 120. Cf. William Telford, *The Theology of the Gospel of Mark* (Cambridge; New York: Cambridge University Press, 1999), 38–39; Mitchell Alexander Esswein, "The One God and the Lord Jesus

climax portraying Jesus's death (15:39).⁹ Between these narrative bookends, Jesus is identified as God's unique Son by the divine voice from heaven (1:11; 9:7), by demons (3:11; 5:7; cf. 1:34), and by Jesus himself (12:6; 13:32; 14:61–62).¹⁰ This title is not the only identity marker of Jesus, but it is the most programmatic and structurally obvious identifier in a book that continually shows its readers how the human contemporaries of Jesus—in contrast to various beings of the spiritual realm—were stumped by the question of his identity.¹¹ Furthermore, "Son of God" is never used in the Hellenistic sense of a so-called *theos anēr* (divine man) who achieves progressive deification or is adopted into a divine panoply like a Greek deity.¹² Rather, the filial relationship of the Father and the Son comes from a Semitic view of the unique Son of God having heavenly origins beyond any adopted king of Israel,¹³ sets the tone for the entire narrative, and therefore keeps the divine identity of Jesus constantly within the vision of Mark's readers.

This Markan emphasis on Jesus's divine identity does not deny the stark humanity revealed in him who is called the Son of God.¹⁴ Mark is *additionally* well-known for exposing Jesus's raw humanity in the narrative,¹⁵ epitomized in Mark's application of the Isaianic "suffering servant" texts to Jesus and his ministry.¹⁶

Ironically, however, even the emphatic title, Son of *Man*, while overtly acknowledging Jesus's humanity (including his subordinate mediatorial agency), is typically employed as a descriptor of Jesus's *divine* nature and attributes.¹⁷ As the Danielic Son of Man, Jesus is Lord of the (i.e., YHWH's) Sabbath, has the authority to forgive sins committed

---

Christ: An Exegetical Examination of the High Christology Found in Paul, Mark and John" (MA Thesis, University of Georgia, 2012), 44; Craig A. Evans, *Mark 8:27–16:20* (Nashville, TN: Thomas Nelson, 2001), lxxix; David E. Garland, *A Theology of Mark's Gospel* (Grand Rapids, MI: Zondervan, 2015), 196–97.

9   Cf. Philip G. Davis, "Mark's Christological Paradox," *JSNT* 35 (1989): 14.
10 Cf. Blomberg, *Jesus and the Gospels*, 132; Evans, *Mark 8:27–16:20*, lxxix; D. Edmond Hiebert, *The Gospel of Mark* (Greenville, SC: Bob Jones University Press, 1994), 13–14.
11 Schnabel, *Mark*, 6, summarizes, "The question of Jesus' identity is like the proverbial red thread that runs through Mark's Gospel (cf. 1:27; 2:7; 4–41; 6:3, 14–16; 8:27–28, 29; 14:61–62)." Cf. Richard Bauckham, "Markan Christology According to Richard Hays: Some Addenda," *JTI* 11.1 (2017): 21; Kingsbury, *The Christology of Mark's Gospel*, 145; Joel Marcus, *Mark 8–16* (New Haven, CT: Yale University Press, 2009), 611; Mark L. Strauss, *Four Portraits, One Jesus*, 2nd ed. (Grand Rapids, MI: Zondervan, 2020), 240–41.
12 Cf. Achtemeier, "Mark, Gospel Of," 551; Kingsbury, *The Christology of Mark's Gospel*, 25–27.
13 Cf. Taylor, *The Gospel According to Mark*, 55, 65; Boring, *Mark*, 251; Joshua E. Leim, "In the Glory of His Father: Intertextuality and the Apocalyptic Son of Man in the Gospel of Mark," *JTI* 7.2 (2013): 213.
14 Cf. James R. Edwards, *The Gospel According to Mark* (Grand Rapids, MI; Leicester, England: Eerdmans; Apollos, 2002), 13; Ralph Martin, *Mark: Evangelist and Theologian* (Grand Rapids, MI: Zondervan, 1972), 139.
15 Cf. Swete, *Commentary on Mark*, xciv. So also, other commentators argue for Mark's presentation of Jesus as both genuinely human and genuinely divine: e.g., A. E. J. Rawlinson, *St. Mark* (London: Methuen & Co. Ltd., 1925), l–lii; Strauss, *Four Portraits, One Jesus*, 240; Taylor, *The Gospel According to Mark*, 121.
16 So, Boring, *Mark*, 253. Cf. Timothy C. Gray, *The Temple in the Gospel of Mark* (Tübingen: Mohr Siebeck, 2008), 127.
17 Boring, *Mark*, 252, summarizes, "The Christological language of the Son of Man sayings is thoroughly theocentric." Cf. Gray, *The Temple in the Gospel of Mark*, 57; Leim, "In the Glory of His Father," 226; Telford, *The Theology of the Gospel of Mark*, 41; Blomberg, *Jesus and the Gospels*, 472–73.

against God, commands YHWH's angels, gathers all humanity, and reigns/judges from the divine throne of the Ancient of Days.[18] earlier attempts by some scholars to find the meaning of "son of man" in a generic view of mankind, Jesus's use is clearly illeistic,[19] as evidenced in his frequent allusions to other Danielic terminology for himself. While avoiding the self-designation of some common messianic titles (likely due to contemporary connotations of a political revolutionary), Jesus delineated messianism as his own fulfillment of the Danielic Son of Man, who is more than an earthly Israelite king: he is God's heavenly king, who sits not merely on the Davidic throne but at the authoritative "right hand" of God's throne, exercising sovereignty over all nations.[20] Thus, the kingdom of God is ruled by the Son of Man.[21]

Further interwoven strands include the following. The Jesus portrayed by Mark fulfills the functions and works of God and is identified by metaphors unique to God.[22] Christophanies replace (or fulfill) theophanies.[23] The supernatural power of Jesus evidences his coming/presence as the coming/presence of YHWH, the embodiment of YHWH in human form.[24] Even the discipleship theme in Mark, which is thought by some to be the key feature and/or purpose of the book, is founded on the high Christology of Jesus's divine identity, since "the way" that Jesus takes in leading his disciples is first mapped out as the way of YHWH (Mark 1:2–3).[25] Jesus shares with

---

[18] Cf. Bayer, *A Theology of Mark*, 48, 58; Leim, "In the Glory of His Father," 216–26; Martin, *Mark*, 191.

[19] For a study of illeistic language employed in the OT by YHWH and in the NT by Jesus, see Roderick Elledge, *Use of the Third Person for Self-Reference by Jesus and Yahweh: A Study of Illeism in the Bible and Ancient Near Eastern Texts and Its Implications for Christology* (London; New York: T&T Clark, 2017).

[20] Leim, "In the Glory of His Father," 221, notes, "What is striking is that in Mark 8:38, the Son of Man is ashamed not of idolatry and adultery against YHWH but of sins such as these committed against himself, the eschatological bridegroom (2:19), whereas such transgression violates Israel's covenant with YHWH, Israel's husband (e.g., Hos 1:2; Jer 2:2). The same shame that idolatry against YHWH elicits now transfers to those who deny association with the Son of Man.... In Daniel, the Son of Man comes to the Ancient of Days and is 'given' (ἐδόθη) glory. In Mark 8:38, however, the coming of the Son of Man is the revelation of his Father's glory in which he already shares." Cf. Bayer, *A Theology of Mark*, 35, 38, 45, 58–59.

[21] Gray, *The Temple in the Gospel of Mark*, 57–58, notes, "Jesus' opening proclamation of the ἡ βασιλεία τοῦ θεοῦ in Mark 1:15 is now further explained as Jesus being the one who possesses the ἐξουσία of the kingdom. In Daniel, the motif of kingdom is permeated with eschatology; it is not accidental that 'kingdom' and 'authority' are interchangeable in LXX Daniel. In Mark the same is true. Jesus ushers in the kingdom, which is identical to his authority, both of which are signs of God's eschatological initiative." Cf. Dorothy Lee, "Christological Identity and Authority in the Gospel of Mark," *Phronema* 33.1 (2018): 3–4; Boring, *Mark*, 252.

[22] See, for example, Michael Tait, *Jesus, the Divine Bridegroom, in Mark 2:18–22* (Rome: Gregorian & Biblical Press, 2010), 43, 133. Blomberg, *Jesus and the Gospels*, 469, notes similar features of the Gospels in general. See, Boring, *Mark*, 249–57, for a helpful discussion of Christological titles and metaphors in Mark.

[23] Jesus's walking on the sea and his transfiguration are a couple of the more prominent examples. Cf. Leim, "In the Glory of His Father," 224–28.

[24] Cf. Moritz, "Mark, Book Of," 23; Leim, "In the Glory of His Father," 232; Gray, *The Temple in the Gospel of Mark*, 23.

[25] Joel Marcus, *The Way of the Lord* (London; New York: T&T Clark, 2004), 29, 33–41, argues persuasively that "the genitive κυρίου ('of the Lord') should be taken as a subjective rather than an objective genitive," setting up the interpretation that Jesus himself is the promised fulfillment of the Isaian return of YHWH to/for his people. Cf. Gray, *The Temple in the Gospel of Mark*, 23.

his Father the divine identity as YHWH.[26] The Markan Gospel, contrary to the critical consensus of some former generations, is bursting with themes displaying a high Christology.[27] Just as Mark's portrayal of Jesus's lowly humanity cannot be denied, so Mark's portrayal of Jesus sharing the identity of YHWH must not be ignored.[28] This high Christology is supported all-the-more by Mark's extensive use of OT YHWH-texts applied to Jesus.

Markan Cases of Old Testament YHWH-Texts Applied to Jesus

Mark 1:2–3

The first instance of Mark's application of YHWH-texts to Jesus is immediate.[29] In the place of the lengthy introductions provided by the other three Gospels, Mark provides his concise incipit (1:1) then promptly proceeds to use YHWH-texts to identify Jesus (1:2–3).[30] The effect is a literary "one-two punch" that sets the Christological tone for the rest of the Gospel.[31] Some scholars have doubted that Mark's opening title for Jesus—Son of God—pertains to divine identity (or divine nature) rather than to adoptive agency.[32] But the debate appears to be settled at once by Mark's deliberate identification of Jesus as YHWH.[33] As Daniel Johansson comments, "The first instance

---

[26] Cf. Leim, "In the Glory of His Father," 214, 232; Boring, *Mark*, 252; Daniel Johansson, "Kyrios in the Gospel of Mark," *JSNT* 33.1 (2010): 120–21.

[27] Cf. Taylor, *The Gospel According to Mark*, 121; Timothy J. Geddert, "The Implied YHWH Christology of Mark's Gospel: Mark's Challenge to the Reader to 'Connect the Dots,'" *BBR* 25.3 (2015): 327; Tait, *Jesus, the Divine Bridegroom*, 17, 314. Michael Kok, "Marking a Difference: The Gospel of Mark and the 'Early High Christology' Paradigm," *JJMJS* 3 (2016): 104, 124, on the other hand, is one who argues that "Mark's Gospel exemplifies an anomalous datum against the early high Christology paradigm," preferring the term "divine agency" to "divine identity."

[28] Cf. Geddert, "Implied YHWH Christology," 339; contra Kok, "Marking a Difference," 124.

[29] This is not to say that the uninitiated reader would catch this connection in a first reading of Mark 1:1–4. It is not until 1:9 that Mark specifically connects the OT references to Jesus. Cf. Johansson, "Kyrios in the Gospel of Mark," 105; Rodney J. Decker, *Mark 1–8: A Handbook on the Greek Text* (Waco, TX: Baylor University Press, 2014), 5.

[30] James A. Brooks, *Mark*, NAC (Nashville, TN: Broadman, 1991), 40, thinks Jesus and the NT writers "often reinterpreted" OT references, which leads him to make an ambiguous evaluation of these initial YHWH-texts. Similarly, Kok, "Marking a Difference," 121, states without specificity, "Mark ties Jesus' mission closely with the divine purposes." But others see the placement of the cluster immediately after the incipit as significant for higher Christological interpretation: e.g., Stein, *Mark*, 42; Rikk Watts, "Rule of the Community and Mark 1:1–13: Preparing the Way in the Wilderness," in *Reading Mark in Context*, ed. Ben C. Blackwell, John K. Goodrich, and Jason Maston (Grand Rapids, MI: Zondervan, 2018), 41.

[31] Similarly, Strauss, *Mark*, 67; Boring, *Mark*, 36. Compare also, Rikk E. Watts, *Isaiah's New Exodus in Mark* (Grand Rapids, MI: Baker, 1997), 90, and Rikk E. Watts, "Mark," in *Commentary on the New Testament Use of the Old Testament*, ed. G. K. Beale and D. A. Carson (Grand Rapids, MI: Baker Academic, 2007), 119.

[32] See discussion above on "Mark's Christology." Cf. Stein, *Mark*, 41; Schnabel, *Mark*, 38.

[33] J. R. Daniel Kirk, *A Man Attested by God* (Grand Rapids, MI: Eerdmans, 2016), 494–95, again equivocates: "Confronted with the possibility of applying scriptural texts to Jesus that would directly identify Jesus with God, Mark instead changes those texts so that no such direct identification is made.... [P]laying the role of God on earth, as that role is prophesied by Isaiah and Malachi, does in fact establish Jesus as a unique agent of the dawning eschatological age. The idealized human paradigm allows us to say that God is visiting the people through Jesus, who is the agent identified

of κύριος, which refers to both God and Jesus (Mk 1.3), is seen as the key to Mark's κύριος Christology."[34]

"As it is written" (1:2) ties a cluster of quoted YHWH-texts—Isaiah 40:3, Malachi 3:1, and Exodus 23:20—to Jesus.[35] This structural move is not only programmatic for the rest of Mark's Gospel,[36] but, if any form of Markan priority is correct, then the emphatic placement of these OT quotations in the *beginning* of "the beginning of the Gospel of Jesus Christ, the Son of God" (Mark 1:1) could have impressed every other canonical Evangelist to include as vital the same YHWH-text connections to Jesus in his own presentation.[37] In any event, the remarkable nature of this early identification of Jesus with YHWH cannot be ignored without missing the authorial meaning and metanarratival purpose of Mark's Gospel.[38]

---

with God's actions on the earth." Kirk's view is problematic, however, since the "changes" Mark makes to these YHWH-texts effectively equate Jesus with the "Lord" (YHWH) of their original contexts. YHWH both sends the messenger (John) and arrives after the messenger. Thus (and in light of the overarching Scriptural portrayal of God as triune), the Lord who sends can certainly use pronouns to differentiate himself from the Lord whose way is prepared. Unfortunately, Kirk's paradigm *a priori* rules out Mark's conspicuous application to "directly identify Jesus with God." Nor does he adequately explain why Mark, a monotheist, chose YHWH-texts to introduce and identify Jesus in the first place. (See next footnote, as well.)

[34] Johansson, "Kyrios in the Gospel of Mark," 101. Cf. Moritz, "Mark, Book Of," 481. Bauckham, "Markan Christology According to Richard Hays," 25, adds an important clarification: "By calling Jesus κύριος in contexts where the word was recognized as a substitute for the divine name, early Christians indicated clearly that Jesus shared the divine identity of God his Father. But they did not want to say that Jesus was simply identical with God his Father. The word *God* could all-too-easily imply either that or that Jesus was a subordinate god. By substituting 'his' for 'our God' in his citation of Isa 40:3, Mark was actually ruling out a possible reading of that verse that would distinguish 'the Lord' and 'our God' as two divinities" (emphasis Bauckham).

[35] Virtually all commentators identify Isa 40:3 and Mal 3:1 as sources of Mark's quotation, while many include Exod 23:20. However, Rawlinson, *St. Mark*, 5, thought "a very early copyist, who was more interested in fulfilments of Scriptural prophecy than the Evangelist himself" added the Mal 3:1 allusion due to Matthew's influence. Bauckham, "Markan Christology According to Richard Hays," 23–24, is one who is "doubtful" about any reference to Exod 23:20 because, "the only point at which Mark 1:2 corresponds to Exod 23:20 and not to Mal 3:1 is in the phrase πρὸ προσώπου σου ('before your face'), which Mark places after τὸν ἄγγελόν μου whereas Mal 3:1 has 'before my face' (נפל, πρὸ προσώπου μου) after 'way' (דרך, ὁδόν). Mark or his source could well have made these changes to Mal 3:1 without reference to Exod 23:20. . . . If Mark's text in 1:2 is influenced by Exod 23:20, then the context in Exod 23:20 has been ignored, for the 'you' in Exod 23:20–22 is very clearly Israel." However, while it is possible that Mark was not thinking of the Exodus reference when he cited Malachi and Isaiah, it is very likely that both prophetic passages are in typological continuity with Exod 23—something Mark likely understood in light of the new exodus motif continued throughout his Gospel.

[36] Cf. Robert A. Guelich, *Mark 1–8:26*, WBC (Waco, TX: Word, 1989), 12; Watts, "Rule of the Community and Mark 1:1–13," 45.

[37] And, as Stein, *Mark*, 43, points out, "The Isaiah quotation (1:3) is associated with John in all four Gospel accounts (Matt. 3:3; Luke 3:4; John 1:23), and there is no reason to deny that this came from John's own understanding of his ministry, as John 1:23 claims (cf. Luke 1:76)."

[38] The metanarrative into which Mark includes his Gospel is the redemptive history of the OT with YHWH as its center. Edwards, *The Gospel According to Mark*, 28, writes, "The introductory tapestry of OT quotations not only links the person and ministry of Jesus inseparably with the preceding revelation of God in the OT, but it makes the person and ministry of Jesus nonunderstandable apart from it. From a Christian theological perspective, this unites the NT uniquely and inseparably to the OT. The gospel is understandable only as the completion of something that God began in the history of Israel." Cf. Watts, "Mark," 119, and Watts, "Rule of the Community and Mark 1:1–13," 44–45.

Mark's attachment of just one of the authors ("Isaiah the prophet"; 1:2) to the entire cluster is no oversight but representative of the conflation.[39] There may be multiple reasons why Mark credited Isaiah alone for a catena of texts, but perhaps the most intentional was to highlight Isaiah's context as an interpretive key to the cluster and, therefore, to Mark's Gospel as a whole.[40] By quoting Isa 40:3 Mark has apparently latched onto the Isaian theme of a new exodus from exile, which is frequently intermixed by promises of both YHWH's personal coming and the redemptive ministry of YHWH's "suffering servant" (e.g., 26:20; 35:2, 4; 40:3–5, 9–10; 42:1–6; 49:1–6; 52:7–8; 52:13–53:12; 59:15–20; 66:12–16).[41] Mark's additional quotation of Malachi only underscores the Isaian promises, since Malachi's own purpose for writing, when the return from exile did not see the immediate arrival of YHWH and his servant, was to reiterate YHWH's Isaian promises.[42] Mark's new exodus motif is further corroborated by his allusion to the work of YHWH's messenger in the first Exodus (Exod 23:20) in whom resides YHWH's "name"[43] and the authority to pardon sins (23:21), a prerogative YHWH himself later enacts for his people in the context of the Isaian quote (Isa 40:2).[44]

Thus, the gathered cluster represents a theologically charged history:[45] the first exodus is the pattern of a second exodus, which YHWH had promised his people

---

[39] Cf. Schnabel, *Mark*, 39; Marcus, *Mark 8–16*, 147; Stein, *Mark*, 42–43; Watts, "Rule of the Community and Mark 1:1–13," 41.

[40] Edwards, *The Gospel According to Mark*, 27, with perhaps some speculation is nevertheless on track when he writes, "The Isaiah quotation in v. 3 was deemed the defining element of the tapestry of quotations. Thus, the whole is attributed to Isaiah, who was considered the greatest of the prophets, and whose authority in the early church superseded that of both Exodus and Malachi." Cf. Watts, *Isaiah's New Exodus in Mark*, whose entire study shows Mark's proclivity for Isaiah; but see, in particular, 138–39.

[41] For comments and examples of the Isaian new exodus in Mark, see, Joseph Addison Alexander, *The Gospel According to Mark*, repr. of 1858 Charles Scribner and Co. (Grand Rapids, MI: Baker, 1980), 3; Marie-Joseph Lagrange, *Évangile Selon Saint Marc*, 6th ed. (Paris: Librairie Lecoffre J. Gabalda et Cie, 1942), 5; Watts, *Isaiah's New Exodus in Mark*, 90; Watts, "Mark," 113–14; Johansson, "Kyrios in the Gospel of Mark," 63.

[42] Cf. Richard M. Blaylock, "My Messenger, the LORD, and the Messenger of the Covenant: Malachi 3:1 Revisited," *SBJT* 20.3 (2016): 84–85. Watts, "Mark," 116, writes, "Malachi addresses the disappointment attending the apparent failure of Isaiah's new exodus, Ezekiel's temple vision, the promised prosperity of Haggai, and the restorationist hopes of Zechariah." Cf. Watts, *Isaiah's New Exodus in Mark*, 67–68, 90, 370.

[43] The relationship between the Exodus and the new exodus is typological. Unlike the human messenger of Isa 40:3 and Mal 3:1 who was to go before YHWH, the divine messenger of Exod 23:20 went before the Israelites. Cf. Guelich, *Mark 1–8:26*, 11; Strauss, *Mark*, 62; Richard T. France, *The Gospel of Mark* (Grand Rapids, MI; Cambridge, UK: Eerdmans, 2014), 64. Edwards, *The Gospel According to Mark*, 27, notes, "the 'messenger' who will lead the people is not a human guide or even Moses, but a divine messenger of Yahweh." Another typological difference is pointed out by Watts, *Isaiah's New Exodus in Mark*, 72: in Exodus 23 the messenger preceded Yahweh's dispossession of Israel's enemies; in Malachi 3 the messenger would precede Yahweh's dispossession of Israel itself (as the cultic-civic center of God's people).

[44] Lagrange, *Évangile Selon Saint Marc*, 5, mentions the contextual "remission of sin" in passing; most commentators pass over it altogether. But the Isaianic new exodus theme, with the prominent place of the "Suffering Servant's" redemptive work on behalf of God's people, is poignantly stressed in Mark's Gospel by Jesus himself at 10:45, where he connects the exalted Son of Man with "serving" by giving up his life as a ransom in the stead of "many" (a clear allusion to the Servant's work in Isa 53).

[45] Indeed, the opening verses are Christological in application, but, as Geddert, "Implied YHWH Christology," 334, notes of the theological origins of the cluster, "All three OT texts that Mark combines ... speak of preparations for the coming of Yhwh."

during (ca. Isaiah) and after (ca. Malachi) their second captivity/exile.[46] Mark's blunt purpose is to show how Jesus is the redemptive-historical fulfiller of YHWH's OT promise of that expected new deliverance.[47] During the prophetic era as represented by "Isaiah the prophet" Israel was taught to readjust her focus and expectations on the return of YHWH and his servant/messiah.[48] This dual promise of redemption by YHWH and also by his servant, Mark interprets, is fulfilled in Jesus.[49] Astonishingly, in addition to wearing the Servant's shoes, Jesus wears YHWH's shoes.[50] Jesus is both Lord and Servant of the Lord (cf. "Lord and Christ" in Peter's parallel, Acts 2:36).[51] Mark, therefore, follows both aspects of the promise. But his Gospel's opening emphasis is that the way of YHWH is embodied in the way of Jesus.[52] In the light of such fulfillment Mark can confidently apply OT YHWH-texts to Jesus—and he does so with immediacy.

---

[46] The republished dissertation of Watts, *Isaiah's New Exodus in Mark*, is especially insightful on these connections. Cf. Watts, "Mark," 113–20.

[47] Lagrange, *Évangile Selon Saint Marc*, 4, notes the surprising Christological amplification of the Isaian text, "C'est Iahvé qui devait ramener son peuple de Babylone; Jésus jouera ce rôle dans une circonstance encore plus solennelle : il est identifié au Seigneur" (It was Yahweh who was to bring his people back from Babylon; Jesus will play this role in an even more solemn circumstance: he is identified with the Lord).

[48] Alexander, *The Gospel According to Mark*, 3, as long ago as 1858, summarized the Isaian background of Mark's cluster: "Isaiah's words are commonly referred to the return from Babylon, of which, however, there is no express mention in the text or context. The image really presented to the prophet is that of God returning to Jerusalem, revisiting his people, as he did in every signal manifestation of his presence, but above all at the advent of Messiah, and the opening of the new dispensation, of which John the Baptist was the herald and forerunner." Cf. Adolf Schlatter, *Markus: der Evangelist für die Griechen*, 2nd ed. (Stuttgart: Calwer Verl, 1984), 15.

[49] Despite much critical attention paid to John (as "my messenger" and the "voice of one crying in the wilderness"), the OT texts and Mark's use of them zero in on the coming of YHWH. Cf. Edward, *The Gospel According to Mark*, 27–28; Watts, *Isaiah's New Exodus in Mark*, 87–88.

[50] Watts, "Mark," 119, notes, "Substituting *autou*, referring to Jesus, for Isa. 40:3's *tou theou hēmōn* ... Mark makes the forthright claim that Israel's new-exodus hopes have been inaugurated in Jesus: he is the one through whom Yahweh's delivering personal presence and kingly reign is manifest (1:15)." Cf. Adela Yarbro Collins, *Mark* (Minneapolis, MN: Fortress Press, 2007), 148.

[51] Kelli S. O'Brien, "Hints and Fragments: The Use of Scripture in Mark 1,2–3 and the Dead Sea Scrolls," in *Reading the Gospel of Mark in the Twenty-First Century*, ed. Geert Van Oyen (Leuven, Belgium: Peeters, 2019), 305, 312, sees mostly a low Christology in Mark (even in the titles Son of Man, Son of God, and Lord), but finds a high Christology in Mark's OT citations, concluding that there is a "sort of profound identification between Jesus and God" though "not definitive." But a greater recognition of Mark's high Christology throughout his Gospel may be recognized when divine identity and divine agency are not pitted against one another: Isaiah envisions the coming the YHWH and his Servant; Mark sees the fulfillment of both in Jesus.

[52] Boring, *Mark*, 37, writes, "The way of the Lord is not the ethical pattern the Lord wants people to follow, but the Lord's own way, which he himself walks at the head of his redeemed people. For Mark, 'the Lord' whose way is to be prepared is the Lord Jesus." Boring's understanding is to be preferred to that of John R. Donahue and Daniel J. Harrington, *The Gospel of Mark*, Sacra Pagina 2 (Collegeville, MN: Liturgical Press, 2002), 61, who interpret the Lord's way as a Markan theme with the double meaning of "a path or journey" and "the journey toward discipleship," a merely ethical interpretation (rightly dismissed by Boring). Schnabel, *Mark*, 40, more accurately writes, "The promised coming of God has taken place in the coming of Jesus. Where and when Jesus acts, God acts." The substitution of Jesus for YHWH, however, is a statement of identity, not mere agency.

Mark 1:7-8

Verses seven and eight of chapter one contain at least two complementary allusions to OT YHWH-texts which Mark—in quoting John the Baptist—combines for heightened effect. In v. 7, if "the mightier one coming" (Ἔρχεται ὁ ἰσχυρότερός) is not a general allusion to OT prophecies of YHWH's eschatological coming to his people in power/might and glory (e.g., Isa 63:1; Ezek 43:3–9),[53] then the speech of John may be alluding specifically to Isa 40:10. This option is the most likely source behind the claim in Mark 1:7 not only because it contains the specific dual features of YHWH's personal "coming" with "might" (Κύριος Κύριος μετὰ ἰσχύος ἔρχεται; LXX) but it appears in the same chapter of Isaiah just quoted in Mark's opening identification of Jesus (1:3; cf. Isa 40:3). Thus, in Mark's context, Jesus is the mightier one who is *coming*—confirmed by the subsequent narrative marker in 1:9: "In those days Jesus *came*."[54] Furthermore, "[t]his description of Jesus anticipates the compact one-verse parable in 3:27, where Jesus refers to himself as the only one powerful enough to bind the strong one, Satan."[55]

John the Baptist's explanatory statement of why the coming one was mightier than he draws attention to their categorically distinct baptisms: John baptized penitent sinners (1:4–5) in mere water; the mightier one coming would baptize them in the Holy Spirit.[56] YHWH "baptized" no one in the OT. However, John transparently uses the language of his own public ministry of symbolic external washing in water to draw into contrast the well-known prophetic promise that YHWH would "pour out" his Spirit to cleanse and effect an internal renewal of the hearts of his people in the eschaton (e.g., Isa 44:3; Ezek 36:25–27; 39:29).[57] Mark's readers are expected to recognize this background, especially since they have just been told that John is the prophetic "voice" preceding YHWH's arrival (1:3–4).[58]

If the Baptist in Mark's Gospel did not allude generally to OT prophetic promises of YHWH to bestow his Spirit on his people, then he may have been referring to Ezek

---

[53] Garland, *A Theology of Mark's Gospel*, 211, notes how the general OT use of "mighty one" for YHWH has christological significance here.
[54] Cf. France, *Divine Government*, 101, and France, *The Gospel of Mark*, 72.
[55] Edwards, *The Gospel According to Mark*, 33.
[56] Donahue and Harrington, *The Gospel of Mark*, 64, argue, "the Holy Spirit is not so much a person, as in later Trinitarian theology, as it is God's power and spirit that effect holiness." However, Jesus's baptizing "in/by the Holy Spirit (ἐν πνεύματι ἁγίῳ)" is metaphorical and not meant to be pressed as an argument against the Spirit's personhood, a stance echoed in the next pericope where the Spirit descends (metaphorically) like a dove from heaven. Furthermore, as Decker, *Mark 1–8*, 11, notes for usage options with the dative case here, the grammar is not the decisive element, but the larger context of Mark. The Baptist's lesser-to-greater argument contains precisely the notion that, while John's instrument of washing the penitent sinner was mere water and therefore symbolic, Jesus's agent of washing would be the promised person of the Holy Spirit and therefore an effectual reality. The contrast implies a difference between outer/physical and inner/spiritual washing, because only a divine Person (i.e., the Holy Spirit) can cleanse and renew the heart, as John's likely OT background in Ezek 36:25–27 and perhaps other passages demonstrate.
[57] Cf. Hooker, *The Gospel According to St. Mark*, 38; France, *Divine Government*, 101; Hiebert, *The Gospel of Mark*, 30; Schnabel, *Mark*, 43. France, *The Gospel of Mark*, 72, notes that the Spirit's bestowal in the OT background of John's statement is not impersonal but the personal coming of YHWH.
[58] Cf. Schnabel, *Mark*, 43; France, *Divine Government*, 101.

36:25–27 specifically.[59] In this new covenant passage, YHWH promised Israel he would (metaphorically) "sprinkle clean water" on them to "cleanse" them from all their iniquities/idolatries, he would grant them "a new heart and a new spirit," and he would place "[his] Spirit within [them]" so they would take care to obey him. Thus, Ezekiel laid out the background of the Baptist's contrast between an outward (i.e., symbolic) sprinkling/washing with water versus the inward (i.e., real) cleansing/renewal by the indwelling Holy Spirit. Another passage providing some background for John may have been Joel 2:28–29 (LXX, 3:1–2) in which YHWH promised to "pour out [his] Spirit" on all members of his new covenant—an action that Peter saw as implemented by the risen and exalted Jesus (cf. Acts 2).[60] In Mark 1:8, both the Baptist and his OT sources connect YHWH's bestowal of the Holy Spirit with his eschatological salvation from sin and presence with his people.[61] The astonishing clarification in Mark's narrative is that YHWH, the mightier one who would baptize God's people in the Holy Spirit, had arrived in the sandals of a man.[62] Here again is a Markan case of OT YHWH-texts applied to Jesus.[63]

Mark 1:10–11

The next case may seem less certain, but it is worthy of consideration. Mark alludes again to the Isaianic coming of YHWH in his narrative description of "the heavens being torn open and the Spirit descending on [σχιζομένους τοὺς οὐρανοὺς καὶ τὸ πνεῦμα … καταβαῖνον εἰς]" Jesus at his baptism (1:10). Because of Mark's previous citation of Isaiah and multiple allusions to Isaiah, this detail is almost certainly an allusion to Isa 64:1 (MT 63:19b), in which the prophet cries out to YHWH, "O that you would tear open the heavens and descend [לוא קרעת שמים ירדת]."[64] The pertinent issue

---

[59] Marcus, *Mark 8–16*, follows Guelich (25) in stating, "Ezek 36:25–27 provides an especially striking parallel [with Mark 1:8]." Similarly, Donahue and Harrington, *The Gospel of Mark*, 64, call Ezek 36:25–26 "[t]he closest OT parallel to Mark 1:8." Collins, *Mark*, 146, while arguing for an earlier form of the saying which contrasted water and fire, nevertheless sees the association of "water and spirit" in Ezek 36.

[60] Marcus, *Mark 1–8*, 152, appears to reference the Joel-Acts connection. For a more direct statement of connection, see Hiebert, *The Gospel of Mark*, 30.

[61] Similarly, Schnabel, *Mark*, 43.

[62] Boring, *Mark*, 42, sees Jesus here operating "as the functional equivalent of God." Hooker, *The Gospel According to St. Mark*, 39, summarizes Mark 1:7–8 well, if a bit too tentatively: "In Mark's account of John's preaching we find ideas which, like the quotations from Malachi and Isaiah, were used in the Old Testament with reference to God himself. It is God who is the Mighty One, in whose presence John might well feel unworthy; it is God who comes in judgement; it is God who pours out the Spirit. Some of these ideas were, of course, transferred in time to a Messiah who was expected to act as God's vicegerent. The reference here to sandals certainly suggests a human figure, but anthropomorphic metaphors concerning God are common in the Old Testament, and it seems at least possible that John was expecting, not a Messiah, but the advent of God himself." See also, Edwards, *The Gospel According to Mark*, 33; Schnabel, *Mark*, 43.

[63] This is implied if not stated in Riemer Roukema, *Jesus, Gnosis and Dogma*, trans. Saskia Deventer-Metz (London; New York: T&T Clark, 2010), 29; Garland, *A Theology of Mark's Gospel*, 211; France, *Divine Government*, 101; Schnabel, *Mark*, 43.

[64] Cf. Hooker, *The Gospel According to St. Mark*, 46; Watts, "Mark," 120–22; Garland, *A Theology of Mark's Gospel*, 214. Marcus, *Mark 1–8*, 165–66, interprets the eschatological significance of this event, but without clarity on the Isaian expectation of YHWH's personal descent.

here is how the *descent of YHWH* in Isaiah, the *descent of the Spirit* in Mark, and the theophanic Spirit ("as a dove") descending *to Jesus* [εἰς αὐτόν] are connected and intended to be understood.[65]

Critical scholars tend to view Jesus's baptismal scene as a portrayal of divine adoption, in which a merely human Jesus was chosen by God to be his representative "son" and/or was entered into and animated by a divine spirit (as in Gnosticism).[66] But such a Greek construct does not fit well with Mark's Jewish narrative. All Markan events leading to this scene emphasize the coming of YHWH as fulfilled in Jesus. The Isaian background alluded to in Mark 1:10 simply confirms the same expectation of YHWH's coming (descent). The Markan descent of the Spirit, therefore, was not a contradiction of the Isaian descent of YHWH (for YHWH and the Holy Spirit essentially cannot be separated), but rather revealed *how* YHWH could fulfill such an expectation. The Spirit's coming upon/to Jesus "as a dove" through the rent heavens is surely theophanic:[67] God himself visibly appeared and came down from heaven to Jesus, signifying and affirming Jesus's own divine identity. That is why the heavenly voice in the next verse does not introduce a new functional relationship (adopted sonship) but declares an ontological relationship (affirmed sonship).[68]

Some scholars believe Ps 2:7 is the primary background to the divine voice pronouncing in Mark 1:11, "You are my beloved son; with you I am well-pleased."[69] However, Psalm 2—a coronation psalm of Israel's king anointed to the functional status of YHWH's royal "son" and typologically anticipating the final Davidic King/Son—lacks the unique descriptor "beloved/only" (found rather in Gen 22:2, 12, 16), as

---

[65] Boring, *Mark*, 46, recognizes here Mark's "predilection for Isaiah." Strauss, *Mark*, 72, understands the ripping open of the heavens to indicate "a theophany, or revelation of God," not merely the sending of an agent.

[66] Bart D. Ehrman, *The Orthodox Corruption of Scripture* (New York: Oxford University Press, 2011), 165, thinks Mark "does little to discourage the Gnostic understanding of the event, that the dove represents the divine Christ who descended from the heavenly realm and entered into Jesus, empowering him for his ministry." Cf. Bruce J. Malina and Richard L. Rohrbaugh, *Social-Science Commentary on the Synoptic Gospels*, 2nd ed. (Minneapolis, MN: Fortress Press, 2003). Kok, "Marking a Difference," 118, asserts that the heavenly voice signifies Jesus's adoption, not (as M. Eugene Boring argues) a declaration of Jesus's identity. Marcus, *Mark 1–8*, 162, notes that Israel, angels, and kings have also been called sons of YHWH, though this does not preclude a unique sonship of Jesus. Hooker, *The Gospel According to St. Mark*, 48, had earlier pointed out, however, that the heavenly voice does not express an adoption formula: "Even if Mark had Ps. 2.7 in mind, however, there is no reason to suppose that he thought of the words in this way; it is far more likely that he interpreted them simply as a declaration of Jesus' identity. Certainly Matthew and Luke do not seem to have understood the words as an adoption formula, for they see no difficulty in using them after their own birth narratives – something especially striking if we accept the 'western' text of Luke 3.22 ('today I have begotten you'). Moreover, the repetition of the words in Mark 9.7 shows clearly that he regards them as a declaration and not as an adoption."

[67] Cf. Strauss, *Mark*, 72.

[68] Cf. C. E. B. Cranfield, *The Gospel According to Mark* (London; New York: Cambridge University Press, 1959), 55; I. Howard Marshall, "Son of God or Servant of Yahweh?—A Reconsideration of Mark I. 11," *NTS* 15.3 (1969): 336; M. Eugene Boring, "Markan Christology: God-Language for Jesus?," *NTS* 45 (1999), 465.

[69] E.g., Nicholas Perrin, *Jesus the Priest* (Grand Rapids, MI: Baker, 2018), 70, who believes the Markan text is clearly linked to Psalm 2:7 (and Gen 22:2), but not so clearly to Isa 42:1. Rawlinson, *St. Mark*, 10, was one in a long line of scholars seeing more general allusions, stating that Mark 1:10–11 "is built up out of two or more O.T. passages (Ps ii 7; Is xliv 2: cf. Is xlii 1; Gen xxii 2 (LXX))."

well as the phrase "with you I am well-pleased" (a more apparent allusion to Isa 42:1).[70] Thus, the potentially adoptionist language from Ps 2:7 ("Today, I have begotten you") is excluded from the Markan Divine speech, while an affirmation of Jesus's ontological identity is emphasized: *my beloved/unique Son*.[71] Significantly, the voice from heaven makes the same ontological affirmation later at Jesus's transfiguration (9:7), "This is my beloved Son," thus indicating again not a new function but a recognized identity for Jesus.[72]

It is more likely that the Markan divine voice is focusing on Jesus as the Isaian Servant (and one cannot lightly dismiss Isaiah's anticipation of a divine Son: Isa 7:14; 9:6).[73] Not only does the Isaian YHWH in 42:1 express the sentiment of the Markan divine Voice (the Servant is the one "in whom my soul delights"), but the very next phrase identifies the Servant as the one upon whom YHWH has put his Spirit.[74] For these reasons the baptismal scene of Jesus more closely ties him to the Isaian servant of YHWH, anointed and empowered by the Holy Spirit as the unique and beloved Son of God.[75] In summary, if Mark 1:10 can be said to apply an OT YHWH-text to Jesus, it is by Trinitarian implication: the rending of the heavens and descent of YHWH longed for in Isaiah's final appeal (64:1) is affirmed by the voice (*Father*) claiming filial identity with Jesus (*Son*) and visually depicted by the *Holy Spirit*.[76] YHWH thus affirmed the reality of his descent and presence to be found in Jesus.[77]

---

[70] Cf. Marshall, "Son of God or Servant of Yahweh?," 336; Cranfield, *The Gospel According to Mark*, 55; Boring, *Mark*, 45.

[71] For the interchangeableness of the translation descriptors, "unique/only" and "beloved," see Cranfield, *The Gospel According to Mark*, 55; Boring, *Mark*, 45–46. For the "omission" of adoptionist language in the Markan divine voice, see Larry W. Hurtado, "Early Christological Interpretation of the Messianic Psalms," *Salmanticensis* 64 (2017): 90–91; Boring, "Markan Christology," 465.

[72] Cf. Hooker, *The Gospel According to St. Mark*, 48; Boring, "Markan Christology," 465; Hurtado, "Early Christological Interpretation of the Messianic Psalms," 91. For an attempt to counter Boring's argument that a second divine pronouncement in Mark 9:7 confirms that adoption was not intended in either Jesus's baptism or his transfiguration, see Kok, "Marking a Difference," 118.

[73] Watts, "Mark," 129, holds that Ps 2 and Isa 42 each play significant parts here in referencing the Davidic King and the Suffering Servant, respectively. But Watts gives a more extensive Isaian background. Boring, *Mark*, 45–46, notes that YHWH's Spirit in Isaiah ties together both coming king and suffering servant.

[74] Cf. Marcus, *Mark 1–8*, 163; Boring, *Mark*, 45–46.

[75] Perrin, *Jesus the Priest*, 70, is "disinclined" to see Isa 42:1 "as a scriptural backdrop to the heavenly voice," because the term *son* does not appear there. However, the term *beloved* does not appear in Ps 2 (while the phrase "in whom I delight" in Isa 42:1 does seem to be referenced by the Markan divine Voice), and the broader Isaian backdrop in fact does expect a royal divine son (7:14; 9:6–7). Furthermore, in Isa 42:1 YHWH gives his Spirit to his Servant. Cf. Boring, *Mark*, 45–46.

[76] Cranfield, *The Gospel According to Mark*, 55, believed the divine Voice revealed Jesus's "already existing filial consciousness." Cf. Watts, "Mark," 122. Hiebert, *The Gospel of Mark*, 34, could conclude, "In the baptismal scene, we have a clear manifestation of the Trinity."

[77] Cf. Strauss, *Mark*, 72. Watts, "Mark," 122, comments, "Because Mark's story concerns Isaiah's delayed new exodus, with John the Baptist as Malachi's preparatory Elijah, the rending of the heavens at Jesus' baptism constitutes Yahweh's long-awaited response. Isaiah's final lament has been answered: God has come down to deliver his people, baring his mighty arm to do 'awesome things that we did not expect.' Christologically, just as Isa. 40 and Mal. 3 anticipated the coming not of a messianic figure, but of God himself, so too Isa. 64. Jesus is identified not merely as Yahweh's agent, but in some mysterious way with Yahweh's very presence, whose coming, eschatologically, inaugurates that great and terrible day of the Lord (Mal. 4:5) and the beginnings of the new heaven and the new earth (Isa. 65:17–25; 66:10–14, 18–24)."

Mark 1:17

Jesus's initial calling of disciples contains unusual elements that evidence a divine rather than human prerogative.[78] Unlike OT prophets and Second Temple rabbis who were invariably chosen by their students to follow, Jesus chooses who will follow him.[79] The demand itself is more than peculiar when one realizes that Jesus would deliberately gather twelve disciples (transparently the beginnings of YHWH's renewed Israel) not around the law or the temple but around himself.[80] His demand was "follow me," a prerogative of YHWH.[81] And he couched that demand in a metaphor used in the Jewish Scriptures by YHWH alone: "I will make you fishers of men" (Mark 1:17).[82]

Although the concept of YHWH catching people like one catches fish can be found in more than one OT passage (cf. Jer 16:16; Ezek 29:4–5; Amos 4:2; Hab 1:14–17), only in Jer 16:16 does YHWH say he would commission "many fishers" to catch other people.[83] Some scholars doubt that Jesus (and/or Mark) alluded to this YHWH-text in Jeremiah, because the Jeremiah context is one of gathering Israel for eschatological judgment.[84] Indeed, it is argued that all the OT metaphors of God as fishing/hunting or of sending out fishers/hunters speak negatively of judgment and therefore have nothing to do with Jesus's positive use of the figure in Mark 1:17.[85] But immediately preceding YHWH's fishing mission of judgment in Jer 16:16–18 he had promised restoration to the scattered of Israel (16:14–15), and immediately following YHWH's gathering by

---

[78] Geddert, "Implied YHWH Christology," 335, includes this verse as part of an ongoing Markan theme of Jesus exercising divine prerogatives as God: 1:17; 2:14; 3:13, 34–35; 6:7, 11; 8:34, 38; 10:21, 29.
[79] Cf. David E. Garland, *Mark*, NIVAC (Grand Rapids, MI: Zondervan, 1996), 69–70; Stein, *Mark*, 78.
[80] Cf. Garland, *A Theology of Mark's Gospel*, 265; Geddert, "Implied YHWH Christology," 335.
[81] Cf. Marcus, *Mark 1–8*, 185. Boring, "Markan Christology," 465, writes, "The call of the disciples is what God does to make people prophets, not what rabbis do to make people disciples. The claim is absolute, asking what only God can ask, idolatrous if not ultimately God's claim (cf. 8:34; 10.17–22; 12.44; 14.3–9)." See also, Garland, *Mark*, 69, and Garland, *A Theology of Mark's Gospel*, 265.
[82] Garland, *A Theology of Mark's Gospel*, comments, "The verb 'I will make you' (ASV) in 1:17 occurs throughout the OT on the lips of God as a promise.... When Jesus says to the first disciples, 'I will make you to become fishers of men' (ASV), he is speaking as God speaks." Stein, *Mark*, 78, adds that the phrase "[come] after me" implies a calling of service to Jesus, not an equal partnership.
[83] The Amos passage portrays fishers who hook and drag away the "cows of Bashan"—Samaritan women made wealthy by exploiting the poor. But those fishers come from other nations to enslave the "cows" rather than to gather them to YHWH. Ezekiel and Habakkuk depict YHWH himself fishing or hunting down men for judgment. Thus, the Jeremiah passage is the clearest parallel to Jesus's statement in Mark 1:17. Scholars who note Jer 16:16 as the background here include Rawlinson, *St. Mark*, 15; Bayer, *A Theology of Mark*, 100; Carl Judson Davis, *The Name and Way of the Lord* (Sheffield, England: Sheffield Academic, 1996), 182. Scholars who point to multiple OT passages as general background of Jesus's statement here include William L. Lane, *The Gospel According to Mark* (Grand Rapids, MI: Eerdmans, 1974), 67; Garland, *Mark*, 69. Schnabel, *Mark*, 53–54, perplexingly concludes "The phrase, 'fishers of people'... has no obvious parallels in the Old Testament, Jewish or Greco-Roman sources."
[84] Cf. Taylor, *The Gospel According to Mark*, 169; Hooker, *The Gospel According to St. Mark*, 60; Donahue and Harrington, *The Gospel of Mark*, 74.
[85] See, Cranfield, *The Gospel According to Mark*, 70; Guelich, *Mark 1–8:26*, 51; Donahue and Harrington, *The Gospel of Mark*, 74; Stein, *Mark*, 78. Strauss, *Mark*, 83, follows the same notion that OT references about fishing for people are "always in the context of impending judgment," but then surmises, "Jesus reverses this image to one of salvation. To fish for people is to rescue them from sin and death by calling them into God's kingdom."

his fishers/hunters Jeremiah would be joined by the nations who repudiate the idols of their fathers and are made to "know" the power and the name of YHWH (16:19–21).[86]

Thus, YHWH's sending of fishers to gather men for judgment comes in the midst of restoration, falling in line with common prophetic descriptions of "the Day of the LORD." As Jer 16:16 depicted YHWH promising to commission fishers to gather people to himself for judgment and salvation, so Mark 1:17 depicts Jesus commissioning his disciples as fishers to gather people (by implication) to himself.[87]

Mark 1:25

Following the divine Voice at Jesus's baptism, the first words spoken to the Markan Jesus are those of another transcendent being, an unclean spirit, whom Jesus "rebuked ... saying, 'Be muzzled, and come out of him!'" Unclean spirits, or demons, are not only among the several creatures and forces rebuked by YHWH in the OT, but they are rebuked by YHWH alone.[88] Furthermore, the authority to rebuke fallen angels/demons was the prerogative of YHWH, not even angels.[89] In Mark 1:25 Jesus takes that divine prerogative for himself.

While scholars may doubt that Jesus was identifying himself with YHWH by the exorcism of a demon in this passage—after all, exorcism was also practiced by his disciples—there are several indicators to the contrary.[90] First, the previous applications of YHWH-texts to Jesus (1:2, 3, 7, 8, 10, 11, 17) prepare the reader for more of the same. Second, as a transcendent being, the unclean spirit reveals transcendent knowledge identifying Jesus with YHWH as the judge of demons and "the Holy One of God."[91]

---

[86] Marcus, *Mark 1–8*, 185, after listing several options, writes, "There may not be any need to choose among these different interpretations; the disciples' fishing for people is probably a multivalent image that includes their future missionary preaching, their future teaching, and their future exorcisms (cf. 3:14–15; 6:7, 12–13, 30; 13:9–10), all of which are understood as a participation in God's eschatological war against demonic forces." Bayer, *A Theology of Mark*, 100, also finds more than negative judgment in the Jeremian passage. Garland, *A Theology of Mark's Gospel*, 265, adds that Jesus's promissory language, "I will make you," is the language of YHWH.

[87] Cf. Marcus, *Mark 1–8*, 185; Garland, *Mark*, 69–70; Bayer, *A Theology of Mark*, 100; Geddert, "Implied YHWH Christology," 335.

[88] Bauckham, "Markan Christology According to Richard Hays," 29, notes on the Markan choice of *rebuke* (ἐπιτιμάω), "It is the equivalent of the Hebrew גער, which is often used in the Hebrew Bible of God's power to rebuke and to subdue the cosmic elements, especially the sea imagined as a hostile force of chaos. Used in that sense, only God appears as the subject of this verb." Cf. Schnabel, *Mark*, 58. Donahue and Harrington, *The Gospel of Mark*, 80–81, note a variety of uses for both גער and ἐπιτιμάω, although it remains true that YHWH alone "rebukes" (or exorcises) demonic beings in the OT.

[89] Cf. Bauckham, "Markan Christology According to Richard Hays," 29–30.

[90] Cf. Donahue and Harrington, *The Gospel of Mark*, 80–81, for varied examples of "rebuking" in Scripture and Second Temple literature. The critical point here, however, is that the rebuking of the unclean spirit in Mark 1:25 was considered the prerogative of YHWH, since in the Jewish Scriptures only he was able to command and exorcise unclean spirits.

[91] Berthold W. Köber, "Jesus—Der Heilige Gottes: Die Heiligkeit Jesu Im Zeugnis Der Synoptiker in Ihrer Bedeutung Für Theologie Und Glauben," *EvT* 62.4 (2002): 316, interprets from the demonic testimony here "dass Jesus an der Heiligkeit Jahwes und damit an Jahwe selbst Anteil hat [that Jesus shares in the holiness of Yahweh and thus in Yahweh himself]." Context is everything, since the concept of the "holy one" may be used of God, saints, or angels. Cf. Hooker, *The Gospel According to St. Mark*, 64–65; Strauss, *Mark*, 92–93. Thus, when the unclean spirit calls Jesus "the holy one of God

Third, the categorically supra-human "authority" of Jesus frames the pericope as the interpreted meaning of this exorcism (1:22, 27).[92] Fourth, Jesus does not effect the exorcism by incantation, ritual, evoking the divine name, or a petitioning prayer, but by his own authoritative word.[93] The meaning of Jesus's rebuke of the unclean spirit, then, is that Jesus possesses divine authority in himself to command and judge the enemies of YHWH.[94] He is not portrayed as a mere agent, as his disciples are when Jesus later grants them authority to exorcise demons.[95] Rather, Jesus's rebuke of the unclean spirit is a participation in the prerogative of YHWH as found the Jewish Scriptures (e.g., Zech 3:2; Ps 68:30; 106:9).

Mark 2:5–12

One common approach to Jesus's claim to forgive the sins of the paralytic is to place Jesus in the category of priests (or other representatives) who act as God's agents in pronouncing God's forgiveness.[96] But does the Markan narrative allow for that interpretation?[97] It appears, rather, that several features of Mark's narrative mitigate

---

[ὁ ἅγιος τοῦ θεοῦ]" it parallels the heavenly voice which had just called Jesus "the Son of Me [God], the beloved one [ὁ υἱός μου ὁ ἀγαπητός]." Boring, "Markan Christology," 466, also points out that, while it is not determinative of ontology, the demon's opening question to Jesus, Τί ἡμῖν καὶ σοί, implies a significant categorical difference between them. As argued above, the unique sonship of Jesus does not emphasize function, but ontology. So, too, features in the current pericope around 1:25 support the view that Jesus is uniquely and ontologically "the holy one" as YHWH is "the holy one."

[92] This pericope opens with the people astonished at the authority of Jesus above the (human) scribes (1:22) and closes with their astonishment of his authority over unclean spirits (1:27). Boring, *Mark*, 63, notes how the categorically high authority of Jesus is a frequent theme of Mark. Collins, *Mark*, 174, interprets the authority as "rooted in Jesus' appointment as the messiah and his endowment with the Holy Spirit." But her view downplays the stated concern of the unclean spirit, who recognized Jesus's identity as the eschatological judge, whose unassailable word would destroy demons.

[93] Boring, *Mark*, 63, 65, comments, "In Judaism, the divine authority is mediated by the Torah, which then must be interpreted through debate and voting by qualified scholars. For Mark, God's authority is mediated by the word of Jesus, who simply pronounces. . . . Jesus operates entirely by his powerful word. There is only his *rebuke* and his *command*" (emphasis Boring). See also, Strauss, *Mark*, 93; Bauckham, "Markan Christology According to Richard Hays," 30.

[94] Donahue and Harrington, *The Gospel of Mark*, 80, point out the legal implications of the language here. Cf. Bauckham, "Markan Christology According to Richard Hays," 30.

[95] Strauss, *Mark*, 93, notes, "Yet unlike other exorcists, Jesus does not use spells, rituals, or incantations to coerce demons into submission. His own authority is enough; he speaks and the demon obeys." Cf. Boring, *Mark*, 65.

[96] Various interpretations of Jesus forgiving as a mere representative of God include those of Malina and Rohrbaugh, *Social-Science Commentary on the Synoptic Gospels*, 154; Edwin K. Broadhead, *Teaching with Authority* (Sheffield: Sheffield Academic, 1992), 79; Collins, *Mark*, 185–86; Robert Walter Funk and Roy W. Hoover, eds., *The Five Gospels* (Toronto; New York: Macmillan, 1993), 44.

[97] The following argument will, of course, answer "no." Stephen T. Davis, " 'Who Can Forgive Sins but God Alone?': Jesus, Forgiveness, and Divinity," in *The Multivalence of Biblical Texts and Theological Meanings*, ed. Christine Helmer (Atlanta, GA: Society of Biblical Literature, 2006), 121, summarizes a glaring problem with the view that Jesus was acting as a mere representative of God: "It would hardly amount to blasphemy simply to assure repentant sinners that God has forgiven them."

against seeing Jesus as a mere representative of YHWH and instead portray him as self-consciously exercising the prerogatives of YHWH.[98]

At the center of the controversy is Jesus's pronouncement to a paralytic, "Son, your sins are forgiven [Τέκνον, ἀφίενταί σου αἱ ἁμαρτίαι]" (Mark 2:5).[99] Despite a shared view among commentators that Jesus's use of the "divine passive" here implied he was speaking on behalf of God as a third party representative, the rest of Mark's narration rebuts that interpretive option.[100] The passive voice does not require a source of forgiveness other than Jesus.[101] Moreover, Jesus identifies that source with his third-person illeism, "the Son of Man" (his favorite self-designation; Mark 2:10), as the subject.[102] Thus, while Jesus does not remove God/YHWH from being the source of forgiveness, he does specify that source to be himself.[103]

Numerous other details of the Markan account support the view that Jesus was claiming the OT prerogative of YHWH to forgive sins[104] (and very possibly, with Ps 103:3 in view[105]). First, that prerogative is exactly what the scribes understood Jesus to be claiming when they accused him of blasphemy: their criticism is formulated as "Who can forgive sins but God alone?" (Mark 1:7b),[106] an apparent allusion to the

---

[98] This is not to deny that Jesus appears as both YHWH and YHWH's representative in this passage. Some scholars come close to stating this view, restraining themselves by the "ambiguity" of the text (Marcus, *Mark 1–8*, 224; cf. Hooker, *The Gospel According to St. Mark*, 87–88). The question is not whether Jesus fills a functional role as God's representative—he does—but whether Jesus is also identified ontologically with YHWH—he is.

[99] Joachim Gnilka, *Das Evangelium Nach Markus (Mk 1–8,26)* (Zürich: Neukirchener, 1978), 100, calls Jesus's authoritative pronouncement of forgiveness in 2:5 "die Quintessenz der Perikope [the quintessence of the pericope]." Collins, *Mark*, 185, notes, "Although the passive voice implies that it is God who forgives, the simple declaration 'your sins are forgiven' (ἀφίενταί σου αἱ ἁμαρτίαι) is unusual in the context of Jewish tradition."

[100] Cf. Brooks, *Mark*, 58; Stein, *Mark*, 118–19.

[101] Cf. Cranfield, *The Gospel According to Mark*, 99; Gundry, *Mark*, 112, Hiebert, *The Gospel of Mark*, 67; Strauss, *Mark*, 121.

[102] This is the first of fourteen occurrences in Mark of Jesus's favorite self-designation, "the Son of Man." Stein, *Mark*, 121, argues compellingly that it is authentic to Jesus. Cf. Edwards, *The Gospel According to Mark*, 80; France, *The Gospel of Mark*, 127; Schnabel, *Mark*, 67.

[103] Contra Malina and Rohrbaugh, *Social-Science Commentary on the Synoptic Gospels*, 154. Like many, Decker, *Mark 1–8*, 52, notes that Jesus uses the Son of Man title exclusively for himself. Cf. France, *The Gospel of Mark*, 127–28.

[104] Most commentators describe Jesus as exercising a "divine prerogative" (or similar expression). E.g., Swete, *Commentary on Mark*, 35; Rawlinson, *St. Mark*, 24; Cranfield, *The Gospel According to Mark*, 99; Taylor, *The Gospel According to Mark*, 196; Gnilka, *Das Evangelium Nach Markus (Mk 1–8,26)*, 100–1; Hiebert, *The Gospel of Mark*, 67; France, *The Gospel of Mark*, 129; Watts, "Mark," 131; Stein, *Mark*, 119; Richard B. Hays, *Echoes of Scripture in the Gospels* (Waco, TX: Baylor University Press, 2016), 65; Schnabel, *Mark*, 67.

[105] Frederick J. Gaiser, "'Your Sins Are Forgiven. . . . Stand Up and Walk': A Theological Reading of Mark 2:1–12 in the Light of Psalm 103," *ExAud* 21 (2005): esp. 71, 82, argues convincingly for the primacy of Psalm 103 as background for Jesus both healing and forgiving the paralytic. Watts, "Mark," 131, 133, favors a continuing Isaian new exodus theme as background (e.g., Isa 33:24; 43:25; 44:22–24). Stein, *Mark*, 115, represents many scholars who see a more generalized reference to OT connections of sin and sickness, forgiveness and healing (e.g., Ps 41:3–4; 103:3; Isa 33:24; 38:17; 57:18–19; Hos 14:4). However, the appeal of Ps 103:3 is its clear parallelism between YHWH's forgiveness of sins and healing of diseases: it is unlikely that Jesus was unaware of these paired divine prerogatives when he proceeded to pair them himself.

[106] A great many scholars interpret the scribes' accusation of blasphemy against Jesus as an indicator of Jesus's indirect claim to deity. Cf. Swete, *Commentary on Mark*, 35; Cranfield, *The Gospel According to Mark*, 99; Gundry, *Mark*, 112; Davis, "Who Can Forgive Sins but God Alone?," 122; Watts, "Mark,"

monotheistic expression in the *Shema*.¹⁰⁷ Second, Jesus responded by claiming to know the (unspoken) accusation of blasphemy residing in their hearts, implying divine knowledge of their thoughts.¹⁰⁸ Third, Jesus did not deny or qualify that he personally possessed the divine prerogative to forgive sins, but instead moved to demonstrate the truth of it.¹⁰⁹ Fourth, Jesus both predicted and proved his authority to forgive by demonstrating his authority to heal.¹¹⁰ His use of a *qal wahomer* argument proved that his claim to forgive went beyond mere words, since his claim to heal could be empirically verified.¹¹¹ Fifth, his reference to the Son of Man having authority "on the earth" does not indicate a delegated human authority¹¹² but the universal divine authority of the Daniel 7 figure standing in their midst.¹¹³ Blomberg asks, "Why add 'on earth' unless he was more than an ordinary earth-dweller?"¹¹⁴ Sixth, Jesus rendered efficacious forgiveness in the present, proven by his efficacious healing in the present,¹¹⁵

133; Strauss, *Mark*, 121–22; Schnabel, *Mark*, 66; Hays, *Echoes of Scripture in the Gospels*, 65; Richard J. Bauckham, "Christology," *Dictionary of Jesus and the Gospels*, 128; Crispin H. T. Fletcher-Louis, "A New Explanation of Christological Origins: A Review of the Work of Larry W. Hurtado," *TynBul* 60.2 (2009): 174; Blomberg, *New Testament Theology*, 45; Simon J. Gathercole, "The Trinity in the Synoptic Gospels and Acts," in *The Oxford Handbook of the Trinity*, ed. Gilles Emery and Matthew Levering (Oxford; New York: Oxford University Press, 2011), 59; Boring, "Markan Christology," 466.

¹⁰⁷ Cf. Marcus, *Mark 1–8*, 222; Strauss, *Mark*, 122; Schnabel, *Mark*, 67; Bauckham, "Markan Christology According to Richard Hays," 28; Gathercole, "The Trinity in the Synoptic Gospels and Acts," 56.

¹⁰⁸ Strauss, *Mark*, 122, writes, "There is heavy irony here. Even as the religious leaders are scoffing at Jesus' claim to divine authority, he is reading their minds—demonstrating a prerogative of God!" Cf. Gnilka, *Das Evangelium Nach Markus (Mk 1–8,26)*, 100; Marcus, *Mark 1–8*, 222; Schnabel, *Mark*, 67.

¹⁰⁹ Cf. Geddert, "Implied YHWH Christology," 330; Watts, "Mark," 133; Stein, *Mark*, 118–19.

¹¹⁰ Cf. Geddert, "Implied YHWH Christology," 331; Gaiser, "Your Sins Are Forgiven," 83; Cranfield, *The Gospel According to Mark*, 98; Taylor, *The Gospel According to Mark*, 195; Strauss, *Mark*, 121.

¹¹¹ Cf. Taylor, *The Gospel According to Mark*, 197; Hiebert, *The Gospel of Mark*, 68; Watts, "Mark," 133; Strauss, *Mark*, 122.

¹¹² J. R. Daniel Kirk, *A Man Attested by God*, 281, claims to allow for a full integration of the facts within a divine Christology view, yet asserts that his "idealized human paradigm" still makes better sense of this passage. Ironically, Dan G. McCartney, "Ecce Homo: The Coming of the Kingdom as the Restoration of Human Vicegerency," *WTJ* 56 (1994), 12 n29, whom Kirk (xii) credits with inspiring his human-only view of Jesus, distinguishes Jesus's authority to forgive sins from any delegated authority "because Jesus 'the Man' was also divine; no one can forgive offenses against someone else."

¹¹³ It is not enough to say with Joel Marcus, "Authority to Forgive Sins upon the Earth: The Shema in the Gospel of Mark," in *The Gospels and the Scriptures of Israel*, ed. Craig A. Evans and W. Richard Stegner (Sheffield, England: Sheffield Academic, 1994), 204, that Jesus was "acting as the earthly plenipotentiary of the one who forgives them *in heaven*" (emphasis Marcus), or, Marcus, *Mark 1–8*, 223, that "the heavenly God ... has delegated his power of absolution to a 'Son of Man' who carries out his gracious will in the early sphere." The references to "in heaven" and "on earth" do not bifurcate the authority of a heavenly God and an earthly Jesus but rather show Jesus's divine authority as the heavenly Son of Man to be on the earth as well as in heaven. His authority to judge includes authority to forgive, and it is not restricted to the earth but is cosmic in nature. Cf. France, *The Gospel of Mark*, 129; Geerhardus Vos, *The Self-Disclosure of Jesus*, ed. Johannes G. Vos (Phillipsburg, NJ: P&R, 2002), 86; Davis, "Who Can Forgive Sins but God Alone?," 122; Craig A. Evans, "Jesus' Self-Designation 'The Son of Man' and the Recognition of His Divinity," in *The Trinity*, ed. Stephen T. Davis, Daniel Kendall, and Gerald O'Collins (Oxford; New York: Oxford University Press, 1999), 37; Kristian A. Bendoraitis, "The Parables of Enoch and Mark 1:14–2:12: The Authoritative Son of Man," in *Reading Mark in Context*, ed. Ben C. Blackwell, John K. Goodrich, and Jason Maston (Grand Rapids, MI: Zondervan, 2018), 53; Simon J. Gathercole, *The Preexistent Son* (Grand Rapids, MI: Eerdmans, 2006), 58.

¹¹⁴ Blomberg, *Jesus and the Gospels*, 468.

¹¹⁵ So, Gundry, *Mark*, 112: "The present tense of ἀφίενται most naturally means that Jesus pronounces the forgiveness as taking place at this very moment and therefore as being effected by his pronouncement (cf. Acts 9:34). So we do not have a miracle at least not yet—but a word, an authoritative word of sins being forgiven on the spot."

dramatically showing his authority to bypass the temple and its sacrifices to secure forgiveness for sinners.[116] The basis of such a unilateral pardon bypassing YHWH's cultic requirements will be indicated later when Jesus includes in his prerogatives as "the Son of Man" a categorically unique sacrifice: "to give his life as a ransom for many" (10:45)—a clear allusion to the effectually redemptive sacrifice of the Isaian Servant (Isa 53:12).[117] Seventh, the pericope ends with witnesses glorifying *God* for the acts of *Jesus*—another Markan clue to his divine identity.[118]

It may be debatable whether Mark 2:5–12 is applying a specific OT YHWH-text, such as Ps 103:3, to Jesus.[119] It is not debatable that numerous OT texts attribute the source of all healing and forgiveness to YHWH.[120] Therefore, this Markan pericope at least can be connected to YHWH-texts generally, if not to one text specifically. Jesus's claim, the scribes' accusation, Jesus's counter-claim with healing miracle, as well as other features chosen to be included by Mark, all point to Jesus acting as YHWH does in YHWH-texts.[121]

Mark 2:19–20

The next clear case of YHWH-texts applied to Jesus comes in an episode of Jewish fasting. When Jesus was asked why he and his disciples did not join the disciples of John and the Pharisees in fasting, he said it was because "the bridegroom [ὁ νυμφίος] is with them.... they have the bridegroom [τὸν νυμφίον] with them" (Mark 2:19).[122] It was only when "the bridegroom [ὁ νυμφίος] is taken away" that Jesus's disciples would fast (2:20).[123]

---

[116] Blomberg, *A New Testament Theology*, 45, notes, "the temple priests regularly assured those who brought animals to sacrifice that their sins were forgiven. But the priests were properly credentialed, and the worshipers were following proper legal procedure. Jesus is a merely self-styled rabbi, not an authorized priest, and the healed man has offered no sacrifices in the Temple. Only God could legitimately bypass the very process he himself established and credibly declare the man's sins pardoned." Likewise, see Garland, *A Theology of Mark's Gospel*, 284, and Garland, *Mark*, 94.

[117] Cf. Strauss, *Mark*, 122; Evans, "Jesus' Self-Designation 'The Son of Man' and the Recognition of His Divinity," 33, 44.

[118] Some scholars seem reluctant to acknowledge the Markan identification of Jesus as God. Marcus, *Mark 1–8*, 224; Boring, "Markan Christology," 466.

[119] The position taken here on the likely connection between YHWH's actions in Ps 103:3 and Jesus's actions in Mark 2:5–12 is similar to that of Gaiser, "Your Sins Are Forgiven," e.g., 71, 82.

[120] Watts, "Mark," 131, and Hays, *Echoes of Scripture in the Gospels*, 65, lean toward an Isaian background (e.g., Isa 43:25) patterned after Exod 34:6–7. Other interpreters point to various passages (including Mic 7:18–19; Hos 14:4; Ps 41:4; 103:3; Isa 33:24; 38:17; Jer 31:3; the book of Job) as contributing to a general OT teaching that YHWH alone is the healer and forgiver of his people. Cf. Garland, *A Theology of Mark's Gospel*, 112; Schnabel, *Mark*, 66; Gathercole, "The Trinity in the Synoptic Gospels and Acts," 58.

[121] Marcus, *Mark 1–8*, 224, while not necessarily in agreement with this statement, nevertheless sees the targeted issue of the passage: "It is significant that this first Markan controversy story, which has been placed deliberately at the beginning of 2:1–3:6 by Mark, is overtly Christological; it concerns not simply the question of Jesus' behavior but also and more particularly the issue of his identity." Gathercole, *The Preexistent Son*, 57, writes, "Mark 2:1–12 is probably the most popular passage in the Synoptic Gospels used in support of a divine Christology. This is not without some justification."

[122] France, *The Gospel of Mark*, 139, is surely correct that Jesus's emphasis here is on the bridegroom's identity rather than on the wedding event.

[123] Boring, *Mark*, 86, and Strauss, *Mark*, 139, note that Jesus's description of the bridegroom about to be "taken away [ἀπαρθῇ]" from his disciples may reflect the phrase in Isa 53:8 where the suffering servant is "taken away [αἴρεται, LXX]" from the earth.

Jesus's triply-emphatic self-identification as *the* bridegroom is an allusion to a cluster of OT texts giving YHWH alone that title and role.[124] While it may be that Jesus has a particular passage in mind, the YHWH-as-bridegroom theme runs throughout the Prophets[125] (particularly Isaiah).[126] Some passages refer to YHWH as the past, present, or future bridegroom/husband of Israel (e.g., Isa 54:5; 61:10; 62:5; Hos 2:7; Joel 1:8); some refer to Israel as the past, present, or future bride/wife/beloved of YHWH (e.g., Isa 5:1; 54:6; Hos 2:2); some imply a past or present marriage between YHWH and Israel by accusations of Israel's adultery/whoredom or unfaithfulness to her covenant with YHWH (Isa 50:1; Ezek 16:15, 22-41; Hos 2:2-13; 9:1).[127] Significantly, YHWH himself promised to become the bridegroom/husband of his redeemed people in the eschaton (Isa 54:1-8; 62:4-5; Hos 2:16-20), culminating in a banquet or wedding feast (Isa 25:6-8; Jer 31:10-14; cf. Jer 7:34; 25:10; 33:11).[128] The non-fasting of Jesus's disciples while he is present with them is explainable if Jesus is YHWH, the OT bridegroom, whose presence is the occasion of eschatological feasting.[129] Otherwise, his disciples' non-fasting becomes difficult to explain.[130]

Even the messiah was not identified as the future bridegroom/husband of God's people in Jewish writings before Jesus.[131] This makes Jesus's self-identification here all the more significant: as *the* bridegroom, he claims a major eschatological role for himself that is exclusive to YHWH.[132] And the triple-tradition claim (cf. Matt 9:15; Luke 5:34-35) is surely authentic, since its doctrine is paralleled in John (3:29; cf. Rev 19:7-9) and even in Paul (2 Cor 11:2; Eph 5:22-33), implying that Paul's source for this significant identification of Jesus was likely in the Jesus tradition he received from the

---

[124] Edwards, *The Gospel According to Mark*, 90, writes, "The imagery of the bridegroom recalls not a messianic function but the person of God himself. In this suggestive metaphor Jesus continues, naturally and without arrogance, to presume the prerogatives of God to himself." Cf. Cranfield, *The Gospel According to Mark*, 110.

[125] Cf. Cranfield, *The Gospel According to Mark*, 110; Hooker, *The Gospel According to St. Mark*, 100; Donahue and Harrington, *The Gospel of Mark*, 107; Ben Witherington, *The Christology of Jesus* (Minneapolis, MN: Fortress, 1997), 212.

[126] Some commentators find Isa 62:5 to be very (or most) significant to the background of Jesus's self-identification as bridegroom. E.g., Marcus, *Mark 1-8*, 237; Collins, *Mark*, 199; Garland, *A Theology of Mark's Gospel*, 305.

[127] The passages listed indicate that the YHWH-Israel "marriage" is a prevalent metaphorical theme in the OT. Cf. Swete, *Commentary on Mark*, 44. For a significant study tracking Israel's breaking of the covenant and unfaithfulness to YHWH in "marriage," see Raymond C. Ortlund, *God's Unfaithful Wife* (Leicester, England: Apollos; Downers Grove, IL: InterVarsity, 2002).

[128] Cf. Strauss, *Mark*, 139; France, *The Gospel of Mark*, 139; Stein, *Mark*, 137.

[129] Cf. Witherington, *The Christology of Jesus*, 80; Strauss, *Mark*, 139; Schnabel, *Mark*, 74-75.

[130] Funk and Hoover, *The Five Gospels*, 47, deny the self-identification of Jesus as the Bridegroom/YHWH from the Jewish Scriptures and rather invent an anachronistic explanation for Jesus's teaching on fasting. Collins, *Mark*, 199, is closer to the mark: "The focus on the bridegroom, rather than on the wedding feast, turns the attention of the audience to Jesus. Further, it implies that the presence of Jesus is equivalent to the presence of God."

[131] Marcus, *Mark 1-8*, 237, notes, "In Jewish sources, however, 'bridegroom' as a metaphor for the Messiah is not attested until the sixth-to-seventh-century work *Pesiqta Rabbati*." Cf. Cranfield, *The Gospel According to Mark*, 110; Hooker, *The Gospel According to St. Mark*, 100; Gundry, *Mark*, 136; France, *The Gospel of Mark*, 139; Donahue and Harrington, *The Gospel of Mark*, 107; Stein, *Mark*, 137; Witherington, *The Christology of Jesus*, 212.

[132] Cf. Edwards, *The Gospel According to Mark*, 90; Ortlund, *God's Unfaithful Wife*, 138.

risen Christ and the Apostles (cf. 1 Cor 11:23; 15:3, 8; Gal 1:18–2:9).[133] Thus, the OT promise of YHWH to be the bridegroom of a new people in the eschaton is clearly taken over by Jesus in Mark 2:19–20, the tradition of which may be the basis for the more fully-orbed NT doctrine of the marriage between Christ and the Church (cf. Eph 5:22–33; Rev 19:7–9).[134]

Mark 2:28

Jesus's claim to be "Lord of the Sabbath" is a transparent allusion to YHWH's lordship over the Jewish Sabbath as delineated in the OT.[135] The Sabbath was set apart by YHWH at the completion of creation (Gen 2:3–4) and emphasized in the Law by YHWH as fourth of the Ten Words (Exod 20:8–11; Deut 5:12–15), making Sabbath-breaking an egregious offense against YHWH personally (Exod 31:13–14; Ezek 20:13).[136] Sabbaths were to be kept "to/for YHWH" (Exod 16:25; Lev 23:3), because he owned them (i.e., "my Sabbaths"; Exod 31:13; Lev 19:3, 30).[137] It is this fundamental background that lay behind Jesus's claim to be Lord of the Sabbath.

Not only has the *title* "Lord" (κύριος) already been established in Mark's opening (1:3) as a reverent substitute for the divine name in OT YHWH-texts, but the *meaning* of the term in this context must include that of "owner or master" of the Sabbath.[138] It cannot here take a mundane meaning, such as "sir." The full title, "Lord of the Sabbath," indicates authority over the Sabbath and, therefore, over the Law—expanding on the authority to forgive sins that Jesus claimed in 2:10.[139] This is supported by the καί

---

[133] Collins, *Mark*, 199, notes, "it is clear that the allegorical complex of images in Mark 2:19 was already known to Paul. He portrays himself as the best man, who plays a role in the wooing and betrothal of the bride: Christ as the bridegroom and the members of the Corinthian community as the bride (2 Cor 11:2)." Gundry, *Mark*, 136, argues that the source of Jesus's bridegroom sayings must predate the NT passages (i.e., John 3:28–29; 2 Cor 11:2; Eph 5:22–33; Rev 19:7; 21:2, 9), which show a developed focus on the bride rather than the bridegroom.

[134] Cf. Gundry, *Mark*, 136; Marcus, *Mark 1–8*, 237; Edwards, *The Gospel According to Mark*, 90; Stein, *Mark*, 137; Schnabel, *Mark*, 74–75; Philip B. Payne, "Jesus' Implicit Claim to Deity in His Parables," *TJ* 2 (1981): 11–12; Witherington, *The Christology of Jesus*, 212.

[135] Geoffrey Grogan, "New Testament Christology—or New Testament Christologies?," *Themelios* 25.1 (1999), 71, calls it "a monumental claim to assert lordship over the God-Instituted Sabbath." Stein, *Mark*, 148, writes, "The audacity of this claim should not be missed." France, *The Gospel of Mark*, 148, quips, "Once again, the 'messianic secret' is strained to the limits."

[136] Edwards, *The Gospel According to Mark*, 97, captures this astonishing allusion of Jesus: "God, as we noted earlier, had instituted the Sabbath (Gen 2:3), and Jesus now presumes preeminence over it! Once again Jesus puts himself squarely in the place of God." Cf. Stein, *Mark*, 150; Strauss, *Mark*, 149.

[137] Cf. Gundry, *Mark*, 148; France, *The Gospel of Mark*, 148; Schnabel, *Mark*, 78.

[138] Swete, *Commentary on Mark*, 50, believed "owner" was a better gloss than "master." Decker, *Mark 1–8*, 67, and Edwin Keith Broadhead, *Naming Jesus* (Sheffield, England: Sheffield Academic, 1999), 139, prefer "master." I. H. Marshall, "Jesus as Lord: The Development of the Concept," in *Eschatology and the New Testament*, ed. W. Hulitt Gloer (Peabody, MA: Hendrickson, 1988), 137, writes, "Here 'lord' is not a title but more a description of a function. Nor is it used absolutely to mean 'the lord' but relatively to refer to the lord of the Sabbath. It is a tremendous assertion to make. What kind of man is it who can claim lordship over the Sabbath? Was not this the prerogative of God? Moreover, it is the Son of man of whom this is said. Here we have a link between Son of man and κύριος that could be significant." But Marshall's either/or distinction is unnecessary; Jesus assumes both a divine title and divine function. Cf. Johansson, "Kyrios in the Gospel of Mark," 112.

[139] Cf. Paul J. Achtemeier, "'He Taught Them Many Things': Reflections on Marcan Christology," *CBQ* 42.4 (1980): 471; Strauss, *Mark*, 149; Stein, *Mark*, 150.

inserted within the title to imply the universal scope of Jesus's authority: he is "Lord *even* of the Sabbath [κύριός ἐστιν ... καὶ τοῦ σαββάτου]," since he is Lord (YHWH) over all things.[140]

This second use of the "the Son of Man" title in Mark 2:28 must be connected to the first use in 2:10.[141] Jesus's first use highlighted the Son of Man's "authority" on earth (ἐξουσίαν ἔχει ὁ υἱὸς τοῦ ἀνθρώπου ἐπὶ τῆς γῆς); his use in this verse extends the Son of Man's authority as "Lord" over God's signature institution since the creation—the Sabbath.[142] "Son of Man" cannot be a reference to humanity in general (nor to an Israelite subset of humanity), but is a continuing allusion to the Danielic figure who was to be granted universal and eternal authority ("his dominion is an everlasting dominion" [שלטן עלם שלטנה]) by the Ancient of Days (Dan 7:13–14).[143] Thus, as "the Lord of the Sabbath" the Son of Man would eclipse all Davidic/messianic authority (Mark 2:23–28) in the dominion to be granted by the Ancient of Days.[144]

In terms of the Markan narrative, Jesus is introduced as the Son of God (1:1), appears as Lord (=YHWH; 1:3), will wash repentant sinners with God's Holy Spirit (1:8), is claimed as God's Son by the heavenly voice (1:11), announces the eschatological fulfillment of God's kingdom (1:15), demonstrates "authority" over demonic enemies of God (1:27), heals and thereby demonstrates "authority" that only God has to forgive sins (2:7, 10), claims the prerogative of YHWH as the eschatological bridegroom (2:19–20), and now claims the prerogative of YHWH to rule the Sabbath as its Lord

---

[140] Cf. France, *The Gospel of Mark*, 148; Schlatter, *Markus*, 77; Stein, *Mark*, 149. John M. Frame, *Systematic Theology* (Phillipsburg, NJ: P&R, 2013), 453, remarks, "This is an astonishing claim. In the OT, the Sabbath was the day that Yahweh claimed for himself, over against all human interests."

[141] Cf. Johansson, "Kyrios in the Gospel of Mark," 112. Edwards, *The Gospel According to Mark*, 97, adds that the definite article implies the unique vocation of Jesus, who is *the* (Danielic) Son of Man.

[142] Cf. France, *The Gospel of Mark*, 148; Schnabel, *Mark*, 78.

[143] The impact of critical scholarship can be seen generally in interpreters before 1980 and in the lingering dénouement of the Jesus Seminar members. Seminar leaders Funk and Hoover, *The Five Gospels*, 49, believed that verses 27 and 28 "could have circulated independently" and that "[t]he phrase 'son of Adam' in v. 28 is generic: it is parallel with 'Adam and Eve' in v. 27 and means the same thing—a member of the human race," a view that led them to doubt the veracity of the event and to speculate that "Jesus gives a radical reinterpretation of the creation story (Gen 1:26; Ps 8:4–8): the dominion God gave humankind over all earthly beings is extended even to the Sabbath day." One can see the earlier critical impact on Rawlinson, *St. Mark* (1925), 34, Cranfield, *The Gospel According to Mark* (1959), 118, and Taylor, *The Gospel According to Mark* (1966), 220, who all called verse 28 a "Christian comment" (from Mark or the tradition he received) on verse 27, although Rawlinson admitted it would have been unlikely for Jesus to say that humanity was "lord" of the God-instituted Sabbath. Achtemeier, "'He Taught Them Many Things'" (1980), 471, too, followed suit in thinking the original "son of man" saying from Jesus would have reflected merely Psalm 8 (not Dan 7) and addressed how "the person is superior to the Sabbath" and "can act with some degree of sovereignty relative to it." More recent scholarship, however, is less speculative of Jesus's "original" sayings, recognizing the importance of the Danielic Son of Man background. Edwards, *The Gospel According to Mark*, 97, writes, "If 'Son of Man' means simply 'man,' then v. 28 is not an answer to the Pharisees but a mere tautology. Finally, there are no instances of the use of 'Son of Man' in the Gospels with reference to humanity in general. Here, as always when 'Son of Man' appears on the lips of Jesus, it carries the definite article, '*the* Son of Man,' referring to Jesus' unique vocation as the Son of Man with divine authority and power from Dan 7:14" (emphasis Edwards). Cf. Johansson, "Kyrios in the Gospel of Mark," 112. Regarding a possible allusion to Ps 8 in addition to Dan 7, cf. Strauss, *Mark*, 146; Hooker, *The Gospel According to St. Mark*, 104–5; France, *The Gospel of Mark*, 147; Stein, *Mark*, 149.

[144] Cf. Schlatter, *Markus*, 77; Achtemeier, "'He Taught Them Many Things,'" 471; Strauss, *Mark*, 149.

(2:28). It is unlikely, given this flow in the Markan narrative, that Jesus is claiming anything less than identity with/as YHWH.[145] It is thus apparent that Jesus is alluding to OT YHWH-texts in his self-identification as "Lord of the Sabbath."

Mark 3:27

When Jesus depicts the defeat of the "strong man" (Satan) by one who is able to bind and plunder him, he not only builds on the Baptist's description of him (Jesus) as "the stronger one" (Mark 1:7) who had just definitively defeated the devil (1:13), but also alludes to an OT description of God.[146] YHWH is the only one stronger than the devil and able to bind him and to plunder his "possessions," which in the Markan context are people possessed or held captive by demons.[147] This theme may be based on multiple OT passages (e.g., Ps 68:18; Isa 24:21-23), but the explanation of Jesus for his exorcisms in Mark 3:27 is a likely allusion to Isa 49:24-25.[148]

Isaiah 49 describes the restoration of Israel with new exodus imagery and climaxes in the parallel taking//rescue of the captives//prey from the mighty (man)//a tyrant (49:24-25) by YHWH the Savior, Redeemer, Mighty One (49:26).[149] Although Mark 3:27 uses some different vocabulary, the allusion to Isa 49:24-25 is fairly certain.[150] Mark has already made allusions to the Isaian new exodus, so the reader must be on the alert for more.[151] In fact, Jesus appears to include the Isaian imagery of 53:12 with its prediction of the Servant dividing the spoils (plunder) of the strong,[152] making this another case in which Jesus can allude to himself as both YHWH and the Servant of YHWH. And, although Jesus uses "possessions" [σκεύη] to refer to people, the term is entirely appropriate in a parable on demon-possession.[153] The self-conscious point of Jesus is that he himself fills the role of YHWH, who was expected in the eschaton[154] to bind the devil/strong man and to free those who are held captive in the devil's

---

[145] Cf. France, *The Gospel of Mark*, 148; Stein, *Mark*, 150; Strauss, *Mark*, 150.
[146] Cf. Boring, *Mark*, 108; Garland, *Mark*, 132; Hooker, *The Gospel According to St. Mark*, 116; Edwards, *The Gospel According to Mark*, 122; Marcus, *Mark 1-8*, 283; Watts, *Isaiah's New Exodus in Mark*, 154, 156.
[147] Cf. Marcus, *Mark 1-8*, 283.
[148] Many commentators recognize the allusion to Isa 49. E.g., Hooker, *The Gospel According to St. Mark*, 116; Garland, *Mark*, 132; Marcus, *Mark 1-8*, 283; Watts, "Mark," 146.
[149] Cf. Boring, *Mark*, 108; Watts, *Isaiah's New Exodus in Mark*, esp. 149-52.
[150] Cf. Watts, *Isaiah's New Exodus in Mark*, 147-50; Watts, "Mark," 146; Hooker, *The Gospel According to St. Mark*, 116; France, *The Gospel of Mark*, 173.
[151] Cf. Watts, *Isaiah's New Exodus in Mark*, 156.
[152] Cf. Watts, *Isaiah's New Exodus in Mark*, 151-52; Watts, "Mark," 146; Boring, *Mark*, 108.
[153] Cf. France, *The Gospel of Mark*, 173; Hooker, *The Gospel According to St. Mark*, 116.
[154] Marcus, *Mark 1-8*, 283, writes, "In these Old Testament traditions the strong liberator is God himself, and it is possible that this is the original meaning of 3:27 in Jesus' mouth. In the Markan context, however, the juxtaposition with 3:22-26 secures an identification of Satan's antagonist as Jesus, and this identification is confirmed by the larger Gospel context, in which John the Baptist has identified Jesus as 'the Stronger One' (1:7). Far from being in league with Satan, then, Jesus is the one who liberates human beings from his control. His exorcisms are a sign that God's new age is dawning and that he is the appointed agent for its advent (cf. As. Mos. 10:1); they are not just isolated instances of a powerful spirit besting other spirits but part of a decisive, coordinated attack on the entire structure of evil in the universe...." Cf. Watts, *Isaiah's New Exodus in Mark*, 152; Watts, "Mark."

"house."¹⁵⁵ Thus, Mark 3:27 alludes to an OT YHWH-text (Isa 49:24–25) and applies it to Jesus.

Mark 4:37–41

This passage is on the clearer end of the spectrum of Markan allusions to YHWH-texts applied to Jesus, as evidenced by the plethora of scholars who comment on the connection.¹⁵⁶ In the OT, it is YHWH alone who can stir up or calm the sea with a command/rebuke (Exod 15:8; Ps 89:9; 104:6–7; 106:9).¹⁵⁷ He not only created and circumscribed the waters by his divine word (Gen 1:2–10; Ps 29:3; Jer 5:22), he also delivers people from chaotic waters, both literally and figuratively (Gen 8:1; Exod 15:10–11; Ps 69:1–2; Isa 51:10). As God the Creator, he is by definition over nature, i.e., *supernatural*, in his being and actions (traditionally, his "person and work").¹⁵⁸ Supernatural acts in Scripture, therefore, run contrary to primitive interpretations of world mysteries since they are events intrinsic to, and inseparable from, the super-nature of nature's superior Maker.¹⁵⁹

---

¹⁵⁵ Jesus's self-conscious fulfilling of YHWH's two-pronged role (binding Satan, freeing captive people) is well stated in Edwards, *The Gospel According to Mark*, 122: "He alludes to himself as the 'Mighty One,' as prophesied by John the Baptizer (1:7), who fulfills Yahweh's mission of plundering the house of the oppressor and liberating his captives (Tob 3:17). The parable of v. 27, which is also carefully preserved in the *Gospel of Thomas* 35, offers an unusually clear insight into Jesus' self-understanding. As the Son of God, Jesus does something *for* humanity before doing something *to* it. He must liberate humanity from the power of evil (1 John 3:8) before restoring it to the image of God" (emphasis Edwards). Cf. Garland, *Mark*, 132.

¹⁵⁶ Dozens of commentators will be cited throughout this section. Cf. Boring, "Markan Christology," 466, who simply remarks that the phenomenon is "often noted" by exegetes.

¹⁵⁷ Cf. Paul J Achtemeier, "Person and Deed: Jesus and the Storm-Tossed Sea," *Int* 16.2 (1962): 174–75; Edwards, *The Gospel According to Mark*, 150; Gnilka, *Das Evangelium Nach Markus (Mk 1–8,26)*, 196; Donahue and Harrington, *The Gospel of Mark*, 160; Strauss, *Mark*, 208; Schnabel, *Mark*, 114–15.

¹⁵⁸ France, *The Gospel of Mark*, 221, notes, "Together with 6:45–52 (the other lake miracle), this pericope places Jesus in a more starkly 'supernatural' light even than the healing miracles. Control of the elements is even more extraordinary and inexplicable than the restoration of suffering human beings, and is in the OT a frequently noted attribute of God in distinction from human beings."

¹⁵⁹ Malina and Rohrbaugh, *Social-Science Commentary on the Synoptic Gospels*, 164, espouse a common misunderstanding: "In Israel they [the wind and the sea] were believed to be controlled by spirits or demons, while non-Israelites personified them as deities who manifested themselves in the action of winds and seas." Gundry, *Mark*, 240, soundly rebuts that misunderstanding: "The usual cross-references to Rev 16:5; *Jub.* 2:2; *1 Enoch* 60:16; 61:10; 66:1–2; 69:22; *2 Enoch* 19:4 do not hit the mark of associating sea storms with malevolent demons; for in those passages the angels of the wind and water do God's bidding ... and in *1 Enoch* 101:4–7 God himself sends the sea storm (cf. also Exod 15:10; Josh 24:7; Pss 29:3–9; 77:17–20 [16–19]; 104:3–4; Jonah 1:4; Job 26:12 [the last only if we translate with 'stirs up'])... Jesus' personification of the wind and sea need not demonize them any more than his personification of the barren fig tree (11:14) will demonize it. The fact that despite his shutting up demons in Mark 1:25, 34; 3:12, the verb σιωπάω never occurs in those passages and does not encourage a demonic understanding of his silencing the sea. Hence, we should not think of him as exorcising demons of the wind and sea, but should think instead of language that emphasizes his power by echoing not only the accounts of exorcisms but also OT passages concerning God's rebuking and stilling the sea (Job 26:11–12 [translating with "stills" rather than with "stirs up," which would disturb the synonymous parallelism]; Pss 65:8[7]; 66:6; 106:9; 107:29–30; Nah 1:4 [cf. 2 Macc 9:8; 1QH 6:23–27] plus many more passages dealing in general with God's control over the sea." Cf. Gnilka, *Das Evangelium Nach Markus (Mk 1–8,26)*, 196; Taylor, *The Gospel According to Mark*, 275.

Many OT passages contribute to the background of Jesus's calming of the storm in Mark 4:37–41,[160] but two YHWH-texts are most obvious: Ps 107:23–32 and Jonah 1:4–16.[161] It is more likely that the generalized text of Ps 107 was written prior to the prophet Jonah and, therefore, sets an interpretive trajectory that leads to both events detailed in Jonah 1 and Mark 4.

In Ps 107:25, YHWH's wondrous works include his command of the stormy wind to increase the waves of the sea. Unidentified sailors in YHWH's storm find that "their soul melts" (v. 26) and "all their wisdom is swallowed up" (v. 27), before they cry out to YHWH in their trouble and he delivers them from their distress (v. 28) by quieting the storm and hushing the waves (v. 29). In the end, the sailors respond in relief with thanks and praise to YHWH (vv. 30–32). The narrative in Mark 4 is clearly parallel:[162] a windstorm and high breaking waves cause the fearful disciples to call out to Jesus, who commands the wind and the sea to be still. A tell-tale difference, however, is that the fearful sailors (disciples) rescued by Jesus do not respond with thanks and praise, but with great fear—not of YHWH but of *Jesus*, whose identity becomes the focus of the entire passage (Mark 4:41; see below).

The allusions of Mark to Jonah—both comparisons and contrasts—may be more numerous.[163] It is difficult to miss the Jonah–Mark parallels, as laid out in Table 3:2. At least two transparent parallels inform Mark's readers that Jesus was assuming the role of YHWH in this event.[164] First, although the pagan sailors in Jonah's ship reverently "called out to YHWH" for rescue from perishing (Jon 1:14), the disciples addressed Jesus as a mere "teacher" and were perturbed with him—as the captain was with Jonah!—for sleeping when they needed rescue from perishing (Mark 4:38).[165]

---

[160] Some texts have been listed already. For similar lists and comments, see, Guelich, *Mark 1–8:26*, 267; Boring, *Mark*, 143; Garland, *A Theology of Mark's Gospel*, 123; James R. Harrison, "Modern Scholarship and the 'Nature' Miracles: A Defense of Their Historicity and Affirmation of Jesus' Deity," *RTR* 72.2 (2013): 96.

[161] Cf. Hooker, *The Gospel According to St. Mark*, 138–39, who adds Exod 14:21–31 to the background; Edwards, *The Gospel According to Mark*, 148; Gathercole, *The Preexistent Son*, 63.

[162] Thomas G. Weinandy, *Jesus Becoming Jesus* (Washington, DC: Catholic University of America Press, 2018), 129, calls the scene in Mark "almost a literal enactment of Psalm 107"; France, *The Gospel of Mark*, 221, concludes that Ps 107:23–32 "must surely have been in Mark's mind." Donahue and Harrington, *The Gospel of Mark*, 160, write that "Mark's narrative virtually paraphrases" the psalmist; and Strauss, *Mark*, 208, similarly writes that "Psalm 107:23–29 sounds almost like a poetic paraphrase" of the Markan narrative. Dennis E. Johnson, *Walking with Jesus Through His Word* (Phillipsburg, NJ: P&R, 2015), 115, comments on the expected response to the disciples' rhetorical question ("Who then is this . . .?") in Mark 4:41: "Psalm 107 had given the answer: This is the Lord. . . ."

[163] See especially, Elizabeth Struthers Malbon, "Jonah, Jesus, Gentiles, and the Sea: Markan Narrative Intersections," in *Reading the Gospel of Mark in the Twenty-First Century*, ed. Geert Van Oyen (Leuven, Belgium: Peeters, 2019), 251–95. Cf. Hooker, *The Gospel According to St. Mark*, 140. Harrison, "Modern Scholarship and the 'Nature' Miracles," 96, argues that Jonah is the only historical narrative in the OT background of Mark.

[164] This is not to say there are only two contrasts/ironies between the two narratives, but that the following two examples show a conspicuous connection being made between YHWH and Jesus. For other narrative contrasts between Jonah and Mark, see Boring, *Mark*, 146–47; Malbon, "Jonah, Jesus, Gentiles, and the Sea," 269, 289.

[165] Marcus, *Mark 1–8*, 333, notes the ironic effect here: "Indeed, even the sleeping of Jesus is part of his likeness with God. In ancient Near Eastern myths the supreme deity is often portrayed as sleeping as a sign of his sovereignty: there are no enemies powerful enough to disturb his slumber. . . . Old

Table 3.2 YHWH-Jesus Parallels in the Storms of Jonah and Mark

	Jonah		Mark
1:3	He went down to Joppa and found a ship	4:36	they took him with them in the boat
1:4	YHWH hurled a great wind upon the sea there was a mighty storm on the sea so that the ship threatened to break up	4:37	And a great windstorm arose, waves were breaking into the boat
1:5	the sailors were afraid, and each called out his god.		
	...But Jonah...was asleep.	4:38	But [Jesus] was...asleep....
1:6	So the captain came and said to him,		And they woke him and said to him,
	"What do you mean, you sleeper? Arise, call out to your god that we may not perish."		"Teacher, do you not care that we are perishing?"
1:9	...[Jonah] said..."I fear YHWH...who made the sea...."		
1:14	Therefore they called out to YHWH, "O YHWH, let us not perish for this man's life."	4:38	They woke him and said to him, "Teacher, don't you care we are perishing?"
1:15	They picked up Jonah and hurled him into the sea, the sea ceased from its raging.	4:39	And he awoke and rebuked the wind and said to the sea, "Peace! Be still!" the wind ceased; there was great calm.
		4:40	He said to them, "Why are you so afraid? Have you still no faith?"
1:16	Then the men feared YHWH exceedingly, and they offered a sacrifice to YHWH and made vows.	4:41	And they were filled with great fear and said to each other, "Who then is this, that even wind and sea obey him?"

In other words, where one would expect the disciples to "call out to YHWH" they unknowingly did so by speaking to Jesus, who in turn showed no personal need to call out to YHWH but exhibited his own power over the elements as only YHWH could.[166] Second, the disciples' failure to understand Jesus's divine identity is emphasized again in the contrasting conclusions: although the sailors in Jonah's boat "greatly feared"

Testament adaptations of this idea, however, turn God's sleeping into a cause for concern; Israel calls on him to awaken, arise, and come to his people's aid." Cf. Collins, *Mark*, 260. Malbon, "Jonah, Jesus, Gentiles, and the Sea," 269, notes the vast difference in responses to the sailors' desperate pleas to avoid perishing: "[Jonah's] request that he be thrown overboard into the sea or [Jesus's] command the sea to be still." Thus, the difference is between placating YHWH and acting as YHWH. Harrison, "Modern Scholarship and the 'Nature' Miracles," 96, rightly points out that the "highly unflattering portrait of the disciples in vv. 38b, 40, and 41 is undoubtedly authentic" and "more resembles eyewitness testimony than literary invention or theological elaboration."

[166] Cf. Weinandy, *Jesus Becoming Jesus*, 129. Geddert, "Implied YHWH Christology," 332, thinks the disciples may have expected Jesus to call out to God, as the Joppa captain had expected of Jonah. In any case, Jesus astonished them by commanding the wind and waves rather than petitioning God to do so.

YHWH and then worshiped him, the disciples "greatly feared" Jesus[167] and yet asked the obtuse question: "Who then is this, that even the wind and the sea obey him?" The Markan reader knows the answer is YHWH,[168] who, as Jesus, had just questioned their lack of faith (4:40).

Despite interpretive attempts to deny that the disciples' question was an inquiry into Jesus's identity, the Markan context with its allusions to YHWH-texts rules against it.[169] Not only does Jesus do what YHWH does, but the disciples' question—*Who then is this?*—ensures that the YHWH-identity of Jesus is front and center in the pericope.[170] This should be no surprise, since the divine identity of Jesus is a driving theme in Mark, implied in a string of identity questions tied to supernatural deeds and divine titles.[171] In the calming of the storm, then, Jesus speaks and acts as God, not man.[172] His personal word of power over creation transcends explanations of agency or delegation.[173] In fact,

---

[167] The parallel of "great fear" between the Joppan sailors and Jesus's disciples is surely deliberate. Cf. Edwards, *The Gospel According to Mark*, 151; Malbon, "Jonah, Jesus, Gentiles, and the Sea," 272. Decker, *Mark 1–8*, 115, tracks a Markan theme of fearing Jesus akin to the OT "fear of the LORD."

[168] Cf. Strauss, *Mark*, 209; Hooker, *The Gospel According to St. Mark*, 140; Garland, *A Theology of Mark's Gospel*, 123.

[169] Malina and Rohrbaugh, *Social-Science Commentary on the Synoptic Gospels*, 164, assert, "The disciples' question in v. 41 is not one of 'identity' as a modern reader would assume. It is one of status or honor. It asks about Jesus' location in the hierarchy of powers." But their distinction is problematic, unless "status and honor" can be separated from the intrinsic identity of YHWH. And, as Garland, *A Theology of Mark's Gospel*, 292, points out, "The question 'What is this?' (1:27) now shifts to 'Who is this?' "—increasing the emphasis on Jesus's identity in this passage. Even if one could prove as true the questionable theory that Second Temple Jews accepted pagan views of a "hierarchy of powers" (Malina and Rohrbaugh, 164), the answer to the disciples' question still could not be any lesser being than YHWH. Cf. Richard B Hays, *Reading Backwards* (London: SPCK, 2015), 22.

[170] Curiously, Malbon, "Jonah, Jesus, Gentiles, and the Sea," 270, 289, in an otherwise informative essay, sees Jesus merely "acting as God's delegate," teaching the lesson of God's mercy to the Gentiles "not as God, but as a follower of God who understands God and acts in accordance with that understanding." This seems to fly in the face of the identity question following a clear demonstration of divine power, since the question and the fear behind it are not justified if Jesus is merely exemplifying how to follow God. Other commentators are more on target in recognizing that the identity question is meant to provoke a recognition of Jesus's divinity. Cf. Gundry, *Mark*, 240; Edwards, *The Gospel According to Mark*, 150–51; Strauss, *Mark*, 209; Weinandy, *Jesus Becoming Jesus*, 129.

[171] Cf. Stein, *Mark*, 246, who writes, "Mark intends his readers to reflect on who this Jesus is who possesses divine authority over nature itself. Mark's answer to this question is found throughout his Gospel. Jesus is the Christ (1:1; 8:29), the Son of God (1:1; 3:11; 15:39), the Beloved Son (1:11; 9:7), the Holy One of God (1:24), the Son of the Most High God (5:7), the Son (13:32), the Son of the Blessed (14:61–62), the Son of Man (2:10, 28; 8:31, 38; etc.), the King of the Jews (15:26, 32)." Cf. France, *The Gospel of Mark*, 221; Strauss, *Mark*, 209; Weinandy, *Jesus Becoming Jesus*, 129; Hays, *Echoes of Scripture in the Gospels*, 66.

[172] Collins, *Mark*, 260, appropriately assesses Mark's portrayal: "The narrative thus portrays Jesus behaving not like a devout human person but like God, who caused the sea to cease from its raging in the Jonah story. Thus, Jesus is portrayed not so much as a human being who has trust in God's power to save, but as a divine being. The amazement of the disciples is intelligible in light of the cultural context and parallel texts: they have God manifest in the boat with them!" Cf. Boring, *Mark*, 146–47; Schnabel, *Mark*, 115.

[173] Contra Malbon, "Jonah, Jesus, Gentiles, and the Sea," 289, who calls it "faulty logic" to conclude that "Jesus is God" from this context; he is rather "acting as God's delegate." Donahue and Harrington, *The Gospel of Mark*, 161, think "Mark's readers would be led to see that Jesus is the agent of God's power." While one can maintain that the Jesus is both YHWH and YHWH's agent, their statement seems too weak as a summary of this passage; Moses and Elijah were also agents of God's power, but Jesus clearly transcends their agency. Other commentators more accurately describe the unmediated and personal power of Jesus as that of God himself. Cf. Edwards, *The Gospel According to Mark*, 148–51; Hays, *Reading Backwards*, 123.

Jesus's divine identity as revealed in a unilateral act of divine power and authority is the point of the passage.[174] The reader has already been conditioned in Mark to see Jesus assuming the roles and prerogatives of YHWH, and this passage further confirms a pattern of OT YHWH-texts applied to Jesus.[175]

Mark 6:34–44

The biblical theology of Mark 6:34–44 recalls at least two important clusters of OT YHWH-texts now being applied to Jesus. They can be grouped around the orienting statement of Jesus's compassion for the crowds who were "like sheep without a shepherd" (v. 34) and the subsequent narrative of Jesus feeding the five thousand (vv. 35–44).[176]

The metaphor of sheep lacking a shepherd has an extensive OT background.[177] As an important precursor, in Jacob's blessings of his progeny he both identified God as his own shepherd (Gen 48:15) and appeared to predict the rise of a shepherd from God (Gen 49:24; cf. 49:10). However, the first use of the particular metaphor later picked up by Mark comes when Joshua is chosen by YHWH to succeed Moses in leading the people "so that the congregation of YHWH may not be as sheep having no shepherd" (Num 27:17).[178] YHWH later commanded the judges to shepherd his people (cf. 1 Chr 17:6; 2 Sam 7:11), but shepherding language truly came alive during the period of the kings, particularly with regard to David who had once been a literal shepherd.[179] After the failure of the people's choice of a king (Saul, instead of YHWH!), YHWH chose David to be the faithful shepherd of Israel (cf. 2 Sam 5:2; Ps 78:70–72)[180] and the

---

[174] Cf. Gnilka, *Das Evangelium Nach Markus (Mk 1–8,26)*, 196; Hooker, *The Gospel According to St. Mark*, 140; Edwards, *The Gospel According to Mark*, 148–49; Stein, *Mark*, 246.

[175] The YHWH-Jesus connection has prompted several ways of expressing its ramifications. Marcus, *Mark 1-8*, describes the Markan Jesus as "similar to the OT God" and the subject of "a high Christology that goes a long way toward equating Jesus with the OT God." Edwards, *The Gospel According to Mark*, 151, writes that since "Jesus does again what only God can do," his followers should "recognize in Jesus the same presence of God." Boring, *Mark*, 147, writes, "Jesus' calming of the storm casts him in the role of God." Geddert, "Implied YHWH Christology," 124, concludes, "Only God can calm the angry sea—so Jesus does (4:39). I do not think it is a stretch to claim that in Mark there are at least ten texts designed to communicate to the reader: If you have eyes to see it, you can recognize in Jesus the very person of God!"

[176] The second cluster revolves mostly around YHWH's miraculous provision of quail and manna (meat and bread) during the forty-years wandering of the wilderness generation as depicted primarily in the book of Exodus. The first cluster has roots in Genesis and is found throughout the OT. Numerous commentators have brought together short lists of the first cluster. E.g., Cranfield, *The Gospel According to Mark*, 217; Hiebert, *The Gospel of Mark*, 176; Stein, *Mark*, 313; Marcus, *Mark 1–8*, 406.

[177] Cf. Guelich, *Mark 1–8:26*, 340; Donahue and Harrington, *The Gospel of Mark*, 205; Stein, *Mark*, 313.

[178] Schnabel, *Mark*, 150, is correct when he writes of Mark 6:34, "The verbal parallels are closest with Numbers 27:17; the thematic connection, in the context of Jesus' proclamation of the coming of the kingdom of God, is strongest with Ezekiel 34:1–16." Cf. Marcus, *Mark 1–8*, 406; Collins, *Mark*, 319; Stein, *Mark*, 313; Boring, *Mark*, 182–83.

[179] Collins, *Mark*, 319, writes, "The expression 'sheep without shepherd' is most frequently used in the Bible of a people without a king. The motif of the people lacking a shepherd here could be a hint that Jesus is the messiah of Israel, the king whom they need."

[180] Cf. Boring, *Mark*, 183; Stein, *Mark*, 313.

messianic precursor of YHWH's final shepherd/king (cf. 2 Sam 7:11–16; Ps 132:11–12; Jer 23:1–6; Ezek 34:23–24; Mic 5:2–4).[181]

Self-evidently, however, the universal and eternal aspects of the final shepherd's reign could only be filled by YHWH himself[182]—reinforcing the fact that Israel had erred in demanding a human king to lead them "like all the nations" (cf. 1 Sam 8:4–7). Thus, the Psalms and the Prophets are rich both in declaring the *transcendent status* of YHWH as Shepherd (e.g., Pss 23:1–2; 28:9; 80:1–2; Jer 17:16) and in predicting the *personal arrival* of YHWH as Shepherd (Isa 40:10–11; Ezek 34:11–22, 31; Mic 2:12–13; 7:14; cf. Mal 3:1–2). Until then, God's people could be described as "sheep that have no shepherd" either when they had no representative king or when the king they had was evil (cf. 1 Kgs 22:17; 2 Chr 18:16; cf. Ezek 34:1–10).[183] And so, the once-rejected kingship of YHWH ultimately would be realized and consummated in the eschaton when YHWH himself would be present with his people and permanently solve their problem of "wandering like sheep . . . for lack of a shepherd" (Zech 10:2; cf. Ezek 34:1–31).

Therefore, Mark's description of Jesus having compassion on the people because they were like sheep without a shepherd continues the OT narrative and becomes more than a simple affirmation that Jesus felt pity for suffering people.[184] Rather, harkening back to a second cluster of YHWH-texts, Jesus proceeded to demonstrate his compassion with Torah-like teaching and Exodus-like feeding of the five thousand (i.e., just as YHWH had provided meat and bread), strongly suggesting that the promised divine Shepherd had arrived.[185] Jesus was fulfilling the work begun in all of Israel's shepherds, including Moses and David, because in his compassion for YHWH's shepherdless sheep he acted unilaterally as the ultimate Shepherd to teach, feed, satisfy, and comfort them.[186]

---

[181] Cf. Collins, *Mark*, 319; Stein, *Mark*, 313; Schnabel, *Mark*, 150; Boring, *Mark*, 183.

[182] Boring, *Mark*, 183, notes, "Israelite and Judean kings were charged to represent God's rule among the people, but human kingship failed; God is the true king / shepherd of Israel (Gen 48:15; 49:24; Pss 23:1; 28:9; 80:1; Isa 40:11) and will replace defective and perverse human shepherds (Jer 23:1–4; Ezek 34) by establishing his own kingship in power, either by coming himself or by sending an eschatological king / shepherd (Isa 40:11; 49:9–10; Jer 31:10; Ezek 34:5, 8, 15, 23–24; Mic 5:1–4; Matt 2:6)." Boring's summary is insightful, although his last "either/or" phrase would more accurately reflect the biblical passages he notes if it were changed to "both/and."

[183] Cf. Marcus, *Mark 1–8*, 406; Donahue and Harrington, *The Gospel of Mark*, 205; Schnabel, *Mark*, 149–50; Boring, *Mark*, 182–83.

[184] Cranfield, *The Gospel According to Mark*, 216, notes, "In the N.T. σπλαγχνίζομαι is only used of Jesus, apart from three occasions on which it occurs on his lips with reference to figures in parables that have a close connection with himself (Mt. xviii. 27, Lk. x. 33, xv. 20). It denotes not a mere sentiment, but a pity which expresses itself in active assistance." Cf. Guelich, *Mark 1–8:26*; Strauss, *Mark*, 274; France, *The Gospel of Mark*, 265.

[185] Boring, *Mark*, 183, also notes, "'Torah' was often symbolized by 'bread' (Prov 9:5; Deut 8:3; Philo, *Names* 259–60; *Gen. Rab.* 43:6; 54:1; 70:5; cf. the development of this theme in John 6). Thus the shepherd of Ps 23, as understood in some streams of first-century Judaism, is the eschatological shepherd who will give ultimate 'rest' (cf. the sought rest of v. 35 above and Heb 4:1–11), will lead in paths of righteousness by his teaching of Torah, will make the people recline on the green grass, and will prepare a table, that is, celebrate the eschatological banquet in the wilderness. All these motifs are found in Mark's story and illustrate that the feeding story is incorporated within this image of Jesus as eschatological teacher." On the demonstration of Jesus's compassion as evidence of divine shepherding, see also, Watts, *Isaiah's New Exodus in Mark*, 177–78; Marcus, *Mark 1–8*, 406.

[186] Cf. Edwards, *The Gospel According to Mark*, 195; Watts, "Mark," 161; Hays, *Reading Backwards*, 23; Hays, *Echoes of Scripture in the Gospels*, 70.

Other allusions fill out the Markan fulfillment patterned in YHWH's Exodus provisions, including the emphasis on the "wilderness" location (vv. 31, 32, 35; cf. Exod 16:1, 3, 10) and the arrangement in groups of fifty and one hundred (v. 40; cf. Exod 18:21, 25).[187] More to the point is the manner of the feeding itself: as Moses had questioned YHWH on how he was supposed to feed the Israelites (Num 11:13, 21–22; cf. Ps 78:19–20), so the disciples questioned Jesus on how they were supposed to feed the crowds.[188] Thus, when Jesus himself produced plentiful meat and bread to satisfy the crowds, he was assuming the role of YHWH who satisfied the hunger of Israel in the wilderness with meat and "bread from heaven" (Exod 16:4; cf. John 6:31–35).[189]

It must be granted that the eternal kingdom to be shepherded by the royal Son of David was not consummated in Mark 6:34–44, since he was soon crucified. But this, too, was predicted in the Prophets, who depicted YHWH as mysteriously striking down the eschatological shepherd and scattering the sheep (Zech 13:7; cf. 12:10) before the sheep would be refined and ultimately declare, "YHWH is my God" (Zech 13:9; cf. Ezek 34:30–31). Since this predicted interlude of the eschatological shepherd's sacrifice precedes the eschatological banquet in the Prophets (Isa 25:6–8; 53:12; Ezek 34:13–14, 29–31), the relatively meager fare of the feeding of the five thousand appears to be a mere foretaste and down-payment of Jesus for the feast of the consummation.[190] In any event, it remains clear that Mark 6:34–44 harkens back to at least two clusters of YHWH-texts—those depicting YHWH's future presence as the solution to his people being "like sheep without a shepherd," and those describing YHWH's miraculous provision of meat and bread in the wilderness—portraying Jesus in the eschatological role of YHWH.

Mark 6:48–52

This pericope is clearly meant to advance Mark's theme of the divine identity of Jesus by using a "constellation of OT texts."[191] Mark presents Jesus as the God of the OT both

---

[187] Several incidental parallels between the wilderness feedings and the feeding of the five thousand are picked up by commentators. E.g., Cranfield, *The Gospel According to Mark*, 222; Edwards, *The Gospel According to Mark*, 195; Brooks, *Mark*, 108; Garland, *A Theology of Mark's Gospel*, 290; Watts, *Isaiah's New Exodus in Mark*, 178–79; Boring, *Mark*, 186.

[188] Lane, *The Gospel According to Mark*, 228, and Watts, *Isaiah's New Exodus in Mark*, 178, are unsure of a deliberate allusion here, but the miracle of Jesus is categorically the same as YHWH's miraculous provision of meat and bread, and the entire scene contains too many other coincidental features to be unintended.

[189] Cf. Strauss, *Mark*, 279. Stein, *Mark*, 317–18, also points out the thread of connection running through the miracle feeding of Elijah in 2 Kgs 4:42–44, in which a meager amount of bread satisfied one hundred men with some left over. But he rightly concludes that the Exodus provisions are the primary background to the feeding here, since Jesus's greatness is being highlighted.

[190] Cf. Lane, *The Gospel According to Mark*, 232; Strauss, *Mark*, 276–79; Boring, *Mark*, 183, 186.

[191] Dane Ortlund, "The Old Testament Background and Eschatological Significance of Jesus Walking on the Sea (Mark 6:45–52)," *Neot* 46.2 (2012): 320. On Mark's advancing or emphasizing of the divine identity of Jesus, see, Weinandy, *Jesus Becoming Jesus*, 129; William Hendriksen, *Exposition of the Gospel According to Mark* (Grand Rapids, MI: Baker, 1975), 263; Hooker, *The Gospel According to St. Mark*, 169; Stein, *Mark*, 328; Holly Beers, "4QConsolations and Mark 6:30–56: Images of a New Exodus," in *Reading Mark in Context*, ed. Ben C. Blackwell, John K. Goodrich, and Jason Maston (Grand Rapids, MI: Zondervan, 2018), 103.

functionally and essentially.[192] More than an agent of God like Moses, Jesus attests to his transcendent deity by unilateral supernatural acts and self-identification as YHWH.[193] This is accomplished and confirmed by multiple allusions to YHWH-texts applied to Jesus for the same revelatory event.

While several features of the narrative harken back to OT YHWH-texts, two are most evident of the Markan agenda to portray the divine identity of Jesus.[194] The first is the central miracle of Jesus walking on the stormy sea, an action in Scripture that only YHWH can do.[195] Most commentators recognize Job 9:8—"who alone stretched out the heavens and tread the waves of the sea"—as the primary interpretive authority behind Jesus's action.[196] Even so, every OT reference to walking on water or controlling the elements describes YHWH.[197] Thus, it is doubtful that any early reader

---

[192] Or, in the words of Edwards, *The Gospel According to Mark*, 198, "Thus Jesus not only walks in God's stead, but he also takes his name." Collins, *Mark*, 335, however, refers to "the assimilation of Jesus to God in this passage," and holds, "awareness of these intertextual connections is not necessary for the audience to realize that Jesus is being portrayed here as divine in a functional, not necessarily in a metaphysical sense." But this interpretation seems easily rebutted by Gathercole, *The Preexistent Son*, 65: "Thus far, the majority of the discussion has been concerned with Jesus' exercise of divine functions. Some of these could conceivably be interpreted simply as Jesus acting on God's behalf. As we have seen however, this runs into difficulty when the functions are specifically predicated in the OT as uniquely God's."

[193] Cf. Hooker, *The Gospel According to St. Mark*, 169; Garland, *Mark*, 264; Edwards, *The Gospel According to Mark*, 198–99; Stein, *Mark*, 328; Garland, *A Theology of Mark's Gospel*, 294, 299; Schnabel, *Mark*, 138; Beers, "4QConsolations and Mark 6:30–56," 104–5; Harrison, "Modern Scholarship and the 'Nature' Miracles," 101.

[194] Note, for example, Bauckham, "Christology," 128, who summarizes the passage with the central epiphanic features of Jesus (a) trampling the waves and (b) making his self-declaration.

[195] Numerous commentators point out that treading on the waves is an action attributed only to God/YHWH in the OT. E.g., Hooker, *The Gospel According to St. Mark*, 169; Gundry, *Mark*, 336; Garland, *Mark*, 262; Marcus, *Mark 1–8*, 432; Boring, *Mark*, 189; Strauss, *Mark*, 285; Garland, *A Theology of Mark's Gospel*, 130, 294; Schnabel, *Mark*, 156; Beers, "4QConsolations and Mark 6:30–56," 104; Roukema, *Jesus, Gnosis and Dogma*, 29.

[196] Cf. Gundry, *Mark*, 336; Edwards, *The Gospel According to Mark*, 199; Collins, *Mark*, 336–37; Ortlund, "The Old Testament Background and Eschatological Significance of Jesus Walking on the Sea (Mark 6:45–52)," 325; Strauss, *Mark*, 285; Schnabel, *Mark*, 156; Hays, *Reading Backwards*, 24; Hays, *Echoes of Scripture in the Gospels*, 71–72; Gathercole, *The Preexistent Son*, 63; Richard B. Hays, "Can the Gospels Teach Us How to Read the Old Testament?," *ProEccl* 11.4 (2002): 409–10.

[197] Other passages are either less specific than Job 9:8, or they allude more specifically to the sea crossing of the Exodus: Job 38:16; Ps 77:19–20; Isa 43:16; 51:9–10; Hab 3:15. But always, YHWH performs the miracle, not Moses or another human agent. Cf. Garland, *Mark*, 262; Boring, "Markan Christology," 467. Collins, *Mark*, 328–29, notes that ancient Greek and Roman traditions depict their own gods who control the sea (e.g., Poseidon, Neptune), showing that "Jewish, Greek, and Roman traditions thus all included a portrayal of a deity controlling wind and sea and making a path through the sea." In her interpretation of the present passage she writes, 334, "Jesus' depiction as 'walking on the sea' ... reveals that he is the agent of God who can perform deeds like those of the God of the Hebrew Bible. It also suggests that he is a king who, by divine power, can walk on water, unlike arrogant rulers who only vainly imagine that they can." But this interpretation falls short of the point of Mark's description in the light of the Jewish background: unlike the pagan deities mentioned, the Hebrew God was not restricted to controlling a portion of the natural world but can tread the waves because he created the heavens and the earth and has no rival. The key to understanding Jesus's action is the exclusivity of Job's claim: the Hebrew God "alone stretched out the heavens and tramples the waves of the sea" (Job 9:8). Although Peter's brief walk on the water in the Matthean account was by means of faith, it was on the basis of Jesus's authoritative command, "Come" (Matt 14:29). Again, Jesus is depicted as much more than God's agent.

of Mark would have attributed Jesus's actions to human agency or to a naturalistic explanation.[198] Rather, Jesus is portrayed as filling the shoes of YHWH by his own creative-redemptive power.[199]

The second feature of this narrative that clearly harkens back to YHWH-texts is the revelation of Jesus at the crucial moment of his self-identification. In response to the screams of terror from the disciples who imagined he was a ghost, Jesus spoke immediate words of comfort: "Take heart: I am. Do not be afraid [Θαρσεῖτε, ἐγώ εἰμι: μὴ φοβεῖσθε]."[200] While the phrase ἐγώ εἰμι can be grammatically translated, "It is I," this is unlikely contextually, as Jesus was concurrently treading the waves and voicing this identifying claim as the basis for two commands to abandon their fear.[201] If Jesus were a mere man who had no ability to walk on water or control creation, his words would hardly be a comfort. Rather, ἐγώ εἰμι must be interpreted in harmony with its OT background as the abbreviated explanation of the revelatory name *YHWH*, revealed in Exod 3:14, and translated emphatically as "I am."[202]

---

[198] Some commentators are apt to dismiss supernatural features out-of-hand: e.g., Funk and Hoover, *The Five Gospels*, 66. Others assume that an allegorical interpretation is intended: e.g., Malina and Rohrbaugh, *Social-Science Commentary on the Synoptic Gospels*, 173. France, *The Gospel of Mark*, 270, however, responds well to naturalistic interpretations: "The suggestion that Jesus may have walked on a submerged sandbank which happened to be conveniently located (or was 'wading through the surf near the hidden shore', V. Taylor) takes no account of the actual nature of the lake of Galilee, nor of the fact that fishermen who knew the lake well would not be likely to be impressed. Mark tells us that Jesus walked on the lake, and we have no way of getting behind his account to suggest any other explanation for what he clearly understood to be a supernatural feat." Cf. Schnabel, *Mark*, 138.

[199] Günther Juncker, "Jesus and the Angel of the Lord: An Old Testament Paradigm for New Testament Christology" (PhD diss., Trinity Evangelical Theological Seminary, 2001), 348, notes, "God's mastery over the sea is depicted in relation to two OT traditions: the creation tradition and the exodus tradition." Cf. Garland, *Mark*, 262; Lee, "Christological Identity and Authority in the Gospel of Mark," 13.

[200] Some scholars point out the significant connection between Jesus's commands of comfort and his claim of divine identity. E.g., Hays, "Can the Gospels Teach Us How to Read the Old Testament?," 411; Ortlund, "The Old Testament Background and Eschatological Significance of Jesus Walking on the Sea (Mark 6:45–52)," 326; Garland, *A Theology of Mark's Gospel*, 297.

[201] "I am" sayings of YHWH in the OT are frequently accompanied by comforting/commanding words not to fear, particularly among the Songs of Isaiah (e.g., 41:4; 43:11, 13, 25; 46:4; 48:12; 51:12). Cf. Lane, *The Gospel According to Mark*, 237; Gundry, *Mark*, 337; Ortlund, "The Old Testament Background and Eschatological Significance of Jesus Walking on the Sea (Mark 6:45–52)," 326; Beers, "4QConsolations and Mark 6:30–56," 104–5; Hays, *Echoes of Scripture in the Gospels*, 72–73; D. A. Carson, " 'I AM' Sayings," *Dictionary of Biblical Theology*, 411; Weinandy, *Jesus Becoming Jesus*, 434.

[202] See the discussion of the divine name in the introductory chapter. Marcus, *Mark 1–8*, 427, 432, here comments, "The OT texts in which God identifies himself by means of *egō eimi* (Exod 3:14; Deut 32.39; Isa 41:4; 43:10–11; cf. Isa 47:8,10) are the most important background for the weighty NT usages of the phrase (besides our passage, cf. especially John 8:58 and 18:6); this background is especially relevant for our passage because so many other features of the pericope are evocative of the OT God (walking on the waters, passing by, reassuring adherents, conquering the storm.... These OT texts are all based on Exod 3:14, in which God reveals that his name is *egō eimi ho ōn*, 'I am the One who is,' a name denoting his active, upholding, uncircumscribed, everlasting presence, which allows no rival force to withstand it (cf. Childs, *Exodus*, 61–70).... Although, therefore, Mark never explicitly says that Jesus is divine, he comes very close to doing so here, and this high evaluation of Jesus is consonant with indicators elsewhere in the Gospel (cf. e.g. 4:35–41; 14:61–62)." Cf. Lane, *The Gospel According to Mark*, 237; Boring, *Mark*, 190; Stein, *Mark*, 326; Strauss, *Mark*, 286; Beers, "4QConsolations and Mark 6:30–56," 104–5; Hays, *Echoes of Scripture in the Gospels*, 72–73; Weinandy, *Jesus Becoming Jesus*, 434. Scholars who doubt the intended connection of Jesus's self-identification with the divine name include Decker, *Mark 1–8*, 176; Schnabel, *Mark*, 157.

The descriptions of Jesus walking on water and self-identifying as YHWH are more than enough to recognize in this pericope a deliberate intent to identify Jesus with YHWH.[203] But multiple other features of the Markan narrative add support to the view that Mark intended to paint a portrait of the highest Christology.[204] Not only does Jesus's mere presence calm the storm (apparently, he can merely *will* his supernatural power and need not speak), but there are other likely allusions to YHWH-texts applied to Jesus. The peculiar phrase that Jesus meant to "pass by" his disciples [καὶ ἤθελεν παρελθεῖν αὐτούς] appears to have no satisfactory explanation,[205] unless it is connected with OT theophanies of YHWH "passing by" his chosen representatives to display his glory and announce his identity.[206] The intended epiphany is confirmed by Jesus's subsequent self-identification, ἐγώ εἰμι, which makes more sense as YHWH-speech—"I am"—rather than an anticlimactic, "It is I."[207] This is further supported by the bracketing phrases, "take courage" and "be not afraid," which are also common in YHWH-speech, especially in terrifying moments of theophany.[208]

---

[203] Similarly, Gundry, *Mark*, 341; Stein, *Mark*, 326.

[204] In addition to features mentioned below, see more parallels in Juncker, "Jesus and the Angel of the Lord: An Old Testament Paradigm for New Testament Christology," 348–49.

[205] Rawlinson, *St. Mark*, 89, indeed, finds the phrase perplexing. J. R. Daniel Kirk, *A Man Attested by God*, 454, on the other hand, perplexingly asserts, "Jesus's intention to pass the disciples by, in the context of Mark's Gospel, can only signal that he intends to resume the proper place of leader whom his disciples are following." William Richard Stegner, "Jesus' Walking on the Water: Mark 6.45–52," in *The Gospels and the Scriptures of Israel* (Sheffield, England: Sheffield Academic, 1994), 232–33, discusses other minority views, which are not as compelling as the epiphanic view discussed below.

[206] The comments of Marcus, *Mark 1–8*, 426, generally reflect the divine epiphany view of a number of scholars: "the background to this strange feature of the narrative is to be found in Exod 33:17–34:8, where God reveals his glory to Moses by *passing by* him; this tradition became so important that it was reworked in the story of God's self-revelation to Elijah in 1 Kgs 19:11–13 (see Heil, *Jesus Walking*, 69–71). Under the impact of these passages the verb *parelthein* ('to pass, to pass by') became almost a technical term for a divine epiphany in the Septuagint; in Dan 12:1 and Gen 32:31–32 LXX, for example, it was inserted into contexts that lacked it in the MT. (Interestingly, the Genesis text, like Mark 6:48, combines an epiphanic usage of *parelthein* with a symbolic reference to dawn.) Mark, similarly, has introduced the motif of Jesus 'passing by' into the narrative of the walking on the water because of its epiphanic connotation, but since he needs to end the story by having Jesus united with the disciples in the boat, he writes only that Jesus *wanted* to pass them, not that he *did* so" (emphasis Marcus). Cf. Stein, *Mark*, 324–25; Lane, *The Gospel According to Mark*, 236; Broadhead, *Teaching with Authority*, 125; Gundry, *Mark*, 336; Garland, *A Theology of Mark's Gospel*, 130, 295; Edwards, *The Gospel According to Mark*, 199; Collins, *Mark*, 334; Ortlund, "The Old Testament Background and Eschatological Significance of Jesus Walking on the Sea (Mark 6:45–52)" 323–24; Schnabel, *Mark*, 157; Beers, "4QConsolations and Mark 6:30–56," 105; Roukema, *Jesus, Gnosis and Dogma*, 29; Watts, *Isaiah's New Exodus in Mark*, 231; Hays, "Can the Gospels Teach Us How to Read the Old Testament?," 410–11.

[207] Cf. Guelich, *Mark 1–8:26*, 353; Broadhead, *Teaching with Authority*, 125; Marcus, *Mark 1–8*, 432. Those who think it is "unlikely" that that ἐγώ εἰμι is a theophanic formula include, Strauss, *Mark*, 286–87; Decker, *Mark 1–8*, 176.

[208] The close connection between "I Am" and "be not afraid" is especially noticeable in Isaiah (e.g., 41:4; 43:11, 13, 25; 46:4; 48:12; 51:12). Cf. Watts, *Isaiah's New Exodus in Mark*, 161; Boring, *Mark*, 190. General statements on the connection may be found in several other scholars, including, Lane, *The Gospel According to Mark*, 237; Marcus, *Mark 1–8*, 434; Stein, *Mark*, 325; Garland, *A Theology of Mark's Gospel*, 297; Beers, "4QConsolations and Mark 6:30–56," 104–5. An indirect argument for Jesus using YHWH-language when he says, "Take courage—I AM—be not afraid," is present in the bias of Funk and Hoover, *The Five Gospels*, 66, whose presumptive practice was to rule as inauthentic any words of Jesus attesting to his divinity.

In summary, there is a "constellation" of YHWH-texts alluded to in this pericope. When Jesus walked on the sea he did what only YHWH could do. When he then identified himself, he used YHWH-language to do so.[209] When Mark described Jesus's intent to "pass by" the disciples, an intended theophany is more likely than an awkward oddity.[210] And when the raging sea was calmed by the mere presence of Jesus in the boat, the reader is led to recognize the power and presence of YHWH embodied in Jesus.[211] Mark 6:48–52 simply cannot be understood apart from its application of YHWH-texts to Jesus.[212]

Mark 7:32–37

Although other biblical figures besides Jesus are described as performing miracles of healing, clues in this passage lead its readers to recognize in Jesus the personal presence of YHWH as the healer of the deaf-mute man. The same NT *hapax legomenon* occurring in Mark 7:32 (μογιλάλον, *stammerer*) occurs as an OT *hapax* in Isa 35:6 (LXX, μογιλάλων), strongly suggesting a "deliberate allusion."[213] This connection is significant, since Isa 35 is a major prophetic description of new creation realities accompanying the eschatological coming of YHWH:[214] eyes and ears shall be opened, the lame shall leap, and the stammering tongue shall speak/sing (35:5–6), when YHWH comes to save and to be seen by his needy and anxious people (35:2–4).[215] That Jesus healed a man whose speech impediment was accompanied by deafness only strengthens the allusion to these verses promising YHWH's personal presence to heal these very ailments.[216]

---

[209] Cf. Gundry, *Mark*, 337; Stein, *Mark*, 328; Garland, *A Theology of Mark's Gospel*, 297; Hays, "Can the Gospels Teach Us How to Read the Old Testament?," 411; Boring, *Mark*, 190.

[210] Cf. Guelich, *Mark 1–8:26*, 353; Hooker, *The Gospel According to St. Mark*, 169; Gundry, *Mark*, 341; Marcus, *Mark 1–8*, 432; Donahue and Harrington, *The Gospel of Mark*, 213; Boring, *Mark*, 189–90; Ortlund, "The Old Testament Background and Eschatological Significance of Jesus Walking on the Sea (Mark 6:45–52)," 32–26; Garland, *A Theology of Mark's Gospel*, 297.

[211] Cf. Gundry, *Mark*, 337; Boring, *Mark*, 190; Stein, *Mark*, 328; Beers, "4QConsolations and Mark 6:30–56," 105.

[212] Cf. Geddert, "Implied YHWH Christology," 327, 333; Harrison, "Modern Scholarship and the 'Nature' Miracles," 101; Hays, *Reading Backwards*, 26, 28. Garland, *A Theology of Mark's Gospel*, 299.

[213] Cf. France, *The Gospel of Mark*, 302; Edwards, *The Gospel According to Mark*, 224; Collins, *Mark*, 375–76; Stein, *Mark*, 356; Hiebert, *The Gospel of Mark*, 213; Geddert, "Implied YHWH Christology," 338; Hays, *Echoes of Scripture in the Gospels*, 74. Garland, *A Theology of Mark's Gospel*, 289, rightly notes that Jesus's healing miracle "harks back" to Exod 4:11: "Then YHWH said to him [Moses], 'Who has made man's mouth? Who makes him mute, or deaf, or seeing, or blind? Is it not I, YHWH?'" But while this is thematically the case, it is more likely (based on the same *hapax* and the promise of healing) that Isaiah 35 is most obvious to Mark's readership.

[214] Cf. Edwards, *The Gospel According to Mark*, 224–25; Collins, *Mark*, 375–76; Garland, *A Theology of Mark's Gospel*, 289.

[215] Boring, *Mark*, 216, comments, "There is no reference to the man's faith. This story as a whole reflects the promise of salvation in Isa 35:4–6, when 'He [God] himself will come' and heal those who are deaf, blind, and lack understanding, and give them hearing, sight, and the power to speak clearly." Others point out the poetic and metaphorical language of the Isaian background predicting the messianic or eschatological feature being fulfilled in Jesus: e.g., Brooks, *Mark*, 123; Marcus, *Mark 1–8*, 481; Edwards, *The Gospel According to Mark*, 224–25; Strauss, *Mark*, 325.

[216] Stein, *Mark*, 356, questions whether "Isa. 35:5–6 and Mark 8:22–26 were tied together in the pre-Markan tradition," since the healing of the blind and lame also appears in Isaiah but not here in Mark. But the unusually specific connection of μογιλάλων/μογιλάλον between the two passages seems too weighty to be a coincidence. Furthermore, Mark's readers are well aware that Jesus also healed the blind and the lame. It would be unnecessary and stretch credulity for the deaf/stammering man to be blind and lame, too, in order to confirm a connection to the Isaian promise.

Specifics of this Markan account are not found in other Gospels, leading some scholars to speculate that Matthew and Luke were hesitant to include a story containing "magical elements."[217] But such a view is dubious. That Jesus put his fingers in the ears and touched the tongue of a deaf/stammering man was not only a transparent communiqué of what he was about to do (i.e., heal the man's blocked hearing and stammering speech), but it recalls the OT wonders accomplished by "the finger(s) of God" (Exod 8:19; 31:18; Ps 8:3), a connection to Jesus that he himself made explicit on another occasion (Luke 11:20).[218] His use of spittle need not be dismissed as superstition either, but fits well as a cultural indicator that Jesus himself would be the source of the man's cure.[219] And, although his heavenward gaze surely implied some level of communion with his Father, the healing occurred upon Jesus's personal command over nature. Thus, the "agency" of Jesus appears more divine than human.[220] This may be supported further by a common observation that the verdict of Jesus's audience that he did "all things well [καλῶς πάντα]" (Mark 7:37) echoes the divine verdict at creation that "everything . . . (was very) good [τὰ πάντα . . . καλὰ]" (Gen 1:31, LXX).[221]

Here again is a Markan snapshot of Jesus that alludes to multiple YHWH-texts, though its focus is surely on the fulfillment of YHWH's promised coming in Isa 35:5–6 to heal his deaf and speech-handicapped people.[222] And yet, this specific physical healing by Jesus is significant to the surrounding contours of Mark's Gospel, in which the followers of Jesus must spiritually be able to hear him and to speak honorably of Jesus/God (Mark 7:14, 6–7).[223]

Mark 8:1–10

Jesus's miraculous feeding of the four thousand is another allusion to YHWH's wilderness feedings of Israel, recalling the same clusters of YHWH-texts (see discussion on Mark 6:34–44). In fact, Mark (like Matthew) records two miraculous

---

[217] Collins, *Mark*, 369, wonders if Matthew and Luke were trying to avoid Mark's "magical elements." Cranfield, *The Gospel According to Mark*, 251, provides a sufficient answer. See also the subsequent discussion on the probable purpose of Jesus touching the man's ears and tongue with his fingers.
[218] Cf. Boring, *Mark*, 217.
[219] Cf. Cranfield, *The Gospel According to Mark*, 251.
[220] Collins, *Mark*, 376, interprets from the OT echoes in Mark's narrative that Jesus is God's agent of eschatological renewal. Hays, *Echoes of Scripture in the Gospels*, 74, however, points out that "the *agent* of the healing and restoring action in Isaiah 35 is none other than God himself" (emphasis Hays). Cf. Edwards, *The Gospel According to Mark*, 225.
[221] Many commentators have noted this connection here. Scholars who are confident of a Markan (re-)creational echo of Genesis 1 include, Marcus, *Mark 1–8*, 480–81; Boring, *Mark*, 218; Garland, *A Theology of Mark's Gospel*, 289; Geddert, "Implied YHWH Christology," 338. Scholars who think an echo of Genesis 1 is at least possible include, Cranfield, *The Gospel According to Mark*, 251; Brooks, *Mark*, 123; Collins, *Mark*, 376; Strauss, *Mark*, 324; Schnabel, *Mark*, 178.
[222] Similarly, Edwards, *The Gospel According to Mark*, 224–25; Strauss, *Mark*, 325.
[223] Boring, *Mark*, 216, perceptively notes, "The Markan Jesus has repeatedly called for authentic hearing (4:3, 9, 20, 23, 24; 6:11; 7:14). Now, for the first time in the Gospel, Jesus heals a deaf person, showing that as the lack of hearing is divine judgment (cf. 4:10–12), so the ability to hear is divine gift; neither deafness nor perceptive hearing is simply a matter of human choice; each lies in the hand of the sovereign God (cf. Exod 4:11). So also the inability to speak coherently is a serious malady (cf. 9:5–6; 14:40) that only God can heal." Cf. Joel F. Williams, *Mark*, EGGNT (Nashville, TN: B&H Academic, 2020), 129.

feedings (6:30–44; 8:1–10) following the OT pattern of two recorded feedings (Exod 16; Num 11).[224] Other Markan features recalling YHWH's feeding of the Israelites include the hungry crowds, the question of how they are to be fed, the wilderness location, the two elements of meat and bread, and the miraculous divine provision that proves more than satisfying to the recipients of the meal.[225] These and other details remind the reader of both YHWH's miraculous provisions to Israel and Jesus's previous miraculous provision to the five thousand.[226]

Despite numerous parallels with the previous feeding miracle, the feeding of the four thousand is not a duplicate of the same tradition but an advance on the revelation of Jesus's divine identity.[227] The new crowd is largely Gentile rather than Jewish,[228] drawing to mind OT promises of YHWH's eschatological banquet for the nations (e.g., Isa 2:2; 25:6; 49:6; Mic 4:1–2).[229] This is underscored by Jesus's comment in Mark 8:2, "I have compassion on the crowd," which builds upon the Markan comment on the previous feeding: "he had compassion on them, because they were like sheep without a shepherd" (6:34).[230] The sheep/shepherd motif had alluded to YHWH's compassionate rule over Israel; here, the compassionate rule of Jesus extends to the nations.[231] Like YHWH, Jesus satisfies the hunger of all peoples, both physically and spiritually, both in history and in the age to come (cf. Isa 25:6–8; Jon 4:2, 10–11; Mark 6:42; 7:26–29; 8:8, 14–21, 34–38).[232]

---

[224] Cf. Marcus, *Mark 1–8*, 495.
[225] Cf. Hooker, *The Gospel According to St. Mark*, 190; Marcus, *Mark 1–8*, 495; Boring, *Mark*, 219; Collins, *Mark*, 380; Stein, *Mark*, 371.
[226] Cf. Marcus, *Mark 1–8*, 495.
[227] Cf. Edwards, *The Gospel According to Mark*, 228; Strauss, *Mark*, 335. For an argument on the historicity of the second feeding, see Hiebert, *The Gospel of Mark*, 216.
[228] For an argument giving nine reasons from the context that Gentiles are in view in the feeding of the four thousand, see Boring, *Mark*, 219–21. Others defending the view of a largely Gentile crowd include France, *The Gospel of Mark*, 305; Hiebert, *The Gospel of Mark*, 216–17; Strauss, *Mark*, 335. It is significant that the feeding of the four thousand occurs soon after Jesus's discussion with the Syrophoenician woman of the "bread" Jesus/God gives to all people (Mark 7:24–30). For an opposing argument, see Stein, *Mark*, 367.
[229] Strauss, *Mark*, 335, writes, "The inclusion of the nations is not surprising in a passage with such strong eschatological implication. Mark's favorite prophet, Isaiah, envisioned the day when the nations would stream to the mountain of the Lord to learn his ways and to worship him (Isa 2:2–3; cf. Mic 4:1–2); the messianic banquet is not for Israel alone, but 'for all peoples' everywhere (Isa 25:6). God's salvation is destined to go forth to the ends of the earth (49:6; Acts 1:8), to those who are near as well as those who are 'far off'' (Acts 2:39)." Cf. Schnabel, *Mark*, 181.
[230] Cf. Strauss, *Mark*, 335; Schnabel, *Mark*, 181.
[231] Hiebert, *The Gospel of Mark*, 216, observes, "only on this occasion is Jesus recorded as using this verb ['have compassion'] of Himself (Matt. 15:32). Mark elsewhere used it three times of Jesus (1:41; 6:34; 9:22)." Cf. Schnabel, *Mark*, 181.
[232] Stein, *Mark*, 371, writes, "The question 'How will anyone be able here in the desert to provide these people with bread?' is meant to elicit the response, 'No human being can. Yet just as God was able to feed the children of Israel with manna in the wilderness, so the Son of God is able to do the same.'" Cf. Boring, *Mark*, 219–20; Edwards, *The Gospel According to Mark*, 228.

Mark 8:38 (see on 14:62 with 13:26–27)

Mark 9:1–8

Jesus's transfiguration harkens back to YHWH's Sinai theophany, begging the first observers, and now readers, to interpret the meaning of his epiphany in that light.[233] Parallels include a delay of six days, the high mountain location, the brightness of the transfigured Jesus, the appearance of the Sinai/Horeb figures (Moses and Elijah), the overshadowing cloud of God's presence (*shekinah*), God's revelatory identification, and the requirement to obey the word of YHWH/Jesus.[234] The important interpretive question is whether the Markan parallels are meant to portray Jesus as merely a prophet in the line of Moses and Elijah or (also) as the embodied presence of YHWH.[235]

Certainly, the divine voice at Jesus's transfiguration connects Jesus's authority with that of Moses and subsequent prophets, portraying Jesus as the fulfillment of YHWH's promise in Deut 18:15–22 of a consummate prophet.[236] But several features of Mark's narrative depict Jesus as exalted above the OT prophets and even equal to God.[237] The nature of the transfiguration itself alludes more to classic YHWH-texts than to

---

[233] France, *The Gospel of Mark*, 348, 354–55, summarizes well: "Mark's narrative does not reproduce exactly the Exodus story, but there are enough verbal and conceptual echoes to trigger thoughts of a new Sinai experience, and perhaps of Jesus as a new Moses (see on v. 4). The fact that Elijah also met with God on the same mountain (1 Ki. 19:8–18) reinforces the link.... While a cloud is a frequent theophanic motif in the OT (Ex.13:21–22; 33:9–10; 40:34–38; 1 Ki. 8:10–11, etc.), the echoes here are more specifically of the Sinai narratives, in the coming of a cloud on the mountain (Ex. 19:16; 24:15–16) and the voice of God speaking from the cloud (Ex. 19:9; 24:16; 24:18–25:1; 34:5)." Marcus, *Mark 8–16*, 631, concludes, "But the most important biblical background is that of Moses' ascent of Sinai after six days (Exod 24:16), since Mosaic symbolism runs all through our passage." Cf. Hooker, *The Gospel According to St. Mark*, 215–18. Despite these stark connections, Collins, *Mark*, 419, asserts a Hellenistic and Roman influence.

[234] Some of these features are discussed in Hooker, *The Gospel According to St. Mark*, 215–18; Brooks, *Mark*, 143; Hiebert, *The Gospel of Mark*, 246; Edwards, *The Gospel According to Mark*, 262–69; France, *The Gospel of Mark*, 348, 354; Boring, *Mark*, 261; Marcus, *Mark 8–16*, 631–35; Garland, *A Theology of Mark's Gospel*, 304–5.

[235] See discussion in the next paragraph. Also, Edwards, *The Gospel According to Mark*, 265, answers this dilemma in part: "According to Deut 18:15, 18, a passage that is recalled in v. 7, Moses is considered the prototype of the eschatological Prophet, and Moses is frequently regarded as the representative figure of the prophetic tradition in Judaism. Likewise, Elijah was associated with Mt. Sinai (1 Kgs 19:1–9), where he also received the word of God, though in a different fashion from Moses. Although the NIV introduces 'Elijah and Moses' equally in v. 4, the Greek has Elijah appearing *with* Moses, which seems to imply a certain subordination of Elijah to Moses. In only one passage do Elijah and Moses appear together before the Day of Yahweh. In Mal 4:4–6, Israel is commanded to remember the 'instruction' (Heb. *torah*) of God's servant Moses. Immediately following, Elijah is introduced as the prophet who turns the hearts of people to repentance on the Day of Yahweh. The appearance of Moses and Elijah in the transfiguration narrative likely recalls this passage and their prophetic roles as joint preparers of the final Prophet to come (so Deut 18:15, 18 [see also 4Q175, lines 5–8]; Mal 4:5–6). Their joint preparation for Jesus is further signified by Mark's description of them 'talking with Jesus'; that is, they hold an audience with Jesus as a superior." Juncker, "Jesus and the Angel of the Lord," 376, also points out, "The transfigured Jesus does not resemble Moses or Elijah on the mountain; he resembles God himself on the mountain (cf. Deut 33:2; Hab 3:3–4)."

[236] Cf. Hooker, *The Gospel According to St. Mark*, 218; Brooks, *Mark*, 143; Edwards, *The Gospel According to Mark*, 265–66; Marcus, *Mark 8–16*, 634.

[237] Cf. Edwards, *The Gospel According to Mark*, 265–66; Hooker, *The Gospel According to St. Mark*, 218.

descriptions of human or angelic figures.[238] Jesus's transformation mirrors the Ancient of Days (Dan 7:9) as least as much as it does the Son of Man (7:13).[239] Likewise, Psalm 104:1–2 depicts YHWH as "clothed with splendor and majesty, covering yourself with light as with a garment," envisaging the Jesus of Markan description, rather than subservient angels from whom Jesus was just distinguished (Mark 8:38).[240]

Although the cloud of divine presence (*shekinah*) overshadowed Moses and Elijah as well as Jesus,[241] the voice from the cloud singled out Jesus as "my beloved Son"—categorically superior to the prophets—and as the disciples' standard of authority ("listen to him").[242] Thus, in the narrative parallels, Jesus replaces Sinai's stone tablets (YHWH's Law) as the divine standard requiring human obedience.[243] Furthermore, Peter's misguided offer to build three tabernacles for Jesus, Moses, and Elijah was answered, ironically, with God leaving Jesus "alone" as the implied true tabernacle, since the divine presence in the cloud had just singled out the authority (with divine

---

[238] Cf. Sigurd Grindheim, "Sirach and Mark 8:27–9:13: Elijah and the Eschaton," in *Reading Mark in Context*, ed. Ben C. Blackwell, John K. Goodrich, and Jason Maston (Grand Rapids, MI: Zondervan, 2018), 133–34; J. Ryan Lister, *The Presence of God* (Wheaton, IL: Crossway, 2015), 260; France, *The Gospel of Mark*, 347, 351, 354; Boring, *Mark*, 261.

[239] It is striking that in Daniel, the Ancient of Days possesses snow white clothing (7:9) and the Son of Man comes with heavenly clouds (7:13). In Mark, it is Jesus whose clothing is bleach white (9:3) and the divine voice that speaks from the overshadowing cloud. Grindheim, "Sirach and Mark 8:27–9:13," 134, writes, "In the Old Testament there is only one character that stands out because of his extraordinary white attire . . . (Dan 7:9)." Cf. Juncker, "Jesus and the Angel of the Lord," 376.

[240] Cf. Schnabel, *Mark*, 209; France, *The Gospel of Mark*, 351. Contextually, the unnatural brightness of Jesus's transfigured glory is divine rather than angelic (Mark 8:38).

[241] Since the disciples heard the voice come out of the cloud (clearly harkening back to the OT glory-cloud of the *shekinah*, or God's manifest presence; e.g., Exod 24:16; 40:35), those who were overshadowed must have been Jesus and the two OT prophets. Cf. Rawlinson, *St. Mark*, 120; Hooker, *The Gospel According to St. Mark*, 217–18. That the cloud could possess both concealing and revealing purposes is likely and not contradictory; the Voice was unseen, though revelatory, while Jesus's identity was both mysterious and disclosed. Cf. Cranfield, *The Gospel According to Mark*, 295; Brooks, *Mark*, 143. The *shekinah* epiphany was a theophany, not a misplaced resurrection scene. Cf. Strauss, *Mark*, 381–82.

[242] Boring, "Markan Christology," 468, writes, "It is sometimes claimed that the mighty deeds accomplished by the Markan Jesus are nothing beyond what Spirit-endowed prophets such as Elijah had accomplished, and do not call for 'divine' categories with which to interpret him. . . . It is possible to construct a chronological 'career' of Jesus from 'ordinary' human being to Spirit-empowered human being who is killed and then exalted by God to transcendent status, which fits 'human' and 'divine' 'natures' into a chronological scheme. . . . But in the transfiguration story Mark presents this option in the examples of Moses and Elijah, and explicitly rejects it. Likewise, he pointedly places the 'son' in a different category than the prophet-servants of 12.1–11." Cf. Edwards, *The Gospel According to Mark*, 265–68; Stein, *Mark*, 418–19. Collins, *Mark*, 422, adds that Elijah and Moses were not transfigured, but merely appeared. Curiously, Malina and Rohrbaugh, *Social-Science Commentary on the Synoptic Gospels*, 183, downplay the transcendence in Jesus's transfiguration to create maxims foreign to the text.

[243] Garland, *A Theology of Mark's Gospel*, 304–5, writes, "This account can be compared with the giving of the Ten Commandments on Mount Sinai. God begins with the formula of self-introduction, 'I am the Lord your God,' and then gives the Decalogue (Exod 20:1–17). In this instance, God introduces his Son and demands that they listen to him. This command implies that [quoting Schweizer, *Mark*, 183] 'his instruction is to be seen on a level with God's commandments. His words, like God's word, "will not pass away" (Mark 13,31).' The command to listen also resonates with the fundamental confession of Israel that begins, 'Hear, O Israel' (Deut 6:4). Jesus is the Son of God, and humans must listen to him alone." Cf. Hooker, *The Gospel According to St. Mark*, 218; France, *The Gospel of Mark*, 354; Lee, "Christological Identity and Authority in the Gospel of Mark," 7.

presence?) in Jesus.[244] Far from being an adoptive statement, the words of the divine voice confirm the transfiguration as a theophany.[245] Thus, Jesus had been correct six days earlier to predict that some of the disciples (i.e., Peter, James, and John) would personally witness the reign of God in power (Mark 9:1).[246]

In summary, Jesus is depicted as the locus of divine presence (*shekinah*), the embodied fulfillment of YHWH's promises to dwell with his people, and the personal Power of God's kingdom, at his transfiguration.[247] This is accomplished, in large part, by allusions to OT YHWH-texts of Sinai theophanies and other descriptions of YHWH (see, esp., Exod 24:15–16; 34:4–9; 40:35; Ps 104:1–2; Dan 7:9).[248]

Mark 9:19, 37; 10:18–21; 11:9–10, 15–17; 12:35–37; 13:3–6

Before addressing two major cases remaining in Mark (first, 13:31; second, 14:62 with the thematic parallels of 8:38 and 13:26–27), it seems incumbent to mention a variety of interim texts carrying possible allusions to OT YHWH-texts being applied to Jesus. There is some narrative distance between the previously addressed passage (9:1–8) and the next one (13:26–27), but this should not give the impression that Mark's Christological tone has diminished. On the contrary, while the following examples may appear to possess weaker OT ties than most of those previously mentioned, their frequency and variety support the contention that Mark portrays Jesus as the embodiment of YHWH, even if on the level of "echoes." Briefly, here are several possible YHWH-text allusions in these interim Markan chapters:

---

[244] Edwards, *The Gospel According to Mark*, 266–67, writes, "As a hollow mortal in the searing light of the eternal, Peter suggests building shelters. Peter's proposal, especially in light of Mark's editorial comment that 'he did not know what to say,' is often thought foolish. The suggestion was not foolish in one sense, however, for Judaism held onto the hope that God would once again tabernacle with his people as in the Exodus.... What Peter must come to understand, however, is that God is providing his own tabernacle in which to dwell. Origen remarked that the cloud replaced the tents that Peter proposed. That is close but not correct. Before Peter's very eyes God's dwelling with humanity is present, for Jesus is the new tabernacle of God dwelling with humanity. Peter cannot establish Jesus; rather, it is Jesus who establishes Peter by his call to discipleship (1:17) and fellowship to be *with him* (3:14). The revelation of Jesus' divine nature before the disciples attests that 'the dwelling place of God is with men, and he will live with them' (Rev 21:3). The transfiguration draws Mark's Christology remarkably close to John's understanding of the Incarnation, 'The Word became flesh and lived [Gk. *skēnoun*, lit. "tabernacled"] for a while among us' (1:14)" (emphasis Edwards). Many scholars also note the unique or divine authority of Jesus as identified by the divine voice: Stein, *Mark*, 418; Hooker, *The Gospel According to St. Mark*, 218; Garland, *A Theology of Mark's Gospel*, 303–4; Grindheim, "Sirach and Mark 8:27–9:13," 133; Lister, *The Presence of God*, 263.

[245] See, Boring, "Markan Christology," 467–68. Cf. Collins, *Mark*, 422; Juncker, "Jesus and the Angel of the Lord," 381.

[246] Cf. France, *The Gospel of Mark*, 346; Stein, *Mark*, 419–20.

[247] Cf. Lister, *The Presence of God*, 259–60; Hooker, *The Gospel According to St. Mark*, 217–18; Brooks, *Mark*, 143; Edwards, *The Gospel According to Mark*, 266; France, *The Gospel of Mark*, 346.

[248] Cf. Lister, *The Presence of God*, 259; Hiebert, *The Gospel of Mark*, 247.

- 9:19 appears to depict Jesus using the lament language of YHWH from Num 14:11 (and Deut 32:20?) to decry unbelief in himself.[249]
- 9:37 seems to imply that Jesus equates his "name" with God's name (YHWH), since receiving him is to receive God.[250]
- 10:18–21 cannot be a denial of Jesus's goodness within the Markan narrative (cf. 1:24; 3:4); thus, it is likely both an affirmation of YHWH's oneness (echoing the *Shema*)[251] and the inclusion of Jesus, who is the authoritative source and means of salvation, within the oneness of YHWH (cf. 2:7). The "one" God and the "one" thing lacking coalesce in Jesus.[252]
- 11:9–10 implicitly places Jesus in the position of YHWH who was the original saving addressee of the idiomatic acclamation, *Hosanna* ("save, please"; Ps 118:25–26; cf. 148:1).[253] This is supported in the context by Jesus's "coming" to the temple from the Mount of Olives as Israel's Lord and King, another allusion to the "way" of YHWH (Zech 9:9; 14:4; Mal 3:1).[254]

---

[249] Cf. Boring, *Mark*, 273–74; Strauss, *Mark*, 397; Edwards, *The Gospel According to Mark*, 278; Marcus, *Mark 8–16*, 653, 661; Hooker, *The Gospel According to St. Mark*, 223.

[250] Schnabel, *Mark*, 223–24, also notes, "The notion that Jesus was 'sent' occurs only here in Mark. For Jesus' conviction that he has to fulfil a mission see 8:31; 9:12; cf. 10:33–34, 38, 45. His assertion that to receive him means to receive God does not necessarily imply divinity, since an envoy can represent the one who commissions him without equal status. But at the time when Mark wrote, the assertion that receiving Jesus means receiving God would indeed have indicated Jesus' divine dignity. Given this meaning, the notion of being sent by God presupposes that Jesus was with God before he was sent, which implies Jesus' pre-existence." Cf. Stein, *Mark*, 451; Schlatter, *Markus*, 177.

[251] So, Marcus, "Authority to Forgive Sins upon the Earth: The Shema in the Gospel of Mark," 209–10; Edwards, *The Gospel According to Mark*, 310; Boring, *Mark*, 294; Marcus, *Mark 8–16*, 721; Strauss, *Mark*, 440–41; Bauckham, "Markan Christology According to Richard Hays," 31.

[252] Geddert, "Implied YHWH Christology," 328, writes, "The logic of the text calls readers to choose between two options: Jesus is denying that he is good; Jesus is implying that he is God. Mark's Gospel gives us no basis whatsoever for the first option. The second is supported by multiple features of this text, so that it would be the preferred option, even if no other texts in this Gospel supported it, and that is far from the case." Cf. Edwards, *The Gospel According to Mark*, 312; Strauss, *Mark*, 441; Marcus, "Authority to Forgive Sins upon the Earth," 209–10; Bauckham, "Markan Christology According to Richard Hays," 31.

[253] Alexander, *The Gospel According to Mark*, 301, also points out that Jesus's own name is etymologically related to this acclamation, strengthening the case that Jesus is YHWH come to save. Cf. Roukema, *Jesus, Gnosis and Dogma*, 30; Marcus, *Mark 8–16*, 774, 779; Collins, *Mark*, 519–20; Stein, *Mark*, 505. Malina and Rohrbaugh, *Social-Science Commentary on the Synoptic Gospels*, 195, call Jesus here, "God's proxy" and "broker of divine resources." However, the evidence in the passage appears to imply divine identity and not merely divine agency.

[254] Edwards, *The Gospel According to Mark*, 334–35, writes, "At the fall of Jerusalem in 586 B.C. Ezekiel had a vision of the glory of the Lord departing from Jerusalem and settling on the Mount of Olives (Ezek 11:23). According to Zech 14:4 the Mount of Olives would be the site of final judgment, and the rabbis and Josephus (*Ant.* 20.169) associated it with the coming of the Messiah. Mark, who seldom mentions place names, may mention the Mount of Olives here in order to associate its messianic significance with Jesus' entry into Jerusalem.... Mark calls God 'Lord' not infrequently (1:3; 11:19; 12:11, 29, 30, 36), but the word scarcely refers to God in this instance.... The most obvious referent of *kyrios*, therefore, is Jesus. On occasion in Mark Jesus refers to himself as 'Lord' or uses the term in relation to himself (2:28; 5:19; 12:36, 37), and it appears that he does so here again. His hearers, of course, may have understood the term in the sense of 'master,' but the use of *kyrios* rather than 'I' or even 'Son of Man' appears to be another instance of Jesus' *exousia*, that is, his presumption to divine authority." Various ways in which Jesus is connected to YHWH in this pericope are discussed by several scholars: e.g., Johansson, "Kyrios in the Gospel of Mark," 114–15; Davis, *The Name and Way of the Lord*, 166; Swete, *Commentary on Mark*, 251; Geddert, "Implied

- 11:15–17 shows Jesus acting and speaking like YHWH in his cleansing of the temple (Hos 9:15; Zech 14:21; Mal 3:1–3)[255] and perhaps in his personal reference to the temple as "my house" (Isa 56:7; cf. Jer 7:11).[256]
- 12:35–37 apparently shows Jesus implying his equality with YHWH by applying the transcendent second "Lord" of Ps 110:1 to himself.[257]
- 13:3–6 may imply that many false teachers of the eschaton would claim the divine authority of Jesus by coming in his "name."[258]

Mark 13:26–27 (see on 14:62 with 8:38)

Mark 13:31

The next Markan application of YHWH-texts to Jesus perhaps possesses greater clarity than those cases in the previous section and, therefore, warrants a separate section for discussion. Jesus made the astonishing claim, "Heaven and earth will pass away, but my words will not pass away" (Mark 13:31). Although his words echo several OT YHWH-texts (incl. Pss 102:25–27; 119:89; Isa 51:6; 54:10), it is likely that Jesus was alluding

---

YHWH Christology," 114; Hooker, *The Gospel According to St. Mark*, 258; Evans, *Mark 8:27–16:20*, 141; Collins, *Mark*, 517–18; Stein, *Mark*, 504; Boring, *Mark*, 313–15; Roukema, *Jesus, Gnosis and Dogma*, 30–31; France, *The Gospel of Mark*, 432.

[255] Cf. France, *The Gospel of Mark*, 438; Martin, *Mark*, 224; Strauss, *Mark*, 500.

[256] Cf. Martin, *Mark*, 224; France, *The Gospel of Mark*, 445; Richard N. Longenecker, *Biblical Exegesis in the Apostolic Period*, 2nd ed. (Grand Rapids, MI: Eerdmans; Vancouver, Canada: Regent, 1999), 42; Collins, *Mark*, 531; Stein, *Mark*, 522; Strauss, *Mark*, 500.

[257] Although in Psalm 110, the first "Lord" translates *YHWH* and second translates *Adonai*, they are both translated with *kurios* in the NT, not only blurring their OT distinction but emphasizing the equality with YHWH of the "Lord" who sits at God's right hand until all his enemies are subdued. The different titles for "lord" need not be opposed, however; Hebrew *Adon* (or the Aramaic *Mar*) was a common substitute for the divine name, particularly in speech, and so here of Jesus's (likely) Aramaic speech. And the contexts of both Ps 110 and Jesus's claim here in Mark depict the second "Lord" as transcendent and co-equal with God; he must be more than a man. Cf. France, *The Gospel of Mark*, 487–88; Bauckham, "Markan Christology According to Richard Hays," 31–32; Boring, *Mark*, 349; Ben Witherington III and Kazuhiko Yamazaki-Ransom, "Lord," *Dictionary of Jesus and the Gospels*, 529; Blomberg, *Jesus and the Gospels*, 475; Marcus, *Mark 8–16*, 850–51; Schnabel, *Mark*, 307; Kärkkäinen, Veli-Matti, *Christology*, 20–21. James D. G Dunn, *Unity and Diversity in the New Testament* (London: SCM Press, 2006), 54, however, questions here whether Jesus "thought of the Messiah as a divine figure." Similarly, Ferdinand Hahn, *The Titles of Jesus in Christology* (London: Lutterworth, 1969), 107, thought that here in Mark "a stage of tradition is discernible in which the kyrios title is not understood as a predicate implying divine dignity," and yet, "the fact cannot be overlooked that now Jesus … bears a title primarily applied to God."

[258] Several scholars believe that the phrase ἐγώ εἰμι in Mark 13:6 implies the predicate "the Christ" (as found in Matt 24:5) or, simply, "he." See, Hooker, *The Gospel According to St. Mark*, 307; France, *The Gospel of Mark*, 510; Collins, *Mark*, 604; Stein, *Mark*, 598; Carson, "'I AM' Sayings," 411; Schnabel, *Mark*, 318. Several others, however, entertain the possibility of an implied reference to divine self-identity mirroring that of "Jesus" which incorporates the name YHWH. Cf. Cranfield, *The Gospel According to Mark*, 395; Brooks, *Mark*, 209; Edwards, *The Gospel According to Mark*, 391; Boring, "Markan Christology," 469. Another feature of the pericope which may support a divine use of the "I am" phrase by false teachers imitating Jesus is the peculiar detail that Jesus was sitting "on the Mount of Olives opposite the temple" (Mark 13:3), recalling YHWH's past departure from, and future coming to, the Mount of Olives (Ezek 11:23; Zech 14:4). Cf. Edwards, *The Gospel According to Mark*, 389; Boring, *Mark*, 353; Marcus, *Mark 8–16*, 869; Harriman, "The King Arrives, but for What Purpose?," 288–89, 295.

specifically to Isa 40:8,[259] in which a contrast is made between the temporal things of creation (flesh/people, grass/flower) and the eternal word of God. The implication is that, as YHWH's word is more enduring than the vegetation and humanity he created, so Jesus's words are more enduring than heaven and earth.[260] In fact, Jesus ramped up the comparison, apparently to accentuate the absolute divine authority of his words.[261]

Some scholars have interpreted Jesus's claim here to be hyperbole or on the creature level of prophets/teachers or angels who speak representatively for God.[262] But applying a YHWH-text to oneself would be a bizarre and blasphemous method of hyperbole, and Jesus was clearly speaking for himself ("my words").[263] He unambiguously equated his own speech with God's.[264] Other features of the passage also bear this out. In the previous pericope, Jesus had predicted the eschatological coming of the Son of Man with theophanic glory-clouds and angels (13:26–27; see discussion in the following section). So, when Jesus asserted that certain signs would show "he is near, at the very gates" (13:29), his "words that will not pass away" (13:31) must include his prediction of a future coming as identifiably theophanic, in light of both the OT *history* of YHWH's theophanic self-disclosures (e.g., Exod 34:5–8; Num 9:15–22; Ezek 30:3) and OT *prophecy* of YHWH's theophanic coming (e.g., Joel 2:30–31; Zeph 1:14–18; Mal 3:1–3).[265] In other words, the

---

[259] Many commentators see Isa 40:8 as the primary background of Jesus's statement: e.g., Hooker, *The Gospel According to St. Mark*, 321; Boring, *Mark*, 376; David B. Capes, *Old Testament Yahweh Texts in Paul's Christology* (Tübingen, Germany: J. C. B. Mohr [Paul Siebeck]; reprinted 2017, Baylor University Press, Waco, TX, 1992), 179; Davis, *The Name and Way of the Lord*, 182; R. T. France, *Jesus and the Old Testament* (Grand Rapids, MI: Baker, 1982), 150. Other commentators see a cluster of OT texts (usually including Isa 40:8) as background: e.g., Rawlinson, *St. Mark*, 192; Cranfield, *The Gospel According to Mark*, 409; Marcus, *Mark 8–16*, 918; Strauss, *Mark*, 595; perhaps Garland, *A Theology of Mark's Gospel*, 307; Donahue and Harrington, *The Gospel of Mark*, 376.

[260] This point is expressed in similar ways by the commentators. Cf. Cranfield, *The Gospel According to Mark*, 409; Michael Green, "Jesus in the New Testament," in *The Truth of God Incarnate* (Grand Rapids, MI: Eerdmans, 1977), 34; Boring, *Mark*, 31; Stein, *Mark*, 619; Marcus, *Mark 8–16*, 917; Strauss, *Mark*, 595; Garland, *A Theology of Mark's Gospel*, 307.

[261] France, *Jesus and the Old Testament*, 150, notes, "In Jesus' saying, however, the contrast is stronger; grass and flowers are replaced by heaven and earth.... The claim is a daring one." Cf. Stein, *Mark*, 619; Hooker, *The Gospel According to St. Mark*, 321; France, *Divine Government*, 102; Schnabel, *Mark*, 336.

[262] Malina and Rohrbaugh, *Social-Science Commentary on the Synoptic Gospels*, 207, for example, think Jesus's words here "function like a word of honor." However, they seem unaware that Jesus's claim is a transparent application of a YHWH-text to himself rather than a hypothetical oath formula. Donahue and Harrington, *The Gospel of Mark*, 376, comment that Jesus's claim "serves to underscore the authority of Jesus as a teacher," and Collins, *Mark*, 617, parallels Jesus's speech to angelic speech in Rev 19:9 and 22:6. But Jesus's emphasis on "my words" as more sure than heaven and earth is simply not to be found in any other human agent in Scripture, and in the Revelation passages, the speaking angels carefully specify that their words come not from themselves but from God. All interpretations of Jesus's claim in Mark 13:31 fall short of its meaning when his allusion to Isa 40:8 is not given its due. Cf. Marcus, *Mark 8–16*, 918.

[263] Cf. Boring, "Markan Christology," 469.

[264] Cf. R. T. France, "The Worship of Jesus: A Neglected Factor in Christological Debate?," in *Christ the Lord*, ed. Harold H. Rowdon (Leicester, England; Downers Grove, IL: InterVarsity, 1982), 28; Boring, "Markan Christology," 469.

[265] Gundry, *Mark*, 788, notes, "In a number of OT passages the Day of the Lord is said to be near (Isa 13:6; Jer 31:16; Ezek 30:3; Joel 1:15; 2:1; Obad 15; Zeph 1:7, 14; cf. Jer 31:16 LXX). But in Mark 13:29 it is the Son of man who will be near when the events of vv 14–23 are taking place." Cf. Stein, *Mark*, 620.

context of Jesus's claim to divine speech (Mark 13:31) includes the prediction of his divine parousia (13:26, 29).[266]

Jesus's implication that his words are YHWH's words is supported by contemporary Jewish-Christian thought in Gospel parallels. What was incontrovertible for first-century Jews like Jesus is the eternal nature of God's Law, which will outlast heaven and earth (Matt 5:18; Luke 16:17).[267] If this was indeed Jesus's view of God's Law, then the Markan Jesus was equating his own teaching with YHWH's eternal Law.[268] In another first-century parallel, Jas 5:4, 7 referred to the coming of *the Lord of hosts* (a common OT YHWH-title) as "the Judge standing at the doors [ὁ κριτὴς πρὸ τῶν θυρῶν ἕστηκεν]" (5:9), while the Markan Jesus described *himself* as "near, at the doors [ἐγγύς ἐστιν ἐπὶ θύραις]" (Mark 13:29)[269]—another hint in this context of Jesus's self-perceived divine identity. Thus, not only does Jesus's specific claim in Mark 13:31 apply a YHWH-text(s) to himself, but the surrounding context[270] strongly supports that application.

Mark 14:62 (with 8:38; 13:26–27)

A threefold conglomerate of Jesus's parallel claims to his immanent enthronement and consummate parousia is presented here as a final Markan example of applying OT YHWH-texts to Jesus. Various parallels may be seen in the layout of Table 3.3.

Table 3.3 Parallels and Developments in Jesus' Parousia Predictions in Mark

(1) Mark 8:38	**(2) Mark 13:26–27**	**(3) Mark 14:62**
For whoever is ashamed of me and my words in this adulterous and sinful generation, of him will the Son of Man also be ashamed when he comes in the glory of his Father with the holy angels.	And then they will see the Son of Man coming in clouds with great power and glory. And then he will send out the angels and gather the elect from the four winds, from the ends of the earth to the ends of heaven.	I AM, and you will see the Son of Man seated at the right hand of Power, and coming with the clouds of heaven.

---

[266] Stein, *Mark*, 620, represents many scholars who rightly understand Jesus's words to include his symbolic "coming" in judgment upon Jerusalem in 70 AD (cf. 13:30: "this generation"). This view, however, does not negate the consummate fulfillment of Jesus's claim to come "in clouds with great power and glory" (13:26) and to gather "his elect" (13:37).
[267] Cf. France, *The Gospel of Mark*, 540; Garland, *A Theology of Mark's Gospel*, 307.
[268] Cf. Hooker, *The Gospel According to St. Mark*, 321; France, *The Gospel of Mark*, 540; Garland, *A Theology of Mark's Gospel*, 307; Schnabel, *Mark*, 336.
[269] Being or standing "at the doors" implies the coming/presence of someone rather than something. Cf. Hooker, *The Gospel According to St. Mark*, 321; Marcus, *Mark 8–16*, 911.
[270] Sigurd Grindheim, *God's Equal* (London; New York: T&T Clark, 2011), 185–86, gives a sufficient answer to the concern that the subsequent verse (Mark 13:32) contradicts this one: "When it comes to power and authority, Jesus freely acted as if there was no distinction between himself and the Father. The power and authority that belonged to the Father also belonged to him, not by virtue of appointment, but by virtue of who he was. At the same time, Jesus claimed to act in perfect obedience to the Father and to submit to his will. Read in this light, his claim to ignorance is understandable. He awaited his Father's command to initiate the apocalyptic events he had outlined in his speech. Jesus' claim to ignorance is not a claim out of inability, but a claim out of deference."

Obvious connections include Jesus's illeistic self-designation as the Son of Man, his "coming," which some would see (or be shamed by), and various accompanying features of his coming, such as *glory*, *clouds*, *power*, and *angels*. But there is a certain development in these revelations that may be more clearly observed when they are addressed in their Markan order.

(1) Jesus's claims in Mark 8:38 appear to anticipate the transfiguration in the next scene (9:1–8), but they also allude to OT texts of YHWH's eschatological advent. Some scholars see Dan 7:9–14 as the most influential background to Jesus's Son of Man prediction:[271] key correspondences include the Son of Man figure, his "coming" (to the Ancient of Days; 7:13), and the glory he possesses. Others believe Zech 14:5 is primary:[272] key correspondences include the "coming" of YHWH (to earth; cf. 14:4, 9) and accompanying angels or holy ones. As documented in several earlier examples, Mark often clusters YHWH-texts for application to Jesus. It may be that both the coming of the Son of Man to the Ancient of Days for exaltation in divine glory (Dan 7:13) and the coming of YHWH with an entourage to judge the earth (Zech 14:4–5)—and possibly other texts anticipating an eschatological coming or day of YHWH (e.g., Isa 59:19; 66:18–20; Joel 2:31)—are subsumed into Jesus's trajectory for the Son of Man.[273] The salient point for this study is not which YHWH-text is most prominent in Jesus's allusion but that he alludes to YHWH-texts at all in order to identify himself and to predict his eschatological endeavors. Even the portion of Mark 8:38 not shared by the subsequent parallels in 13:26–27 and 14:62—"whoever is ashamed of me and my words in this adulterous and sinful generation, of him will the Son of Man also be ashamed when he comes"—implies Jesus's divine identity by alluding to YHWH-texts in its radical claim to put to shame (ἐπαισχυνθήσεται) those who reject *Jesus's words* (NB: Jer 8:9, in which "wise" leaders who reject *YHWH's word* shall be put to shame [ᾐσχύνθησαν]; cf. Deut 32:5, 20; Ps 78:8; Isa 1:2–4; Hos 2:4).[274] In summary, the most

---

[271] E.g., France, *Divine Government*, 80–81; Edwards, *The Gospel According to Mark*, 260; James W. Voelz and Christopher Wright Mitchell, *Mark 8:27–16:8* (Saint Louis, MO: Concordia, 2019), 632–34.

[272] E.g., Harriman, "The King Arrives, but for What Purpose?," 286; Paul Sloan, "The Return of the Shepherd: Zechariah 13:7–14:6 as an Interpretive Framework for Mark 13," in *Ancient Readers and Their Scriptures*, ed. Garrick V. Allen and John Anthony Dunne (Leiden; Boston: Brill, 2019), 152–56. Sloan, 153–55, gives five reasons to assume the influence of Zech 14:5 on Mark 8:3. Strauss, *Mark*, 374–75, does not specify a Zechariah connection but nevertheless interprets Jesus's "coming" here as culminating in his Second Advent.

[273] Cf. Harriman, "The King Arrives, but for What Purpose?," 286. Lamar Williamson, *Mark*, (Atlanta, GA: J. Knox Press, 1983), 155, comments, "The transfiguration (9:2–8) confirms but does not complete the Parousia hope." Schnabel, *Mark*, 206, represents several commentators who recognize the Second Advent in this verse because of its judgment motif, but neglect to note its ties to Zech 14:5.

[274] Not only does Jesus claim ultimately to judge the rejecters of his word, but the reason he identifies for their spurning of him (being "an adulterous and sinful generation") harkens back to Jesus's claim to be the divine bridegroom (Mark 2:19–20). Marcus, *Mark 8–16*, 619, comments, "In the LXX, as Bultmann ('*Aischynō*,' 189–91) points out, God is usually the subject of *aischynein*, and the 'shame' he brings is His judgment (e.g., Pss 44:9 [43:8 LXX]; 119:31,116 [118:31, 116 LXX])." The Markan Jesus as Son of Man, therefore, takes over part of the judging role of the OT God, just as he shares in his 'Father's' glory." Cf. Schnabel, *Mark*, 205–6; Maria Horstmann, *Studien Zur Markinischen Christologie: Mk 8,27–9,13* (Münster: Aschendorff, 1969), 47; Donahue and Harrington, *The Gospel of Mark*, 264; Voelz and Mitchell, *Mark 8:27–16:8*, 632–34; Mary Healy, *The Gospel of Mark* (Grand Rapids, MI: Baker Academic, 2008), 170; Strauss, *Mark*, 374–75.

likely OT allusions appropriated here by Jesus—Zech 14:5, Dan 7:13-14; Jer 8:9—are all YHWH-texts.[275]

(2) Mark 13:26-27 reiterates some of the features in 8:38, including the Son of Man figure, his "coming" in/with glory, and his close association with the (holy) angels. But Jesus advances his portrayal in several ways. An ambiguous "they," Jesus claims, shall "see" the coming Son of Man; if the parallel be pressed, then the "adulterous and sinful generation" of 8:38 are the "they" of 13:26. It would make sense that those who shall be shamed (judged) by Jesus shall "see" him in some sense.[276] Also, the coming of Jesus "in the glory of his Father" (8:38) is restated as his unmistakably theophanic coming "in clouds with great power and glory" (13:26).[277] Since, as many commentators recognize, Jesus was alluding to OT manifestations of YHWH, it is likely that he understood by "his Father's glory" the glory-cloud manifestation of God's localized presence (*shekinah*) often featured in OT theophanies (e.g., Exod 16:10; 19:9, 16, 19; Num 10:34; Pss 63:2; 97:2)[278] and predicted to feature in YHWH's eschatological coming with judgment and salvation (e.g., Isa 4:5; 13:9-13; 24:17-23; Dan 7:13-14; Joel 2:30-31; Hag 2:6-9).[279] Finally, the angels accompanying the Son of Man in 8:38 are tellingly *sent by him* to heaven and earth to gather the elect, apparently, *to himself*.[280] The language appears to exceed (but may include) an effectual call producing Christian converts[281]—some of the elect are gathered *from heaven*—and to culminate in a final gathering of the elect at Jesus's consummate Parousia.[282] The cosmic scope of the gathering carried out by Jesus points to the same cosmic gathering promised to be carried out by YHWH (cf.

---

[275] Daniel 7:13-14 is the only passage here that is debatable as a YHWH-text, since the Danielic Son of Man appears as an agent who is "given" his absolute authority. But, as argued earlier in the opening on Mark's Christology and at other points, agency and voluntary submission to his "Father" does not necessarily reduce the "Son (of Man)" to a creaturely nature. Rather, divine qualities tend to be accentuated in Jesus's descriptions of the Son of Man. Cf. Leim, "In the Glory of His Father," 225-26.

[276] France, *The Gospel of Mark*, 535, represents the view that what some of Jesus's listeners would "see" were political and religious ramifications of Jesus's Danielic exaltation after his resurrection. Strauss, *Mark*, 591-92, represents the view that some of Jesus's listeners would literally see his consummate Parousia. Neither interpretation negates Jesus's personal claims to carry out divine judgment, fulfilling the prerogative of YHWH.

[277] Cf. Marcus, *Mark 8-16*, 908; Schnabel, *Mark*, 332-33; Adams, "The Coming of the Son of Man in Mark's Gospel," 57-58.

[278] E.g., Taylor, *The Gospel According to Mark*, 518; Gundry, *Mark*, 745; Marcus, *Mark 8-16*, 908; Harriman, "The King Arrives, but for What Purpose?," 293-94; Adams, "The Coming of the Son of Man in Mark's Gospel," 57.

[279] Cf. Rawlinson, *St. Mark*, 190; Stein, *Mark*, 615-16; Strauss, *Mark*, 592; Schnabel, *Mark*, 331-32; Sloan, "Return of the Shepherd," 152-53.

[280] Cf. Gundry, *Mark*, 745; Edwards, *The Gospel According to Mark*, 404; Marcus, *Mark 8-16*, 909; Garland, *Mark*, 306; Geddert, "Implied YHWH Christology," 337; Harriman, "The King Arrives, but for What Purpose?," 290, 295-96; Schnabel, *Mark*, 332; Adams, "The Coming of the Son of Man in Mark's Gospel," 58; Sloan, "Return of the Shepherd," 152-56.

[281] Some scholars lean toward a figurative interpretation of "earth and heaven" as a merism for "everywhere" and thus suggest Jesus was describing an ongoing gathering of converts to faith in Jesus through the spread of the Gospel. Cf. Rawlinson, *St. Mark*, 190-91; France, *The Gospel of Mark*, 532, 536.

[282] Most scholars believe that the universal gathering of the elect points beyond the Danielic enthronement scene to the final Parousia of the Son of Man at the consummation. Cf. Stein, *Mark*, 615; Strauss, *Mark*, 592; Schnabel, *Mark*, 333; Sloan, "Return of the Shepherd," 156-58; Healy, *The Gospel of Mark*, 269; Voelz and Mitchell, *Mark 8:27-16:8*, 968-69. If Jesus was telescoping significant

Deut 30:4; Isa 11:11–12; 43:5–7; 66:18–20; Jer 23:3; Ezek 11:16–17; Zech 14:1–9).[283] In particular, when Jesus promises to "gather his elect from the four winds ... of heaven" at his coming, it is difficult to miss his allusion to Zech 2:6, in which YHWH had promised to "come" and dwell in the midst of Zion's citizens (2:10) whom he had previously scattered like "the four winds of the heavens."[284] Jesus places himself in the role of YHWH as both the gatherer and the focus of the gathering.[285]

(3) Jesus's final parallel description in the series (14:62) again contains some features shared with the previous two descriptions, including the Son of Man self-designation, his "coming" with heaven's clouds, and his visibility to his present audience (at least to the high priest and the Jewish leaders [Sanhedrin?]; cf. 14:62: "you [*pl*] shall see"[286]). If Jesus was describing the same event(s), then those who will see his coming, formerly called "this adulterous and sinful generation" (8:38) and "they" (13:26), now include the Jewish leaders who were condemning him to death. Thus he predicts the ironic reversal that he will judge those who were judging him.[287] Jesus also parallels his coming "in the glory of His Father" (8:38) and "in clouds with great power and glory" (13:26) now "with the clouds of heaven" (14:62), "heaven" standing as a circumlocution for *YHWH* and the entire phrase reminiscent of the *shekinah*, or manifest divine presence.[288]

---

events in his eschatological predictions of Mark 8:38; 13:24–27; 14:62—e.g., his theophanic transfiguration, his resurrection and heavenly exaltation/enthronement to God's right hand, his destruction of Jerusalem and the Temple, his cosmic reign in the spread of the Gospel, his gathering of the elect both in the Church Age and at his Parousia, his judgment of the world on "the Day of the Lord"—it would not be unusual. Prophetic foreshortening is common in Scripture.

[283] Many commentators note that OT promises of YHWH to gather dispersed Jews from the nations/ends of the earth is the background of Jesus's claim to gather his elect (i.e., Christians) from the nations/ends of the earth. Cf. Marcus, *Mark 8–16*, 909; Gundry, *Mark*, 745; Stein, *Mark*, 615; Strauss, *Mark*, 592; Schnabel, *Mark*, 331–32; Lee, "Christological Identity and Authority in the Gospel of Mark," 14; Healy, *The Gospel of Mark*, 269–70; Sloan, "Return of the Shepherd," 155–58. Adams, "The Coming of the Son of Man in Mark's Gospel," 58–59, summarizes, "The gathering together of the dispersed people of God is a prominent element of Old Testament hope. The wording of verse 27 echoes Deuteronomy 13:7; 30:4 and Zechariah 2:6. These texts refer to the gathering of Jewish exiles out of their far-flung places of captivity. But in Mark, 'the elect' extends beyond the elect of Israel. Thus the language of universality drawn from these texts functions to indicate the redeemed company is made up of people from all nations (cf. 13:10). The thought here, especially in view of the mention of glory in verse 26, is very close to Isaiah 66:18, in which the Lord declares: 'I am coming to gather all nations and tongues; and they shall come and shall see my glory.'"

[284] Sloan, "Return of the Shepherd," 152, writes, "Proportionate space has not been devoted to the fact that the Son of Man comes *with angels*, and that he comes *to gather the elect*. The latter features evoke two theophanic scenes from Zech 14:5 and 2:10, respectively" (emphasis Sloan). See Sloan's extended discussion, 152–58. Cf. Watts, "Mark," 227; Gundry, *Mark*, 745; Edwards, *The Gospel According to Mark*, 404; France, *The Gospel of Mark*, 536; Stein, *Mark*, 615; Marcus, *Mark 8–16*, 909; Harriman, "The King Arrives, but for What Purpose?," 296; Adams, "The Coming of the Son of Man in Mark's Gospel," 58.

[285] Cf. Edwards, *The Gospel According to Mark*, 404; Donahue and Harrington, *The Gospel of Mark*, 374–75; Marcus, *Mark 8–16*, 909; Harriman, "The King Arrives, but for What Purpose?," 290, 297–98; Lee, "Christological Identity and Authority in the Gospel of Mark," 14.

[286] Cf. Voelz and Mitchell, *Mark 8:27–16:8*, 1095.

[287] Cf. France, *The Gospel of Mark*, 616; Geddert, "Implied YHWH Christology," 338; Schnabel, *Mark*, 386; Perrin, *Jesus the Priest*, 277; J. Scott Duvall and J. Daniel Hays, *God's Relational Presence* (Grand Rapids, MI: Baker Academic, 2019), 194; Healy, *The Gospel of Mark*, 300.

[288] Collins, *Mark*, 706, calls the phrase "typical of divine beings"—to which arises the question, *Who then would be in view for Jesus, a monotheistic Jew*? Since YHWH alone rides the clouds in Judaism,

A significant addition to the parallel is the description of the Son of Man to be "seated at the right hand of Power" (14:62).[289] This feature strikingly identifies the exalted "Lord" (*adonai*) of Ps 110:1 with the exalted Son of Man in Dan 7:13–14.[290] In both passages, the figure in view is enthroned with sovereign authority equal to that of YHWH.[291] Such an implication is likely the reason Jesus was accused of blasphemy by the high priest (14:63–64),[292] although some commentators believe the charge stemmed from Jesus's possible use of the divine name when he began his response with "I am [ἐγώ εἰμι]" (Mark 14:62).[293] While there remains disagreement among the scholars as to whether Jesus was referring merely to his heavenly exaltation ("seated at the right hand

---

Jesus here must be depicting himself (the Son of Man) as YHWH. R. Kendall Soulen, "'Hallowed by Thy Name!': The Theological Significance of the Avoidance of God's Name in the New Testament," in *Strangers in a Strange Land*, ed. Lucy Lind Hogan and D. William Faupel (Lexington, KY: Emeth Press, 2009), 145–46, points out that this pericope is stocked with circumlocutions (or "buffer language"), such as, "the Blessed" (14:61), "the Power" and (possibly) "Heaven" or Jesus's ambiguous "I am" (14:62), demonstrating what was surely a first century Judaic practice of avoiding the divine Name. The practice by Jesus for himself only emphasizes a claim to his divine identity.

[289] For discussions on the circumlocution of "the Power" for God in the OT and the significance of Jesus's connection here in Mark, see, Richard J. Bauckham, "The Power and the Glory: The Rendering of Psalm 110:1 in Mark 14:62," in *From Creation to New Creation*, ed. Daniel M. Gurtner and Benjamin L. Gladd (Peabody, MA: Hendrickson, 2013), 95–96; Robert H. Gundry, "Jesus' Supposed Blasphemy (Mark 14:61b–64)," *BBR* 18.1 (2008): 886. Cf. Cranfield, *The Gospel According to Mark*, 445; Lane, *The Gospel According to Mark*, 537; Voelz and Mitchell, *Mark 8:27–16:8*, 1096.

[290] For various expressions of how the figures are related, see, Lane, *The Gospel According to Mark*, 537; Garland, *Mark*, 563; Edwards, *The Gospel According to Mark*, 447; France, *The Gospel of Mark*, 612; Bauckham, "Markan Christology According to Richard Hays," 32; Broadhead, *Naming Jesus*, 142; Adams, "The Coming of the Son of Man in Mark's Gospel," 59–60; John J. R. Lee, "The Divinity of Jesus and the Uniqueness of God: Are They Compatible? A Reflection on High Christology and Monotheism in Mark's Gospel," *MJT* 15.1 (2016): 89.

[291] Cf. Bayer, *A Theology of Mark*, 56; Lee, "The Divinity of Jesus and the Uniqueness of God: Are They Compatible?," 89; France, *The Gospel of Mark*, 612; Watts, "Mark," 234; Bauckham, "The Power and the Glory," 95; Bauckham, "Markan Christology According to Richard Hays," 32; Adams, "The Coming of the Son of Man in Mark's Gospel," 60–61.

[292] Many scholars believe the blasphemy accusation was based on broad or general claims made by Jesus to share God's authority (as applied by Ps 110:1 and Dan 7:13–14), rather than on pronunciation of, or claim to, the divine name. Cf. E. Earle Ellis, "Deity Christology in Mark 14:58," in *Jesus of Nazareth*, ed. Joel B. Green and Max Turner (Grand Rapids, MI: Eerdmans; Carlisle, UK: Paternoster, 1994), 197; Garland, *Mark*, 562; Evans, *Mark 8:27–16:20*, 456–57; Edwards, *The Gospel According to Mark*, 449; France, *The Gospel of Mark*, 615–16; Boring, *Mark*, 414–15; Collins, *Mark*, 706; Stein, *Mark*, 686; Marcus, *Mark 8–16*, 1008; Schnabel, *Mark*, 386; Perrin, *Jesus the Priest*, 277; Bauckham, "Christology," 128; Lee, "The Divinity of Jesus and the Uniqueness of God: Are They Compatible?," 89.

[293] Some scholars believe, or express the possibility, that Jesus was alluding to the divine name here, thus implying his divine identity. E.g., Alexander, *The Gospel According to Mark*, 402; Hooker, *The Gospel According to St. Mark*, 360–62; Brooks, *Mark*, 243; Edwards, *The Gospel According to Mark*, 447; Geddert, "Implied YHWH Christology," 338; Norm Mundhenk, "Jesus Is Lord: The Tetragrammaton in Bible Translation," *BT* 61.2 (2010): 60; Healy, *The Gospel of Mark*, 300. Others, often arguing from the Matthean parallel and/or a less attested Markan variant, believe Jesus was not alluding to the divine name but simply answering, "(You say that) I am (the Christ, the Son of the Blessed One)." E.g., Taylor, *The Gospel According to Mark*, 568; Hendriksen, *Exposition of the Gospel According to Mark*, 612; Gundry, *Mark*, 910; Evans, *Mark 8:27–16:20*, 450; Collins, *Mark*, 704; Stein, *Mark*, 684, 686; Voelz and Mitchell, *Mark 8:27–16:8*, 1095. And still others recognize an allusion to the divine name in the text, but attribute the ambiguity to Mark or a Markan editor rather than to Jesus. Cf. Boring, *Mark*, 413–14; Marcus, *Mark 8–16*, 1005–6. The bottom line for the present study is that Jesus may have alluded to the divine name in his self-description before the Sanhedrin, but his combining of Ps 110:1 and Dan 7:13 to identify himself with YHWH by a shared cosmic authority is much more conclusive.

of power") or also to his earthly Parousia ("and coming with the clouds of heaven"),[294] neither interpretation affects the significance of his use of OT YHWH-texts to identify himself as both a peer of YHWH and a participant in YHWH's identity.[295]

In summary, numerous YHWH-texts lie behind the claims in Jesus's parallel statements in Mark 8:38; 13:26–27, and 14:62.[296] And yet, some specific allusions may be confidently identified. (A) Mark 8:38 contains discernable allusions to Jer 8:9, Dan 7:13–14, and Zech 14:5. (B) Mark 13:26–27 also picks up Dan 7:13–14, but adds the promise of YHWH's coming/presence and cosmic gathering as epitomized in Zech 2:6–10. And (C) Mark 14:62 again alludes to Dan 7:13–14, while incorporating Ps 110:1. In each case, the claims of Jesus would be blasphemous—even for an agent of YHWH—unless Jesus meant for his listeners to recognize in his own person the truth of his divine identity shared with monotheistic Judaism's God, YHWH.[297]

Conclusion

Conventionalized views of Mark's Gospel having a low Christology ought to be rejected. Although Markan style and titular Christology may initially appear less theological than those of John and, debatably, the other Synoptics, the Markan narrative clearly tells a different story. Mark portrays Jesus not only as YHWH's peer but as participant in the divine identity through his frequent application of OT YHWH-texts to Jesus.

This biblical-theological study has examined at least nineteen Markan passages to confirm the ubiquity of this phenomenon in the Second Gospel. It is incumbent upon NT scholars to recognize this theological current in order to understand and describe an accurate Christology of Mark. The neglect of YHWH-texts applied to Jesus in

---

[294] Some commentators see enthronement (not an earthward *parousia*) in both phrases, due to the background in Daniel. E.g., Taylor, *The Gospel According to Mark*, 569; France, *Divine Government*, 77. More interpreters, however, see both enthronement ("seated") and descent ("coming with the heavenly clouds" as viewed from the earthbound perspective of Jesus's audience, and paralleled with Mark 8:38; 13:26–27) in the claims of Jesus. E.g., Stein, *Mark*, 684; Hiebert, *The Gospel of Mark*, 432; Strauss, *Mark*, 657; Broadhead, *Naming Jesus*, 142; Adams, "The Coming of the Son of Man in Mark's Gospel," 59–60; Duvall and Hays, *God's Relational Presence*, 194; Healy, *The Gospel of Mark*, 300; Watts, *Isaiah's New Exodus in Mark*, 286. Unusually, Evans, *Mark 8:27–16:20*, 452, interprets the verbs *seated* and *coming* together as a moving throne, perhaps chariot-like, descending to earth.

[295] Cf. Bauckham, "Markan Christology According to Richard Hays," 32; Bayer, *A Theology of Mark*, 56; Lane, *The Gospel According to Mark*, 537; Marcus, *Mark 8–16*, 1008.

[296] Adams, "The Coming of the Son of Man in Mark's Gospel," 60, offers the following "discourse concept" of the three parallel passages in Mark: "The coming Son of Man is the exalted Jesus (14:62). He comes, at the close of history (13:24), from his heavenly seat of power (14:62), as the divine warrior (8:38), at the head of an angelic force (8:38; 13:27) to effect judgement (8:38; 14:62) and to rescue the elect (13:27). His coming is visible (13:26; 14:62) and its effects are global (13:27) and cosmic (13:24–25)." Of course, other scholars would question the omission of the transfiguration, resurrection, destruction of the Temple/Jerusalem, and perhaps other significant events from Adams's "concept."

[297] Similarly, Geddert, "Implied YHWH Christologyxs," 338.

the Second Gospel can only produce a deficient understanding of the first-century view of Jesus. And if scholarly opinion is correct that Mark is indeed the earliest Gospel, likely written in the generation of those who personally knew Jesus, then it is all the more incumbent upon NT scholars not to ignore the plethora of Markan cases but rather to consider how Jesus shaped the view his followers (and biographers) had of him.

4

Luke's Application of YHWH-Texts to Jesus

The Gospel of Luke is the most distinct Gospel among its Synoptic counterparts.[1] Roughly one-half of Luke is unique to itself.[2] And, although the Third Evangelist possesses eighty more verses (1,136 more words in NA27) than does Matthew, Luke has about 150 fewer verse parallels with Mark than does Matthew.[3] Furthermore, the Gospel of Luke

> opens with a unique infancy narrative (chaps. 1–2), and Jesus commences his ministry with an inaugural sermon not recorded elsewhere (4:14–30). Luke also reports five miracle stories and a whopping seventeen parables not recounted anywhere else. Jesus's words from the cross are completely unique in this Gospel. . . . And Luke provides us with our only account of Jesus's ascension (or our only two accounts, since the story is repeated later in Acts 1:6–11).[4]

In this light, the application of OT YHWH-texts to Jesus will only increase in significance, if the phenomenon occurs not only in Lukan parallels with the other Synoptic Gospels but also within his own unique material.

Despite its relative uniqueness among the Synoptics, Luke clearly shares with its counterparts the same genre and overarching purpose.[5] Beyond an ancient literary *bios*, Luke's portrait of Jesus is a theological biography of "good news" (i.e., *gospel*; cf. Luke

---

[1] See below on Luke's unique content. A more obvious distinction is that Luke is the only Gospel having "an explicit sequel, Acts" (Robert J. Cara, "Luke," in *A Biblical-Theological Introduction to the New Testament*, ed. Michael J. Kruger (Wheaton, IL: Crossway, 2016), 93). Regarding Luke's unique style, see, Archibald Thomas Robertson, *The Gospel According to Luke*, vol. 2 of *Word Pictures in the New Testament* (Nashville, TN: Broadman, 1930), xiii.

[2] Cf. Mark Allan Powell, *Introducing the New Testament*, 2nd ed. (Grand Rapids, MI: Baker Academic, 2018), 166; Mark L. Strauss, *Four Portraits, One Jesus*, 2nd ed. (Grand Rapids, MI: Zondervan, 2020), 316. Cf. James R. Edwards, *The Gospel According to Luke* (Grand Rapids, MI: Eerdmans, 2015), 295; Arthur A. Just, *Luke 9:51–24:53* (St. Louis, MO: Concordia, 1997), 420.

[3] Cf. Powell, *Introducing the New Testament*, 170; Luke Timothy Johnson, *The Gospel of Luke* (Collegeville, MN: Liturgical Press, 1991), 1.

[4] Powell, *Introducing the New Testament*, 166–67. For similar observations on material unique to Luke, see, Cara, "Luke," 93; Charles A. Kimball, *Jesus' Exposition of the Old Testament in Luke's Gospel* (Sheffield, England: JSOT Press, 1994), 11; Sam Rogers, "Jesus' Identity in the Sabbath Miracles in the Gospel of Luke," *Africanus* 8.2 (2016): 29.

[5] In fact, all of the "Gospels" are well-labeled since the identity and acts of Jesus upon whom they focus constitute and determine the "good news" (= *gospel*). For similarities in genre and/or purpose among the Evangelists, see also, Robert H. Stein, *Luke*, NAC (Nashville, TN: Broadman, 1992), 48; Pablo T. Gadenz, *The Gospel of Luke* (Grand Rapids, MI: Baker Academic, 2018), 22; Adrian M. Leske, "The

2:10; 4:18).[6] As a Gospel, Luke does not merely record the life of its Hero, but situates that Life within God's redemptive-historical purposes for the world.[7] Luke, in particular among the Evangelists, emphasizes Jesus as the *Savior* of Israel and the Gentiles/world (1:69, 71; 2:11, 30–32, 38; 3:6; cf. 1:47)[8] who continues and consummates the OT metanarrative (cf. 1:1–4; 24:26–27, 44–48).[9] This is *God's* metanarrative but it centers on the ongoing work and self-declared identity of *Jesus*, as the opening statement of Luke's sequel implies (Acts 1:1).[10] For Luke, therefore, Jesus's recent appearance in and to Israel cannot be understood apart from his present exaltation to heaven and his sending of the Spirit to God's New Covenant people, the Church (Luke 3:16; 22:20; 24:49; Acts 1:5, 8; 2:33; cf. Luke 11:13; 12:12; Acts 2:2–4, 16–21, 33–36).[11]

Influence of Isaiah 40–66 on Christology in Matthew and Luke: A Comparison," in *Society of Biblical Literature 1994 Seminar Papers*, ed. Eugene H. Lovering Jr. (Atlanta, GA: SBL Press, 1994), 902; Alan J. Thompson, *Luke* (Nashville, TN: B&H Academic, 2017), 6.

[6] Cf. Darrell L. Bock, *A Theology of Luke and Acts* (Grand Rapids, MI: Zondervan, 2012), 45–46; I. Howard Marshall, *Luke: Historian and Theologian* (Grand Rapids, MI: Academie Books, 1989), 19; Stephen I. Wright, "Luke," in *Theological Interpretation of the New Testament*, ed. Kevin J. Vanhoozer (Grand Rapids, MI: Baker Academic, 2008), 51, 57; Johnson, *The Gospel of Luke*, 1; Arthur A. Just, *Luke 1:1–9:50* (St. Louis, MO: Concordia, 1996), 20.

[7] For similar descriptions of the Lukan Jesus as positioned within the larger redemptive-historical narrative of Scripture, see, I. Howard Marshall, *The Gospel of Luke* (Grand Rapids, MI: Eerdmans, 1978), 35; Joel B. Green, *The Theology of the Gospel of Luke* (Cambridge; New York: Cambridge University Press, 1995), 26; Bock, *A Theology of Luke and Acts*, 30, 45–56; Joshua W. Jipp, "The Beginnings of a Theology of Luke-Acts: Divine Activity and Human Response," *JTI* 8.1 (2014): 31; David W. Pao and Eckhard J. Schnabel, "Luke," in *Commentary on the New Testament Use of the Old Testament*, ed. G. K. Beale and D. A. Carson (Grand Rapids, MI: Baker Academic, 2007), 251.

[8] The Lukan emphasis on Jesus as *savior* in God's global redemptive purposes is noted by numerous scholars. See, Alan Culpepper, "The Gospel of Luke: Introduction, Commentary, and Reflections," in *The New Interpreter's Bible*, ed. Leander E. Keck (Nashville, TN: Abingdon, 1995), 19; Joel B. Green, "Luke, Gospel Of," in *Dictionary of Jesus and the Gospels*, ed. Joel B. Green, Jeannine K. Brown, and Nicholas Perrin, 2nd ed. (Downers Grove, IL; Nottingham, England: IVP Academic, 2013), 546; Craig L. Blomberg, *Jesus and the Gospels*, 2nd ed. (Nottingham, England: Apollos; Downers Grove, IL: InterVarsity Press, 2009), 165; Joseph A. Fitzmyer, *The Gospel According to Luke I–IX* (Garden City, NY: Doubleday, 1970), 192; Johnson, *The Gospel of Luke*, 23; Gary M. Burge and Gene L. Green, *The New Testament in Antiquity*, 2nd ed. (Grand Rapids, MI: Zondervan, 2020), 249; John T. Carroll, *Luke* (Louisville, KY: Westminster John Knox, 2012), 12; Marshall, *Luke*, 19; Dario Tokić, "Božje Opraštanje u Evanđelju Po Luki," *Bogoslovska Smotra* 82.3 (2012): 733; François Bovon, *Luke 1: A Commentary on the Gospel of Luke 1:1–9:50*, trans. Christine M. Thomas (Minneapolis, MN: Fortress, 2002), 5; Gadenz, *The Gospel of Luke*, 22; Strauss, *Four Portraits, One Jesus*, 342; Cara, "Luke," 93.

[9] Strauss, *Four Portraits, One Jesus*, 342, writes, "The central theme of Luke-Act is *the arrival of God's salvation, available now to people everywhere.* ... By fulfilling the promises to Israel, Jesus becomes Savior of the whole world. ... The whole of Jesus' life and ministry is the fulfillment of prophecy. All of Scripture finds its culmination in him (cf. 24:27)" (emphasis Strauss). Cf. Richard B. Hays, *Echoes of Scripture in the Gospels* (Waco, TX: Baylor University Press, 2016), 191–92; Pao and Schnabel, "Luke," 251–52; G. K. Beale and Benjamin L. Gladd, *The Story Retold* (Downers Grove, IL: IVP Academic, 2020), 100, 105; Blomberg, *Jesus and the Gospels*, 165; Cara, "Luke," 93; David E. Garland, *Luke* (Grand Rapids, MI: Zondervan, 2011), 37; Johnson, *The Gospel of Luke*, 10.

[10] Cf. Culpepper, "The Gospel of Luke," 13; Alfred Plummer, *The Gospel According to St. Luke*, ed. Charles Augustus Briggs, Samuel Rolles Driver, and Alfred Plummer, 6th ed. (New York: Charles Scribner's Sons, 1903), xxxvi. Luke locates Jesus at the center of God's story. Cf. Bock, *A Theology of Luke and Acts*, 29–30; Carroll, *Luke*, 12; Fitzmyer, *The Gospel According to Luke*, 192; Green, "Luke, Gospel Of," 547; Jerome Kodell, "The Theology of Luke in Recent Study," *BTB* 1.2 (1971): 124.

[11] The promise of the Spirit for God's people in the eschaton has wide OT roots (e.g., Num 11:29; Isa 42:1, 6; 49:6, 8; 59:20–21; Jer 31:31–34; Ezek 36:27; 37:14; Joel 2:28–32; Zech 12:10), which Luke links to Jesus in both his earthly ministry and subsequent heavenly reign. Cf. Vincent Taylor, *Behind the Third Gospel* (Oxford: Oxford University Press, 1926), 268; Edward Earle Ellis, *The Gospel of Luke*, rev. ed. (Grand Rapids, MI: Eerdmans, 1974), 10; Bock, *A Theology of Luke and Acts*, 30.

Luke's Christology

A high Christology is presupposed in Luke's theological narrative of Jesus.[12] The familiar miracle echoed (cf. Gen 21:1–7) in the *human* birth of John is soon eclipsed by staggering echoes in the *divine* birth of Jesus. John was conceived and born because God opened a post-menopausal womb for an elderly couple (Luke 1:7–20), but Jesus was conceived and born of a virgin by the overshadowing presence and power of God (Luke 1:34–37; cf. Gen 1:2; 1 Kgs 8:10–11; Isa 7:14). Thus, the divine nature and heavenly origin of Jesus informed his pre-birth titles: "the Son of the Most High" (1:32), "the Son of God" (1:35), "my [Elizabeth's] Lord" (1:43), "the Most High" (1:76), "the Lord" (1:76), "the Arising ... from on high" (1:79), "Christ the Lord" (2:11).[13] Furthermore, Luke portrays the incarnate Son of God as the embodied visitation of YHWH to his eschatological people (1:68, 78; 7:16; 19:44; cf. Mal 3:1–5; 4:1–6).[14] In contrast, John's relative greatness is not innate but derivative as the privileged human herald of the divine "Lord" (1:17, 76; 3:4).

Luke's narrative continues with the divine sonship (3:22, 38; 4:9, 41; 8:28; 9:35; 10:22; 20:13; 22:70)[15] and divine lordship (5:8; 6:5, 46; 10:17; 13:25; 20:42, 44)[16] of Jesus

---

[12] Cf. Hays, *Echoes of Scripture in the Gospels*, 262; Robert F. O'Toole, "How Does Luke Portray Jesus as Servant of YHWH," *Bib* 81.3 (2000): 225; Christopher Kavin Rowe, *Early Narrative Christology* (Berlin; New York: Walter de Gruyter, 2006), 27–28; Mark L. Strauss, "Christology and Christological Purpose in the Synoptic Gospels: A Study of Unity in Diversity," in *Reconsidering the Relationship between Biblical and Systematic Theology in the New Testament*, ed. Benjamin E. Reynolds, Brian Lugioyo, and Kevin J. Vanhoozer (Tübingen, Germany: Mohr Siebeck, 2014), 58–59. For a view doubtful of a high Christology in Luke, see Christopher M. Tuckett, "The Christology of Luke-Acts," in *The Unity of Luke-Acts*, ed. Giuseppe Alberigo (Leuven, Belgium: Leuven University Press, 1999), 157–58.

[13] Cf. Nina Henrichs-Tarasenkova, *Luke's Christology of Divine Identity* (New York: Bloomsbury T&T Clark, 2016), 172, 194; Beale and Gladd, *The Story Retold*, 105; O'Toole, "How Does Luke Portray Jesus as Servant of YHWH," 225; Rowe, *Early Narrative Christology*, 27.

[14] Cf. Gregory R. Lanier, "Luke's Distinctive Use of the Temple: Portraying the Divine Visitation," *JTS* 65.2 (2014): 447; Rowe, *Early Narrative Christology*, 200; Henrichs-Tarasenkova, *Luke's Christology of Divine Identity*, 172; J. Scott Duvall and J. Daniel Hays, *God's Relational Presence* (Grand Rapids, MI: Baker Academic, 2019), 203; Green, *The Theology of the Gospel of Luke*, 61; Hays, *Echoes of Scripture in the Gospels*, 243; O'Toole, "How Does Luke Portray Jesus as Servant of YHWH," 225; Aída Besançon Spencer, "'Fear' as a Witness to Jesus in Luke's Gospel," *BBR* 2 (1992): 69. Carl R. Holladay, *Introduction to the New Testament*, reference ed. (Waco, TX: Baylor University Press, 2017), 271, is too ambiguous: "Jesus himself symbolizes God's presence among the people because he is so closely identified with the Father (10:21–22)."

[15] Cf. Duvall and Hays, *God's Relational Presence*, 203; Holladay, *Introduction to the New Testament*, 261.

[16] Rowe, *Early Narrative Christology*, 27, 31–32, 200, underscores the narrative significance in Luke's use of "Lord" for Jesus. Similarly, see Hays, *Echoes of Scripture in the Gospels*, 253. Tuckett, "The Christology of Luke-Acts," 157–58, believes the argument for a high Christology from Luke's use of κύριος is "not entirely convincing" because it downplays Luke's use of Χριστός for Jesus. But it is difficult to see how an emphasis on one title must cancel the usage of another title. Cannot the human Messiah also be the divine Lord? Scholars have long recognized that the lordship of Jesus in the Third Gospel cannot be reduced to mere politeness or respect on the human level. Cf. Taylor, *Behind the Third Gospel*, 265–66; Culpepper, "The Gospel of Luke," 16; Darrell L. Bock, *Luke* (Downers Grove, IL: InterVarsity Press, 1994), 31; I. Howard Marshall, "The Christology of Luke's Gospel and Acts," in *Contours of Christology in the New Testament*, ed. Richard N. Longenecker (Grand Rapids, MI: Eerdmans, 2005), 126, 144–45; Duvall and Hays, *God's Relational Presence*, 203.

never far from the storyline. The identity of Jesus is, in fact, the key to Luke's narrative.[17] Although Jesus can call John the greatest figure in old covenant history (7:28), John can say he is not worthy to untie the sandals of Jesus (3:16). Further indications of Jesus's divine identity include his supernatural power (4:41; 5:13), his unsurpassed personal authority (6:5; 7:48–49), his reception of worship (17:15–18; 24:52), his exaltation to God's throne (24:51; cf. 20:41–44; Acts 1:2, 9–11), and his sending of God's promised Spirit to the people of God for the eschatological age (Luke 3:16; 24:49; cf. Acts 1:4–5, 8).[18] Like the other canonical Gospels, Luke clearly portrays the humanity of Jesus (Luke 2:40; 22:44).[19] But Jesus's humanity is asserted alongside his divine identity without any sense of conflict.[20] There can be no surprise, then, that within the milieu of Luke's understanding of Jesus he frequently applies OT YHWH-texts to Jesus.[21]

Lukan Cases of Old Testament YHWH-Texts Applied to Jesus

Luke 1:17, 76; 3:4–6; 7:26–27

One of Luke's first applications of YHWH-texts to Jesus is an allusion in 1:17 that is confirmed by parallel allusions and quotations in 1:76, 3:4–6, and 7:26–27.[22] Each of the four texts shall be examined separately in Lukan order, before general observations are made tying them together. All are applications of Mal 3:1 and/or Isa 40:3(–5) to Jesus, but may allude to other YHWH-texts as well.[23]

Luke 1:17

The significance of this verse in the purpose of Luke's Gospel should not be underestimated. The words come from the angel Gabriel who dwells in God's presence

---

[17] Cf. Culpepper, "The Gospel of Luke," 13; Green, *The Theology of the Gospel of Luke*, 61. François Bovon, *Luke the Theologian*, 2nd ed. (Waco, TX: Baylor University Press, 2006), 181, refuses to speak of "an identification of Jesus with God" or "an assimilation of Jesus into Yahweh," since, "Luke always respects a certain distance between the Father and the Son." But identifying Jesus with YHWH/God does not imply assimilation; neither does it exclude a distinction between Father and Son. It remains the case that the divine identity of Jesus is continually implied in Luke's Gospel. See also, Hays, *Echoes of Scripture in the Gospels*, 243–44; Green, "Luke, Gospel Of," 547.

[18] Divine actions, titles, and prerogatives abound in Luke's life of Jesus. Cf. Henrichs-Tarasenkova, *Luke's Christology of Divine Identity*, 171–72; Fitzmyer, *The Gospel According to Luke*, 193–94; Hays, *Echoes of Scripture in the Gospels*, 244, 259; Jipp, "The Beginnings of a Theology of Luke-Acts," 34; Dennis E. Johnson, "Jesus Against the Idols: The Use of Isaianic Servant Songs in the Missiology of Acts," *WTJ* 52 (1990): 352–53; O'Toole, "How Does Luke Portray Jesus as Servant of YHWH," 225; Spencer, "'Fear' as a Witness to Jesus in Luke's Gospel," 69; Stein, *Luke*, 48; Strauss, "Christology and Christological Purpose in the Synoptic Gospels," 59.

[19] Cf. Fitzmyer, *The Gospel According to Luke*, 192; Rowe, *Early Narrative Christology*, 28.

[20] Cf. Rowe, *Early Narrative Christology*, 28; Hays, *Echoes of Scripture in the Gospels*, 253, 280.

[21] Or, to say it another way: Luke's application of OT YHWH-texts to Jesus is a narratively natural way to portray the divine identity of Jesus. Cf. Hays, *Echoes of Scripture in the Gospels*, 262.

[22] Cf. Thompson, *Luke*, 18; Stein, *Luke*, 76.

[23] Cf. Plummer, *The Gospel According to St. Luke*, 15; Robertson, *Luke*, 11; Stein, *Luke*, 76; Bock, *Luke*, 90; Bovon, *Luke 1*, 37; Riemer Roukema, *Jesus, Gnosis and Dogma*, trans. Saskia Deventer-Metz (London; New York: T&T Clark, 2010), 36.

(1:11, 19) and close out the opening speech in a series of divine revelations leading to the incarnation and birth of Jesus. Verse seventeen functions programmatically, not just for the birth narratives, but for the entire Gospel. It locates new and miraculous developments from God within the continuing flow of redemptive history. Significantly, the angel's announcement ties YHWH's last promise in the Hebrew Scriptures (Mal 4:5–6) with the first fulfillment in Luke's narrative (Luke 1:13–17): before his personal coming for judgment YHWH[24] would send "Elijah the prophet" to turn the hearts of faithless fathers and children in repentance for reconciliation.[25]

But Gabriel's allusions take in more than YHWH's final words in Malachi.[26] His claim that "he (John) will go before him (God)" refers to YHWH's promise in Mal 3:1, "I will send my messenger ... before me."[27] And the purpose Gabriel gives for God's coming, "to make ready for the Lord a people prepared," also alludes to Mal 3:1, "my messenger ... will prepare the way before me," and (likely) Isa 40:3, "A voice cries, '... prepare the way of YHWH.'"[28] It matters little that in the OT the forerunner prepares *the way* for YHWH, while in Luke the forerunner prepares *a people* for the Lord.[29] They are one and the same activity, since leveling the way in the wilderness is a figure for removing the obstacle of unrepentant hearts in God's people (cf. Mal 4:6; Isa 40:2–3; Luke 1:17; 3:3).[30] John's task would be to make people ready for God's arrival.[31]

And that is the crux of Gabriel's allusion. The angel identifies Zechariah's yet unconceived son as the promised forerunner of "the Lord" *God* (=YHWH), when in Luke's continuing narrative John turns out to be the forerunner of "the Lord" *Jesus*[32]

---

[24] "The great and awesome Day of YHWH" is the looming expectation of Malachi's final verses (4:5–6 Eng; 3:22–23 LXX). The prophet anticipates the coming in judgment of God himself. Cf. Fitzmyer, *The Gospel According to Luke*, 327; Markus Öhler, "The Expectation of Elijah and the Presence of the Kingdom of God," *JBL* 118.3 (1999): 469; Edwards, *The Gospel According to Luke*, 38.

[25] Luke's presentation identifies John as the Elijah-like figure of Malachian expectation who would prepare the people for YHWH's arrival by calling for their repentance ("turning"). Cf. Walter Grundmann, *Das Evangelium Nach Lukas*, 2nd rev. ed. (Berlin: Evangelische Verlagsanstalt, 1966), 51; John Nolland, *Luke 1–9:20* (Nashville, TN: Nelson, 2000), 31; Fred B. Craddock, *Luke* (Louisville, KY: John Knox Press, 1990), 26; Bock, *Luke*, 88, 91.

[26] Not only do Gabriel's allusions extend beyond Mal 4:5–6 to Mal 3:1 and Isa 40:3 (see below), but they may bring in Mal 2:6 and Isa 43:7. Cf. Bock, *Luke*, 87, 90–91.

[27] Scholars are virtually unanimous in understanding Malachi's messenger as the forerunner of YHWH/God. Cf. Grundmann, *Das Evangelium Nach Lukas*, 51; Plummer, *The Gospel According to St. Luke*, 15; Robertson, *Luke*, 11; Ellis, *The Gospel of Luke*, 70; Marshall, *The Gospel of Luke*, 58; Bock, *Luke*, 87; Just, *Luke 1:1–9:50*, 56; Garland, *Luke*, 67–68; Edwards, *The Gospel According to Luke*, 38; Carl Judson Davis, *The Name and Way of the Lord* (Sheffield, England: Sheffield Academic Press, 1996), 99. Bart D. Ehrman, *The Orthodox Corruption of Scripture* (New York: Oxford University Press, 2011), 99, notes that a few manuscripts of Luke 1:15 have the *nomina sacra* for "God" rather than "Lord," evidencing a change by Christians "to emphasize the orthodox view that this one born of a virgin was in fact God." This may be true. It is reasonable to postulate that a Christian copyist(s) sought to make explicit that which he believed to be implicit in the text he received.

[28] Cf. Pao and Schnabel, "Luke," 258; Stein, *Luke*, 76; Culpepper, "The Gospel of Luke," 47.

[29] Cf. Stein, *Luke*, 76; Bock, *Luke*, 90.

[30] Cf. Bock, *Luke*, 87, 90–91.

[31] Joel B. Green, *The Gospel of Luke* (Grand Rapids, MI: Eerdmans, 1997), 76; Bock, *Luke*, 90–91; Öhler, "The Expectation of Elijah and the Presence of the Kingdom of God," 469.

[32] Scholars differ on whether Jesus is meant to be understood here as YHWH or YHWH's agent (or both!). But virtually all interpreters agree that Luke portrays Jesus as filling the predicted role of

(cf. subsequent uses of κύριος for Jesus: 1:43; 2:11; 3:4 with 16, 22). If this initial case of YHWH-texts applied to Jesus seems unconvincing,[33] it is greatly strengthened by the following allusions to the same YHWH-texts in Luke's continuing narrative.[34]

Luke 1:76

After the birth of John, his father Zechariah no longer doubted Gabriel's announcement. Rather, he joined the angelic chorus, in part, by alluding to the same YHWH-texts used by Gabriel in 1:17 to identify Jesus in relation to John.[35] In fact, his allusions increase in clarity.[36] Zechariah describes the forerunning task of John as going "before the Lord to prepare his ways"—a greater verbal similarity than Luke 1:17 to both Mal 3:1 and Isa 40:3.[37] As in these OT passages, "the Lord" in 1:76 can only be YHWH,[38] "the God of Israel," as Zechariah identified him in the opening of his prophesy (Luke 1:68).[39] Zechariah clarifies that he has YHWH in mind by paralleling "the Most High" (a common circumlocution for YHWH; cf. 2 Sam 22:14; Ps 7:17) with "the Lord."

YHWH in Mal 3:1 and Isa 40:3. Cf. Fitzmyer, *The Gospel According to Luke*, 327; Marshall, *The Gospel of Luke*, 58; Stein, *Luke*, 76; Bock, *Luke*, 88, 90–91; Garland, *Luke*, 67–68; Steven J. Beardsley, "Luke's Narrative Agenda: The Use of Κύριος within Luke-Acts to Proclaim the Identity of Jesus" (PhD diss., Temple University, 2012), 120–21; Edwards, *The Gospel According to Luke*, 38; Caleb T. Friedeman, "The Revelation of the Messiah: The Christological Mystery of Luke 1–2 and Its Unveiling in Luke-Acts" (PhD diss., Wheaton College, 2018), 74; Richard B. Hays, *Reading Backwards* (London: SPCK, 2015), 65; Roukema, *Jesus, Gnosis and Dogma*, 36; Ehrman, *The Orthodox Corruption of Scripture*, 99.

[33] Fitzmyer, *The Gospel According to Luke*, 327, comments that Jesus "cannot be meant here, since Zechariah is told nothing of the birth of yet another child in God's plan." But, of course, the narrative delay to reveal Jesus as the "Lord" whom John "goes before" to "prepare his way" only strengthens Jesus's identification with/as YHWH.

[34] Cf. Beardsley, "Luke's Narrative Agenda," 120–21; Friedeman, "The Revelation of the Messiah," 74.

[35] Cf. Green, *The Gospel of Luke*, 118; Pao and Schnabel, "Luke," 265; Nolland, *Luke 1–9:20*, 88; Bock, *Luke*, 188.

[36] Cf. Carroll, *Luke*, 60; Green, *The Gospel of Luke*, 118; R. T. France, *Luke* (Grand Rapids, MI: Baker, 2013), 28. Friedeman, "The Revelation of the Messiah," 99, however, still finds here "a veiled divine Christology."

[37] Many scholars recognize here Zechariah's allusions to Malachi and/or Isaiah. E.g., Roukema, *Jesus, Gnosis and Dogma*, 36; Fitzmyer, *The Gospel According to Luke*, 385; Gregory R. Lanier, *Old Testament Conceptual Metaphors and the Christology of Luke's Gospel* (New York: Bloomsbury Academic, 2018), 122; Edwards, *The Gospel According to Luke*, 63; Diane G. Chen, *Luke* (Eugene, OR: Cascade Books, 2017), 28.

[38] Cf. Plummer, *The Gospel According to St. Luke*, 42; Robertson, *Luke*, 19; France, *Luke*, 28; Lanier, "Luke's Distinctive Use of the Temple," 450; Chen, *Luke*, 28.

[39] Cf. Hays, *Echoes of Scripture in the Gospels*, 258. Marshall, *The Gospel of Luke*, 93, on the other hand, writes, "For Christian readers κυρίου would presumably refer to Jesus; the mention of God in v. 78 need not mean that κυρίου refers to God here. It is not clear, however, whether Zechariah was thinking of the Messiah here (as Elizabeth did, 1:43) or of God (so Vielhauer, 40)." But this seems to strain the evidence; "the mention of God" in 1:68 (and the parallel with "the Most High" in 1:76) is better understood as Zechariah's (and Luke's) *confirmation* that "the Lord" refers to God/YHWH. Bock, *Luke*, 188, 191, rightly holds firm that *the Lord* before whom John prepares the way can only be *the God of Israel* mentioned in 1:68. But instead of identifying Jesus with YHWH, Bock unnecessarily turns his discussion to Jesus's agency as "a new figure" (*the rising sun from on high*) introduced in 1:79. Without denying the messianic agency of Jesus, it seems best to emphasize his divine identity in accordance with Luke's narrative presentation of Jesus as "the Lord" (=YHWH) of the YHWH-texts, Mal 3:1 and Isa 40:3.

However, it is contextually clearer here (1:76) than it was in Gabriel's announcement (1:17) that *Jesus* is "the Lord" for whom John would prepare the way.[40] The preborn Jesus had just been identified as Elizabeth's "Lord" (1:43) and is about to be called "Christ the Lord" (2:11).[41] But these bracketing uses only support the more transparent message of Zechariah's prophecy: as John would fulfill the role of *YHWH's forerunner* to prepare his ways, so Jesus would fulfill the role of *YHWH himself*[42] to "visit us from on high" (1:78).[43] This joint fulfillment will be underscored yet two more times in Luke (3:4–6; 7:26–27).[44]

Luke 3:4–6

This formal citation of a YHWH-text (Isa 40:3–5) is the first of its kind in Luke, but was already anticipated (Luke 1:17, 76) and will receive attention again later in the narrative (7:26–27).[45] Its importance here is underscored not only in the fact that every Evangelist refers to the same YHWH-text (cf. Matt 3:3; Mark 1:2–3; John 1:23)[46] but in that Luke records the most extensive citation.[47] By going beyond Isa 40:3—the limit of the other three Evangelists—to include verses 4–5, Luke highlights the preparatory nature of John's message,[48] the universal nature of YHWH's salvation,[49] and the

---

[40] Cf. Nolland, *Luke 1–9:20*, 88–89; Green, *The Gospel of Luke*, 118; Edwards, *The Gospel According to Luke*, 63; Hays, *Reading Backwards*, 62–63, and Hays, *Echoes of Scripture in the Gospels*, 248; Marshall, *The Gospel of Luke*, 93. Others who make the connection for both Luke 1:17 and 1:76 to Mal 3:1 and/or Isa 40:3 include, Stein, *Luke*, 101; Bock, *Luke*, 188; Pao and Schnabel, "Luke," 265; Roukema, *Jesus, Gnosis and Dogma*, 36.

[41] Cf. Fitzmyer, *The Gospel According to Luke*, 385–86; Green, *The Gospel of Luke*, 118; Carroll, *Luke*, 60; Thompson, *Luke*, 38.

[42] Many scholars see here in Luke's narrative a deliberate identification of Jesus with "the Lord" (=YHWH) of Isaiah and Malachi. Cf. Fitzmyer, *The Gospel According to Luke*, 385–86; Edwards, *The Gospel According to Luke*, 63; Lanier, *Old Testament Conceptual Metaphors and the Christology of Luke's Gospel*, 122. Hays, *Reading Backwards*, 68, concludes, "Thus, Luke leads the reader to perceive that John's vocation to 'go before the face of *the Lord* to prepare his way' (1:76) will in fact portend the coming and *visitation* not of some intermediary but of none other than Israel's God" (emphasis Hays).

[43] See comments in the section on Luke 1:78. Cf. Hays, *Echoes of Scripture in the Gospels*, 258; Thompson, *Luke*, 38–39; Henrichs-Tarasenkova, *Luke's Christology of Divine Identity*, 158; Friedemann, "The Revelation of the Messiah," 98–99.

[44] E.g., Green, *The Gospel of Luke*, 118.

[45] Cf. Edwards, *The Gospel According to Luke*, 109; Pao and Schnabel, "Luke," 275–76; Rowe, *Early Narrative Christology*, 76.

[46] Cf. Leon Morris, *Luke*, 2nd ed. (Downers Grove, IL: IVP Academic, 1988), 112; Stein, *Luke*, 129; Gadenz, *The Gospel of Luke*, 83; Jeannine K. Brown, *The Gospels as Stories* (Grand Rapids, MI: Baker Academic, 2020), 51.

[47] Culpepper, "The Gospel of Luke," 81; Peter Böhlemann, *Jesus Und Der Täufer* (Cambridge; New York: Cambridge University Press, 1997), 50; France, *Luke*, 51; Edwards, *The Gospel According to Luke*, 109; Strauss, *Four Portraits, One Jesus*, 322.

[48] Many scholars recognize the language of repentance or moral preparation in the extra verses quoted by Luke (Isa 40:4–5)—especially in anticipation of the juxtaposed baptisms of John and Jesus (Luke 3:7–17). Cf. Bovon, *Luke 1*, 121; Plummer, *The Gospel According to St. Luke*, 87; Nolland, *Luke 1–9:20*, 144; Stein, *Luke*, 129; Bock, *Luke*, 291–93; Dietrich Rusam, *Das Alte Testament Bei Lukas* (Berlin; New York: Walter de Gruyter, 2003), 159.

[49] Luke's inclusion of the Isaianic phrase, "all flesh shall see" (40:5) the salvation of God, fits well with the prominent theme in Luke of the good news of God's salvation in Jesus spreading beyond Israel. Cf. Grundmann, *Das Evangelium Nach Lukas*, 102; Nolland, *Luke 1–9:20*, 145; Culpepper, "The Gospel of Luke," 81; Just, *Luke 1:1–9:50*, 151; France, *Luke*, 52; Hays, *Echoes of Scripture in the Gospels*, 248; Strauss, *Four Portraits, One Jesus*, 322; Brown, *The Gospels as Stories*, 51.

narrative continuity between YHWH's promises in Isaiah and Jesus's fulfillment of those promises in Luke.⁵⁰

The crux interpretum of Luke 3:4–6 is what to think of the Baptist's substitution of "him" for "God." In Isa 40:3, the forerunner of YHWH calls upon the people to straighten the roads "of our God" (τοῦ θεοῦ ἡμῶν, LXX). In Luke (and the other Synoptics), the forerunner of the Lord calls upon the people to straighten the roads "of him" (αὐτοῦ). Some scholars see this change as a Christianizing of the text, a transfer from YHWH to Jesus in meaning or application.⁵¹ Others maintain (often for the sake of integrity) that "his" paths can only be interpreted to mean YHWH's paths, as in the cited original text, so that its application to Jesus implies representative agency.⁵² But both views presuppose a distinction between YHWH and Jesus that is demanded neither by the citation nor by Luke's narrative.

A better interpretation understands Luke to be affirming YHWH's personal fulfillment of Isaiah's prophecy, while simultaneously identifying Jesus as YHWH.⁵³ This makes good sense when one considers the options. If Luke had retained "God" in his citation, then his audience might not realize he was including Jesus in the divine identity. And if he had exchanged "God" for "Jesus," then his audience might have separated the two and assumed that Jesus was merely an agent for God. But Luke used the more ambiguous pronoun (in fact, αὐτοῦ is recorded by all the Synoptists),⁵⁴ which can perform the double duty of (1) affirming the personal fulfillment of the Isaianic promise by YHWH and (2) identifying the embodied presence of YHWH as Jesus.⁵⁵

---

⁵⁰ Luke's wider quotation suggests an even wider context of Isaiah, particularly YHWH's coming with universal judgment and redemption in Isa 40–66. Cf. Bock, *Luke*, 291; Green, *The Gospel of Luke*, 171; Pao and Schnabel, "Luke," 275–76. Hays, *Echoes of Scripture in the Gospels*, 148–49, perceptively adds, "The most significant observation here is that in Luke 3:1–6, Luke has taken the keynote passage from Isaiah 40 that declares the salvific coming of Israel's God and worked it narratively into an announcement of the imminent coming of Jesus as the one who would bring 'the salvation of God' (Luke 3:6; citing Isa 40:5 LXX). Considering the full content of Isaiah 40, this identification of Jesus as the one in whom 'all flesh will see the salvation of God' is hermeneutically momentous. For it is precisely in Isaiah 40 that we find one of the most radical declarations in all of Scripture of the *incomparability* of God ... (Isa 40:25) ... (Isa 40:9–10a)" (emphasis Hays).

⁵¹ Apparently, Nolland, *Luke 1–9:20*, 143; Bovon, *Luke 1*, 121; Chen, *Luke*, 48.

⁵² Cf. Plummer, *The Gospel According to St. Luke*, 87. Bock, *Luke*, 293, explains, "When one puts 3:6 with 3:15–16, Luke is saying that God's salvation is seen in the Spirit baptism that Christ brings. This idea parallels the infancy section; namely, that in Christ the salvation of *God* comes (2:26, 30). Luke's presentation of salvation is consistent. John, the herald of God, calls for moral preparation in the wilderness before God brings his salvation in Messiah. God again is at work, bringing his promise to pass. What people see—and are to see—in Jesus are the hand and coming of God himself" (emphasis Bock). Bock's view could be understood as the view defended in this study, except that he stops short of saying that Jesus is identified with/as YHWH.

⁵³ See especially, Rowe, *Early Narrative Christology*, 77; Hays, *Echoes of Scripture in the Gospels*, 247–48; Gadenz, *The Gospel of Luke*, 83. Cf. France, *Luke*, 51–52; William Childs Robinson, *Our Lord* (Grand Rapids, MI: Eerdmans, 1937), 133–34; David K. Bernard, *The Glory of God in the Face of Jesus Christ* (Blandford Forum, Dorset, UK: Deo Publishing, 2016), 84.

⁵⁴ Cf. Rowe, *Early Narrative Christology*, 71–72; Hays, *Reading Backwards*, 62–63.

⁵⁵ Similary, Rowe, *Early Narrative Christology*, 77; Hays, *Echoes of Scripture in the Gospels*, 247–48.

If the Baptist and the Evangelists all believed that Jesus was the embodiment of YHWH for whom his people must prepare themselves, then it would not be surprising for them to apply Isa 40:3 to Jesus.[56] If they did not believe it, then the application of this YHWH-text to Jesus would make no obvious sense and only foster unnecessary confusion. Thus, the ambiguity of the substituted pronoun evidences a deliberate choice to identify Jesus unambiguously as YHWH.[57]

Luke 7:26–27

In a fourth Lukan reference to the same thematic set of YHWH-texts, Jesus himself makes the quotation ("it is written"). Most commentators agree that Jesus specifically referenced Mal 3:1, but with likely allusions to the thematic background found in Exod 23:20, Isa 40:3, and/or the contextual parallel in Mal 4:5.[58] Connections between these passages can be observed in Table 4.1.

Table 4.1 YHWH-Texts in the Background of Luke 7:26–27

	Sender	Sent One	Preparer(s)	Prepared	Other Features
Exodus 23:20–21:	YHWH	Angel (Messenger)	YHWH	A place	The angel protects YHWH's people
Isaiah 40:3–5:	YHWH	Voice in the Wilderness	People of YHWH	Way of YHWH	The preparation is for God / His coming
Malachi 3:1:	YHWH	Messenger	Messenger	Way before YHWH	Adonai / Messenger comes in judgment
Malachi 4:5–6:	YHWH	Elijah the Prophet	Elijah the Prophet	Hearts of the People	Preparation is for the Coming Day of YHWH
Luke 7:26–27:	The Lord	Messenger, Prophet = John	Messenger, Prophet = John	"Your Way Before You"	"You" (singular) attests to the role of YHWH

This passage may be the most difficult of the four in Luke (cf. 1:17, 76; 3:4–6; 7:26–27) to interpret, primarily because the quotation by Jesus appears to turn two characters into three.[59] Whereas Mal 3:1 says, "Behold, I send my messenger, and he will prepare the way before me," Jesus quotes the passage with the curious adjustment, "Behold, I send my messenger before your face, who will prepare your way before you."[60] In Malachi, the

---

[56] Cf. Fitzmyer, *The Gospel According to Luke*, 461, with skepticism. Others are less skeptical: e.g., Rowe, *Early Narrative Christology*, 71–72, 77; Hays, *Echoes of Scripture in the Gospels*, 247–49.
[57] Cf. Garland, *Luke*, 155; Hays, *Reading Backwards*, 62; Rowe, *Early Narrative Christology*, 71–72, 77.
[58] Cf. Grundmann, *Das Evangelium Nach Lukas*, 165; Marshall, *The Gospel of Luke*, 295–96; Nolland, *Luke 1–9:20*, 337, 339; Johnson, *The Gospel of Luke*, 123; Bock, *Luke*, 673; Culpepper, "The Gospel of Luke," 163–64; Just, *Luke 1:1–9:50*, 312; Green, *The Gospel of Luke*, 298; Pao and Schnabel, "Luke," 300; Garland, *Luke*, 313; France, *Luke*, 130; Stanley E. Porter, "Composite Citations in Luke-Acts," in *New Testament Uses*, vol. 2 of *Composite Citations in Antiquity* (New York: T&T Clark, 2018), 69.
[59] However, cf. Marshall, *The Gospel of Luke*, 296; Bock, *Luke*, 674.
[60] Many commentators believe that Jesus incorporated Exod 23:20 with his quotation of Mal 3:1. But there is disagreement on what this might mean. See, for example, Bock, *Luke*, 673–74; Green, *The Gospel of Luke*, 298; France, *Luke*, 130.

characters are YHWH and his messenger, while in Luke, the characters are YHWH, his messenger, and "you" (singular).[61]

But it is not difficult to see in Jesus's application that the "new" character addressed by YHWH has assumed YHWH's role from the original text.[62] In Mal 3:1 (and 4:5; Isa 40:3), YHWH's messenger prepares the way for YHWH, while in Jesus's quotation YHWH's messenger prepares the way for the figure YHWH addresses.[63] Since he identifies John the Baptist as the messenger, Jesus implies that he himself is the one addressed by YHWH as "you."[64] Therefore, Jesus claims, albeit indirectly, the role of YHWH from Mal 3:1.[65] By this point in the narrative, however, it comes as no surprise. Gabriel, Zechariah, and John had all previously made the same application. Jesus simply confirms it—although his claim likely functions as the authoritative climax to the thematic series.[66]

In summary, Luke 1:17, 76; 3:4-6; 7:26-27 together apply the OT YHWH-texts Isa 40:3-5 and Mal 3:1 to Jesus (with Exod 23:20 and Mal 4:5 also informing the background).[67] As the prophets looked forward to the eschatological coming of YHWH to bring salvation and judgment, Isaiah and Malachi in particular predicted a forerunner to announce YHWH's visitation.[68] All four Evangelists identify that forerunner as John the Baptist, effectively placing Jesus in the role of YHWH. This identification of Jesus as YHWH is especially acute in Luke's Gospel, where the

---

[61] Bock, *Luke*, 674, argues "that the pronoun is a reference to the nation as a collective singular ... and thus the prophet prepares the nation for God's coming in Messiah." But, Thompson, *Luke*, 121, answers, "The ref. to Mal 3:1 (cf. 1:17, 76; 3:4; Mark 1:2), however, indicates that the messenger (i.e., Elijah = John) goes before Yahweh, and Jesus replaces the coming of Yahweh here (Fitzmyer 674; Marshall 296; Nolland 337; Pao and Schnabel 303a)." Thus, the parallel in Luke 1:17 and 7:27 is not between "a people" and "you," but between "the Lord" and "you." Jesus interprets Mal 3:1 as YHWH sending John before the face of YHWH (i.e., Jesus).

[62] Cf. Pao and Schnabel, "Luke," 303. Nolland, *Luke 1-9:20*, 339, rightly acknowledges that Mal 3:1 anticipates "very directly a coming of God." But he unnecessarily alters that interpretation to posit—from a perceived influence of Exod 23:20 on Jesus's words—the coming of "a mysteriously shrouded eschatological figure."

[63] Fitzmyer, *The Gospel According to Luke*, 674, represents some scholars who believe "the words are to be understood as a quotation of Mal 3:1, slightly influenced by the wording of Exod 23:20," but that, "Isa 40:3 has had no influence here." Pao and Schnabel, "Luke," 303, represent many scholars who assume the singular pronoun in Luke 7:27 refers to the Messiah. This may be a true implication. However, such a view is problematic, since no OT prophecy describes a forerunner of the messiah, and the primary text Jesus quotes here, Mal 3:1, predicts that the forerunner prepares the way for YHWH.

[64] Cf. Nolland, *Luke 1-9:20*, 337; Pao and Schnabel, "Luke," 303; France, *Luke*, 130; Thompson, *Luke*, 121.

[65] Cf. Pao and Schnabel, "Luke," 303; Stein, *Luke*, 230.

[66] Cf. Green, *The Gospel of Luke*, 298.

[67] Comments from various scholars on the thematic connections of Luke 1:17, 76; 3:4-6; 7:27 to the YHWH-texts mentioned here may be found throughout this section. For thematic connections found especially in this final parallel in 7:27, see, for example, Nolland, *Luke 1-9:20*, 337; Culpepper, "The Gospel of Luke," 163-64; Green, *The Gospel of Luke*, 298.

[68] Admittedly, as Nolland, *Luke 1-9:20*, 337, 339, writes concerning Jesus's quotation in Luke 7:27, "Mal 3:1 is the controlling citation ... quoted in a form influenced by Exod 23:20." Cf. Green, *The Gospel of Luke*, 298-99. And yet, even in Luke 7:27 the connection to Isaiah remains in the background due to John's previous quotation of Isaiah 40:3-5 in Luke 3:4-6 and the close thematic tie between Malachi 3 and Isaiah 40 of the eschatological coming of YHWH. Cf. France, *Luke*, 130.

application of these YHWH-texts to Jesus are emphasized by thematic repetition in the speeches of Gabriel, Zechariah, John, and Jesus himself.

Luke 1:68, 78; 7:16; 19:44

Not only does Luke's Gospel highlight on four occasions *the way of the Lord* prepared by his forerunner, but it highlights on four more occasions *the visitation of the Lord* to his people.[69] These two themes clearly overlap and combine for a remarkably emphatic presentation of Jesus as the Lord (=YHWH) of the OT. Although the case is sometimes made that YHWH has "visited" his people representatively through Jesus as God's mere agent, a better case can be made that Luke presents Jesus as the personal visitation of YHWH.[70] This is true in part because all four Lukan passages which identify Jesus with the divine visitation (1:68, 78; 7:16; 19:44) apply YHWH-texts to do so.[71]

Luke 1:68

The first two references in Luke of God's visitation to his people appear as bookends in Zechariah's prophecy (Luke 1:68, 78).[72] This *inclusio* strongly implies that Zechariah's amazement over John's birth is eclipsed by his elation over the long-awaited occasion to which John's birth points: the redemptive visitation of YHWH.[73]

Zechariah opens his Spirit-filled prophecy (1:67) blessing "the Lord God of Israel, for he has visited and made redemption [ἐπεσκέψατο καὶ ἐποίησεν λύτρωσιν] for his people" (1:68) by raising up Jesus as "a horn of salvation" (1:69).[74] The broad concept of God's visitation to people on earth has an extensive OT background.[75] The specific

---

[69] Among the many scholars who note Luke's fourfold use of "visitation" in 1:68, 78; 7:16; 19:44 are Johnson, *The Gospel of Luke*, 32; Bock, *Luke*, 178; Lanier, *Old Testament Conceptual Metaphors and the Christology of Luke's Gospel*, 39.

[70] This is not to pit the two against each other. But commentators who emphasize the messianic agency of Jesus may at times downplay the expectations in the Lukan texts of YHWH's personal presence. Cf. Bock, *Luke*, 178–79; Green, *The Gospel of Luke*, 115. Instead, one might paraphrase verses 68–69 by saying that YHWH himself has arrived to redeem his people as the promised Davidic King.

[71] See below for examples of YHWH-texts likely in the background of Zechariah's statement in Luke 1:68. Cf. Lanier, *Old Testament Conceptual Metaphors and the Christology of Luke's Gospel*, 39–40. Nolland, *Luke 1–9:20*, 91, is one of many who find a probable allusion in Luke 1:68 to Ps 106:4.

[72] Similarly, Craddock, *Luke*, 32, 76–79; Adelbert Denaux, "The Theme of Divine Visits and Human (In)Hospitality in Luke-Acts: Its Old Testament and Graeco-Roman Antecedents," in *The Unity of Luke-Acts*, ed. Joseph Verheyden (Leuven, Belgium: Leuven University Press, 1999), 275.

[73] Carroll, *Luke*, 58, comments, "The first two metaphors, visitation and redemption, express one idea (i.e., hendiadys): God has visited the people for the purpose of redeeming them. In the LXX the verb *episkeptesthai* (visit), which may also mean 'look upon,' signifies divine presence to judge (Exod 32:34) or deliver the people (e.g., Gen 21:1; Exod 4:31; Ruth 1:6; Ps 105 [106E]:4; it reappears in the future tense in Luke 1:78). Zechariah envisages a divine visitation to save...." Cf. Fitzmyer, *The Gospel According to Luke*, 382; Stein, *Luke*, 99; Thompson, *Luke*, 36.

[74] Green, *The Gospel of Luke*, 115, comments that God's visitation and his raising of the Davidic savior are presented as two affirmations of one divine act. Furthermore, the fact that YHWH is the "horn of salvation" for David in Ps 18:2 supports the interpretation that Jesus (as the "horn of salvation" in Luke 1:69) stands in the place of YHWH. The aorists appear to function like prophetic perfects ("he has visited and accomplished redemption"). Similarly, Stein, *Luke*, 99; Bock, *Luke*, 178.

[75] Cf. Johnson, *The Gospel of Luke*, 45–56; Bock, *Luke*, 178; Edwards, *The Gospel According to Luke*, 62; Lanier, *Old Testament Conceptual Metaphors and the Christology of Luke's Gospel*, 39–40.

Lukan term (ἐπισκέπτομαι) was often used in the LXX to express God's historical intervention to bless/save or to curse/punish (e.g., Ruth 1:6; 1 Sam 2:21; Ps 65:9; Isa 29:6; Jer 15:15).[76] More significantly, however, it was used in reference to the theophanic visitation of YHWH during the Exodus (cf. Gen 50:24–25; Exod 3:16; 4:31; 13:19).[77] Thus, it appears that the Lukan narrative ties the manifest visitation of YHWH in the glory-cloud with the manifest visitation of YHWH in Jesus.[78] This is supported by OT prophetic expectations of YHWH's "visitation" in the eschaton to render both punishment (cf. Isa 29:6; Jer 23:2) and salvation (cf. Ezek 34:11; Zeph 2:7).[79] Zechariah's own prophecy will emphasize the saving features[80] of God's eschatological visitation (see comments below). But Zechariah makes it clear from the start that—as the horn (i.e., power) of salvation[81]—Jesus was "raised up" to effectuate the promised visitation of "the Lord God of Israel" (=YHWH; Luke 1:68–69).[82]

Luke 1:78

The closing bracket of Zechariah's prophetic *inclusio*[83] not only confirms Jesus as "the Lord God of Israel" in the opening bracket (1:68) who has come to visit his people, but

---

[76] More literally, ἐπισκέπτομαι refers to the personal inspection or examination of persons with a view toward acting upon the findings with favor or with judgment. That is why the neutral term *visit(ation)* is often appropriate in English translations. For discussions of this term, see Robertson, *Luke*, 18; Fitzmyer, *The Gospel According to Luke*, 382–83; Nolland, *Luke 1–9:20*, 86; Johnson, *The Gospel of Luke*, 45–46; Bovon, *Luke 1*, 72; Pao and Schnabel, "Luke," 263; Carroll, *Luke*, 58; Edwards, *The Gospel According to Luke*, 62; Lanier, *Old Testament Conceptual Metaphors and the Christology of Luke's Gospel*, 39–40.

[77] Cf. Johnson, *The Gospel of Luke*, 45–46; Pao and Schnabel, "Luke," 263; Edwards, *The Gospel According to Luke*, 62; Hays, *Echoes of Scripture in the Gospels*, 257; Lanier, *Old Testament Conceptual Metaphors and the Christology of Luke's Gospel*, 39.

[78] Edwards, *The Gospel According to Luke*, 62, does not specify the YHWH-Jesus connection but writes perceptively, "God's supreme visitation in the OT was the saving deliverance of the exodus (Gen 50:24–25; Exod 3:16). Israel's experience of the divine was thus not a mere 'God consciousness' but a concrete historical revelation of God in space and time. God visits his people to redeem them (v. 68), and he redeems them so they may serve him (v. 74)." Luke is surely portraying Jesus as the "concrete historical revelation of God" visiting his people.

[79] Cf. Bovon, *Luke 1*, 72; Nolland, *Luke 1–9:20*, 91; Pao and Schnabel, "Luke," 263.

[80] Cf. Johnson, *The Gospel of Luke*, 45–46; Plummer, *The Gospel According to St. Luke*, 40; Grundmann, *Das Evangelium Nach Lukas*, 71; Carroll, *Luke*, 58; Thompson, *Luke*, 36.

[81] YHWH is David's "horn of salvation" in Ps 18:2, another YHWH-text likely applied to Jesus as the "horn of salvation" in Luke 1:69. In any case, since an animal's horn was thought to display and symbolize its power, Jesus is apparently portrayed here as God's power/locus of salvation. Cf. Ellis, *The Gospel of Luke*, 78; Nolland, *Luke 1–9:20*, 91; Craddock, *Luke*, 33; Edwards, *The Gospel According to Luke*, 62.

[82] "Raised up" likely refers to the incarnation and not the resurrection at this point, although it may be suggestive of both. Cf. Just, *Luke 1:1–9:50*, 94; Green, *The Gospel of Luke*, 115. The most probable YHWH-texts behind Zechariah's prophetic opening in Luke 1:68–69 are Ps 106:4 (cf. "visit," "salvation," "your people") and Ps 18:2 ("horn of salvation"). Or, Zechariah simply applies the general prophetic expectation of YHWH's eschatological visitation (e.g., Isa 23:17; Ezek 34:11; Zeph 2:7) to Jesus of Nazareth.

[83] Zechariah's *inclusio* framed by "visit" (ἐπισκέπτομαι) in 1:68, 78 goes unidentified by most commentators. But the thematic or double reference to divine visitation garners various comments. Cf. Nolland, *Luke 1–9:20*, 90; Bock, *Luke*, 188–89; Just, *Luke 1:1–9:50*, 95; Edwards, *The Gospel According to Luke*, 64; Henrichs-Tarasenkova, *Luke's Christology of Divine Identity*, 158; Lanier, *Old Testament Conceptual Metaphors and the Christology of Luke's Gospel*, 83; Denaux, "The Theme of Divine Visits and Human (In)Hospitality in Luke-Acts," 275.

it closes the door on viewing him as anyone less than God.[84] Accordingly, the only visitor who can meet the character description of Luke 1:78–79 is the divine visitor of OT YHWH-texts.[85] There are multiple reasons for this.

First, the one who "visits us" is identified as coming "from on high" (ἐξ ὕψους; 1:78)—a clear designation of his heavenly origin[86]—implying deity and pre-existence.[87] Second, he is identified as the "Arising One" (ἀνατολή)[88] of messianic prophecy,[89] who

---

[84] See fuller argument below. Cf. France, *Luke*, 28; Hays, *Echoes of Scripture in the Gospels*, 258; Henrichs-Tarasenkova, *Luke's Christology of Divine Identity*, 158; Lanier, *Old Testament Conceptual Metaphors and the Christology of Luke's Gospel*, 122.

[85] Henrichs-Tarasenkova, *Luke's Christology of Divine Identity*, 158, writes, "even though it is not wrong to read 1.79 messianically since one can find references in the OT to the Davidic messiah as a light that shines on both Jews (Isa. 9.2 [9.1, LXX]) and Gentiles (42.6) who sit in the darkness, Luke discourages his readers from understanding Jesus as a mere Davidide. Not only does he attribute to Jesus the function of visitation (ἐπισκέψεται, Lk. 1.79; cf. 7.16; Acts 15.14), which earlier in the Benedictus he attributed to YHWH himself (Lk. 1.68) and which in the OT is attributed to YHWH alone (e.g., Gen. 21.1; Exod. 4.31; 1 Sam. 2.21; Lam. 4.22), but also he echoes in his description of Jesus' function OT passages that identify the one who brings light, peace, and, therefore, salvation with YHWH himself (Isa. 42.6–7; Ps. 107.10–14) or with one who is more than a mere Davidide (Isa. 9.6–7)." Cf. Nolland, *Luke 1–9:20*, 89; Lanier, *Old Testament Conceptual Metaphors and the Christology of Luke's Gospel*, 81–82, 117–18, 122.

[86] Paul Winter, "Two Notes on Luke I, II With Regard To The Theory Of 'Imitation Hebraisms,'" *ST* 7.2 (1953): 160, argues that, contextually and literarily, "ἀνατολὴ ἐξ ὕψους is most improbable as a figurative expression for a messiah; the metaphor cannot possibly be applied to any one but to God." Simon J. Gathercole, "The Heavenly Ἀνατολή (Luke 1:78–9)," *JTS* 56.2 (2005): 476–77, points out that the phrase ἐξ ὕψους in LXX refers to God's dwelling place (not God himself) and the only other Lukan occurrence of the phrase (24:49) confirms this meaning. Gregory R. Lanier, "'From God' or 'from Heaven'? Ἐξ Ὕψους in Luke 1,78," *Bib* 97.1 (2016): 127, adds, "An analysis of ~ 280 instances of ὕψος and ~ 230 of ὕψιστος in the relevant Jewish/Christian sources suggests that while ὕψιστος often refers to God, ὕψος never does. The ἀνατολή should be understood as coming 'from heaven.'" Thus, Luke 1:78 does not teach the *agency* of the Rising One (i.e., from God), but his *origin* (i.e., from heaven), implying his divine identity.

[87] Cf. Friedeman, "The Revelation of the Messiah," 98–99; Nolland, *Luke 1–9:20*, 90; Hays, *Echoes of Scripture in the Gospels*, 258; Thompson, *Luke*, 38–39. Bovon, *Luke 1*, 76, and Carroll, *Luke*, 62, appear to equivocate on the clarity of Zechariah's statement that the ἀνατολή comes from the abode of God and bears his identifying title.

[88] Some commentators suppose that ἀνατολή carries layered meaning or multiple meanings, particularly relating to plant growth ("branch, shoot") or astral movement ("sunrise, shining star"), which in turn can stand for time ("dawn") or place ("east"). Thus, Luke 1:78, which may seem to favor the meaning "sunrise" in its context, also alludes to messianic "branch" prophecies of Jer 23:5; Zech 3:8; 6:12. E.g., Marshall, *The Gospel of Luke*, 95; Chen, *Luke*, 28–29. However, as Gregory R. Lanier, "The Curious Case of צֶמַח and Ἀνατολή: An Inquiry into Septuagint Translation Patterns," *JBL* 134.3 (2015): 527, has shown, ἀνατολή is an appropriate Greek (LXX) gloss of צֶמַח in those Hebrew passages because of their semantic overlap "relating to the process or final product of the arising, emergence, or growth of a given entity: new vegetation from the ground, bodily tissue, and (for ἀνατολή/ἀνατέλλω) luminary bodies or rivers." Others who note the fundamental meaning of ἀνατολή as "rising" include Nolland, *Luke 1–9:20*, 89–90; Edwards, *The Gospel According to Luke*, 64. Thus, ἀνατολή does not inherently refer to light/luminaries but to the arising/emergence of the object(s) in view. In Luke 1:78, Jesus is "(an/the) Arising One" (Lanier, 527) who, astonishingly, because of God's tender mercy, visits earth from heaven.

[89] The messianic "branch" prophecies (Jer 23:5; Zech 3:8; 6:12; cf. Ps 132:17; Isa 11:1; Jer 33:15 [not in LXX]) lie behind Luke 1:78. Ironically, the connection is obscured by the gloss "branch" for the Hebrew term, צֶמַח, which more generally refers to the *emergence or arising* of something/someone. Thus, the LXX uses ἀνατολή to highlight the nature of the Messiah when translating these prophesies. The thought behind צֶמַח /ἀνατολή is not that messiah grows like a branch or shines like the sun at dawn, but that he arises/emerges. For the semantic ranges of these terms, see Lanier, "The Curious

also possesses divine attributes and identity.⁹⁰ Third, since he is distinguished from the "child" (John) who goes before him (1:76), the visiting one (Jesus) possesses the other divine titles in the immediate context: *the Most High*; *the Lord*; *God* (1:76, 78).⁹¹ Fourth, although John would declare the knowledge of salvation by God's forgiveness of sins (thus preparing the Lord's ways; 1:76–77), Jesus the Arising (One) would give light to those sitting in darkness and death (1:78–79)—another allusion to YHWH's eschatological forgiveness for salvation in the new covenant.⁹² As Bock puts it, "John will proclaim salvation, but Jesus can take them into it."⁹³

In short, YHWH-texts applied to Jesus as the "visitor" of Zechariah's prophecy (e.g., Ezek 34:11; Zeph 2:7; cf. Luke 1:78) are here supported by allusions to several other YHWH-texts applied to Jesus (e.g., Isa 40:3; 9:2, 7; 60:1–3; Jer 23:5–6; Isa 42:16). These applications make it difficult to interpret Jesus's identity as anyone less than YHWH in Zechariah's prophetic fulfillment of YHWH's visitation.⁹⁴

Luke 7:16

The third Lukan mention of God's visitation, like the first two (1:68, 78),⁹⁵ occurs in a fulfillment pericope that includes YHWH's messenger preparing his way (7:16; cf. 7:27), which highlights, again, that *the way of the Lord* and *the visitation of God* are not

---

Case of צמח and Ἀνατολή," especially, 513–27. Scholars who find in Jesus messianic fulfillment of the "branch" passages above (and/or who think Luke 1:78 alludes to messianic luminary passages, such as Num 24:17; Mic 4:2; cf. Rev 22:16), include Stein, *Luke*, 101; Bock, *Luke*, 191–93; Carroll, *Luke*, 61–62; Edwards, *The Gospel According to Luke*, 64.

⁹⁰ Virtually all commentators recognize ἀνατολή as a messianic title/descriptor of Jesus. The issue here, however, is whether the "visitation" of the ἀνατολή as Jesus means he is merely the representative of YHWH or also the embodied presence of YHWH. For Jesus as a mere agent, see, Fitzmyer, *The Gospel According to Luke*, 387; Carroll, *Luke*, 61. For Jesus as both the messianic agent and the personal presence of YHWH, see, Henrichs-Tarasenkova, *Luke's Christology of Divine Identity*, 158; Lanier, *Old Testament Conceptual Metaphors and the Christology of Luke's Gospel*, 117–18; Friedeman, "The Revelation of the Messiah," 98–99.

⁹¹ See similar comments in Lanier, *Old Testament Conceptual Metaphors and the Christology of Luke's Gospel*, 117–18; Nolland, *Luke 1–9:20*, 89–90, 92; Green, *The Gospel of Luke*, 119.

⁹² Bovon, *Luke 1*, 76, is not alone when he writes, "Readers of v. 78 will think of Ps 107(LXX 106):10 and the beginning of the messianic oracle in Isa 9:2 (LXX 9:1). The eschatological light of the Messiah suddenly illumines the dark world of the dying." Cf. Fitzmyer, *The Gospel According to Luke*, 388; Marshall, *The Gospel of Luke*, 95; Nolland, *Luke 1–9:20*, 92; Stein, *Luke*, 101; Bock, *Luke*, 189, 193–94; Edwards, *The Gospel According to Luke*, 64; Chen, *Luke*, 28–29. Lanier, *Old Testament Conceptual Metaphors and the Christology of Luke's Gospel*, 118, however, believes that ἐπιφᾶναι should be translated as "appear, show oneself" rather than "give light, shine." If he is correct, this meaning could further support the interpretation of Jesus as the embodiment of YHWH, the Emerging One (ἀνατολή) who visits and appears from on high.

⁹³ Bock, *Luke*, 194.

⁹⁴ Cf. Henrichs-Tarasenkova, *Luke's Christology of Divine Identity*, 158; Lanier, *Old Testament Conceptual Metaphors and the Christology of Luke's Gospel*, 126; France, *Luke*, 28; Hays, *Echoes of Scripture in the Gospels*, 258; Denaux, "The Theme of Divine Visits and Human (In)Hospitality in Luke-Acts," 275–76; Gathercole, "The Heavenly Ἀνατολή (Luke 1:78–9)," 475, 477.

⁹⁵ Many scholars acknowledge this thematic connection, some adding Luke 19:44 and Acts 15:14. Cf. Craddock, *Luke*, 97; Johnson, *The Gospel of Luke*, 119; Bock, *Luke*, 654; Culpepper, "The Gospel of Luke," 158; Rowe, *Early Narrative Christology*, 120–21; Beardsley, "Luke's Narrative Agenda," 146; Strauss, "Christology and Christological Purpose in the Synoptic Gospels," 58; Edwards, *The Gospel According to Luke*, 216; Robert Brent Graves, *The God of Two Testaments*, rev. ed. (Hazelwood, MO: Word Aflame Press, 2000), 257.

only two perspectives on the same event but are both fulfilled in Jesus. This reference to God's visitation of his people (Ἐπεσκέψατο ὁ θεὸς τὸν λαὸν αὐτοῦ) continues to recall OT predictions of YHWH's eschatological visitation (e.g., Ezek 34:11; Zeph 2:7).[96]

The unique features of this occurrence only serve to underscore what has now become a central Lukan theme: God has visited his people in the person of Jesus.[97] This time, the claim is found on the lips of a "considerable crowd" (7:12), who had just witnessed Jesus raise the dead son of a widow at Nain (7:13–15). Several additional clues in the text communicate that God's "visitation" is meant to be taken as personal and not merely as representative. Luke as narrator now identifies Jesus as "the Lord" (7:13).[98] Jesus appears to render divine compassion.[99] Unlike the miracle after which this one is certainly patterned—Elijah's raising of a widow's dead son (1 Kgs 17:17–24)[100]—Jesus does not follow a ritual and call upon YHWH to raise the dead, but personally commands the dead to life (Luke 7:14).[101] Thus, Jesus proves to be not only "a great prophet," but someone much greater than Elijah (who prefigured the mere prophet John instead).[102] Luke allows the crowd to instruct his readers on Jesus's identity: being struck with fear,[103] "they glorified God" and ultimately concluded, "God has visited his people" (7:16).[104]

Luke 19:44

The fourth Lukan reference to God's visitation in the person of Jesus[105] occurs on the lips of Jesus himself in the final week of his ministry (19:44). Although God is not

---

[96] And, of course, the anticipated visitation of God in the eschaton that is found in the Prophets has its basis in YHWH's manifest presence/interventions in Israel's ancient history (e.g., Gen 21:1; Exod 4:31; Ruth 1:6; Ps 106:4). Cf. Stein, *Luke*, 223; Bock, *Luke*, 654; Gadenz, *The Gospel of Luke*, 67; Hays, *Reading Backwards*, 67.

[97] More than any other Evangelist Luke presents Jesus's ministry in OT terminology of YHWH's arrival: 1:16–17, 68, 76, 78; 3:4–6; 7:16, 26–27; 19:44. Cf. Duvall and Hays, *God's Relational Presence*, 203; Hays, *Echoes of Scripture in the Gospels*, 243; Lanier, "Luke's Distinctive Use of the Temple," 447–48.

[98] Beardsley, "Luke's Narrative Agenda," 146, comments: "Jesus is not simply an agent of God, he is ὁ κύριος." Cf. Rowe, *Early Narrative Christology*, 121; Pao and Schnabel, "Luke," 299; Edwards, *The Gospel According to Luke*, 214; Gadenz, *The Gospel of Luke*, 144.

[99] Edwards, *The Gospel According to Luke*, 214, sees an allusion here to YHWH's compassion on the broken-hearted in Isa 54:7–10. Rowe, *Early Narrative Christology*, 120, notes shared parallels between Luke 1:78 and 7:13, 16 with both God's/Jesus's compassion and God's visitation. Cf. Beardsley, "Luke's Narrative Agenda," 146.

[100] And, perhaps less allusive is Elisha's raising of the Shunammite woman's son in 2 Kgs 4:32–37. Cf. Stein, *Luke*, 223; Pao and Schnabel, "Luke," 299; Chen, *Luke*, 96–97; Gadenz, *The Gospel of Luke*, 144.

[101] Cf. Plummer, *The Gospel According to St. Luke*, 199–200; Chen, *Luke*, 97.

[102] Cf. Pao and Schnabel, "Luke," 299; Chen, *Luke*, 97; Gadenz, *The Gospel of Luke*, 144.

[103] Cf. Denaux, "The Theme of Divine Visits and Human (In)Hospitality in Luke-Acts," 276.

[104] Edwards, *The Gospel According to Luke*, 214, comments, "The Greek word for 'come to help' (*episkeptesthai*) was the first (1:68) and last word (1:78) of Zechariah's song in the infancy narrative. Its subject is God—not a distant and uninvolved God—but the God who visits, even intrudes into, his creation in grace in order to 'redeem' (1:68) and raise up a 'horn of salvation' (1:69) for his people 'from heaven' (1:78). The exclamation of the people in v. 16 is a confession of faith that, in the raising of the boy in Nain, this prophet from Capernaum is the fulfillment of the longing of Israel for God's eschatological intervention of salvation." Cf. Beale and Gladd, *The Story Retold*, 113.

[105] Certainly, to say God has visited his people "in" Jesus—like the Pauline phrase, "God was ... in Christ" (2 Cor 5:19) —may be nuanced either as God *being* in Jesus (identity) or *acting* in Jesus (agency). Denaux, "The Theme of Divine Visits and Human (In)Hospitality in Luke-Acts," 276–77, appears to keep the ambiguity. Others, however, believe that Jesus here is claiming divine identity. Cf. Hays, *Reading Backwards*, 68; Thompson, *Luke*, 310.

explicitly named, he is implied as the divine visitor both by Luke's previous references to God's visitation (1:68, 78, 7:16) and by Jesus's allusion to YHWH-texts predicting God's personal visitation in the eschaton (e.g., Ezek 34:11; Zeph 2:7).[106]

At first, Jesus connects the "visitation" with his peace-making ministry (Luke 19:42),[107] which is time-marked as "this day" (19:42) and "the time of your visitation (τὸν καιρὸν τῆς ἐπισκοπῆς σου)" (19:44).[108] Since, however, the citizens of "the city" Jerusalem (19:41) displayed a blind ignorance (19:42, 44) of God's visitation of *peace*, Jesus applied to them prophecies of God's visitation of *punishment*.[109] His reference to the besieging of Jerusalem by her enemies (19:43) recalls predictions of YHWH's eschatological visitation with the same results (cf. Isa 29:6; Jer 6:15).[110] Similarly, Jesus's references to their enemies tearing down their children, as well as every stone of their city (Luke 19:44), recalls more predictions of YHWH's visitation in judgment against both Jerusalem/Israel and her enemy nations (cf. Ps 137:9; Hos 13:16; Jer 26:18; Ezek 4:1–3).[111] In effect, Jesus laments[112] that Jerusalem's rejection of his peaceful visitation earns them God's wrathful visitation.[113] Thus, in the Lukan use of OT YHWH-texts, the visitation of God is (initially) fulfilled in the public ministry of Jesus.[114] He is, by implication, YHWH embodied.

---

[106] Thompson, *Luke*, 310, translates Luke 19:44 to reflect God's personal visitation. Cf. Edwards, *The Gospel According to Luke*, 551; Garland, *Luke*, 774.

[107] The time-bound visitation of Jesus (cf. next footnote) is here marked by peace (Luke 19:42), which underscores the redemptive/saving purpose of his first advent. Cf. Plummer, *The Gospel According to St. Luke*, 452; Green, *The Gospel of Luke*, 689–90; François Bovon, *Luke 3: A Commentary on the Gospel of Luke 19:28–24:53*, trans. James Crouch (Minneapolis, MN: Fortress Press, 2012), 19; Edwards, *The Gospel According to Luke*, 551; Hays, *Echoes of Scripture in the Gospels*, 258; Thompson, *Luke*, 310.

[108] Joseph A. Fitzmyer, ed., *The Gospel According to Luke X–XXIV* (Garden City, NY: Doubleday, 1985), 1259, called it "the period of opportunity." Cf. Morris, *Luke*, 297–98; John Nolland, *Luke 18:35–24:53* (Dallas, TX: Word, 1993), 932; Johnson, *The Gospel of Luke*, 299; Green, *The Gospel of Luke*, 689; Garland, *Luke*, 773; Thompson, *Luke*, 310; Denaux, "The Theme of Divine Visits and Human (In)Hospitality in Luke-Acts," 277.

[109] Cf. Johnson, *The Gospel of Luke*, 299; Garland, *Luke*, 774; William Hendriksen, *Exposition of the Gospel According to Luke* (Grand Rapids, MI: Baker, 1978), 879; Morris, *Luke*, 297–98; Green, *The Gospel of Luke*, 689–91; Adelbert Denaux, "A Stranger in the City: A Contribution to the Study of the Narrative Christology in Luke's Gospel," *LS* 30 (2005): 270; Edwards, *The Gospel According to Luke*, 551; Klyne Snodgrass, *Stories with Intent*, 2nd ed. (Grand Rapids, MI: Eerdmans, 2018), 539.

[110] Jesus's phrase in Luke 19:44, "the time of your visitation (τὸν καιρὸν τῆς ἐπισκοπῆς σου)," may actually allude to the phrase in Jer 6:15, "at the time of their visitation (LXX: ἐν καιρῷ ἐπισκοπῆς αὐτῶν)," in which YHWH describes his own coming/visitation in judgment. Cf. Fitzmyer, *The Gospel According to Luke*, 1259; Nolland, *Luke 18:35–24:53*, 932; Johnson, *The Gospel of Luke*, 299; Culpepper, "The Gospel of Luke," 372; Gadenz, *The Gospel of Luke*, 328.

[111] Cf. Culpepper, "The Gospel of Luke," 372; Morris, *Luke*, 297–98; Edwards, *The Gospel According to Luke*, 551.

[112] Culpepper, "The Gospel of Luke," 372, notes, "Jesus' weeping over the city also evokes echoes of his earlier lament in Luke 13:34–35 ... [and anticipates] 23:28–31 ... Jesus' lament over Jerusalem, therefore, is part of the theme of lament over Israel's failure that runs through Luke and Acts (cf. Luke's use of the Isaianic judgment oracle in Acts 28:24–28)." The Lukan portrayal of Jesus in lament reveals the compassionate YHWH rather than a "weeping prophet" like Jeremiah, contra Stephen Voorwinde, "Jesus' Tears—Human or Divine?," *RTR* 56.2 (1997): 76. Cf. Hays, *Echoes of Scripture in the Gospels*, 258.

[113] Cf. Pao and Schnabel, "Luke," 357; Garland, *Luke*, 774; Edwards, *The Gospel According to Luke*, 551.

[114] Similarly, Graves, *The God of Two Testaments*, 257; Green, *The Gospel of Luke*, 691; Gadenz, *The Gospel of Luke*, 328.

Thematic Trajectory of the Lukan Birth Narrative

It is difficult to underestimate the thematic significance in Luke's Gospel of the coming of YHWH in the person of Jesus.[115] Like the other three canonical Gospels (cf. Matt 3:3; Mark 1:2–3; John 1:23), Luke uses YHWH-texts (i.e., Mal 3:1; Isa 40:3) to identify John the Baptist as YHWH's messenger "Elijah" and, therefore, to identify Jesus as YHWH.[116] But, like no other Gospel, Luke makes that identification at least four times (1:17, 76; 3:4–6; 7:27; cf. 2:30–31; 3:16–17). Additionally, like no other Gospel, Luke applies YHWH-texts of God's redemptive "visitation" in the eschaton (e.g., Zeph 2:7; Ezek 34:11) to Jesus another four times (Luke 1:68, 78; 7:16; 19:44).[117] The ease and frequency with which Luke incorporates these complementary themes in the narrative suggests that he assumed Jesus was the embodiment of YHWH.[118] These early threads set a thematic trajectory for the rest of Luke's Gospel in which the reader must look out for more of the same: Jesus as God come to earth in a saving visitation of his people. The application of YHWH-texts to Jesus would be only natural within such a trajectory.

Luke 3:16–17

Previous exegesis of the Markan parallel (Mark 1:7–8) contains many observations pertinent to Luke 3:16–17, so discussion here will be succinct. The Baptist compares and contrasts himself to Jesus in three important ways that apply OT YHWH-texts to Jesus. First, Jesus is "the mightier one to come [ἔρχεται . . . ὁ ἰσχυρότερός]" (Luke 3:16), which harkens back to the promise of Isa 40:10 that "the Lord (Heb: יהוה) comes/shall come with might (LXX: κύριος μετὰ ἰσχύος ἔρχεται)."[119] Second, Jesus would not baptize with John's water, a mere symbol, but with the Holy Spirit and fire (Luke 3:16), an act of power which harkens back to YHWH's promise to pour out his Spirit in the eschaton (e.g., Isa 44:3; Ezek 36:25–27)[120] and may be linked to salvific purifying fire (cf. Isa 4:4; Mal 3:1–3), although John proceeds to highlight judgment fire (Luke 3:17; cf. Isa 30:27–28, 33).[121]

---

[115] Garland, *Luke*, 774, comments, "The 'time [or season] of your visitation' refers in the Old Testament to the coming of God, whether for rescue (see Gen 21:1; 50:24–25; Exod 3:16; 4:31; 13:19; Jer 15:15; Ps 106:4) or for judgment (Isa 10:3; Jer 6:15; 10:15). The statement reflects a high Christology, since it is Jesus who visits Jerusalem."

[116] Johnson, *The Gospel of Luke*, 301–2, sees more significance of Malachi 3 in the wider Lukan narrative.

[117] Cf. Johnson, *The Gospel of Luke*, 299; Garland, *Luke*, 774; Nolland, *Luke 18:35–24:53*, 930.

[118] Cf. Hays, *Reading Backwards*, 68; Garland, *Luke*, 774.

[119] Although commentators are nearly unanimous that "the strong(er) one" of OT background is a description of YHWH (as found in passages such as Deut 10:17; 2 Sam 22:33; Ps 18:32; Isa 11:2; 28:2; 49:26; Jer 50:34), they frequently claim that the descriptor in Luke 3:16 either cannot refer to God or is merely used in some lesser messianic sense. Cf. Marshall, *The Gospel of Luke*, 146; Nolland, *Luke 1–9:20*, 151; Bock, *Luke*, 320; Bovon, *Luke 1*, 126; Hans Klein, *Das Lukasevangelium* (Göttingen: Vandenhoeck und Ruprecht, 2006), 167; Pao and Schnabel, "Luke," 279. Edwards, *The Gospel According to Luke*, 113–14, rightly sees a more direct identification of Jesus with YHWH.

[120] Cf. Matthew Steven Godshall, "The Messiah and the Outpouring of the Holy Spirit: The Christological Significance of Jesus as Giver of the Spirit in Luke-Acts" (PhD diss., Southern Baptist Theological Seminary, 2013), 189–90, 193; J. Daryl Charles, "The 'Coming One'/'Stronger One' and His Baptism: Matt 3:11–12, Mark 1:8, Luke 3:16–17," *The Journal of the Society for Pentecostal Studies* 11.1 (1989): 40, 43–45.

[121] Some scholars understand "fire" here as metaphorical of divine purification of the believer, being parallel with the cleansing of the believer by baptism with the Holy Spirit. Cf. Plummer, *The Gospel According to St. Luke*, 95; Morris, *Luke*, 115; Klein, *Das Lukasevangelium*, 167. Other scholars believe

Third, Jesus not only owns the winnowing fork, threshing floor, and storage barn of eschatological separation,[122] "but he will burn the chaff with unquenchable fire (τὸ δὲ ἄχυρον κατακαύσει πυρὶ ἀσβέστῳ)" (Luke 3:17), a clear allusion of YHWH's prerogative of final judgment (Isa 66:15–16) and its result for the rebellious: "and their fire shall not be quenched (καὶ τὸ πῦρ αὐτῶν οὐ σβεσθήσεται)" (66:24).[123] Thus, Luke portrays John as identifying Jesus with a compilation of OT YHWH-texts.

Luke 5:10

Whether or not Luke 5:1–11 forms a triple tradition parallel with Matt 4:18–22 and Mark 1:16–20, it bears additional features and nuances worthy of commentary beyond that offered previously on Mark 1:17.[124] The climax of the scene occurs when Jesus tells Simon in verse 10, "from now on you will be capturing men alive (ἀπὸ τοῦ νῦν ἀνθρώπους ἔσῃ ζωγρῶν)." As noted in the explanation of Mark's account, this commissioning by Jesus harkens back to YHWH's commissioning of fishers and hunters of men in the OT—most notably in Jer 16:16.[125] And while in Jeremiah the capture of idolaters may appear to be for the purpose of retribution alone (16:17–18), the broader context predicts both Israel's restoration to the land (Jer 16:15) and the nations' awareness of their guilty idolatry when they come to know YHWH's power and name (16:19–21).[126] In Luke, the emphasis of Jesus is clearly positive, as he uses a term for catching men *alive* (or, perhaps, *for life*).[127] But the key to understanding Jesus's declaration is in his presumption to determine the disciples' future role of capturing people precisely as YHWH had promised he would do post-Exile.

Other features of this Lukan pericope confirm that Jesus was applying a YHWH-text(s) with YHWH-prerogatives to himself. Before the "astonishing" catch of "a large number of fish" (Luke 5:9, 6) Simon addressed Jesus as "master" (Ἐπιστάτα; 5:5), but

---

"fire" refers to the eschatological fire that both purifies the believer and punishes the wicked. Cf. Nolland, *Luke 1–9:20*, 153, 155; Garland, *Luke*, 159; Charles, "The 'Coming One'/'Stronger One' and His Baptism," 40, 49.

[122] Charles, "The 'Coming One'/'Stronger One' and His Baptism," 48, sees the possessive pronouns as marking divine attributes of Jesus. Furthermore, John may be alluding to specific YHWH-texts in his claim about Jesus: e.g., Isa 41:15–16; Jer 15:7.

[123] Cf. Marshall, *The Gospel of Luke*, 148; Bock, *Luke*, 324–25.

[124] Some scholars believe that Luke describes a different event here than the one described in Matthew and Mark: e.g., Robert L. Thomas and Stanley N. Gundry, *A Harmony of the Gospels* (Chicago, IL: Moody, 1978), 8; Hendriksen, *Luke*, 285. Other scholars believe the more likely view that all the Synoptics are referring to the same event: e.g., James R. Harrison, "Modern Scholarship and the 'Nature' Miracles: A Defense of Their Historicity and Affirmation of Jesus' Deity," *RTR* 72.2 (2013): 89–90; Marshall, *The Gospel of Luke*, 199–206; Garland, *Luke*, 227–29. Despite acknowledging multiple attestation of the fishing metaphor in the Gospels, including parallels to John 21:1–11, Robert Walter Funk and Roy W. Hoover, eds., *The Five Gospels*, 282, perplexingly assert, "the saying in this form would not have circulated in the oral tradition outside this story and so does not go back to Jesus."

[125] Cf. France, *Luke*, 82. Some scholars suggest a broader OT background for the phrase, including passages such as Amos 4:2 and Hab 1:14–15 with Jer 16:16: e.g., Fitzmyer, *The Gospel According to Luke*, 569; Pao and Schnabel, "Luke," 292. But Jer 16:16 is most likely the background.

[126] Similarly, Fitzmyer, *The Gospel According to Luke*, 569.

[127] Cf. Fitzmyer, *The Gospel According to Luke*, 568; Morris, *Luke*, 133; Just, *Luke 1:1–9:50*, 209; Green, *The Gospel of Luke*, 234–35; Pao and Schnabel, "Luke," 292; France, *Luke*, 82.

afterward as "Lord" (κύριε; 5:8)—hinting at the divine identity of Jesus already in view by use of the term in 1:43 and 2:11.[128] This high Christology is bolstered by both the obeisance and the confession of guilt by Simon Peter toward Jesus, "Depart from me, for I am a sinful man" (5:8), which echo the obeisance and confessions of OT saints who found themselves in YHWH's presence (e.g., Ezek 1:28; Isa 6:5).[129] Jesus's initial command precipitating the miracle (5:4) and his follow-up command not to fear him (5:10) only add to the pericope's perspective that Jesus acted as YHWH acts.[130] Thus, when Jesus defined his disciples' future occupation as "catching men alive," multiple features within the Lukan account support Jesus's application of a YHWH-text (Jer 16:16) to himself.[131]

Luke 5:20–26 and 7:47–50

Luke's account of Jesus healing and forgiving the paralytic has been addressed at its parallels in Matt 9:2–7 and Mark 2:5–12, and so it will be addressed only briefly here. However, comments will be included on an entirely distinct (but thematically related) Lukan pericope at 7:36–50,[132] which records another instance of Jesus forgiving sins committed against God and thereby alluding to OT YHWH-texts.

Luke 5:20–26

The narrative flow of this important pericope shows (a) Jesus pronouncing forgiveness of a man's sins,[133] (b) the religious authorities charging Jesus with blasphemy since "God alone" can forgive sins,[134] (c) Jesus countering with a rhetorical question on whether it is easier to declare forgiveness or to heal the man, and (d) Jesus healing the man before the leaders can answer that merely declaring forgiveness would be easier.[135]

---

[128] Cf. Garland, *Luke*, 228; Morris, *Luke*, 134; Rowe, *Early Narrative Christology*, 85–86; Edwards, *The Gospel According to Luke*, 155–56.

[129] Most commentators note that Peter's response to Jesus shows his recognition of personal sinfulness in the divine presence (as is common in OT scenes). Cf. Marshall, *The Gospel of Luke*, 204–5; Hendriksen, *Luke*, 284; Morris, *Luke*, 133–34; Stein, *Luke*, 169; Garland, *Luke*, 228; Chen, *Luke*, 69; Gadenz, *The Gospel of Luke*, 112–13. Funk and Hoover, *The Five Gospels*, 282, however, propose without evidence and contrary to each Evangelist that Peter's response originally belonged after his denial of Jesus.

[130] Rowe, *Early Narrative Christology*, 88, argues against the use of κύριε as merely a polite address. Cf. Henrichs-Tarasenkova, *Luke's Christology of Divine Identity*, 188; Roch A. Kereszty, *Jesus Christ*, rev. ed. (New York: Alba House, 2002), 174–75.

[131] Similarly, Henrichs-Tarasenkova, *Luke's Christology of Divine Identity*.

[132] See discussion below on Luke 7:47–50. Cf. Bock, *Luke*, 484; Richard J. Bauckham, "Christology," *Dictionary of Jesus and the Gospels*, 131.

[133] The pronouncement is clearly on Jesus's own authority. Cf. Nolland, *Luke 1–9:20*, 235; Stein, *Luke*, 176–78; Edwards, *The Gospel According to Luke*, 166.

[134] Cf. Edwards, *The Gospel According to Luke*, 167; Plummer, *The Gospel According to St. Luke*, 155; Morris, *Luke*, 138; Nolland, *Luke 1–9:20*, 236; Stein, *Luke*, 176–77; Bock, *Luke*, 482; Just, *Luke 1:1–9:50*, 229; France, *Luke*, 89; Hays, *Echoes of Scripture in the Gospels*, 255. Funk and Hoover, *The Five Gospels*, 283, however, appear wide of the mark when they speculate, "It is possible that Jesus is here claiming that all sons of Adam (not the apocalyptic figure of Daniel 7) can forgive sins."

[135] Cf. Marshall, *The Gospel of Luke*, 216; Morris, *Luke*, 138; Green, *The Gospel of Luke*, 242–43.

Based in this series of interactions ending with an unequivocally divine miracle (5:25–26),[136] Jesus was able to tell his critics, "the Son of Man has authority on earth to forgive sins" (5:24).[137]

Thus, as with its Synoptic parallels, this Lukan account demonstrates that the conflict between Jesus and the religious authorities was centered on Jesus's exercise of YHWH's prerogative to forgive sins committed against YHWH.[138] Although Ps 103:2–3 is a likely candidate for allusion in Jesus's demonstrative claim both to heal disease and to forgive sin, there may be other YHWH-texts in the background of Jesus's claim.[139] However, no priest, angel, or other agent of God in the Scriptures ever forgave sins on his own authority, as Jesus does in this passage.[140] The argument that Jesus employed a divine passive in Luke 5:20 (ἀφέωνταί σοι αἱ ἁμαρτίαι σου: "your sins have been forgiven you [*by God*]") to point away from himself and highlight what God had done falls flat on Jesus's central claim in 5:24.[141] His audience certainly knew that he was claiming to forgive sins on his own authority (the accusation of blasphemy underscores it),[142] and, rather than deny their charge, Jesus emphasized his personal authority to forgive sins.[143]

Luke's surrounding narration clearly supports this understanding by describing Jesus as possessing "the power of the Lord" (5:17),[144] knowing the thoughts of his critics (5:22),[145] and demonstrating his authority to heal and forgive such that both the healed paralytic and all those witnessing the miracle glorified *God* (5:25, 26).[146] The climactic

---

[136] As Garland, *Luke*, 243, observes, "Jesus' power to heal is eroding their influence."

[137] Since the authority given to the Son of Man in Dan 7:13–14 encompasses everlasting dominion of all earthly kingdoms, it surely includes the authority to pardon sinners on the earth. For other comments on the first occurrence of the Son of Man title in Luke and its implications for Jesus's authority, see Marshall, *The Gospel of Luke*, 215–16; Klein, *Das Lukasevangelium*, 221; Rowe, *Early Narrative Christology*, 104–5; Edwards, *The Gospel According to Luke*, 168–69; Thompson, *Luke*, 90–91.

[138] Edwards, *The Gospel According to Luke*, 166–67, comments, "It is, of course, the prerogative of a mortal to forgive sins against himself, but the sin in this instance is not against Jesus. Jesus forgives sins of another, which can only be God's prerogative." Cf. Hendriksen, *Luke*, 297; Stein, *Luke*, 178; France, *Luke*, 89; Charles L. Quarles, "Lord or Legend: Jesus as the Messianic Son of Man," *JETS* 62.1 (2019): 107.

[139] E.g., Exod 34:6–7; Pss 103:12; 130:4; Isa 43:25; 44:22; 55:6–7; Jer 31:34; Mic 7:18. Cf. Hendriksen, *Luke*, 297; Pao and Schnabel, "Luke," 292; Edwards, *The Gospel According to Luke*, 167.

[140] Garland, *Luke*, 242–43, adds, "This forgiveness is not connected to any atoning rituals and circumvents the temple cult. It helps clarify that the leper's return to the priests was simply a requirement for him to be reintegrated into society and not a theological necessity." Rowe, *Early Narrative Christology*, 103–4, argues, "the charge would never have arisen in this precise form on the presupposition of an agent-like Christology. An agent of God does not constitute a rival to God's uniqueness as the only God." Cf. Edwards, *The Gospel According to Luke*, 166.

[141] Stein, *Luke*, 176, comments, "This is not to be understood as a 'divine passive' or circumlocution for 'God forgives you.' This is evident from the following verses (esp. 5:24) where Jesus' words are understood to be an implicit claim of equality with God (5:21; 7:49; cf. John 5:18; 10:33), i.e., Jesus himself is understood as having forgiven the man his sins." Cf. Just, *Luke 1:1–9:50*, 225. For commentators who emphasize Jesus's use of the divine passive, see Carroll, *Luke*, 130–31; Chen, *Luke*, 76.

[142] Cf. Plummer, *The Gospel According to St. Luke*, 155; Just, *Luke 1:1–9:50*, 229; France, *Luke*, 89; Edwards, *The Gospel According to Luke*, 167.

[143] Cf. Plummer, *The Gospel According to St. Luke*, 155.

[144] Cf. Klein, *Das Lukasevangelium*, 221; Stein, *Luke*, 178; Rowe, *Early Narrative Christology*, 104–5.

[145] Cf. Just, *Luke 1:1–9:50*, 225.

[146] Cf. Nolland, *Luke 1–9:20*, 238; Rowe, *Early Narrative Christology*, 105.

question of the critics—"Who can forgive sins but God alone?"—identifies the burning theme of the passage[147] and implies that Jesus had boldly taken upon himself this monotheistic prerogative of YHWH as found in the OT Scriptures.[148]

Luke 7:47–50

Luke alone includes an additional story of forgiveness to "a woman of the city who was a sinner (γυνὴ ἥτις ἦν ἐν τῇ πόλει ἁμαρτωλός)."[149] Although some scholars believe Luke has misplaced a tradition that the other Evangelists describe as a pre-burial anointing (Matt 26:1–13; Mark 14:3–9; John 12:2–8), it is clear that Luke describes a distinct event (with distinct place, time, characters, and purpose)[150] that highlights again Jesus's divine authority to forgive sins.

The focus of Luke 7:47–50, like that in 5:17–26, is on Jesus's declaration—"Your sins are forgiven" (Ἀφέωνταί σου αἱ ἁμαρτίαι; 7:48)[151]—and the subsequent question of shock in 7:49: "Who is this, who even forgives sins?"[152] The question recalls Mic 7:18: "Who is a God like you, pardoning iniquity ...?"[153] Jesus's divine identity, which is implied in the answer to the rhetorical question, is central to the entire pericope.[154] The dinner host doubted in his mind that Jesus could even be identified as a prophet, because (he thought) Jesus seemed oblivious to the fact that the woman touching him was "a sinner" (ἁμαρτωλός; 7:39).[155] But since Jesus knew that his host's view of his

---

[147] Cf. Edwards, *The Gospel According to Luke*, 166–67; Stein, *Luke*, 177; Bock, *Luke*, 482; Morris, *Luke*, 138.

[148] Many scholars recognize that Jesus was taking to himself the divine prerogative of forgiving sins committed against God: e.g., Stein, *Luke*, 178; France, *Luke*, 89; Edwards, *The Gospel According to Luke*, 166; Quarles, "Lord or Legend," 107; Geoffrey Grogan, "New Testament Christology—or New Testament Christologies?," *Them* 25.1 (1999): 71–72. Some scholars also point out a possible allusion in Luke 5:21 (μόνος ὁ θεός) to the Jewish monotheistic *Shema* (cf. Deut 6:4; κύριος εἷς ἐστιν): e.g., Simon J. Gathercole, "The Trinity in the Synoptic Gospels and Acts," in *The Oxford Handbook of the Trinity*, eds. Gilles Emery and Matthew Levering (Oxford; New York: Oxford University Press, 2011), 56; Hays, *Echoes of Scripture in the Gospels*, 225.

[149] Cf. Bauckham, "Christology," 131.

[150] Cf. Johnson, *The Gospel of Luke*, 128–29. Perhaps what is thought to be the greatest argument for Luke's "misplaced story" is that the host in Luke 7 bears the same name (Simon) as the host in the burial anointing stories. But there are at least eight different "Simons" in the NT (cf. Matt 4:18; 10:4; 13:55; 26:6/Mark 14:3; Matt 27:32; John 6:71; Acts 8:9; 9:43), implying that there could easily be a ninth in this passage. Numerous differences between accounts trump the argument that the same (common) name refers to the same person.

[151] The perfect passive indicates that the woman was then in a state of forgiveness. While it is unclear when her forgiveness began, it is clear that Jesus authoritatively declared it to be so. Cf. Grundmann, *Das Evangelium Nach Lukas*, 172–73; Bock, *Luke*, 703; Nolland, *Luke 1–9:20*, 359. Some commentators believe that Jesus was acting merely as a spokesman/agent because he used a divine passive: e.g., Malina and Rohrbaugh, *Social-Science Commentary on the Synoptic Gospels*, 256; Carroll, *Luke*, 180. But their view overlooks the central point of the passage (Who is *Jesus* that he can forgive sins?) and must accuse the questioners of asking the wrong question.

[152] Cf. Stein, *Luke*, 238; Garland, *Luke*, 330; Thompson, *Luke*, 126; Bauckham, "Christology," 131.

[153] Cf. Gathercole, "The Trinity in the Synoptic Gospels and Acts," 59.

[154] Cf. Culpepper, "The Gospel of Luke," 171; Stein, *Luke*, 238. Contra Malina and Rohrbaugh, *Social-Science Commentary on the Synoptic Gospels*, 256.

[155] Bock, *Luke*, 706, however, notes how the narrative implies that Jesus is much more than a prophet. Cf. Garland, *Luke*, 330.

identity was grossly deficient, Jesus told him the parable of two debtors, in which the debtor who was forgiven the most loved his benefactor the most.[156] The applicatory key to Jesus's parable is that the benefactor who forgave his debtors symbolized God.[157] Thus, when the sinful woman expressed her great love for Jesus she was expressing her great love to God.[158] This identification of the forgiving moneylender (God) with Jesus confirms that in Jesus's use of the "divine passive" he was referring to himself as the source of the woman's forgiveness.[159] He portrayed himself as the God who forgives great sinners. And he proceeded to emphasize his divine prerogative to forgive sins against God by declaring to the woman, "Your faith has saved you; go in peace" (7:50), where both the means (faith) and result (peace) of her forgiveness were delineated by Jesus's authoritative word.

Conspicuously absent from the account (except, tellingly, by symbolic parallel in Jesus's parable) is any deference to God as the woman's forgiver (as in 2 Sam 12:13; Pss 32:1–2; 130:7–8; Isa 40:2). Similarly conspicuous is the absence of the temple, priests, or sacrifices showing any instrumental means of her divine pardon (as in Lev 4:35; 16:30; cf. Heb 9:22).[160] Rather, Jesus relied on his own authority to declare forgiveness of this sinner, just as YHWH had declared forgiveness of sinners in the OT (e.g., Isa 43:25; Jer 31:34; 33:8).[161] For this reason, Jesus's two declarations of a sinful woman's forgiveness in Luke 7:47, 48 allude to OT YHWH-texts that assumed the same prerogative. Furthermore, the question posed in 7:49 likely harkens back to the specific YHWH-text, Mic 7:18.[162] Thus, a combination of YHWH-texts becomes the background for Jesus's claim.

Luke 5:34–35

Jesus's self-identification as "the bridegroom" occurs in all the Synoptics (cf. Matt 9:15; Mark 2:19–20; Luke 5:34–35; the Baptist used the title for Jesus in John 3:29).[163] Since the Markan account has been addressed sufficiently, bare comments shall be offered here.

In the OT, YHWH alone is identified as the bridegroom of his people Israel and of his future people in the eschaton.[164] The messiah is never called a

---

[156] Cf. Snodgrass, *Stories with Intent*, 89; Philip B. Payne, "Jesus' Implicit Claim to Deity in His Parables," *TJ* 2 (1981): 13.
[157] Cf. Just, *Luke 1:1–9:50*, 325.
[158] Cf. Payne, "Jesus' Implicit Claim to Deity in His Parables," 13; Just, *Luke 1:1–9:50*, 325; Snodgrass, *Stories with Intent*, 90.
[159] Cf. Just, *Luke 1:1–9:50*, 325; Snodgrass, *Stories with Intent*, 89–90; Thompson, *Luke*, 126.
[160] Cf. Beale and Gladd, *The Story Retold*, 113; Garland, *Luke*, 330–31; Bock, *Luke*, 705; Snodgrass, *Stories with Intent*, 90. Likewise, within the narrative flow of this scene Jesus is portrayed as more than a mediating prophet (cf. Luke 7:39).
[161] Similarly, Bauckham, "Christology," 131; Nolland, *Luke 1–9:20*, 359; Just, *Luke 1:1–9:50*, 325.
[162] Cf. Gathercole, "The Trinity in the Synoptic Gospels and Acts," 58.
[163] Several scholars point out that, while John refers to a separate event from that of the Synoptic Gospels, all four Evangelists record usage of "the bridegroom" for Jesus. E.g., Bock, *Luke*, 516–17; Edwards, *The Gospel According to Luke*, 173.
[164] E.g., Isa 54:1–6; 62:4–5; Jer 2:32; 31:32; Hos 2:14–23. Cf. Marshall, *The Gospel of Luke*, 225; Hendriksen, *Luke*, 309; Johnson, *The Gospel of Luke*, 98; Bock, *Luke*, 516; Pao and Schnabel, "Luke," 293; Edwards, *The Gospel According to Luke*, 173–74.

bridegroom.¹⁶⁵ Since the presence of YHWH as bridegroom would mark the eschatological celebration (Isa 61:10–62:5; Hos 2:14–23; cf. Isa 25:6–9; Jer 31:10–14),¹⁶⁶ Jesus's assumption that his disciples would feast while he was there and fast when he was taken away implies that he saw himself as YHWH.¹⁶⁷ There should be no doubt, therefore, that in calling himself "the bridegroom," whose presence calls for feasting by the wedding guests, Jesus was applying OT YHWH-texts to himself.¹⁶⁸

Luke 6:5

Jesus's claim in Luke 6:5 to be "Lord of the Sabbath" (Κύριός . . . τοῦ σαββάτου), like his earlier claim to be "the bridegroom" of his disciples, also has triple attestation in the Synoptic Gospels.¹⁶⁹ Since extensive comments have already been made on Matt 12:8 and Mark 2:28, this section shall be brief.

Luke chose to omit Mark's purpose statement of the Sabbath (Mark 2:27), possibly to intensify the focus on Jesus's lordship.¹⁷⁰ The emphatic placement of κύριος supports this interpretation;¹⁷¹ Luke's account could be translated, "the Lord of the Sabbath is the Son of Man,"¹⁷² or, more interpretively, "Just who is Lord of the Sabbath? The Son of Man is!"¹⁷³ Since YHWH was the sole creator (Gen 2:2–3),¹⁷⁴ legislator (Exod

---

[165] Cf. Fitzmyer, *The Gospel According to Luke*, 599; Marshall, *The Gospel of Luke*, 225; Stein, *Luke*, 185; Edwards, *The Gospel According to Luke*, 173. Pao and Schnabel, "Luke," 293, note, "it is only in later traditions that this metaphor is applied to the Messiah (cf. 2 Cor. 11:2; Eph. 5:25–27; Rev. 19:7–10; 21:2; *Pirqe R. El.* 4; *Pesiq. Rab.* 149a)."

[166] For comments on the eschatological banquet and/or bridegroom's wedding feast, see Nolland, *Luke 1–9:20*, 248; Green, *The Gospel of Luke*, 249; Garland, *Luke*, 253; Payne, "Jesus' Implicit Claim to Deity in His Parables," 11–12.

[167] As Edwards, *The Gospel According to Luke*, 173–74, writes, "nowhere in the OT is the Messiah presented as a bridegroom, and only rarely so outside the OT. This does not diminish its Christological significance, however, for in the OT God is not infrequently described as Israel's husband and lover (Isa 5:1; 54:5–6; 62:4–5; Ezek 16:6–8; Hos 2:19). The same nuptial imagery increases in later Judaism. In this stunning metaphor, which appears in all four Gospels, Jesus does not allude to his messianic office, but presumes the prerogatives of God himself. Similar to the forgiveness of sins in 5:24, Jesus invites hearers to supply their own answer to his identity. Both episodes, powerfully though implicitly, provoke hearers to recognize that, in the mission of Jesus, the *person* of God is present" (emphasis Edwards). Similarly, see Payne, "Jesus' Implicit Claim to Deity in His Parables," 11–12; Marshall, *The Gospel of Luke*, 225; Garland, *Luke*, 253; Gadenz, *The Gospel of Luke*, 120–21.

[168] Further NT teaching that the church is the bride of Christ is simply more evidence and application of the divine bridegroom theme in the Gospels. Cf. Hendriksen, *Luke*, 309; Green, *The Gospel of Luke*, 249; Garland, *Luke*, 253; Gadenz, *The Gospel of Luke*, 120–21.

[169] Cf. Quarles, "Lord or Legend," 107.

[170] Several commentators interpret the omission as bringing more focus to the Christological importance of Jesus's statement: e.g., Bock, *Luke*, 526; Rowe, *Early Narrative Christology*, 107–8; Hays, *Echoes of Scripture in the Gospels*, 255.

[171] Cf. Plummer, *The Gospel According to St. Luke*, 168; Rowe, *Early Narrative Christology*, 107; Edwards, *The Gospel According to Luke*, 180; Thompson, *Luke*, 98.

[172] Rowe, *Early Narrative Christology*, 108.

[173] Edwards, *The Gospel According to Luke*, 180. Green, *The Gospel of Luke*, 254, therefore, appears to land shy of the intended meaning when he says Jesus's claim "designates Jesus as God's authorized agent to determine what was appropriate on the Sabbath." There is neither an authorization nor an agent mentioned in Jesus's claim to be the Sabbath's Lord.

[174] Cf. Edwards, *The Gospel According to Luke*, 179; Gadenz, *The Gospel of Luke*, 123. Thomas G. Weinandy, *Jesus Becoming Jesus* (Washington DC: Catholic University of America, 2018), 133, adds that Jesus elsewhere healed on the Sabbath, thus "undertaking the new work of new creation."

20:8–11),¹⁷⁵ and owner (Exod 31:13) of the Sabbath, Jesus appeared to be claiming divine authority as the Sabbath's Lord.¹⁷⁶ Thus, as the Danielic Son of Man to whom the Ancient of Days bestows everlasting dominion over all earthly realms (Dan 7:13–14), Jesus found it fitting not only to claim authority to forgive sins committed against YHWH (Luke 5:24) but to claim lordship over YHWH's Sabbath (6:5).¹⁷⁷ Such a claim, at minimum, would have had in mind Exod 20:8–11, which portrays YHWH alone as Lord of the Sabbath.¹⁷⁸

Luke 6:46

The vocative doublet, "Lord Lord" (κύριε κύριε), has been addressed more fully in Matthew where it occurs three times (Matt 7:21, 22; 25:11).¹⁷⁹ Nevertheless, the only other NT occurrence here in Luke 6:46 makes it worth revisiting. The pericope of Luke 6:46–49 parallels that of Matthew 7:21–27, but it is decidedly shorter and uses a second person rather than Matthew's third person perspective.¹⁸⁰ But the meaning remains the same: anyone who addresses Jesus as "Lord Lord"¹⁸¹ and yet does not obey his words is a fool who will reap great ruin in his fall (Luke 6:49; cf. Matt 7:23, 27, in which rejection by Jesus parallels the great fall).

The key to understanding the severe consequences of disobeying Jesus's words lies in the unique identity of the one being addressed by the hypothetical hypocrite.¹⁸² The double vocative, κύριε κύριε, was not an emphatic repetition for heightened emotion,¹⁸³

---

[175] Keeping the institution of the Sabbath was commanded in Israel's *Torah*, specifically, as fourth of the Ten Commandments. Astonishingly, Jesus was claiming authority over God's Law. Cf. Plummer, *The Gospel According to St. Luke*, 168; Garland, *Luke*, 263; Grogan, "New Testament Christology—or New Testament Christologies?," 72. Morris, *Luke*, 143, appears to write tongue-in-cheek when he understates, "This is a staggering claim, for the sabbath was of divine institution (Exod. 20:8–11). To be lord of a divine ordinance is to have a very high place indeed."

[176] On the importance of Luke's emphatic κύριος within his unique presentation, see Rowe, *Early Narrative Christology*, 108.

[177] Cf. Gadenz, *The Gospel of Luke*, 123; Morris, *Luke*, 143; Edwards, *The Gospel According to Luke*, 179.

[178] Similarly, Marshall, *The Gospel of Luke*, 233; Morris, *Luke*, 143.

[179] In addition to the previous discussion at Matt 7:21–22, see especially, Quarles, *A Theology of Matthew*, 142–43; Staples, "'Lord, Lord': Jesus as YHWH in Matthew and Luke," 1–19; Daniel Isaac Block, *Covenant* (Grand Rapids, MI: Baker Academic, 2021), 468–69.

[180] Cf. Bock, *Luke*, 619; Staples, "'Lord, Lord': Jesus as YHWH in Matthew and Luke," 17. Block, *Covenant*, 468, however, observes, "although Luke offers a drastically abbreviated version of Matthew 7:21–27, he fleshes out the meaning of the expression by declaring its opposite."

[181] Technically, there should be no comma separating the doublet, since it represents the divine name rather than an emphatic repetition. Cf. Staples, "'Lord, Lord': Jesus as YHWH in Matthew and Luke," 19 n87.

[182] As Block, *Covenant*, 468–69, writes, "Remarkably, in both Matthew 7:21–22 and Luke 6:46 Jesus identified himself as the divine addressee.... In declaring the contrasting fates of those who act upon the words that *he* spoke ... Jesus did not speak as a divinely commissioned prophet rather than a false prophet, nor did he speak in the name of God; he spoke as God" (emphasis Block). Cf. Gadenz, *The Gospel of Luke*, 136. P. Maurice Casey, *From Jewish Prophet to Gentile God* (Cambridge, UK: James Clarke & Co.; Louisville, KY: Westminster/John Knox Press, 1991), 68, however, falters by overlooking the septuagintal significance of "κύριε κύριε" and asserting a post-Easter origin for the use of κύριος. Similarly, Malina and Rohrbaugh, *Social-Science Commentary on the Synoptic Gospels*, 251, fall shy of the divine significance embedded in the double vocative.

[183] The double vocative in Luke 6:46 is often assumed to be an expression of deep pathos. Cf. Grundmann, *Das Evangelium Nach Lukas*, 154; Thompson, *Luke*, 110–11. Staples, "'Lord, Lord': Jesus as YHWH in Matthew and Luke," 2–3, 14–15, 18, however, argues compellingly against that assumption.

but a common surrogate for the divine name in the LXX.¹⁸⁴ The Greek word for "Lord" (κύριος) served double duty to translate the Hebrew אדני יהוה, "(my) Lord YHWH," or slight variants as a way to avoid pronouncing the divine name.¹⁸⁵ This background for Jesus's illustration reveals that the hypocrite whose house (i.e., life) falls into ruin merely gives lip service to Jesus as "Lord YHWH" but does not embrace and obey Jesus as the Lord YHWH.¹⁸⁶ Thus, behind Jesus's claim are a good many YHWH-texts in which OT saints (e.g., Moses, Gideon, David, Amos) had addressed YHWH as אדני יהוה and the LXX had translated with κύριε κύριε ("Lord Lord").¹⁸⁷ Staples writes, "it is hard to escape the conclusion that these verses thereby place a self-referential use of the divine name on Jesus' lips, an echo any first-century reader familiar with the Greek Bible would be unlikely to miss."¹⁸⁸ It is profoundly detrimental to Christological studies that here many modern readers miss Jesus's self-referential and emphatic appellation of the divine name.

Luke 8:22–25

Luke's account of Jesus calming the storm (8:22–25), while shorter than Mark's account (4:35–41), is slightly longer than Matthew's account (8:18, 23–27) and contains its own unique features.¹⁸⁹ The disciples address Jesus with the titular doublet, "Master, Master" (Ἐπιστάτα ἐπιστάτα; Luke 8:24), rather than the singular title "Teacher" (Διδάσκαλε;

---

[184] Cf. Quarles, *A Theology of Matthew*, 142; Staples, "'Lord, Lord': Jesus as YHWH in Matthew and Luke," 3, 11–14, 18–19; Block, *Covenant*, 468.

[185] Staples, "'Lord, Lord': Jesus as YHWH in Matthew and Luke," 8, 10–11, notes, "This combination [of יהוה אדנא] (and its variants) occurs 319 times in the Masoretic Text.... This use of the single κύριος eventually became the most common solution for rendering יהוה אדנא and its variants elsewhere in the LXX (196 times in Rahlfs), though given the tendency of some early manuscripts to leave a space where the Tetragram appears (e.g. P.Ryl. III.458), one wonders whether many of these examples of a single κύριος were the result of such spaces (or perhaps dots or some other placeholder) eventually dropping out in the process of transmission.... The scribal reserve towards repetition observed in the transmission history further highlights just how distinctive the double κύριος sounded when it was retained. The distinctiveness of this repetition is further reinforced by the fact that *in every extant example in pre-Talmudic Jewish literature outside the Gospels, the double κύριος serves as a Greek rendering of* יהוה אדנא" (emphasis Staples). Cf. Quarles, *A Theology of Matthew*, 142; Block, *Covenant*, 468.

[186] Gadenz, *The Gospel of Luke*, 136, comments, "whereas Old Testament teaching on the two ways involves doing what God has commanded, now Jesus says: **do what I command**. Teaching with such authority is only possible for one who is **Lord, Lord**, like the God who revealed himself to Moses (Exod 34:6)" (emphasis Gadenz). Cf. Bock, *Luke*, 621; Block, *Covenant*, 469; Staples, "'Lord, Lord': Jesus as YHWH in Matthew and Luke," 18.

[187] See a list of eighteen occurrences in Quarles, *A Theology of Matthew*, 142 n18. Cf. Staples, "'Lord, Lord': Jesus as YHWH in Matthew and Luke," 2, 12.

[188] Staples, "'Lord, Lord': Jesus as YHWH in Matthew and Luke," 19. Cf. Quarles, *A Theology of Matthew*, 142–43; Block, *Covenant*, 468–69.

[189] Luke uses ninety-four Greek words in his account, Mark 118, and Matthew eighty-five. Cf. Nolland, *Luke 1–9:20*, 400; Hays, *Echoes of Scripture in the Gospels*, 255. Culpepper, "The Gospel of Luke," 184, observes, "This is the only sea miracle in Luke, in contrast to Mark and Matthew, which also report Jesus' walking on the water (Matt 14:22–33; Mark 6:45–52; cf. John 6:16–21)."

Mark 4:38) or "Lord" (Κύριε; Matt 8:25).[190] Luke leaves out the adjective, "great" (μέγας), which is favored by both Matthew (8:24, 26) and Mark (4:37, 39).[191]

More importantly, however, Luke employs two terms not found in the other Synoptics that are used in the LXX version of the storm calmed by YHWH in the Book of Jonah (κινδυνεύω: "to be in danger"; Jonah 1:4; Luke 8:23; and κλύδων: "billow, surging wave"; Jonah 1:4, 11, 12; Luke 8:24).[192] These lexical ties support the view that Jesus's actions as described in Luke were meant to be viewed in light of YHWH's actions as described in Jonah.[193] Several points of contact between the stilling of the storm in Jonah 1:3–16 and that in Luke 8:22–25 may be found in the previous commentary on Mark 4:36–41. But two parallels of particular significance are the sailors' pleas to YHWH/Jesus for rescue from perishing (Jonah 1:14; Luke 8:24),[194] and the awesome calming of the tempest by YHWH/Jesus (Jonah 1:15; Luke 8:24).[195] The implication that Jesus is YHWH, who alone can calm the sea and rescue the perishing,[196] is further confirmed when the disciples respond to Jesus with fear—just as Jonah's shipmates had responded to YHWH with fear (Jonah 1:16; Luke 8:25).[197]

A vital key to interpreting the Lukan passage is the direction given by the disciples' question, "Who then is this who commands even the winds and the water—and they listen to him?!" (8:25).[198] Their conundrum was not about *how* Jesus could demonstrate God's power (as a divinely appointed agent), but about *who* Jesus was ontologically.[199] The disciples were Jewish monotheists. And yet, Jesus spoke, behaved, and effected supernatural miracles with the "power of the Lord" (cf. 5:17) as if he were God

---

[190] Cf. Hays, *Echoes of Scripture in the Gospels*, 255; Gadenz, *The Gospel of Luke*, 163. Edwards, *The Gospel According to Luke*, 245, points out, "The word for 'Master,' *epistatēs*, occurs in the NT only in Luke, always in reference to Jesus, and all save one from the mouth of disciples."

[191] Cf. Nolland, *Luke 1–9:20*, 400.

[192] Cf. Just, *Luke 1:1–9:50*, 358.

[193] Cf. Just, *Luke 1:1–9:50*, 358–59; Edwards, *The Gospel According to Luke*, 245–46.

[194] Cf. Edwards, *The Gospel According to Luke*, 245; Gadenz, *The Gospel of Luke*, 163.

[195] Cf. Edwards, *The Gospel According to Luke*, 245–46; Garland, *Luke*, 356.

[196] Channing L. Crisler, *Echoes of Lament and the Christology of Luke* (University of Sheffield: Sheffield Phoenix Press, 2020), 181, writes, "Jesus' ability to answer a lament at sea by commanding the winds and the waves is only paralleled by Yhwh himself (Ps. 106.23–29 LXX)."

[197] Green, *The Gospel of Luke*, 334, writes, "Jesus' companions in the boat react as they would to a theophany, with fear; but their amazement, followed by their uncertainty about Jesus' identity, indicates that they do not yet fathom what they have seen." Cf. Chen, *Luke*, 114; Hendriksen, *Luke*, 441; Morris, *Luke*, 174; Nolland, *Luke 1–9:20*, 400–1; Stein, *Luke*, 254; Klein, *Das Lukasevangelium*, 314; Thompson, *Luke*, 137–38.

[198] Hays, *Echoes of Scripture in the Gospels*, 255, calls it "the looming theological question of Jesus' identity." Cf. Morris, *Luke*, 174; Stein, *Luke*, 253; Edwards, *The Gospel According to Luke*, 246; Thompson, *Luke*, 138; Garland, *Luke*, 357.

[199] Most commentators recognize the disciples' *Who?* question as underscoring Jesus's identity. Cf. Nolland, *Luke 1–9:20*, 401; Stein, *Luke*, 253; Hays, *Echoes of Scripture in the Gospels*, 255; Thompson, *Luke*, 138; Chen, *Luke*, 114. Malina and Rohrbaugh, *Social-Science Commentary on the Synoptic Gospels*, 259, however, assert, "The disciples' question in this verse is not one of 'identity' as a modem reader would assume. It is one of status or honor.... It asks about Jesus' location in the hierarchy of powers." Their interpretation appears to err by overemphasizing Greco-Roman thought and overlooking the Jewish Scriptures, since OT YHWH-texts clearly inform Jesus's actions and their Lukan portrayal.

himself.²⁰⁰ He harnessed the raging elements, as YHWH had done in Jonah and as only YHWH does elsewhere in Scripture (e.g., Pss 89:9; 104:6–7; 107:23–30).²⁰¹ The disciples' question, in effect, invites its hearers to apply OT YHWH-texts to Jesus as the supernatural master of the natural elements.

Luke 9:26–36

Jesus's transfiguration has been treated in the comments at Mark 9:1–8. However, since Luke's account includes two verses not found in either Matthew or Mark, and since the application of OT YHWH-texts to Jesus may at first seem incongruent to an event in which Jesus appears distinct from the divine voice, a discussion of Luke 9:28–36 seems necessary to this study. Jesus's prediction of his glorious coming in 9:26–27 shall be treated in this section, as well.

Luke's account of the Transfiguration, like those of Matthew and Mark, is prefaced by Jesus's predictions of (1) the glorious coming of the Son of Man and (2) the beholding of God's kingdom by "some of those who are standing here" prior to their deaths (9:26–27).²⁰² Many scholars agree that the Transfiguration immediately follows these predictions in all the Synoptic Gospels as their partial and/or proleptic fulfillment—particularly of Jesus's second prediction that some of his disciples would be eyewitnesses of God's kingdom.²⁰³

The Lukan account is unique in that what the other Synoptists describe as the Son the Man coming "in the glory of his Father" (ἐν τῇ δόξῃ τοῦ πατρὸς αὐτοῦ; Matt 16:27; Mark 8:38), Luke describes as the Son of Man coming "in his glory, and that of the Father" (ἐν τῇ δόξῃ αὐτοῦ καὶ τοῦ πατρός; Luke 9:26).²⁰⁴ Luke's emphasis on Jesus coming in *his own* glory cannot be a grammatical ambiguity or copyist error, since he repeats the phrase "his glory" as part of his unique material in 9:31–32.²⁰⁵ Thus, by recording Jesus's prediction that some of his disciples would not die "until they *see* God's kingdom" (9:27), and then narrating that three of them "*saw* his glory" (9:32), Luke confirmed the identity of the Son of Man in his glory (9:26) as the transfigured Jesus (9:32).²⁰⁶ Allusively, therefore, Luke connected YHWH-texts of the Exodus (esp.

---

²⁰⁰ Cf. Fitzmyer, *The Gospel According to Luke*, 728; Nolland, *Luke 1–9:20*, 400; Green, *The Gospel of Luke*, 333; Klein, *Das Lukasevangelium*, 314; Edwards, *The Gospel According to Luke*, 244; Chen, *Luke*, 113.
²⁰¹ Cf. Nolland, *Luke 1–9:20*, 401; Grundmann, *Das Evangelium Nach Lukas*, 180; Fitzmyer, *The Gospel According to Luke*, 728, 730; Stein, *Luke*, 253; Bock, *Luke*, 762; Culpepper, "The Gospel of Luke," 184; Pao and Schnabel, "Luke," 308; Edwards, *The Gospel According to Luke*, 246; Chen, *Luke*, 113–14; Gadenz, *The Gospel of Luke*, 163.
²⁰² Gadenz, *The Gospel of Luke*, 183, notes, "This is the first time that Jesus mentions his second coming (12:40; 17:24; 18:8; 21:27). It is also the clearest allusion so far to the figure mentioned in Daniel."
²⁰³ Cf. Ellis, *The Gospel of Luke*, 142; Johnson, *The Gospel of Luke*, 152, 156; Green, *The Gospel of Luke*, 380; David L. Jeffrey, *Luke* (Grand Rapids, MI: Brazos, 2012), 141.
²⁰⁴ Cf. Fitzmyer, *The Gospel According to Luke*, 789; Johnson, *The Gospel of Luke*, 152; Edwards, *The Gospel According to Luke*, 277. Stein, *Luke*, 280, interprets, "Luke heightened the Christological nature of this saying by attributing personal glory to Jesus (Luke 21:27; 24:26)."
²⁰⁵ Cf. Arthur Michael Ramsey, *The Glory of God and the Transfiguration of Christ* (London; New York; Toronto: Longmans, Green and Co., 1949), 40; Johnson, *The Gospel of Luke*, 156.
²⁰⁶ Cf. Edwards, *The Gospel According to Luke*, 277; Marshall, *The Gospel of Luke*, 376; Johnson, *The Gospel of Luke*, 156. Contra Malina and Rohrbaugh, *Social-Science Commentary on the Synoptic Gospels*, 264.

Exod 24:1–2, 15–18; 34:4–7, 29–35) and the Danielic Son of Man (esp. Dan 7:9–10, 13–14), and applied both backgrounds to Jesus.²⁰⁷

The rest of the Lukan account supports this. Not only does the Transfiguration prediction in 9:26–27 recall Dan 7:9–14 (cf. overlapping terminology: son of man; came/coming; glory; myriads/angels; kingdom), but the Transfiguration narrative in 9:28–36 incorporates Danielic descriptions of YHWH (the Ancient of Days) for Jesus. Luke writes of Jesus, "his clothing became dazzling white" (ὁ ἱματισμὸς αὐτοῦ λευκὸς ἐξαστράπτων; 9:29), recalling what Daniel wrote of the Ancient of Days, "his garment was white as snow" (τὸ ἔνδυμα αὐτοῦ λευκὸν ὡσεὶ χιών; Dan 7:9).²⁰⁸ Likewise, the cloud of God's presence from which the divine voice exalts Jesus (Luke 9:34–35) recalls the clouds that would accompany the Danielic Son of Man (Dan 7:13).²⁰⁹ The narrative end of the Transfiguration—"when the voice had spoken, Jesus was found alone"— points to Jesus as the ultimate tabernacle of God's presence, the one to whom the glory-cloud attested and whose identity was far greater than Peter had imagined (9:33).²¹⁰ In other words, in the Lukan narrative Jesus's identity includes both the Danielic Son of Man and the Ancient of Days (YHWH).²¹¹

Transfiguration allusions to YHWH at the Exodus abound, as well.²¹² As Moses ascended a mountain with three companions to meet with YHWH in the glory-cloud,

---

²⁰⁷ Similarly, Johnson, *The Gospel of Luke*, 153–54; Ellis, *The Gospel of Luke*, 142; Pao and Schnabel, "Luke," 311.

²⁰⁸ Cf. Gadenz, *The Gospel of Luke*, 185; Johnson, *The Gospel of Luke*, 133; perhaps also, Grundmann, *Das Evangelium Nach Lukas*, 192; Marshall, *The Gospel of Luke*, 382. Klein, *Das Lukasevangelium*, 346, likens Jesus in his glory to the angels. But that misses the narrative emphasis of Jesus having his own glory (Luke 9:26, 32; cf. 24:26). Furthermore, in the Matthean parallel the angels belong to Jesus: Matt 16:27. He is not one of them; he is their Lord.

²⁰⁹ Cf. Green, *The Gospel of Luke*, 375. Of course, the glory-cloud is also a prime feature at Sinai and throughout the Exodus: cf. John Nolland, *Luke 9:21–18:34* (Nashville, TN: Nelson, 2008), 501; Johnson, *The Gospel of Luke*, 153; Pao and Schnabel, "Luke," 311. This is because the glory-cloud was a visible representation of God's presence: cf. Fitzmyer, *The Gospel According to Luke*, 802; Morris, *Luke*, 191; Garland, *Luke*, 395. Thus, the glory-cloud would also mark the unique presence of God in the tabernacle/temple: cf. Jeffrey, *Luke*, 141; Edwards, *The Gospel According to Luke*, 283–84; Gadenz, *The Gospel of Luke*, 187.

²¹⁰ Cf. Edwards, *The Gospel According to Luke*, 283–84; Gadenz, *The Gospel of Luke*, 187.

²¹¹ Quarles, "Lord or Legend," 111, adds that the two figures were even identified as one in a (likely) pre-Christian version of Daniel: "The Old Greek text of Dan 7:9–14 contains a reading different from that which appears in the MT and Theodotian. Both the MT and Theodotian's version distinguish the Son of Man from the Ancient of Days. In the Old Greek text, the Ancient of Days and the 'one like a son of man' refer to one being, rather than to two separate beings.... καὶ ὡς παλαιὸς ἡμερῶν παρῆν... and he was coming like the Ancient of Days.... This reading is supported by the earliest known manuscript of the LXX, MS 967, which dates to the second century. Although some scholars argue that the Septuagint reading is a product of unintentional scribal error which mistook ἕως for ὡς most critics now conclude that the original Greek translation equated the Son of Man and Ancient of Days to express a carefully thought-out interpretation of the Aramaic text."

²¹² Since Luke reveals the topic of discussion between Jesus and his prophetic predecessors, Moses and Elijah, as "his [Jesus's] exodus" (τὴν ἔξοδον αὐτοῦ; Luke 9:31), many scholars recognize a deliberate comparison between Jesus's Transfiguration and Israel's Exodus/deliverance by the manifest presence of YHWH. Cf. Craddock, *Luke*, 133–34; Johnson, *The Gospel of Luke*, 153; Culpepper, "The Gospel of Luke," 206–7; Just, *Luke 1:1–9:50*, 402; Green, *The Gospel of Luke*, 377; Pao and Schnabel, "Luke," 311; Edwards, *The Gospel According to Luke*, 282; Chen, *Luke*, 131; Susan Maxwell, Booth, *The Tabernacling Presence of God* (Eugene, OR: Wipf & Stock, 2015), 132.

so did Jesus.[213] But the merely human Moses, a type, was eclipsed by the ontologically superior Jesus.[214] Moses' face reflected the glory of YHWH (Exod 34:29–35; cf. 2 Cor 3:7, 13), but Jesus's face exuded his own glory (Luke 9:29, 32; cf. 2 Cor 3:18; 4:4, 6).[215] Moses (and the Israelites from a distance) witnessed light flashes (LXX: ἀστραπαί) from the cloud of YHWH's presence (Exod 19:16; cf. 20:18–21), but light was flashing from (ἐξαστράπτων) the very clothing Jesus wore (Luke 9:29).[216] The voice from the cloud before Aaron, Nadab, and Abihu spoke to Moses as mediator of the divine Law, but the voice from the cloud before Peter, James, and John told them to obey the words of Jesus as God's Son.[217] The mediatorial agency of Jesus as the fulfillment of a "new Moses" is not thereby denied, but the qualitatively higher authority of Jesus eclipsed that of even the greatest human prophets, Moses and Elijah.[218] The Transfiguration was essentially portrayed as a theophany.[219] This is achieved in part—and not so subtly—by applying OT YHWH-texts to Jesus.

---

[213] Cf. Fitzmyer, *The Gospel According to Luke*, 802; Nolland, *Luke 9:21–18:34*, 501, 503; Craddock, *Luke*, 133; Johnson, *The Gospel of Luke*, 153–54; Just, *Luke 1:1–9:50*, 402; Edwards, *The Gospel According to Luke*, 284; J. Ryan Lister, *The Presence of God* (Wheaton, IL: Crossway, 2015), 259–60.

[214] Similarly, Nolland, *Luke 9:21–18:34*, 503; Gadenz, *The Gospel of Luke*, 185; Beale and Gladd, *The Story Retold*, 114–15.

[215] Cf. Stein, *Luke*, 284; Green, *The Gospel of Luke*, 380; Garland, *Luke*, 392; Jeffrey, *Luke*, 141; Beale and Gladd, *The Story Retold*, 115.

[216] Nolland, *Luke 9:21–18:34*, 498, comments, "Much more economically than Mark, Luke has Jesus' garments becoming λευκὸς ἐξαστράπτων, 'a white that flashes [like lightning].' The verb here is used in the LXX of Ezek 1:4, 7 in connection with outskirts of God's glory, as Ezekiel sees God upon his throne. It occurs also in the LXX of Dan 12:6, with reference to the splendid heavenly figure encountered by Daniel in a vision." Cf. Johnson, *The Gospel of Luke*, 152; Garland, *Luke*, 392; Booth, *The Tabernacling Presence of God*, 132.

[217] The command of the divine voice to Jesus's disciples, "Listen to him!," recalls Moses' prediction to the Israelites that YHWH would "raise up for you a prophet like me.... [and] you shall listen to him!" (Deut 18:15). Cf. Fitzmyer, *The Gospel According to Luke*, 803; Johnson, *The Gospel of Luke*, 156; Pao and Schnabel, "Luke," 312. The divine voice makes clear, however, that Jesus eclipses the merely human prophets, Moses and Elijah, because Jesus is God's "chosen (i.e., fore-loved)" *Son*, implying pre-existent divinity in his absolute authority. Cf. Bovon, *Luke 1: A Commentary on the Gospel of Luke 1:1–9:50*, 379; Garland, *Luke*, 397–98; Chen, *Luke*, 131.

[218] Cf. Garland, *Luke*, 397–98; Stein, *Luke*, 286; Fitzmyer, *The Gospel According to Luke*, 803; Nolland, *Luke 9:21–18:34*, 503; Craddock, *Luke*, 134; Bovon, *Luke 1*, 378–79.

[219] This is not to deny the obvious theophany of the glory-cloud from which came the divine voice. It is merely to point out that in the Transfiguration Jesus emanated his own glory (like the Ancient of Days in Daniel 7 and YHWH at Sinai) and was confirmed by the divine Voice to have an authority greater than the greatest prophets. Johnson, *The Gospel of Luke*, 152, perhaps under-interprets the Transfiguration as a kratophany, although conceptually the manifestation of the sacred may overlap with the manifestation of deity. Lanier, "Luke's Distinctive Use of the Temple," 452–53, is certainly correct to connect the Transfiguration of Jesus with the Lukan theme of divine visitation by Jesus. Similarly, Edwards, *The Gospel According to Luke*, 284, correctly interprets the Transfiguration as showing Jesus to be the (true) tabernacle/temple of divine presence. Cf. Gadenz, *The Gospel of Luke*, 187; Beale and Gladd, *The Story Retold*, 114–15; Lister, *The Presence of God*, 259–60, 263. In multiple ways, therefore, the Transfiguration may be called a theophany.

Luke 11:20–23

Luke's account of Jesus's claim to conquer "the strong man"[220] (11:17–23) is longer than Mark's account (3:23–27; see discussion at Mark 3:27) and differs from Matthew's account (12:25–30) in surprising ways.[221] These differences are partly explained by an increase in allusions to OT YHWH-texts applied to Jesus in the Lukan pericope. Allusions revolve around three phrases from Jesus's speech: "the finger of God" (11:20), "the mightier one" (11:22), and "whoever does not gather with me scatters" (11:23). Each phrase of itself could appear ambiguous to the reader. But as a part of a cluster, each phrase strengthens the likelihood of allusion to YHWH-texts by the others.

Luke is the only Evangelist to use the phrase "by the finger of God" (ἐν δακτύλῳ θεοῦ), which is all the more peculiar since Matthew's parallel has "by the Spirit of God" (ἐν πνεύματι θεοῦ; Matt 12:28)—a rendering which seems more in line with Lukan theology.[222] But this unexpected verbal choice, whether original to Jesus or interpretive of Luke,[223] only strengthens the probability that Luke deliberately identified Jesus with YHWH by allusions to OT YHWH-texts.[224] In the OT, "the finger(s) of God" refers to YHWH's personal power and authority in creation (Ps 8:3), miracles (Exod 8:19), and written revelation (Exod 31:18; Deut 9:10; cf. Dan 5:5, 25–28).[225] Many commentators believe that Jesus's use of the phrase for himself harkens back specifically to YHWH's redemptive miracles of the ten plagues (cf. Exod 8:19),[226] although some believe Jesus

---

[220] Not many scholars deny that Jesus was describing himself as the "mightier one" in Luke 11:22, since the point of his illustration was to explain why he had just cast out a demon. Cf. Marshall, *The Gospel of Luke*, 478.

[221] Many scholars recognize a triple tradition parallel here of the same event: e.g., Kurt Aland, ed., *Synopsis Quattuor Evangeliorum*, 2nd ed. (Stuttgart, Germany: Deutsche Bibelgesellschaft, 1985), 165–76, 558. Some scholars, however, surmise that Luke's account must be describing a separate incident: e.g., Thomas and Gundry, *A Harmony of the Gospels*, 9, 11, 77–78, and especially, 139. The position taken here is that the Synoptic writers have described the same event. However, separating Luke's account from the others does not alter the argument that his narrative appears to apply OT YHWH-texts to Jesus in a generous fashion.

[222] Morris, *Luke*, 216, merely calls this difference "rather curious." Johnson, *The Gospel of Luke*, 181, believes it is unexpected, except that Luke is making "a deliberate allusion to Exod 8:19."

[223] Many commentators believe that Luke's "finger of God" is original: e.g., Ellis, *The Gospel of Luke*, 167; Stein, *Luke*, 331; François Bovon, *Luke 2*, trans. Donald S. Deer (Minneapolis, MN: Fortress Press, 2013), 121. Nolland, *Luke 9:21–18:34*, 639, however, believes Luke altered the text.

[224] Garland, *Luke*, 483, citing Edward J. Woods, *The Finger of God and Pneumatology in Luke-Acts* (Sheffield, UK: Sheffield Academic Press, 2001), 243, adds, "The phrase 'the finger of God' derives from the Old Testament; there are 'no *known* convincing parallels' to this expression in Greek or Roman literature" (emphasis Woods).

[225] Sigurd Grindheim, *God's Equal* (London; New York: T&T Clark, 2011), 30, interprets the phrase as "sovereign intervention"; Green, *The Gospel of Luke*, 457, as "active power"; Garland, *Luke*, 483, as "creative power." Stein, *Luke*, 331, comments that both *Spirit of God* (Matt 12:28) and *finger of God* (Luke 11:20) "refer to God's power."

[226] Cf. Ellis, *The Gospel of Luke*, 167; Nolland, *Luke 9:21–18:34*, 639; Johnson, *The Gospel of Luke*, 181; Green, *The Gospel of Luke*, 457; Pao and Schnabel, "Luke," 323; Edwards, *The Gospel According to Luke*, 345; Thompson, *Luke*, 188; Grindheim, *God's Equal*, 30. Jeffrey, *Luke*, 159, however, suggests that Dan 5:5–6, 24–28, is "perhaps yet more pertinent in this context."

was laying claim to a greater creative and redemptive authority.[227] Since "the finger of God" in the OT always refers to the personal intervention of YHWH and not to the instrumentality of creature-agents,[228] it seems clear that Jesus was claiming for himself the prerogative of divine sovereignty even over the supernatural powers of Satan.[229]

Jesus's description in Luke 11:21–22 of "a mightier one" (ἰσχυρότερος) who conquers "the mighty one" (ὁ ἰσχυρός) appears to be another allusion to OT YHWH-texts.[230] The primary source is most likely Isa 49:24–26, in which YHWH promised that the prey/captives (= children of Israel in exile) "shall be saved from the mighty one" (παρὰ ἰσχύοντος σωθήσεται; LXX) so that "all flesh shall know that I am YHWH your Savior, and your Redeemer, the Mighty One (ἰσχύος) of Jacob."[231] Apparently, Jesus used this self-identifying promise of YHWH to rescue Israelites from bondage to the mighty one (Babylon) to explain how he was able to rescue an Israelite from bondage to the mighty one (Beelzebul).[232] The Lukan addition of Jesus claiming to take the mighty man's armor and distribute his spoil (Luke 11:22) may also be a play on Isa 53:12, in which the Servant of YHWH would divide his spoil among "the many" who (because the Servant bore their iniquities; cf. 53:11) are then ironically recast as "the mighty ones."[233]

Finally, Jesus concluded his strong man illustration by identifying himself as the defining figure of God's mission in what seems to be more allusions to YHWH-texts. First, Jesus's words, "Whoever is not with me is against me" (Luke 11:23a), echo the sentiment of YHWH to Joshua (Josh 5:13; cf. 6:2), revealing that the only two categories

---

[227] Garland, *Luke*, 483, comments, "Both of these contexts [i.e., the ten plagues in Exod 8:19 and the ten words in Exod 31:18; Deut 9:10] may provide a backdrop for understanding Jesus' phrase. The first allusion points to the self-evident nature of Jesus exorcisms that anyone should recognize. They are proof of God's creative power working in human affairs. The second allusion underscores the revelatory character of Jesus' exorcisms that is comparable to God's writing the two tablets of the covenant. These two allusions combined suggest that Jesus' exorcisms reveal God's majesty and creative power." Cf. Grindheim, *God's Equal*, 30, 39.

[228] Edward J. Woods, *The "Finger of God" and Pneumatology in Luke-Acts* (Sheffield, UK: Sheffield Academic Press, 2001), 245, argues "for the *double* nuanced meaning for the 'finger of God' at Lk. 11.20, involving both the meaning of 'deliverance power' recalling Exod. 8.19, and God's 'covenantal revelation' of his Law as at Deut. 9.10" (emphasis Woods). If these nuances do exist, they would seem to imply Jesus's personal intervention (visitation) as YHWH.

[229] Cf. Ben Witherington, *The Christology of Jesus* (Minneapolis, MN: Fortress Press, 1997), 203–4; Grindheim, *God's Equal*, 6, 39; Edwards, *The Gospel According to Luke*, 345.

[230] Cf. Bovon, *Luke 9:51–19:27*, 122; Edwards, *The Gospel According to Luke*, 346.

[231] Cf. Pao and Schnabel, "Luke," 323–24; Bovon, *Luke 9:51–19:27*, 122; Edwards, *The Gospel According to Luke*, 345.

[232] Most interpreters understand Jesus to be portraying himself as the stronger one who plunders Satan the strong one. Cf. Marshall, *The Gospel of Luke*, 478; Morris, *Luke*, 215–16; Green, *The Gospel of Luke*, 458; Carroll, *Luke*, 256; Bovon, *Luke 9:51–19:27*, 122; Edwards, *The Gospel According to Luke*, 345–46; Weinandy, *Jesus Becoming Jesus*, 140; Grindheim, *God's Equal*, 30, 39.

[233] The verbal comparisons seem to support this allusion. Luke 11:22 has "a stronger one ... his spoils he distributes" (ἰσχυρότερος ... τὰ σκῦλα αὐτοῦ διαδίδωσιν), which is not far from Isa 53:12: "of the strong ones he divides the spoils" (τῶν ἰσχυρῶν μεριεῖ σκῦλα). Cf. Nolland, *Luke 9:21–18:34*, 642; Pao and Schnabel, "Luke," 324. Hendriksen, *Luke*, 621, sees a conceptual connection to Ps 68:18, though this seems less probable.

of humanity are defined with reference to YHWH/Jesus.[234] Second, and more likely, Jesus identified himself with YHWH as the gatherer of his people in the eschaton. His language in Luke 11:23b harkens back to the Prophets, where YHWH promised to gather personally his scattered people/sheep (e.g., Isa 56:8; Jer 23:1–3; Ezek 34:11–13, 20–24). Jesus appears to place himself in the position of YHWH by allusion to these texts, as well as those previously mentioned in the current pericope.[235]

Luke 12:49

Jesus's purpose statement, "I came to cast fire upon the earth" (Πῦρ ἦλθον βαλεῖν ἐπὶ τὴν γῆν), is unique to Luke among the Gospels.[236] But it would have sounded familiar to his Jewish disciples as an allusion to OT YHWH-texts.[237] The image recalls fiery judgments upon Sodom and Gomorrah (Gen 19:24), Korah's 250 rebels against Moses (Num 16:35; Ps 78:21), Ahab's 450 prophets of Baal (1 Kg 18:38), and Ahaziah's 100 messengers for Baal-zebub (2 Kgs 1:2–16).[238] David, Isaiah, and YHWH himself in the prophets predicted that YHWH would send or rain down fire from heaven as part of his judgment on the wicked of the earth (cf. Ps 11:6; Isa 66:15–16; Ezek 38:22; 39:6; Amos 1:4, 7, 10, 12; 2:2, 5; Zeph 3:8; Mal 3:1–2; 4:1).[239] There are several reasons to believe that Jesus was claiming YHWH's prerogative as divine Judge by applying such texts as these to himself.[240]

First, Jesus's claim to have *come* for the purpose of casting fire implies both an otherworldly origin and preexistence.[241] Second, his claimed prerogative is

---

[234] Edwards, *The Gospel According to Luke*, 346, comments, "The present saying ... is in fact an example of 'implicit Christology,' i.e., a claim Jesus makes of himself that no human being could make of himself or herself. Jesus places himself in a separate class from disciples, for only Jesus can bind the strong man (v. 22; Mark 3:27)." Cf. Green, *The Gospel of Luke*, 458. This point is strengthened by the NT (Jude 1:9) affirmation of the OT (Zech 3:2) that the high angel Michael dared not attempt to rebuke Satan, let alone overthrow him. Apparently, Jesus enjoys a greater authority/identity than even the greatest angel.

[235] Cf. Weinandy, *Jesus Becoming Jesus*, 140, commenting on the Matthean parallel. Many scholars recognize OT prerogatives of YHWH here applied to Jesus: e.g., Witherington, *The Christology of Jesus*, 203–4; Edwards, *The Gospel According to Luke*, 346; Grindheim, *God's Equal*, 30, 39, 42, 59.

[236] Cf. Marshall, *The Gospel of Luke*, 545. Nolland, *Luke 9:21–18:34*, 707–8, discusses possible origins.

[237] See discussion below. Also, the likelihood of the disciples knowing this background is supported by the prior request of James and John to "tell fire to come down from heaven and consume" a non-receptive Samaritan village (Luke 9:54). Cf. Bovon, *Luke 9:51–19:27*, 249. The vast difference, however, is between the disciples requesting permission from Jesus (who rebuked them for it; 9:54–55) and Jesus claiming the prerogative for himself (12:49).

[238] Scholars differ over which OT event(s) may supply the primary allusion to Jesus's claim: e.g., Strauss, "Christology and Christological Purpose in the Synoptic Gospels," 58, suggests Gen 19:24; Johnson, *The Gospel of Luke*, 207, suggests 1 Kgs 18:36–40 and 2 Kgs 1:10, 12, 14; Bovon, *Luke 9:51–19:27*, 249, suggests Gen 19:24 and 2 Kgs 1:10–24.

[239] A variety of other scholars emphasize an OT prophetic background to Jesus's claim: e.g., Hendriksen, *Luke*, 82; Pao and Schnabel, "Luke," 332; Chen, *Luke*, 188.

[240] Cf. Nolland, *Luke 9:21–18:34*, 708; Hendriksen, *Luke*, 682; Bock, *Luke*, 1192. Edwards, *The Gospel According to Luke*, 384.

[241] Simon J. Gathercole, *The Preexistent Son: Recovering the Christologies of Matthew, Mark, and Luke* (Grand Rapids, MI: Eerdmans, 2006), 161–63, writes, "This saying from Luke 12.49 is one of those which is most clearly undergirded by a theology of preexistence. Not only does it share the features

Luke's Application of YHWH-Texts to Jesus 151

unquestionably that of adjudicating the Final Assize: Jesus himself is the one who casts the divine fire of judgment, and the whole earth is the scope of his jurisdiction.[242] Third, Jesus chose several verbal and conceptual connections to YHWH-texts of Judgment.[243] Greek terms reflecting LXX terminology include the same terms for "come" (e.g., Isa 66:15; Mal 4:1), "fire" (e.g., Ps 11:6; Ezek 38:22), "kindle" (e.g., Amos 1:14; Mal 4:1), "upon" (e.g., Ps 78:21; Amos 1:4, 7, 10, 12), and "the earth" (e.g., Deut 32:22; Zeph 3:8). Conceptually, "casting" fire echoes YHWH's "sending" (e.g., Ezek 39:5; Amos 2:2, 5) and "raining down" (e.g., Gen 19:24; Ps 11:6) fire. Fourth, Jesus's delay in kindling the fire of Judgment was due to his own impending "baptism," which images death by drowning in an overwhelming catastrophe and/or divine judgment (cf. Gen 6:5–8, 17; 7:20–23; Ps 18:4; 42:7; 69:1–2, 14–15; Isa 30:27–28; 43:2; Jon 2:3–6).[244] And fifth, the *completion* (cf. Luke 12:50: ἕως ὅτου τελεσθῇ; "until it should be finished")[245] of Jesus's "baptism" (death by overwhelming punishment)[246] grounds his judicial role[247] to divide even biological families into two classes of humanity—something only YHWH does (cf. Mic 7:5–7; Mal 4:6).[248] Thus, the entire pericope supports Jesus's claim, "I have

---

of the 'I have come' sayings ... but is seems to provide even more explicit indication by making casting fire upon the earth the goal of Jesus' coming.... Jesus' coming means his bringing something to the world from the outside. (Would it make sense to talk of 'casting' onto the earth from the earth?) In any case, the sheer scale of the claim to be bringing divine judgment of such a catastrophic kind also points to an extremely exalted status for Jesus. He clearly stands, here, over against the rest of humanity." Cf. Stein, *Luke*, 365; Thompson, *Luke*, 214; Stephen J. Wellum, "The Deity of Christ in the Synoptic Gospels," in *The Deity of Christ*, ed. Christopher W. Morgan and Robert A. Peterson (Wheaton, IL: Crossway, 2011), 86.

[242] Cf. Bock, *Luke*, 1192; Gathercole, *The Preexistent Son*, 162; Bovon, *Luke 9:51–19:27*, 249; Edwards, *The Gospel According to Luke*, 384. This focus on Final Judgment, however, does not deny that some purgation and purification are accomplished by Christ between his atoning death and Parousia. Rather, as the passage implies by Jesus's division of families, the fire Jesus would kindle after his judicial death ("baptism"; 12:50) would burn until its consummate manifestation at the Great Assize. Cf. Nolland, *Luke 9:21–18:34*, 708, 710.

[243] Gathercole, *The Preexistent Son*, 162, underscores the primary implication of Jesus's verbal allusions to YHWH-texts here: "Although Elijah is able on one occasion to call down fire from heaven, he merely prays for it; he is not himself the bringer or the sender. As a result, the claim to be able to *bring* fire to the earth is an implicit claim, if anything, to divine rather than prophetic identity. In fact, the closest parallels to the action of Jesus described here are perhaps also the coming of the Lord with fire in Micah 1 or, more probably, the Lord's destruction of Sodom and Gomorrah in Genesis 19." Similarly, see Wellum, "The Deity of Christ in the Synoptic Gospels," 86–87.

[244] Cf. Bock, *Luke*, 1194; Plummer, *The Gospel According to St. Luke*, 334; Stein, *Luke*, 365; Garland, *Luke*, 530; Edwards, *The Gospel According to Luke*, 384; Chen, *Luke*, 188.

[245] Cf. Nolland, *Luke 9:21–18:34*, 709; Bock, *Luke*, 1193; Garland, *Luke*, 530.

[246] Cf. Chen, *Luke*, 188; Plummer, *The Gospel According to St. Luke*, 334; Garland, *Luke*, 530; Edwards, *The Gospel According to Luke*, 384.

[247] Edwards, *The Gospel According to Luke*, 384, writes, "The use of 'baptism' as a metaphor of Jesus' impending death is evidence that he foresaw both his death in Jerusalem and its atoning significance (Mark 10:45). The death of Jesus in Jerusalem is a precondition of the coming fire, and like 'fire,' 'baptism' inaugurates the fulfillment of God s will. Vv. 49–50 are an important window into Jesus' Christological self-understanding, for he is conscious that his person and mission cannot be separated from the ultimate 'fire' and 'baptism' to which the world will be subjected." Cf. Marshall, *The Gospel of Luke*, 547.

[248] Stein, *Luke*, 365, comments, "This verse alludes to Mic 7:6 and gives specific examples of the forthcoming division. No doubt Luke would have seen in this a fulfillment of Scripture.... The implied Christology of this passage should not be overlooked. Once again Jesus was speaking of his divine mission. 'I have come'; 'I have a baptism'; 'I came to bring.' Luke clearly understood Jesus as the

come to cast fire upon the earth," as an allusion to YHWH-texts bearing application to himself.[249]

Luke 13:34

The wording of Jesus's lament in Luke 13:34 is virtually the same as that in Matthew 23:37.[250] Jesus's central allusion to YHWH-texts is found in his expressed desire to gather Jerusalem's children as a hen gathers her brood under her wings.[251] Theoretically, this claim could have been expressed by a mere leader—a prophet, priest, or king—of Israel, except that the Lukan context demands understanding Jesus's words as the personal desire of YHWH.[252]

First, YHWH is the only OT figure who compared his relationship to Israel as that of a mother bird to her young.[253] He introduced the figure to describe himself bearing the Israelites on eagles' wings during the Exodus (Exod 19:4)—a thought repeated in the Song of Moses (Deut 32:11) and serving as inspiration for Israel's worship of YHWH who provided refuge in the shelter of his wings (cf. Pss 17:8; 36:7; 57:1; 61:4; 63:7; 91:4). Second, Jesus claimed that his desire to gather his people ("Jerusalem") to himself ("under her wings") was a longstanding concern with repeated attempts ("How often . . .!").[254] On the surface, Jesus's expression of frequency does not make sense of

---

one who has come in fulfillment of the OT. He was also the one over whom all humanity is divided. Not only did Jesus bring division in this life, but this division continues in eternity, for the final judgment is dependent upon one's attitude toward Jesus (Luke 12:8–9; 9:26). Again the question must be raised, Who is this who makes such claims?" Cf. Nolland, *Luke 9:21–18:34*, 709–10; Bock, *Luke*, 1192–93, 1195.

[249] For similar conclusions, see Gathercole, *The Preexistent Son*, 162; Wellum, "The Deity of Christ in the Synoptic Gospels," 86; Edwards, *The Gospel According to Luke*, 384.

[250] Cf. Gathercole, *The Preexistent Son*, 220; Jonathan Rowlands, "Jesus and the Wings of YHWH: Bird Imagery in the Lament over Jerusalem (Matt 23:37–39; Luke 13:34–35)," *NovT* 61 (2019): 115.

[251] Virtually every commentator ties Jesus's hen-with-wings metaphor for himself to similar OT metaphors for YHWH: e.g., Grundmann, *Das Evangelium Nach Lukas*, 289; Marshall, *The Gospel of Luke*, 575–76; Nolland, *Luke 9:21–18:34*, 742; Johnson, *The Gospel of Luke*, 218–19; Stein, *Luke*, 384; Bock, *Luke*, 1249; Culpepper, "The Gospel of Luke," 282; Green, *The Gospel of Luke*, 539; Klein, *Das Lukasevangelium*, 494; Pao and Schnabel, "Luke," 336; Bovon, *Luke 9:51–19:27*, 328; Edwards, *The Gospel According to Luke*, 407; Hays, *Echoes of Scripture in the Gospels*, 261; Thompson, *Luke*, 227; Chen, *Luke*, 199; Lanier, *Old Testament Conceptual Metaphors and the Christology of Luke's Gospel*, 167; Gadenz, *The Gospel of Luke*, 262.

[252] See supporting arguments below. Rowlands, "Jesus and the Wings of YHWH," 132–33, summarizes, "Jesus claims to *be* YHWH, not merely to be acting on the part of YHWH or to be an emissary for YHWH. This claim is *ontological* rather than *economic*; it primarily concerns who Jesus *is*, not what he *does*. . . . How reasonable is it to suggest the evangelists used this imagery to portray Jesus as YHWH? I suggest it is preferable to alternative readings since it has greater explanatory power regarding the bird imagery. . . . The image of a protective bird in the HB is only ever used to refer to YHWH himself and never to any intermediaries of YHWH" (emphasis Rowlands).

[253] Cf. Rowlands, "Jesus and the Wings of YHWH," 133; Chen, *Luke*, 199.

[254] Hays, *Echoes of Scripture in the Gospels*, 261, captures the sense well when he writes, "[Jesus's] lament portrays Jerusalem as rejecting the protection he has repeatedly sought to give (even though Luke's narrative makes no mention of any previous visits by Jesus to Jerusalem!), just as Israel in Deuteronomy 32 is portrayed as a stubborn people who have forgotten the God who gave them birth (Deut 32:15–18). Who then should we understand to be the speaker in Luke 13:34? These daring words can hardly be merely the complaint of a rejected prophet. They are nothing other than a cry from the heart of Israel's God."

the Lukan narrative, in which no visit of Jesus to Jerusalem as an adult has yet been recorded.[255] However, in the Lukan metanarrative, which has been emphasizing the visitation of YHWH to Israel (Luke 1:68, 78; 7:16; cf. 19:44) in the preexistent "Lord" Jesus (1:17, 43, 76; 2:11; 3:4-6; 7:26-27), Jesus's claim only verifies the big picture: YHWH has come again to his people in Jesus, yet they have largely refused to come under his protection.[256]

Third, Jesus's lament echoes the laments of YHWH for his people to return to him.[257] Fourth, Jesus lamented the persecutions and murders of the Old Covenant prophets as if he himself had sent the prophets and then arrived as their superior.[258] This interpretation is shortly confirmed by Jesus's Parable of the Wicked Tenants (20:9-18)[259] and the resultant opposition against Jesus by Jerusalem's leaders (20:19-20). And fifth, Jesus's use of Ps 118 implied that he himself had forsaken Jerusalem's "house" (whether that be the temple, city, or nation)[260] and would remain unseen by them until they declared that he was coming in the name of the Lord/YHWH (Luke 13:35).[261] These features support the interpretation that Jesus identified as YHWH by applying YHWH-texts, such as Deut 32:11 and Ps 91:4, to himself.[262]

Luke 17:20-37; 21:25-28; 22:69-70

Luke records three major occasions of Jesus making eschatological predictions after his pre-Transfiguration prediction in 9:26-27.[263] Although each prediction varies as to its contextual audience—Jesus's disciples (17:22), a crowd at the temple (21:1), and the Sanhedrin after his arrest (22:66)—they display a thematic overlap which may be

---

[255] Cf. Gathercole, *The Preexistent Son*, 220; Hays, *Echoes of Scripture in the Gospels*, 261. Furthermore, the Matthean parallel more clearly ties Jesus's frequent attempts to gather his people with the generations of prophets who preceded his coming (cf. Matt 23:29-37).

[256] Cf. Stein, *Luke*, 384; Bock, *Luke*, 1249; Culpepper, "The Gospel of Luke," 282; Klein, *Das Lukasevangelium*, 494; Garland, *Luke*, 560; Snodgrass, *Stories with Intent*, 316.

[257] The background surely includes both YHWH's promise to gather Israel (e.g., Deut 30:1-5; Isa 11:12; Jer 29:14) and Israel's ongoing refusal to return/be gathered to YHWH (e.g., Amos 4:6, 8, 9, 10, 11; Hos 7:10; Jer 3:10, 22). Cf. Edwards, *The Gospel According to Luke*, 407; Garland, *Luke*, 560; Hays, *Echoes of Scripture in the Gospels*, 260-61. Significantly, the next profound lament of Jesus over Jerusalem (Luke 19:41-44) faults the people for not recognizing "the time of your [divine] visitation."

[258] Cf. Thompson, *Luke*, 227. Gathercole, *The Preexistent Son*, 220-21, believes Luke's account portrays Jesus more as a prophet than does Matthew's account, in which Jesus claims to have *sent* the prophets (Matt 23:34). This is true. And yet Luke's portrayal still includes Jesus's claim to have often desired to gather Jerusalem under his own protection—something far beyond the pale of any OT prophet's proclamation and prerogative.

[259] Cf. Bock, *Luke*, 1249; Snodgrass, *Stories with Intent*, 283.

[260] Cf. Fitzmyer, *The Gospel According to Luke*, 1035; Edwards, *The Gospel According to Luke*, 408.

[261] Cf. Rowe, *Early Narrative Christology*, 200; Edwards, *The Gospel According to Luke*, 408; Gathercole, *The Preexistent Son*, 220.

[262] Similarly, Johnson, *The Gospel of Luke*, 218-19; Nolland, *Luke 9:21-18:34*, 742; Hays, *Echoes of Scripture in the Gospels*, 261; Thompson, *Luke*, 227; Lanier, *Old Testament Conceptual Metaphors and the Christology of Luke's Gospel*, 167.

[263] This is not to deny other occasions in Luke when Jesus predicted future events (e.g., 12:8-9, 35-40; 18:7-8, 31-34; 21:34-36), but to acknowledge similarities in emphasis and intensity between these later occasions. Culpepper, "The Gospel of Luke," 332, points out, "These pictures of judgment stand in a series of such warnings in Luke (e.g., 3:17; 6:24-26, 46-49; 10:13-15; 11:29-32; 12:1-3, 49-59; 13:1-9, 34-35)."

summarized as the Son of Man *revealed* (17:30), the Son of Man *coming* (21:27), and the Son the Man *seated* (22:69). Since they are thematically intertwined and collectively allude to OT YHWH-texts, each shall be addressed here in its Lukan sequence.

Luke 17:20–37

This is the longest of Jesus's Son of Man prophecies in the Third Gospel. Jesus first noted the invisible presence of God's reign (17:20–21), before describing its consummate manifestation in judgment by the Son of Man (17:22–37). He clearly referred to the day(s) of the Son of Man (17:22, 24, 26, 30, 31—five rapid mentions) with allusions to the OT Day of YHWH.[264] He characterized "that Day" (17:31) with recognizable theophanic features—the whole sky lit up as with lightning, fire and sulfur rained from heaven (17:24, 29)—to explain how "the Son of Man is revealed" (17:30) "in his Day" (17:24).[265] Other allusions further confirm that Jesus's "Day" includes the Final Assize.[266] As with the destructive fire and sulfur of Lot's time, the Son of Man's "Day" will be like the destructive flood of Noah's time and will feature scavenger birds feeding on human corpses, a signature feature of YHWH's judgments (e.g., Jer 19:7; Ezek 32:4). While all of these elements of Jesus's prophecy imply that he fills the role of YHWH as universal Judge, the centerpiece of the prophecy is the *revealing* of the Son of Man—i.e., Jesus—in his divine identity by theophanic features.[267]

Luke 21:25–28

This passage follows a specific prediction of Jerusalem's destruction (21:20–24) with a more general prediction of cosmic upheaval.[268] And while the cosmic language surely includes Jerusalem, its allusion to YHWH-texts identifies Jesus as universal Judge (cf. "the inhabited earth," 21:26). The centerpiece of this pericope is the bold allusion to Dan 7:13 in Jesus's prediction, "they will see the Son of Man coming in a cloud with

---

[264] Cf. Nolland, *Luke 9:21–18:34*, 859; Bock, *Luke*, 1430; Thompson, *Luke*, 273; Chen, *Luke*, 236.

[265] Crispin H. T. Fletcher-Louis, *Christological Origins*, vol. 1 of *Jesus Monotheism* (Eugene, OR: Wipf & Stock, 2015), 187, notes, "The prediction that at his coming the Son of Man will be like lightning that lights up the whole world (in Matt 24:27) or the whole sky (in the parallel Luke 17:24) is particularly reminiscent of Ps 97:4: 'His (*Yhwh's*—vv. 1, 9, 12) lightnings light up the world, the earth sees and trembles' (see also Pss 18:13–14; 144:6; Zech 9:14)." Cf. Nolland, *Luke 9:21–18:34*, 859; Bock, *Luke*, 1429; Pao and Schnabel, "Luke," 346–47; Garland, *Luke*, 699.

[266] See, Stein, *Luke*, 443.

[267] Garland, *Luke*, 699, notes, "While the parallel saying in Matt 24:27 compares the lightning to 'the coming of the Son of Man,' Luke compares it to the Son of Man himself. Lightning accompanies God's appearances on earth in Exod 19:16–24; 2 Sam 22:15; Pss 18:14; 77:18 (see also *2 Bar.* 53:5–10), and Luke emphasizes the glorification of the Son of Man (see 9:29, where in the transfiguration his garments became 'as a flash of lightning'). Like lightning, the Son of Man's arrival will be sudden, eye-catching, glorious, frightening, and celestial." See also, Bock, *Luke*, 1429–30; Fletcher-Louis, *Christological Origins*, 187; Pao and Schnabel, "Luke," 346–47.

[268] Cf. Green, *The Gospel of Luke*, 740; Carroll, *Luke*, 420; Edwards, *The Gospel According to Luke*, 607.

power and great glory" (Luke 21:27).[269] Although most translations of Daniel distinguish between "one like a Son of Man" and "the Ancient of Days," they may not have been distinguished originally.[270]

More certain, however, is the sharing of YHWH's characteristics and prerogatives with the Son of Man, such that Jesus's claim implies that he is YHWH's equal.[271] The coming of Jesus "in a cloud with power and great glory" (21:27) implies a divine visitation, a prominent Lukan theme.[272] The cosmic portents surrounding Jesus's coming ("signs in sun and moon and stars ... the roaring of the sea and the waves ... the powers of the heavens ... shaken"; 21:25–26) recall portents of divine intervention and judgment.[273] The response of humanity to Jesus's coming ("distress of nations in perplexity ... people fainting with fear and with foreboding of what is coming on the world ... they will see the Son of Man coming"; 21:25–27) further suggests a visitation of God.[274] Or, to put it another way, nothing in Jesus's description of his coming suggests the advent of a creature, whether human or angelic.[275] But the key of this prophecy is in the *coming* of the Son of Man—i.e., Jesus—to punish or to redeem those who dwell "on the earth" (21:25).[276] This is confirmed by Jesus after his fig tree illustration (12:29–33), when he reiterated that "that Day" (21:34) of cosmic judgment "will come upon all who dwell on the face of the whole earth" (21:35), making it vital for his disciples to pray for "strength to escape all these things ... and to stand before the Son of Man" (21:36). Thus, Jesus shall judge as YHWH.[277]

---

[269] Commentators invariably note here the strong allusion in Jesus's self-identifying prophecy in Luke 21:27 to the Danielic Son of Man in Dan 7:13–14: e.g., Darrell L. Bock, "Proclamation from Prophecy and Pattern: Lucan Old Testament Christology" (PhD diss., University of Aberdeen, 1987), 136; Nolland, *Luke 9:21–18:34*, 1006; Stein, *Luke*, 525; Kimball, *Jesus' Exposition of the Old Testament in Luke's Gospel*, 196; Pao and Schnabel, "Luke," 378; Garland, *Luke*, 835; Edwards, *The Gospel According to Luke*, 607–8.

[270] See earlier comments at Luke 9:26–36 on the possibility that the Danielic Son of Man was originally identified "as" the Ancient of Days. Cf. Quarles, "Lord or Legend," 111.

[271] Similarly, Kimball, *Jesus' Exposition of the Old Testament in Luke's Gospel*, 196; Garland, *Luke*, 835; Carroll, *Luke*, 420; Edwards, *The Gospel According to Luke*, 607–8; Nolland, *Luke 9:21–18:34*, 1007; Bock, "Proclamation from Prophecy and Pattern," 136–37.

[272] Passages using the language of visitation include Luke 1:68, 78; 7:16; 19:44. Regarding the Danielic language of coming in a cloud, see, Kimball, *Jesus' Exposition of the Old Testament in Luke's Gospel*, 193–94; Garland, *Luke*, 835; Edwards, *The Gospel According to Luke*, 608; Pao and Schnabel, "Luke," 378; Thompson, *Luke*, 335.

[273] Green, *The Gospel of Luke*, 740, comments, "Thus, the OT is the source for this mural's astral phenomena ('signs in the sun, the moon, and the stars ... the powers of the heavens will be shaken' – vv 25–26), distress and confusion among the nations (v 25), the roaring of the sea (v 25), and the fear of the people (v 26). It is of no little consequence that, especially when read against the background of their OT precursors, these images portend the advent of the Day of the Lord and, so, portray the coming of the Son of Man as a theophany." See also, Nolland, *Luke 9:21–18:34*, 1005–7; Kimball, *Jesus' Exposition of the Old Testament in Luke's Gospel*, 192–93; Culpepper, "The Gospel of Luke," 407; Pao and Schnabel, "Luke," 378; Carroll, *Luke*, 420.

[274] Cf. Edwards, *The Gospel According to Luke*, 608; Green, *The Gospel of Luke*, 740; Carroll, *Luke*, 420.

[275] Cf. Bock, "Proclamation from Prophecy and Pattern," 136–37; Bock, *Luke*, 1685–86; Kimball, *Jesus' Exposition of the Old Testament in Luke's Gospel*, 196.

[276] Cf. Bock, "Proclamation from Prophecy and Pattern," 137; Nolland, *Luke 9:21–18:34*, 1007; Stein, *Luke*, 523–25; Kimball, *Jesus' Exposition of the Old Testament in Luke's Gospel*, 193–94; Carroll, *Luke*, 420; Edwards, *The Gospel According to Luke*, 607–8.

[277] Cf. Kimball, *Jesus' Exposition of the Old Testament in Luke's Gospel*, 196.

Luke 22:69–70

This passage is the climax of Jesus's Son-of-Man prophecies in Luke, in which he overtly revealed his divine status before the Sanhedrin.[278] Jesus here envisioned the Son of Man "seated at the right hand of the power of God"—a clear allusion not only to the enthronement prophecy of Dan 7:13–14, but also to its Davidic precursor in Ps 110:1.[279] As occupant of the throne of God, Jesus did indeed make himself equal with God.[280] Moreover, he appeared to take the Divine Name for himself by alluding to its Greek reflection in the emphatic phrase, "I am" (ἐγώ εἰμι).[281] With skillful irony Jesus agreed that his accusers correctly called him "the Son of God" (even though he had used "the Son of Man") by his appropriation of "I am" to happily confirm that divine identification.[282]

In summary, Jesus's three major predictions of the Son of Man in Luke (after the Transfiguration) display his divine identity largely through the application of OT YHWH-texts.[283] First, the *revealing* of the Son of Man (Luke 17:30) picks up OT types and predictions of the revealing/visibility of YHWH (e.g., Exod 19:16; Ps 97:4; Ezek 1:4).[284] This includes the "Day" of the Son of Man (Luke 17:24, 30, 31; cf. 17:22, 26; 21:24) employed like the Day of the YHWH (cf. Isa 13:6; Joel 2:1–2; Mal 4:5).[285] Second, the *coming* of the Son of Man (Luke 21:27) fulfills OT expectations of the coming/

---

[278] That the Sanhedrin recognized in Jesus's words a claim to divinity or equality with God is generally noted by the commentators. Cf. Plummer, *The Gospel According to St. Luke*, 519; Ellis, *The Gospel of Luke*, 263; Edwards, *The Gospel According to Luke*, 661; Thompson, *Luke*, 355; Chen, *Luke*, 291; Pao and Schnabel, "Luke," 392. Funk and Hoover, *The Five Gospels*, 393, admit something of the author's high view of Jesus, but simply reject it as impossibly the view of the historical Jesus.

[279] Cf. Fitzmyer, *The Gospel According to Luke*, 1462; Pao and Schnabel, "Luke," 391; Edwards, *The Gospel According to Luke*, 659; Thompson, *Luke*, 355; Porter, "Composite Citations in Luke-Acts," 81.

[280] Thompson, *Luke*, 355, summarizes, "'at the right hand of the power of God' . . . is a circumlocution for the sovereign rule of God in which Jesus is both identified with God the Father and yet is distinct from him (see 20:42). The allusion to Ps 110:1 (and Dan 7:13) together with the use of the term δύναμις in the context of a trial before the ruling council (22:66) emphasizes where the true locus of divine authority resides. Jesus is actually the Judge over them." Cf. Morris, *Luke*, 336; Pao and Schnabel, "Luke," 391; Jeffrey, *Luke*, 265.

[281] Some writers who find Jesus's use of ἐγώ εἰμι here either ambiguous or suggestive of the Divine Name include Johnson, *The Gospel of Luke*, 360; Bovon, *Luke 9:51–19:27*, 246; Chen, *Luke*, 291; John G. Napier, "The Christological Significance of the Name Yahweh" (ThM thesis, Dallas Theological Seminary, 1979), 21–23.

[282] Cf. Edwards, *The Gospel According to Luke*, 661–62; Robertson, *Luke*, 277; Plummer, *The Gospel According to St. Luke*, 519; Ellis, *The Gospel of Luke*, 263; Napier, "The Christological Significance of the Name Yahweh," 23; Johnson, *The Gospel of Luke*, 360; Bovon, Luke, 246; Chen, *Luke*, 291.

[283] Fletcher-Louis, *Christological Origins*, 188, claims, "What is remarkable about all these Gospel texts [including Luke 17:24] is the fact that *it is only with the Son of Man title that we have a clear citation or allusion to a scriptural Yhwh text in the service of a Yhwh-Kyrios Christology*. We never find Jesus connected in this way to scriptural *Yhwh-Kyrios* texts through his identity as a prophet, the messiah (*christos*), a son of David, the Son of God title, or even the word 'Lord'" (emphasis Fletcher-Louis). Unfortunately, Fletcher-Louis's claim that even the Christological title "Lord" never alludes to OT YHWH-texts seems odd in the light of passages such as Luke 1:76; 3:4; 6:5, 46. The point is well-taken, however, that Jesus clearly portrayed the Son of Man with allusions to YHWH-texts, in effect claiming the highest possible Christology.

[284] Cf. Bock, *Luke*, 1429–30; Pao and Schnabel, "Luke," 346.

[285] Cf. Nolland, *Luke 9:21–18:34*, 859; Bock, *Luke*, 1430; Chen, *Luke*, 236.

presence of YHWH (e.g., Isa 64:1; Zech 14:5; Zeph 3:15, 17). This connection is confirmed particularly by Jesus's allusion to his coming as the Danielic Son of Man (Dan 7:13–14), who bears characteristics and prerogatives of YHWH. Third, the *session* of the Son of Man (Luke 22:69) parallels OT descriptions and predictions of YHWH as the enthroned Judge of the earth (Ps 9:7–8; 45:6; Isa 37:16). However, when Jesus applied to himself the conspicuous enthronement passages of Ps 110:1 and Dan 7:13–14—in which David's Lord (the Son of Man) shares YHWH's throne—he made clear that his own future enthronement would be to the throne of YHWH himself. Ironically, Jesus anticipated in his enthronement "at the right hand of God's power" the authority to judge all the earth (Luke 22:69; Ps 110:1; Dan 7:13–14)—including the Sanhedrin—who mistakenly presumed to be his judges and misused his words against him (Luke 22:71).[286]

Luke 19:9–10

Luke is the only Evangelist to record Jesus's purpose statement that he (as the Son of Man) "came ... to seek and to save the lost" (ἦλθεν ... ζητῆσαι καὶ σῶσαι τὸ ἀπολωλός; Luke 19:10).[287] Scholars overwhelmingly recognize in Jesus's claim an allusion to YHWH's shepherding declaration in Ezekiel 34.[288] In Ezekiel's vivid portrayal, YHWH derided the failed "shepherds of Israel" for feeding themselves and scattering the sheep (Ezek 34:1–10).[289] Key phrases in YHWH's indictment of Israel's unfaithful kings and religious leaders include, "you have not sought the lost" (τὸ ἀπολωλὸς οὐκ ἐζητήσατε; 34:4), "I myself will seek out my sheep" (ἐγὼ ἐκζητήσω τὰ πρόβατά μου; 34:11), "I will seek the lost" (Τὸ ἀπολωλὸς ζητήσω; 34:16), and "I will save my sheep" (σώσω τὰ πρόβατά μου; 34:22).[290] Thus, Jesus's claim to seek and to save the lost draws heavily from these YHWH-texts.

Some scholars emphasize from Ezekiel 34 that YHWH predicted his appointment of a Davidic "servant" and "prince" to be the "one shepherd" (34:23–24) who would represent him to his "rescued/saved" (34:10, 12, 23) eschatological people.[291] This messianic representation is certainly a crucial feature of Ezekiel's prophecy without

---

[286] Cf. Pao and Schnabel, "Luke," 391; Jeffrey, *Luke*, 265; Thompson, *Luke*, 355.

[287] A similar "I came to ..." purpose statement in Luke occurs at 5:32. Cf. Wellum, "The Deity of Christ in the Synoptic Gospels," 86.

[288] Among many others, see, R. T. France, *Jesus and the Old Testament* (Grand Rapids, MI: Baker, 1982), 156; Dennis Edward Johnson, "Immutability and Incarnation: An Historical and Theological Study of the Concepts of Christ's Divine Unchangeability and His Human Development" (PhD diss., Fuller Theological Seminary, 1984), 448–49; Fitzmyer, *The Gospel According to Luke*, 1226; Green, *The Gospel of Luke*, 673; Gathercole, *The Preexistent Son*, 168–69; Nolland, *Luke 18:35–24:53*, 906–7.

[289] Cf. France, *Luke*, 299; Green, *The Gospel of Luke*, 673; Andrew T. Abernethy and Greg Goswell, *God's Messiah in the Old Testament* (Grand Rapids, MI: Baker Academic, 2020), 229.

[290] Ezekiel 34:16 is typically selected by commentators as the main source of Jesus's claim in Luke 19:10. E.g., Pao and Schnabel, "Luke," 354; France, *Luke*, 299; Thompson, *Luke*, 297. Outside Ezekiel, Isa 40:11 may be the closest runner-up thematically.

[291] E.g., Nolland, *Luke 18:35–24:53*, 906, 908; Green, *The Gospel of Luke*, 673; Gadenz, *The Gospel of Luke*, 317.

which it cannot be properly understood.[292] But Jesus selected the language of YHWH rather than that of the Messiah to describe his missional role in Luke 19:10.[293] Both of Jesus's verbs (ζητῆσαι καὶ σῶσαι) reflect the personal actions of YHWH ("seek" in Ezek 34:4, 11, 16; "save" in 34:22) rather than those of the Davidic Messiah, whose job description focused rather on feeding and ruling/shepherding God's people (34:23–24).[294] Like YHWH, Jesus also called the recipients of his saving mission "the lost" (34:4, 16; Luke 19:10).[295] Furthermore, Jesus had just described Zacchaeus's repentant response to his call as "salvation" coming to "the house" of a "son of Abraham" (19:9)—much like YHWH's decree to "save" his flock and "judge between (true) sheep and (false) sheep" (Ezek 34:22), i.e., YHWH's "human sheep" of "the house of Israel" (34:30–31).[296]

Finally, Jesus's expressed visitation, "For the Son of Man came to..." (19:10), makes greater sense of a presumed preexistence than of a mere change in earthly location.[297] These factors support strong allusions in Jesus's words (19:9–10) to YHWH's words (Ezek 34) and make it difficult to imagine that Jesus thought of himself as anyone less than YHWH. Abernethy and Goswell summarize, "Jesus is not claiming to be the Davidic shepherd who tends the flock (as per most scholars) but the Divine Shepherd who saves."[298]

---

[292] Bock, *A Theology of Luke and Acts*, 196, writes, "Jesus becomes the instrument through whom God works." Abernethy and Goswell, *God's Messiah in the Old Testament*, 229, rightly expand, "Jesus is depicted as the shepherd-king who comes to seek and to save the lost in Luke 19:10, a verse that appears to sum up the message of salvation in Luke's Gospel as a whole, but understanding what is said here depends on Ezek. 34:16, 22 ('I [YHWH] will seek the lost.... I will rescue [save] my flock'). Jesus is not claiming to be the Davidic shepherd who tends the flock (as per most scholars) but the Divine Shepherd who saves."

[293] Johnson, "Immutability and Incarnation," 449, brings in Jesus's prior parable of the lost sheep in Luke 15:3–7, when he remarks, "It would take no great leap of allegorical imagination to see that Jesus, not they, was acting the role of Yahweh in seeking out the lost (cf. Luke 19:10) and bringing them home to a joyful celebration." Cf. France, *Jesus and the Old Testament*, 156; Abernethy and Goswell, *God's Messiah in the Old Testament*, 229–30; Gathercole, *The Preexistent Son*, 169; Thompson, *Luke*, 297.

[294] Geerhardus Vos, "Seeking and Saving the Lost: Luke 19:10," *Kerux* 7.1 (1992): 7, writes, "Seeking and saving are acts in which God puts forth his omniscience and omnipotence, the searcher of hearts and the Lord of spirits. To these divine prerogatives the 'Son of Man' lays claim in the pursuit of his task." Gathercole, *The Preexistent Son*, adds simply, "prophets do not save." Cf. Abernethy and Goswell, *God's Messiah in the Old Testament*, 229–30; Wellum, "The Deity of Christ in the Synoptic Gospels," 86–87.

[295] Cf. Abernethy and Goswell, *God's Messiah in the Old Testament*, 229–30; Garland, *Luke*, 750–51; Thompson, *Luke*, 297.

[296] Cf. Nolland, *Luke 18:35–24:53*, 908. Garland, *Luke*, 750–51, comments, "Zacchaeus only wanted 'to see' Jesus, but he finds one who was on a quest for him. Jesus seeks to gather him in as a shepherd gathers lost sheep (Ezek 34:11–16, which uses the image to refer to God). The reason why it is 'necessary' for him to stay with Zacchaeus (19:5) is because his divine mission to seek the lost requires it. When finally he sees Jesus, he learns who he truly is—the rescuer of the lost, the restorer of dignity, his Savior."

[297] Cf. Vos, "Seeking and Saving the Lost," 3; France, *Jesus and the Old Testament*, 156; Gathercole, *The Preexistent Son*, 169; Strauss, "Christology and Christological Purpose in the Synoptic Gospels," 58.

[298] Abernethy and Goswell, *God's Messiah in the Old Testament*, 229. Cf. Johnson, "Immutability and Incarnation," 448–49; G. W. Grogan, "The New Testament Interpretation of the Old Testament: A Comparative Study," *TynBul* 18 (1967): 75; R. T. France, "Development in New Testament Christology," in *Crisis in Christology*, ed. William R. Farmer (Livonia, MI: Dove Booksellers, 1995), 73; Strauss, "Christology and Christological Purpose in the Synoptic Gospels," 58; Wellum, "The Deity of Christ in the Synoptic Gospels," 86–87.

Luke 20:17-18

Since the Matthean account of Jesus referring to himself as the "stone" of OT prophecy was previously addressed at Matt 21:42-45, comments here will be brief.[299] After Jesus told the parable of the vineyard owner who sent his servants *and even his son* to reclaim his vineyard (a variation on Isa 5:1-7), he then alluded to himself with a medley of OT "stone passages."[300] In Luke 20:17, Jesus quoted verbatim the portrait in Ps 118:22[301] (also alluded to in Isa 28:16).[302] Then, in Luke 20:18, Jesus used the language of Isa 8:15 and Dan 2:34-35, 44-45 to portray himself and his actions even further.[303] The basic intertextualizations appear in Table 4.2.[304]

Table 4.2 YHWH-Text Cluster behind Luke 20:17-18

Luke 20:17	quotes	Ps 118:22	alluded to by	Isa 28:16
Luke 20:18			alludes to	Isa 8:15 and Dan 2:34-35, 44-45

Scholars generally recognize that Jesus used this thematic cluster of "stone passages" to identify himself and his ministry.[305] The cluster of texts comes in two waves—in relation to Jesus's two statements—which show an advancement of meaning in accordance with much Hebrew parallelism.[306] In Luke 20:17, Jesus referred to stone passages which harbor some ambiguity about whom they represent. But in 20:18, Jesus referred to stone passages which identify YHWH as the "stone" who breaks and crushes his enemies.[307] Thus, in poetic fashion it appears that Jesus made a clever reveal that as the stone/cornerstone/rock of OT prophecy he fills the role of YHWH.[308]

---

[299] Mark 12:10-11 is also parallel. Cf. Stein, *Luke*, 493.

[300] Cf. Fitzmyer, *The Gospel According to Luke*, 1281; Stein, *Luke*, 495; Culpepper, "The Gospel of Luke," 382-83. Some scholars believe the transition from the vineyard parable to the stone passages was further facilitated by a wordplay on the Hebrew terms for *son* (בֵּן) and *stone* (אֶבֶן). E.g., Edwards, *The Gospel According to Luke*, 570; Kimball, *Jesus' Exposition of the Old Testament in Luke's Gospel*, 159-60.

[301] The LXX reference is Ps 117:22. Cf. Edwards, *The Gospel According to Luke*, 570.

[302] Hendriksen, *Luke*, 894, and Fitzmyer, *The Gospel According to Luke*, 1286, note both Ps 118:22 and Isa 28:16 in the background of Luke 20:17, while most other commentators note only Ps 118:22.

[303] Cf. Hendriksen, *Luke*, 895; Morris, *Luke*, 304; Nolland, *Luke 18:35–24:53*, 953; Stein, *Luke*, 493; Culpepper, "The Gospel of Luke," 382; Pao and Schnabel, "Luke," 362-63; France, *Luke*, 317; Snodgrass, *Stories with Intent*, 290-91.

[304] It may be that Simeon also alluded to the stone passage of Isa 8:15 when he told Mary that Jesus would cause "the fall and rising of many in Israel" (Luke 2:34). Cf. Fitzmyer, *The Gospel According to Luke*, 1286; Stein, *Luke*, 493; Culpepper, "The Gospel of Luke," 382; France, *Luke*, 317; Edwards, *The Gospel According to Luke*, 570.

[305] Cf. Kimball, *Jesus' Exposition of the Old Testament in Luke's Gospel*, 159; Culpepper, "The Gospel of Luke," 382; Pao and Schnabel, "Luke," 363.

[306] Similarly, Lanier, *Old Testament Conceptual Metaphors and the Christology of Luke's Gospel*, 213.

[307] Cf. France, *Luke*, 317; Stein, *Luke*, 493; Lanier, *Old Testament Conceptual Metaphors and the Christology of Luke's Gospel*, 213-14.

[308] Cf. France, *Jesus and the Old Testament*, 152-53; France, *Luke*, 317; Lanier, *Old Testament Conceptual Metaphors and the Christology of Luke's Gospel*, 213-14.

Luke 21:33

"Heaven and earth shall pass away, but my words shall not pass away."[309] Luke 21:33 and Mark 13:31 are verbatim; Matt 24:35 is nearly so.[310] Understandably, this triple-tradition claim from Jesus would have been memorable—both for its pithy parallelism and for its bold meaning.[311] There can be little doubt that Jesus was alluding to similar claims made by or about YHWH.[312] In particular, Isa 40:8 uses a parallelism that may be the primary basis of Jesus's own contrast—"the grass withers, the flower fades, but the word of our God will stand forever"—although Jesus's statement boldly heightened that contrast.[313]

Additional YHWH-texts likely contributed to the thought in Jesus's expression.[314] Ps 102:25–27 teaches that earth and heaven will pass away, but YHWH himself remains the same forever. Verses 89 and 160 of Ps 119 claim that YHWH's word is fixed in the heavens and endures forever. YHWH says in Isa 51:6 that while the heavens and

---

[309] Although the focus here remains on Jesus's allusion to YHWH-texts, his statement was not a disconnected platitude but a vital element in the narrative. Jesus had already warned his disciples not to be ashamed of his words in the light of his glorious coming (Luke 9:26). As he further speaks of his coming (21:25–27) and their need to be ready for the suddenness of that Day (21:26–36), he reiterates the supreme and eternal authority of his own words (21:33). Cf. Stein, *Luke*, 528; Nolland, *Luke 18:35–24:53*, 1010. But it is not merely his eschatological predictions that are unbreakable. All his personal speech ("my words")—like God's law (16:17)—is more durable than creation itself. Cf. France, *Jesus and the Old Testament*, 151; Thompson, *Luke*, 336.

[310] Cf. Aland, *Synopsis Quattuor Evangeliorum*, 406; Klein, *Das Lukasevangelium*, 652; Stein, *Luke*, 528; Hays, *Echoes of Scripture in the Gospels*, 255–56. Manuscript evidence for both Mark and Luke favors exact statements with future middle indicatives: ὁ οὐρανὸς καὶ ἡ γῆ παρελεύσονται, οἱ δὲ λόγοι μου οὐ μὴ παρελεύσονται. Matthew paraphrases the second verbal thought with an aorist active subjunctive: ὁ οὐρανὸς καὶ ἡ γῆ παρελεύσεται, οἱ δὲ λόγοι μου οὐ μὴ παρέλθωσιν. However, there may be no discernable difference in sense between the two renderings.

[311] Similarly, see France, *Jesus and the Old Testament*, 151; Thompson, *Luke*, 336. Funk and Hoover, *The Five Gospels*, 385, reported from the Jesus Seminar, "While Jesus did use oaths upon occasion (as in Mark 8:12, Scholars Version), the Fellows decided by an overwhelming majority that this one must have been supplied by a Christian author as a conclusion to this entire discourse." But their judgment seems to ignore the evidence of its triple testimony, memorable pith, radical personal claim, and (argued below) its transparent allusion to OT YHWH-texts—all features that support authenticity from Jesus himself.

[312] This point is made to varying degrees by numerous scholars: e.g., France, *Jesus and the Old Testament*, 151; Fitzmyer, *The Gospel According to Luke*, 1353; Nolland, *Luke 18:35–24:53*, 1010; Stein, *Luke*, 528; David B. Capes, *The Divine Christ* (Grand Rapids, MI: Baker Academic, 2018), 178; Bock, *Luke*, 1692; Culpepper, "The Gospel of Luke," 409; Green, *The Gospel of Luke*, 742; Pao and Schnabel, "Luke," 379; Edwards, *The Gospel According to Luke*, 610; Hays, *Echoes of Scripture in the Gospels*, 255–56; Thompson, *Luke*, 336.

[313] Some scholars emphasize Isa 40:8 as a source for Jesus: e.g., Daniel Doriani, "The Deity of Christ in the Synoptic Gospels," *JETS* 37.3 (1994): 347; Hays, *Echoes of Scripture in the Gospels*, 255; David B. Capes, *Old Testament Yahweh Texts in Paul's Christology* (Tübingen, Germany: Mohr (Paul Siebeck), 1992; repr., Waco, TX: Baylor University Press, 2017), 179. Other scholars simply list Isa 40:8 first among possible sources: e.g., Fitzmyer, *The Gospel According to Luke*, 1353; Nolland, *Luke 18:35–24:53*, 1010; Culpepper, "The Gospel of Luke," 409. France, *Jesus and the Old Testament*, 151, notes how Jesus likely strengthened the reference to Isa 40:8 by heightening the contrast.

[314] The YHWH-texts under discussion are listed in whole or in part by various commentators. Cf. France, *Jesus and the Old Testament*, 151; Fitzmyer, *The Gospel According to Luke*, 1353–54; Stein, *Luke*, 528; Nolland, *Luke 18:35–24:53*, 1010; Bock, *Luke*, 1692; Culpepper, "The Gospel of Luke," 409; Green, *The Gospel of Luke*, 742; Pao and Schnabel, "Luke," 379; Edwards, *The Gospel According to Luke*, 610; Thompson, *Luke*, 336.

the earth will vanish and wear out, his salvation and righteousness shall never end. And YHWH adds in Isa 55:10–11 that as precipitation from heaven produces seed and bread from the earth, so YHWH's spoken word shall not fail to accomplish his purpose. The significance of these texts is that they highlight the eternal and effectual qualities of YHWH's word, which Jesus then claims for his own words.[315] Jesus did not identify his speech as the representative communiqué of a prophet, but baldly equated his own words with the word of YHWH by clear allusion to OT YHWH-texts.[316]

Luke 24:44–49

Other possible allusions to YHWH-texts might have been included in this chapter (see conclusion below). Significantly, however, this survey closes with YHWH-texts applied to Jesus in a uniquely Lukan account of Jesus's pre-ascended self-revelation to his disciples. Although several features surrounding this scene draw attention to the deity of Christ, Luke 24:44–49 functions as the revelatory climax of Jesus's divine identity in the Third Gospel.[317] And Jesus reveals his divinity in large part through the application of OT YHWH-texts to himself.[318]

Several significant themes culminate in Jesus's final Lukan speech. Just as Jesus had mysteriously "opened" the eyes of the two disciples on the road to Emmaus (24:31) and had "opened" the Scriptures to them (24:32), so Jesus eventually "opened" the minds of all his disciples to understand the Scriptures (24:45).[319] Similarly, Jesus explained

---

[315] Morris, *Luke*, 318, summarizes well: "Jesus' words have a permanence that does not attach to this material universe." Scholars generally highlight the permanence, certainty, eternality, authority, immutability, and/or indestructibility of YHWH's/Jesus's words as the implication of Jesus's claim in Luke 21:33. See, France, *Jesus and the Old Testament*, 151; Fitzmyer, *The Gospel According to Luke*, 1353–54; Bock, *Luke*, 1692; Doriani, "The Deity of Christ in the Synoptic Gospels," 347; Green, *The Gospel of Luke*, 742; Klein, *Das Lukasevangelium*, 652; Pao and Schnabel, "Luke," 379; Bovon, *Luke 3*, 121; France, *Luke*, 335; Edwards, *The Gospel According to Luke*, 610; Hays, *Echoes of Scripture in the Gospels*, 255; Thompson, *Luke*, 336; Capes, *The Divine Christ*, 178.

[316] As Edwards, *The Gospel According to Luke*, comments, "For Jesus to assert that his words will outlive heaven and earth is a remarkable claim of authority. The only being who could reasonably make such a claim is God (Isa 51:6). If Jesus' words will outlive the cosmos, then in ways that we who are bound to the treadmill of time cannot understand, his words encompass past, present, and future." Cf. France, *Jesus and the Old Testament*, 151; Capes, *Old Testament Yahweh Texts in Paul's Christology*, 179; Pao and Schnabel, "Luke," 379.

[317] Revealing the true identity of Jesus is the grand purpose of all the Gospels, in which the disciples consistently prove themselves confused until Jesus's post-resurrection appearances and teachings. Luke is no exception: although his readers can see the divine identity of Jesus throughout the narrative, it is not until the conclusion that Jesus's divine self-understanding is fully revealed and understood by his followers. Cf. Denaux, "A Stranger in the City," 256–57. Contrarywise, Funk and Hoover, *The Five Gospels*, 399, assert that the words of Jesus here were a later invention. But the Lukan narrative only makes sense if Jesus actually spoke the words in this account. It seems contradictory to hold that "independent sayings" of Jesus are more authentic than his conversations that naturally cohere in the recorded narrative.

[318] J. R. Daniel Kirk, *A Man Attested by God*, 25, 537, criticizes the (divine) christological reading by Richard B. Hays of Luke 24 by claiming that Jesus was referring instead to his (human) rejection, suffering, and death as the subject of all the Scriptures. But Kirk's bifurcation is unwarranted and overlooks the extensive YHWH-text background of Luke 24:44–49, including Jesus's personal claim to send the Holy Spirit to empower his disciples as his own witnesses (see discussion below for the YWHW-text significance of these claims).

[319] Cf. Robertson, *Luke*, 296–97; Marshall, *The Gospel of Luke*, 905; Bovon, *Luke 3*, 375.

both to the Two (24:25–27, 32) and to the Eleven-plus (24:44–47) that he himself is the key theme of all Scripture—a radical hermeneutic that assumes both the objective centrality and subjective authority of YHWH.[320] Thus, Jesus interpreted "all that the prophets have spoken" about himself (24:25, 27) by "my words that I have spoken to you" (24:44)—likely including the witness of YHWH-texts to himself.[321] Furthermore, when Jesus claimed that the forgiveness of sins would be proclaimed to all nations ἐπὶ τῷ ὀνόματι αὐτοῦ (literally, "on the name of him," i.e., *Jesus* as the sacrificed and risen Christ; 24:47), he appeared to add to the variety of ways in Luke that he bore the *name* of YHWH (e.g. 1:31; 2:21; 9:48, 49; 10:17; 13:35; 19:38; 21:8, 17; cf. 1:49; 5:20–24; 7:47–50; 11:2). Finally, Jesus's outwardly superfluous comment that his disciples were "witnesses" of his redemptive work (24:48) was more deeply a claim to his own divine authority. Indeed, Jesus later clarified in the Lukan corpus, "you are *my* witnesses" (Acts 1:8), which is an allusion to YHWH's predicted possession of eschatological witnesses in Isa 43:10, 12; 44:8.[322]

These themes running through the final words of Jesus in Luke's Gospel point to his divine identity. But in this pericope, Jesus's clearest appropriation of YHWH-texts appears in his final declaration: "I am sending the promise of my Father upon you. But stay in the city until you are clothed with power from on high" (24:49).[323] For Jesus, the Father's "promise" was equivalent to the "power" that he (Jesus) would send. Both terms are metaphorical for the Holy Spirit.[324] Luke's Gospel (with its sequel) is renowned for its emphasis on the Spirit and his power, largely because of these concluding words from Jesus. But the key to their interpretation lies in Jesus's claim that he himself would send the Holy Spirit "from on high" to clothe his followers.[325] Each major element of Jesus's claim in Luke 24:49 alludes to OT YHWH-texts:

---

[320] Nearly a century ago, Robertson, *Luke*, 294, quipped, "Jesus found himself in the Old Testament, a thing that some modern scholars do not seem able to do." Cf. Edwards, *The Gospel According to Luke*, 721–22, 733–34; Hays, *Reading Backwards*, 14; Napier, "The Christological Significance of the Name Yahweh," iii–iv; Stephen J. Wellum, "From Alpha to Omega: A Biblical-Theological Approach to God the Son Incarnate," *JETS* 63.1 (2020): 82.

[321] Edwards, *The Gospel According to Luke*, 733–34, comments, "The commission begins in v. 44 by appealing to Jesus' earthly teaching. 'These are my words' (NIV 'This is what I told you') is shifted emphatically to the head of the sentence. Its Greek form is a clarion echo of the Hebrew 'These are the words,' which characteristically introduces divine revelation in the OT (e.g., Exod 19:6; 35:1; Deut 1:1; Isa 42:5; Zech 8:16)."

[322] Dennis E. Johnson, *The Message of Acts in the History of Redemption* (Phillipsburg, NJ: P&R, 1997), 34–50, insightfully shows how the mission of Jesus's disciples in the Book of Acts follows the commission of YHWH's eschatological "witnesses" in Isaiah. Marshall, *The Gospel of Luke*, 48, is one of several commentators who see the books of Luke and Acts linked by Jesus's appointment of the disciples as his "witnesses."

[323] Stein, *Luke*, 621, comments, "The verb is a futuristic present (literally 'I am sending') that emphasizes the certainty of what God was about to do."

[324] Cf. Plummer, *The Gospel According to St. Luke*, 563; Marshall, *The Gospel of Luke*, 907; Stein, *Luke*, 621; Nolland, *Luke 18:35–24:53*, 1220; Green, *The Gospel of Luke*, 859; Pao and Schnabel, "Luke," 402; Garland, *Luke*, 969; Godshall, "The Messiah and the Outpouring of the Holy Spirit," 208.

[325] For Jesus himself to send YHWH's promised Holy Spirit "from on high" carries too many clues to interpret his words other than that of him taking YHWH's position and prerogative. Similarly, see, Godshall, "The Messiah and the Outpouring of the Holy Spirit," 208–9; Hays, *Reading Backwards*, 71; and, possibly, Denaux, "A Stranger in the City," 266; Green, *The Gospel of Luke*, 859.

- God the Father's promise of the Spirit: e.g., Isa 44:3; Joel 2:28–29; cf. Luke 11:13.[326]
- YHWH to pour out/send the Holy Spirit: e.g., Ezek 39:29; Joel 2:28–29.[327]
- The Spirit to come upon/clothe YHWH's people: e.g., Isa 32:15; 44:3; cf. 61:10.[328]
- The Spirit to empower people to do YHWH's will: e.g., Ezek 36:27; Joel 2:28–29.[329]

While other texts may serve as further background to Jesus's claims in this pericope, the YHWH-texts noted above appear to be the clearest allusions in light of Jesus's chosen terminology.[330] The most significant feature of these references is that they all were originally YHWH-texts. The claim of Jesus to be the heavenly sender of God's promised Holy Spirit finds no OT parallel in human agents or angels.[331] It is no wonder, therefore, that Luke's concluding scene depicts the disciples worshiping Jesus at his ascension, which is all the more significant since Jesus had previously limited monotheistic worship to YHWH (Luke 4:8).[332]

Conclusion

The Gospel According to Luke contains numerous cases of OT YHWH-texts applied to Jesus. Some of these cases run parallel to cases in Matthew and/or Mark. But many others are unique to Luke, demonstrating that the Third Evangelist did not parrot his likely predecessors but intuitively employed the same phenomenon that is found in their accounts of Jesus.

The unique material and sheer length of Luke's Gospel help explain why it contains so many examples of the YHWH-text phenomenon. Given the ubiquity of the phenomenon across all the Gospels, Luke's relatively larger tally of texts may be expected, since his Gospel is longer. In fact, the frequency of the phenomenon in Luke implies a strong probability that he recorded other cases not addressed in this chapter. Some of the passages which warrant further investigation include the following:

---

[326] Cf. Stein, *Luke*, 621; Godshall, "The Messiah and the Outpouring of the Holy Spirit, 208, 216."

[327] Hays, *Reading Backwards*, 71, captures the point here: "How can [Jesus] promise, after the resurrection, to send power from on high ('the promise of the Father') upon his followers (24:49) and then, in the dramatic opening scenes of Acts, fulfill that promise by pouring out the Holy Spirit (Acts 2:33)? Even more than the power to forgive sins or still storms, surely the power to send the Spirit is a prerogative that belongs exclusively to God." Cf. Denaux, "A Stranger in the City," 266.

[328] Cf. Marshall, *The Gospel of Luke*, 907; Stein, *Luke*, 621.

[329] Cf. Nolland, *Luke 18:35–24:53*, 1220; Garland, *Luke*, 969.

[330] Several commentators focus on the following four YHWH-texts as the most significant background to Jesus's claim in Luke 24:49: Isa 32:15; 44:3; Ezek 39:29; Joel 2:28–29. E.g., Marshall, *The Gospel of Luke*, 907; Nolland, *Luke 18:35–24:53*, 1220; Pao and Schnabel, "Luke," 402; Godshall, "The Messiah and the Outpouring of the Holy Spirit," 208. Other scholars have underscored a primarily Isaian background. E.g., Johnson, *The Message of Acts in the History of Redemption*, 35–49; Hays, *Echoes of Scripture in the Gospels*, 263–64.

[331] Similarly, Godshall, "The Messiah and the Outpouring of the Holy Spirit," 212–13.

[332] Cf. Stein, *Luke*, 624–25; Marshall, *The Gospel of Luke*, 910; Gathercole, "The Trinity in the Synoptic Gospels and Acts," 60; Garland, *Luke*, 970; Godshall, "The Messiah and the Outpouring of the Holy Spirit," 214–15; Strauss, "Christology and Christological Purpose in the Synoptic Gospels," 58.

- In Luke 2:25–32, Jesus is called "the Consolation of Israel" (echoing Isa 52:9) and YHWH's visible "Salvation" (echoing Isa 52:10), as well as "light" and "glory"—all titular descriptions which may be appropriated from YHWH-texts.
- In Luke 9:12–17, Jesus feeds the 5,000 in a "desolate place," reminiscent of YHWH feeding the Israelites in the wilderness.[333] (The Synoptic parallel in Mark 6:34–44 was treated in the previous chapter.)
- In Luke 9:41–43, Jesus addressed an Israelite crowd as a "faithless and twisted generation" with whom he was burdened to bear—language quite similar to YHWH's lament over Israel in Deut 32:5, 20.[334]
- In Luke 19:46, Jesus quoted YHWH-text Isa 56:7 with some ambiguity. He may have personalized YHWH's words when he referred to "my house . . . of prayer."[335] If so, then Jesus's descent from the Mount of Olives to the temple (Luke 19:37, 45) also may have enacted a temporary reversal of YHWH's OT departure from the temple (cf. Ezek 11:23).[336]
- In Luke 23:42, the plea of a crucified criminal next to Jesus, "Remember me," sounds very much like a prayer to YHWH,[337] and Jesus's response sounds very much like that of one in YHWH's position of authority to decide who enters the "kingdom" and "Paradise."[338]

Since the potential seems high for the existence of other Lukan applications of OT YHWH-texts to Jesus, this study may best be characterized as "complete" rather than "exhaustive." (The same description must hold true for the previous chapters on Matthew and Mark.) Nevertheless, the numerous cases addressed here secure the highest possible Christology. While there can be no doubt that Luke faithfully described a very human Jesus (cf. 2:7, 40; 4:2; 22:42–44; 23:46), his extensive application of OT YHWH-texts to Jesus shows conclusively that he also portrayed Jesus as the divine Lord. It remains now to summarize this phenomenon in all of the Synoptic Gospels and to consider some of its ramifications.

---

[333] See, e.g., France, *Luke*, 161; Chen, *Luke*, 126–27.
[334] Cf. Marshall, *The Gospel of Luke*, 391–92; Green, *The Gospel of Luke*, 389; France, *Luke*, 172.
[335] Cf. Edwards, *The Gospel According to Luke*, 556.
[336] Cf. Lanier, "Luke's Distinctive Use of the Temple," 457–58.
[337] Cf. Green, *The Gospel of Luke*, 822; Garland, *Luke*, 925–26.
[338] Cf. Edwards, *The Gospel According to Luke*, 692; Thompson, *Luke*, 366.

5

Realizations and Ramifications

The following conclusion shall now address some realizations and ramifications (i.e., observable data and their implications) of the preceding biblical-theological study. There are many. However, for the sake of thematic focus and clarity, five examples of each shall be addressed.

Five Realizations from This Study

1. The Practice Is Remarkably Frequent in the Synoptic Gospels

The application of OT YHWH-texts to Jesus in the Synoptic Gospels is an astonishingly frequent phenomenon. Numerically, each of the Synoptics appears to have employed the phenomenon well over twenty times. If suggestions made earlier in this study of other possible cases are added, then Mark's Gospel provides about thirty cases, while Matthew and Luke have close to forty occurrences each.

Table 5.1 lists the passages (some containing multiple occurrences of OT YHWH-texts applied to Jesus) that were treated in this study. Likely parallels can be seen sharing the same line, while unique passages remain alone on a line. Bold references mark passages formally addressed in this study, while parenthetic references mark untreated parallels or briefly mentioned passages that likely apply OT YHWH-texts to Jesus. These data indicate not only a radical hermeneutical practice but the astonishing frequency of the practice by the Synoptists. Such sizable results imply a significance which cannot be overlooked in Christological studies without severe truncation of the biblical portrayal of Jesus.[1]

---

[1] Significant ramifications shall be discussed below. But historically, there has been no consensus among scholars on the significance of the phenomenon. For example, C. M. Tuckett, *Christology and the New Testament* (Louisville, KY: Westminster John Knox Press, 2001), 59, after acknowledging the phenomenon in Paul, nevertheless writes, "the application of Old Testament Yahweh-texts to Jesus should not be overpressed. How far New Testament writers were aware of, and explicitly used, the contexts of Old Testament verses they cited is a much-debated issue." Perhaps Tuckett's skepticism would diminish in view of the current study. John R. W. Stott, *The Authentic Jesus* (Basingstoke, UK: Marshalls, 1985), 33, appears to have had sharper understanding of the phenomenon: "This transfer of God-titles and God-texts from Yahweh to Jesus has an unavoidable implication. It identifies Jesus as God, who is able to save and who is worthy of worship. That the early Christians acted on this conviction is incontrovertible."

Table 5.1 List of Passages Addressed (or Paralleled) in this Study

Key Phrase(s) / Topic(s)	Matthew	Mark	Luke
God with us	1:23	—	—
The way of the Lord	3:3	1:2–3	1:17, 76; 3:4–6 (par); 7:26–27
God's Visitation	—	—	1:68, 78; 7:16; 19:44
Baptize with the Holy Spirit	(3:11–12)	1:7–8	3:16–17
Heavens torn; my beloved Son	(3:16–17)	1:10–11	(3:21–22)
Fishers of men	(4:19)	1:17	5:10
Rebuking demons	—	1:25	(4:33–36)
Lord, Lord	7:21–22 (w/ 25:11)	—	6:46
Lord, save/have mercy	8:25; 14:30; 15:22 17:15; 20:30–31	(9:22; 10:47–48)	(16:24; 17:13; 18:38–39)
Your sins are forgiven	9:2	2:5–12	5:20–26 (with 7:47–50)
Bridegroom with them	(9:15)	2:19–20	5:34–35
Lord of the Sabbath	12:8	2:28	6:5
Bind strong man by Spirit/finger of God	(12:28–29)	3:27	11:20–23
"Perishing"; commanding wind and sea	(8:24–27)	4:37–41	8:22–25
Sheep w/o shepherd; feeding 5,000	(14:14–21)	6:34–44	(9:12–17; see conclusion)
My messenger before me	11:10	—	7:26–28 (see 1:17)
I will give you rest	11:28	—	—
Walking on the sea; "I Am"	14:25–27	6:48–52	—
Opened ears, released tongue	—	7:32–37	—
Compassion; feeding 4,000	(15:32–38)	8:1–10	—
Coming w/ angels, glory	16:27	8:38 (see 14:62)	9:26–27
Transfiguration	(17:1–8)	9:1–8	9:28–36
How long? My name; God alone good; follow Me; hosanna; My house; Lord to my Lord: I AM		9:19, 37; 10:18–21 11:9–10, 15–17 12:35–37; 13:3–6	
I came to cast fire on the earth	—	—	12:49
How often! as hen gathers under wings	(23:37)	—	13:34
Son of Man came to seek & save the lost	—	—	19:9–10
My words shall not pass away	24:35	13:31	21:33
Gathered in my name; there I am	18:20	—	—
Out of mouths of infants...praise	21:16	—	—
Stone passages	21:42–45	(12:10–11)	20:17–18
In glory, w/ angels; gather nations	24:30–31 (w/ 25:31–32)	13:26–27 (see 14:62)	21:25–28 (see 17:20–37)
Seated at right hand, coming on clouds	26:64	14:62	22:69–70 (par?)
All authority; I am with you	28:18–20	—	—
Sending promise from on high	—	—	24:44–49

2. The Practice Is Varied in Its Approaches and Practitioners

The YHWH-text phenomenon is employed in a variety of forms by a variety of characters. There appears to be no unique formula or signifier. Rather, OT YHWH-texts are applied to Jesus in a seemingly unbridled fashion. There are formal quotations (e.g., Mark 1:2), allusions (e.g., Matt 11:28), and, perhaps, "echoes" (e.g., Luke 7:16). A few applications are verbatim, while the majority are allusions often found in the form of paraphrases, catch-phrases, and/or titles unique to YHWH. Some occurrences are revealed by the narrator's descriptive details, while many others are broadcasted through the speech of varied actors within the narrative—including Jesus, the divine voice, demonic beings, prophetic characters, disciples, crowds, and (even) human antagonists. The rule seems to be there is no rule. The phenomenon occurs so frequently that it appears naturally in the storyline (see below, "Five Ramifications").

A corollary to this variety in forms is that the use of allusions does not necessarily evidence lesser significance than the use of quotations. Some allusions—such as Jesus walking on the sea (Mark 6:48–49; cf. Job 9:8), lamenting, "How often would I have gathered your children together as a hen gathers her brood under her wings, and you were not willing!" (Matt 23:37b; cf. Ps 91:4; Deut 32:11, 15), and asserting, "Heaven and earth will pass away, but my words will not pass away" (Luke 21:33; cf. Isa 40:8)— clearly portray Jesus in the role of YHWH by allusion to YHWH-unique texts. Readers aware of the OT metanarrative would find these specific allusions just as compelling as formal citations in their application of YHWH-texts to Jesus.[2]

The frequent *Who is this?* question in the Gospels only supports this observation.[3] Jesus's enactment of YHWH-texts (through speech and actions unique to YHWH)

---

[2] R. T. France, *Jesus and the Old Testament* (Grand Rapids, MI: Baker, 1982), 14–15, is worth quoting again: "We shall not confine our attention to formal quotations of the Old Testament. The tendency to do so has marred some recent work, for it inevitably results in an incomplete picture. To discover how Jesus understood and used the Old Testament, we must go beyond verbatim quotations, whether introduced by a set formula or not, to include references to Old Testament teaching or events, verbal allusions, and even, in a few cases, significant actions which seem to have been intended to call attention to prophecies of the Old Testament. The importance of the less formal allusions in particular is that they often betray the Old Testament models around which the speaker's or writer's thinking formed itself and in many cases they are deliberately framed to suggest a particular Old Testament passage or idea."

[3] M. David Litwa, "Iesus Deus: The Early Christian Depiction of Jesus as a Mediterranean God" (PhD diss., University of Virginia, 2013), 150–51, appears to contradict himself when he comments, "The language and themes of the Synoptic writers indicate that demonstrating the divinity of Jesus was not their central concern. Jesus' titles 'son of man' and 'son of god,' scholars have pointed out, are multivalent and complex, and do not automatically amount to the meaning of 'god' or 'divine being.' The idea that Jesus' divinity is implied in many Synoptic stories may be true (e.g., the forgiveness of sins, the healings, the stilling of the sea), but ambiguity remains and results in the notorious indecisiveness of the Synoptic disciples themselves: 'Who then is this?' (Mark 4:41). The story of Jesus' transfiguration, however, throws a question mark against the mere humanity of Jesus. This story—shared by all Synoptic writers—uses language and imagery that recall epiphanies of gods and goddesses in the ancient Mediterranean world." Contra Litwa, the Synoptics are filled with language and themes demonstrating the divinity of Jesus as a concern vital to their narrative. This is done in large part by the frequent application of OT YHWH-texts to Jesus, which underscores that Jesus's transfiguration and his other supernatural acts do not "recall epiphanies of gods and goddesses in the ancient Mediterranean [i.e., Hellenistic] world" but instead recall the promises and actions of YHWH from the *Jewish* Scriptures. Thus, every *Who is this?* question in the Synoptics, while displaying the mental perplexity of the speaker(s), is recounted to emphasize the divine identity of Jesus. Only the confused questioners do not understand what Jesus, the authors, and the readers know about Jesus's divine identity through a wide application of YHWH-texts to himself.

often elicited questions from various bystanders and recipients of his actions regarding his identity (e.g., Matt 8:27; 11:2–3; 12:23; 21:10; Mark 1:27; 2:7; 4:41; 11:28; Luke 5:21; 7:49; 8:25; 9:9), which Jesus himself often provoked people to consider (e.g., Matt 12:6; 16:13–15; 22:45; Mark 2:9–11; 8:27–29; 10:18; 12:35–37; Luke 9:18–20; 12:8–10; 18:19). It is no wonder that the Synoptics are filled with allusions to OT YHWH-texts, when the constant undercurrent driving their narratives is the question of Jesus's unique identity.

3. The Practice Appears Ubiquitously in All Parts of All the Synoptics

Old Testament YHWH-texts applied to Jesus appear ubiquitously in all sections of all the Synoptic Gospels. Not only are YHWH-texts often applied to Jesus in the Synoptics, they occur in double and triple tradition parallels, as well as in passages unique to each Evangelist (possibly even Mark, which has relatively little unique material).

Some cases unique to each Synoptist:
Matt 11:28; 21:16; 28:18–20
Mark 2:27; 7:32–37
Luke 1:68, 78; 12:49; 24:44–49

Furthermore, the application of YHWH-texts to Jesus occurs frequently in both "Q" and "non-Q" material (potentially calling into question the existence of Q as a distinctive and separate source from the Synoptists themselves).

Some cases in Q:
Matt 3:11–12 // Mark 1:7–8 // Luke 3:16–17
Matt 7:21–22 // Luke 6:46
Matt 11:10 // Luke 7:27
Matt 12:29–30 // Mark 3:27 // Luke 11:21–23
Matt 23:37 // Luke 13:34

Some cases not in Q:
Matt 3:3 // Mark 1:2–3 // Luke 3:4–6
Matt 4:19 // Mark 1:17 // Luke 5:10
Matt 12:8 // Mark 2:28 // Luke 6:5
Matt 21:42–45 // Mark 12:10–11 // Luke 20:17–18
Matt 24:35 // Mark 13:31 // Luke 21:33

If any of the Synoptics contain portions created by different editors, the YHWH-text phenomenon apparently does not attest to it. Rather, the ubiquity of the practice— particularly in the unique material of each Gospel—suggests the construction of a continuous storyline by a single author for each distinctive account. And yet, the three are united in their multifaceted portrayal of Jesus.[4]

---

[4] Similarly, Craig L. Blomberg, "Where Do We Start Studying Jesus?," in *Jesus Under Fire*, ed. Michael J. Wilkins and J. P. Moreland (Grand Rapids, MI: Zondervan, 1995), 39, comments, "All three Synoptic Gospels (like John) have Jesus calling himself the Son of Man, which notwithstanding protracted debate as to its origin, almost certainly harks back to the human figure of Daniel 7:13–14, who is

4. The Practice Includes Sources from All Genres of the Jewish Scriptures

The Synoptic Gospels apply to Jesus a large number of OT YHWH-texts, several of which repeatedly, from all major divisions and genres of the Jewish Scriptures. This comports well with the hermeneutic of Jesus in Luke 24:27: "And beginning with Moses and all the Prophets, he interpreted to them in all the Scriptures the things concerning himself," and further in 24:44: "everything written about me in the Law of Moses and the Prophets and the Psalms must be fulfilled" (cf. John 5:39). A sampling of certain and probable YHWH-text applications from the chapter on Mark's Gospel alone shows significant sourcing from each of Jesus's three divisions of the Jewish Scriptures:

> **The Law of Moses:** Gen 2:3; 49:24; Exod 3:14; 19:16; 20:8–11; 23:20; 24:15–16; 31:13–14; 34:4–9; 40:35; Lev 19:3, 30; 23:3; Num 11:13–14, 21–23; 14:11; Deut 6:4; 30:4; 32:39; 33:2–3.
>
> **The Psalms (i.e., Writings):** Job 9:8–11; Pss 23:1–2; 28:8–9; 68:30; 78:8, 19–20; 80:1–2; 89:9; 103:3; 104:1–2; 106:9; 107:23–32; 110:1; 118:25–26.
>
> **The Prophets:** 1 Kgs 19:11; Isa 11:11–12; 24:21–23; 25:6–8; 35:4–6; 40:3–5, 10–11; 41:4; 43:5–7, 10–11, 13, 25; 44:3; 46:4; 48:12; 49:24–26; 51:12; 54:5; 64:1; Jer 8:9; 16:16; 23:3; 31:10–14; Ezek 11:16–17, 23; 34:11–22, 30–31; 36:25–27; 39:29; Dan 7:9–10, 13–14; Hos 2:16–20; Joel 2:28–29; Jon 1:4–16; Mic 2:12–13; 7:14; Hab 3:3–4; Zech 2:6, 10; 3:2; 14:4–5, 9; Mal 3:1–3; 4:5–6.

These lists reveal numerous textual examples from each major section of the Jewish Scriptures, nicely matching the claim of Jesus that all parts of the Scriptures speak of him.[5] Moreover, some of the deepest pools from which YHWH-texts were *repeatedly* drawn also attest to Jesus's threefold sourcing: the Law (e.g., Exod 3:13–14; Deut 6:4); the Psalms (e.g., Pss 2:6–7; 110:1); the Prophets (e.g., Isa 40:3; Dan 7:13–14).[6]

---

nevertheless present in God's divine throne-room receiving universal authority and an everlasting kingdom. The Jesus of the Synoptics also accepts worship (Matt. 14:33), forgives sins (Mark 2:5), announces that people's final destinies will be based on their response to him (Mark 8:38; Luke 12:8–10), and applies metaphors to himself, particularly in his parables, that in the Old Testament are often applied to Yahweh (Lord of the harvest, shepherd, sower, vineyard owner, bridegroom, rock, etc.)."

[5] Similarly, Richard B. Hays, "Figural Exegesis and the Retrospective Re-Cognition of Israel's Story," *BBR* 29.1 (2019): 43.

[6] Matthew Barrett, *Canon, Covenant and Christology* (Downers Grove, IL: IVP Academic, 2020), 287, for example, underscores the radical nature of Synoptists' use of Ps 110:1 for Jesus when he writes, "Out of its twenty-one uses in the New Testament, seven come from the Gospels . . . all seven can be found in the Synoptics . . . which once again reiterates Stuhlmacher's point that a high Christology is not original to John. That Psalm 110 is absent from Judaic literature but pervades the New Testament canon says something. This 'difference simply reflects the fact that early Christians used the text to say something about Jesus which Second temple Jewish literature is not interested in saying about anyone: that he participates in the unique divine sovereignty over all things' [quotation of Richard Bauckham, *Jesus and the God of Israel* (Eerdmans, 2008), 22]."

5. The Synoptics Apply Both YHWH-Texts and Messianic Texts to Jesus

The application of YHWH-texts to Jesus appears in tandem with the application of messianic texts to Jesus, yet with no sense of contradiction between the two strands of fulfillment.[7] The two greatest eschatological promises in the OT may be the coming/presence of YHWH and the coming/presence of the Messiah. This study has not denied the latter, but has simply focused on how the former is supported by the application of OT YHWH-texts to Jesus.

Does the OT portray the Messiah as human or divine? Scholars are divided over the answer to that question. But the short answer is surely that messianic prophecies most often portray or imply the humanity of the Messiah as God's agent raised up to deliver and rule God's people. Thus, many alternate titles for the Messiah—Servant of YHWH, Son of Man, Son of David, Shepherd/King of Israel, Prophet like Moses, etc.—can suggest (even highlight) a human nature and identity for YHWH's Anointed One.[8] Although good arguments may be made for the expectation of a divine Messiah, there can be no doubt that the OT also anticipates the appearance of a human figure who is exalted by God to an eternal throne.

The question of a divine Messiah, however, is overshadowed by YHWH's promises to come personally and dwell in the midst of his people.[9] The surprise of the Synoptic Gospels is that Jesus claims (and is consistently portrayed as) the fulfillment of both lines of promises. There is no question that he is the human Messiah (leaving open the question of the Messiah's deity). But with the frequent application of YHWH-texts to Jesus, there is also no question in the Synoptic portrayals of Jesus that he is the embodiment of YHWH.[10] Therefore (and in view of Luke 24:25–27, 44–47), just as Jesus certainly expected his disciples to see him in OT *messiah*-texts, so also the data of this study loudly suggest that Jesus expected his disciples to see him in OT *YHWH*-texts.

It is true that Luke's readers are not made privy to specific interpretive examples in Jesus's discussion with the Emmaus travelers (cf. 24:27). But the whole of Luke's Gospel had already portrayed Jesus demonstrating his OT hermeneutic. He freely received and applied both messianic texts (e.g., 4:18–19; 10:22–23; 18:38–41) and YHWH-texts (e.g., 5:24; 6:46; 13:34) to himself. The same phenomenon can easily be shown to be the practice of Jesus in the Gospels of Matthew and Mark.

This dual-fulfillment portrayal undermines the fundamental assumption of works like J. R. Daniel Kirk's, *A Man Attested by God*. When Kirk argues that the Synoptics portray Jesus merely as an idealized human figure without divinity or preexistence,[11] he

---

[7] Cf. Larry W. Hurtado, *Ancient Jewish Monotheism and Early Christian Jesus-Devotion* (Waco, TX: Baylor University Press, 2017), 88, 93.

[8] As previously noted of several passages, the title "Son of *Man*" overtly calls attention to the humanity of the Messiah. Nevertheless, its Danielic sourcing portrays this figure with divine attributes and prerogatives. Crispin H. T. Fletcher-Louis, *Jesus Monotheism* (Eugene, OR: Wipf & Stock, 2015), 188, concludes that the Son of Man title is the only messianic title used by the Gospels that alludes to YHWH-texts "*in the service of a Yhwh Kyrios Christology*. We never find Jesus connected in this way to scriptural *Yhwh-Kyrios* texts through his identity as a prophet, the messiah (*christos*), a son of David, the Son of God title, or even 'Lord'" (emphasis Fletcher-Crispin). This is an overstated conclusion in view of how often "Lord" is used of Jesus with reference to YHWH-texts, but his point

overlooks a wealth of YHWH-text revelations. His stark error is in applying an either/or rubric to the both/and portrayal of Jesus in the Gospels.[12] Jesus is portrayed as both the anointed human agent and the personal embodiment of YHWH. Recognition of this dual portrayal comes from watching how the Synoptists apply both OT messiah-texts and OT YHWH-texts to Jesus, rather than by imposing an external paradigm onto their theological biographies. But by imposing his paradigm Kirk must then equivocate on what it means for Jesus to share the divine identity[13] and to do works

---

supports the fact that sometimes there is no sharp distinction in Scripture between the role of YHWH and his Messiah. Here, it is sufficient to note that, without negating the truth of the Messiah's divine nature, the OT Scriptures generally emphasize his humanity. The more revolutionary surprise of the Synoptics, however, is Jesus's identification with both messianic texts and YHWH-texts.

[9] Similarly, N. T. Wright, "Son of God and Christian Origins," in *Son of God*, ed. G. V. Allen et al. (University Park, PA: Eisenbrauns, 2019), 130–31.

[10] Cf. Benjamin Breckinridge Warfield, *The Person and Work of Christ*, (Philadelphia, PA: P&R Publishing, 1950), 58–59, 253–54, 255. John Hick, "The Logic of God Incarnate," *RelS* 25.4 (1989): 414–15, 420, on the other hand, appears to overlook the YHWH-text phenomenon in the Synoptics.

[11] E.g., Kirk, *A Man Attested by God*, 3, 23, 45.

[12] E.g., Kirk, *A Man Attested by God*, 516: "Indeed, what the passion narrative shows us in clearest terms is that the Jesus of Mark's story so fully embodies the person of the suffering Davidic king, and of the suffering servant, that he stands entirely on the human side of the divine-human divide." Censure of Kirk's either/or paradigm is common among his reviewers: e.g., Elizabeth E. Shively, "Review of A Man Attested By God by J. R. Daniel Kirk," *JETS* 60.3 (2017); 639; David B. Capes, "Review of A Man Attested By God by J. R. Daniel Kirk," *Int* 72.4 (2019); 443; Simon J. Gathercole, "Review of A Man Attested By God by J. R. Daniel Kirk," *SJT* 71.1 (2018); 104; Joshua Leim, "Theological Hermeneutics, Exegesis, and J. R. Daniel Kirk's A Man Attested by God," *JTI* 15.1 (2021); 28, 40; Mark Proctor, "Kirk's Assessment of Lukan Christology," *PRSt* 46.1 (2019); 99. In response, Kirk, "Still A Man Attested by God: A Response to Proctor, Thurman, and Wardle," *PRSt* 46.1 (2019); 112–13, acknowledges this common critique before issuing a challenge: "If someone wishes to argue for both/and, divine and human, this is going to have to come from fresh arguments or a different set of data. But I would also discourage scholars from looking. In my estimation, the stories work better when read as testimony to the myriad ways in which Jesus is messiah, savior, and otherwise the fulfillment of humanity's ruling and saving purposes." Kirk's answer to his critics utterly fails to address their concern. And since Kirk overlooks the vast majority of OT YHWH-texts applied to Jesus addressed in this study, he misses numerous "fresh arguments" against his view and (perplexingly) discourages other scholars from seeking such arguments, as well. Kirk's response to his critics reveals again the severe hermeneutical bias he utilized to assert his thesis.

[13] E.g., Kirk, *A Man Attested by God*, 263, argues that Mark portrays Jesus as "a specially designated human person embodying the divine prerogatives rather than a human embodiment of Israel's God as such." But divine prerogatives (by definition) belong to God alone. Jesus could walk on water by his own authority as God; Peter could walk on water by Jesus's authority as God to grant that miracle. But this is far from saying that Peter embodied divine prerogatives. Kirk apparently senses the equivocation when he adds that Jesus is not the embodiment of God "as such." Does he mean that Jesus is sort of (or seems to be) the embodiment of God, but not really? Kirk is equivocating. Elsewhere, 405, Kirk asserts that YHWH-text applications to Jesus must be portraying Jesus as a merely human messiah because it is "not the ontology of Jesus as God or the unity of Jesus with/as YHWH that is articulated." But this assertion is hard to swallow. Jesus (and the Evangelists) had an abundance of OT messiah-texts he could have appropriated to himself in order to affirm his human identity (ontology)—and sometimes he did!—but on numerous occasions he (and/or the Evangelists) chose to appropriate YHWH-texts to himself, affirming his divine identity (ontology). Kirk's loyalty to his paradigm sees more troubled waters of equivocation when he writes, 570, 579, "Idealized human Christology is a wide-ranging paradigm that accounts for Christological claims that reach as high as heaven – without thereby demanding the further inference that the character is thought to be preexistent or an earthly apparition of someone who is, inherently, Israel's God. The exalted place occupied by idealized humans makes it difficult to even articulate what would be entailed in the

that only God can do.[14] By definition and logic, if Jesus is creator and governs all things, he cannot then be one of those created and governed things (as a merely human agent, no matter how idealized), but rather the one God of biblical monotheism.

Illustrative of a better approach than Kirk's either/or reading of Jesus's identity as merely an "ideal human figure" is Channing Crisler's both/and reading of Jesus's identity as the "righteous ideal lamenter."[15] Crisler notes how Jesus is portrayed, particularly in Luke's Gospel, as both the ideal human lamenter and the embodied divine lamenter (who also answers the laments of God's people).[16] Not only did Jesus lament as the representative man (e.g., Luke 22:42–44; 18:7–8), but Jesus spoke as YHWH the lamenter (e.g., Luke 9:41–43; 13:34–35; 19:41–44) and YHWH the answerer of laments (e.g., Luke 5:8–10; 7:12–16, 8:24–25). And these instances are only a small subset of the many messianic-texts and YHWH-texts applied to Jesus in the Synoptic Gospels.

Five Ramifications from This Study

1. The Practice Implies an Early Origin and Deliberate Employment

The frequent application of OT YHWH-texts to Jesus in the Synoptic Gospels argues for their early origin and deliberate employment. This common practice in the earliest

---

appearance of a divine being who causes us to reimagine the inherent identity of Israel's God.... If we neglect to develop a broader theology of Jesus as idealized human being ... [w]e are left with a story that backs itself into a corner, was never able to construct a human character capable of fulfilling the quest that drives the narrative, and thus had to surrender its major plot line in favor of a divine entrance from outside to rescue those trapped within the confines of the unfolding script." Thus, Kirk recognizes Christological claims that reach as high as heaven, making it difficult for Kirk to imagine what it would be like if Israel's God actually did make an appearance. However, if one sets aside the constraints of Kirk's either/or paradigm, then it becomes transparent that Jesus himself fully articulated what is entailed in the appearance of Israel's God. YHWH-texts applied to Jesus overwhelmingly support this. Cf. James B. Prothro, "Review of *A Man Attested By God: The Human Jesus of the Synoptic Gospels*," *Logia* 29.3 (2020), 47, who also finds "Kirk's treatment of Old Testament YHWH-texts applied to Jesus ... underwhelming." Furthermore, Kirk oddly believes it is necessary for a human character to drive the Synoptic narrative rather than to "surrender" the major plot line to a divine entrance and rescue "from outside." But why the paradigmatic necessity to keep Jesus merely human? He is still a man, even if he is also YHWH in the flesh. And why is a divine entrance into the human story a surrender of the plot line? Is not the central theme of the Synoptics (and NT Christianity) God's intrusive rescue of fallen humans because they cannot save themselves? Ironically, to follow Kirk's paradigm would seem to gut the major plot line from the Synoptic narrative.

[14] E.g., Kirk, *A Man Attested by God*, 4, writes that in Scripture "human figures are variously represented as playing roles otherwise belonging to God alone ... such humans can be depicted as the very embodiment of God, God's visible representation, God's voice, the exhibition of God's rule and majesty." But how does a man play a role belonging to "God alone," if he is not also God? Is there no distinction between delegated representational roles for God's human agents and inherently divine prerogatives/roles for God alone? Richard Bauckham, "Is 'High Human Christology' Sufficient? A Critical Response to J. R. Daniel Kirk's, *A Man Attested by God*," *BBR* 27.4 (2017), esp. 508, 511, 517, criticizes Kirk for not making a distinction between merely human agents of God (who rule over some things) and Jesus (who rules over all things). The Scriptures present the sovereignty of angels and human kings as derived and limited by God, while they present the sovereignty of Jesus as instrinsic and unlimited, the kind of absolute rule possessed by YHWH alone.

[15] E.g., Channing L. Crisler, *Echoes of Lament and the Christology of Luke*, 238–39.

[16] E.g., Channing L. Crisler, *Echoes of Lament and the Christology of Luke*, 152–53, 192, 203, 221, 241.

Evangelists makes it difficult to imagine that their numerous occurrences were tacked on by later generations of the church or that Matthew, Mark, and Luke all employed the practice unintentionally or carelessly.

Paul's practice of applying OT YHWH-texts to Jesus as freely as he applied YHWH-texts to God has been irrefutably described in the study by Capes.[17] And since the Pauline corpus was penned in the 50s and 60s AD, its use of YHWH-texts for Jesus (bolstered by early creedal formulations for Jesus as "Lord," i.e., YHWH) was settled in the mind of Paul and his contemporaries by that time.[18] Although the epistles of Paul were occasioned by the missionary developments of his later ministry, they reflect the radical doctrinal shift that took place at his conversion likely within two years of the death and resurrection of Jesus.[19] Paul's doctrinal timeline, which includes personal discussions with the apostles Peter and James within the first decade of Jesus's departure (Gal 1:18–19) and personal confirmation fourteen years later with the apostolic "pillars" James, Peter, and John (Gal 2:1, 9), does not allow for an extended development or plethora of Christological views in the early church. Rather, Paul's timeline from conversion to doctrinal codification in his Epistles supports a very early unity among the first generation of Christian leaders as to the divine lordship of Jesus.[20]

Similarly, since Luke's Gospel is generally considered to be the last of the Synoptics to be written—and since Luke's sequel (Acts) concludes abruptly with events occurring around AD 62—it may be that his Gospel was written no later than AD 62, which implies that the Gospels of Mark and Matthew could have begun circulating in the AD 50s.[21] This possible timeline would place all of the synoptic Evangelists during the first generation of the Church after Christ's death and resurrection and, in fact, would place them among Jesus's personal disciples and/or eyewitnesses of his resurrection or (at least) among the contemporaries of living apostles and eyewitnesses.[22]

Furthermore, if the Synoptics were all written in the 50s or early 60s, then much of their first readership could attest to their veracity. This would mean that, in sync with Paul, the Synoptists were liberally applying OT YHWH-texts to Jesus within the first generation of Jesus's post-resurrection followers. In other words, the YHWH-text phenomenon in the Synoptic Gospels is not explained well by a theory of changing oral traditions eventually gathered and edited by communities in generations removed

---

[17] David B. Capes, *Old Testament Yahweh Texts in Paul's Christology* (Tübingen, Germany: J. C. B. Mohr (Paul Siebeck), 1992; repr. 2017, Baylor University Press, Waco, TX).
[18] For comments on the established creedal use of "Jesus is Lord" antedating Paul's letters, see, Vincent Taylor, *The Names of Jesus* (London: Macmillan & Co. Ltd., 1953), 47; Hurtado, *Ancient Jewish Monotheism and Early Christian Jesus-Devotion*, 203.
[19] Cf. Larry W. Hurtado, *Lord Jesus Christ* (Grand Rapids, MI: Eerdmans, 2003), 83.
[20] Cf. I. Howard Marshall, "The Development of Christology in the Early Church," *TynBul* 18 (1967), 84–85; Michael Welker, *God the Revealed* (Grand Rapids, MI: Eerdmans, 2013), 74–75; David B. Capes, *The Divine Christ* (Grand Rapids, MI: Baker Academic, 2018), 182–83.
[21] Cf. Blomberg, "Where Do We Start Studying Jesus?," 29. Although there could have been theological reasons for Luke to stop his narrative with Paul still under house arrest while the Gospel was spreading "unhindered" (Acts 28:31), there would surely have been profound exhortational reasons to record a thriving Christian movement after the death of Paul and the destruction of Jerusalem. But they are not included. Therefore, the Book of Acts likely began circulating before those major events and near the time of its narrative ending in the late 60s.
[22] Similarly, Craig S. Keener, *Christobiography* (Grand Rapids, MI: Eerdmans, 2019), 498.

from Jesus, but rather as the confirmable testimonies of apostles and/or eyewitnesses circulated with the oversight of apostolic authority.[23]

The frequency of the YHWH-text phenomenon in all of the Synoptic accounts further testifies to their authorial intent. Matthew, Mark, and Luke cannot have been jointly careless or uniformly ignorant of their numerous blunders, if they did not intend their readers to see Jesus as the embodiment of YHWH.[24] Rather, the Synoptists demonstrate a deliberate—even, aggressive—practice of applying OT YHWH-texts to Jesus. They have a demonstrable agenda, which they play out over and over in each of their Gospels: *Jesus must be understood as YHWH in the flesh.* Their first readership, bathed in first century Jewish expectation of YHWH's coming, may have detected that truth as easily as modern readership now detects it in the prologue of John's Gospel.

2. The Evidence Suggests that Jesus Is the Source of the Practice

The ubiquitous nature of the YHWH-text phenomenon in the Synoptics, particularly since it is regularly employed by Jesus, suggests that Jesus himself is the source of the practice.[25] Embedded within each of the Synoptic accounts are various declarations and deeds of Jesus himself recalling YHWH-texts. He self-identifies as YHWH by the application of OT revelation unique to YHWH. And his practice is surely the basis for each Evangelist applying YHWH-texts to Jesus throughout their own narrative descriptions and (sometimes unwittingly) from the speeches of other characters.[26]

Not only can the Synoptics reader see Jesus repeatedly alluding to OT YHWH-texts to reveal his identity, but he can see Jesus claim himself as the hermeneutical key to understanding the entire OT revelation. The implications of Luke 24 (cf. John 5:39) cannot be exaggerated. The OT is the story of YHWH's dealings with Israel and the nations in the light of his identity as sole Creator and Redeemer of the universe. YHWH is the Maker and Ruler of all. There is none like him. He not only orchestrates all history, he is the central figure of his own special revelation (i.e., the Jewish Scriptures). Within Israel's story, YHWH is the true center and chief Actor. He is the hermeneutical key to understanding both general and special revelation.

---

[23] Cf. Richard Bauckham, "The Gospels as Testimony to Jesus Christ: A Contemporary View of Their Historical Value," in *The Oxford Handbook of Christology*, ed. Francesca Murphy (Oxford; New York: Oxford University Press, 2015), 57, 67, 69; N. T. Wright, *The New Testament and the People of God* (Minneapolis, MN: Fortress Press, 1992), 421.

[24] Capes, *The Divine Christ*, 173, reasons similarly for YHWH-texts in Paul: "It may be one thing to 'slip up' and link Christ with God's name in a single text; but Paul programmatically read texts containing the divine name in relation to Jesus over and over again in a variety of contexts. And we should not forget that Paul was reading these texts in relation to a man of recent history, not a religious figure from two thousand years ago. This is a remarkable development that took place within only a few years of Jesus's execution."

[25] Similarly, Carl F. H. Henry, "The Identity of Jesus of Nazareth," *CTR* 6.1 (1992): 127.

[26] C. H. Dodd, *According to the Scriptures*, 110, argues that the surprising application of Psalm 110, the Son of Man in Daniel, and various other OT passages to Jesus in the Gospels must have come from Jesus himself. Andrew Ter Ern Loke, *The Origin of Divine Christology*, 137–39, 144–45, 200–1, adds that Jesus's first disciples likely would not have defended his divine identity unless he had convinced them of it himself by word and deed. The numerous applications of OT YHWH-texts to Jesus in the Synoptics testify to this conviction.

But Jesus could claim that he is the true center and hermeneutical key to understanding the (Jewish) Scriptures. The Scriptures are all, in every part, about *him* (24:27, 44). Such a claim would be transparently ludicrous, if not made by God. Thus, Jesus opens the door (as he "opened the Scriptures" and "opened the minds" of his disciples; 24:32, 45) to see him as YHWH in the Scriptures.[27] He therefore justifies (in Luke's final chapter) his public practice of applying YHWH-texts to himself (as recorded in Luke's previous chapters).

Jesus's own practice speaks volumes about his self-consciousness and self-identity.[28] He implies, by what he presumes is a natural and legitimate appropriation of OT YHWH-texts to himself, that he eclipses God's Law and God's Temple (Matt 12:8; Mark 13:31; Luke 9:26-36),[29] as well as God's prophets, priests, and kings (Matt 16:27; Mark 2:5; Luke 3:4-6; cf. Matt 12:41-42). While it is true that no mortal can plumb the depths of the psyche of Jesus, nevertheless, Jesus has willingly disclosed his self-understanding at many points. And by referencing YHWH-texts to explain his person and work, Jesus self-consciously claims the identity and prerogatives of YHWH. This is the unified testimony of the Synoptists—a unity which itself is an argument that Jesus is the source of their application of YHWH-texts to him. Thus, the Synoptists followed their Lord even in his Christological use of the OT.[30]

3. The Synoptics Rival John's High Christology by This Practice

The YHWH-text phenomenon in the Synoptic Gospels implies a united Christology as high as that of John's Gospel. Gospels criticism of the nineteenth and twentieth centuries generally sees the Synoptics as having a low Christology (Jesus as merely human) and John as having a high Christology (Jesus as not merely human, but also divine).[31] But

---

[27] While numerous studies may be cited to demonstrate the validity of seeing Jesus as YHWH in the Jewish Scriptures, here are two brief examples which demonstrate complementary approaches: Philip B. Payne, "Jesus' Implicit Claim to Deity in His Parables," *TJ* 2 (1981): 3-23; Daniel Doriani, "The Deity of Christ in the Synoptic Gospels," *JETS* 37.3 (1994): 333-50.

[28] It is true that Jesus's self-consciousness "is not available to us" (Stephen J. Wellum, "The Deity of Christ in the Synoptic Gospels" in Christopher W. Morgan and Robert A. Peterson, *The Deity of Christ* (Wheaton, IL: Crossway), 62). However, aspects of his thinking are certainly available to us by his self-identifying and revelatory choices, which include the self-application of various OT YHWH-texts.

[29] Cf. N. T. Wright, *Jesus and the Victory of God* (Minneapolis, MN: Fortress Press, 1996), 653.

[30] Cf. F. F. Bruce, *Jesus, Lord and Savior* (Downers Grove, IL: InterVarsity Press, 1986), 204.

[31] Although it is variously expressed, the critical view often appears as mere assertion and without any recognition of the YHWH-text phenomenon: e.g., Hick, "The Logic of God Incarnate," 420, asserts, "Thus even if one were to grant the possibility of God becoming incarnate, on the Fourth Gospel model, as a physically human being who is at least sometimes conscious of being divine, eternal, omnipotent and omniscient, this would not be the Jesus whom historical research has glimpsed through the synoptic gospels." P. Maurice Casey, *From Jewish Prophet to Gentile God* (Louisville, KY: Westminster/Knox Press, 1991), 166, further asserts, "We have found these beliefs only in the Johannine literature, and we must take seriously the obverse of this fact—most New Testament writers did not believe that Jesus was incarnate and divine. Neither did Jesus of Nazareth, nor did the first apostles." Harold Bloom, *Jesus and Yahweh* (New York: Riverhead Books, 2007), 5, on a more popular level asserts, "I cannot recall a single passage in the Synoptic Gospels that unequivocally identifies Jesus as God: such status comes to him only in John." None of these assertions appears to show any awareness of the ubiquitous YHWH-text phenomenon in the Synoptics.

the data of this study exposes this critical view as biased thinking that neglects large portions of the evidence to the contrary. In particular, advocates of a low Christology in the Synoptics have largely overlooked the numerous ways and occasions in which the Synoptics have applied OT YHWH-texts to Jesus.

All the Synoptics, as well as John, use the same classic OT promises of YHWH coming to his people—Isa 40:3 and Mal 3:1—to identify Jesus.[32] Although John opens his Gospel with a theological treatise of Jesus as God in the flesh (John 1:1–18), Matthew and Luke both portray the same divine incarnation, in large part, through the application of OT YHWH-texts to Jesus in his virgin birth narratives (cf. Matt 1:21–25; 2:5–6; Luke 1:31–35, 68, 76–79).[33] Likewise, although it is often claimed that John's Gospel alone applied the divine Name to Jesus through the use of "I am" statements, the claim is misleading, since the feature is alive and well in the Synoptic records (Matt 14:27; Mark 6:50; 13:6; 14:62; Luke 21:8; 22:70).[34] It is more accurate to say that John recounted more instances than Luke did of Jesus's "I am" sayings—just as Luke recounted more instances than John did of applying to Jesus both YHWH's promise to visit his people (Luke 1:68, 78; 7:16; 19:44) and YHWH's way being prepared for his coming (1:17, 76; 3:4–6; 7:26–27). Even if the Synoptics contained no "I am" statements, that would not negate the high Christology underscored by the numerous other occasions in which they apply OT YHWH-texts to Jesus.[35]

The long-held critical bifurcation of the Synoptics and John in terms of low and high Christologies should have been abandoned long ago. And the YHWH-text phenomenon helps to explain why. Most scholars acknowledge a relatively later date of writing for John's Gospel: traditional scholarship believes the Synoptics began circulating in the 50s or 60s and John in the 80s or 90s, while more critical scholarship tends to place the Synoptic writings in the 70s to 90s and John in the 90s or early second century. Although the evidence mentioned above favors the traditional timeline, even if the critical timeline were correct, the documents themselves argue against a development of low to high Christology between the Synoptics and John. This developmental view is now difficult to defend, since all of the canonical Gospels

---

[32] Henry, "The Identity of Jesus of Nazareth," 126, writes, "The critical effort to set the Synoptics over against the Fourth Gospel in respect to affirmation of the deity of Jesus Christ was unavailing. Even the least dogmatic of the Synoptics, the Gospel of Mark, which uses the Old Testament references sparingly, nonetheless opens with two Old Testament passages (Isa 40:3; Mal 3:1) that speak of the messenger who prepares for the historical arrival of the Lord." Cf. Norm Mundhenk, "Jesus Is Lord: The Tetragrammaton in Bible Translation," *BT* 61.2 (2010): 55–56; N. T. Wright, "Pictures, Stories, and the Cross: Where Do the Echoes Lead?" *JTI* 11.1 (2017): 49.

[33] Cf. Blomberg, "Where Do We Start Studying Jesus?," 39.

[34] James D. G. Dunn, *Jesus According to the New Testament* (Grand Rapids, MI: Eerdmans, 2019), 54–55, follows a long line of claimants when he writes, "It is a striking fact that these 'I am' sayings appear only in the Fourth Gospel. It is almost impossible to believe that there were such sayings in the Jesus tradition, sayings that Jesus was remembered as uttering about himself, and yet all three synoptic evangelists ignored them completely." Fortunately, some commentators reject Dunn's fallacy and have pointed out several occurrences in the Synoptics of Jesus making "I am" statements: e.g., Dean L. Overman, *A Case for the Divinity of Jesus* (Lanham, MD: Rowman & Littlefield, 2009), 58–59; Riemer Roukema, *Jesus, Gnosis and Dogma* (New York: T&T Clark, 2010), 42–43.

[35] Cf. Blomberg, "Where Do We Start Studying Jesus?," 39.

frequently apply OT YHWH-texts to Jesus, thus demonstrating that none of the Evangelists possessed a low Christology.[36]

Furthermore, the transparent theological agenda of John's Gospel (along with his epistles) was not merely to prove the deity of Jesus but to prove his *humanity*, as docetic and proto-Gnostic influences became an increasing threat to settled Christian doctrine.[37] In other words, John's prologue and subsequent narrative did not seek to change what was an already established Christology of Jesus's divine identity, but rather to reassert against an apparent docetism that Jesus could not be reduced to a divine spirit being (similar to the "Jesus" in the Gospel of Thomas) and was indeed the Word who *became flesh* (John 1:14). John's uniqueness among the Evangelists likely evidences, in part, the later time period during which he wrote. But differences between John's Gospel and the Synoptics do not bear out Christological development, but rather Christological defense against *cultural* changes. Jesus is portrayed as God and Man in the Synoptics, as well as in John. Ironically (for the critical scholar), Synoptic applications of OT YHWH-texts applied to Jesus testify to an early high Christology, and Johannine emphases on the *incarnation* show a later defense of Jesus's humanity.[38]

4. The Practice Reveals Jesus as the Central Figure of the Scriptures

The YHWH-text phenomenon reveals the person and work of Jesus as the crescendo of the metanarrative continued from the Jewish Scriptures. The Bible's story of all things begins with the creation and ends with the new creation. However, that is not the biblical-theological center of the metanarrative. God is the center: "In the beginning, God..." (Gen 1:1). He is the Creator, Judge, Redeemer, and Ruler from creation to new creation. The presence of YHWH as the Triune God in creation leads eventually to the presence of YHWH as the Triune God in the new creation. In between, YHWH manifests his relational and saving presence for the benefit of various Patriarchs and their descendants (particularly, Israel)[39] and, through a

---

[36] Barrett, *Canon, Covenant and Christology*, 288, rightly notes, "[O]ne must remember that the Synoptics need not move into an excursus on the person of Jesus to present a high view of his divinity and pre-existence. By portraying, in narrative format, the *works* Jesus performs, the Synoptics teach Jesus' divine identity just as much as John" (emphasis Barrett).

[37] Similarly, Capes, *Old Testament Yahweh Texts in Paul's Christology*, 182–83.

[38] P. Maurice Casey, "The Deification of Jesus," in *1994 Seminar Papers*, ed. Eugene H. Lovering Jr. (Chicago, IL: Scholar's Press, 1994), 706, posits a three-stage Christology in which the third stage occurs only after the destruction of Jerusalem and "the Johannine community quarreled with 'the Jews' so decisively that they took on Gentile self-identification. At this stage also, they dropped the boundary marker of Jewish monotheism, and hailed Jesus as God with such clarity and determination that 'the Jews' accused them of blasphemy." But the death-knell to Casey's developmental theory of Christology is found in the early ubiquitous application of OT YHWH-texts to Jesus by the Synoptists long before John wrote his Gospel. Kevin J. Vanhoozer, *Is There a Meaning in This Text?* (Grand Rapids, MI: Zondervan, 2009), 291, identifies the root of the critics' problem: "In the case of the Gospels, the texts are the only access we have to the events in question. It should be evident that the skeptical critic stands at a distinct disadvantage to the believer when it comes to apprehending the subject matter of the Gospels: 'The attempt to get behind these testimonies does not enable us to say more but to say less than they do.' For too long, biblical critics have sought to understand the biblical text by ignoring its plain testimony and instead attempting to cross-examine extra-textual witnesses (e.g., other ancient literary sources, archaeological evidence, etc.). This, as I have argued, takes us as far as thin description only; for, inasmuch as one distrusts testimony, one removes the most important means of knowing what the Bible is about."

climactic crisis of sacrifice and judgment to address his people's faithless sin (Isa 53; Zech 12:10; 13:7), he promises his saving presence in spiritually new ways for his post-exilic gathered people (Isa 59:20–21; Jer 32:37–40; Ezek 36:24–28). YHWH compares his redemptive new-creational relationship with his eschatological people to a marriage which can never again be broken (Jer 31:31–34; Hos 2:19–20). Thus, his manifest presence with his redeemed people shall never end (Ezek 37:26–28; Zech 2:10–11).

Jesus, by application of various OT YHWH-texts, claims that his appearance within that metanarrative is that of YHWH redeeming his people after the exile in order to gather them for the new creation (e.g., Matt 11:28; 28:18–20; Mark 1:17; Luke 13:34). For a time, then, YHWH visited his people in his manifest personal presence (i.e., in Jesus)[40] for the purpose of accomplishing salvation for sinners by giving his life as their ransom (Matt 20:28; Mark 10:45). And, having accomplished the promised redemption before returning to his exalted state, Jesus promised his continuing divine presence by the Holy Spirit until he returns visibly to judge all peoples and to dwell forever with his redeemed people in the glory of his personal manifest presence.[41]

Much more could be added to fill out the details of the biblical metanarrative.[42] But the application of OT YHWH-texts to Jesus in the Synoptic Gospels underscores that Jesus is the embodied presence of YHWH in a sweeping two-act play that is divided by his divine incarnation.[43] Jesus, as portrayed by the Evangelists, understood himself to be the long-expected coming/presence of YHWH. To miss this continuity is to ignore the Scriptures of Act One (the OT) and to atomize the Scriptures of Act Two (the NT).[44]

---

[39] Cf. C. John Collins, "How the New Testament Quotes and Interprets the Old Testament," in *Understanding Scripture*, ed. Wayne A. Grudem, C. John Collins, and Thomas R. Schreiner (Wheaton, IL: Crossway, 2012), 186; N. T. Wright, "'The Evangelists' Use of the Old Testament as an Implicit Overarching Narrative," in *Biblical Interpretation and Method*, ed. K. J. Dell and P. M. Joyce (Oxford: Oxford University Press, 2013), 195.

[40] This is especially pronounced in Matthew's Immanuel theme (1:23; 18:20; 28:18–20). Cf. Ryan Lister, *The Presence of God* (Wheaton, IL: Crossway, 2015), 255; Richard B. Hays, *Echoes of Scripture in the Gospels* (Waco, TX: Baylor University Press, 2016), 162–63. Luke's divine visitation passages also come to mind (1:68, 78; 7:16; 19:44). Ultimately, however, YHWH's embodied presence in Jesus is implied in all Synoptic YHWH-text applications.

[41] Jesus implied that he was the embodiment of YHWH not only in his first advent, but during his absence and when he would personally return in his second advent (e.g., Matt 7:21–22; 25:31–33; Luke 5:24, 35; 9:26; 24:49). His embodiment is thus everywhere assumed while not explicitly described during the mystery of his first earthly advent. Cf. Richard B. Hays, *Reading Backwards* (London: SPCK Publishing, 2015), 31.

[42] Richard J. Bauckham, "Christology," *Dictionary of Jesus and the Gospels*, 126, explains what he calls "Metanarratival Christology." Other scholars have suggested metanarratival themes (such as the divine name, the temple, and the covenantal storyline) that clearly overlap thematically with the relational presence of YHWH/Jesus with his people. See, Oskar Grether, *Name Und Wort Gottes Im Alten Testament* (Giessen, Germany: Alfred Töppelmann, 1934), 183; N. T. Wright, "Jesus' Self-Understanding," in *The Incarnation*, ed. S. T. Davis, D. Kendall, and G. O'Collins (Oxford: Oxford University Press, 2002), 56–57; Stephen J. Wellum, *Christ Alone* (Grand Rapids, MI: Zondervan, 2017), 50–51.

[43] The illustration of the Old and New Testaments as a two-act play was ably posed by John Bright, *The Kingdom of God in Bible and Church* (London: Lutterworth Press, 1955), 200. Cf. Alec Motyer, *Look to the Rock* (Leicester, England: InterVarsity Press, 1996), 20. Similarly, see, Hays, *Reading Backwards*, 14–16.

[44] Similarly, N. T. Wright, "Kingdom Come: The Public Meaning of the Gospels," *ChrCent* 125.12 (2008): 30.

Each part explains the other and points to the creative mind of one ultimate Author and Actor.[45] The claims of Jesus cannot be explained by, nor attached to, Hellenistic religions, because the YHWH-texts in which they are saturated are thoroughly Jewish and serve as the basis for Jesus's manifest "coming"—just as YHWH had promised to do in Act One of the drama.[46] Act Two centers on Jesus's fulfillment and completion of the redemptive-historical metanarrative.[47] The Synoptics, in particular, all pick up where the OT left off in order to reveal Jesus as the promised coming/presence of YHWH.[48] Jesus is the key that unlocks YHWH's personal promises of OT eschatology.[49] In this light, YHWH-texts applied to Jesus can be seen simply as a natural expression of the promise/fulfillment structure connecting the Two Testaments.

5. The Data Encourage Pursuits in Other Vital Christological Studies

The data from this study encourage additional biblical-theological studies that could significantly impact future understanding and approaches to Christology. Three suggestions follow.

First, there are large portions of the NT which need to be included in future YHWH-text inquiries. David B. Capes has focused on Paul; this study has focused on the Synoptic Gospels. But additional light needs to be shed on the practice in the General Epistles, whether as a whole or by distinct authors, such as the Petrine or Johannine Epistles. Large tracts, like Hebrews, Acts, and Revelation seem crucial for this inquiry, as does John's Gospel (which would clearly be valuable for comparison with the practice in the Synoptics). Comparisons of YHWH-text applications by author (e.g., Paul to John, or Peter to the Author of Hebrews), by genre (e.g., epistles to Gospels, or narratives to apocalyptic), or by date (e.g., James or early Paul to the Johannine corpus) may also prove valuable for understanding the interpretive phenomenon and early Christological themes and emphases.

Second, this study encourages inquiries into the intertextual hermeneutics of the NT use of the OT. In particular, granting that Jesus applied OT YHWH-texts to himself, in what ways did he do so? And why did others (e.g., Paul, the Synoptists)

---

[45] Cf. G. K. Beale, *Handbook on the New Testament Use of the Old Testament* (Grand Rapids, MI: Baker Academic, 2012), 97; Hays, "Figural Exegesis and the Retrospective Re-Cognition of Israel's Story," 44, 46.

[46] Contra Wilhelm Bousset, *Kyrios Christos*, trans. John E. Steely (Nashville, TN: Abingdon Press, 1970), 128, 134, 149–51; and contra Lawrence M. Wills, "Wisdom and Word among the Hellenistic Saviors: The Function of Literacy," *JSP* 24.2 (2014): 123, 140–41. Michael F. Bird, "The Peril of Modernizing Jesus and the Crisis of Not Contemporizing the Christ," *EQ* 78.4 (2006): 310, navigates to a more balanced corrective. Cf. Capes, *The Divine Christ*, 32, 43–44.

[47] Cf. Beale, *Handbook on the New Testament Use of the Old Testament*, 97; Bauckham, "Christology," 125–27; Wright, "Pictures, Stories, and the Cross," 50.

[48] Cf. Christopher J. H. Wright, "Christ and the Old Testament," *JTI* 2.1 (2008): 12–13; N. T. Wright, *The New Testament and the People of God*, 396–97.

[49] Cf. N. T. Wright, "The Biblical Formation of a Doctrine of Christ," in *Who Do You Say That I Am?*, ed. Donald Armstrong (Grand Rapids, MI: Eerdmans, 1999), 64–65.

believe they were justified to follow suit?⁵⁰ Does this mean the modern interpreter is justified (as presumed in this study) to do the same? And how does this form of intertextuality relate to interpretive "meaning" and "significance." Is Kevin Vanhoozer correct to say that "meaning" is the author's intended meaning, while "significance" is the author's extended meaning?[51] Does this help explain the practice of the application of YHWH-texts to Jesus? If so, how? Are YHWH-text applications to Jesus in the NT the inspired "extended meaning" (significance) of the "authorial meaning" of OT texts concerning YHWH? Why or why not?[52]

And third, does the YHWH-text phenomenon help solve the problem of a "center" in biblical theology? Current scholarship appears to frown on the search for an overarching theme or subject of the entire Bible and generally posits the weaving together of multiple subjects and themes. Does the Synoptic practice of applying OT YHWH-texts to Jesus address the current consensus? Do Jesus's claims in Luke 24 sound different in the light of the YHWH-text phenomenon?[53] And does Richard Bauckham's conceptual expression of Jesus "sharing in the divine identity" make any contribution here?[54] If Jesus can self-identify as YHWH, does this not lead to some manner of a Christological or Trinitarian "center" in biblical theology?

These suggestions for further study reflect the central importance of their Subject, who is "Christ the Lord" (Luke 2:11), and of whom his Spirit-indwelt people confess, "Jesus is Lord" (1 Cor 12:3; cf. Rom 10:9). The significance of this NT creedal claim is filled-out by acknowledging that the NT Lord is the OT YHWH. Similarly, the great significance of OT YHWH-texts applied to Jesus in the Synoptic Gospels is that the ubiquitous practice identifies Jesus as the embodied presence of YHWH.

---

[50] Grant R. Osborne, "History and Theology in the Synoptic Gospels," *TJ* 24NS (2003): 7, in another context, rightly reminds the Synoptics reader that portraying Jesus truly required the Evangelists to write theologized history. Wright, *The New Testament and the People of God*, 402–3, clarifies that the Evangelists did not produce anachronistic accounts of Jesus, but continued the history of Israel with the historical advent of Jesus as the basis of their theology.

[51] Vanhoozer, *Is There a Meaning in This Text?*, 262, 264–65, further describes how "significance" as a kind of *sensus plenior* of the NT also argues for one divine Author of the Scriptures.

[52] The YHWH-text phenomenon as practiced by NT writers is clearly meant to fill out the meaning of the OT texts that apply to Jesus. Hindsight (aided by the NT inspired interpretation and application of OT texts) adds greater understanding. The NT in particular often provides a "thick" interpretation of OT texts which possessed a relatively "thin" meaning in their original contexts: cf. Beale, *Handbook on the New Testament Use of the Old Testament*, 27; Stephen J. Wellum, *God the Son Incarnate* (Wheaton, IL: Crossway, 2016), 87. Progressive revelation, by definition, reveals more meaning and significance without contradicting the originally intended meaning.

[53] G. W. Grogan, "The New Testament Interpretation of the Old Testament: A Comparative Study," *TynBul* 18 (1967): 73, points out the radical nature of Jesus's self-definitive hermeneutic to the OT: "The Rabbinic concentration of attention upon the Law was replaced by Him with a Christocentric interpretation of the Old Testament (Mt. 26:54–56; Lk. 4:16–21; 24:25–27, 44–47; Jn. 5:38–40)." Cf. Roch A. Kereszty, *Jesus Christ*, rev. and updated ed. (New York: Alba House, 2002); Wright, "Christ and the Old Testament," 12–15.

[54] E.g., Richard Bauckham, *God Crucified* (Grand Rapids, MI: Eerdmans, 1998), 42: "Once we have rid ourselves of the prejudice that high Christology must speak of Christ's divine nature, we can see the obvious fact that the Christology of divine identity common to the whole New Testament is the highest Christology of all. It identifies Jesus as intrinsic to who God is."

Bibliography

Abba, Raymond. "The Divine Name Yahweh." *Journal of Biblical Literature* 80.4 (1961): 320–28.
Abernethy, Andrew T., and Greg Goswell. *God's Messiah in the Old Testament: Expectations of a Coming King.* Grand Rapids, MI: Baker Academic, 2020.
Achtemeier, Paul J. "Gospel Miracle Tradition and the Divine Man." *Interpretation* 26.2 (1972): 174–97.
Achtemeier, Paul J. "'He Taught Them Many Things': Reflections on Marcan Christology." *Catholic Biblical Quarterly* 42.4 (1980): 465–81.
Achtemeier, Paul J. "Mark, Gospel Of." Pages 541–57 in vol. 4 of *The Anchor Bible Dictionary* 6 vols. New York: Doubleday, 1992.
Achtemeier, Paul J. "Person and Deed: Jesus and the Storm-Tossed Sea." *Interpretation* 16.2 (1962): 169–76.
Adams, Edward. "The Coming of the Son of Man in Mark's Gospel." *Tyndale Bulletin* 56.1 (2005): 39–61.
Aland, Kurt, ed. *Synopsis Quattuor Evangeliorum.* 2nd ed. Stuttgart: Deutsche Bibelgesellschaft, 1985.
Albright, W. F., and C. S. Mann. *Matthew.* AB. Garden City, NY: Doubleday, 1971.
Alexander, Joseph Addison. *The Gospel According to Mark.* New York: Charles Scribner, 1858. Repr., Grand Rapids, MI: Baker Books, 1980.
Allen, Leslie C. *Psalms 101–150.* Rev. ed. WBC 21. Nashville, TN: Nelson, 2002.
Allison, Dale C., Jr. "The Embodiment of God's Will: Jesus in Matthew." Pages 117–32 in *Seeking the Identity of Jesus: A Pilgrimage.* Edited by Beverly Roberts Gaventa and Richard B. Hays. Grand Rapids, MI: Eerdmans, 2008.
Baird, William. *From Jonathan Edwards to Rudolf Bultmann.* Vol. 2 of *History of New Testament Research.* Minneapolis, MN: Fortress, 2003.
Baker, David W. "God, Names Of." Pages 359–68 in *Dictionary of the Old Testament: Pentateuch.* Downers Grove, IL: InterVarsity Press, 2003.
Barker, Joel D. "Day of the Lord." Pages 132–43 in *Dictionary of the Old Testament Prophets.* Downers Grove, IL: InterVarsity Press, 2012.
Barrett, Matthew. *Canon, Covenant and Christology: Rethinking Jesus and the Scriptures of Israel.* Downers Grove, IL: IVP Academic, 2020.
Bauckham, Richard. "Biblical Theology and the Problems of Monotheism." Pages 187–232 in *Out of Egypt: Biblical Theology and Biblical Interpretation.* Edited by Craig G. Bartholomew et al. Milton Keynes, UK: Paternoster; Grand Rapids, MI: Zondervan, 2004.
Bauckham, Richard. "Christology." Pages 125–34 in *Dictionary of Jesus and the Gospels.* 2nd ed. Downers Grove, IL: InterVarsity Press, 2013.
Bauckham, Richard. *God Crucified: Monotheism and Christology in the New Testament.* Grand Rapids, MI: Eerdmans, 1998.
Bauckham, Richard. "The Gospel of John and the Synoptic Problem." Pages 657–88 in *New Studies in the Synoptic Problem.* Edited by P. Foster et al. Leuven; Paris; Walpole: Peeters, 2011.

Bauckham, Richard. "The Gospels as Testimony to Jesus Christ: A Contemporary View of Their Historical Value." Pages 55–71 in *The Oxford Handbook of Christology*. Edited by Francesca Murphy. Oxford; New York: Oxford University Press, 2015.

Bauckham, Richard. "The Incarnation and the Cosmic Christ." Pages 25–57 in *Incarnation: On the Scope and Depth of Christology*. Edited by Niels Henrik Gregersen. Minneapolis, MN: Fortress, 2015.

Bauckham, Richard. "Is 'High Human Christology' Sufficient? A Critical Response to J. R. Daniel Kirk's *A Man Attested by God*." *Bulletin for Biblical Research* 27.4 (2017): 503–25.

Bauckham, Richard. *Jesus and the Eyewitnesses: The Gospels as Eyewitness Testimony*. 2nd ed. Grand Rapids, MI: Eerdmans, 2017.

Bauckham, Richard. *Jesus and the God of Israel: God Crucified and Other Studies on the New Testament's Christology of Divine Identity*. Grand Rapids, MI: Eerdmans, 2008.

Bauckham, Richard. "Jesus, Worship Of." Pages 812–19 in vol. 3 of *The Anchor Bible Dictionary*. Edited by David Noel Freedman. 6 vols. New York: Doubleday, 1992.

Bauckham, Richard. "Markan Christology According to Richard Hays: Some Addenda." *Journal of Theological Interpretation* 11.1 (2017): 21–36.

Bauckham, Richard. "The Power and the Glory: The Rendering of Psalm 110:1 in Mark 14:62." Pages 83–101 in *From Creation to New Creation: Biblical Theology and Exegesis*. Edited by Daniel M. Gurtner and Benjamin L. Gladd. Peabody, MA: Hendrickson, 2013.

Bauer, David R. *The Gospel of the Son of God: An Introduction to Matthew*. Downers Grove, IL: IVP Academic, 2019.

Bayer, Hans F. *A Theology of Mark: The Dynamic Between Christology and Authentic Discipleship*. Phillipsburg, PA: P&R, 2012.

Beale, G. K. *Handbook on the New Testament Use of the Old Testament: Exegesis and Interpretation*. Grand Rapids, MI: Baker Academic, 2012.

Beale, G. K., and Benjamin L. Gladd. *The Story Retold: A Biblical-Theological Introduction to the New Testament*. Downers Grove, IL: IVP Academic, 2020.

Beardsley, Steven J. "Luke's Narrative Agenda: The Use of Κύριος within Luke-Acts to Proclaim the Identity of Jesus." PhD diss., Temple University, 2012.

Beare, Francis Wright. *The Gospel According to Matthew: Translation, Introduction, and Commentary*. San Francisco: Harper & Row, 1982.

Beers, Holly. "4QConsolations and Mark 6:30–56: Images of a New Exodus." Pages 100–107 in *Reading Mark in Context: Jesus and Second Temple Judaism*. Edited by Ben C. Blackwell, John K. Goodrich, and Jason Maston. Grand Rapids, MI: Zondervan, 2018.

Bendoraitis, Kristian A. "The Parables of Enoch and Mark 1:14–2:12: The Authoritative Son of Man." Pages 48–54 in *Reading Mark in Context: Jesus and Second Temple Judaism*. Edited by Ben C. Blackwell, John K. Goodrich, and Jason Maston. Grand Rapids, MI: Zondervan, 2018.

Bernard, David K. *The Glory of God in the Face of Jesus Christ: Deification of Jesus in Early Christian Discourse*. Blandford Forum, UK: Deo, 2016.

Bird, Michael F. "The Peril of Modernizing Jesus and the Crisis of Not Contemporizing the Christ." *Evangelical Quarterly* 78.4 (2006): 291–312.

Black, Matthew. "The Christological Use of the Old Testament in the New Testament." *New Testament Studies* 18.1 (1971): 1–14.

Blaising, Craig A. "The Day of the Lord: Theme and Pattern in Biblical Theology." *Bibliotheca Sacra* 169 (2012): 3–19.

Blaylock, Richard M. "My Messenger, the LORD, and the Messenger of the Covenant: Malachi 3:1 Revisited." *Southern Baptist Journal of Theology* 20.3 (2016): 69–95.

Block, Daniel I. *Covenant: The Framework of God's Grand Plan of Redemption*. Grand Rapids, MI: Baker Academic, 2021.

Block, Daniel I. "How Many Is God? An Investigation into the Meaning of Deuteronomy 6:4–5." *Journal of the Evangelical Theological Society* 47.2 (2004): 193–212.

Blomberg, Craig L. *The Historical Reliability of the Gospels*. 2nd ed. Nottingham, UK: Apollos; Downers Grove, IL: IVP Academic, 2007.

Blomberg, Craig L. *Jesus and the Gospels*. 2nd ed. Nottingham, UK: Apollos; Downers Grove, IL: InterVarsity Press, 2009.

Blomberg, Craig L. "Matthew." Pages 1–109 in *Commentary on the New Testament Use of the Old Testament*. Edited by G. K. Beale and D. A. Carson. Grand Rapids, MI: Baker Academic; Nottingham, UK: Apollos, 2007.

Blomberg, Craig L. *Matthew*. NAC 22. Nashville, TN: Broadman & Holman, 1992.

Blomberg, Craig L. *A New Testament Theology*. Waco, TX: Baylor University Press, 2018.

Blomberg, Craig L. *The Historical Reliability of the Gospels*. 2nd ed. Nottingham, UK: Apollos; Downers Grove, IL: IVP Academic, 2007.

Blomberg, Craig L. "Where Do We Start Studying Jesus?" Pages 17–50 in *Jesus Under Fire: Modern Scholarship Reinvents the Historical Jesus*. Edited by Michael J. Wilkins and J. P. Moreland. Grand Rapids, MI: Zondervan, 1995.

Bloom, Harold. *Jesus and Yahweh: The Names Divine*. New York: Riverhead Books, 2007.

Bock, Darrell L. *Luke*. IVPNTC 3. Downers Grove, IL: InterVarsity Press, 1994.

Bock, Darrell L. "Proclamation from Prophecy and Pattern: Lucan Old Testament Christology." PhD diss., University of Aberdeen, 1987.

Bock, Darrell L. "Son of Man." Pages 894–900 in *Dictionary of Jesus and the Gospels*. 2nd ed. Downers Grove, IL: IVP Academic, 2013.

Bock, Darrell L. *A Theology of Luke and Acts: Biblical Theology of the New Testament*. Grand Rapids, MI: Zondervan, 2012.

Boers, Hendrikus. "Where Christology Is Real." *Interpretation* 26.2 (1972): 300–327.

Böhlemann, Peter. *Jesus Und Der Täufer: Schlüssel Zur Theologie Und Ethik Des Lukas*. Cambridge; New York: Cambridge University Press, 1997.

Böhler, Dieter. "Mose Als Empfänger Der Offenbarung Des Namens JHWH Und Urheber Des Namens 'Jesus.'" *Theologie und Philosophie* 89.4 (2014): 585–89.

Booth, Susan Maxwell. *The Tabernacling Presence of God: Mission and Gospel Witness*. Eugene, OR: Wipf & Stock, 2015.

Boring, M. Eugene. *Mark: A Commentary*. NTL. Louisville, KY: Westminster John Knox, 2006.

Boring, M. Eugene. "Markan Christology: God-Language for Jesus?" *New Testament Studies* 45 (1999): 451–71.

Bornkamm, Günther. *Jesus von Nazareth*. Stuttgart: Kohlhammer, 1956.

Böttrich, Christfried. "'Gott Und Retter': Gottesprädikationen in Christologischen Titeln." *Neue Zeitschrift für systematische Theologie und Religionsphilosophie* 42.3 (2000): 217–36.

Bousset, Wilhelm. *Kyrios Christos: A History of the Belief in Christ from the Beginnings of Christianity to Irenaeus*. Translated by John E. Steely. Nashville, TN: Abingdon, 1970.

Bousset, Wilhelm. *Kyrios Christos: Geschichte Des Christusglaubens von Den Anfängen Des Christentums Bis Irenäus*. 5th ed. Göttingen: Vandenhoeck & Ruprecht, 1965.

Bovon, François. *Luke*. 3 vols. Hermeneia. Translated by Christine M. Thomas, Donald S. Deer, and James Crouch. Minneapolis, MN: Fortress, 2002–2013.

Bovon, François. *Luke the Theologian: Fifty-Five Years of Research (1950–2005)*. 2nd rev. ed. Waco, TX: Baylor University Press, 2006.
Bovon, François. "Premiéres Christologies: Exaltation et Incarnation, Ou de Pâques â Noël." *Études Théologiques et Religieuses* 85.2 (2010): 185–200.
Bowman, Robert M., and J. Ed Komoszewski. *Putting Jesus in His Place: The Case for the Deity of Christ*. Grand Rapids, MI: Kregel, 2007.
Bright, John. *The Kingdom of God in Bible and Church*. London: Lutterworth, 1955.
Broadhead, Edwin K. *Teaching with Authority: Miracles and Christology in the Gospel of Mark*. Sheffield, UK: Sheffield Academic, 1992.
Broadhead, Edwin Keith. *Naming Jesus: Titular Christology in the Gospel of Mark*. Sheffield, UK: Sheffield Academic, 1999.
Brooks, James A. *Mark*. NAC 23. Nashville, TN: Broadman & Holman, 1991.
Brown, Colin. "Quest of the Historical Jesus." Pages 718–56 in *Dictionary of Jesus and the Gospels*. 2nd ed. Nottingham, UK; Downers Grove, IL: IVP Academic, 2013.
Brown, Jeannine K. *The Gospels as Stories: A Narrative Approach to Matthew, Mark, Luke, and John*. Grand Rapids, MI: Baker Academic, 2020.
Bruce, F. F. *Jesus, Lord & Savior*. Downers Grove, IL: InterVarsity Press, 1986.
Bullinger, E. W., ed. *The Companion Bible*. Grand Rapids, MI: Kregel, 1990.
Bultmann, Rudolf. "Introductory Word." Pages 7–9 in *Wilhelm Bousset's Kyrios Christos*. Translated by John E. Steely. 5th ed. Nashville, TN: Abingdon, 1970.
Burge, Gary M., and Gene L. Green. *The New Testament in Antiquity: A Survey of the New Testament Within Its Cultural Contexts*. 2nd ed. Grand Rapids, MI: Zondervan, 2020.
Byrne, Máire. *The Names of God in Judaism, Christianity and Islam: A Basis for Interfaith Dialogue*. London; New York: Continuum, 2011.
Capes, David B. *The Divine Christ: Paul, the Lord Jesus, and the Scriptures of Israel*. Grand Rapids, MI: Baker Academic, 2018.
Capes, David B. "Intertextual Echoes in the Matthean Baptismal Narrative." *Bulletin for Biblical Research* 9 (1999): 37–49.
Capes, David B. *Old Testament Yahweh Texts in Paul's Christology*. Tübingen: Mohr Siebeck, 1992. Repr., Waco, TX: Baylor University Press, 2017.
Capes, David B. "Paul's Use of Old Testament Yahweh-Texts and Its Implications for His Christology." PhD diss., Southwestern Baptist Theological Seminary, 1990.
Capes, David B. "Review of *A Man Attested By God* by J. R. Daniel Kirk." *Interpretation* 72.4 (2018): 442–44.
Capes, David B. "YHWH and His Messiah: Pauline Exegesis and the Divine Christ." *Horizons in Biblical Theology* 16.2 (1994): 121–43.
Cara, Robert J. "Luke." Pages 93–113 in *A Biblical-Theological Introduction to the New Testament*. Edited by Michael J. Kruger. Wheaton, IL: Crossway, 2016.
Carroll, John T. *Luke: A Commentary*. NTL. Louisville, KY: Westminster John Knox, 2012.
Carson, D. A. "Christological Ambiguities in the Gospel of Matthew." Pages 97–114 in *Christ the Lord: Studies in Christology Presented to Donald Guthrie*. Edited by Harold H. Rowdon. Leicester, UK; Downers Grove, IL: InterVarsity Press, 1982.
Carson, D. A. *The God Who Is There: Finding Your Place in God's Story*. Grand Rapids, MI: Baker Books, 2010.
Carson, D. A. "'I AM' Sayings." Page 411 in *Evangelical Dictionary of Biblical Theology*. 3rd ed. Grand Rapids, MI: Baker Academic, 2017.
Carson, D. A. "Matthew." Pages 23–670 in *Matthew–Mark*. Vol. 9 of *The Expositor's Bible Commentary*. Edited by Tremper III Longman and David E. Garland. Rev. ed. Grand Rapids, MI: Zondervan, 2010.

Casey, P. Maurice. *From Jewish Prophet to Gentile God: The Origins and Development of New Testament Christology*. Cambridge: Clarke & Co.; Louisville, KY: Westminster John Knox, 1991.

Casey, P. Maurice. "The Deification of Jesus." Pages 697–714 in *Society of Biblical Literature 1994 Seminar Papers*. SBLSPS 33. Chicago: Scholar's Press, 1994.

Charles, J. Daryl. "The 'Coming One'/'Stronger One' and His Baptism: Matt 3:11–12, Mark 1:8, Luke 3:16–17." *The Journal of the Society for Pentecostal Studies* 11.1 (1989): 37–50.

Chen, Diane G. *Luke: A New Covenant Commentary*. Eugene, OR: Cascade, 2017.

Childs, Brevard S. *Biblical Theology in Crisis*. Philadelphia: Westminster, 1970.

Clark, Henry B. "Albert Schweitzer's Understanding of Jesus as the Christ." *The Christian Scholar* 45.3 (1962): 230–37.

Cole, Graham A. *The God Who Became Human: A Biblical Theology of Incarnation*. Downers Grove, IL: InterVarsity Press, 2013.

Collins, Adela Yarbro. *Mark: A Commentary*. Hermeneia. Minneapolis, MN: Fortress, 2007.

Collins, Adela Yarbro. "The Worship of Jesus and the Imperial Cult." Pages 234–57 in *The Jewish Roots of Christological Monotheism*. Edited by Carey C. Newman, James R. Davila, and Gladys S. Lewis. Leiden; Boston: Brill, 1999.

Collins, C. John. "How the New Testament Quotes and Interprets the Old Testament." Pages 181–97 in *Understanding Scripture: An Overview of the Bible's Origin, Reliability, and Meaning*. Edited by Wayne A. Grudem, C. John Collins, and Thomas R. Schreiner. Wheaton, IL: Crossway, 2012.

Cox, Steven L., and Kendell H. Easley. *Harmony of the Gospels*. Nashville, TN: Holman, 2007.

Craddock, Fred B. *Luke*. IBC. Louisville, KY: John Knox, 1990.

Cranfield, C. E. B. *The Gospel According to Mark: An Introduction and Commentary*. CGTC. London; New York: Cambridge University Press, 1959.

Cranfield, C. E. B. "The Witness of the New Testament to Christ." Pages 73–91 in *Essays in Christology for Karl Barth*. Edited by T. H. L. Parker. London: Lutterworth, 1956.

Crisler, Channing L. *Echoes of Lament and the Christology of Luke*. Sheffield, UK: Sheffield Phoenix, 2020.

Cullmann, Oscar. "All Who Call on the Name of Our Lord Jesus Christ." Translated by A. Anderson Swidler. *Journal of Ecumenical Studies* 1.1 (1964): 1–21.

Cullmann, Oscar. *The Christology of the New Testament*. Translated by Shirley C. Guthrie and Charles A. M. Hall. Rev. ed. Philadephia: Westminster, 1963.

Cullmann, Oscar. *Early Christian Worship*. Philadelphia: Westminster, 1953.

Cullmann, Oscar. "'Kyrios' as Designation for the Oral Tradition Concerning Jesus." *Scottish Journal of Theology* 3.2 (1950): 180–97.

Culpepper, R. Alan. "Fulfilment of Scripture and Jesus' Teachings in Matthew." *In die Skriflig* 49.2 (2015): 1–8.

Culpepper, R. Alan. "The Gospel of Luke: Introduction, Commentary, and Reflections." Pages 1–490 in *Luke–John*. Vol. 8 of *The New Interpreter's Bible*. Edited by Leander E. Keck. Nashville, TN: Abingdon, 1995.

Davies, W. D., and Dale C. Allison. *A Critical and Exegetical Commentary on the Gospel According to Saint Matthew*. 3 vols. ICC. London; New York: T&T Clark, 2004.

Davis, Carl Judson. *The Name and Way of the Lord: Old Testament Themes, New Testament Christology*. Sheffield, UK: Sheffield Academic, 1996.

Davis, Philip G. "Mark's Christological Paradox." *Journal for the Study of the New Testament* 35 (1989): 3–18.

Davis, Stephen T. "'Who Can Forgive Sins but God Alone?': Jesus, Forgiveness, and Divinity." Pages 113–23 in *The Multivalence of Biblical Texts and Theological Meanings*. Edited by Christine Helmer. Atlanta, GA: Society of Biblical Literature, 2006.

Decker, Rodney J. *Mark 1–8: A Handbook on the Greek Text*. Waco, TX: Baylor University Press, 2014.

DeClaissé-Walford, Nancy L., Rolf A. Jacobson, and Beth LaNeel Tanner. *The Book of Psalms*. NICOT. Grand Rapids, MI: Eerdmans, 2014.

Denaux, Adelbert. "A Stranger in the City: A Contribution to the Study of the Narrative Christology in Luke's Gospel." *Louvain Studies* 30 (2005): 255–75.

Denaux, Adelbert. "The Theme of Divine Visits and Human (In)Hospitality in Luke-Acts: Its Old Testament and Graeco-Roman Antecedents." Pages 255–79 in *The Unity of Luke-Acts*. Edited by Joseph Verheyden. Leuven: Leuven University Press, 1999.

Dennis, J. A. "Glory." Pages 313–15 in *Dictionary of Jesus and the Gospels*. 2nd ed. Downers Grove, IL: IVP Academic, 2013.

DeYoung, James B. "The Function of Malachi 3.1 in Matthew 11.10: Kingdom Reality as the Hermeneutic of Jesus." Pages 66–91 in *The Gospels and the Scriptures of Israel*. Edited by Craig A. Evans and W. Richard Stegner. Sheffield, UK: Sheffield Academic, 1994.

Dodd, C. H. *According to the Scriptures: The Sub-Structure of New Testament Theology*. London: Nisbet and Company, 1952.

Donahue, John R., and Daniel J. Harrington. *The Gospel of Mark*. SP 2. Collegeville, MN: Liturgical Press, 2002.

Doriani, Daniel. "The Deity of Christ in the Synoptic Gospels." *Journal of the Evangelical Theological Society* 37.3 (1994): 333–50.

Dungan, David L. *A History of the Synoptic Problem: The Canon, the Text, the Composition, and the Interpretation of the Gospels*. New York: Doubleday, 1999.

Dunn, James D. G. *Jesus According to the New Testament*. Grand Rapids, MI: Eerdmans, 2019.

Dunn, James D. G. *Unity and Diversity in the New Testament: An Inquiry into the Character of Earliest Christianity*. London: SCM, 2006.

Duvall, J. Scott, and J. Daniel Hays. *God's Relational Presence: The Cohesive Center of Biblical Theology*. Grand Rapids, MI: Baker Academic, 2019.

Eckman, Edward W. "The Identification of Christ with Yahweh by New Testament Writers." *Gordon Review* 7.4 (1964): 143–53.

Edwards, James R. *The Gospel According to Luke*. PNTC. Grand Rapids, MI; Cambridge: Eerdmans; Nottingham, UK: Apollos, 2015.

Edwards, James R. *The Gospel According to Mark*. PNTC. Grand Rapids, MI; Cambridge: Eerdmans; Leicester: Apollos, 2002.

Ehrman, Bart D. *The Orthodox Corruption of Scripture: The Effect of Early Christological Controversies on the Text of the New Testament*. New York: Oxford University Press, 2011.

Ehrman, Bart D., and Zlatko Pleše, eds. *The Apocryphal Gospels: Texts and Translations*. New York: Oxford University Press, 2011.

Elledge, Ervin Roderick. "The Illeism of Jesus and Jahweh: A Study of the Use of the Third-Person Self-Reference in the Bible and Ancient Near Eastern Texts and Its Implications for Christology." PhD diss., Southern Baptist Theological Seminary, 2015.

Elledge, Ervin Roderick. *Use of the Third Person for Self-Reference by Jesus and Yahweh: A Study of Illeism in the Bible and Ancient Near Eastern Texts and Its Implications for Christology*. London; New York: T&T Clark, 2017.

Ellis, E. Earle. "Deity Christology in Mark 14:58." Pages 192–203 in *Jesus of Nazareth: Lord and Christ*. Edited by Joel B. Green and Max Turner. Grand Rapids, MI: Eerdmans; Carlisle: Paternoster, 1994.

Ellis, E. Earle. *The Gospel of Luke*. Rev. ed. Grand Rapids, MI: Eerdmans, 1974.

Erickson, Millard J. *The Word Became Flesh*. Grand Rapids, MI: Baker Books, 1991.

Esswein, Mitchell Alexander. "The One God and the Lord Jesus Christ: An Exegetical Examination of the High Christology Found in Paul, Mark and John." MA thesis, University of Georgia, 2012.

Evans, Craig A. "Jesus' Self-Designation 'The Son of Man' and the Recognition of His Divinity." Pages 29–47 in *The Trinity: An Interdisciplinary Symposium on the Trinity*. Edited by Stephen T. Davis, Daniel Kendall, and Gerald O'Collins. Oxford; New York: Oxford University Press, 1999.

Evans, Craig A. *Mark 8:27–16:20*. WBC 34B. Nashville, TN: Nelson, 2001.

Farnell, F. David. "The Synoptic Gospels in the Ancient Church: The Testimony to the Priority of Matthew's Gospel." *The Master's Seminary Journal* 10.1 (1999): 53–86.

Fitzmyer, Joseph A. *The Gospel According to Luke*. 2 vols. AB 28–28A. Garden City, NY: Doubleday, 1970–1985.

Fletcher-Louis, Crispin H. T. *Jesus Monotheism*. Eugene, OR: Wipf & Stock, 2015.

Fletcher-Louis, Crispin H. T. "A New Explanation of Christological Origins: A Review of the Work of Larry W. Hurtado." *Tyndale Bulletin* 60.2 (2009): 161–205.

Ford, J. Massingberd. "'He That Cometh' and the Divine Name (Apocalypse 1, 4. 8; 4, 8)." *Journal for the Study of Judaism in the Persian, Hellenistic, and Roman Period* 1.2 (1970): 144–47.

Frame, John M. *The Doctrine of God*. Phillipsburg, NJ: P&R, 2002.

Frame, John M. *A History of Western Philosophy and Theology*. Phillipsburg, NJ: P&R, 2015.

Frame, John M. *Systematic Theology: An Introduction to Christian Belief*. Phillipsburg, NJ: P&R, 2013.

France, R. T. "Development in New Testament Christology." Pages 63–82 in *Crisis in Christology: Essays in Quest of Resolution*. Edited by William R. Farmer. Livonia, MI: Dove Booksellers, 1995.

France, R. T. *Divine Government: God's Kingship in the Gospel of Mark*. London: SPCK, 1990.

France, R. T. *The Gospel of Mark: A Commentary on the Greek Text*. NIGTC. Grand Rapids, MI; Cambridge: Eerdmans, 2002.

France, R. T. *The Gospel of Matthew*. NICNT. Grand Rapids, MI: Eerdmans, 2007.

France, R. T. *Jesus and the Old Testament: His Application of Old Testament Passages to Himself and His Mission*. Grand Rapids, MI: Baker Books, 1982.

France, R. T. *Luke*. TTC. Grand Rapids, MI: Baker Books, 2013.

France, R. T. "The Worship of Jesus: A Neglected Factor in Christological Debate?" Pages 17–36 in *Christ the Lord: Studies in Christology Presented to Donald Guthrie*. Edited by Harold H. Rowdon. Leicester, UK; Downers Grove, IL: InterVarsity Press, 1982.

Fredriksen, Paula. *When Christians Were Jews: The First Generation*. New Haven, CT: Yale University Press, 2018.

Freedman, David Noel, ed. *The Anchor Bible Dictionary*. 6 vols. New York: Doubleday, 1992.

Friedeman, Caleb T. "The Revelation of the Messiah: The Christological Mystery of Luke 1–2 and Its Unveiling in Luke-Acts." PhD diss., Wheaton College, 2018.

Funk, Robert. "The Jesus Seminar and the Quest." Pages 130–39 in *Jesus Then & Now: Images of Jesus in History and Christology*. Edited by Marvin Meyer and Charles Hughes. Harrisburg, PA: Trinity Press International, 2001.

Funk, Robert Walter, and Roy W. Hoover, eds. *The Five Gospels: The Search for the Authentic Words of Jesus: New Translation and Commentary.* New York; Toronto: Macmillan, 1993.
Gadenz, Pablo T. *The Gospel of Luke.* Grand Rapids, MI: Baker Academic, 2018.
Gaiser, Frederick J. "'Your Sins Are Forgiven. . . . Stand Up and Walk': A Theological Reading of Mark 2:1–12 in the Light of Psalm 103." *Ex Auditu* 21 (2005): 71–87.
Garber, Zev. "Teaching the Shema (Torah and Testament): Text, Translation, Tradition." *Biblical Theology Bulletin* 48.3 (2018): 143–47.
Garland, David E. *Luke.* ZECNT 3. Grand Rapids, MI: Zondervan, 2011.
Garland, David E. *Mark.* NIVAC. Grand Rapids, MI: Zondervan, 1996.
Garland, David E. *A Theology of Mark's Gospel: Good News About Jesus the Messiah, the Son of God.* Grand Rapids, MI: Zondervan, 2015.
Gathercole, Simon J. *The Composition of the Gospel of Thomas: Original Language and Influences.* Cambridge; New York: Cambridge University Press, 2012.
Gathercole, Simon J. "The Heavenly Ἀνατολή (Luke 1:78–9)." *Journal of Theological Studies* 56.2 (2005): 471–88.
Gathercole, Simon J. *The Preexistent Son: Recovering the Christologies of Matthew, Mark, and Luke.* Grand Rapids, MI: Eerdmans, 2006.
Gathercole, Simon J. "Review of *A Man Attested By God* by J. R. Daniel Kirk." *Scottish Journal of Theology* 71.1 (2018), 102–4.
Gathercole, Simon J. "The Trinity in the Synoptic Gospels and Acts." Pages 55–68 in *The Oxford Handbook of the Trinity*. Edited by Gilles Emery and Matthew Levering. Oxford; New York: Oxford University Press, 2011.
Geddert, Timothy J. "The Implied YHWH Christology of Mark's Gospel: Mark's Challenge to the Reader to 'Connect the Dots.'" *Bulletin for Biblical Research* 25.3 (2015): 325–40.
Gieschen, Charles A. "Confronting Current Christological Controversy." *Concordia Theological Quarterly* 69.1 (2005): 3–32.
Gieschen, Charles A. "The Divine Name in Ante-Nicene Christology." *Vigiliae Christianae* 57.2 (2003): 115–58.
Gnilka, Joachim. *Das Evangelium nach Markus (Mk 1–8,26).* EKKNT 2. Zürich; Neukirchen-Vluyn: Neukirchener Verlag, 1978.
Gnilka, Joachim. *Jesus Christus nach frühen Zeugnissen des Glauben.* Munich: Kösel-Verlag, 1970.
Godshall, Matthew Steven. "The Messiah and the Outpouring of the Holy Spirit: The Christological Significance of Jesus as Giver of the Spirit in Luke-Acts." PhD diss., Southern Baptist Theological Seminary, 2013.
Graves, Robert Brent. *The God of Two Testaments.* Rev. ed. Hazelwood, MO: Word Aflame, 2000.
Gray, Timothy C. *The Temple in the Gospel of Mark: A Study in Its Narrative Role.* Tübingen: Mohr Siebeck, 2008.
Green, Joel B. *The Gospel of Luke.* NICNT. Grand Rapids, MI: Eerdmans, 1997.
Green, Joel B. "Luke, Gospel Of." Pages 540–52 in *Dictionary of Jesus and the Gospels.* 2nd ed. Nottingham, UK; Downers Grove, IL; IVP Academic, 2013.
Green, Joel B. *The Theology of the Gospel of Luke.* Cambridge; New York: Cambridge University Press, 1995.
Green, Joel B., Jeannine K. Brown, and Nicholas Perrin, ed. *Dictionary of Jesus and the Gospels.* Nottingham, UK; Downers Grove, IL: IVP Academic, 2013.
Green, Michael, ed. "Jesus in the New Testament." Pages 17–57 in *The Truth of God Incarnate.* Grand Rapids, MI: Eerdmans, 1977.

Grether, Oskar. *Name und Wort Gottes im Alten Testament*. Giessen: Töpelmann, 1934.
Grindheim, Sigurd. *God's Equal: What Can We Know About Jesus' Self-Understanding?* London; New York: T&T Clark, 2011.
Grindheim, Sigurd. "Sirach and Mark 8:27-9:13: Elijah and the Eschaton." Pages 130-36 in *Reading Mark in Context: Jesus and Second Temple Judaism*. Edited by Ben C. Blackwell, John K. Goodrich, and Jason Maston. Grand Rapids, MI: Zondervan, 2018.
Grogan, G. W. "The New Testament Interpretation of the Old Testament: A Comparative Study." *Tyndale Bulletin* 18 (1967): 54-76.
Grogan, Geoffrey. "New Testament Christology—or New Testament Christologies?" *Themelios* 25.1 (1999): 60-73.
Grundmann, Walter. *Das Evangelium Nach Lukas*. 2nd ed. Berlin: Evangelische Verlagsanstalt, 1966.
Guelich, Robert A. *Mark 1-8:26*. WBC 34A. Waco, TX: Word, 1989.
Guillet, Jacques. "Jesus (Name Of)." Pages 263-65 in *Dictionary of Biblical Theology*. Edited by Xavier Léon Dufour. Translated by Joseph R. Sweeny. 2nd ed. New York: Seabury, 1973.
Gundry, Robert H. "Jesus' Supposed Blasphemy (Mark 14:61b-64)." *Bulletin for Biblical Research* 18.1 (2008): 131-33.
Gundry, Robert H. *Mark: A Commentary on His Apology for the Cross*. Grand Rapids, MI: Eerdmans, 1993.
Gundry, Robert H. *The Use of the Old Testament in St. Matthew's Gospel, With Special Reference to the Messianic Hope*. Leiden: Brill, 1967.
Hagner, Donald A. *Matthew*. 2 vols. WBC 33A-B. Nashville, TN: Word, 1993; Dallas: Word, 1995.
Hahn, Ferdinand. *The Titles of Jesus in Christology: Their History in Early Christianity*. London: Lutterworth, 1969.
Hare, Douglas R. A. *Matthew*. IBC. Louisville, KY: Westminster John Knox, 1993.
Harriman, K. R. "The King Arrives, but for What Purpose? The Christological Use of Zechariah 13-14 in Mark 13." *Journal of Theological Interpretation* 10.2 (2016): 283-98.
Harrington, Daniel J. *The Gospel of Matthew*. SP 1. Collegeville, MN: Liturgical Press, 1991.
Harris, Murray J. *Jesus as God: The New Testament Use of Theos in Reference to Jesus*. Grand Rapids, MI: Baker Books, 1992.
Harrison, Everett F. "Jesus." Pages 297-98 in *Baker's Dictionary of Theology*. Grand Rapids, MI: Baker Books, 1960.
Harrison, Everett F., Geoffrey W. Bromiley, and F. H. Carl Henry, eds *Baker's Dictionary of Theology*. Grand Rapids, MI: Baker Books, 1960.
Harrison, James R. "Modern Scholarship and the 'Nature' Miracles: A Defense of Their Historicity and Affirmation of Jesus' Deity." *Reformed Theological Review* 72.2 (2013): 86-102.
Hays, Richard B. "Can Narrative Criticism Recover the Theological Unity of Scripture?" *Journal of Theological Interpretation* 2.2 (2008): 193-211.
Hays, Richard B. "Can the Gospels Teach Us How to Read the Old Testament?" *Pro Ecclesia* 11.4 (2002): 402-18.
Hays, Richard B. *Echoes of Scripture in the Gospels*. Waco, TX: Baylor University Press, 2016.
Hays, Richard B. *Echoes of Scripture in the Letters of Paul*. New Haven, CT: Yale University Press, 1989.
Hays, Richard B. "Figural Exegesis and the Retrospective Re-Cognition of Israel's Story." *Bulletin for Biblical Research* 29.1 (2019): 32-48.

Hays, Richard B. "The Liberation of Israel in Luke-Acts: Intertextual Narration as Countercultural Practice." Pages 101–17 in *Reading the Bible Intertextually*. Edited by Richard B. Hays and Leroy A. Huizenga Alkier. Waco, TX: Baylor University Press, 2009.

Hays, Richard B. *Reading Backwards: Figural Christology and the Fourfold Gospel Witness*. London: SPCK, 2015.

Healy, Mary. *The Gospel of Mark*. Grand Rapids, MI: Baker Academic, 2008.

Hendriksen, William. *Exposition of the Gospel According to Luke*. Grand Rapids, MI: Baker Books, 1978.

Hendriksen, William. *Exposition of the Gospel According to Mark*. Grand Rapids, MI: Baker Books, 1975.

Hendriksen, William. *Exposition of the Gospel According to Matthew*. Grand Rapids, MI: Baker Books, 1984.

Hengel, Martin. *Studies in Early Christology*. London; New York: T&T Clark, 2004.

Henrichs-Tarasenkova, Nina. *Luke's Christology of Divine Identity*. New York: T&T Clark, 2016.

Henry, Carl F. H. "The Identity of Jesus of Nazareth." *Criswell Theological Review* 6.1 (1992): 91–130.

Hick, John. "The Logic of God Incarnate." *Religious Studies* 25.4 (1989): 409–23.

Hidalgo, Esteban J. "The Shema Through the Ages: A Pre-Modern History of Its Interpretation." *Andrews University Seminary Student Journal* 2.2 (2016): 13–34.

Hiebert, D. Edmond. *The Gospel of Mark: An Expositional Commentary*. Greenville, SC: Bob Jones University Press, 1994.

Holladay, Carl R. *Introduction to the New Testament*. Waco, TX: Baylor University Press, 2017.

Hooker, Morna D. "'Who Can This Be?' The Christology of Mark's Gospel." Pages 79–99 in *Contours of Christology in the New Testament*. Edited by Richard N. Longenecker. Grand Rapids, MI: Eerdmans, 2005.

Hooker, Morna Dorothy. *The Gospel According to St. Mark*. Peabody, MA: Hendrickson, 1991.

Horstmann, Maria. *Studien Zur Markinischen Christologie: Mk 8,27–9,13 Als Zugang Zum Christusbild Des Zweiten Evangeliums*. Münster: Aschendorff, 1969.

Howard, George. "The Tetragram and the New Testament." *Journal of Biblical Literature* 96.1 (1977): 63–83.

Hurtado, Larry W. "Early Christological Interpretation of the Messianic Psalms." *Salmanticensis* 64 (2017): 73–100.

Hurtado, Larry W. *Lord Jesus Christ: Devotion to Jesus in Earliest Christianity*. Grand Rapids, MI: Eerdmans, 2003.

Hurtado, Larry W. *One God, One Lord: Early Christian Devotion and Ancient Jewish Monotheism*. 3rd ed. London; New York: T&T Clark, 2015.

Hurtado, Larry W. "YHWH's Return to Zion: A New Catalyst for Earliest High Christology?" Pages 75–95 in *Ancient Jewish Monotheism and Early Christian Jesus-Devotion: The Context and Character of Christological Faith*. Edited by Larry W. Hurtado, April D. DeConick, and David B. Capes. Waco, TX: Baylor University Press, 2017.

Hurtado, Larry W., April D. DeConick, and David B. Capes, eds *Ancient Jewish Monotheism and Early Christian Jesus-Devotion: The Context and Character of Christological Faith*. Waco, TX: Baylor University Press, 2017.

Hylton, Michael Antony. "Reflections on the Use of the Name Yahuwah (Yahweh) or IAO in the Early Church Communities." *International Journal of Humanities and Social Science* 3.4 (2013): 91–97.

Isbell, Charles D. "The Divine Name היהא as a Symbol of Presence in Israelite Tradition." *Hebrew Annual Review* 2 (1978): 101–18.

Jeffrey, David L. *Luke*. Grand Rapids, MI: Brazos, 2012.

Jipp, Joshua W. "The Beginnings of a Theology of Luke-Acts: Divine Activity and Human Response." *Journal of Theological Interpretation* 8.1 (2014): 23–43.

Jobes, Karen H., and Moisés Silva. *Invitation to the Septuagint*. 2nd ed. Grand Rapids, MI: Baker Academic, 2015.

Johansson, Daniel. "Kyrios in the Gospel of Mark." *Journal for the Study of the New Testament* 33.1 (2010): 101–24.

Johnson, Dennis E. *Him We Proclaim: Preaching Christ from All the Scriptures*. Phillipsburg, NJ: P&R, 2007.

Johnson, Dennis E. "Immutability and Incarnation: An Historical and Theological Study of the Concepts of Christ's Divine Unchangeability and His Human Development." PhD diss., Fuller Theological Seminary, 1984.

Johnson, Dennis E. "Jesus Against the Idols: The Use of Isaianic Servant Songs in the Missiology of Acts." *Westminster Theological Journal* 52 (1990): 343–53.

Johnson, Dennis E. *The Message of Acts in the History of Redemption*. Phillipsburg, NJ: P&R, 1997.

Johnson, Dennis E. *Walking with Jesus Through His Word: Discovering Christ in All the Scriptures*. Phillipsburg, NJ: P&R, 2015.

Johnson, Luke Timothy. *The Gospel of Luke*. Collegeville, MN: Liturgical Press, 1991.

Johnson, Luke Timothy. "The Jesus Seminar's Misguided Quest for the Historical Jesus." *Christian Century* 113.1 (1994): 16–22.

Johnson, S. Lewis. *The Old Testament in the New: An Argument for Biblical Inspiration*. Grand Rapids, MI: Zondervan, 1980.

Juncker, Günther. "Jesus and the Angel of the Lord: An Old Testament Paradigm for New Testament Christology." PhD diss., Trinity Evangelical Theological Seminary, 2001.

Just, Arthur A. *Luke*. 2 vols. ConcC. St. Louis, MO: Concordia, 1996–1997.

Just, Felix. "'Have No Fear! Do Not Be Afraid!'" *Catholic Resources for Bible, Liturgy, Art, and Theology*. Updated 15 June 2021. http://catholic-resources.org/Bible/HaveNoFear.htm.

Kähler, Martin. *The So-Called Historical Jesus and the Historic, Biblical Christ*. Translated by Carl E. Braaten. Philadelphia: Fortress, 1964.

Kaiser, Walter C. Jr. *The Uses of the Old Testament in the New*. Chicago: Moody, 1985.

Kärkkäinen, Veli-Matti, *Christology: A Global Introduction*. Grand Rapids, MI: Baker Academic, 2003.

Käsemann, Ernst. "Das Problem Des Historischen Jesus." *Zeitschrift für Theologie und Kirche* 51 (1954): 125–53.

Käsemann, Ernst. "The Problem of the Historical Jesus." Pages 15–47 in *Essays on New Testament Themes*. Translated by W. J. Montague. Naperville, IL: Allenson, 1964.

Keener, Craig S. *Christobiography: Memory, History, and the Reliability of the Gospels*. Grand Rapids, MI: Eerdmans, 2019.

Keener, Craig S. *A Commentary on the Gospel of Matthew*. Grand Rapids, MI: Eerdmans, 1999.

Kennedy, Joel. *The Recapitulation of Israel: Use of Israel's History in Matthew 1:1–4:11*. Tübingen: Mohr Siebeck, 2008.

Kereszty, Roch A. *Jesus Christ: Fundamentals of Christology*. Rev. ed. New York: Alba House, 2002.

Kimball, Charles A. *Jesus' Exposition of the Old Testament in Luke's Gospel*. Sheffield, UK: JSOT Press, 1994.

Kingsbury, Jack Dean. *The Christology of Mark's Gospel*. Philadelphia: Fortress, 1983.

Kingsbury, Jack Dean. *Matthew: Structure, Christology, Kingdom*. Philadelphia: Fortress, 1975.

Kingsbury, Jack Dean. "The Title 'Kyrios' in Matthew's Gospel." *Journal of Biblical Literature* 94.2 (1975): 246–55.

Kirk, J. R. Daniel. *A Man Attested by God: The Human Jesus of the Synoptic Gospels*. Grand Rapids, MI: Eerdmans, 2016.

Kirk, J. R. Daniel. "Still A Man Attested by God: A Response to Proctor, Thurman, and Wardle." *Perspectives in Religious Studies* 46.1 (2029): 111–16.

Kirk, J. R. Daniel, and Stephen L. Young. "'I Will Set His Hand to the Sea': Psalm 88:26 LXX and Christology in Mark." *Journal of Biblical Literature* 133.2 (2014): 333–40.

Klein, Hans. *Das Lukasevangelium*. Göttingen: Vandenhoeck & Ruprecht, 2006.

Kline, Meredith G. "Primal Parousia." *Westminster Theological Journal* 40.2 (1978): 245–80.

Köber, Berthold W. "Jesus—Der Heilige Gottes: Die Heiligkeit Jesu Im Zeugnis Der Synoptiker in Ihrer Bedeutung Für Theologie Und Glauben." *Evangelische Theologie* 62.4 (2002): 304–17.

Kodell, Jerome. "The Theology of Luke in Recent Study." *Biblical Theology Bulletin* 1.2 (1971): 115–44.

Kok, Michael. "Marking a Difference: The Gospel of Mark and the 'Early High Christology' Paradigm." *Journal of the Jesus Movement in Its Jewish Setting* 3 (2016): 102–24.

Kramer, Werner. *Christ, Lord, Son of God*. Translated by Brian Hardy. Chatham, UK: SCM Press, 1966.

Lagrange, Marie-Joseph. *Évangile Selon Saint Marc*. 6th ed. Paris: Librairie Lecoffre, 1942.

Lane, William L. *The Gospel According to Mark: The English Text with Introduction, Exposition, and Notes*. NICNT. Grand Rapids, MI: Eerdmans, 1974.

Lanier, Gregory R. "The Curious Case of צמח and Ἀνατολή: An Inquiry into Septuagint Translation Patterns." *Journal of Biblical Literature* 134.3 (2015): 505–27.

Lanier, Gregory R. "'From God' or 'from Heaven'? Ἐξ Ὕψους in Luke 1,78." *Biblica* 97.1 (2016): 121–27.

Lanier, Gregory R. "Luke's Distinctive Use of the Temple: Portraying the Divine Visitation." *Journal of Theological Studies* 65.2 (2014): 433–62.

Lanier, Gregory R. *Old Testament Conceptual Metaphors and the Christology of Luke's Gospel*. New York: Bloomsbury Academic, 2018.

Lee, Dorothy. "Christological Identity and Authority in the Gospel of Mark." *Phronema* 33.1 (2018): 1–19.

Lee, John J. R. "The Divinity of Jesus and the Uniqueness of God: Are They Compatible? A Reflection on High Christology and Monotheism in Mark's Gospel." *Midwestern Journal of Theology* 15.1 (2016): 84–100.

Leim, Joshua E. "In the Glory of His Father: Intertextuality and the Apocalyptic Son of Man in the Gospel of Mark." *Journal of Theological Interpretation* 7.2 (2013): 213–32.

Leim, Joshua E. *Matthew's Theological Grammar: The Father and the Son*. Tübingen: Mohr Siebeck, 2015.

Leim, Joshua E. "Theological Hermeneutics, Exegesis, and J. R. Daniel Kirk's *A Man Attested by God*." *Journal of Theological Interpretation* 15.1 (2021): 22–43.

Léon-Dufour, Xavier, ed. *Dictionary of Biblical Theology*. Translated by Joseph R. Sweeny et al. 2nd ed. New York: Seabury, 1973.

Léon-Dufour, Xavier. "Jesus Christ." Pages 265–72 in *Dictionary of Biblical Theology*. Translated by Edward M. Stewart. 2nd ed. New York: Seabury, 1973.

Leske, Adrian M. "The Influence of Isaiah 40–66 on Christology in Matthew and Luke: A Comparison." Pages 897–916 in *Society of Biblical Literature 1994 Seminar Papers*. SBLSPS 33. Chicago: Scholars Press, 1994.

Lessing, Gotthold Ephraim. "On the Proof of the Spirit and of Power." Pages 83–88 in *Lessing: Philosophical and Theological Writings*. Edited and translated by H. B. Nisbet. Cambridge; New York: Cambridge University Press, 2005.

Lister, J. Ryan. *The Presence of God: Its Place in the Storyline of Scripture and the Story of Our Lives*. Wheaton, IL: Crossway, 2015.

Litwa, M. David. "Iesus Deus: The Early Christian Depiction of Jesus as a Mediterranean God." PhD diss., University of Virginia, 2013.

Loewen, Jacob A. "The Names of God in the Old Testament." *Biblical Translator* 35.2 (1984): 201–7.

Loke, Andrew Ter Ern. *The Origin of Divine Christology*. New York: Cambridge University Press, 2017.

Longenecker, Richard N. *Biblical Exegesis in the Apostolic Period*. 2nd ed. Grand Rapids, MI: Eerdmans; Vancouver: Regent College Publishing, 1999.

Luz, Ulrich. *Das Evangelium Nach Matthäus (Mt 1–7)*. EKKNT 1. Zürich: Benziger; Neukirchen-Vluyn: Neukirchener Verlag, 1985.

Luz, Ulrich. *Matthew 1–7: A Commentary*. Translated by James E. Crouch. Rev. ed. Hermeneia. Minneapolis, MN: Fortress, 2007.

Luz, Ulrich. *Matthew 8–20: A Commentary*. Translated by James E. Crouch. Hermeneia. Minneapolis, MN: Fortress, 2001.

Luz, Ulrich. *Matthew 21–28: A Commentary*. Translated by James E. Crouch and Wilhelm C. Linss. Hermeneia. Minneapolis, MN: Fortress, 2005.

Luz, Ulrich. *The Theology of the Gospel of Matthew*. Translated by J. Bradford Robinson. Cambridge; New York: Cambridge University Press, 1995.

MacDonald, Nathan. *Deuteronomy and the Meaning of "Monotheism."* 2nd ed. Tübingen: Mohr Siebeck, 2012.

Macfarland, Charles S. *Jesus and the Prophets*. New York; London: Putnam's Sons, 1905.

Machen, J. Gresham. *The Origin of Paul's Religion*. Grand Rapids, MI: Eerdmans, 1925.

MacWhorter, Alexander. *Jahveh Christ, or, The Memorial Name*. Boston: Gould & Lincoln, 1857.

Malbon, Elizabeth Struthers. "Jonah, Jesus, Gentiles, and the Sea: Markan Narrative Intersections." Pages 251–95 in *Reading the Gospel of Mark in the Twenty-First Century: Method and Meaning*. Edited by Geert Van Oyen. Leuven: Peeters, 2019.

Malina, Bruce J., and Richard L. Rohrbaugh. *Social-Science Commentary on the Synoptic Gospels*. 2nd ed. Minneapolis, MN: Fortress, 2003.

Marcus, Joel. "Authority to Forgive Sins upon the Earth: The Shema in the Gospel of Mark." Pages 196–211 in *The Gospels and the Scriptures of Israel*. Edited by Craig A. Evans and W. Richard Stegner. Sheffield, UK: Sheffield Academic, 1994.

Marcus, Joel. *Mark 1–8: A New Translation with Introduction and Commentary*. AB 27. New York: Doubleday, 2000.

Marcus, Joel. *Mark 8–16: A New Translation with Introduction and Commentary*. AB 27A. New Haven, CT: Yale University Press, 2009.

Marcus, Joel. *The Way of the Lord: Christological Exegesis of the Old Testament in the Gospel of Mark*. London; New York: T&T Clark, 2004.

Marshall, I. Howard. "The Christology of Luke's Gospel and Acts." Pages 122–47 in *Contours of Christology in the New Testament*. Edited by Richard N. Longenecker. Grand Rapids, MI: Eerdmans, 2005.

Marshall, I. Howard. "The Development of Christology in the Early Church." *Tyndale Bulletin* 18 (1967): 77–93.

Marshall, I. Howard. *The Gospel of Luke: A Commentary on the Greek Text*. NIGTC. Grand Rapids, MI: Eerdmans, 1978.

Marshall, I. Howard. "Jesus as Lord: The Development of the Concept." Pages 129–45 in *Eschatology and the New Testament: Essays in Honor of George Raymond Beasley-Murray*. Edited by W. Hulitt Gloer. Peabody, MA: Hendrickson, 1988.

Marshall, I. Howard. "Jesus Christ, Titles Of." Pages 584–93 in *New Bible Dictionary*. Edited by James D. Douglas et al. 2nd ed. Leicester, UK; Downers Grove, IL: InterVarsity Press, 1992.

Marshall, I. Howard. *Luke: Historian and Theologian*. Grand Rapids, MI: Academie Books, 1989.

Marshall, I. Howard. *The Origins of New Testament Christology*. Downers Grove, IL: InterVarsity Press, 1976.

Marshall, I. Howard. "Son of God or Servant of Yahweh?—A Reconsideration of Mark I.11." *New Testament Studies* 15.3 (1969): 326–36.

Martin, Ralph. *Mark: Evangelist and Theologian*. Grand Rapids, MI: Zondervan, 1972.

Marxsen, Willi. *Mark the Evangelist: Studies on the Redaction History of the Gospel*. Translated by James Boyce et al. Nashville, TN: Abingdon, 1969.

McCartney, Dan G. "Ecce Homo: The Coming of the Kingdom as the Restoration of Human Vicegerency." *Westminster Theological Journal* 56 (1994): 1–21.

McComiskey, Thomas Edward. "God, Names Of." Pages 349–52 in *Evangelical Dictionary of Theology*. 3rd ed. Grand Rapids, MI: Baker Academic, 2017.

McNeile, A. H. *The Gospel According to St. Matthew: The Greek Text with Introduction, Notes, and Indices*. Grand Rapids, MI: Baker Books, 1980.

Menken, Maarten J. J. "The Psalms in Matthew's Gospel." Pages 61–82 in *The Psalms in the New Testament*. Edited by Steve Moyise and Maarten J. J. Menken. London; New York: T&T Clark, 2004.

Moo, Douglas J. "The Christology of the Early Pauline Letters." Pages 169–92 in *Contours of Christology in the New Testament*. Edited by Richard N. Longenecker. Grand Rapids, MI: Eerdmans, 2005.

Moritz, Thorsten. "Mark, Book Of." Pages 480–85 in *Dictionary for Theological Interpretation of the Bible*. Edited by Kevin J. Vanhoozer. London: SPCK; Grand Rapids, MI: Baker Academic, 2005.

Morris, Leon. *The Gospel According to Matthew*. PNTC. Grand Rapids, MI: Eerdmans; Leicester, UK: InterVarsity Press, 1992.

Morris, Leon. *Luke*. TNTC 3. 2nd ed. Downers Grove, IL: IVP Academic, 1988.

Motyer, Alec. *Look to the Rock: An Old Testament Background to Our Understanding of Christ*. Leicester, UK: InterVarsity Press, 1996.

Moyise, Steve. *The Old Testament in the New: An Introduction*. 2nd ed. London: T&T Clark, 2015.

Mundhenk, Norm. "Jesus Is Lord: The Tetragrammaton in Bible Translation." *Bible Translator* 61.2 (2010): 55–63.

Napier, John G. "The Christological Significance of the Name Yahweh." ThM thesis, Dallas Theological Seminary, 1979.
Nolland, John. *The Gospel of Matthew: A Commentary on the Greek Text*. NIGTC. Grand Rapids, MI: Eerdmans; Bletchley, UK: Paternoster, 2005.
Nolland, John. *Luke 1–9:20*. WBC 35A. Nashville, TN: Nelson, 2000.
Nolland, John. *Luke 9:21–18:34*. WBC 35B. Nashville, TN: Nelson, 2008.
Nolland, John. *Luke 18:35–24:53*. WBC 35C. Dallas: Word, 1993.
O'Brien, Kelli S. "Hints and Fragments: The Use of Scripture in Mark 1,2–3 and the Dead Sea Scrolls." Pages 297–313 in *Reading the Gospel of Mark in the Twenty-First Century: Method and Meaning*. Edited by Geert Van Oyen. Leuven: Peeters, 2019.
Öhler, Markus. "The Expectation of Elijah and the Presence of the Kingdom of God." *Journal of Biblical Literature* 118.3 (1999): 461–76.
Orr, James. "Jesus Christ." *ISBE* 3 (1956): 1624–68.
Ortlund, Dane. "The Old Testament Background and Eschatological Significance of Jesus Walking on the Sea (Mark 6:45–52)." *Neotestamentica* 46.2 (2012): 319–37.
Ortlund, Raymond C. *God's Unfaithful Wife: A Biblical Theology of Spiritual Adultery*. Leicester, UK: Apollos; Downers Grove, IL: InterVarsity Press, 2002.
Osborne, Grant R. "History and Theology in the Synoptic Gospels." *Trinity Journal* 24NS (2003): 5–22.
Osborne, Grant R. *Matthew*. ZECNT. Grand Rapids, MI: Zondervan, 2010.
Oswalt, John. *The Book of Isaiah: Chapters 1–39*. NICOT. Grand Rapids, MI: Eerdmans, 1986.
O'Toole, Robert F. "How Does Luke Portray Jesus as Servant of YHWH." *Biblica* 81.3 (2000): 328–46.
Overman, Dean L. *A Case for the Divinity of Jesus: Examining the Earliest Evidence*. Lanham, MD: Rowman & Littlefield, 2009.
Pao, David W., and Eckhard J. Schnabel. "Luke." Pages 251–414 in *Commentary on the New Testament Use of the Old Testament*. Edited by G. K. Beale and D. A. Carson. Grand Rapids, MI: Baker Academic, 2007.
Payne, Philip B. "Jesus' Implicit Claim to Deity in His Parables." *Trinity Journal* 2 (1981): 3–23.
Perrin, Nicholas. *Jesus the Priest*. Grand Rapids, MI: Baker Books, 2018.
Perrin, Nicholas. "Mark, Gospel Of." Pages 553–66 in *Dictionary of Jesus and the Gospels*. Nottingham, UK; Downers Grove, IL: IVP Academic, 2013.
Peterson, Robert A. "Toward a Systematic Theology of the Deity of Christ." Pages 193–227 in *The Deity of Christ*. Edited by Christopher W. Morgan and Robert A. Peterson. Wheaton, IL: Crossway, 2011.
Plummer, Alfred. *The Gospel According to St. Luke*. 6th ed. ICC. New York: Scribner's Sons, 1903.
Porter, Stanley E. "Composite Citations in Luke-Acts." Pages 62–93 in *New Testament Uses*. Edited by Sean A. Adams and Seth M. Ehorn. Vol. 2 of *Composite Citations in Antiquity*. New York: T&T Clark, 2018.
Porter, Stanley E. *Sacred Tradition in the New Testament: Tracing Old Testament Themes in the Gospels and Epistles*. Grand Rapids, MI: Baker Academic, 2016.
Powell, Mark Allan. *Introducing the New Testament: A Historical, Literary, and Theological Survey*. 2nd ed. Grand Rapids, MI: Baker Academic, 2018.
Powery, Emerson B. *Jesus Reads Scripture: The Function of Jesus' Use of Scripture in the Synoptic Gospels*. Leiden: Brill, 2003.

Proctor, Mark. "Kirk's Assessment of Lukan Christology." *Perspectives in Religious Studies* 46.1 (2019): 95–101.
Prothro, James B. "Review of *A Man Attested By God* by J. R. Daniel Kirk." *Logia* 29.3 (2020): 47–48.
Quarles, Charles L. "Lord or Legend: Jesus as the Messianic Son of Man." *Journal of the Evangelical Theological Society* 62.1 (2019): 103–24.
Quarles, Charles L. *Matthew*. EGGNT. Nashville, TN: B&H Academic, 2017.
Quarles, Charles L. *A Theology of Matthew: Jesus Revealed as Deliverer, King, and Incarnate Creator*. Phillipsburg, NJ: P&R, 2013.
Ramsey, Arthur Michael. *The Glory of God and the Transfiguration of Christ*. London; New York; Toronto: Longmans, Green, 1949.
Rawlinson, A. E. J. *The New Testament Doctrine of the Christ*. London: Longmans, Green, 1926.
Rawlinson, A. E. J. *St. Mark: With Introduction, Commentary and Additional Notes*. London: Methuen, 1925.
Reimarus, Hermann Samuel. *Fragments from Reimarus*. Edited by Charles Voysey. Translated by anonymous. 1879. Repr., Lexington, KY: American Theological Library, 1962.
Reimarus, Hermann Samuel. *The Goal of Jesus and His Disciples*. Translated by George Wesley Buchanan. Leiden: Brill, 1970.
Reymond, Robert L. *Jesus, Divine Messiah: The New Testament Witness*. Phillipsburg, NJ: P&R, 1990.
Reynolds, Benjamin E. "The 'One Like a Son of Man' According to the Old Greek of Daniel 7,13–14." *Biblica* 89 (2008): 70–80.
Ridderbos, Herman N. *Matthew*. BSC. Grand Rapids, MI: Zondervan, 1987.
Robertson, Archibald Thomas. *The Gospel According to Luke*. Vol. 2 of *Word Pictures in the New Testament*. Nashville, TN: Broadman, 1930.
Robinson, William Childs. *Our Lord: An Affirmation of the Deity of Christ*. Grand Rapids, MI: Eerdmans, 1937.
Rogers, Sam. "Jesus' Identity in the Sabbath Miracles in the Gospel of Luke." *Africanus* 8.2 (2016): 26–37.
Rösel, Martin. "The Reading and Translation of the Divine Name in the Masoretic Tradition and the Greek Pentateuch." *Journal for the Study of the Old Testament* 31.4 (2007): 411–28.
Roukema, Riemer. *Jesus, Gnosis and Dogma*. Translated by Saskia Deventer-Metz. London; New York: T&T Clark, 2010.
Rowe, C. Kavin. *Early Narrative Christology: The Lord in the Gospel of Luke*. Berlin; New York: Walter de Gruyter, 2006.
Rowe, C. Kavin. "Romans 10:13: What Is the Name of the Lord?" *Horizons in Biblical Theology* 22.2 (2000): 135–73.
Rowlands, Jonathan. "Jesus and the Wings of YHWH: Bird Imagery in the Lament over Jerusalem (Matt 23:37–39; Luke 13:34–35)." *Novum Testamentum* 61 (2019): 115–36.
Royse, James R. "Philo, Κυριος, and the Tetragrammaton." Pages 167–83 in *Heirs of the Septuagint: Philo, Hellenistic Judaism, and Early Christianity*. Edited by David T. Runia, David M. Hay, and David Winston. Atlanta, GA: Scholars Press, 1991.
Rusam, Dietrich. *Das Alte Testament Bei Lukas*. Berlin; New York: Walter de Gruyter, 2003.
Schlatter, Adolf. *Der Evangelist Matthäus: Seine Sprache, Sein Ziel, Seine Selbständigkeit*. Stuttgart: Calwer, 1963.
Schlatter, Adolf. *Markus: der Evangelist für die Griechen*. 2nd ed. Stuttgart: Calwer, 1984.

Schnabel, Eckhard J. *Mark: An Introduction and Commentary*. TNTC 2. Downers Grove, IL: IVP Academic, 2017.

Schnackenburg, Rudolf. *The Gospel of Matthew*. Translated by Robert R. Barr. Grand Rapids, MI: Eerdmans, 2002.

Schreiner, Thomas R. *The King in His Beauty: A Biblical Theology of the Old and New Testaments*. Grand Rapids, MI: Baker Academic, 2013.

Schweitzer, Albert. *Geschichte Der Leben-Jesu-Forschung*. 2nd ed. Tübingen: Mohr Siebeck, 1913.

Schweitzer, Albert. *The Quest of the Historical Jesus: A Critical Study of Its Progress from Reimarus to Wrede*. Translated by W. Montgomery. London: Black, 1952.

Schweitzer, Albert. *Von Reimarus Zu Wrede*. Tübingen: Mohr Siebeck, 1906.

Serle, Ambrose. *Horae Solitariae*. 3rd ed. London: Mills, 1804.

Shaw, Frank. *Earliest Non-Mystical Jewish Use of Ιαω*. Leuven; Walpole: Peeters, 2014.

Shaw, Frank. "The Transition of Ιαω from Non-Mystical to Mystical Use and Its Implications for Scholarship." *Biblische Notizen* 176 (2018): 65–87.

Shively, Elizabeth E. "Review of *A Man Attested By God* by J. R. Daniel Kirk." *Journal of the Evangelical Theological Society* 60.3 (2017): 637–39.

Sloan, Paul. "The Return of the Shepherd: Zechariah 13:7–14:6 as an Interpretive Framework for Mark 13." Pages 128–58 in *Ancient Readers and Their Scriptures: Engaging the Hebrew Bible in Early Judaism and Christianity*. Edited by Garrick V. Allen and John Anthony Dunne. Leiden; Boston: Brill, 2019.

Small, Rusty N. "What Was Spoken Through the Prophet Isaiah: Matthew's Use of Isaiah to Reveal Matthew's Christology." PhD diss., Southeastern Baptist Theological Seminary, 2012.

Smith, Gary V. *Isaiah 1–39*. NAC 15A. Nashville, TN: Broadman & Holman, 2007.

Snodgrass, Klyne. *Stories with Intent: A Comprehensive Guide to the Parables of Jesus*. 2nd ed. Grand Rapids, MI: Eerdmans, 2018.

Soulen, R. Kendall. *The Divine Name(s) and the Holy Trinity*. Louisville, KY: Westminster John Knox, 2011.

Soulen, R. Kendall. "'Hallowed by Thy Name!': The Theological Significance of the Avoidance of God's Name in the New Testament." Pages 145–49 in *Strangers in a Strange Land*. Edited by Lucy Lind Hogan and D. William Faupel. Lexington, KY: Emeth, 2009.

Soulen, R. Kendall. "Jesus and the Divine Name." *Union Seminary Quarterly Review* 65.1–2 (2015): 47–58.

Soulen, R. Kendall. "The Name of the Holy Trinity: A Triune Name." *Theology Today* 59.2 (2002): 244–61.

Spadaro, Martin C. *Reading Matthew as the Climactic Fulfillment of the Hebrew Story*. Eugene, OR: Wipf & Stock, 2015.

Spencer, Aída Besançon. "'Fear' as a Witness to Jesus in Luke's Gospel." *Bulletin for Biblical Research* 2 (1992): 59–73.

Staples, Jason A. "'Lord, Lord': Jesus as YHWH in Matthew and Luke." *New Testament Studies* 64 (2018): 1–19.

Stegner, William Richard. "Jesus' Walking on the Water: Mark 6.45–52." Pages 212–34 in *The Gospels and the Scriptures of Israel*. Edited by Craig A. Evans and W. Richard Stegner. Sheffield, UK: Sheffield Academic, 1994.

Stein, Robert H. "The 'Criteria' for Authenticity." Pages 225–63 in *Gospel Perspectives: Studies of History and Tradition in the Four Gospels*. Edited by R. T. France and David Wenham. Sheffield, UK: JSOT Press, 1983.

Stein, Robert H. *Luke*. NAC 24. Nashville, TN: Broadman & Holman, 1992.
Stein, Robert H. *Mark*. BECNT. Grand Rapids, MI: Baker Academic, 2008.
Stendahl, Krister. *The School of St. Matthew and Its Use of the Old Testament*. 2nd ed. Philadelphia: Fortress, 1968.
Stonehouse, Ned Bernard. *The Witness of Matthew and Mark to Christ*. Philadelphia: Presbyterian Guardian, 1944.
Stott, John R. W. *The Authentic Jesus: A Response to Current Scepticism in the Church*. Basingstoke: Marshalls, 1985.
Strauss, David Friedrich. *The Life of Jesus, Critically Examined*. Translated by Mary Ann Evans, a.k.a. George Eliot. 1846. Repr., Philadelphia: Fortress, 1973.
Strauss, Mark L. "Christology and Christological Purpose in the Synoptic Gospels: A Study of Unity in Diversity." Pages 41–62 in *Reconsidering the Relationship between Biblical and Systematic Theology in the New Testament*. Edited by Benjamin E. Reynolds, Brian Lugioyo, and Kevin J. Vanhoozer. Tübingen: Mohr Siebeck, 2014.
Strauss, Mark L. *Four Portraits, One Jesus: A Survey of Jesus and the Gospels*. 2nd ed. Grand Rapids, MI: Zondervan, 2020.
Strauss, Mark L. *Mark*. ZECNT. Grand Rapids, MI: Zondervan, 2014.
Subramanian, J. Samuel. *The Synoptic Gospels and the Psalms as Prophecy*. London; New York: T&T Clark, 2007.
Swete, Henry Barclay. *Commentary on Mark: The Greek Text with Introduction Notes and Indexes*. Repr. of *The Gospel According to Mark*, London: Macmillan, 1913. Grand Rapids, MI: Kregel, 1977.
Swete, Henry Barclay, and Richard Rusden Ottley. *An Introduction to the Old Testament in Greek*. 2nd ed. Cambridge: Cambridge University Press, 1914.
Tait, Michael. *Jesus, the Divine Bridegroom, in Mark 2:18–22: Mark's Christology Upgraded*. Rome: Gregorian & Biblical Press, 2010.
Tasker, R. V. G. *The Old Testament in the New Testament*. 2nd ed. London: SCM, 1954.
Taylor, Vincent. *Behind the Third Gospel: A Study of the Proto-Luke Hypothesis*. Oxford: Oxford University Press, 1926.
Taylor, Vincent. *The Gospel According to Mark: The Greek Text with Introduction, Notes, and Indexes*. 2nd ed. New York: St. Martin's, 1966.
Taylor, Vincent. *The Names of Jesus*. London: Macmillan, 1953.
Telford, William. *The Theology of the Gospel of Mark*. Cambridge; New York: Cambridge University Press, 1999.
Thielman, Frank S. "Evangelicals and the Jesus Quest: Some Problems of Historical and Theological Method." *Churchman* 115.1 (2001): 61–73.
Thomas, Robert L., and Stanley N. Gundry. *A Harmony of the Gospels*. Chicago: Moody, 1978.
Thompson, Alan J. *Luke*. EGGNT. Nashville, TN: Broadman & Holman, 2017.
Thompson, Henry O. "Yahweh." *ABD* 6: 1011–12.
Tokić, Dario. "Božje Opraštanje u Evandelju Po Luki." *Bogoslovska Smotra* 82.3 (2012): 731–41.
Tov, Emanuel. "P. Vindob. G 39777 (Symmachus) and the Use of the Divine Names in Greek Scripture Texts." *Academia.edu*. Online forum: https://www.academia.edu/29198634/293._P._Vindob._G_39777_Symmachus_and_the_Use_of_the_Divine_Names_in_Greek_Scripture_Texts_http_orion.mscc.huji.ac.il_symposiums_15th_papers_Tov.pdf.
Tov, Emanuel. "The Greek Biblical Texts from the Judean Desert." Pages 97–122 in *The Bible as Book: The Transmission of the Greek Text*. Edited by Scot McKendrick and Orlaith A. O'Sullivan. New Castle, DE: Oak Knoll, 2003.

Toy, Crawford Howell. *Quotations in the New Testament*. New York: Scribner's Sons, 1884.
Treier, Daniel J. and Walter A. Elwell, eds *Evangelical Dictionary of Biblical Theology*. 3rd ed. Grand Rapids, MI: Baker Academic, 2017.
Tuckett, Christopher M. *Christology and the New Testament: Jesus and His Earliest Followers*. Louisville, KY: Westminster John Knox, 2001.
Tuckett, Christopher M. "The Christology of Luke-Acts." Pages 133–64 in *The Unity of Luke-Acts*. Edited by Giuseppe Alberigo. Leuven: Leuven University Press, 1999.
Turner, David L. *Matthew*. BECNT. Grand Rapids, MI: Baker Academic, 2008.
Vander Hart, Mark D. "The Transition of the Old Testament Day of the LORD into the New Testament Day of the Lord Jesus Christ." *Mid-America Journal of Theology* 9.1 (1993): 3–25.
Vanhoozer, Kevin J. *Is There a Meaning in This Text?: The Bible, the Reader, and the Morality of Literary Knowledge*. Grand Rapids, MI: Zondervan, 2009.
Vasileiadis, Pavlos D. "Exodus 3:14 as an Explanation of the Tetragrammaton: What If the Septuagint Rendering Had No Platonic Nuances?" *Biblische Notizen* 183 (2019): 101–28.
Vasileiadis, Pavlos D. "The God Iao and His Connection with the Biblical God, with Special Emphasis on the Manuscript 4QpapLXXLevb." *Vetus Testamentum et Hellas* 4 (2017): 21–51.
Vasileiadis, Pavlos D., and Nehemia Gordon. "Transmission of the Tetragrammaton in Judeo-Greek and Christian Sources." *Accademia: Revue de La Société Marsile Ficin* 18 (2019): 1–18.
Vermeylen, Jacques. "Name." Pages 1093–95 in *Encyclopedia of Christian Theology*. Edited by Jean-Yves Lacoste. New York; London: Routledge, 2005.
Viljoen, Francois P. "The Superior Authority of Jesus in Matthew to Interpret the Torah." *In die Skriflig* 50.2 (2016): 1–7.
Voelz, James W., and Christopher Wright Mitchell. *Mark 8:27–16:8*. ConcC. Saint Louis, MO: Concordia, 2019.
Voorwinde, Stephen. "Jesus' Tears—Human or Divine?" *Reformed Theological Review* 56.2 (1997): 68–81.
Vos, Geerhardus. "The Kyrios Christos Controversy." *Princeton Theological Review* 15.1 (1917): 21–89.
Vos, Geerhardus. "Seeking and Saving the Lost: Luke 19:10." *Kerux* 7.1 (1992): 1–19.
Vos, Geerhardus. *The Self-Disclosure of Jesus: The Modern Debate About the Messianic Consciousness*. Edited by Johannes G. Vos. Phillipsburg, NJ: P&R, 2002.
Warfield, Benjamin B. *The Lord of Glory*. New York: American Tract Society, 1907.
Warfield, Benjamin B. *The Person and Work of Christ*. Philadelphia: P&R, 1950.
Watts, John D. W. *Isaiah 1–33*. 2nd ed. WBC 24. Nashville, TN: Nelson, 1999.
Watts, Rikk E. "Immanuel: Virgin Birth Proof Text or Programmatic Warning of Things to Come (Isa 7:14 in Matt 1:23)?" Pages 92–113 in *From Prophecy to Testament: The Function of the Old Testament in the New*. Edited by Craig A. Evans. Peabody, MA: Hendrickson, 2004.
Watts, Rikk E. *Isaiah's New Exodus in Mark*. Grand Rapids, MI: Baker Books, 1997.
Watts, Rikk E. "Mark." Pages 111–249 in *Commentary on the New Testament Use of the Old Testament*. Edited by G. K. Beale and D. A. Carson. Grand Rapids, MI: Baker Academic, 2007.
Watts, Rikk E. "Rule of the Community and Mark 1:1–13: Preparing the Way in the Wilderness." Pages 41–47 in *Reading Mark in Context: Jesus and Second Temple Judaism*. Edited by Ben C. Blackwell, John K. Goodrich, and Jason Maston. Grand Rapids, MI: Zondervan, 2018.

Weinandy, Thomas G. *Jesus Becoming Jesus: A Theological Interpretation of the Synoptic Gospels*. Washington, DC: Catholic University of America Press, 2018.
Welker, Michael. *God the Revealed: Christology*. Grand Rapids, MI: Eerdmans, 2013.
Wellum, Stephen J. *Christ Alone: The Uniqueness of Jesus as Savior: What the Reformers Taught . . . and Why It Still Matters*. Grand Rapids, MI: Zondervan, 2017.
Wellum, Stephen J. "The Deity of Christ in the Synoptic Gospels." Pages 61–89 in *The Deity of Christ*. Edited by Christopher W. Morgan and Robert A. Peterson. Theology in Community. Wheaton, IL: Crossway, 2011.
Wellum, Stephen J. "From Alpha to Omega: A Biblical-Theological Approach to God the Son Incarnate." *Journal of the Evangelical Theological Society* 63.1 (2020): 71–94.
Wellum, Stephen J. *God the Son Incarnate: The Doctrine of Christ*. Wheaton, IL: Crossway, 2016.
Wenham, John William. *Redating Matthew, Mark & Luke: A Fresh Assault on the Synoptic Problem*. Downers Grove, IL: InterVarsity Press, 1992.
Wilkinson, Robert J. *Tetragrammaton: Western Christians and the Hebrew Name of God: From the Beginnings to the Seventeenth Century*. Leiden; Boston: Brill, 2015.
Williams, Joel F. *Mark*. EGGNT. Nashville, TN: Broadman & Holman, 2020.
Williamson, Lamar. *Mark*. IBC. Atlanta, GA: John Knox, 1983.
Wills, Lawrence M. "Wisdom and Word among the Hellenistic Saviors: The Function of Literacy." *Journal for the Study of the Pseudepigrapha* 24.2 (2014): 118–48.
Winn, Adam. *The Purpose of Mark's Gospel: An Early Christian Response to Roman Imperial Propaganda*. Tübingen: Mohr Siebeck, 2008.
Winter, Paul. "Two Notes On Luke I, II With Regard To The Theory Of 'Imitation Hebraisms.'" *Studia Theologica* 7.2 (1953): 158–65.
Witherington, Ben, III. *The Christology of Jesus*. Minneapolis, MN: Fortress, 1997.
Witherington, Ben, III, and Kazuhiko Yamazaki-Ransom. "Lord." Pages 526–35 in *Dictionary of Jesus and the Gospels*. Nottingham, UK; Downers Grove, IL: IVP Academic, 2013.
Woods, Edward J. *The "Finger of God" and Pneumatology in Luke-Acts*. Sheffield, UK: Sheffield Academic, 2001.
Wrede, William. *Das Messiasgeheimnis in Den Evangelien*. 2nd ed. Göttingen: Vandenhoeck & Ruprecht, 1963.
Wrede, William. *The Messianic Secret*. Translated by J. C. G. Greig. Cambridge; London: Clarke, 1971.
Wright, Christopher J. H. "Christ and the Old Testament." *Journal of Theological Interpretation* 2.1 (2008): 11–16.
Wright, N. T. "The Biblical Formation of a Doctrine of Christ." Pages 47–68 in *Who Do You Say That I Am? Christology and the Church*. Edited by Donald Armstrong. Grand Rapids, MI: Eerdmans, 1999.
Wright, N. T. *The Climax of the Covenant: Christ and the Law in Pauline Theology*. Minneapolis, MN: Fortress, 1993.
Wright, N. T. "'The Evangelists' Use of the Old Testament as an Implicit Overarching Narrative.'" Pages 189–200 in *Biblical Interpretation and Method: Studies in Honour of John Barton*. Edited by K. J. Dell and P. M. Joyce. Oxford: Oxford University Press, 2013.
Wright, N. T. "Five Gospels but No Gospel: Jesus and the Seminar." Pages 115–57 in *Crisis in Christology: Essays in Quest of Resolution*. Edited by William R. Farmer. Livonia, MI: Dove Booksellers, 1995.
Wright, N. T. "The Historical Jesus and Christian Theology." *Sewanee Theological Review* 39.4 (1996): 404–12.
Wright, N. T. "Jesus and the Identity of God." *Ex Auditu* 14 (1988): 42–56.

Wright, N. T. *Jesus and the Victory of God*. Minneapolis, MN: Fortress, 1996.
Wright, N. T. "Jesus' Self-Understanding." Pages 47–61 in *The Incarnation*. Edited by S. T. Davis, D. Kendall, and G. O'Collins. Oxford: Oxford University Press, 2002.
Wright, N. T. "Kingdom Come: The Public Meaning of the Gospels." *Christian Century* 125.12 (2008): 29–34.
Wright, N. T. *The New Testament and the People of God*. Minneapolis, MN: Fortress, 1992.
Wright, N. T. "The New, Unimproved Jesus." *Christianity Today* 37.10 (1993): 22–26.
Wright, N. T. "One God, One Lord." *Christian Century* 130.4 (2013): 22–25, 27.
Wright, N. T. "Pictures, Stories, and the Cross: Where Do the Echoes Lead?" *Journal of Theological Interpretation* 11.1 (2017): 49–68.
Wright, N. T. *The Resurrection of the Son of God*. Minneapolis, MN: Fortress, 2008.
Wright, N. T. "Son of God and Christian Origins." Pages 118–34 in *Son of God: Divine Sonship in Jewish and Christian Antiquity*. Edited by G. V. Allen, K. Akagi, P. Sloan, and M. Nevader. University Park, PA: Eisenbrauns, 2019.
Wright, Stephen I. "Luke." Pages 50–59 in *Theological Interpretation of the New Testament*. Edited by Kevin J. Vanhoozer. Grand Rapids, MI: Baker Academic, 2008.
Yarbrough, Robert W. "Jesus Christ, Name and Titles Of." Pages 406–12 in *Evangelical Dictionary of Biblical Theology*. Edited by Walter A. Elwell. Grand Rapids, MI: Baker Books, 1996.
Zahn, Theodore. "The Adoration of Jesus in the Apostolic Age." Translated by C. J. H. Ropes. *Bibliotheca Sacra* 51 (1894): 314–30, 389–406.
Zahn, Theodore. *Die Anbetung Jesu Im Zeitalter Der Apostel*. 5th ed. Leipzig: Deichert, 1910.

Subject Index

Abba, Raymond 3, 5–6
Abernethy, Andrew T. 157–58
Achtemeier, Paul J. 18, 72–73, 90–91, 93
Adams, Edward 114–17
adoption theory 43, 73, 75, 81–82, 108
  see also Son of God
agent/s
  angels as 11, 138
  Holy Spirit as 79, 81
  humans as 11, 27, 65, 75, 85, 96, 100, 111, 138, 149, 163, 171–72
  Jesus as unique/chief 26–27, 34, 42–43, 49, 64, 73, 75, 92, 96, 114, 124, 129
  Jesus not merely an 26–27, 30, 46–47, 49, 53, 59, 78, 82, 85, 96, 100–1, 111, 126, 129, 131–33, 138–39, 141, 144, 147, 171–72
  see also divine agency; mediator
Aland, Kurt 148, 160
Albright, W. F. 41, 58, 61
Alexander, Joseph Addison 77–78, 109, 116
Allen, Leslie C. 63
Allison, Dale C., Jr. 44, 47–48, 51–56, 58, 64–65
Ancient of Days 59–60, 65–67, 74, 91, 107, 113, 142, 146–47, 155
appearing of the Lord/YHWH in
  the eschaton 6, 78, 114–15, 133, 154, 179
  Jesus 15, 17, 31–33, 54–55, 58, 68, 78, 82, 91, 96, 114–15, 120, 130, 132, 146, 154, 161, 171–72, 178–79
  manifestations 5–6, 32, 60, 81–82, 107, 114, 130, 133, 146, 154, 177, 179
  see also theophany
  see also coming; presence
appellations/surrogates for YHWH 7–9, 13, 143

Baird, William 21
Baker, David W. 4
Barker, Joel D. 6
Barrett, Matthew 169, 177
Bauckham, Richard 10–12, **25–27**, 34, 42, 73, 76, 84–85, 87, 100, 109–10, 116–17, 137, 139–40, 169, 172, 174, 178–80
Bauer, David R. 42–45, 47
Bayer, Hans F. 72, 74, 83–84, 116–17
Beale, Gregory K. 36–37, 47, 49, 75, 120–21, 133, 140, 147, 179–80
Beardsley, Steven J. 124, 132–33
Beare, Francis Wright 45, 48, 51, 59, 61
Beers, Holly 99–103
Bendoraitis, Kristian A. 87
Bernard, David K. 126
biblical theology 24–25, 97, 180
bios/βιός 72, 119
  see also theological biography
Bird, Michael F. 179
birth narratives 45, 71, 81, 121, 123, 135, 176
Black, Matthew 23–24
Blaising, Craig A. 6
Blaylock, Richard M. 77
Block, Daniel I. 12, 142–43
Blomberg, Craig L. 23, 43, 47, 49, 51, 53–54, 57–59, 63, 65, 67, 72–74, 87–88, 110, 120, 168, 173, 176
Bloom, Harold 175
Bock, Darrell L. 59, 120–30, 132–33, 135–37, 139–43, 145, 150–56, 158, 160–61
Boers, Hendrikus 24
Böhlemann, Peter 125
Böhler, Dieter 61
Booth, Susan Maxwell 146–47
Boring, M. Eugene 72–75, 78, 80–83, 85, 87–88, 92–94, 96–111, 116
Bornkamm, Günther 23

Böttrich, Christfried 15, 44
Bousset, Wilhelm **21–23**, 24–25, 32, 34–35, 179
Bovon, François 8, 120, 122, 125–26, 130–32, 134–35, 147–52, 156, 161
Bowman, Robert M. 12, 49
branch 131–32
   see also Jesus as the Arising/Emerging One
Bright, John 178
Broadhead, Edwin Keith 7, 10, 85, 90, 102, 116–17
Brooks, James A. 75, 86, 99, 103–4, 106–8, 110, 116
Brown, Colin 19
Brown, Jeannine K. 125
Bruce, F. F. 175
Bullinger, E. W. 4
Bultmann, Rudolf 21–24, 35, 113
Burge, Gary M. 120
Byrne, Máire 6

Capes, David B. 2–3, 13–14, 25, **31–33**, 34, 39, 47, 54, 64–66, 111, 160–61, 171, 173–74, 177, 179
Cara, Robert J. 119–20
Carroll, John R. 120, 124–25, 129–32, 138–39, 149, 154–55
Carson, D. A. 45, 48–49, 51–52, 54–55, 60–64, 66–67, 101, 110
Casey, P. Maurice 11, 17, 35, 142, 175, 177
Charles, J. Daryl 135–36
Chen, Diane G. 124, 126, 131–33, 137–38, 144–47, 150–52, 154, 156, 164
Chiasm; Bookends 14, 43, 47, 61, 72–73, 129
Childs, Brevard S. 24, 101
Christ of faith, see Jesus of history
Christological
   monotheism 26–27, 29, 32–33
   studies 2, 10, 18–25, 35–36, 39, 143, 165, 179–80
Christophany 74
   see also incarnation; Jesus as the embodied presence of YHWH
circumlocution 13–14, 99, 115–16, 124, 138, 156
Clark, Henry B. 21

clouds; glory-cloud 5, 60, 66–67, 106–8, 111–15, 117, 130, 146–47, 154–55, 166
Cole, Graham A. 42
Collins, Adela Yarbro 11, 78, 80, 85–86, 89–90, 95–98, 100, 102–11, 115–16
Collins, C. John 1, 37, 178
coming/arrival of
   Jesus 4, 15, 28, 42–43, 49, 54, 59, 65–67, 74, 78–79, 81, 111–15, 117, 126, 128, 133–35, 145, 153, 155, 157–58, 160, 176, 178, 180
   the Lord/YHWH 1, 6, 15, 28, 33–34, 42, 49, 54, 60, 66, 74, 77–81, 98, 103, 106, 112–13, 123, 126–28, 133–35, 151, 154, 176, 178
   the Son of Man/Messiah 1, 28, 42–43, 49, 59–60, 65, 74, 77–78, 107, 109, 111–17, 131, 145, 154–58
   see also Son of Man
   see also day of the Lord; divine visitation
consummation 6, 38, 98–99, 112, 114, 154
   see also eschatological . . .
covenant(s) 2, 5–6, 11–12, 54–55, 61, 64, 68, 74, 89, 122, 149, 153, 178
   see also New Covenant
Craddock, Fred B. 123, 129–30, 132, 146–47
Cranfield, C. E. B. 12, 81–83, 86–87, 89, 91, 97–99, 104, 107, 110–11, 116
creator-creature distinction 2, 10–11, 27, 62, 64, 93, 149, 172
cries for salvation/mercy 51–52, 44, 51, 58, 94–95, 109, 144, 164
   see also Jesus answers prayers/laments
Crisler, Channing L. 144, 172
critical theories 19–25, 27–32, 34–36, 39, 42, 45–46, 48, 72, 75, 78, 81, 91, 161, 171–72, 175–77
Cullmann, Oscar 12, 23
Culpepper, R. Alan 44, 120–23, 125, 127–28, 132, 134, 139, 143, 145–46, 152–53, 155, 159–60

dating the Gospels 90, 174–76, 179
Davidic King 1, 14, 23, 42–43, 46, 62–63, 74, 81–82, 91, 97–99, 129–31, 156, 158, 170–71

see also enthronement; Messiah; shepherd; Son of David
Davies, W. D. 47–48, 51–56, 58, 64–65
Davis, Carl Judson 15, 83, 109, 111, 123
Davis, Philip G. 73
Davis, Stephen T. 85–87, 178
day of the Lord/YHWH 5–6, 12, 33, 42, 48, 55, 66, 82, 84, 91, 106, 111, 113, 115, 123, 127, 154–56, 160
Dead Sea Scrolls/DSS 8–9, 48, 78
Decker, Rodney J. 75, 79, 86, 90, 96, 101–2
DeClaissé-Walford, Nancy L. 63
Denaux, Adelbert 129–30, 132–34, 161–63
Dennis, J. A. 60
DeYoung, James B. 54
divine
    agency/agent 18, 21, 75, 78, 100, 104, 109, 117, 123, 144, 170
    authority 17, 27–28, 30, 44, 50–51, 53, 56–58, 60–61, 64–65, 67, 73–74, 77, 84–85, 87–88, 90–91, 96–97, 100, 106–12, 116, 122, 137–40, 142–43, 147–49, 156–57, 160–62, 164, 166, 169, 171
    see also sections on Jesus; YHWH
    Christology 27, 29, 36. 81, 87–88, 124
    see also Christological monotheism
    compassion 97–98, 105, 133–34, 166
    embodiment, *see* embodiment
    forgiveness, *see* Jesus forgives sins
    identity 2, 26–27, 30–35, 43, 45, 47–48, 51, 58, 68–69, 73–76, 78, 81, 88, 95–97, 99–101, 105, 112–13, 116–17, 121–22, 124, 126, 133, 137, 139, 154, 156, 161–62, 167, 171, 174, 177, 180
    incarnation, *see* incarnation
    initiative 6, 42, 47, 57, 68, 74, 112
    intervention 42, 58, 130, 133, 148–49, 155
    lament 109, 134, 152–53, 164, 167, 172
    see also Jesus answers prayers/laments
    lordship 2–3, 17–19, 22, 33, 51, 56, 58, 67, 90, 112, 121, 141–42, 158, 169, 173
    see also Jesus as the Lord; "Jesus is Lord," Lord of the Sabbath
    kingship/kingdom, *see* divine sovereignty/rule; Jesus as the King; kingdom of God
    manifestation 4–6, 15, 31–33, 55, 60, 78, 82, 96, 107, 114–15, 130, 133, 146–47, 177–79
    see also theophany, Christophany
    name 1–14, 18, 21–22, 32–33, 43, 45–47, 49–50, 52, 58–59, 61, 66–68, 76, 84–85, 90, 101, 109–10, 116, 142–43, 153, 156, 162, 174, 176, 178
    see also YHWH; Tetragrammaton
    nature 69, 73, 75, 108, 121, 171, 180
    see also divine identity
    ontology/being 4, 11, 56, 81–82, 85–86, 96, 115, 144, 147, 152, 167, 171–72
    see also divine identity
    Parousia, *see* Parousia; coming of
    passive 86, 138–40
    power 46–47, 51, 58, 67, 79, 84, 96–97, 100, 130, 144, 148, 157–58, 175
    see also divine authority; Jesus as omnipotent; etc.
    prerogatives 2, 4, 17, 27–28, 30, 35, 39, 44, 46, 48, 51–54, 56–57, 59–60, 63–65, 75, 77–78, 83–94, 97, 99, 113–15, 122–25, 127–28, 136, 138–41, 149–51, 153–55, 157–59, 162–63, 167, 170–72, 175
    presence, *see* presence of God
    Shepherd, *see* shepherd; Jesus as the shepherd
    sonship, *see* Son of God
    sovereignty/rule 11–12, 28, 44, 55–59, 74, 91, 94, 98, 104–5, 116, 148–49, 156, 169, 172, 174, 177
    see also divine authority; Jesus as Lord; kingdom of God; etc.
    speech 22, 53, 64–65, 82–83, 85–86, 96, 102, 106–7, 110–12, 142, 151–52, 160–61, 167
    see also Jesus as the authority; word of God
    throne, enthronement 44, 56, 60, 65–67, 74, 110, 112, 115–17, 122, 147, 156–57, 166, 169–70

visitation 5, 30, 33, 38, 47, 75, 78, 121, 125, 128–35, 147, 149, 153, 155, 158, 166, 176, 178
  see also coming of the Lord/YHWH
Dodd, C. H. 24, 38, 174
Donahue, John R. 78–80, 83–85, 89, 93–94, 96–98, 103, 111, 113, 115
Doriani, Daniel 44, 160–61, 175
Dungan, David L. 41
Dunn, James D. G. 110, 176
Duvall, J. Scott 115, 117, 121, 133

Eckman, Edward W. 49
Edwards, James R. 73, 76–77, 79–80, 86, 89–94, 96–100, 102–10, 113–16, 119, 123–25, 129–35, 137–42, 144–56, 159–62, 164
Ehrman, Bart D. 81, 123–24
Elledge, Ervin Roderick 13, 74
Ellis, E. Earle 32, 116, 120, 123, 130, 135, 146, 148, 156
embodiment/embodied presence of YHWH 28–31, 34, 45–47, 59, 74, 78, 103, 106, 108, 121, 126–27, 132, 134–35, 170–72, 174, 178, 180
Emmanuel, *see* Immanuel
enthronement, *see* divine throne
epiphany 31, 100, 102, 106–7, 167
  see also divine manifestation; theophany; Christophany
Erickson, Millard J. 64–65
eschatological
  banquet/wedding feast 43, 50, 89, 98–99, 105, 141
  gathering/harvest 65–66, 74, 83–84, 112, 114–15, 117, 150, 152–53, 158, 166–67, 169, 178
  judgment, *see* final judgment
Esswein, Mitchell Alexander 72
Evans, Craig A. 54, 73, 87–88, 110, 116–17

Farnell, F. David 41
Father, *see* God the Father
feeding miracles 97–99, 104–05, 164, 166
final judgment 6, 12, 15, 17, 33, 42, 44–45, 49–50, 53, 59–61, 65–66, 74, 80, 83–84, 87, 109, 112–15, 117, 123, 127–28, 130, 134–36, 151–55, 157, 178
finger of God, *see* hand/finger of God
fishers of men 83–84, 136–37, 166
Fitzmyer, Joseph A. 120, 122–25, 127–30, 132, 134, 136, 141, 145–47, 153, 156–57, 159–61
Fletcher-Louis, Crispin H. T. 13, 87, 154, 156, 170
Ford, J. Massingberd 17
forgiveness/pardon, *see* Jesus forgives sins
Frame, John M. 2, 19, 49, 56–57, 91
France, Richard T. 18, 36–38, 44, 47, 49–50, 54, 57, 60, 62–66, 68, 71, 77, 79–80, 86–94, 96, 98, 101, 103, 105–8, 110–17, 124–28, 131–32, 136–39, 157–61, 164, 167, 174
Fredriksen, Paula 11
Friedeman, Caleb T. 124–25, 131–32
Funk, Robert Walter 24–25, 85, 89, 91, 101–2, 136–37, 156, 160–61

Gadenz, Pablo T. 119–20, 125–26, 133–34, 137, 141–47, 152, 157
Gaiser, Frederick J. 86–88
Garber, Zev 3, 8
Garland, David 73, 79–80, 83–84, 88–89, 92–94, 96, 99–104, 106–8, 111–12, 114, 116, 120, 123–23, 127, 134–42, 144, 146–49, 151, 153–55, 158, 162–64
Gathercole, Simon J. 36, 44–45, 50, 52, 56–57, 87–88, 94, 100, 131–32, 139–40, 150–53, 157–58, 163, 171
Gathering, *see* eschatological gathering/ harvest
Geddert, Timothy J. 53, 58, 75, 77, 83–84, 87, 95, 97, 103–4, 109, 114–17
Gieschen, Charles A. 18, 61, 68
Gladd, Benjamin L. 120–21, 133, 140, 147
glory-cloud, *see* clouds
Gnilka, Joachim 42, 86–87, 93, 97
God the Father; God as Father 12–14, 21, 27, 33, 43, 46–47, 50, 55–56, 60, 67–68, 73–76, 82, 104, 112–15, 121–22, 145, 156, 162–63
God with us, *see* Immanuel; presence of God

Godshall, Matthew Steven 135, 162–63
Gordon, Nehemia 9
Goswell, Greg 157–58
Graves, Robert Brent 132, 134
Gray, Timothy C. 73–74
Great Commission 67–68
Green, Gene L. 120
Green, Joel B. 120–30, 132, 134, 136–37, 141, 144–50, 152, 154–55, 157, 160–62, 164
Green, Michael 111
Grether, Oskar 178
Grindheim, Sigurd 44, 107–8, 112, 148–50
Grogan, Geoffrey W. 90, 139, 142, 158, 180
Grundmann, Walter 123, 125, 127, 130, 139, 142, 145–46, 152
Guelich, Robert A. 76–77, 80, 83, 94, 97–98, 102–3
Guillet, Jacques 46
Gundry, Robert H. 54–55, 86–87, 89, 93, 96, 100–3, 111, 114–16
Gundry, Stanley N. 136, 148

Hagner, Donald A. 47, 53–58, 61–62, 64, 66–68
Hahn, Ferdinand 7, 43, 51, 110
hand/finger of God 63, 67, 74, 104, 110, 112, 115–16, 126, 148–49, 156–57, 166
hapax legomenon 103
Hare, Douglas R. A. 53, 56, 58
Harriman, K. R. 110, 113–15
Harrington, Daniel J. 52–53, 57–58, 64–65, 67–68, 78–80, 83–85, 89, 93–94, 96–98, 103, 111, 113, 115
Harris, Murray J. 4, 7
Harrison, Everett F. 44
Harrison, James R. 17, 94–95, 100, 103, 136
Harvest, *see* eschatological gathering/harvest
Hays, J. Daniel 115, 117, 121, 133
Hays, Richard B. 25, **29–31**, 34, 37, 39, 43–45, 47, 52, 56, 64–66, 68, 86–88, 96, 98, 100–4, 120–22, 124–27, 130–35, 137, 139, 141, 143–44, 152–53, 160–63, 169, 178–79
Healy, Mary 113–17

Hendriksen, William 59, 99, 116, 134, 136–38, 140–41, 144, 149–50, 159
Hengel, Martin 13
Henrichs-Tarasenkova, Nina 121–22, 125, 130–32, 137
Henry, Carl F. H. 174, 176
Hick, John 171, 175
Hidalgo, Esteban 12
Hiebert, D. Edmond 73, 79–80, 82, 86–87, 97, 103, 105–6, 108, 117
high Christology 2, 10, 26–27, 31–32, 43, 45, 47, 63, 68, 74–75, 78, 97, 121, 135, 137, 169, 175–77, 180
higher criticism, *see* critical theories
historical Jesus, *see* quests for the historical Jesus
Holladay, Carl R. 121
Holy Spirit as the
 agent of baptism/cleansing 69, 79–80, 91, 126, 135, 163, 166
 creator; agent/giver of life 5, 21, 46, 69
 gift of God; given/sent 69, 79–80, 120, 122, 135, 161–63
 power of God 82, 85, 107, 135, 148, 161–63, 166
 presence of God in/with his people 6, 46, 68, 80, 120, 162–63, 178, 180
 promise of God 79–80, 120, 122, 162–63, 178
 revealer/teacher of truth 19, 129, 180
 third member of the Trinity 47, 67–68, 79, 81
Hooker, Morna D. 71–72, 79–84, 86, 89, 91–92, 94, 96–97, 99–100, 103, 105–12, 116
Hoover, Roy W. 24–25, 85, 89, 91, 101–2, 136–37, 156, 160–61
Horstmann, Maria 113
Howard, George 8–9
human agents 11, 27, 30, 42, 47, 49, 65, 75, 85, 96, 100, 111, 117, 132, 138–39, 141, 149, 163, 170–72
Hurtado, Larry W. 11, **25–26**, 32, 34, 42–44, 54, 82, 87, 170, 173
Hylton, Michael Antony 8–10

"I AM" statements 3, 17–18, 24, 31, 58–59, 101–2, 110, 112, 116, 156, 166, 176
identity, *see* divine identity
illeism 13, 74, 86, 113
immanence, *see* transcendence and immanence
Immanuel 43, 45–47, 60, 68, 178
  see also Jesus as God with us; presence of God
incarnation 18, 21, 29, 47, 69, 108, 121, 123, 130, 172, 174–78
  see also embodiment
inclusio; bookends 14, 43, 47, 61, 73, 129–30
intermediary, *see* mediator
Isbell, Charles D. 5–6

Jacobson, Rolf A. 63
Jeffrey, David L. 145–48, 156–57
Jesus
  accepts worship 21, 30–31, 43, 51, 63, 122, 163, 169
  accused of blasphemy 35, 52, 85–87, 116, 137–38
  answers prayers/laments 21, 51–52, 82, 144, 172
  baptizes with/in the Holy Spirit 79–80, 125–26, 135, 166
  bears/takes the divine name, *YHWH* 44, 46, 50, 58, 61, 109, 162
  birth narrative(s) of 45–46, 71, 81, 121, 123–24, 135, 176
  casts/rains fire on the earth 150–52, 154, 166
  chooses/commands disciples 58, 67–68, 83, 101, 108, 136–37, 150, 162
  comes in (his) Glory 60, 65–66, 112, 114–15, 145–46, 178
  commands/rebukes demons 84–85, 91–92, 148, 166
  commissions witnesses 145, 161–62; cf. 30
  divides humanity into two categories 65–66, 136, 151–52
  does what only YHWH can do 28, 30, 83, 88, 91, 95, 100, 103–4, 145, 151, 167, 171–72
  emanates light/lightning 107–8, 147, 154, 164
  feared by men 94–96, 101, 133, 144, 155
  forgives sins 35, 44, 52–53, 73, 77, 85–88, 90–91, 132, 137–42, 162–63, 166–67, 169
  fulfills YHWH's prerogatives, *see* divine prerogatives
  included in the divine identity, *see* divine identity
  laments as YHWH, *see* divine lament
  ontology of, *see* divine ontology
  raises the dead 24, 133
  self-consciousness/self-understanding of 28, 43, 50, 82, 86, 92–93, 141, 151, 161, 175
  self-disclosure/self-revelation of 16, 20–21, 28, 30, 32, 50, 58–59, 161, 175
  self-identity of 24–25, 28, 32, 49, 56, 59, 89, 92, 100–2, 140, 149, 155, 174–75, 180
    see also divine identity
  shares YHWH's attributes/characteristics 14, 34, 64, 73, 93, 132, 155, 157, 170
  speaks eternal/ultimate words 44, 64, 110–13, 160–62, 166–67
    see also Jesus as the authority

Jesus as
  divine; deity 14, 19, 21, 27, 32–34, 43, 51, 53, 61, 64, 67, 83, 96, 133, 135, 142, 161, 165, 167, 171, 176–77
    see also divine identity; divine ontology
  enthroned/exalted to God's throne 31–33, 44, 46–47, 56, 59–60, 65–67, 74, 80, 112–17, 120, 122, 156–57, 169–70, 178
  God with us 31, 43, 45–47, 56, 60–61, 166
    see also Immanuel
  man/human 32–33, 43, 73, 75, 81, 122, 164, 167, 170–71, 177
    see also incarnation
  omnipotent 44, 46, 67, 85, 91, 93, 156, 162–63
  omnipresent 47, 61, 67–68

omniscient 50, 87, 112, 158
preexistent 131, 150, 153, 158
risen/resurrected 23, 26–27, 29, 32–34, 38, 61–62, 68, 80, 90, 114–15, 117, 130, 161–63, 173
self-existent 1, 59
superior to angels 14, 112
superior to Moses/Elijah/the Prophets 106–7, 147, 153, 175

Jesus as the
arbiter/interpreter of scripture 10, 17, 44, 56–57, 64–65, 128, 142, 160
Arising/Emerging One 121, 131–32
atoning/substitutionary sacrifice 88, 99, 151, 162, 178
authority over
  angels and demons 17, 28, 30, 60, 74, 84–85, 91, 114, 149–50
  humanity 50, 53, 64, 73–74, 77, 83, 87–88, 91, 106–7, 116, 138–40, 142–43, 147, 156–57, 164
  nature/the elements 44, 51, 58, 87, 96–97, 100, 138, 171
  Satan/the devil/the "strong man" 79, 92–93, 148–50, 166
  the universe/heaven and earth 56, 59, 67–68, 91, 116, 161, 169
branch, *see* Jesus as the Arising/Emerging One
bridegroom/husband of God's people 74–75, 88–91, 113, 140–41, 166, 169
center of biblical theology; key to scripture 28, 38, 76, 120, 122, 161–62, 174–75, 177–79
coming One 6, 21, 33, 64, 79, 117, 135–36
  see also Son of Man coming
creator 1–2, 57, 60, 64, 93, 100, 103, 111, 141–42, 172
embodied presence of YHWH, *see* embodiment; incarnation
equal/peer of YHWH 34, 43–44, 47, 54, 56, 59–60, 65–66, 69, 106, 110, 116–17, 138, 155–56
giver of rest 55–57, 98, 166
healer of the sick 44, 53, 86–88, 91, 103–4, 137–38, 141, 167
hen/bird gathering/protecting chicks 152, 166–67
horn of salvation 129–30, 133
judge of humanity 2, 15, 17, 32, 42, 44–45, 50, 53, 59–61, 65–66, 69, 74, 80, 85, 87, 112–15, 117, 129, 150, 154–58, 177–78
  see also final judgment
king of
  David's/Messiah's kingdom 14, 28, 42, 46, 81–82, 96–99, 108, 129, 158, 170–71
  God's kingdom 14, 50, 59–60, 63, 67, 74, 78, 108, 138, 145, 158, 164, 169, 172
  heaven and earth/the universe 42, 46, 60, 99, 138, 172
  see also divine throne; Jesus as the authority
lawgiver; law's authority 15, 65, 90, 107, 112, 142, 147, 160, 175, 180
Lord 2, 18–21, 33–35
  see also authority; Lord
mediator 32, 45, 56, 68, 73, 85, 147
Messiah/Christ, *see* Messiah
mightier/stronger one 79–80, 92, 111, 135–36, 148–49
object/recipient of worship 1, 11, 21, 25–26, 30–32, 34, 43, 51, 56, 63, 68–69, 122, 137, 163, 169
prophet like Moses 106, 147, 170
ransom/redeemer 2, 21, 44, 47, 61, 77, 88, 92, 129–30, 149, 155, 178
savior/deliverer from
  physical harm 42, 51–52, 58, 103, 166
  sin and judgment 17, 35, 42, 46–47, 50, 78, 82, 109, 129, 157–58, 166, 170, 172
sender/giver of the Holy Spirit 69, 79–80, 120, 122, 162–63
servant of the Lord 26, 42, 73, 77–78, 82, 88, 92, 121, 149, 170–71
shepherd 42, 97–99, 105, 157–58, 166, 169–70
  see also Jesus as the King
stone/cornerstone/rock 15, 63, 159, 166, 169

tabernacle/temple of God 28, 30, 43, 56–57, 63, 83, 88, 107–8, 138, 140, 146–47, 175
telos of God's narrative/purposes 38, 41, 76, 179
"Jesus is Lord" 19, 23, 34–35, 73, 173, 180
Jesus of history, Christ of faith 19, 23–25, 36, 72
see also quests
Jesus Seminar 24–25, 28
Jewish monotheism, see monotheism; Christological monotheism
Jipp, Joshua W. 120, 122
Jobes, Karen H. 7–8
Johansson, Daniel 75–77, 90–91, 109
Johnson, Dennis E. 2, 37, 44, 94, 122, 157–58, 162–63
Johnson, Luke Timothy 25, 119–20, 127, 129–30, 132, 134–35, 139–40, 145–48, 150, 152–53, 156
Johnson, S. Lewis 36
Juncker, Günther 44, 101–2, 106–8
Just, Arthur A. 119–20, 123, 125, 127, 130, 136–38, 140, 144, 146–47
Just, Felix 58

Kähler, Martin 19
Kaiser, Walter C. 36
Kärkkäinen, Veli-Matti 110
Käsemann, Ernst 23
Keener, Craig S. 47, 54, 58, 65–67, 173
Kennedy, Joel 41–42, 46
Kereszty, Roch A. 4, 137, 180
Kimball, Charles A. 119, 155, 159
kingdom of God 14, 50, 59–60, 63, 67, 74, 83, 91, 97, 99, 108, 138, 145–46, 164, 169
see also divine sovereignty; Jesus as the King
Kingsbury, Jack Dean 44–45, 51, 57, 72–73
Kirk, J. R. Daniel 2, 11, 35, 58, 61, 75–76, 87, 102, 161, 170–72
Klein, Hans 135, 138, 144–46, 152–53, 160–61
Kline, Meredith G. 5
Köber, Berthold W. 84
Kodell, Jerome 120
Kok, Michael 75, 81–82
Komoszewski, J. Ed 12, 49

Kramer, Werner 24
kurie kurie (κύριε κύριε), see "Lord Lord"
kurios (κύριος) 7–10, 13–14, 18, 22, 31, 33, 42, 45, 50–51, 76, 110
see also Lord; Jesus as Lord

Lagrange, Marie-Joseph 77–78
Lament, see divine lament
Lane, William L. 83, 99, 101–2, 116–17
Lanier, Gregory R. 121, 124–25, 129–33, 147, 152–53, 159, 164
Law, see Torah
Lee, Dorothy 74, 101, 107, 115
Lee, John J. R. 116
Leim, Joshua E. 43, 58, 73–75, 114, 171
Léon-Dufour, Xavier 67
Leske, Adrian M. 119
Lessing, Gotthold Ephraim 19–20, 24
Lessing's Ditch 19, 24
Lister, J. Ryan 5–6, 107–8, 147, 178
Litwa, M. David 167
Loewen, Jacob A. 4
Loke, Andrew Ter Ern 174
Longenecker, Richard N. 36, 38, 110
Lord, see YHWH; Jesus; *kurios*; divine name
"Lord Lord" 17, 49–51, 142–43, 166
Lord of the Sabbath 17, 56–57, 73, 90–92, 141–42, 166
lordship, see divine lordship
low Christology 33, 78, 117, 175–77
Luz, Ulrich 42–43, 47–48
LXX, see Septuagint

McCartney, Dan G. 87
McComiskey, Thomas Edward 3–4, 6
MacDonald, Nathan 11
Macfarland, Charles S. 53
Machen, J. Gresham 23, 44
McNeile, A. H. 50, 57, 60
MacWhorter, Alexander 21
Malbon, Elizabeth Struthers 94–96
Malina, Bruce J. 81, 85–86, 93, 96, 101, 107, 109, 111, 139, 142, 144–45
manifestation, see divine manifestation
Mann, C. S. 41, 58, 61
Marcus, Joel 71, 73–74, 77, 80–84, 86–90, 92, 94, 97–98, 100–6, 109–17

Marshall, I. Howard 19, 24, 44, 81–82, 90, 120–21, 123–25, 127–28, 131–32, 135–38, 140–42, 145–46, 148–52, 161–65, 173
Martin, Ralph 73–74, 110
Marxsen, Willi 72
mediator; intermediary 27, 29–30, 32, 45, 53, 56, 67–68, 73, 80, 85, 96, 140, 147, 152
  see also agent
Menken, Maarten J. J. 44, 60, 62–63
Messiah/anointed One 1, 20, 23–24, 27, 29, 32–34, 38, 42–43, 54, 63, 66, 78, 80, 82, 85, 89, 97, 109–10, 121, 124–26, 128, 131–32, 140–41, 156, 158, 170–71
  see also Son of David; servant of the Lord
messianic
  fulfillment 28–29, 42, 98, 109, 131–32, 170
  prophecy/promises 6, 28, 42, 98, 103, 105, 131–32, 157, 170
  texts 10, 15, 98, 105, 131–32, 157, 170–72
metalepsis 31
metanarrative/storyline of scripture 6, 28, 30, 36, 38, 41–42, 178–79
Mitchell, Christopher Wright 113–16
monotheism 1–2, 8, 10–12, 18, 22, 26–27, 29, 32–34, 39, 47, 76, 87, 115, 117 139, 144, 163, 172
  see also Christological monotheism
Moo, Douglas J. 18
Moritz, Thorsten 72, 74, 76
Morris, Leon 48, 53–55, 61–62, 125, 134–37, 139, 142, 144, 146, 148–49, 156, 159, 161
Most High; from on high 14, 96, 121, 124–25, 131–32, 162–63, 166
Motyer, Alec 178
Moyise, Steve 36
Mundhenk, Norm 9–10, 116, 176

name, *see* divine name
Napier, John G. 156, 162
new
  covenant 6, 53, 55, 61, 68, 80, 120, 132
  creation 55, 103, 141, 177–78

exodus 76–77, 82, 86, 92
Moses 56, 100, 106, 147
New Testament use of the Old Testament 18, 30, 36–39, 179–80
Nolland, John 60, 64–65, 123–32, 134–41, 143–60, 162–63

O'Brien, Kelli S. 78
Öhler, Markus 123
ontology, *see* divine ontology
Orr, James 44
Ortlund, Dane 99–103
Ortlund, Raymond C. 89
Osborne, Grant R. 56, 59–60, 64–65, 180
Oswalt, John 46
O'Toole, Robert F. 121–22
Overman, Dean L. 176

Pao, David W. 120, 123–28, 130, 133–36, 138, 140–41, 145–50, 152, 154–57, 159–63
Parousia 112–15, 117, 145, 151, 178
  see also coming; Jesus as the coming One
Payne, Philip B. 90, 140–41, 175
Perrin, Nicholas 72, 81–82, 115–16
Peterson, Robert A. 50
Pleše, Zlatko 36
Plummer, Alfred 120, 122–26, 130, 133–35, 137–38, 141–42, 151, 156, 162
Porter, Stanley E. 37
Powell, Mark Allan 119
power of God, *see* divine power; divine authority
Powery, Emerson B. 48
prayer, *see* Jesus answers prayers/laments
preexistence, *see* Jesus as preexistent
prerogatives of YHWH/God, *see* divine prerogatives
presence of
  God/YHWH 3–6, 15, 28, 30–31, 33, 43–44, 46–47, 55–56, 58–62, 68, 74, 78, 80, 82, 89, 97, 99, 101, 103, 106–8, 114–15, 117, 121–22, 126, 129, 132–33, 137, 141, 147, 157, 170, 177–80
  the Holy Spirit 5–6, 68, 80, 114, 121, 177–78

the Son/Jesus 15, 28, 30–31, 33, 43–44, 46–47, 55–56, 58–62, 68, 74, 78, 82, 89, 97, 99, 101–3, 106, 108, 114–15, 117, 126, 132, 137, 141, 147, 157, 170, 177–80
  see also divine manifestation; embodiment
Proctor, Mark 171
promise of the Holy Spirit, *see* Holy Spirit
promissory markers 5–6, 84
Prothro, James B. 172

"Q" (*Quelle*) 71, 168
Quarles, Charles L. 46–49, 52–53, 57–59, 61, 65–66, 68, 138–39, 141–43, 146, 155
quests of the historical Jesus 20–25, 27–28, 34

Ramsey, Arthur Michael 145
Rawlinson, Alfred E. J. 23, 73, 76, 81, 83, 86, 91, 102, 107, 111, 114
Reimarus, Hermann Samuel 20
representative 11, 49, 59, 63, 81, 85–86, 98, 102, 109, 111, 126, 129, 132–33, 146, 157, 161, 172
  see also agent; divine agent; mediator; Messiah
revealing, revelation, *see* appearing of the Lord
revelatory acts/events 3, 6, 30, 32, 100, 106–7, 149, 161, 175
Reymond, Robert L. 57
Reynolds, Benjamin E. 59
Ridderbos, Herman N. 47, 51, 54, 56
Right Hand (of Power) 44, 66, 110, 112, 115–16, 156–57, 166
Robertson, Archibald Thomas 119, 122–24, 130, 156, 161–62
Robinson, William Childs 126
Rogers, Sam 119
Rohrbaugh, Richard L. 81, 85–86, 93, 96, 101, 107, 109, 111, 139, 142, 144–45
Rösel, Martin 8–9
Roukema, Riemer 80, 100, 102, 109–10, 122, 124–25, 176
Rowe, C. Kavin 4, 121–22, 125–27, 132–33, 137–38, 141–42, 153

Rowlands, Jonathan 152
Royce, James R. 8
Rusam, Dietrich 125

Schlatter, Adolf 49, 67, 78, 91, 109
Schnabel, Eckhard J. 71–73, 75, 77–80, 83–84, 86–91, 93, 96–98, 100–2, 104–5, 107, 109–16, 120, 123–28, 130, 133–36, 138, 140–41, 145–50, 152, 154–57, 159–63
Schnackenburg, Rudolf 56, 58, 61
Schreiner, Thomas R. 48, 53
Schweitzer, Albert 20–21, 25
Septuagint (LXX) 7–10, 18, 37, 48–51, 57, 59, 62, 74, 102, 113, 126, 129–31, 142–44, 146–47, 151
Serle, Ambrose 21
servant of the Lord, *see* Jesus as the servant of the Lord; Messiah
Shaw, Frank 8–9
sheep without a shepherd 97–99, 105, 166
shekinah 5, 47, 59–60, 107, 115
Shema 10–12, 26–27, 29, 33, 87, 109, 139
shepherd 42, 97–99, 105, 157–58, 166, 169–70
Shively, Elizabeth E. 171
Silva, Moisés 7–8
Sloan, Paul 113–15
Small, Rusty N. 57
Smith, Gary V. 46
Snodgrass, Klyne 134, 140, 153, 159
Son of David 14, 24, 42–43, 46, 62–63, 74, 81–82, 91, 99, 129, 131, 156–58, 170–71
Son of God 1, 13, 43, 66, 68, 73, 76, 78, 82, 91, 93, 96, 105, 107, 121, 147, 156, 170
Son of Man
  coming 59–60, 65, 67, 74, 107, 111–15, 145–46, 154–57, 166
  enthroned/exalted 44, 47, 56, 59–60, 65–66, 74, 114, 116–17, 156–57
  forgiving sins 86–88, 138, 142
  gathering 65, 112, 114–15
  identified with YHWH 17, 44, 56, 59, 66–67, 73–74, 87–88, 107, 112–13, 115–16, 146, 155–57

judging 17, 59–60, 65, 112–17, 154–55, 157
revealed/revealing 74, 154, 156
ruling 44, 59–60, 66–67, 146, 154–55
saving/rescuing 17, 77, 88, 117, 157–58, 166
searching/seeking 17, 157–58, 166
sitting/seated/in session 59, 65–66, 116–17, 156–57
worshiped 11, 68
Son of Man as
   divine 11, 59–60, 66, 73, 88, 90–91, 96, 109, 111–12, 114–16, 146, 154–56, 158, 170
   equal with God/YHWH 44, 47, 56–57, 59–60, 66–67, 86–88, 107, 111–16, 142, 146, 154–58
   Jesus's self-designation 86, 113, 115, 155, 168
   ransom/sacrifice for sinners 77, 88
   ultimate authority 17, 53, 56–57, 59–60, 67–68, 73, 86–87, 90–91, 96, 107, 109, 111, 113–14, 116, 138, 141–42, 154–56, 158, 170
Soulen, R. Kendall 4, 7, 12, 14, 116
Spadaro, Martin C. 41
Spencer, Aída Besançon 121–22
Staples, Jason A. 49–51, 142–43
Stegner, William Richard 102
Stein, Robert H. 23, 75–77, 83, 86–87, 89–92, 96–103, 105, 107–12, 114–17, 119, 122–25, 128–29, 132–33, 137–39, 141, 144–45, 147–48, 151–55, 159–60, 162–63
Stendahl, Krister 42, 54
stone passages, *see* Jesus as the stone
Stonehouse, Ned Bernard 45, 50
Stott, John R. W. 165
Strauss, David Friedrich 20, 25
Strauss, Mark L. 72–73, 75, 77, 81–94, 96, 98–105, 107, 109–11, 113–15, 117, 119–22, 125, 132, 150, 158, 163
Subramanian, J. Samuel 62
surrogates for YHWH, *see* appellations
Swete, Henry Barclay 7, 72–73, 86, 89–90, 109
synoptic problem 41, 71

tabernacle 5, 43, 60, 107–8, 146–47
   see also temple
Tait, Michael 74–75
Tanner, Beth LaNeel 63
Tasker, R. V. G. 36
Taylor, Vincent 19, 24, 72–73, 75, 83, 86–87, 91, 93, 101, 114, 116–17, 120–21, 173
Telford, William 72–73
temple 28, 30, 43, 54, 56–57, 60, 62–63, 77, 83, 88, 109–10, 115, 117, 138, 140, 146–47, 153, 164, 175, 178
   see also tabernacle
Tetragrammaton 3–4, 7–11, 13, 18, 31, 46, 58–59, 61, 116, 143, 176
   see also divine name
theological biography 16, 45, 69, 72, 119, 171
theophany 4–5, 18, 74, 81, 102–3, 106–8, 111, 114–15, 130, 144, 147, 154–55
Thielman, Frank S. 25
Thomas, Robert L. 136, 148
Thompson, Alan J. 120–22, 125, 128–31, 133–34, 138–42, 144, 148, 151–58, 16–61, 164
Thompson, Henry O. 1
throne, *see* divine throne
Tokić, Dario 120
Torah, law of Moses 5, 7, 12, 28, 30, 50, 56, 61, 65, 85, 90, 98, 106–7, 112, 142, 147, 149, 160, 169, 175, 180
Tov, Emanuel 8–9
Toy, Crawford Howell 47–48, 62
transcendence and immanence 3, 6, 11–12, 84, 90, 98, 100, 107, 110
transfiguration 60, 74, 82, 106–8, 113, 115, 117, 145–47, 153–54, 156, 166–67
Trinity/Triune God 21, 47, 67–68, 76, 79–82, 177, 180
Tuckett, Christopher M. 121, 165
Turner, David L. 52, 55, 61, 64–65, 67

Vander Hart, Mark D. 6, 42, 48
Vanhoozer, Kevin J. 177, 180
Vasileiadis, Pavlos D. 7, 9–10

Vermeylen, Jacques 3
Viljoen, Francois P. 45
visitation of the Lord/YHWH, *see* divine visitation
Voelz, James W. 113–16
Voorwinde, Stephen 134
Vos, Geerhardus 22–23, 87, 158

Warfield, Benjamin B. 44, 56, 66, 68, 171
Watts, John D. W. 46
Watts, Rikk E. 43, 75–78, 80, 82, 86–88, 92, 98–99, 102, 115–17
way of the Lord/YHWH 15, 48, 53–55, 64, 74, 76–78, 123–29, 132, 166, 76
Weinandy, Thomas G. 94–96, 99, 101, 141, 149–50
Welker, Michael 173
Wellum, Stephen J. 42–43, 50, 66, 151–52, 157–58, 162, 175, 178, 180
Wenham, John William 41
wilderness feedings, *see* feeding miracles
Wilkinson, Robert J. 3–4, 10
Williams, Joel F. 104
Williamson, Lamar 113
Wills, Lawrence M. 179
Winter, Paul 131
Witherington, Ben, III 8, 89–90, 110, 149–50
Woods, Edward J. 148–49
word of God 64, 93, 106–7, 111–13, 158, 160–61, 164
   see also divine speech
worship
   of Jesus 1, 21–22, 25–26, 30–32, 34, 43, 51, 56, 63, 68–69, 122, 163, 165, 169
   of YHWH 5, 25–26, 30–32, 34, 43, 51, 56, 63, 68, 96, 105, 152, 163, 165
   not of angels/idols/men 11, 31
Wrede, William 20, 72
Wright, Christopher J. H. 179
Wright, N. T. 1, 6, 11, 25, **27–29**, 34, 41–43, 171, 174–76, 178–80
Wright, Stephen I. 120

Yamazaki-Ransom, Kazuhiko 8, 110
Yarbrough, Robert W. 19
YHWH (יהוה) 3–8, 49–50, 135, 143
   see also divine name; divine identity; ancient of days; Jesus
YHWH as
   central to scripture 5, 11, 38, 76, 120, 133, 161–62, 172, 174, 177, 180
   coming, *see* coming; day of the Lord
   embodied, *see* embodiment
   manifested, *see* appearing; divine manifestation
   transcendent and immanent, *see* transcendence
   unique 4, 10–12, 14, 26–27, 37–39, 44, 51, 56–57, 74, 100, 138, 146, 167, 169, 174
   see also divine prerogatives; creator-creature distinction
YHWH's equal/peer 34, 43–44, 47, 54, 59–60, 65, 69, 106, 109–10, 116, 138, 155–56
YHWH's servant, *see* servant of the Lord
YHWH-Text(s)
   definition/description of 1–2, 4, 13–17, 37–39
   origin of NT practice 33, 65, 89–90, 92, 118, 172–75
   parallel to Messiah-texts 6, 28, 42, 131–32, 157, 170–72
   significance of 2, 18–19, 49, 89, 117, 161, 163, 165, 167, 180
   ubiquity/frequency of 14–17, 33, 35, 41, 69, 108, 163, 165–66, 168–69

Zahn, Theodore 21

Scripture Index

Synoptic passages (with pages) examined for YHWH-texts in this study are in bold.

Genesis	4	3:6	54
Ch 1	104	3:7	4
1:1	177	3:12	68
1:1-2	5	3:13-14	169
1:2	121	3:13-15	3
1:2-20	93	3:14	3–4, 10, 59, 101, 169
1:26	91		
1:31	104	3:14-15	3–4, 18, 68
2:2-3	141	3:15	3–4
2:3	57, 90, 169	3:16	130, 135
2:3-4	90	4:11	103–4
3:8	5–6	4:31	129, 130–31, 133, 135
6:5-8	151		
6:17	151	8:19	104, 148–49
7:20-23	151	13:19	130, 135
15:1	58	13:21-22	5, 106
17:8	6	14:19	54
18-19	144	14:21-31	94
Ch 19	151	15:8	93
19:24	150–51	15:10	93
21:1	129, 131, 133, 135	15:10-11	93
21:1-7	121	Ch 16	105
22:2	81	16:1	99
26:24	58, 68	16:3	99
28:13 LXX	58	16:4	99
28:15	68	16:10	99, 114
31:11-13	5	16:23	57
32:31-32 LXX	102	16:25	90
46:3	58	16:40	99
48:15	97–98	18:16-19	5
49:10	97	18:21	99
49:24	97–98, 169	18:25	99
50:24-25	130	19:4	152
		19:6	162
Exodus	77, 97	19:9	106, 114
Ch 3	5	19:16	106, 114, 147, 156, 169
3:2	4		
3:2-6	5	19:16-24	154
3:4	4	19:19	114

20:1-17	107	23:3	57, 90, 169
20:8-11	57, 90, 142, 169	24:15-16	52
20:10	57	26:11-12	6
20:18-21	147		
Ch 23	76–77	**Numbers**	
23:20	54, 76–77, 127–28, 169	9:15-22	111
		10:34	114
23:20-21	127	10:35-36	44
23:20-23	54	Ch 11	105
23:21	77	11:13	99
24:1-2	146	11:13-14	169
24:15-16	106, 169	11:21-22	99
24:15-18	146	11:21-23	169
24:16	106–7	11:29	120
24:18–25:1	106	14:11	109, 169
29:45	6	15:30	52
31:12-17	17	16:35	150
31:13	57, 90, 142	27:17	97
31:13-14	90, 169	35:34	61
31:18	104, 148–49		
32:34	129	**Deuteronomy**	
Ch 33	55	1:1	162
33:9-10	106	1:17	50
33:14	55	5:12-15	90
33:15	54	Ch 6	29
33:17–34:8	102	6:4	107, 139, 169
33:22-23	5	6:4-5	11–12
34:4-7	146	8:3	98
34:4-9	169	9:10	148–49
34:5	106	10:17	135
34:5-8	111	13:7	115
34:5-30	5	18:15	106, 147
34:6	142	18:15-22	106
34:6-7	5, 88, 138	18:18	106
34:8	5	30:1-5	153
34:29-35	146–47	30:4	115, 169
35:1	162	31:6	68
35:2	57	31:7	46
39:5	67	Ch 32	152
40:34-38	106	32:5	113, 164
40:35	107–8, 169	32:11	152–53, 167
		32:15	167
Leviticus		32:15-18	152
3:12	8	32:20	109, 115, 164
4:7	8	32:22	151
4:35	8	32:39	101, 169
16:30	140	32:43 LXX	1, 14
19:3	140	33:2	106
19:30	57, 90, 169	33:2-3	169
	57, 90, 169		

Scripture Index

Joshua
1:5	68
1:9	68
5:13	149
6:2	149
24:7	93

Judges
6:11	5
6:14	5
6:20-24	5

Ruth
1:6	129–30, 133

1 Samuel
2:21	130–31
8:4-7	98

2 Samuel
5:2	97
7:11	97
7:11-16	98
7:14	14
12:13	53, 140
22:14	124
22:15	154
22:33	135

1 Kings
8:10-11	106, 121
17:17-24	133
18:36-40	150
18:38	150
19:1-9	106
19:8-18	106
19:11	169
19:11-13	102
22:17	98

2 Kings
1:2-16	150
1:10	150
1:10-24	150
1:12	150
1:14	150
4:32-37	133
4:42-44	99

1 Chronicles
17:6	97

2 Chronicles 42
18:16	98

Esther 4

Job 88
9:8	14, 57–58, 100, 167
9:8-11	169
26:11-12	93
26:12	93
38:16	57, 100

Psalms 4, 44, 60, 62–63, 82, 98, 169
Ps 2	81–82
2:6-7	169
2:7	14, 81–82
6:2	44, 52
6:3 LXX	52
7:17	124
Ps 8	62, 91
8:1	62
8:2 LXX	62
8:3	62, 104, 148
8:4	62
8:4-8	91
9:7-8	157
9:13	44
11:2 LXX	52
11:6	150–51
12:2	52
17:8	152
18:2	129–30
18:4	151
18:13-14	154
18:14	154
18:16	58
18:32	135
Ps 23	98
23:1	98
23:1-2	98, 169
25:16	44
26:11	44
27:7	44

28:8-9	169	97:4	154, 156
28:9	98	102:25–27	1, 14, 64, 110, 160
29:3	93	102:25-26	64
29:3-9	93	102:26	64–65
30:10	44, 52	102:27	14
31:9	44	Ps 103	86
32:1-2	140	103:2-3	138
32:6	58	103:3	35, 44, 86, 88, 169
36:7	152	103:12	138
40:5 LXX	52	104:1-2	107–8, 169
40:11 LXX	52	104:3-4	93
41:3-4	86	104:4	14
41:4	44, 52, 88	104:6-7	93, 145
41:10	44, 52	105:4 LXX	129
42:7	151	105:47 LXX	52
43:8 LXX	113	106:4	129–30, 133, 135
44:9	113	106:9	85, 93, 169
45:6	157	106:10 LXX	132
45:6-7	14	106:23-29 LXX	144
51:1	44	106:47	52
57:1	44, 152	Ps 107	94
61:4	152	107:10	132
63:2	114	107:10-14	131
63:7	152	107:23-29	94
65:7	93	107:23-30	145
65:8 LXX	93	107:23-32	94, 169
66:6	93	107:25-29	94
68:30	85, 169	107:29-30	93
69:1-2	151	107:30-32	94
69:2	58	110	110, 169, 174
69:14-15	151	110:1	14, 24, 67, 110, 116–17, 156–57, 169
77:16	57		
77:16-20	93		
77:18	154	117:22 LXX	159
77:19	57	117:25 LXX	52
77:19-20	100	118:116 LXX	113
78:8	113, 169	Ps 118	17, 63, 153
78:19-20	99, 169	118:22	159
78:21	150–51	118:22-23	63
78:70-72	97	118:25	52
80:1	98	118:25-26	109, 169
80:1-2	98, 169	118:31 LXX	113
82:1	61	119:31	113
85:3 LXX	52	119:89	64, 110, 160
86:1	44	119:116	113
86:3	52	119:160	160
89:9	93, 145, 169	122:3 LXX	52
91:4	152–53, 167	123:3	52
97:2	114	130:4	138

130:7-8	140	13:6	111, 156
132:11-12	98	13:9-13	114
132:17	131	23:17	130
137:9	134	24:17-20	114
144:6	154	24:21-23	92, 169
148:1	109	25:6	105
		25:6-8	89, 99, 105, 169
Proverbs		25:6-9	141
9:5	98	26:20	77
19:17	66	28:2	135
24:12	60	28:16	159
		29:6	130, 134
Ecclesiastes	4	30:27-28	135, 151
1:1	4	30:33	135
3:10-13	4	32:15	163
5:1	4	33:24	86, 88
		Ch 35	46, 103–4
Song of Solomon	4	35:1-10	46
		35:2	77
Isaiah	6, 46–49, 77–82, 89, 101–3, 126–28, 162	35:2-4	103
		35:4	77
		35:4-6	103, 169
		35:5-6	103–4
1:2-4	113	35:6 LXX	103
2:2	105	37:16	157
2:2-3	105	38:17	86, 88
4:4	135	Ch 40	46, 49, 82, 126, 128
4:5	114	Chs 40-66	120, 126
5:1	89, 141	40:1	64
5:1-7	159	40:1-11	64
Ch 6	60	40:2	53, 77, 140
6:5	137	40:2-3	123
7:14	43, 45–47, 82, 121	40:3	15, 17, 48, 64, 76–79, 122–28, 132, 135, 169, 176
8:5-10	46		
8:12-14	15, 63		
8:14	15	40:3-5	46, 77, 122, 125, 127–28, 169
8:15	159		
9:1 LXX	131–32	40:4	15
9:1-7	46	40:4-5	125
9:2	131–32	40:5	64
9:6	46, 82	40:5 LXX	126
9:6-7	82, 131	40:8	64–65, 111, 160, 167
9:7	46, 132		
9:8	32	40:9-10	126
10:3	135	40:10	79, 135
Ch 11	12	40:10-11	98, 169
11:1	131	40:11	98, 157
11:2	135	40:25	126
11:11-12	115, 169	41:4	101, 169
11:12	153		

41:10	68	53:8	88
41:13	58	53:11	149
41:15-16	136	53:12	88, 92, 99, 149
Ch 42	82	54:1-6	140
42:1	81–82, 120	54:1-8	89
42:1-6	77	54:5	89, 169
42:5	162	54:5-6	141
42:6	120, 131	54:6	89
42:6-7	131	54:7-10	133
42:16	132	54:10	64, 110
43:2	68, 151	55:6-7	138
43:5	68	55:10-11	32, 161
43:5-6	115	56:4	57
43:5-7	115, 169	56:7	110, 164
43:7	123	56:8	150
43:10	162	57:18-19	86
43:10-11	101, 169	59:15-20	77
43:12	162	59:19	113
43:13	169	59:20-21	120, 178
43:16	57, 100	60:1-3	132
43:25	86, 88, 138, 140, 169	60:16	21
		61:10	89
44:3	79, 135, 163, 169	61:10–62:5	141
44:3-5	6	62:4-5	89, 141
44:8	162	62:5	89
44:22	138	63:1	79
44:22-24	86	63:7-9	5, 21
46:4	169	Ch 64	82
47:8	101	64:1	80, 82, 157, 169
47:10	101	61:1-3	21
48:12	169	61:10	89, 163
Ch 49	92	62:4-5	140
49:1-6	77	62:5	89
49:6	105, 120	63:9	54
49:8	120	65:17-25	82
49:9-10	98	66:10-14	82
49:24-25	92–93	66:12-16	77
49:24-26	149, 169	66:15	151
49:26	92, 135	66:15-16	136, 150
50:1	89	66:18	115
51:6	64, 110, 160–61	66:18-20	113, 115
51:9-10	100	66:18-24	82
51:10	93	66:24	136
51:12	169		
52:7-8	77	**Jeremiah**	4, 6, 83–84, 134, 136
52:9	164		
52:10	164	1:19	68
52:13–53:12	77	2:2	74
Ch 53	77, 178	2:32	140

3:10	153	**Lamentations**		
3:22	153	4:22	131	
5:22	93			
6:15	134–35	**Ezekiel**	6, 77, 80, 83, 109, 157	
7:11	110			
7:34	89	Ch 1	60	
8:9	113–14, 117, 169	1:4	147, 156	
10:15	135	1:7	147	
15:7	136	1:28	137	
15:15	130, 135–36	4:1-3	134	
15:20	68	Ch 10	68	
16:14-15	83	11:16-17	115, 169	
16:16	83–84, 136–37, 169	11:23	109–10, 164, 169	
16:16-18	83	16:6-8	141	
16:17-18	136	16:15	89	
16:19-21	84, 136	16:22-42	89	
17:16	98	20:13	90	
19:7	154	29:4-5	83	
23:1-3	150	30:3	111	
23:1-4	98	32:4	154	
23:1-6	98	Ch 34	98, 157–58	
23:2	130	34:1-10	98, 157	
23:3	115, 169	34:1-16	97	
23:5	131	34:1-31	98	
23:5-6	132	34:4	157–58	
25:10	89	34:5	98	
25:31	50	34:8	98	
26:18	134	34:10	157	
29:14	153	34:11	130, 132–35, 157–58	
31:3	88			
31:10	98	34:11-13	150	
31:10-14	89, 141, 169	34:11-16	158	
31:16	111	34:11-22	98, 169	
31:16 LXX	111	34:12	157	
31:25	55	34:13-14	99	
31:31-34	55, 120, 178	34:15	98	
31:32	140	34:16	17, 157–58	
31:33	6	34:20-24	150	
31:33-34	68	34:22	157–58	
31:34	35, 53, 138, 140	34:23	157	
31:35-36	64	34:23-24	98, 157–58	
32:37-40	178	34:29-31	99	
33:8	53, 140	34:30-31	99, 158	
33:11	89	34:30-32	169	
33:15	131	34:31	98	
33:20-21	64	Ch 36	80	
33:25-26	64	36:24-28	178	
42:11	68	36:25-26	80	
50:34	135	36:25-27	79–80, 135, 169	

36:25-29	68	13:16	134
36:27	120, 163	14:4	86, 88
37:14	120		
37:26-27	6	**Joel**	6, 66, 80
37:26-28	6, 178	1:8	89
38:22	150–51	1:15	111
39:5	151	Ch 2	12
39:6	150	2:1	111
39:29	79, 163, 169	2:1-2	156
43:3-9	79	2:27	61
		2:28-29	80, 163, 169
Daniel	59–60, 74, 145–47, 155, 174	2:28-30	120
		2:30-31	111, 114
2:34	63	2:31	113
2:34-35	159	2:32	21, 35
2:44-45	63, 159	3:1-2 LXX	80
5:5	148	3:2	65
5:5-6	148	3:5	46
5:24-28	148		
5:25-28	148	**Amos**	6, 143
Ch 7	44, 87, 91, 137, 147	1:4	150–51
7:9	65–66, 107–8, 146	1:7	150–51
7:9-10	146, 169	1:10	150–51
7:9-14	113, 146	1:12	150–51
7:10	66	1:14	151
7:13	67, 107, 113, 116, 146, 154, 156	2:2	150–51
		2:5	150–51
7:13-14	44, 56, 59–60, 67, 114, 116–17, 138, 142, 146, 155–57, 168–69	4:2	83, 136
		4:6	153
		4:8-11	153
7:14	91		
9:3	107	**Obadiah**	4, 6
12:1	102	1:15	111
12:6	147		
		Jonah	94–96, 144–45
Hosea		Ch 1	94
1:2	74	1:3	95
2:2	89	1:3-6	95
2:2-13	89	1:3-16	144
2:4	113	1:4	93, 95, 144
2:7	89	1:4-16	94, 169
2:14-23	140–41	1:6	95
2:16-20	89, 169	1:9	95
2:19	141	1:11	144
2:19-20	178	1:12	144
7:10	153	1:14	94–95, 144
9:1	89	1:14-16	95
9:15	110	1:15	95, 144
		1:16	95, 144

2:3-6	151	2:10-13	6
4:2	105	3:2	85, 150, 169
4:10-11	105	3:8	131
		4:4-5	169
Micah		4:9	169
Ch 1	151	6:12	131
2:12-13	98, 169	8:16	182
4:1-2	105	9:9	109
4:2	132	9:14	154
5:1-4	98	10:2	98
5:2-4	98	12:10	99, 120, 178
5:2	69	13:7	99
7:5-7	151	13:7–14:6	113, 178
7:6	151	13:9	99
7:14	98, 169	14:1-9	115
7:18	138–40	14:1-21	12
7:18-19	88	14:4	100, 109–10, 113
		14:4-5	113
Nahum		14:5	60, 65–66, 113–15, 117, 157
1:3	67	14:9	12, 66, 113
		14:21	110
Habakkuk	83		
1:14-15	136	**Malachi**	6, 42, 75–78, 80, 124–25, 128
1:14-17	83		
3:3-4	106, 169	2:6	123
3:15	57, 100	2:17	54
		Ch 3	82, 135
Zephaniah	6	3:1	17, 54–55, 62, 76–77, 109, 122–25, 127–28, 135, 176
1:7	111		
1:14	111		
1:14-18	111		
2:7	130, 132–35	3:1-2	98, 150
Ch 3	12	3:1-3	6, 110–11, 135, 169
3:8	150–51	3:1-5	121
3:15	157	3:3	55
3:17	157	Ch 4	12
		4:1	150–51
Haggai	77	4:1-6	6, 121
1:13	68	4:4-6	106
2:4	68	4:5	82, 127–28, 156
2:6-9	114	4:5-6	54–55, 123, 127, 169
		4:6	123, 151
Zechariah	6, 60, 65, 77		
1:16	54	**Matthew**	16, 41–45, 71, 166
2:6	115, 169	1:1	51, 69
2:6-10	117	1:1-7	41
2:10	115, 169	1:18	51, 69
2:10-11	178		

1:18–2:6	42	8:25	51–52, 58, 144, 166
1:20	51	8:26	144
1:21	46–47, 51	8:27	52, 168
1:21-25	176	Ch 9	35
1:22-23	45, 68	**9:2**	**52–53**, 166
1:23	43, **45–48**, 51, 60–61, 166	9:2-7	137
		9:15	89, 140, 166
1:25	46–47	9:18	31
2:2	31, 51, 69	10:4	139
2:5-6	176	10:40-42	43
2:6	69, 98	11:2-3	168
2:11	31	**11:10**	**53–55**, 166, 168
2:15	69	11:25	55
3:1-13	15	11:25-30	47
3:1-17	42	**11:28**	**55–56**, 166–68
3:2	14, 48	11:28-29	56
3:3	**48–49**, 50–51, 55, 64, 76, 125, 135, 166, 168	11:29	55
		12:6	43, 56, 63, 168
		12:8	17, **56–57**, 141, 166, 168, 175
3:11	69		
3:11-12	135, 166, 168	12:23	168
3:11-13	64	12:25-30	148
3:12	69	12:28	148, 178
3:16-17	169	12:28-29	
4:10	12	12:29-30	168
4:18	139	12:41-42	175
4:18-22	136	13:41	60
4:19	166, 168	13:55	139
5:1-2	65	14:1-7	42
5:17	65	14:1-33	24
5:17-18	65	14:14-21	166
5:18	65, 112	14:22	57
6:4	60	14:22-33	43, 143
6:6	60	14:25	57
6:18	60	**14:25–27**	**57–59**
7:3-5	65	14:26	57
7:21	17, 44, 50, 142	14:27	27, 58, 176
7:21-22	**49–51**, 142, 166, 168, 178	14:28-33	58
		14:29	100
7:21-27	142	14:30	52, 58, 166
7:21-29	65	14:33	31, 169
7:22	17, 44, 50, 142	15:22	52, 166
7:23	50, 142	15:25	31
7:27	142	15:32	105
8:2	31	15:32-38	166
8:18	143	16:13-15	168
8:23-27	43, 143	**16:27**	**59–61**, 145, 166, 175
8:24	144		
8:24-27	166	16:27-28	65

18:28	59	26:28	68
17:1-8	166	26:29	43
17:1-13	64	26:54-56	180
17:3-5	65	26:63	66
17:15	52, 166	**26:64**	**66–67**, 166
17:17	43	26:64	67
18:11	17	27:32	139
18:17	31	28:9	31
18:20	43, 47, **61–62**, 166, 178	28:16-20	68
		28:17	31, 68
18:27	98	28:18	47, 67
20:8	60	**28:18–20**	**67–68**, 166, 168. 178
20:20	31		
20:28	178	28:19	47, 61
20:30	52	28:19-20	61
20:30-31	166	28:20	47, 61
20:31	52		
Ch 21	63	**Mark**	16, 71–75, 166
21:9	17	1:1	72, 75–76, 91, 96
21:10	168	1:1-4	75
21:14	62	1:1-9	15
21:16	**62–63**, 166, 168	1:2	76–77, 84, 128, 167
21:23	63	**1:2-3**	49, 74, **75–78**, 125, 135, 166, 168
21:33-41	63		
21:42-45	**63**, 159, 166, 168	1:3	48, 76, 79, 84, 90–91, 109
22:45	168		
23:29-37	153	1:3-4	79
23:34	153	1:4-5	79
23:37	152, 166–68	1:7	79, 84, 86, 92
23:37-39	152	**1:7-8**	**79–80**, 135, 166, 168
24:5	110		
24:25	64	1:8	80, 84, 91, 135
24:27	154	1:9	75, 79
24:30	60	1:10	80–82, 84
24:30-31	166	**1:10-11**	**80–82**, 166
24:31	60	1:11	73, 81, 84, 91, 96
24:35	**64–65**, 160, 166, 168	1:13	92
		1:15	74, 91
24:42	44	1:16-20	136
25:11	17, 44, **49–51**, 142, 166	**1:17**	**83–84**, 136, 166, 168, 178
25:31-32	**65–66**, 166	1:22	85
25:31-33	178	1:24	96, 109
25:34-40	43	**1:25**	**84–85**, 93, 166
25:37	44	1:27	85, 91, 96, 168
25:44	44	1:34	73, 93
25:46	50	Ch 2	35
26:1-13	139	2:1-12	86, 88
26:6	139	2:1-3:6	88

2:5	86, 169, 175	6:34	97, 105
2:5-12	**85–88**, 137, 166	**6:34-44**	**97–99**, 104, 164, 166
2:7	53, 91, 109, 168	6:35	99
2:9-11	168	6:35-44	97
2:10	86, 90–91, 96	6:40	99
2:14	83	6:42	105
2:19	74, 88, 90	6:45-52	99, 143
2:19-20	**88–90**, 91, 113, 140, 166	6:48	14, 102
		6:48-49	167
2:20	88	**6:48-52**	**99–103**, 166
2:23-28	91	6:49	14
2:27	141, 168	6:50	176
2:28	17, **90–92**, 96, 109, 141, 166, 168	7:6-7	104
		7:14	104, 106
3:4	109	7:24-30	105
3:11	73, 96	7:26-29	105
3:12	93	7:32	103
3:13	83	**7:32-37**	**103–4**, 166, 168
3:14-15	84	7:37	104
3:22-26	92	**8:1-10**	**104–5**, 166
3:23-27	148	8:2	105
3:27	79, **92–93**, 148, 150, 166, 168	8:3	113
		8:8	105
3:34-35	83	8:12	160
Ch 4	94	8:14-21	105
4:3	104	8:22-26	103
4:9	104	8:27-29	168
4:10-12	104	8:29	96
4:20	104	8:31	96, 109
4:23	104	8:34	83
4:24	104	8:34-38	105
4:35-41	101	**8:38**	74, 83, 96, 107–8, **112–17**, 145, 166, 169
4:36	95		
4:36-41	144	9:1	108
4:37-41	**93–97**, 166	**9:1-8**	**106–8**, 113, 166
4:37	95	9:2-8	113
4:38	94–95, 144	9:7	73, 82, 96
4:39	95, 97	9:12	109
4:40	95–96	9:19	108–9, 166
4:41	94–95, 167–68	9:22	166
5:7	73, 96	9:37	108–9, 166
5:19	109	10:17-22	83
6:7	83–84	10:18	168
6:11	83, 104	10:18-21	108–9, 166
6:12-13	84	10:21	83
6:30	84	10:29	83
6:30-44	105	10:33-34	109
6:31	99		
6:32	99		

Scripture Index

10:38	109	**Luke**	16–17, 71, 119–22, 166, 173
10:45	88, 109, 151, 178		
10:47-48	166	Chs 1–2	119
11:9	17	1:1-4	120
11:9-10	108–9, 166	1:7-20	121
11:15-17	108, 110, 166	1:11	123
11:19	109	1:13-17	123
11:28	168	1:15	123
12:1-11	107	1:16-17	133
12:6	73	**1:17**	49, 121, **122–24**, 125, 127–28, 135, 153, 166, 176
12:10-11	159, 166, 168		
12:11	109		
12:28-34	12	1:19	123
12:29	12, 109	1:31	46, 162
12:29-30	12	1:31-35	176
12:30	109	132	121
12:32-33	12	1:34-37	121
12:35–37	108, 110, 166, 168	1:35	121
12:36	109	1:43	121, 124–25, 137, 153
12:37	109		
12:44	83	1:47	120
13:3	110	1:49	162
13:3-6	108, 110, 166	1:67	129
13:6	110, 176	**1:68**	47, 121, 124, **129–30**, 131–35, 153, 155, 166, 168, 176, 178
13:9-10	84		
13:10	115		
13:24	117		
13:24-25	117	1:68-69	130
13:24-27	115	1:69	120, 129–30, 133
13:26	112, 114–15, 117	1:71	120
		1:74	130
13:26-27	108, 111, **112–17**, 166	1:76	49, 55, 76, 121–22, **124–25**, 127–28, 132–33, 135, 153, 156, 166, 176
13:27	117		
13:29	111–12		
13:31	65, 107–8, **110–12**, 160, 166, 168, 175	1:76-77	132
		1:76-79	176
13:32	73, 96	**1:78**	121, 125, 129, **130–32**, 133–35, 153, 155, 166, 168, 176, 178
14:3-9	83, 139		
14:11	109		
14:61	116		
14:61-62	73, 96, 101	1:78-79	131–32
14:62	17, 108, **112–17**, 166, 176	1:79	121, 124, 131
		2:7	164
14:63-64	116	2:10	119–20
15:26	96	2:11	120–21, 124–25, 137, 153, 180
15:32	96		
15:39	73, 96	2:21	46, 162
		2:25-32	164

2:26	126	5:24	138, 141–42, 170, 178
2:30	126		
2:30-31	135	5:25	138
2:30-32	120	5:25-26	138
2:34	159	5:26	138
2:38	120	**5:34-35**	89, **140–41**, 166
2:40	122, 164	5:35	178
3:1-6	126	**6:5**	17, 121–22, **141–42**, 156, 166, 168
3:1-22	15		
3:3	123		
3:4	48, 76, 121, 124, 128, 156	6:24-26	153
		6:46	121, **142–43**, 156, 166, 168, 170
3:4-6	49, 122, **125–27**, 128, 133, 135, 153, 166, 168, 175–76		
		6:46-49	142, 153
		6:49	142
3:6	120, 126	Ch 7	139
3:15-16	126	7:12	133
3:16	120, 122, 124, 135	7:12-16	172
3:16-17	**135–36**, 166, 168	7:13	133
3:17	135–36, 153	7:13-15	133
3:21-22	166	7:14	133
3:22	81, 121, 124	**7:16**	47, 121, 129, 131, **132–33**, 134–35, 153, 155, 166–67, 176, 178
3:38	121		
4:2	164		
4:8	163		
4:9	121	**7:26-27**	49, 122, 125, **127–29**, 133, 153, 166, 176
4:14-30	119		
4:16-21	180		
4:18	119–20	7:26-28	166
4:18-19	170	7:27	128, 132, 135, 168
4:33-36	166	7:28	122
4:41	121–22	7:36-50	137
Ch 5	35	7:39	139–40
5:1-11	136	7:47	140
5:4	137	**7:47-50**	137, **139–40**, 162, 166
5:5	136		
5:6	136	7:48	139–40
5:8	121, 137	7:48-49	122
5:8-10	172	7:49	138–40, 168
5:9	136	7:50	140
5:10	**136–37**, 166, 168	8:22-25	**143–45**, 166
5:13	122	8:23	144
5:17	138, 144	8:24	51, 143–44
5:17-26	139	8:24-25	172
5:20	138	8:25	144, 168
5:20-24	162	8:28	121
5:20-26	**137–39**, 166	9:9	168
5:21	138–39, 168	9:12-17	164, 166
5:22	138	9:18-20	168

Scripture Index

9:26	145–46, 152, 160, 178	13:34	**152–53**, 166, 168, 170, 178
9:26-27	145–46, 153, 166	13:34-35	134. 152–53, 172
9:26-36	**145–47**, 155, 175	13:35	17, 153, 162
9:27	145	15:3-7	158
9:28-36	145–46, 166	15:20	98
9:29	146–47, 154	16:17	112, 160
9:31	146	16:24	166
9:31-32	145	17:13	166
9:32	145–47	17:15-18	122
9:33	146	17:20-21	154
9:34-35	146	**17:20-37**	**153–54**, 166
9:35	121	17:22	153–54, 156
9:41-43	164, 172	17:22-37	154
9:48	162	17:24	145, 154, 156
9:49	162	17:26	154, 156
9:54	150	17:29	154
9:54-55	150	17:30	154, 156
10:13-15	153	17:31	154, 156
10:17	121, 162	18:7-8	153, 172
10:21-22	121	18:8	145
10:22	121	18:19	168
10:22-23	170	18:31-34	153
10:25-28	12	18:38-39	166
10:33	98	18:38-41	170
11:2	162	19:5	158
11:12	148	19:9	158
11:13	120, 163	**19:9-10**	17, **157–58**, 166
11:17-23	148	19:10	17, 157–58
11:20	104, 148–49	19:25	155
11:20-23	**148–50**, 166	19:25-26	155
11:21-22	149	19:26	155
11:21-23	168	19:37	164
11:22	148–49	19:38	17, 162
11:23	148–50	19:41	134
11:29-32	153	19:41-44	172
12:1-3	153	19:42	134
12:8-9	152–53	19:43	134
12:8-10	168–69	**19:44**	121, 129, 132, **133–34**, 135, 153, 155, 166, 176, 178
12:12	120		
12:35-40	153		
12:40	145	19:45	164
12:49	**150–52**, 166, 168	19:46	164
		20:9-18	153
12:49-50	151	20:13	121
12:49-59	153	20:17	159
12:50	151	**20:17-18**	**159**, 166, 168
13:1-9	153	20:18	159
13:25	121	20:19-20	153

20:41-44	24, 122	24:49	120, 122, 131, 162–63, 178
20:42	121, 156		
20:44	121	24:51	122
21:1	153	24:52	122
21:8	162, 176		
21:17	162	**John**	1, 16–18, 33, 175–77
21:20-24	154		
21:24	156	1:1-18	176
21:25	155	1:14	32, 44, 108, 177
21:25-26	155	1:19-34	15
21:25-27	155, 160	1:23	48, 76, 125, 135
21:25-28	153, **154–55**, 166	3:28-29	90
		3:29	89, 140
21:26	154	5:18	138
21:26-36	160	5:38-40	180
21:27	145, 154–56	5:39	169, 174
21:29-33	155	Ch 6	98
21:33	**160–61**, 166–68	6:16-21	143
21:34	155	6:31-35	99
21:34-36	153	6:35	17
21:35	155	6:48	17
21:36	155	6:57	14
22:20	68, 120	6:71	139
22:42-44	164, 172	8:58	18, 101
22:44	122	10:30	12, 26
22:66	153, 156	10:33	53, 138
22:69	154, 157	10:38	12
22:69-70	153, **156–57**, 166	11:25-26	24
22:70	17, 121, 176	12:2-8	139
22:71	157	12:13	17
23:28-31	134	14:10	12
23:42	164	14:11	12
23:46	164	14:20	12
Ch 24	161, 174–75, 180	17:21	12
24:25	162	17:23	12
24:25-27	162, 170, 180	18:6	101
24:26	145–46	21:1-11	136
24:26-27	120		
24:27	120, 162, 169–70, 175	**Acts**	23, 119, 173
		1:1	120
24:31	161	1:2	122
24:32	161–62, 175	1:4-5	122
24:44	162, 169, 175	1:5	120
24:44-47	162, 170, 180	1:6-11	119
24:44-48	120	1:8	105, 120, 122, 162
24:44-49	**161–63**, 166, 168	1:9-11	122
24:45	161, 175	Ch 2	80
24:47	162	2:2-4	120
24:48	162	2:16-21	120

Scripture Index

2:33	120, 163	**Galatians**	
2:33-36	120	1:18-19	173
2:36	78	1:18–2:9	90
2:39	105	2:1	173
8:9	139	2:9	173
9:34	87	3:20	12
9:43	139		
15:14	131–32	**Ephesians**	
18:25	15	5:22-33	89–90
18:26	15	5:25-27	141
28:24-28	134		
28:31	173	**Philippians**	
		2:6-11	11, 33
Romans			
2:3	50	**Colossians**	
2:5-6	50	1:15-20	33
6:4	60	1:19	42
10:9	18, 180	1:20	42
10:13	21, 32, 35		
11:36	26	**2 Timothy**	
14:9	19	2:19	32
14:10	50		
14:11	32	**Hebrews**	1, 16
		1:3	44
1 Corinthians		1:5	14
1:31	32	1:5-13	14
2:16	32	1:6	1
5:4	61	1:6-7	14
8:4-6	12	1:8-9	14
8:5-6	12	1:10–12	1, 14
8:6	26, 29, 42	1:13	14
10:26	32	2:9	1
11:23	23, 90	Chs 3–4	55
12:3	19, 180	4:1-11	98
15:3	90	8:10-12	68
15:8	90	9:15	68
16:22	23	9:22	140
			15–16
2 Corinthians		**James**	12, 15
3:7	147	2:19	15
3:7-18	5	4:12	15
3:13	147	5:4	112
3:18	147	5:7	112
4:4	147	5:9	15, 112
4:6	147		
5:19	42, 133	**1 Peter**	15
10:17	32	1:17	50
11:2	89–90, 141	2:8	15
		3:14-15	15

2 Peter
3:16 41

1 John
3:8 93
4:2-3 32–33

2 John
1:7 33

Jude
1:9 15–16
   150

Revelation
1:11 41
16:5 93
19:7 90
19:7-9 89–90
19:9 111
21:2 90
21:3 108
21:9 90
22:6 111
22:16 132
22:18-19 41

www.ingramcontent.com/pod-product-compliance
Lightning Source LLC
Chambersburg PA
CBHW051520230426
43668CB00012B/1685